D1606716

Further praise for J Curve Exposure

"Private Equity worldwide attracts growing amounts of capital that fuels the growth of an industry which probably faces its greatest challenge so far. The buy-out industry has yet to demonstrate the sustainability of the exceptional returns it has produced over the last five years while the venture capital industry has yet to bounce back and produce the sort of premium that its risk levels should command for investors. Against this backdrop, the publication by Pierre-Yves Mathonet and Thomas Meyer provides investors in the asset class with the necessary toolbox to understand its fundamentals and to enable them to apply their own judgment on the market. This should allow both existing and prospective investors to navigate the sometimes complex intricacies of the industry and to construct a robust portfolio at this crucial point of the cycle. Congratulations for this superb new work which, as their first book Beyond the J Curve *will become an industry benchmark."*
—Philippe Poggioli, Managing Partner, Access Capital Partners

"Notwithstanding the attractive returns private equity may offer, there are many potential pitfalls for investors. Mathonet and Meyer have done an excellent job (again) in helping investors avoid such pitfalls and build a robust portfolio of private equity funds. Written for practitioners, their new book, J Curve Exposure *provides a theoretically sound basis for those seeking exposure to this asset class. I can strongly recommend it."*
—Peter Cornelius, Head of Strategy & Economics, AlpInvest Partners

"Brilliant. No other book provides practical tools in private equity funds investments. Together with their first book Beyond the J Curve, *institutional investors are now able to sail out with a compass to navigate the turbulent sea of "private equity funds". I strongly recommend this book for all of investors and especially for Asian investors who are increasing exposures in private equity assets."*
—Kazushige Kobayashi, President & CEO, Alternative Investment Capital

"The commitment of the authors to exploring, rationalising and proposing tools and methods for understanding the Private Equity industry in their second book is proof in itself of the need to permanently monitor, understand and follow the evolution of this industry. I can only praise their hard work and their willingness to make us all benefit from their valuable, wise and professional views."
—Javier Echarri, Secretary General, European Private Equity & Venture Capital Association (EVCA)

J Curve Exposure

For other titles in the Wiley Finance series
please see www.wiley.com/finance

J Curve Exposure

Managing a Portfolio of Venture Capital and Private Equity Funds

Pierre-Yves Mathonet
Thomas Meyer

John Wiley & Sons, Ltd

Other Wiley Editorial Offices

John Wiley & Sons Inc., 111 River Street, Hoboken, NJ 07030, USA

Jossey-Bass, 989 Market Street, San Francisco, CA 94103-1741, USA

Wiley-VCH Verlag GmbH, Boschstr. 12, D-69469 Weinheim, Germany

John Wiley & Sons Australia Ltd, 42 McDougall Street, Milton, Queensland 4064, Australia

John Wiley & Sons (Asia) Pte Ltd, 2 Clementi Loop #02-01, Jin Xing Distripark, Singapore 129809

John Wiley & Sons Canada Ltd, 6045 Freemont Blvd, Mississauga, ONT, L5R 4J3, Canada

Wiley also publishes its books in a variety of electronic formats. Some content that appears in print may not be
available in electronic books.

Anniversary Logo Design: Richard J. Pacifico

Library of Congress Cataloging in Publication Data

Mathonet, Pierre-Yves.
   J Curve exposure : managing a portfolio of venture capital and private equity
funds / Pierre-Yves Mathonet, Thomas Meyer.
     p.   cm.
   Includes bibliographical references and index.
   ISBN 978-0-470-03327-2
   1. Venture capital.   2. Private equity.   3. Portfolio management.   I. Meyer, Thomas, 1959–
II. Title.
   HG4751.M38 2007
   332.6—dc22

                                                  2007038114

British Library Cataloguing in Publication Data

A catalogue record for this book is available from the British Library

ISBN-13 978-0-470-03327-2 (HB)

Typeset in 10/12pt Times by Integra Software Services Pvt. Ltd, Pondicherry, India
Printed and bound in Great Britain by Antony Rowe Ltd, Chippenham, Wiltshire
This book is printed on acid-free paper responsibly manufactured from sustainable forestry
in which at least two trees are planted for each one used for paper production.

P.-Y.M.

To my wife Barbara

T.M.

To my wife Mika Kaneyuki who deserves my heartfelt gratitude for her
love and for encouraging me to work on this book

Contents

List of Boxes

Foreword

Private Equity is possibly more visible now than in any other period in its history. As a consequence, many people today feel entitled to express strong and often radical opinions on the industry. Whilst the variety of opinion is impressive and to a large extent constitutes the proof that the industry has become 'on-exceptional', the lack of depth in some of the more colourful is regrettable and harmful.

In their previous book, 'Beyond the J Curve', Thomas Meyer and Pierre-Yves Mathonet provided readers with an in-depth presentation of the private equity industry. By sharing further their professional experience as investors in the asset class they positively contribute to the current debate. The Private Equity industry is complex and any comment on its operation and/or economic impact should be based on a thorough understanding. New comers in private equity will build such understanding by reading this second book while seasoned readers will be challenged by the approach presented in terms of portfolio construction and notably by the role played by venture capital.

The historical track-record evidence of the Private Equity industry used by the authors in their introduction reveals itself as cleverly entertaining and particularly clarifying in understanding the relevance of the industry business model in its different forms, its adaptation capacity and its intrinsic nature of permanent search for effective investment.

To use the analogy of some of the current opponents of the Private Equity industry, the 'wildest animal in the zoo' is actually one of those rare and old animals which from the start, like the Venetian Merchant, have been able to adapt and evolve to embrace the changing nature of the economy and as a consequence remain relevant, alive and rewarding today.

This Darwinian nature of the industry is further evidenced and very well documented by the authors at the level of individual management companies that go through the private equity cycle from the initial fundraising to the next one. While many teams fail to raise their second fund, new players enter the market on the back of their relevant experience for the foreseeable challenges and opportunities. Understanding this basic principle of permanent adaptation is a sine-qua-non start point for entering the industry.

It is important for institutional investors embracing this asset class to acknowledge that it requires not just a strategic long-term commitment but also a deep understanding, permanent monitoring as well as active building and management of the portfolio. As the authors highlight, it is about building a 'life-time program' of an asset which is core and not peripheral. This book will help investors build the tools for understanding, measuring and managing and diversifying their portfolios with that long-term perspective in mind and away from knee-jerk reactions or fashionable me-too strategies.

Regardless of the future evolution of this permanently changing asset class, the size and scope of the players in this market – from brand names to specialized boutiques – the foreseeable higher liquidity potential and sophistication derived from the combined impact of the secondary market, portfolio management and individual deal management, the tools provided in this book, as well as the in-depth understanding that it facilitates, make it a permanent consultation work to be kept on the office desk.

A thorough reading of this work could also help some of those with extreme opinions to assess the relevance of their views and the impact of what they wish for. I would argue that the Venetian merchant families 'commendas' benefited the whole of Venetian society and not just themselves.

The commitment of the authors to exploring, rationalising and proposing tools and methods for understanding the Private Equity industry in their second book is proof in itself of the need to continually monitor, understand and follow the evolution of this industry. I can only praise their hard work allowing us all to benefit from their valuable, wise and professional views.

Javier Echarri
EVCA SECRETARY GENERAL
Brussels, 31st July 2007

Acknowledgments

There are many people whom we would like to thank for their help in bringing this book to fruition. While we cannot name them all, we would like to express our gratitude to:

- Gauthier Monjanel, from the European Investment Fund's VC Risk Management Team, for co-authoring the chapter on side-funds.
- Olivier Amblard, Deutsche Bank, for co-authoring the chapter on securitisation of private equity funds.
- Paulina Junni, Swedish School of Economics and Business Administration, for co-authoring the chapter on real options.
- Ulrich Brunnhuber, CFA, from the European Investment Bank, for authoring the box on Islamic finance and venture capital.
- Brenlen Jinkens, Director and Todd Konkel, Vice President, Cogent Partners, for having shared with us their expertise on secondary transactions.
- Sven Lahann for testing and implementing many of our concepts and Gabriel Robet for having researched several of our ideas.
- Jérôme Marcelino, Ecole de Commerce Européenne - Lyon, for his research on publicly quoted private equity funds-of-funds.
- Wayne E. Yang from Hamilton Lane and Prof. Dr. Cuno Pümpin, Professor em. for marketing & strategy and chairman of the Institute of Management at the University of St. Gallen (HSG), for their suggestions and valuable comments on early drafts.

We would like also to say a special thank to Dr. Didier Guennoc, Research Director, EVCA, for his longstanding support and collaboration and to Francis Carpenter, Chief Executive, European Investment Fund, for supporting our work. All errors and omissions remain our own responsibility.

Finally, to the John Wiley & Sons team who helped us on the book, including Pete Baker, Commissioning Editor; Chris Swain, Assistant Editor; Finance, Julia Bezzant, Marketing Executive, Samantha Hartley, Content Editor; Viv Wickham, Project Editor and Sunita Jayachandran, Project Manager, Integra, India.

Abbreviations

ABS	Asset Backed Security
AFIC	Association Française des Investisseurs en Capital
BVCA	British Venture Capital Association
CAPM	Capital Asset Pricing Model
CDO	Collateralized Debt Obligation
CFO	Collateralized Fund Obligation
DCF	Discounted Cash Flows
EIF	European Investment Fund
EU	European Union
EVCA	European Venture Capital and Private Equity Association
FLP	First Loss Piece
FOIA	Freedom of Information Act
FoF	Fund-of-Funds
GEM	Grading-based Economic Model
GP	General Partner
IAS	International Accounting Standards
IFRS	International Financial Reporting Standards
IRR	Internal Rate of Return
LBO	Leverage Buyout
LP	Limited Partner
M&A	Mergers and Acquisitions
NAV	Net Asset Value
NPI	Net Paid-In
NPV	Net Present Value
NVCA	National Venture Capital Association
PE	Private Equity
POC	Performance, Operational and Compliance grading
PPM	Private Placement Memorandum
PTPE	Publicly Traded Private Equity
SPV	Special Purpose Vehicle
VaR	Value-at-Risk
VC	Venture Capital

Disclaimer

Private equity firms whose names are mentioned explicitly in this book were taken as representative examples, but are not positively or negatively recommended. Many of the concepts presented here have been researched and developed in the course of our work with the European Investment Fund. However, for this book we have researched private equity market practices and discussed different approaches with industry practitioners. The statement made in this book represents the personal opinion of the authors and does not necessarily reflect the views of the European Investment Fund.

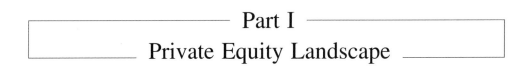

Part I
Private Equity Landscape

1
Introduction

Queen Isabella of Castile essentially did a private equity financing exercise when she purchased an interest in Christopher Columbus' voyage of discovery. '*Lacking the necessary resources, Columbus asked King John II of Portugal in 1484 to back his voyage but was refused. The next year he went to Spain to seek aid of Queen Isabella and King Ferdinand. [. . .] Isabella not only furnished financial support, but also provided management and recruitment assistance. She went even one step further; she allowed Columbus to share in the profits.*'[1] Adding to this analogy: in fact, King John II did the far better due diligence and asked for an independent opinion on this proposal. His experts, correctly, did not agree with Columbus' estimate of the distance to the Indies. Indeed, Columbus erred on the circumference of the Earth and believed that the distance from the Canary Islands to Japan would only be some 3700 kilometers. This is approximately just one-third of the true distance, and Columbus and his crew would have certainly died of thirst and hunger long before reaching the mythical 'Cipangu' mentioned in Marco Polo's travel stories. On the other hand, John's experts were wrong in thinking that the aquatic expanse between Europe and Asia was uninterrupted – clearly showing the limits of experience and historical data in a situation of high uncertainty.

1.1 BARBARIANS, PIRATES AND PRIVATEERS

Not too long ago, private equity investors were vilified as 'Barbarians at the Gate', but this has changed. *The Economist* (2006b) found KKR's Henry Kravis a 'Barbarian no more'. Like the conquistadors following Columbus, such as Hernan Cortés who in later life was appointed Governor and Captain General of the newly conquered territory, private equity firms like KKR, Carlyle or Permira have become respectable, admired and often envied. They create empires of $10 billion or possibly even $100 billion funds, get courted by institutional investors, and recruit the best and the brightest. In the times of Sarbanes-Oxley it is not desirable any more to be CEO of a publicly quoted company – high flyers rather desire heading a private company and becoming a member of this elitist club of the truly rich and powerful. *The Economist* observes that in '*the 1980s private equity was a place for mavericks and outsiders; these days it attracts the most talented members of the business, political and cultural establishment, including many of the world's top managers. Jack Welch, the legendary former boss of GE, is now at Clayton, Dubilier & Rice. Lou Gerstner, who revived IBM, is chairman of Carlyle. Even Bono, the saintly lead singer of rock band U2, is now in the business.*'

---

[1] Quoted from Haemmig (2003).

To some degree over recent years venture capital has remained a poor cousin in this glittering world of private equity. Institutional investors overwhelmingly continue to be skeptical regarding venture capital's prospects and largely ignorant about its business model. To stay with the age of discovery analogy, venture capitalists are still the 'pirates of the carried interest' cruising very different waters – innovation and intangible-based companies in their early stage requiring technical expertise and hands-on involvement rather than the financial engineering typical for targeting large companies with tangible assets. Occasionally they are sent out with government support – a letter of marque – as privateers to battle for the markets of the future. Some succeed and find a treasure or – like Sir Henry Morgan in the 17th century – even build their own little empire, but many go to the gallows (mercifully at least here the analogy does not fully apply).

1.2   A DIFFICULT WORLD TO CONQUER

The focus of this book is institutional investing in private equity, which is mainly through limited partnerships. In his book *The Origins of Western Economic Success*, Meir Kohn explains this structure's medieval roots, where Italian merchant families were financing trade voyages through 'commendas'. In these asymmetric partnerships the 'sleeping partners' were not liable for debt and stayed at home while 'traveling partner' controlled the venture and set sails to search for profitable business. Traveling partners had a lot in common with today's venture capitalist, in the sense that both have, at least initially, little more to offer than their skills and their risk-taking attitude. One may suspect that limited partnerships and similar structures belong to the best ways for skilled and daring professionals to pool funding from wealthy and relatively risk-averse parties for investments in an environment of extreme uncertainty. At the height of Venetian trading power, the sleeping partners made small investments in a large number of commendas to spread the risk, thus resembling today's diversified portfolios of private equity funds held by funds-of-funds and other institutional investors.

1.2.1   Get rich quick?

Private equity firms have moved from the outer fringe to the center of the capitalist system and for institutional investors private equity is becoming an increasingly accepted – although often not wholeheartedly embraced – standard component of their asset allocation. Nevertheless, and despite this kind of investment's long tradition, few publications address the needs of institutions interested in this alternative asset class. Usually start-ups and entrepreneurs and occasionally their financers catch the limelight, but the 'financers of the financers', i.e. the limited partners, are generally forgotten. Most institutions themselves believe that this kind of investing is 'just like any other asset' and do not pay too much attention to this – typically immaterial – part of their activities. However, private equity is a difficult asset class and definitely not a 'get rich quick scheme'. The general claim that private equity historically offered higher returns than the stock markets has to be called into question. The main rationale for investing in this asset class – achieving superior performance through investing into a group of elite funds – is too simplistic.

There is the perception that private equity is an access industry to top-quartile funds. To some degree this is the case, as there is certainly a network of established players, and some industry insiders even predict that the industry will develop into a market where a limited number of proven fund managers are investing on behalf of a few expert investors in their funds. However, the top-quartile promise has to be taken with a huge pinch of salt; in fact, consistently picking above average funds resembles an evolutionary arms race. For simplified illustration: during 2002 and 2003 basically no team that was not a 'proven top-quartile' performer was able to find investors and close their fund. Well, as these vintage years will also by definition have four quartiles, these top performers obviously cannot all be in the first one, essentially rendering meaningless the back-of-the-envelope calculations that aim to support a 'great return potential' usually presented at private equity conferences. Moreover, particularly the experienced investors understand that some degree of experimentation with niche strategies and refreshing with emerging fund managers are an important component of a sustainable private equity investment program.

> *The most important challenge going forward is hence to refine our understanding of what works and what does not work in private equity [. . .] Giving up the illusion of genuinely high private equity returns across the board may be a first step in the process.*
> Gottschalg (2007)

We would argue that you either decide to make a long-term commitment to the asset class and follow a systematic approach or you had better stay out entirely. Industry practitioners believe that investing consistently and continuously probably works best. Private equity is not a sea cruise but a long voyage, such as the ones of Christopher Columbus or Marco Polo.

1.2.2   Chartering a course

The business process underlying a private equity funds investment program is still poorly understood. In addition, 'private equity' as a term spans a very wide range. To discuss all its aspects is not realistic, as it would essentially mean explaining the entire world of modern finance, and instead we therefore focus on venture capital that could arguably be seen as the purest form of private equity. In fact these two terms are often used interchangeably. As this is by definition venturing out into the unknown, we cannot provide a clear map but rather have to reflect on tools that help us to navigate these largely unchartered oceans. Like under a magnifying glass, the problems of institutional investing in venture capital funds provide a case study for analyzing and explaining the essential nuts and bolts of private equity in general. We approach the definition of institutional investing in venture capital funds through defining the boundaries to other segments of the private equity market. Later stage investing, with its increasingly blurred delineation between buyouts and hedge funds, could be seen as one boundary. On the other extreme lies another fuzzy boundary to the informal venture capital market, for example business angels or the famous 'three F's', i.e. family, friends and fools.

Venture capital is about exploration, innovation and discovery. Historically, exploration is often political and associated with development objectives. It is said that in the 15th century Portugal's Henry the Navigator launched the first successful, large-scale research and development organization. These exploration efforts were to some degree also caused by Constantinople having fallen to the Turks and thus had an expressly development purpose. As the Islamic Ottoman Empire for reasons such as religion and politics restricted the flow of commerce to the Christian West, there was a need to find an alternate route to trade valuable commodities such as spices. Consequently, and being aware of the numerous public initiatives, we feel that any discussion of venture capital without acknowledging the role of the government in this market would be incomplete.

1.2.3   Storms and barrier-reefs

In situations where managers cannot rely on quantitative tools, they often tend to base their decisions on gut instinct. Unfortunately, this phenomenon appears to be all too common in venture capital investing. For example, due diligence – or the lack of it – immediately springs to mind. As one of the authors witnessed in 2000, due diligence was often little more than a combination of a job interview with an extended lunch. This has certainly changed, but indiscriminately adding new due diligence criteria does not help if you do not know what you are looking for. In reality, the various limited partners' screening and due diligence processes appear to be very similar. As there is a strong belief that in venture capital 'it's the team', investments are often made on little more than the feel-good factor based on the past performance of individual fund managers. These fund managers tend to be great salespeople and, not just for the inexperienced investors, it is easy to succumb to their charisma.

Another area is inefficient management and monitoring through the private equity fund investment program's lifetime. For a limited partner the problem is to get a sufficient 'real' allocation to private equity – not everything that is committed to a fund is put to work right away. If this does not cause headaches, the institution probably has not allocated enough resources to private equity. To have an impact, the weight of private equity in the portfolio has to be significant. Endowments are known that allocate up to 30% of their assets to buyout and venture capital funds. This creates liquidity risks, as a documented case of a listed private equity fund-of-funds that experienced a 'perfect storm' and was apparently brought to the verge of bankruptcy demonstrates. This case allows us to identify a number of problems and to illustrate the technical questions around the management of a successful private equity funds investment program. Issues surrounding valuation, liquidity management, or investment guidelines provide the relevant questions to be tackled in this book.

1.2.4   Drawing a map

Lack of clarity regarding its business model, the high degree of required judgment and 'rules of thumb' instead of mathematical precision may contribute to the perception that particularly venture capital is highly 'speculative'. The main factors that appear to make institutions shy away from this asset class are an unclear track record of the industry, valuations and risks that are difficult to understand, coupled with a perceived intransparency in the industry, and the significant entry barriers to overcome before tangible results show. There is an increasing recognition that in private equity to date, data of sufficient depth and breadth to 'conduct an accurate, unbiased and comprehensive performance analysis is simply unavailable'.[2]

Indeed, as fund valuations have in many cases little relation to economic reality, frustrated investors feel that there is a lack of transparency. We believe that, for private equity, precise quantification is out of reach in principle. Calls for more data do not necessarily make an appraised asset class more transparent. In fact, many industry experts argue that private equity fund managers are already far more open and responsive vis-à-vis their investors

---

[2] See Gottschalg (2007).

than any publicly listed company. However, the value in venture capital is driven by intangibles such as intellectual property; therefore, assessments tend to extremes between deepest pessimism and unjustified excitement. Because of the long time horizons and due to the nature of investing in innovative technologies, the traditional risk measures fail at capturing the 'unknowns' of an uncertain environment that characterizes this alternative asset class. For venture capital, which is by definition mostly innovation, the environment is continuously evolving and the absence of data restricts the application of a quantitative toolset significantly.

Although it is neither safe nor predictable, there are nevertheless proper management tools for analysis and for managing in uncertain environments. We present approaches for valuation and structuring, and for conducting track record analysis of private equity funds.

1.2.5 Setting out ships and navigating the oceans

Venture capital is not for the 'here and now', it is sowing the seeds for the future and therefore in many ways appeals to dreams. People tend to see the future through 'rose-colored glasses'. There is a demonstrated systematic tendency to be over-optimistic about the outcome of planned actions. One could argue that this uncertainty to a large degree stimulates venture capital. As Columbus demonstrated, not knowing that success is unlikely can in fact help people to embark on journeys that lead to new discoveries.

> *If you want to build a ship, don't drum up people together to collect wood and don't assign them tasks and work, but rather teach them to long for the endless immensity of the sea.*
>
> Antoine de Saint-Exupery

This, however, leads to common errors and biases and it is important to understand the fallacies of decision-making under uncertainty. The tendency to follow moods and fashions, and try to time the market, appears to be ineradicable, but is bound to lead to frustrations. But even if institutions are serious about their venture capital investment programs, these programs tend to follow their own dynamics. In private equity it is difficult to access good funds and to put money to work. Consequently, programs usually need to start on an opportunistic basis. However, over time getting the big picture of the portfolio of funds is becoming increasingly important. The transition from a deal-driven and opportunistic investment style to a portfolio management culture is a challenge, as often evidenced by the lack of structured decision processes, inefficient management of commitments, or over-diversification.

Those that expect a sophisticated portfolio management approach to private equity will usually be disappointed. Very few limited partners use a quantitative approach for their asset allocation strategy, and it is likely that in private equity the response will be the same as not all too long ago was found in a funds-of-hedge-funds survey: that many respondents admitted to having no asset allocation strategy at all.

We draw upon analogies from evolution theory to explain portfolio strategy consideration for a private equity fund investment program and suggest viewing portfolios of funds as evolutionary systems. Indeed, phenomena common for venture capital markets, such as bubbles or general patterns following power laws, characterize economic systems as intrinsically evolutionary. Within such a so-called 'fitness landscape' the simple recipe for creating growth is differentiation, selection, and amplification. We believe that limited partners need checks and balances and for this purpose developed a method for grading – i.e. comparing – funds on a qualitative and quantitative basis pre-investment and throughout their lifetime as a tool to navigate the 'fitness landscape' of the private equity market. Additionally, we look at the real options limited partners have – or could design – to amplify the impact of 'winners' in their portfolios.

1.2.6   Staying on course and moving into calmer waters

Uncertainty in the case of private equity funds also relates to a wide range of possible outcomes, that makes statistical analysis on the individual fund level meaningless. However, after a build-up phase, there is a virtuous circle of well-spread, but not overly diversified, portfolio that allows reasonably continuous and predictable aggregated cash in- and out-flows. Few new annual additions to the portfolio allow you to be selective. A reasonable number of relationships or funds in the overall portfolio give a more or less predictable and steady deal flow and allow an efficient allocation. When looking at a larger population of funds one can again speak about risks that can be managed. We look how this can be done for a portfolio of private equity funds, and how this can be turned into practice through a securitization structure.

There are certainly significant entry barriers to the private equity industry, e.g. a long learning curve and the time before a portfolio of private equity funds has the necessary cruising speed. Limited partners need to build up expertise in portfolio design, due diligence and evaluation, legal structuring, monitoring, liquidity management, workouts, etc. But private equity as a club is not as exclusive as it seems. Launching a funds investment program requires taking a long-term perspective. One cannot get around judgment, expertise and relationships. Institutions that want to become successful players in this exciting market need to build this up – but it is not an insurmountable obstacle.

> *Consequently, practitioners' models rely entirely on intuition, are not validated by any type of established theory and are frequently changed in line with the reality of the market. Academics, in contrast, seek to understand how and why things work, and the only way to explain how things work is often to look back. Consequently, academics' models may be very good at explaining but they are usually very poor at forecasting, with the result that little value is attached to them by practitioners.*
>
> Lhabitant (2004)

In this book we are taking the practitioner's point of view and are targeting commercially oriented institutions that are either already managing or considering setting up a private equity funds investment program. Rather than proposing an 'ideal' program, we are discussing various methods and trade-offs. The techniques we propose here for venture capital can also be used for private equity in general, although for later stage investments other tools could be more meaningful. For the purpose of this book we use the term 'private equity' whenever data, observations or concepts are applicable in general, while we use the term 'venture capital' when we discuss the specific challenges.

Private equity firms whose names are mentioned explicitly in this book were taken as representative examples, but are not positively or negatively recommended. Many of the concepts presented here have been researched and developed in the course of our work with the European Investment Fund. However, for this book we have researched private equity market practices and discussed different approaches with industry practitioners. The statement made in this book represents the personal opinion of the authors and does not necessarily reflect the views of the European Investment Fund.

2
Institutional Investing in Private Equity

In the broad sense, private equity means a security that is not registered and not publicly traded on an exchange. In the USA, private equity securities are exempt from registration with the Securities and Exchange Commission because they are issued in transactions 'not involved in any public offering'. Private equity, including venture capital, is usually considered part of the family of alternative investments and one of the most expensive forms of finance. It provides financing to private firms unable, or unwilling, to seek funding through public equity markets or loans from banks. Active management of portfolio companies and exits form the main drivers of investment returns.

The focus of this book is neither entrepreneurship nor the financing and management of portfolio companies, but institutional investing in the organized private equity market, where professional management is provided by private equity firms as intermediaries. These firms raise pools of capital from institutions such as pension funds, endowments, funds-of-funds, banks, insurance companies, high net worth individuals or family offices as private equity funds for investment in targeted companies. As private equity fund investments are more risky and illiquid than most other asset classes, they are only for those who can afford to have their capital locked in for long periods of time and who are able to risk losing significant amounts of money. Moreover, as private equity funds are also less regulated than ordinary mutual funds, law typically requires that investors have to fulfill certain conditions. As an example, to qualify as an accredited investor in the USA one needs $2.5 million of net worth and exclusive of primary residence, $200 000 of individual income, or $300 000 of joint income with spouse for two documented years and an expectation that such income level will continue. Investments in private equity funds are sold via private placement, and limitations on private placements imposed by the Securities Act have to be obeyed.

Theoretically, due to the high risks and the illiquidity private equity funds should earn a premium over traditional securities, such as stocks and bonds, and thus justify the expectation that annual returns for successful funds range up to 30%. However, based on our own experience and also according to findings of researchers such as Gottschalg (2007), there is little evidence that the average historic performance of private equity is above the returns of truly comparable stock market investments. In other words, investing in private equity, even if it is through professional intermediaries, does not necessarily result in attractive average returns. That raises the question, how can institutions successfully manage portfolios of private equity funds? So far few publications, such as Grabenwarter and Weidig (2005) or Meyer and Mathonet (2005), have touched upon this subject, which we are going to explore in further detail in this book. In this chapter we first look at the dominant form of financial intermediation in private equity, the limited partnership, and then discuss the portfolios of such limited partnerships in the form of a private equity funds investment program.

2.1 LIMITED PARTNERSHIP

Private equity funds fulfill a number of functions. Firstly, they allow pooling of capital for investing in private companies. Secondly, they allow delegating the investment process to fund managers with significant experience and the proper incentives to screen, evaluate and select potential companies with expected high growth opportunities. These managers have the necessary expertise to finance companies that develop new product and technologies and to foster their growth and development by controlling, coaching and monitoring these companies' management. Finally, the fund managers source exit opportunities and realize capital gains on disposing portfolio companies.

Box 2.1:   Basic definitions

For the purpose of this book we use the term **private equity funds investment program** as a generalization for in-house programs, captive or independent fund-of-funds focusing on investments in private equity funds.

Private equity funds are unregistered investment vehicles that pool money to invest in privately held companies. Fund management companies – also referred to as **private equity firms** – set up these funds to attract institutional investors.

As used herein, the term **general partner** refers to the private equity firm as an entity that is legally responsible for managing the fund's investments and who has unlimited personal liability for the debts and obligations when the fund is set up as a limited partnership.

Fund managers are the individuals involved in its day-to-day management. The group of fund managers forms the private equity fund's **management team** that will include the carried interest holders, i.e. those employees or directors of the general that are entitled to share in the 'super profit' made by the fund.

The term **limited partners** refers to the private equity fund's passive investors responsible for the management of a program. Again, we interpret a limited partner as the institution that provides the capital. **Investment managers** are the individuals that represent the limited partner.

The **portfolio companies** are the companies in which a private equity fund has invested and which an **entrepreneur** manages.

Private equity funds are generally structured as limited partnerships. A partnership is simply a contract, whereby two or more individuals consent to carry on an enterprise, contribute to it, by combining property, knowledge or management, and to share its profit. The most basic form of partnership is a general partnership, in which all partners manage the business and are personally liable for its debts, as every partner is both an agent and principal of the firm and may thus bind the firm and the other partners. As these liabilities can be significant, another 'asymmetric' form for investment vehicles has developed: the limited partnership. In this partnership certain limited partners relinquish their ability to manage the business in exchange for limited liability for the partnership's debts. Also, tax and regulatory requirements drive the structuring of these investment vehicles with the additional objectives of transparency (i.e. investors are treated as investing directly in the underlying portfolio companies) and low taxation. See Figure 2.1.

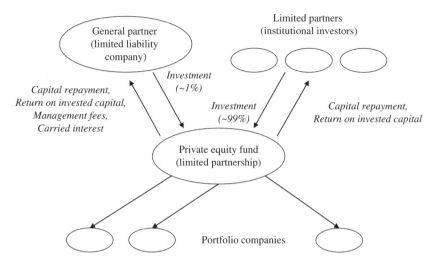

Figure 2.1   Limited partnership structure

While terms and conditions, and investor rights and obligations, were defined in specific non-standard partnership agreements, the limited partnership structure – or comparable structures used in the various jurisdictions – has evolved over the last decades into a 'quasi-standard'.

- Investors are the limited partners and commit a certain amount to the fund. They have little or no influence on the day-to-day management of the fund. However, limited partners are given some oversight of the fund, i.e. by allowing them to sit on advisory boards or on investors committees while still being protected from general liability.
- The fund usually has a contractually limited life of seven to ten years. The fund manager's objective is to realize all investments before or at the liquidation of the partnership. Often there is a provision for an extension of two to three years. The main part of the capital is drawn down during the 'investment period', typically three to five years, where new opportunities are identified. Sometimes there is a provision for an extension of one year. After that, during the 'divestment period', only the existing and successful portfolio companies will be further supported with some follow-on funding provided to extract the maximum value through exits. The manager's efforts during this time are concentrated on realizing or selling the investments.
- The management fees depend on the size of the fund and on the resources required to implement the proposed strategy. They generally range from 2.5% of committed capital for funds of less than €250 million to 1% for the largest buyout funds. The fees are often scaled down once the investment period has been completed and adjusted according to the proportion of the portfolio that has been divested. There are, however, considerable differences from one fund to the next, particularly relating to what the managers do with income and expenses from their investment activity, such as directorship fees or transaction costs. These can have an impact on the returns and often account for material differences between gross and net returns.

- Fund managers earn a relatively low fixed salary and their main incentive is supposed to be the 'carried interest' of, typically, 20% of the profits realized by the fund. Usually carried interest is subject to a 'hurdle rate', so that it only applies once investors have received their capital back and a minimum pre-agreed rate of return. They also often invest a significant share of their personal wealth into the fund to put themselves at risk in case of under-performance and to signal thereby their belief in their success. These incentives motivate fund managers to take large risks when they believe that the potential returns are high, and thus align their interests with those of the limited partners.
- Commitments are drawn down as needed, i.e. 'just-in-time' to make investments or to pay costs, expenses or management fees. Because private equity funds typically do not retain a pool of uninvested capital, their general partners make capital calls when they have identified a company to invest in. Therefore, the main part of the drawdowns is invested immediately. If no suitable investment opportunities are found, funds may even end up reducing the limited partners' commitments.
- When realizations are made, or when interest payments or dividends are received, they are distributed to investors as soon as practical. Thus the fund is 'self-liquidating' as the underlying investments are realized. However, limited partners typically have no right to demand that realizations be made, and these returns are coming mostly in the second half of the fund's lifetime up to its liquidation. Distributions can also be 'in kind' as securities of a portfolio company, normally provided that these securities are publicly tradable.

From a strictly legal viewpoint, in private equity limited partnership shares are illiquid, while in practice secondary transactions occasionally take place. There is a private equity fundraising cycle,[1] and in regular intervals general partners need to return to the capital markets to fundraise for another fund. The future of the general partner depends on the success of this fundraising. If it fails, the lack of a new source of management fees will force the general partner to start to reduce its cost base – until eventually full liquidation – in parallel with the decrease in the management fees received from the old funds under management. Heikkilä (2004) saw this periodical liquidation of private equity funds as essential for the investors, because the exit and re-investment cycle allows them to withdraw capital from less competent fund managers or managers whose industry expertise has become obsolete. It also allows setting back the clock for new investors, who do not need to value and pay for an existing portfolio. The fund management team's track record and reputation is critical for the successful closing of follow-on funds. One private equity firm can act as a 'group', managing several such partnerships in parallel. Typically, limited partnership agreements do not allow follow-on funds with the same strategy by the same manager before the end of the investment period or before a high percentage (usually more than 70%) of the active fund is invested.

For the fund, the 'limited partnership agreement' defines its legal framework and its terms and conditions. It mainly addresses the allocation of capital gains or losses among partners, allocation of interim distributions, management fees to the general partner, possible investment restrictions, and major governance issues. The management company enters into agreements with all employees and with the general partners.

---

[1] It is this cycle that gave its name to the ground-breaking book of Professors Gompers and Lerner of Harvard Business School: *The Venture Capital Cycle.*

The establishment of the first VC limited partnerships in the USA dates back to the late 1950s and 1960s. This model for VC investments is arguably the most successful worldwide and is followed in many international markets. The limited partnership is a result of the extreme information asymmetries and incentive problems that arise in the private equity market.

Beyond such eye-popping returns, the limited partnership proved to be a much more flexible and useful vehicle for venture capital than anything that had been tried before.

Snow (2006)

Although the partnership structure is often seen as an innovation for VC investing, its origins date back to ancient times. For example, partnerships were already referenced in the Mesopotamian Code of Hammurabi, the first written code of laws in human history dating back from the early 2nd millennium BC. Indeed, for unusually large or especially risky enterprises it seems natural to pool resources to better exploit investment opportunities. Any form of equity financing involves a sharing of potential losses as well as of potential gains. Medieval merchants had been combining their capital with other merchants in one way or another, but they also financed their ventures and shared the risk in an asymmetric manner by accepting funds from small investors.

Private partnerships carrying limited liability were unknown in classical Rome, but such contracts could be of either Byzantine or Arabic origin. The profit-and-loss-sharing partnership is embodied in the concept of Islamic finance, where one party provides 100% of the capital and the other, i.e. the 'mudārib', manages the venture using his or her skills. Such 'asymmetric' partnerships were based on a statute in the Code of Justinian and on the Rhodian Sea Law, a 7th century body of regulations governing commercial trade and navigation in the Byzantine Empire. This 'Lex Rhodia' focused on the liability for lost or damaged cargo and divided the cost of the losses among the ship's owner, the owners of the cargo and the passengers, thus serving as a form of insurance against storms and piracy. It was effective until the 12th century and greatly influenced the maritime law of the Italian cities from the 11th century onwards. Partnerships were introduced into Europe as Italian merchants increasingly traded in the Eastern Mediterranean, thus becoming familiar with business practices in this region and adopting the 'commenda'. The commenda contract had a sedentary investor, known as the 'commendator', who advanced capital to a traveling associate, known as a 'tractator'. The commenda combined financing with insurance, as the recipient of the financing was freed from any obligation to the provider of the financing if ship or cargo was lost. The contract ended when profits were distributed after the merchant returned. The commendators, in turn, diversified their risks by entering into commenda contracts with many different merchants.

The commenda not only was a good tool to circumvent restrictive usury laws but also allowed reducing capital risk.[2] It flourished across Europe after its introduction into Italy, but from the mid-13th century onwards it was highly successful in the maritime trade, as it was a convenient way of combining capital with merchant entrepreneurship. The seafaring merchants brought their trade network, nautical experience and considerable leadership for managing their crew into the venture, and for these rare skills they rightfully expected to

---

[2] See Kohn (2003), Hickson and Turner (2005) or Snow (2006).

take a good share of the profits. For example, in a so-called 'unilateral commenda' the merchant added only his own skill and knowledge. In this case the commendator received three-quarters of any profit and the tractator the rest. In the more efficient bilateral commenda the merchant also advanced some capital and in turn could take a higher share of the profits.[3]

Box 2.2:   (Pre-)Islamic finance and venture capital[4]

'*Wer sich selbst und andre kennt,*
Wird auch hier erkennen,
Orient und Okzident,
Sind nicht mehr zu trennen'.[5]

Johann Wolfgang von Goethe (West-Östlicher Divan)

The concept of risk-sharing
Largely driven by the enormous excess liquidity springing from the recent oil-boom, financial concepts and products in the field of Islamic finance have equally boomed in recent years. The market for Islamic bonds (*sukūk*) alone is estimated at $40–50 billion worldwide.[6] No longer a peripheral phenomenon limited to certain countries or groups of people, financial products deemed in *compliance* with the religious precepts of Islamic finance are also being offered by several Western banks or their regional subsidiaries, such as UBS, Citigroup or HSBC.

One conceptual underpinning of Islamic finance is commonly perceived to be the prohibition of interest-taking (*ribā*). While at times in the past this has been interpreted as the prohibition of usury-type interest only, it is now largely accepted to include interest payments that are part of standard Western fixed-income instruments. Durrani and Boocock (2006) point to the fact that also other belief systems, like Christianity or Hinduism, at some point in their history have disallowed the charging of interest. In Islamic finance one common perception is that interest in a standard loan is quasi-risk-free, because the lender is guaranteed a return, independent of whether the underlying business transaction is successful or not. In general, in Islamic finance there is a need for a more direct relationship of risk-sharing between the provider of capital and its user. Durrani and Boocock (2006) argue that '*Islam stresses the need to share rather than transfer [. . .] risk*'. In this wider context then, there appears to be a priori a high degree of compatibility between the notion of risk-taking in venture capital and Islamic finance.

In the wake of the current boom, the variety of Islamic finance products offered is increasing. For example, in 2004 the first fund-of-hedge-funds compliant with the principles of Islamic law, the Sharia, has been introduced in the USA. Similarly,

---

[3] See Hickson and Turner (2005).
[4] We thank Ulrich H. Brunnhuber, CFA who researched and authored this box.
[5] 'He who knows himself and others, / will also recognize here: / Orient and Occident, / can no longer be separated'.
[6] See Bokhari (2007).

the Islamic Development Bank (IDB) in Jeddah had earlier launched a VC fund that targets high-tech firms in Muslim countries. Finally, it appears that historically Arabian (pre-)Islamic contract law has provided at least one of the bases for the partnership structures widely used in venture capital today, in the form of the *mudāraba* contract.[7]

Mudāraba and mushāraka

In light of the above, it is no wonder that Islamic contract law has had a long tradition of defining and sharing investment risks among the relevant parties to a business venture. In fact, according to Choudhury (2001) some of these concepts date back to pre-Islamic days.

A *mudāraba* is a form of commercial contract whereby an investor[8] – or a group of investors – entrust capital to an agent (*mudārib*), who trades in it and then returns the principal along with a predetermined share of the profits to the investors. The investors generally are not liable for any transactions the agent enters into with third parties, beyond the sum of money they provided. The agent, on the other hand, also shares in the success of the business venture based upon a previously agreed share of the profits. However, any losses incurred in the venture are the sole responsibility of the investors, with the agent losing his time and effort, and any anticipated gains she or he would have made had the venture been successful. Furthermore, the agent is also entitled to deduct legitimate business-related expenses from the capital sum provided.

The *mudāraba* form of financing a venture has developed in the context of the pre-Islamic Arabian caravan trade. As such, it appears that its roots are indigenous to the Arabian Peninsula and that it played a critical part in the long-distance caravan trade for the Hejaz region. Numerous prophetic traditions and the extensive treatment of the *mudāraba* structure among Islamic jurists point to an established commercial institution with long experience on the Arabian Peninsula.[9] More importantly, with the Arab conquest, the *mudāraba* spread to Northern Africa and the Near East, and ultimately to Southern Europe. With its introduction as the commenda in the Italian seaports, it laid the foundation for the expansion of European trade in the Middle Ages. In fact, Udovitch has demonstrated a very strong correlation between the structures of the *commenda* and the Arabian *mudāraba*.[10] In Udovitch (1962) he concludes that it 'is the earliest example of a commercial arrangement identical with the later commenda, and containing all its essential features'.

Al-Sarakhsī, a jurist who lived in the 11th century, devoted an entire chapter (*kitāb*) in his legal commentary (*mabsūt*) to treating the *mudāraba* structure of commercial activity. After citing a number of prophetic traditions as a basis, he further argues for the use of this type of commercial contract: 'Because people have a need for this contract. For the owner of capital may not find his way to profitable trading activity, and the person who can find his way to such activity may not have the capital. And

---

[7] See Udovitch (1962) and Durrani and Boocock (2006).
[8] *Rabb al-māl* or owner of the capital.
[9] See Udovitch (1986) and Wakin (1993).
[10] Depending on the school of thought, *mudāraba* contracts are also referred to as *kirād* or *mukārada*. These terms can largely be used interchangeably.

Box 2.2: (Continued)

profit cannot be attained except by means of both of these, that is, capital and trading activity. By permitting this contract, the goal of both parties is attained.'[11]

The separation between capital and labor for a *mudāraba* contract is a critical element in most schools of thought,[12] which is one of the reasons why, for purposes of modern venture capital, the *mudāraba* is combined with another commercial contract, called *mushāraka*, which allows for both parties to provide capital – in modern terms, it would allow the general partner as agent to invest 'hurt money' into the partnership structure as well.

A *mushāraka* – often translated as 'participation financing'[13] – is a contractual partnership with joint participation and exploitation of the capital, and joint participation of the profits and losses. Thus, a *mushāraka* is the classical form of partnership where all parties contribute towards the financing of the business venture. The partners' share of profits are based on a pre-agreed ratio; losses are shared according to each party's investment. The management of the underlying venture can, however, be carried out by just one partner, some or all.

Durrani and Boocock (2006) and Choudhury (2001) have pointed to some short-comings of both the *mudāraba* and the *mushāraka* structure based on some of the underlying principal/agent issues. With some further finetuning they proffer hybrid structures that correct for these problems. Still, *mudāraba* and *mushāraka* (*m&m*) provide the main legal – and historical – basis for VC activity within the precepts of Islamic finance.

Investment restrictions

While the agents in the structures outlined above have considerable freedom in conducting their business, investors can impose certain restrictions. Based on the Islamic belief system, certain industry sectors and/or activities are considered not permissible. They are deemed to be generating profits in a religiously unacceptable manner. Typically, these include some or all of the following: tobacco, alcohol, gambling or gaming activities, pornography, weapons and armament, pork products and conventional financial services. Thus, negative screens are applied much like in the Western tradition. In fact, when comparing the potential investment restrictions found in Western venture capital, the significant overlap of what would typically fall under an exclusion criterion in the Western tradition versus the Islamic finance concept is quite striking.

Some public and private players in the Western venture capital arena also want to be perceived as 'socially responsible investors' and their negative screening lists may, with of course the exception of the prohibition of pork products and conventional financial services, include all of the above. In a venture capital context these exclusion criteria would be placed alongside other aspects in the investment guidelines of the partnership agreement. And in fact, there appears to be a growing number of conventional private

---

[11] Al-Sarakhsī (*Sarakhsī, Mabsūt*, xxii, 19) as cited/translated in Udovitch (1986).
[12] With the exception of the Hanbalī school.
[13] More literally 'sharing', 'participation'.

equity and venture capital funds that have passed compliance tests from an Islamic finance point of view, with only minor adjustments.

In assessing the permissibility of a proposed investment in terms of investment restrictions, Islamic scholars sometimes apply what amounts to a materiality test in the Western accounting tradition. A business activity is considered a core source of revenue or income when it constitutes more than 5% of a company's total revenue or gross income. On the other hand, if an entity's income is derived less than 5% from incidental impermissible activities, such as gambling, alcohol or the production of defense products, then it might be considered acceptable from an Islamic finance point of view. However, that portion of the underlying business activity's income needs to be *purified* by donating it to specified charities. In the absence of uniform standards, the interpretation and application of these investment restrictions can vary between countries and schools of thought.

In the early 20th century increasingly limited partnerships were used in the USA to raise capital for prospecting new oil fields. Finally, in 1959 Draper, Gaither and Anderson adopted this structure and set up what, in all likelihood, was the first limited partnership in the VC industry.[14] The long-term success of this firm, later renamed Draper Fisher Jurvetson, contrasts with the demise of the original non-family venture capital firm American Research and Development (ARD). General George Doriot, the pre-WWII Harvard Business School professor, organized ARD as a publicly traded, closed-end investment company subject to the Investment Company Act of 1940. This closed-end structure was, according to Hsu and Kenney (2004), plagued by three main problems:

(1) Its structure as an investment fund pressured ARD's management to generate a steady stream of cash.
(2) It also inhibited the provision of competitive compensation for ARD's investment professionals. This reduced their incentives and eventually led to their resignation.
(3) Closed-end investment funds often trade at a discount to their value in terms of cash and marketable securities, thus making them targets for corporate raiders.

ARD was a pioneering organization whose business model ultimately failed while the limited partnership had a better fit with the business environment. Indeed, many see the limited partnership as an ideal vehicle for private equity investing. Snow (2006) even mused whether the 'recent surge in public-to-private transactions has led some to wonder whether private limited partnerships are even beginning to challenge the public corporation as a form of corporate governance'.

In essence, terms and conditions aim to align the interests between fund managers and their investors and to discourage 'cheating' (moral hazard), 'lying' (adverse selection) or 'opportunism' (hold-up problem) in whatever form. The limited partnership agreement addresses questions of corporate governance and investor downside protection. For example, the 'key-man' provision caters for investors' concerns that particular people should remain as fund managers. It usually provides that, on a material change in the fund management team, the

---

[14] See Snow (2006).

fund will either be prohibited or suspended from making any new investments and divestment or that it will even be terminated. The 'removal for cause' provision allows investors to terminate a fund or suspend investments in the event of a breach of contract, wilful misconduct, bankruptcy and other defined events. Also, the 'no fault divorce' clause has become standard. It permits the fund's investors to remove the general partner and either terminate the partnership or appoint a new general partner. This clause covers situations at a time after the final closing date where the general partner has not defaulted or breached the terms and conditions of the limited partnership agreement but lost the confidence of its limited partners. Effectuating the removal usually requires an ordinary or special consent and usually, for the no fault divorce clause, will be subject to the general partner receiving compensation. A detailed discussion of all the aspects of limited partnership agreements under the various jurisdictions goes beyond the scope of this book, but in a later chapter we will further describe the mechanics of private equity fund distributions to align interests and create incentives.

While investors certainly have to go 'for the best deal', they need to understand that in a volatile economic environment with continuously changing power between general and limited partners, there are trade-offs between long-term objectives and short-term gains. Consequently, there are a lot of key issues that either cannot be written in contracts or are not enforceable. Therefore, many investor concerns need to be addressed through incentives and through monitoring the fund throughout its lifetime. Incentives have to be designed so that the fund manager's focus is terminal wealth and performance, and that contractual 'loopholes' are not exploited by producing over-optimistic interim results.

2.2   FUNDS-OF-FUNDS

Investing in private equity funds requires a wide-reaching network of contacts to get access to high-quality funds, a trained investment judgment, and the ability to assemble balanced portfolios. Also, the liquidity management is challenging. This demands a full-time team with insight and relationships, adequate resources, access to research databases and models, and skills and experience in due diligence, negotiation and contract structuring. This activity can either be managed in-house, or, as one of the alternatives, the management can be outsourced to a specialist fund-of-funds. A fund-of-funds pools a group of investors and uses the capital to assemble a diversified portfolio of private equity funds. Banks, asset managers, insurance groups or specialists in private equity organize such vehicles. Due to the difficulties and constraints related to the setting up of an in-house program, many institutions follow the outsourcing route.

Funds-of-funds generally mirror the private equity fund structure and are set up as limited partnerships with a general partner managing the day-to-day operations. It is often suspected that the fund-of-funds industry offers poor value to investors. The extra fees charged by funds-of-funds are said to be too high and to outweigh their efficiency gains. For financial institutions willing to take a long-term commitment to this asset class, there will be the question of whether the fund-of-funds is not a 'wasteful' business model and whether the set up of an in-house private equity investment program could avoid the controversial double fees.

2.2.1   Additional layer of management fees

Funds-of-funds are often seen as inefficient because of their additional layer of management fees. Otterlei and Barrington (2003) estimated that they would have to perform 0.7% to

3.4% better to compensate these 'double fees'. However, if the alternative is an in-house program, this argument is questionable. According to Sormani (2005b), the investment in a fund-of-funds is often much cheaper than the costs of managing private equity in-house. Due to the diseconomies of scale, the yearly costs of an internal team can be more than three times higher than the annual fees charged by a fund-of-funds. Finally, for larger institutions, the intermediation through funds-of-funds allows them to focus on their core businesses. This advantage outweighs most cost considerations. Also, investors that consider entering a fund-of-funds should not compare fund-of-funds returns with the underlying returns from private equity funds, but should compare the expected profit from a fund-of-funds investment with the investments that they could make on their own.

> *The conclusion that funds-of-funds provide little value in terms of investment performance [...] requires the incredulous belief that a large, active industry has been built on the sole advantage of mere convenience at the expense of investment under-performance.*
> Ang *et al.* (2005)

Private equity funds are hard to find, hard to evaluate, hard to monitor, have high minimums for commitments, and are often closed to new investors. Funds-of-funds can add value in all these aspects. Main reasons why investors choose them are as an introduction to the asset class to get access to investment expertise and professional resources, for diversification and for scaling their investments, or to get access to top-tier private equity funds.

2.2.2 Jumpstarting the allocation to private equity

For newcomers to the asset class an allocation to funds-of-funds offers the opportunity to instantly access the skill set of sophisticated investors as an efficient way of jumpstarting their private equity investment program. Funds-of-funds have good access to information and professional portfolio management that would otherwise be difficult and expensive to obtain. Through following this route, the investor avoids the burden of research, due diligence, ongoing monitoring, reporting and administration. Often just for these reasons alone the function is outsourced to specialists. As investors become more experienced in the asset class and become more comfortable doing things themselves, the funds-of-funds continuously lose clients. Consequently, they need to offer more value-added services rather than just provide outsourcing services.

However, even for more experienced investors in private equity, investing in a fund-of-funds can make sense, for example to pursue niche strategies in which they lack expertise or as a way to scale their allocation. Some funds-of-funds specialize in certain private equity sectors or geographies, while others follow a more generalist approach. Due to their selection skills and industry contacts, funds-of-funds have additional expertise to make informed judgments on these new firms and in identifying emerging teams. In addition, they are often better skilled and experienced in restructuring failing funds.

2.2.3 Diversification and scaling of investments

A fund-of-funds is seen as a 'safe haven' for private equity investors. It allows them to allocate money among a variety of private equity funds with complementary styles. Especially in new technologies, new teams or emerging markets, a fund-of-funds allows for a reasonable downside protection through diversification. Not surprisingly, various studies[15] show that – because of their diversification – funds-of-funds perform similarly to individual funds, but with less pronounced extremes.

Smaller institutions have difficulties achieving a meaningful level of diversification, while for larger institutions investments in private equity funds may be too cost-intensive, as the size of such investments is too small compared with the significant administration effort. Funds-of-funds can mediate the size issues by 'scaling up' through pooling smaller investors or by 'scaling down' through doing one large commitment to a fund-of-funds. Instead of overburdening a large institutional investor with many small investment decisions, one large commitment to a fund-of-funds is done.

2.2.4   Access to top teams

Securing access to top performing funds has become a major value proposition that investors are looking for in their fund-of-funds managers. Depending on the overall market situation, access to the quality funds can be highly competitive and pose a significant entry barrier for a newcomer to the market. For private equity firms fundraising is a significant burden, and they generally prefer to deal with investors that have a high probability of also backing their future funds. For them a fund-of-funds is a convenient limited partner because it has already pooled various investors and therefore is a source of cheaper and more stable capital. Funds-of-funds are continuously around and speak the 'language' of the industry. Because of their expertise, one expects them to be less likely to succumb to 'herd' mentality. They are more willing to give the fund managers sufficient latitude to focus on their portfolio companies.

Unlike for other institutions, such as pension funds or banks that may have a change of investment strategy imposed on them from higher echelons, for a fund-of-funds private equity is the only business. Funds-of-funds are more likely to be there next time around, as well as tending to have more money at their disposal to commit per fund. A smaller customer base means that a private equity firm has to spend less time fundraising and managing limited partner relationships. Moreover, as industry specialists, funds-of-funds can help fund managers in certain transactions, either through their network or, through co-investing, as provider of additional funding. Because they are perceived to be important limited partners, funds-of-funds can improve terms and conditions of limited partnership agreements, and also exercise a credible threat against fund managers' potential misbehavior. Therefore, their presence is often perceived as a positive signal to all other potential investors.

2.3   PRIVATE EQUITY FUNDS INVESTMENT PROGRAM

Even for large and mature institutional investors in private equity, funds-of-funds can complement their investment strategy by giving them an allocation to niches such as emerging markets. However, the fund-of-funds route leads to a certain loss of control for an institutional investor. Particularly for institutions intending to be long-term players in private equity, it can be meaningful to set up an in-house investment program (Figure 2.2).

---

[15] See, for example, Weidig and Mathonet (2004).

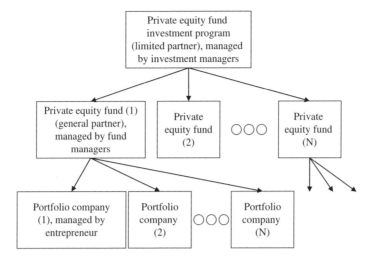

Figure 2.2   Private equity funds investment programs

In the next chapter we discuss the accessible universe of different private equity fund types in more detail.

3
Private Equity Environment

Private equity refers to a multitude of investments with varying risk profiles, liquidity requirements and returns. The main and most important two distinct spheres of private equity are venture capital and buyouts. Venture capital is a subsector of the private equity market providing high-risk, high-reward finance designed for young companies that have different asset structures, cash flows and growth rates than mature companies.

The early modern VC industry could be described as a predominantly American phenomenon. Gompers (2007) traces its origins to the family offices that managed the wealth of high net worth individuals in the last decades of the 19th century and the first decades of the 20th century. Wealthy families such as the Phippes, Rockefellers, Vanderbilts and Whitneys invested in and advised a variety of business enterprises, including the predecessor entities to AT&T, Eastern Airlines and McDonnell–Douglas. Philanthropy and also mankind's eternal dream to 'boldly go where no man has gone before' played and continues to play a role in these activities as well. For example, in the case of SpaceShipOne that completed the first privately funded human spaceflight on 21 June 2004, investor Paul Allen, the co-founder of Microsoft Corporation, was the sponsor behind the project. Gradually, these high net worth individuals began involving outsiders to select and oversee their VC investments. The result of this development was the organized VC market, with funds as the dominant form.

VC fund returns stem from building companies and from managing growth. As a consequence of the problems inherent in the valuation, venture capitalists only do a limited financial due diligence. They typically not only provide financing for building businesses but also industry know-how and management expertise. The investment size can be relatively small – initial stakes in the area of just €100 000 are not uncommon – and are overwhelmingly equity or quasi-equity financed with no or little leverage.[1] To realize investment returns, the focus of their activities is the identification of follow-on investors or the arrangement of 'club-deals'. By nature, venture capital investing must be a long-term investment activity, which also explains why fund managers impose rigid restrictions on the transferability of interests in their funds.

This model is said to work very well in situations of innovation and uncertainty where many potential business ideas might succeed. The best way to deal with this uncertainty is to initially 'bet on every (or many) horse', finance stage-wise and 'ruthlessly' write off investments that do not meet their milestones. Particularly, USA venture capitalists tend to manage narrow portfolios of deep investments. They aim for early stage investments with a high risk premium and manage 'hands-on', i.e. venture capitalists come primarily from technical and operational rather than financial backgrounds. While many fail, the

---

[1] One could argue that there is implicitly 'leverage' through the intensive use of option-like mechanisms and through the fact that there is constrained financing: start-ups are never fully financed and funds do not have the resources to fund all of them.

few successful investments yield, often spectacular, returns. When successful, leading-edge start-ups can reshape entire economies.

Venture capital needs a favorable environment, whereas buyouts also work under adverse economic conditions. Buyout investors target established businesses – generally privately held or spin-outs from public companies – that need financial capital for changing ownership. Venture capital and buyouts form the bulk of a typical institution's private equity portfolio, but in practice the delineation between them and other forms of private equity is less clear. There are significant overlaps between (1) the informal and the organized VC market, (2) venture capital, buyouts and hedge funds, and (3) funds that predominantly invest in equity and the debt financing provided by mezzanine funds and more traditional financial institutions such as banks. Even the line between private equity and public markets is difficult to draw with the private investment in public equity, the public to private transactions and the publicly quoted private equity investments.

3.1   THE INFORMAL VC MARKET

When an entrepreneur gets an idea that could be turned into a business, most of the early financing is out of own pockets or 'sweat equity', because it is very hard to get funding for a risky project at such an early stage. The informal private equity market starts with what is commonly, and not without justification, referred to as 'friends, family and fools', or the 'three F's'.

Business angels or incubators fill the gap in start-up financing between the 'three F's' and the organized private equity market,[2] with investment typically up to €2 million. VC funds provide formal funding for more mature firms with a proven track record. Venture capital – the, according to Sahlman (1990), 'professionally managed pool of capital that is invested in equity-linked securities of private ventures at various stages in their development' – usually invests larger amounts. Business angels and venture capitalists can thus be seen as each other's counterparts or complements, which is also the case in how they make investment decisions and in the value they add to the companies they support. See Figure 3.1.

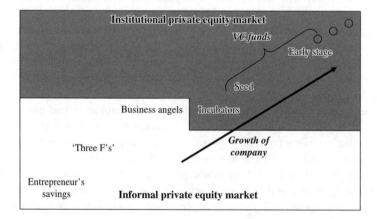

Figure 3.1   Boundary between informal and institutional private equity markets

---

[2] See Amis and Stevenson (2001) or Freear *et al.* (2002).

However, the boundary between the informal and the institutional private equity markets is fuzzy. For example, venture capitalists cooperate with business angels or business angel networks, and business angels occasionally try to set up fund-like vehicles and seek institutional investors themselves. Although venture capitalists and business angels play an important part in the formal and informal sides of the private equity market, there is a range of other more 'mixed' modes of investment that lie somewhere between the formal and informal private equity markets.

3.1.1 Business angels

A business angel can be defined as an individual investor with a certain amount of personal wealth and business skills, who provides capital and support to an early stage company.[3] Simply put, business angels invest money in early stage ventures and receive an equity stake, hoping to get the investment back with profits, or alternatively by lending them money and hoping to receive a full reimbursement of the investment plus interest. This 'angel capital' can help to take the business to the point at which it may be more attractive to a bank or private equity firm. Often entrepreneurs not only need financing but also depend on knowledge and contacts that experienced business angels, who might themselves have been entrepreneurs in the industry earlier, can provide.

Box 3.1: Equity gap

Although helpful at the beginning of the life of the venture, business angels can offer only limited support in terms of equity. Early stage companies are thus often faced with a need for additional equity, once the start-up phase is over and the companies want to make additional investments into equipment, marketing, research, production facilities, etc. in order to expand their business, and it is not uncommon that they turn to venture capitalists for follow-on funding.

According to a study by San José *et al.* (2004) on business angels in Europe, the average amount of money business angels are willing to invest is €470 000, and they ideally invest €75 000 to €100 000 per project. Venture capitalists, on the other hand, usually invest no less than €2 million, and usually come in after the angel investors. This difference between the maximum amounts the business angels are able to invest, and the minimum amount for which venture financing is meaningful, creates an 'equity gap' for early stage companies. Depending on economic conditions, venture capitalists move towards later stage investments, thus increasing this gap to somewhere between €2 million to €5 million. Theoretically the cooperation between business angels and venture capitalists could help to reduce the equity gap.

Unlike venture capitalists, business angels typically do not manage the pooled money of others in a professionally managed fund. San José *et al.* (2004) found that often business angels do not invest alone but rather in groups. In fact, in recent years they have started to organize themselves in networks, both nationally and regionally, aiming to help connect

---

[3] See Rasila *et al.* (2002).

angel investors and start-ups in need of financing to share research and pool their own capital for investment.[4] Although some business angels have even created funds, this type of vehicle still remains relatively unstructured and informal and faces difficulties attracting institutional limited partners.

But the evolution from an informally funded start-up company to a stage where it can be considered by institutional investors is not without its problems. Business angels have, for example, been accused of making investment decisions of too 'fuzzy' or loose criteria, whereas venture capitalists have more rigorous and clearly defined criteria based on which they make their investment decisions. Business angels also tend to have less solid contracts with the companies they invest in, making it sometimes cumbersome for venture capitalists to enforce their strict rules and practices on them. These and other problems make it questionable whether it actually is worthwhile or rather too risky, from an institutional investor's perspective, to engage in more extensive cooperation with business angels.

Business angels take extremely high risks, and thus theoretically should demand a very high return on investment. However, there are also non-financial motives for this activity, such as an opportunity to take an active role in the entrepreneurial process and the joy of helping a young venture grow and develop, or even for philanthropic reasons.[5] In this context the argument brought forward by Fukuyama (1995) springs to mind. In his book *Trust* he investigated the role of 'social capital' in creating prosperity in the context of industry and national contexts. To flourish, he argued, economies need people who can spontaneously form communities and extend trust beyond the clannish bounds of kinship, or the formal claims of contract. Indeed, the business angels in a study by Sørheim (2003) were very concerned with establishing common ground with entrepreneurs and potential co-investors. This can be viewed as a necessary antecedent for long-term trustworthy relationships.

There seems thus to be a need for cooperation between the formal and informal sides on the private equity market from the early stage companies' point of view, i.e. to bridge the capital and knowledge gap. In addition to this it has been argued that many early stage companies would not have survived without the help of business angels, making venture capitalists partly dependent on the supply of ready-to-invest companies that have thrived on support from informal investments. The importance of business angels for the development of a functioning private equity market should not be underestimated, and indeed a number of government initiatives target the creation of this class of investors.

3.1.2 Business incubators

Business incubators are quite similar to business angels in the sense that they offer seed capital and coaching for entrepreneurs with feasible projects in exchange for money and/or equity. They offer a collection of business services to portfolio companies, such as provision of office space, basic information technology-related infrastructure, help in making an effective business plan, administrative services, technical support, mentoring, business networking, or advice on intellectual property and sources of financing. Incubators are usually

---

[4] For example, the European Business Angel Network (EBAN); see www.eban.org.
[5] A survey in France shows that business angels' top three main motivators are (1) seeking added value (34.5%), (2) having fun and (3) helping a sibling create a company. The financial return comes in at fifth place with only 7.8%. See also http://www.eban.org/doc/Rapport Enquete France Angels 2003_EN.ppt. [accessed 30 March 2007].

for-profit firms that take equity or receive a fee for the business services they provide to their clients. They support the entrepreneurial process, helping to increase survival rates for innovative start-up companies. In essence, business incubators could be seen as consulting firms specialized in new firm creation.

In this regard, the several hundred stand-alone incubators established in 1998 and 1999 provide a cautionary tale. These incubators aimed to provide a wide variety of services to entrepreneurial firms, including financing, office space, and assistance in recruiting and operations. Yet despite the excitement they initially engendered, most incubators have failed to successfully birth even a single firm.

Gompers and Lerner (2001)

Business incubators were quite popular in the 1990s dotcom era, but many of them failed. Some were even publicly traded, and their emergence was, according to Gompers and Lerner (2001), 'accompanied by much hoopla, and many traded up to unsustainably high valuations in 1999 and early 2000'. In fact, DiCarlo (2001) found that the companies that have been lumped into the incubator category – CMGI, Internet Capital Group, divine interVentures and Idealab! – 'could use incubation themselves'. These four companies collectively invested billions into countless Internet start-ups with questionable business plans, no profits and, often, no products or revenue. Between January 2000 and January 2001 CMGI, ICG and divine[6] interVentures had lost respectively 96%, 96% and 84% of their market value, whereas Idealab! filed an S-1 for a public offering in early 2000 and withdrew it a little later citing poor market conditions. Gompers and Lerner (2001) or Rasila *et al.* (2002) provide some explanations for the business incubators' high failure rate at that time. Firstly, the set-up and running of the basic infrastructure to support portfolio companies already involves substantial direct costs. In addition, the incentives put in place were questionable. For example, some business incubators asked for a large share of equity in the portfolio companies. Equity stakes that were far higher than venture capitalists normally seek for an early stage financing led to adverse selection.

Apparently, only entrepreneurs who could not raise financing through other avenues were attracted by such incubators. Even in cases where incubators managed to find promising portfolio companies, few investors committed to follow-on financing rounds for these firms. Their concern was that with further dilution the entrepreneurs' stake would prove too small to provide a sufficient degree of motivation. Other incubators took no equity stakes in the portfolio companies at all and therefore had no real vested interest to worry too much about these ventures' long-term success. Finally, to be able to mentor fledgling entrepreneurs, incubator managers would need relevant experience themselves, which too few really had. In line with this, such incubators' own business plans were over-ambitious and based on unrealistic expectations about how many companies they could help at any one time and the range of firms they could support.

Today the surviving business incubators appear to be more careful in their approach. Evaluations of business incubators in Europe and the USA suggest that 90% of incubated start-ups were active and growing after three years of operation, which is a much higher

---

[6] The company's name was properly spelled with a lowercase 'd', because it was felt that having an uppercase 'D' might make it appear that the company was comparing itself to God.

success rate than that observed in start-ups launched without assistance.[7] As business incubators are seen as powerful economic development tools, regional and national government agencies often award financial grants.

3.2 PRIVATE EQUITY AS PART OF ALTERNATIVE ASSETS

Private equity belongs to the so-called alternative assets, i.e. assets 'that have the potential to provide economic value to the owner but are not traditionally considered assets, such as collectibles'.[8] The alternative asset universe comprises, among others, hedge funds, real estate equity funds, oil and gas partnerships, precious metals, art and antiques, fine wines, and even collectibles such as rare stamps, coins or sports cars. Alternative investments depart from traditional investments, i.e. those that are 'mainstream' in the widest sense, for example stocks or bonds, and typically traded on major bourses in the world. Alternative assets are generally more risky and less liquid than traditional assets. Nevertheless, they are no longer the domain of risk-takers or fringe investors, but are rapidly becoming an essential feature of many portfolios.[9]

One driver of this development is that investors expect a diversification of risks. Maintaining a portion of a portfolio in assets that are arguably less correlated with the financial markets can be enticing from a risk control standpoint, especially when financial markets become overvalued. The main motive, however, for investing in alternative assets is their potential for creating increased investment returns. This is mainly due to their often complex nature, making them extremely difficult to analyze. That creates market inefficiencies that can be exploited by firms willing to put in the time and effort to perform the required research. As an alternative asset's investment potential becomes more visible and recognized, more and more investors move in. For example, not too long ago Real Estate Investment Trusts (REITs) were considered to be an alternative asset, but have now gained so much acceptance that they could already be seen as 'mainstream'. Increased demand, on the other hand, leads to declining returns and players in alternative assets move on and search for other avenues.

3.2.1 Comparison of private equity with hedge funds

Consequently, the alternative asset universe in principle is unlimited, but if we look at the major types of funds in private equity, venture capital and buyouts and compare them against hedge funds, we see that in many ways there is a continuum (Table 3.1). While being part of private equity, buyouts to some degree overlap with hedge funds, as they not only share, in the words of *The Economist* (2006a), a *'taste for funny names and fancy fees'*, but also employ strategies that are oriented at investments in companies.

Hedge funds operate within the same regulatory framework as private equity funds and attract the same kind of institutional investors. Both asset classes have in general high minimum investment sums, thus effectively keeping the general public out. Of course, there are clear differences between private equity and hedge funds (Table 3.2).

---

[7] See http://en.wikipedia.org/wiki/Business_incubator [accessed 8 October 2006].
[8] Definition from http://www.investorwords.com/186/alternative_assets.html [accessed 27 January 2007].
[9] See Fraser-Sampson (2006a).

Table 3.1 Comparison company-oriented alternative assets

	VC funds	Buyout funds	Hedge funds
Targeted investments	SMEs	Large companies (private, but also public)	Publicly quoted companies
Instruments	Equity	Equity and debt	All plus derivatives
Investors	Institutions/public sector (government)	Institutions	Institutions
Exposure	Uncertainty	Risk	Risk
Approach	Long-term	Long-term	Short to medium-term
Involvement	Hands-on	Hands-on	Hands-off
Technique	Building company	Improving company	Market play
Drivers	Innovation and company building	Financial engineering and operational improvements	Market inefficiencies and financial engineering

Table 3.2 Private equity and hedge funds in comparison[10]

	Private equity	Hedge funds
Investment philosophy	Long-term investments in promising new and established non-listed companies	Utilization of market opportunities, free choice of investment techniques, such as short selling, leverage and derivatives
Management	Value creation-oriented portfolio management	Financially driven management (trader mindset)
Term	Usually 10 to 12 years	Unlimited
Investors' liquidity	Illiquid investments. Closed-end funds. Distributions are made at the discretion of the general partner	Fairly liquid (including complex derivatives). Open-ended funds, with periodic withdrawals possible
Capital contributions	Based on capital commitment drawdown over time. Fund size capped	100% contribution at subscription date. Fund size not limited
Performance based compensation	Carried interest on realized investments, subject to clawback	Incentive fee taken annually on realized and unrealized gains, no clawback but subject to 'high watermarks'[11]
Valuation	Valuation guidelines. Management fees based on capital commitments	Marked to market. Management fees based on net asset value
Exits	Comparatively difficult	Comparatively easy

---

[10] Based on Avida Advisors (2005) and Geller (2006).

[11] The high watermark refers to the highest peak in value that an investment has reached. It is used in the context of fund manager compensation. The high watermarks ensure that the manager does not get paid performance fees if he loses money but must get the value above the high watermark before receiving a performance bonus. For example, say after reaching a peak a hedge fund loses €10 million in year one, and then makes €15 million in year two. The manager therefore not only reached the high watermark but exceeded it by €5 million (€15 million − €10 million), which is the amount on which the manager gets paid the bonus and not €15 million.

3.2.1.1   Investment philosophy

Private equity funds undertake long-term investments in promising new and established non-listed companies. The business model is based on value creation, i.e. the selection of a management team, a company and a will to build a business. Particularly in venture capital, purely financial approaches do not work and techniques for assessment are mainly qualitative.

Hedge funds, on the other hand, tend to follow short-term strategies such as utilization of market opportunities and inefficiencies. Hedge funds have a free choice of investment techniques, such as short selling, leverage and derivatives, and rely to a large degree on quantitative models.

3.2.1.2   Management

Private equity funds create value through being actively involved in portfolio companies and, even sometimes, influencing its management. They engage in a significant amount of research regarding both the targeted companies and the industries in which they operate. Private equity funds are said to bring the perspective and skill set as 'strategic buyers', i.e. they have longer holding periods and are very interested in the strategic direction of the companies and industries in which they invest. Having said this, critics claim that buyout funds apply basic financial engineering to steady cash flow businesses and that their added value may be overstated.

On the other hand, hedge funds are usually described as having a trader mindset and bringing the perspective and skills of 'financial buyers', always on the look out for the next opportunity. Nevertheless, hedge funds are also increasingly seeking board seats and tying to influence management decisions made by companies in which they have invested.

3.2.1.3   Term

Private equity funds have a contractual lifetime of normally between 10 to 12 years, while that of hedge funds is theoretically unlimited. In practice many hedge funds fail or close shop either when things get too difficult or after their managers had a string of successes and retire.

3.2.1.4   Investors' liquidity

Private equity funds are closed-ended and are binding capital on average for three to five years typically, but potentially as long as ten years. Exits of portfolio companies and the associated distributions are made at the discretion of the general partner, and investors cannot withdraw before the end of the fund's lifetime. Investments are illiquid until an exit event occurs, and even where private equity funds exit a portfolio company though an IPO, they have to wait until the end of the so-called lock-up period before selling or trading company shares.[12]

---

[12] Usually in an initial public offering the lock-up period is determined by the underwriters based on the prevailing market conditions.

Generally, hedge funds trade in very liquid securities and also provide their investors with a lot of liquidity themselves. In theory they are opportunistic investors that will exit quickly and thus the complete antithesis of private equity. Hedge funds are open-ended and can offer rewards sooner as periodic withdrawals are possible. However, funds with more restrictive redemption provisions, such as one or two years' lock-up, can be observed in the market, but they still remain more 'liquid' than private equity funds. Hedge funds have a potential appetite for more short-term private equity strategies such as distressed investments and debt financing. Imitating such private equity strategies for long-term assets with questionable liquidity, such as corporate restructurings, however, is a risky proposition for hedge funds. As their money is short-term this can create a dangerous mismatch of maturities.

3.2.1.5 Capital contributions

Private equity funds only permit capital to be invested during the first few years. Their fund size is capped, and they are limited in their ability to take in new capital. Capital commitments are drawn down over time and re-investments are either not possible or subject to restrictions. Hedge funds require a 100% contribution at subscription date. They typically do not have size caps, and all their capital is available for re-investment.

3.2.1.6 Performance-based compensation

Private equity and hedge funds apply different methods of compensating professionals. Private equity funds have a fixed lifetime, and their value creation tends to show only after several years. They do not get a performance fee until the realization of investments and usually have to return all invested capital before any carried interest is paid to the fund managers. As there can be an influx and outflux of employees at various times during a fund's scheduled term, complex vesting provisions have to be put in place to assure that employees are treated fairly and receive proper incentives.

By contrast, a hedge fund's incentives accrue annually on realized and unrealized gains, and their employees are usually less locked in than their private equity counterparts. Private equity firms are said to be more concerned about the apparently better incentive package for hedge fund professionals than about their direct competition in transactions. Wilshire (2005) quotes an analysis done by Texas Pacific Group on the returns required from a private equity fund to match the same manager compensation (fees and carried interest) of a hedge fund manager (see Table 3.3).

Table 3.3 Private equity fund IRR required to match hedge fund dollars to the general partner

Hedge fund	8%	10%	15%	20%
Private equity fund	13%	14%	19%	24%

For example, a private equity fund would have to produce a return of 19% in order to match the same compensation that a hedge fund would produce with a return of 15%. Nevertheless, with private equity returns tending to be higher, the overall compensation can easily rival and even exceed that of hedge funds, although the fund managers have to be more patient.

3.2.1.7 Valuation

The private equity model is appropriate for assets for which there is no market and which are therefore illiquid and difficult to price. Valuations are based on guidelines rather than a broad consensus and, despite the notions surrounding 'fair value', tend to have a strong conservative bias. Therefore, management fees are typically based on capital commitments.

The majority of hedge fund assets can be priced with accuracy, with valuations subject to more significant scrutiny. This allows marking assets and liabilities to fair value on a periodic basis for purposes of fee calculation and admission or withdrawal of investors. Management and performance fees are determined annually based on the NAV of mostly unrealized investments.

3.2.1.8 Exits

In private equity generating profitable exits is far more difficult than for assets typically held by hedge funds. As equity is an asset with a theoretically unlimited upside, the exit becomes more important the longer the investment horizon. Selling equity, particularly controlling stakes, requires more effort than liquidating debt. As they are operating in public markets, hedge funds have the edge in exit speed and efficiency. Where private equity and hedge funds meet, for example in distressed situations, hedge fund investments, like distressed debt at a discount, are typically self-liquidating.

3.2.2 Encroachment and convergence

Admittedly our comparison between private equity and hedge funds is stereotypical. Hedge funds are not an asset class in the same regard as, say, buyout funds that in terms of structure and transactions types are arguably more standardized. Hedge funds comprise a variety of strategies that have no relevance to one another. Also, the belief that all hedge funds use complex trading strategies is just a broad generalization.[13]

Hybrid strategies and structures have blurred the line between private equity and hedge fund investing. For example, private equity funds also make strategic public investments and have tried to introduce hedge fund-style marked-to-market fees. Hedge funds have increasingly been active in areas that have been traditionally private equity, such as investments in private companies, mezzanine or distressed investing and are beginning to behave less like short-term traders and more like investors. There are rumours that buyout groups that in principle should not engage in hostile raids collude with hedge funds. Allegedly they secretly signed deals to buy shares from hedge funds as such a covert ally could provide a way to get around this obstacle. Some hedge funds have also adopted private equity-like structures like having fixed terms. There are even cross-over funds that combine private equity and hedge fund strategies within a single vehicle with fees and liquidity structure split accordingly. Such hybrids are said to be able to dampen overall risk while improving returns by employing capital more diversely.[14]

---

[13] Even for LTCM (Long-Term Capital Management), the famous hedge fund that collapsed in 1998 and that had employed Nobel laureates Robert Merton and Myron Scholes, market access and privileged information were more relevant than sophisticated models (see Burns, 2002). According to Case (2000), whatever technical advantage LTCM may have had over its competitors lay less in the models employed than in the traders' experience with them. The models apparently dated from the 1970s, and were readily available in the open literature.

[14] See Sormani (2005c).

Wilshire (2005) argues that issues of liquidity, valuation and investment discipline should keep the level of competition from hedge funds to the fringes of the private equity market.

Failure in the hedge fund and private equity world has often been associated with undisciplined behavior.

Wilshire (2005)

There are only a few strategies that allow a move into private equity while remaining disciplined. Consequently, the hedge funds' encroachment in private equity should remain restricted to distressed investments, mezzanine financing and the cross-over between public and private equity. Some believe that the cultures in private equity and hedge funds are likely to remain markedly distinct. As one private equity manager remarked on hedge funds, '*those guys have no idea of what they're getting into [. . .] Taking a company private is very different from trading stock*', whereas hedge fund managers do not hesitate to call the private equity managers 'dinosaurs'.[15]

However, hedge fund houses set up new private equity funds and private equity firms such as Bain Capital, Blackstone, Carlyle or Texas Pacific Group raise hedge funds. Particularly, Blackstone and Carlyle are examples for players that build broader alternative asset platforms and are doing private equity, hedge funds, hedge funds-of-funds, as well as real estate.[16] This also creates synergies on the fundraising side, as in most institutions there is one decision-maker in charge of all alternative assets. Moreover, fund-of-funds groups like Henderson Global Investors or Man Group offer hedge funds, private equity and real estate investments. This constellation makes sense, as this allows optimizing cash flow management. Hedge funds can serve as a supplement to private equity funds to improve their performance, by putting the undrawn commitments to work.[17] Industry experts believe that the convergence is unstoppable. As Axa Private Equity's Stephan Illenberger voiced in a 2006 limited partner conference, in '*10 years we will not speak about private equity anymore [. . .] hedge funds, public and private equity is merging*'.

3.2.3 Distressed assets

Private equity and hedge funds mainly meet in the market for distressed assets. Indeed, it is said that the mindset of hedge fund managers lends itself more to such transactions, as they invest at all levels of a company's capital structure including secured, unsecured debt and derivative instruments. Especially acquiring debt in a poorly performing business at a discount is something where hedge fund players have been active for a long time. Private equity funds, on the other hand, mainly look at turnarounds as an equity opportunity and rather invest behind third-party debt. Nevertheless, the difference is not too pronounced and hedge funds focusing on distressed situations begin to encroach on the space traditionally held by private equity firms.

For companies in financial distress, the original holders often sell the debt or equity to a new set of buyers, such as private equity firms or hedge funds, who then either try to restructure the company or turn it around. Restructuring refers to the rescue and recovery of businesses

---

[15] Quoted from Goldstein (2005).
[16] See AltAssets (2006a).
[17] See Meyer and Mathonet (2005).

close to insolvency or emerging from a formal insolvency process, whereas turnaround usually only refers to improving an under-performing business. 'Restructuring' and 'turnaround' are often used interchangeably, although there is an emerging distinction between the two.

The standard modus operandi for buyout funds is buying excellent assets, with excellent management teams to help them grow and to increase their profitability. By contrast, turnaround usually means buying an under-performing asset and often within a corporate undergoing change to return to a healthy situation. This is typically done by independent chief executives as 'company doctors' with the help of other independent company executives in the turnaround team, that provide industry expertise and specific skills, for example in finance, operations or manufacturing. This activity typically requires time that often goes beyond the usual patience level of hedge funds, while many private equity firms offer turnaround funding.

Box 3.2: Possible candidates for turnaround deals

According to Jon Moulton from Alchemy Partners – a specialist in turnarounds and public to privates in the UK – a private equity deal, to work as a turnaround, needs three factors: the company has to be worth rescuing, the owner and the management must be willing to cede control, and the key issue is that the company must need new capital.

> *'Many companies don't actually need new capital', says Moulton. 'They just need to reassure the banks that they will be repaid in a certain timeframe.'*
> Quoted from Sormani (2005a)

While the turnaround of a loss-making business can be a costly exercise, turnarounds do not necessarily involve a high purchase price. Alchemy, for example, claims that they might buy a business for a few pounds and then invest between £10 million and £30 million to sort it out.[18]

On the other hand, distress of larger corporations is usually approached as a restructuring exercise – often involving redundancies – that usually works quicker than a turnaround. Transactions in the restructuring area include M&A, tender offers, leveraged buyouts, divestitures, spin-offs, equity carve-outs, liquidations or reorganization of a company's operations.

Although companies suffer financial distress mainly during recessions, interesting opportunities can be found in both good and bad economic conditions. Funds specializing in this area provide good diversification within the limited partner's portfolio, and many limited partners have an allocation of around 10% to distressed specialists. Limited partner concerns mainly relate to the complexity of doing distressed transactions that are often time-consuming, result in longer holding periods and can be riskier than more traditional buyouts. Teams need a good track record and have characteristics similar to other buyout firms, but with expertise in the distressed field. They also need an in-depth understanding of local markets and regulatory environment.

---

[18] See Sormani (2005a).

Importing US restructuring practices and applying them to distressed situations across Europe is still problematic. There are different regulatory issues in each country with little harmonization, which presents significant obstacles to company rescue techniques. Although there is some pressure to adopt the US Chapter 11 method of restructuring, there is a natural resistance to change.[19] Limited partners need to focus on local players who know the law in their country, and experienced managers in that niche are rare to find. In fact, it is a small universe with not much competition for deals. Each distressed situation is so unique that it is hard to benchmark, and limited partners will find it nearly impossible to find relevant industry data. Anyway, most of the time these deals are undisclosed so as not to jeopardize the restructuring and turnaround efforts.

3.3   MEZZANINE FINANCING

The term mezzanine generally refers to a layer of financing between a company's senior debt and equity.[20] Structurally, it is subordinate in priority of payment to senior debt, but senior in rank to common stock or equity. As the name suggests, mezzanine finance is a hybrid of debt and equity financing.[21] See Figure 3.2.

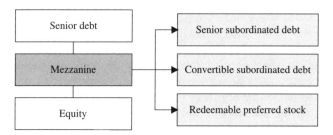

Figure 3.2   Mezzanine financing
Source: Fitch Ratings.

In acquisitions and buyouts, mezzanine can be used to prioritize new owners ahead of existing owners in the event that a bankruptcy occurs. However, it is typically used to finance the expansion of existing companies. Basically it is debt capital that gives the lender the rights to convert to an ownership or equity interest in the company if the loan is not paid back in time and in full. It incorporates equity-based options, such as warrants, with a lower-priority debt. Mezzanine debt is generally the lowest-ranking debt obligation in a borrower's capital structure and contains only a very loose covenant package. It is actually closer to equity than debt, as the debt is usually only of importance in the event of bankruptcy and as it is generally subordinated to debt provided by senior lenders. Depending on how

---

[19] Chapter 11 of the US Bankruptcy Code contains the provisions for court-supervised reorganization of debtor companies. In a Chapter 11 proceeding, the debtor maintains control of the business and usually proposes a plan of reorganization to keep its business alive and pay creditors over time.
[20] In the USA, mezzanine also refers to the funding of venture companies pre-IPO.
[21] In the USA, the typical definition for mezzanine financing is late stage venture capital, for companies expecting to go public usually within six to 12 months, usually so structured to be repaid from proceeds of a public offering, or to establish a floor price for a public offer. In Europe, mezzanine finance has usually been associated with private equity buyouts. The level of mezzanine financing is closely tied to the overall level of M&A activity.

the contract is structured and under certain conditions, mezzanine debt bears the advantage that it accounts, at least partly, for equity in the company's balance sheet or at least for economic capital. For investors, mezzanine returns are higher than senior debt but lower than the returns demanded from private equity funds.

As a quasi-equity product, mezzanine allows the company to retain a more robust capital structure and thus makes it easier to obtain additional standard bank financing. Companies seek mezzanine financing for all kinds of corporate requirements, such as buying out minority shareholders, M&A, launching of new products, or expansion into new countries. To do so, they must demonstrate a history of profitability and a viable expansion plan for the business. Private mezzanine debt securities usually have a maturity of between six and eight years, with little or no amortization. As lenders provide mezzanine debt very quickly and allegedly with comparatively little due diligence and little or no collateral on the part of the borrower, this type of financing is aggressively priced with the lender seeking a return in the 20–30% range. They are highly negotiated instruments and thus illiquid investments with no active market. As a result, any trading usually involves a negotiated process directly involving buyer and seller.

Mezzanine is also some times termed 'sponsorless' due to the absence of a private equity sponsor. It does not require companies to relinquish control or significantly dilute equity and therefore is seen as ideal for profitable companies in need of growth financing. Mezzanine bridges the gap created where banks consider further loans as too risky and where equity is either not available or unwanted. Mezzanine providers often take a minimal equity stake in the company in the form of warrants and, as long as the company performs, are very hands-off investors. They are prepared to lend against the company's business plan and cash flows and, unlike banks, often do not require collateral. Therefore, a company considering mezzanine needs to demonstrate growth in the business plan. For them, mezzanine may be a more expensive but also more flexible solution. Depending on its cash flows, growth potential and financing timeframe, the company can negotiate a higher coupon and fewer warrants or vice versa. It can also avoid giving out warrants entirely if there is a sufficiently strong cash flow to pay dividends instead.

In Europe, mainly banks and independent specialized 'investment boutiques' provide mezzanine capital, whereas in the USA historically insurance companies, pension funds and endowments have been the largest providers. Particularly, insurance companies place great importance on the generation of regular income to reach their goal of paying guaranteed interest. Supply and demand for mezzanine is mainly driven by the commercial banks on the one side and the high yield market on the other. Depending on the economic environment and with increases in corporate defaults commercial banks periodically tighten their lending standards, whereas the usually less expensive high-yield market has an implicit minimum threshold between $125 million and $150 million.[22] Where bank lenders reduce their commitment levels and the high-yield market raises its minimum threshold level, mezzanine can fill the gap. However, a stronger high-yield market has a negative impact on the demand for mezzanine financing.

There is growing convergence between mezzanine financing and private equity, and a number of private equity firms have set up dedicated mezzanine funds. Investors typically expect fairly stable and, on a 'risk-adjusted' basis, more attractive returns compared with

---

[22] See Capital Eyes (2003).

other private equity funds. Mezzanine funds invest by purchasing subordinated debentures with equity warrants from their portfolio companies. To a large degree also the J Curve phenomenon offers an explanation for investors' interest in mezzanine funds. Unlike the typical VC funds, an average-performing mezzanine fund is able to avoid the steep negative returns as it tends to invest in mature companies with predictable cash flows. Investors are attracted by quicker returns compared with buyouts and particularly VC funds. Mezzanine funds generally do not take a very active role on the board of portfolio companies and investing is typically not as resource-intensive as in other private equity funds. Consequently, management fees for mezzanine funds traditionally have been on the low side.

Mezzanine funds earn their return from two main sources. Firstly, they receive regular interest payments, usually quarterly, from their portfolio companies. Secondly, they benefit from the gain on the equity through the so-called 'equity kicker'. The 'equity kicker' is usually a contingent common equity interest, either by way of warrants or a conversion option. In this context the preferred return becomes an important feature. By requiring mezzanine managers to provide this contractual term, limited partners aim to ensure that the general partner shares in partnership profits only if the equity warrants perform well.[23]

Particularly for the European private or family-owned companies in the mid-market, mezzanine is an interesting general financing alternative. An example is Triumph Adler in Germany, which was a turnaround case with €30 million provided in mezzanine.[24] Another case is Italy, where theoretically there is, according to Sormani (2003c), a strong growth potential for buyouts, but where mid-market companies are often wary of taking on private equity backing. Here, like elsewhere in the Southern European countries, managers build a business for the long term and are less inclined to sell a business on. For such companies a more interesting form of raising capital is mezzanine, and seeing the interesting characteristics of mezzanine funds, it cannot come as a surprise that also specialized funds-of-funds have entered the European market.

- In Germany, in 2005 VCM Capital Management and Golding Capital Partners closed two mezzanine funds-of-funds that provided more than €500 million exclusively for investment in Europe and the USA. The first, VCM Golding Mezzanine, closed on €200 million in May 2005, above its original €150 million target. The Europe-focused VCM Golding Mezzanine II was raised in just nine months and closed on €238 million, above its €100 million to €150 million target, indicating the strong institutional investor interest, including pension funds, insurance companies and endowments in Germany, Austria and Switzerland.[25]
- In 2004, Finama Private Equity, a wholly owned subsidiary of France's top mutual company Groupama, launched the first French-based mezzanine fund-of-funds Quartilium Mezzanine focusing on European and US mezzanine funds. The promoters of this vehicle specifically pointed to the possibility of smoothing the J Curve and marketed it as an adequate solution either for a first time investor, or for an investor who has already invested in private equity and wishes to reduce its global risk.
- In 2005 Partners Group also launched its own mezzanine fund-of-funds, Global Mezzanine 2005, for investments across all geographies.

---

[23] The preferred return and related contractual terms are treated differently for venture capital, buyout or mezzanine funds. This subject will be discussed in more detail in a later chapter.
[24] See Hickey (2006).
[25] See AltAssets (2006b).

Also, other players in private equity are seeing the attractions of mezzanine financing (see Figure 3.3). Where equity providers experience lower returns, leveraging limited partnership structures may be a means of satisfying various investor return thresholds. For larger private equity firms, setting up a mezzanine fund alongside their private equity fund can be attractive, particularly as they would not want the mezzanine tranche of their deals to be arranged by a rival. However, investors often see a potential conflict of interest in such 'captive' mezzanine funds and the funds managed by the same firm that provide the equity. Promoters of such captive mezzanine firms counter that in reality few private equity firms regularly compete with one another and that Chinese Walls are put in place. In any case, this discussion demonstrates that despite the lower perceived risks of mezzanine funds, limited partners have to follow the same rigorous due diligence as for all other types of private equity funds.

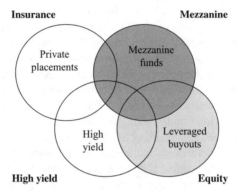

Figure 3.3   US institutions playing in multiple asset classes
Source: Fitch Ratings.

3.4 OVERLAP WITH PUBLIC MARKET

Finally, the dividing line between publicly quoted and private equity is also blurred. Areas of overlap are, for example, private investments in public equity (PIPEs), publicly quoted companies going private, or publicly quoted private equity. PIPE deals involve the selling of publicly traded shares to private investors, rather than to the public through a registered offering. As the sale of the securities is not pre-registered with the Stock Exchange Commission (SEC), they are 'restricted' and cannot be immediately resold by the investors into the public markets. Typically, smaller public companies undertake PIPE transactions and sell shares at a slight discount to the public market price. Significant advantages of PIPEs over traditional public offerings is that they are as predictable as a private placement, that they can be completed rapidly – typically two to three weeks from kick-off to closing – and that they can be executed at reasonable transaction costs. Investors benefit from a nearly liquid security for an attractive price. Moreover, it allows them to acquire a sizeable position in the company without being faced with a rising stock price caused by their own purchases. The selling company typically agrees, as part of the deal, to use its best efforts to register the resale of those restricted securities with the SEC. PIPE transactions come in many varieties, differing in structure and terms of the deal, the securities offered and the investor base. While PIPEs are quite common in the USA, where their frequency follows more or less the ups and downs of the stock markets, they can be illegal in other countries where PIPEs must be preceded by a rights issue. Historically, according to Conza (2002), PIPEs were not sold to traditional private equity investors, but rather to sophisticated public market investors that focused not only on the fundamentals of the company but also on the technical aspects of public market investing dynamics, such as trading volume, float and volatility. However, increasingly private equity firms are making investments in PIPEs.

To the extent that Sarbanes-Oxley causes public companies to be less competitive there is an opportunity for the private equity industry in taking these businesses private and putting some energy back into growing them.

KKR's Henry Kravis (quoted from Demaria, 2005)

Occasionally, private equity investors will acquire all shares of a publicly traded company in a process known as a 'going-private' deal. In recent years, mainly US-based private equity firms have taken many previously public companies such as Hertz, Neiman Marcus, Metro-Goldwyn-Mayer, or Toys 'R' Us private. Some industry experts believe that the Sarbanes-Oxley Act of 2002, also known as 'SOX', is one of the reasons why an increasing number of companies in the USA have been opting to go private. SOX has probably been a factor in this wave of privatizations but, according to Morrow (2005), industry experts, such as Standard & Poor's Chief Economist David Wyss, believe that it is a relatively minor one and rather a transitional phenomenon as companies have been adjusting to a new regulatory environment. It is certainly true that compliance with SOX weighs disproportionately on the smaller public corporations that are operating on thin margins and where the additional cost is a significant percentage of their annual revenues. For such companies going private to avoid SOX costs may be meaningful, which also makes them interesting targets for private equity firms.

Finally, an important area of overlap are publicly quoted venture capital and private equity firms such as 3i Group PLC quoted on the London Stock Exchange (LSE) and part of the FTSE 100 Index, Gewestelijke Investerings Maatschappij Vlaanderen (GIMV) quoted on Euronext Brussels, or Japan Associated Finance Co., Ltd (JAFCO) listed on the Tokyo Stock Exchange. New entrants into the market of quoted private equity vehicles are, for example, KKR Private Equity Investors, a Euronext-listed fund investing in KKR partnerships as well as directly in KKR deals, or Apollo's AP Alternative Assets. Investors can also access private equity through Exchange Traded Funds (ETFs), i.e. vehicles that are tied to the performance of various indices. An example for such an ETF related to private equity is 'Power Shares International Listed Private Equity Portfolio' that focuses on non-US stocks tied to private equity.[26] In the UK, VC trusts are traded on the London Stock Exchange and last but not least there are publicly quoted private equity funds-of-funds, a subject that we will discuss in greater detail in a following chapter.

---

[26] It tracks, among others, the Euronext-listed vehicles of KKR and Apollo, and vehicles associated with 3i and Permira. See Snow (2007).

3.5 CONCLUSION

In this chapter we could only give a broad outline of the private equity universe. Trying to give a complete description of this continuously shifting landscape is bound to fail, as it would essentially require a treatise of the entire world of financing. In many ways the world of private equity resembles an evolutionary arms race, a theme that we will pick up again later in the book.

Instead, we focus in our discussion on the 'plain vanilla' VC fund, which arguably is suited best to explain the principles of institutional investing in the private equity asset class. Moreover, due to the lack of reliable data, VC funds are more challenging from the limited partner's point of view and therefore provide important insights into the management of a private equity fund investment program.

4

Risk Management Lessons from a Listed Private Equity Fund-of-Funds

[Private Equity Holding (PEH)] followed a policy of overcommitting to funds. This went sour when exits dried up and funds, rather than returning cash to PEH, demanded more injections of capital. PEH cut the nominal value of its own shares by 90% last week, in recognition of the severe losses of the last 18 months.

Hutchings (2003)

In this chapter we look at Private Equity Holding AG (PEH), a Swiss private equity fund-of-funds founded in March 1997 and at that time managed by the Vontobel Group. Domiciled in Zug, PEH together with its subsidiaries comprises the Private Equity Group. According to its website, PEH invested '*primarily in top-quality private equity funds with a focus on Western Europe, selectively also on the USA and Israel. In addition to investing through funds, it also makes direct investments in promising companies either together with its partner funds or as pre-IPO financings.*' It was listed on the Swiss Stock Exchange (SWX) only two years after its inception in response to the strong retail investors' demand for VC that characterized this period. PEH had raised almost CHF1.4 billion by 1999, but this impressive start was followed by a deep crisis. For a number of reasons, in 2001 and 2002 it was brought to the verge of illiquidity and had to sell a substantial part of its portfolio, with the associated losses.[1]

We take a brief look at the publicly quoted private equity funds-of-funds market and explain the relevant period of PEH's history. For the purpose of analyzing this type of investment vehicle we discuss ratios as analytical instruments and benchmark PEH against a comparable vehicle, Castle Private Equity (CPE).

4.1 RELEVANCE OF THE PRIVATE EQUITY HOLDING CASE

What explains PEH's crisis and near collapse? At first glance, one is tempted to point to the dotcom bubble and dismiss the whole matter as the inevitable result of a cyclical downturn. Reckless behavior in managing PEH's activities, such as an overly aggressive over-commitment strategy violating own investment guidelines, is another quick – perhaps too quick, and not necessarily accurate – answer.

---

[1] We thank Jérôme Marcelino for his research on Private Equity Holding AG. This chapter is mainly based on his analysis, in Marcelino (2006).

The idea that setbacks are frequently the consequence of mere bad luck is a seductive one. It is psychologically comforting to those who have not themselves experienced disaster, which may be the reason why it is so often offered as a consolation.

Cohen and Gooch (1991)

To some degree, all of these factors are of relevance and the explanation may even be soothing, as it puts the responsibility on human folly. Certainly, a manager of a private equity funds investment program should know that he has to operate in a highly cyclical environment and has to manage accordingly. But is it feasible or meaningful to avoid all risks when being active in – to go with the French expression for venture capital – 'capital risque'? What were the main risks to which PEH was, or was perceived to be, exposed?

- The loss of capital is the typical investor's major concern, and usually a high degree of diversification is seen as the appropriate remedy to protect against this risk. PEH, however, apart from its relatively narrow vintage year spread, was well diversified when it ran into its problems, which may have created a sense of false security.
- We lack insights into the thinking of PEH's management at that time, but the perceived threat of under-performance versus the stock market in general, or other players in private equity in particular, could form part of the explanation of PEH's near downfall. The perceived risk of generating a return below a set threshold, could have brought PEH's management to embark on a so-called 'over-commitment strategy' that, as a consequence, created the critical liquidity shortfall.
- Apparently, and to no small degree, operational risk, i.e. not respecting investment guidelines, contributed to PEH's crisis. At that time, the guidelines might have been more suitable for a portfolio in 'cruising speed', but building up a fund-of-funds is difficult and requires a different approach. Often during this phase the management of a private equity funds investment program may find guidelines overly restrictive and inadequate. Under such circumstances it is all too human to throw some restraints overboard.

The immaturity of the publicly quoted private equity fund-of-funds vehicles, the generally under-developed toolset for their management and the still poor understanding of the technicalities at that time appear to have contributed to many of the issues, and we cannot escape the conclusion that it holds lessons for all investors in private equity funds that have to sail between the Scylla of protecting their capital and the Charybdis of not achieving their target return.

The listed fund-of-funds market is interesting. The problem is that it is totally under-researched.

Urs Wietlisbach, Partners Group (Meek, 2002)

This case study covers the period 1997–2003 and is an 'unauthorized history', but it has to be made clear that there is no intention to come up with a 'villain' whose fault it is that PEH came close to failure. Moreover, PEH managed a turnaround, so this history is by no means a reflection on this company's current status. By definition, private equity is an opaque industry and it can be assumed that many managers of institutional alternative investment programs at that time – the burst of the dotcom bubble – made comparable mistakes. PEH as a listed vehicle simply had the bad luck of being more visible and exposed than others.

However, this case is well documented and, as under a microscope, we can analyze the developing story and draw important lessons for the management of a private equity funds investment program. This analysis is based entirely on publicly available information. It therefore has shortcomings as it lacks insight into other reasons for certain decisions and cannot avoid arguing with hindsight.

4.2   THE SWISS PRIVATE EQUITY FUNDS-OF-FUNDS INDUSTRY

The private equity fund-of-funds concept began to take off in Switzerland in 1996 to 1997. Cowley (2002) explains the size of this industry as a legacy of the country's well-developed banking and financial services industry. There is a comparatively large institutional investment market, and Switzerland has, for a number of years now, represented a deep pool of potential capital for private equity. Its private equity fund-of-funds industry has an international mix of professionals with diverse backgrounds in direct private equity, industry, consulting and investment management that enables fundraising on a global scale through the understanding of local investment cultures. A non-exhaustive list of important players comprises Adveq, Partners Group, Capital Dynamics, Capvent or Unigestion. These players have also been expanding internationally. Adveq created a German subsidiary, Capvent set up offices in London and India, and Unigestion has offices in Munich, Paris and London.

4.2.1   The market for publicly quoted private equity funds-of-funds

One of the most innovative players in this market is the Partners Group. In 2006 it did its own IPO and previously, together with Liechtenstein Global Trust (LGT), launched the listed CPE. Rösch (2000) suggests a spectrum of the Swiss publicly listed private equity fund-of-funds market between CPE and PEH. CPE is described as the 'most conservative' and PEH the 'most aggressive' in this spectrum, but both of them were then seen as meaningful add-ons to portfolios. Another publicly quoted private equity fund-of-funds is ShaPE, backed by Julius Baer and Robeco. Listed private equity funds-of-funds offer liquidity and a quick build-up of a diversified portfolio of private equity funds. They were set up specifically to attract investors such as high net worth individuals wanting to get access to the private equity asset class without going through the set-up of a dedicated program and without being exposed to the illiquidity of unquoted investments.

It is often difficult for institutional investors to get an allocation to private equity, and pension funds in particular need to make a case to regulators for making an investment in an illiquid and risky asset class such as private equity. For example, German insurers and pension fund managers have to invest in private equity products that comply with specific regulatory and legal requirements, such as 'Deckungsstock' and 'Spezialfondsfähigkeit'. Publicly quoted private equity already meets these stringent requirements and addresses the hurdles of regulatory requirements, tax efficiency and transparency. Indeed, pension funds like that of Swissair's flight attendants, that of the city of Basel's personnel or that of the oil company Petroplus invested high amounts in PEH.

Publicly quoted private equity is based on familiar investment trust-like structures and promises liquidity, instant access to a diversified portfolio, and management expertise. Moreover, institutional investors that are new to private equity often use such products to gain an insight into the market before deciding to manage their own fund investments.

4.2.2 Importance for investors

Listed vehicles could be a meaningful way of entering the asset class as they increase flexibility in tactical asset allocations and allow fast exposure to private equity fund investments, while maintaining some degree of liquidity. Whereas in the usual limited partnership structure investors exercise tight control over usage of funding, i.e. strict segregation of management fees from capital calls, in publicly quoted private equity interests are less well aligned and shareholders' control over the usage of the capital is reduced. The influence shareholders have on listed private equity companies cannot be compared to the strong involvement investors exercise (or should exercise) in the case of limited partnerships. PEH is a very rare case, where shareholders' voices helped to drive the change.

Over recent years listed private equity has had its ups and downs. While the sector has begun to gain wider recognition as it offers immediate exposure to the asset class particularly for retail investors, some do not see a huge appetite for listed funds-of-funds. Analysts claim that during 2005 publicly quoted private equity 'returns remain a long way ahead of quoted equity markets',[2] but the point made by Stephan Hepp from Swiss private equity advisory firm SCM remains valid – these vehicles 'display the same characteristics as public stocks because that's what they are [. . .] Any gain that they make is also not necessarily to do with the performance of the underlying investments, but rather a function of market sentiment.'[3]

For publicly quoted private equity liquidity may also be an illusion, as for second-line stocks, share price discounts can make it difficult, if not impossible, to get out without incurring losses. Certainly, in principle the lack of liquidity is priced into the market, but extreme discounts are not unusual. The thin market results in high bid – ask spreads. Again there is often a discount for the majority of such structures, the market price reflecting the relative illiquidity of the market. This can of course go in both directions. If one wants to buy a large position, it will be difficult to find sellers and may therefore take several months while pushing the price up; likewise, if one has a larger position, it may take several months to sell it. The significant discounts on the NAV are said to be comparable to that observed for secondary transactions of unlisted funds. To quote a manager from LGT: 'Listed vehicles do offer liquidity to their investors, but we're not talking about a daily 10% turnover rate [. . .] It's best to think of the liquidity of these vehicles in terms of weeks or months. If you have a larger position in the fund then, obviously, it will take a longer time to sell your shares, three months maybe. Waiting three months to sell and doing so at a significant discount to NAV may leave investors no better off than if they had committed to unlisted private equity and were forced to sell through the traditional secondary market. But that level of liquidity is still significantly higher than the typical ten to 15-year lock-up in traditional private equity structures.'[4] Some publicly listed funds-of-funds, such as AIG Private Equity or Julius Baer's ShaPE, claim that they are more liquid as a sizeable parent company is willing and able to buy back shares if necessary.

According to Meek (2004), the 'fact remains that these vehicles were set up specifically to attract less sophisticated investors, who may not have known much about private equity as an asset class'. This statement may have been true at that time, but recently there has

---

[2] See Brierley and Barnard (2005).
[3] See Meek (2004).
[4] See Meek (2004).

been an increasing institutional interest in managing undrawn commitments of private equity investment programs through investments in publicly quoted private equity.

4.2.3 Growing opportunities

Very often in private equity funds-backed collateralized fund obligations (CFO) – one example is Nomura's SVG Diamond – secondary transactions are foreseen to get a vintage year spread and a mature basic portfolio that already starts to generate some liquidity through re-flows. After the burst of the dotcom bubble, when a lot of institutional investors came to the conclusion that private equity was not for them, savvy investors like Coller, Landmark or Lexington entered the market. They basically ran a 'convergence strategy' – not unlike hedge funds – where fund shares were bought up by investors that were less exposed to short-term liquidity needs, better in assessing the inherent value of the funds, or better in extracting value from these funds. This logic was not difficult to follow and the secondary market also followed its own cycle and quickly became competitive. With fewer institutions forced to sell their stakes in private equity funds, far more competitors were chasing too few deals. To some degree, in the context of such CFOs publicly quoted private equity may be able to act as a substitute for secondary transactions.

Publicly quoted private equity is of relevance in the context of over-commitment strategies – ironically, the cause of PEH's problems – and is becoming increasingly part of an overall asset allocation for private equity funds programs.[5] It is believed that the listed private equity sector has a role to play in providing flexibility and in accelerating exposure to the asset class. It can complement commitments to limited partnerships by giving investors immediate exposure to relatively mature portfolios and be used as another tool to rebalance and finetune a portfolio. In this context, publicly quoted private equity funds-of-funds are interesting not for medium- to long-term potential but as part of a short-term strategy.

Beyond Switzerland, internationally listed vehicles have also become more widespread. To name a few, Schroders Ventures, Pantheon or Standard Life have been active in this market already for some time. In Scandinavia, Amanda Capital Group is a publicly listed private equity fund-of-funds. In 2004, ING launched Australia's first listed vehicle PEAL LIC, and also Macquarie Private Capital Group manages an Australian Stock Exchange-listed private equity fund-of-funds.

4.3 COMMITMENTS AND INVESTMENTS

Before going into the details of PEH's history, it is useful to discuss the difference between commitments and investments and its implications in the context of private equity funds. Commitments constitute a limited partner's obligation to provide a certain amount of capital to a private equity fund when the general partner asks for capital. It has to be made clear that the commitment available for funding will not be needed at once but is drawn down and invested over time. If we plot the average proportion of undrawn commitments,[6] repayments, management fees and investments over the lifetime of a fund (Figure 4.1), we see that their balance follows a quite distinctive lifecycle.

---

[5] See Meyer and Mathonet (2005).
[6] Also often called outstanding commitments.

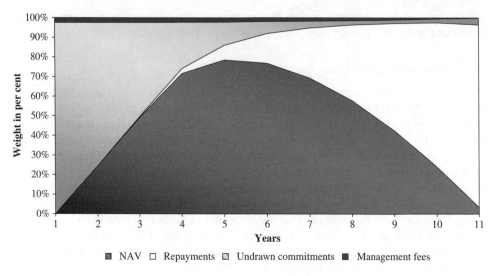

Figure 4.1   Private equity fund lifecycle

4.3.1   Importance of over-commitments

The commitments are indicative for the portfolio composition, whereas investments represent the real allocation of capital and are captured in the NAV. This observation motivates so-called 'over-commitment strategies' for minimizing the opportunity costs of the undrawn capital.

On average, only 20–40% of a limited partner's commitments are invested per year. It generally takes three to six years for a fund to call most of the capital from its investors, depending on the attractiveness of the investment opportunities. On the other hand, funds will start to exit portfolio companies and return money to the limited partners before all the capital has been invested. In practice, these repayments are often netted against capital calls for a fund's new and follow-on investments. As a consequence, the resources available are never completely invested in private equity partnerships. 'Historically, the average exposure ranges from 60 to 70%.'[7] Investors in private equity are looking for abnormal returns higher than in the other traditional asset classes. Therefore, the level of investment has to be raised to 100% by committing more than the available funding. PEH continued its investment pace unabated during its first four years of operation, where investments rose to almost CHF1 billion – about twice as much as commitments.

4.3.2   Best practices

The over-commitment ratio (OCR) gives an insight into PEH's management of its capital and its investment policy:

$$OCR = \frac{\text{total fund commitment}}{\text{shareholders' equity} + \text{long-term debt}}$$

---

[7] From Castle Private Equity AG Annual Report 2000, p. 17.

PEH defined total fund commitments as fair value plus undrawn capital commitments. They are related to the consolidated long-term debt with the shareholders' equity.[8] The formula was taken from the 2005 investment guidelines, though the method used is the same since PEH started its activities:

$$OCR = \frac{\text{undrawn commitment} + \text{fair value of paid-in capital}}{\text{shareholders' equity} + \text{long-term debt}}$$

An OCR of lower than 100% suggests an inefficient use of resources. Above 100%, the ability of an over-committed fund-of-funds like PEH to honor its commitments and to avoid becoming a defaulting investor essentially depends on the reliability of the cash flow forecasting. Opinions vary on what degree of over-commitments would still be seen as prudent. Singleton and Henshilwood (2003) gathered the views of eight leading fund-of-funds managers and gatekeepers. See Table 4.1.

Table 4.1 Over-commitment level

Manager	Level of commitment estimated	Comments
A	Between 150% and 330%	
B	125%	
C	135%	
D	175%	
E	150%	
F	167%	
G	90%	Would top up with listed PE vehicles
H	130%	

Source: Singleton and Henshilwood (2003).

Their view was that 150% of the strategic asset allocation is a suitable target to aim for in terms of commitments. It has to be kept in mind that their poll aimed to research market practices to achieve any given level of strategic asset allocation to private equity, but did not specifically relate to the question of liquidity risk incurred by a fund-of-funds. However, their findings give a feel for the usual over-commitment ratios. With the exception of fund manager 'A', all the others recommended ratios that are clearly below 200%.

4.3.3 Over-commitments and risks

There are two angles to look at when discussing over-commitment strategies. Firstly, over-commitments are necessary to reduce the 'cash drag' from which particularly publicly quoted private equity funds-of-funds suffer. Here investors commit all their capital at once and it needs to be quickly put to work as otherwise only low returns are generated, with negative effect on the total return. As Urs Wietlisbach of Partners Group remarked, 'it's a very difficult thing to get right and requires a huge amount of research and analysis into the historic cash flows in the private equity market'.

---

[8] Here we can notice that, the fair value is used for both the denominator and numerator. As we will see later, valuation is a complex issue in private equity and this has most probably played a role in the (near) fall of PEH.

Secondly, over-commitments are necessary because of the long lead times caused, for example, through sourcing opportunities, conducting due diligence or negotiating the limited partnership agreements. Over the lifetime of a fund the total commitment is generally never fully drawn, occasionally limited partners allow re-investments and most funds ultimately request a maximum of between 80% and 95% of the committed capital, although during market downturns funds often run out of money and approach their investors to raise so-called 'side funds' – a subject we will explore in more detail in a later chapter.

Many saw PEH's aggressive over-commitment strategy to venture backfired and so it was forced to downsize.

Sormani (2003b)

It is clear that one cannot sign for more than one expects to get as returns from the existing portfolio. Consequently, the long-term average return of an asset class puts a ceiling on over-committing.[9] In the case of buyout funds, average returns are higher than those for VC funds where returns also tend to be more cyclical and where liquidity often 'dries up' over protracted periods. Consequently, for VC-focused programs over-commitment ratios would be significantly lower than in the case of later stage private equity. But at the end of the 1990s nobody was too pessimistic about VC returns.

Having said this, over-committing is essentially 'leveraging over time' as it has the same magnifying effect on returns and also – as a result of forced sell-offs – on losses. Generally, the combination of leverage and an illiquid market is highly dangerous. In a liquid market one could be over-committed without any serious harm. If one runs out of resources, one can easily realize assets. But this is just theory, as investor confidence has an impact on liquidity. When markets plunge, there are simply not enough buyers. Even in public markets it is a mistake to believe that they have an obligation to provide buyers to accommodate sellers. Without over-commitments one never gets into the problem of realizing assets. If you are not over-committed you do not run out of liquidity and you cannot be forced to sell – liquidity is irrelevant. But an over-committed private equity fund-of-funds may be forced to sell, which, because of the contractual illiquidity, the thin market for such assets and the negotiation under time pressure, will nearly always result in prices to the seller's disadvantage.

4.4   THE RISE AND (NEAR) FALL OF PRIVATE EQUITY HOLDING

PEH came to the market right in time for an unprecedented boom in VC. 1997 was an exceptional year for the private equity industry, fundraising and investment volume in both the USA and Europe went far beyond previously achieved levels. PEH started with CHF400 million as resources available for investment activities, put the capital provided by investors quickly to work and was able to post profits as soon as at the end of its second financial year.

---

[9] Simplistically one could think of this ceiling as mainly driven by the average percentage of the capital called and the average return for a private equity fund. As on average never more than 90% of the commitment will be 'out of the house' at any point in time (allowing at least approximately 110% over-commitment) and taking the usual – probably too optimistic – assumption of 10% to 15% average return should allow an OCR of between 120% and 125% over the long term.

4.4.1 Opportunities and growth

Within its first three years, PEH's portfolio composition underwent significant changes. From 1997 until 2000 competition for participating in attractive VC funds was becoming more and more intense. We have no indications that this was the case for PEH, but generally there is a danger that under these circumstances management's selectivity when assessing new opportunities slips and that the due diligence conducted is not as rigorous as before. Industry-wide that was especially the case for Internet start-up companies and for the VC funds focusing on that sector during the dotcom bubble.

4.4.1.1 Shift toward VC funds

During its early years, direct investments and loans given to companies had the higher weight in PEH's portfolio. There could be two reasons for this. Firstly, for a first-time fund-of-funds like PEH it could be difficult to get access to high-quality funds – particularly in the overheated market environment during the late 1990s. However, with Vontobel as a highly reputable backer it should not have been too difficult for PEH to get established in the market, and indeed its fund portfolio comprises a number of well-known private equity fund 'brands'. The second, and probably more relevant, reason is the time lag associated with sourcing fund proposals, doing the due diligence, and negotiating the terms and conditions. Most of all, the time when a fund is closed and finally starts its investment activities depends to a large degree on the other limited partners. This, however, characterizes the start-up phase of a fund-of-funds and consequently in 1998 the balance between fund and direct investments was reversed. In fact, direct investments and loans were gradually reduced afterwards and by the end of 2001 represented only 10% of the amounts invested, although PEH continued to achieve most of its returns through its direct investment portfolio.[10]

There were also other shifts in PEH's portfolio composition. In the first year, it had a stronger orientation toward buyouts and balanced funds, but during 1998 it increasingly overweighted venture capital: 'The fund portfolio was expanded in the financial year 1998/99 as planned. In particular, allocations to the venture capital sector were increased, [. . .] as this segment [is seen] as being especially attractive in the medium term.'[11] This trend continued during 1999 when 'the strategic decision to overweight venture funds was systematically implemented'.[12] Initially being oriented toward the later stages and direct investments, it ended up being strongly exposed to VC funds.

As Sormani (2003b) observed in the context of private equity funds-of-funds, the 'only way you can keep investors in a listed vehicle happy is by delivering good news frequently enough to outweigh the bad'. For the average shareholder, valuations in venture capital are difficult to understand and will often be mistrusted. The typically pronounced J Curve development of VC funds' interim valuations in combination with a market downturn can mean the 'death' of a listed vehicle.

---

[10] See Rösch (2000). A detailed analysis of PEH direct investment activities goes beyond the scope of this chapter, however, direct investments are often also seen as another way to manage over-commitments.

[11] Extract from: 'PEH AG, 1998/99 Annual Report', page 4: 'Report on the Financial Year 1998/99'.

[12] Extract from: 'PEH AG, 1999/00 Annual Report', page 7: 'Report on the Financial Year 1999/00'.

4.4.1.2 Taking risks

In the annual report, PEH's management explained that *'the risk to the investor's capital is reduced by diversifying its private equity financings among different sectors, regions, stages of corporate development, types of financing arrangement and the times at which capital is provided'*.[13] It is a fair comment to see this as a very incomplete model of the risks to which a VC fund-of-funds is exposed. As the coming events demonstrated, it notably ignores the timing of the fund portfolio's cash flow patterns and the 'hidden' liabilities implicit in the commitments.

With 246% in 1997, PEH's over-commitment could be seen as extremely high and goes further than the limit of 200% given in PEH's own investment guidelines. For a private equity funds investment program with its long lead times the definition of suitable investment guidelines and adhering to them is not straightforward. These 200% go beyond 'market best practices' of 120–130% and the 150% meanwhile seen as the upper limit.[14]

One could interpret this as an indication for aggressive risk-taking, but during the first years of operation, capital calls will generally only go up gradually and PEH's first challenge was becoming fully invested. Basically, the OCR is often quite high during the fund-of-funds investment phase when capital needs to be quickly put to work. A high OCR itself is not necessarily an indicator for a coming crisis, but it should have been brought downward after the first build-up of the portfolio.

Maintaining a high OCR over longer time periods is implicitly assuming that favorable market conditions would continue. Capital re-flows would have to be sufficient and timely enough to honor the new commitments into which PEH had already entered to keep as fully invested in private equity funds as possible. It has to be kept in mind that there is a time-lag associated with new commitments, and a significant part of PEH's undrawn commitments dated back to previous years but was getting increasingly called by the VC funds.

4.4.1.3 Increasing capital needs

PEH management's market outlook remained optimistic but, although probably not fully clear about the extent of the shortfall, they understood that their expansion strategy had to be funded. To invest as rapidly as PEH did, it had been necessary to make use of the additional authorized capital of CHF75 million in nominal terms. Issued at a premium, CHF444 million additional funding thus became available to the company and by March 2000 the consolidated capital had risen to CHF1390 million. Repayments stemming from the young portfolio of funds were not yet high enough to cover the management fees and other expenses. The year was concluded by a marginal accounting loss of CHF0.27 million – not atypical for a program still in its J Curve and no cause for major concern at that time.

Overall, the over-commitment levels give an indication that PEH was taking significant risks in the management of its portfolio. Nevertheless, the financial statements seemed 'healthy'. At that time, as a result of the capital increase, PEH had become 'one of the biggest private equity investors of its kind in Europe'.[15] Whether this claim is justified is beside the point, as in any case PEH remained a second-line stock in the Swiss stock exchange.

---

[13] Extract from: 'PEH AG, 1999/00 Annual Report', page 5: 'Report on the Financial Year 1999/00'.
[14] In PEH's 2005 investment guidelines the limit for over-commitments was set to 133%.
[15] Extract from: 'PEH AG, 1997/98 Annual Report', page 7: 'Report on the Financial Year 1997/98'.

4.4.2 The 'new economy'

PEH was not alone in its optimism. It was the whole 'zeitgeist' where the 'old economy' was 'blown to bits'. Industry-wide there was a strong belief in the New Economy that took triple-digit return figures as normal instead of seeing them as an indication for unsustainable risk-taking. Still in May 2000, *The Economist* (2000) mused that whether 'the venture boom will continue now that some of the froth has been blown off the stock market is a matter of feverish argument. Optimists note that the IPO market often closes for a while, only to open unscathed when confidence returns. Some indeed see the IPO market as a mere extension of the venture-capital boom, and not its cause.'

4.4.2.1 Follow the crowd

One could describe private equity as 'Granovettarian' sociology where industry players are often personally known to each other, rather than being anonymous, atomistic economic agents.[16] *The Economist* (2000) sees the 'strong personal connections and clusters of like-minded people' as part of the explanation why venture capital in the USA has been so hugely successful in creating new firms. As GartnerG2 research director David Schehr remarked about the New Economy hype: 'How much of it was a much smaller group of people who talked to each other and themselves about this, and how much of it was the press being told by these people that this was the way it is going to be?'[17] They were merely working within a certain environment and were inevitably influenced by that. It is easy, with the benefit of hindsight, to think that people acted unwisely, but predicting the way innovation will have an impact upon the economy is a difficult business in any case. That there was a 'tech bubble' by the end of the 1990s most would have already agreed by then. To quote a developer who worked at boo.com (the over-hyped Internet fashion retailer that went bust with the loss of 300 jobs after only six months as a live site[18]): 'Those of us that had been in the business for a while were worried about it being a bubble. But we worried for so long – in internet time – that by 1999, the worry turned to concern that maybe we were among the ones who didn't "get it", who didn't really understand the power of the net.'

4.4.2.2 How long can it last?

But was the time when the bubble would finally burst really unforeseeable? Certainly one reason for the tech boom during the 1990s was the accelerated business spending in preparation for the Y2K switchover. Whoever witnessed this period, reading memos from one's IT department would have described it, not unlike the end of the first millennium, as a time of sweeping apocalyptic fears and a generalized sense of hysteria. Once New Year had passed without incident, the Last Judgment did not take place, planes still flew, power plants still worked and bills still went out (and unfortunately also arrived) punctually, anybody could have guessed that worldwide nearly all companies would decide that they had spent enough on computer equipment and related services for years to come and would quickly cut their IT budget down to normal amounts. Resulting hiring freezes, layoffs and consolidations

---

[16] Granovetter is a US sociologist famous for his work in networks theory and in economic sociology. The basic argument of his article called 'The strength of weak ties' is that relationships to family members and close friends ('strong ties') will not provide as much diversity of knowledge as the relationship to acquaintances, distant friends and the like ('weak ties').

[17] See Woods (2003).

[18] See Alden (2005). However, at the time of this writing boo.com appears to be back, with the launch of a new site announced.

in many industries eventually would have (and also did in reality) hit the dotcom sector. This argument is not meant to be a serious explanation of the crash post-2000, but shows that it would not have been too far-fetched to come up with such a scenario before the turn of the millennium.[19]

Stulz (2000) remarked, in the context of the failed hedge fund Long-Term Capital Management, that such 'events showed brutally that risk management is part of the social sciences. What makes social sciences different is that their object of study changes continuously, in this case partly as a result of financial innovation. Understanding these changes and how they influence risk is critical in times of great uncertainty. Risk management is not rocket science – it cannot be, since the past does not repeat itself on a sufficiently reliable basis. Future risks cannot be understood without examining the economic forces that shape them – a skill that is not taught in physics departments or engineering schools. However, understanding risks makes sense only if that understanding is used to create value.'

4.4.3 Clouds gathering

The period between April 2000 and March 2001 marks an inflection point, as it was half way between the past successes of PEH and its coming difficulties and was when crucial decisions about the investment strategy were taken.

4.4.3.1 Market downturn

While PEH clearly profited from a booming stock market, a market downturn would have two negative effects. Firstly, proceeds generated by exits through IPO would decrease and such events would become more seldom. Secondly, PEH as a quoted company itself would be unable to raise significant new capital from public markets.

So far every year PEH had invested heavily. Long-term assets were increasing in line with shareholders' equity and net consolidated profits were rising every year. The question is how sustainable such a strategy would be with the over-commitment strategy. Even if PEH's OCR of 166% was already particularly high, at that time the limit was not even reached. This could have created some complacency as PEH saw lower market valuations as attractive investment opportunities. Implicitly it was betting that the market would grow again in the near future and therefore maintained its growth strategy. This was probably the major strategic mistake that led to PEH's coming crisis. In March 2001 profits decreased to reach their 1999 level. This was the first sign of market downturn during the remainder of the year that caused write-downs exceeding investment gains and resulted in a net loss of CHF265 million as at March 2002. Industry insiders saw as the root cause for this development the high degree of over-commitments in combination with a strong VC sector orientation that was hit hardest by the overall economic downturn.

4.4.3.2 Funding problems

Funding was becoming a priority in PEH's strategy, but due to the difficult stock market situation it was not possible to finance the investments by issuing new share capital. Therefore, the current assets were reallocated to support new investments through a reduction

---

[19] However, this interpretation correlates quite closely to the peak of US stock markets. Peak of Dow Jones: 19 January 2000 (closed at: 11 722.98, intraday peak of: 11 908.50). Peak of Nasdaq: 10 March 2000 (closed at: 5048.62, intraday peak of: 5132.52).

of cash and cash equivalents by 89%. Moreover, PEH negotiated a credit facility from Swiss Life/Rentenanstalt of up to CHF500 million to meet additional financing needs. Half of it was used up right away, essentially to pay back short-term borrowings. Almost 90% of PEH current assets were used to enter into new commitments, while the level of undrawn commitments was already too high. As specified in the annual report, 'At the end of the reporting period, the combined equity and borrowings was fully invested with private equity investments amounting to CHF1.62 billion'.[20] The capital raised through the last increase was entirely drawn and deteriorating market conditions created a vicious cycle where issuing further share capital was no longer a viable option. As a result of all these factors, the OCR increased to 202%, i.e. breaking the set limit. Although some funds were sold in the secondary market, there were not many attractive opportunities to exit funds or direct investments, aggravating the 'liquidity squeeze'. As a consequence, and for the first time since PEH started its operations, no additional investments or new commitments were made.

Certainly management misjudgment has to be blamed for creating and deepening PEH's financial distress. A report from independent auditors points to 'misconduct on several instances including transgression of competencies, negligence with regard to duty of care as well as inadequate documentation'.[21] There were apparently also issues related to the relationship between Vontobel and PEH, but the discussion of these events goes beyond the scope of the case study.[22] In June 2001 all agreements with the Vontobel Group were terminated with immediate effect, PEH's Deputy Chairman of the Board and its CEO resigned from their respective functions, and Swiss Life Private Equity Partners AG replaced Vontobel as PEH's manager and advisor.

4.4.3.3   Flexible investment strategy?

PEH's presentation for the press conference held in October 2001 in Zurich gives an insight into their views on the market and the required adjustments.[23] In their diagnostics, during the 'booming 90s', the VC segment of the private equity benefited most, allowing for quick returns through IPOs with IRRs more important than multiples.

Box 4.1:   Stock market view

March 2000
The LPX major market price index is based on the 20 most liquid listed private equity companies worldwide. PEH's share price was trailing the sector during its first year of trading. However, at the end of its third financial year investors seemed to be more convinced of PEH's potential, and from March to August 2000, it outperformed the LPX (Figure 4.2 and 4.3).

---

[20] Extract from: 'PEH AG, 2000/01 Annual Report', page 5: 'Report on the Financial Year 2000/01'.
[21] Extract from: 'PEH AG, 2000/01 Annual Report', page 6: 'Report on the Financial Year 2000/01'.
[22] See Marcelino (2006).
[23] See Keijzer (2001).

Box 4.1: (Continued)

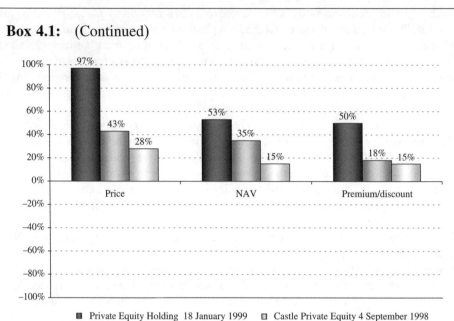

■ Private Equity Holding 18 January 1999   ▣ Castle Private Equity 4 September 1998
□ AIG Private Equity 12 October 1999

Figure 4.2   Fund-of-funds performance from inception through 31 July 2000
Source: Bloomberg, annual reports (see Wietlisbach, 2001).

On 31 March 2000 PEH's share price was CHF605. Earnings per share doubled to CHF34.68 and the market capitalization rose to CHF2722.5 million. The additional authorized capital could be placed in the market with a significant premium.

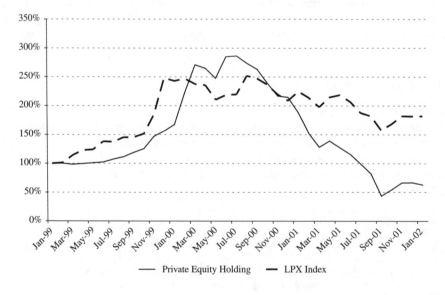

——— Private Equity Holding   ▬ ▬ LPX Index

Figure 4.3   Private Equity Holding vs. LPX Major Market Price Index
Source: Bloomberg.

September 2000

PEH performed poorly with its share price declining by 54.5% to CHF275. The earnings per share were cut to less than half, CHF12.14, and PEH's market capitalization went down to CHF1238 million. After six months of outperforming the LPX, in September 2000 PEH fell below the index. This negative development essentially cut off the option to improve financial health through another capital increase. There is an old saying that even a dead cat will bounce if it is dropped from high enough, and PEH followed this pattern with a short and false recovery, when its share price suddenly increased to CHF250 and for a few days followed the LPX index. However, its share price finally collapsed to its level of January 1999 (Figure 4.4).

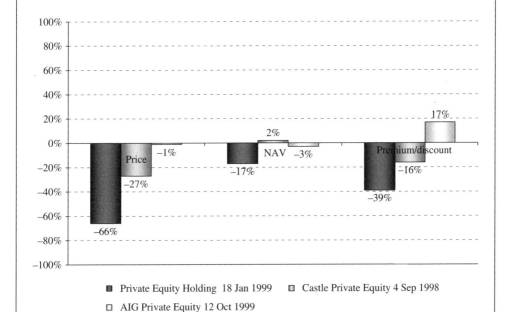

Figure 4.4   Fund-of-funds performance from 1 August 2000 to 31 July 2001
Source: Bloomberg, annual reports (see Wietlisbach, 2001).

The 'new millennium' saw a burst of this speculative bubble. While IPO markets were 'dead', this was not the case for technology. PEH believed that a 'new era will start', but the question was when. Management therefore called for a 'flexible investment strategy' implemented through the so-called '6 C' program, focusing on:

- 'Corporate governance', that required strengthening through introducing a number of oversight bodies.
- 'Costs', with separate budgets for operative expenses (legal fees, tax, audit, transaction costs, administration costs and stronger alignments of interests through performance-based incentive depending on share price development and through introduction of stock options).
- 'Composition' of the portfolio that required an adjustment of asset allocation over the medium term. Follow-on financing for directly held portfolio companies was to be

provided on a selective basis. While the focus remained on venture capital over the medium term, the aim was an above average increase in buyouts. Over-commitments were to be reduced through structured financing or secondary transactions.

- 'Cash flow' was to be put under control by securing long-term financing and through more conservative planning.
- 'Control' was understood to be a weakness and was to be tackled through the introduction of 'state-of-the-art' instruments.
- 'Communication' was to become more transparent and proactive to gain the trust of investors and the public.

Moreover, the merger plans for 5E Holding AG with PEH were suspended. '6 C' was certainly a nice collection of management buzzwords, but these measures apparently had little impact or proved to be too little, too late. As a result of generally difficult financial market conditions, the share price dropped by 58% to CHF116 and PEH's market capitalization fell to CHF522 million.

Box 4.2: Fair value

Being able to trade the shares is important but investors are also concerned whether the share price is trading near its fair value. PEH – like many others – is in this context referring to the NAV as the 'fair value'. That, however, calls for a number of comments. Firstly, a private equity fund's NAV is an accounting figure and – at least at that time – had a clearly conservative bias. EVCA's international fair valuation guidelines were only put in place in 2005; whether they are able to overcome the conservative bias in early stage VC investing is debatable and will be analyzed in more detail later on. Secondly, even if portfolio companies are fairly valued, a private equity fund's fair value is derived from but is not equivalent to the value of the underlying portfolio companies. The NAV leaves out a number of relevant factors, for example the undrawn commitments – which became PEH's Achilles heel – or the fund manager's value added or destroyed. Moreover, the contractual design of a limited partnership agreement means that the option to trade is explicitly given up.[24] In other words, private equity funds need to be valued under a buy-and-hold assumption. One has to differentiate between:

- The accounting-based portfolio valuations reported by the private equity funds held by PEH.
- The 'intrinsic', i.e. economic values of the private equity funds held by PEH.
- PEH's share price, essentially driven by supply and demand of the market.

Monitoring valuations for a portfolio of private equity funds is a significant technical challenge that we will discuss in more detail in the following chapters.

---

[24] See Lerner and Schoar (2002).

4.4.4 Iceberg ahead

However, between 2001 and 2002 PEH's management appear to have generally seen lower market valuations rather as an attractive investment opportunity and they continued their investment pace in the expectation that the market would soon grow again.

After its peak in 2000, fundraising in the private equity market plunged in 2002 by 30% and back to its 1999 level. Strong corrections in the markets occurred and, according to the PricewaterhouseCoopers Money Tree Survey (US Report) for 2001, the average valuation for venture-backed companies declined by 45.5%. The market corrections had the strongest impact on the Internet, telecommunications and software sectors – those areas toward which PEH had been shifting its allocation in previous years. As stressed in its annual report, for PEH the 2001/2002 financial year was the most difficult one to date.

4.4.4.1 Verge of illiquidity

PEH's 2002/2003 annual report stated that the company was brought to 'the verge of illiquidity'.[25] That finally triggered a change in the management. PEH was spun out from Swiss Life Private Equity Partners with the termination of the associated agreements, and the newly created Alpha Associates became its administrator and manager.

With a continuing bear market, IPOs became rare and, associated with the lower number of exits, repayments dried up. Thus, with more funds calling their capital, PEH was becoming dangerously close to being unable to honor these drawdowns. In return this would cause financial distress in those funds and result in further substantial write-downs in PEH's portfolio. For the defaulting investor there are stiff penalties associated with not meeting a drawdown request, such as the termination of the limited partner's right to participate in the fund's future investments, and the loss of entitlement to distributions or income. However, this does not affect its liability for losses or partnership expenses, the mandatory transfer or sale of its partnership interests, the continuing liability for interest in respect of the defaulted amount, or the partial or total forfeiture of the partnership interest. PEH had to find a solution for its liquidity problems and considered several alternative financing routes:

- Renegotiation of financial obligations: despite lowered undrawn commitments, the funding remained insufficient. Furthermore, it would have prevented PEH from accessing additional debt financing. In that market environment it was also not possible to replace Swiss Life with another debt provider.
- Sale of the entire portfolio and liquidation of the company: this option was not considered further, as the total portfolio sale would have barely covered the Swiss Life loan and nothing would have been left for PEH shareholders.
- Retention of the portfolio through an increase of leverage and a new management contract: rejected as well because of the high interest expenses associated with the leverage plus all the additional costs (e.g. transaction costs, issuance of warrants). It would have increased financial risk for shareholders and liquidity and would have been likely to be just an intermediate solution with difficulties resurfacing sooner rather than later.
- Securitization: one of the solutions envisaged by the management was to use securitization. However, due to significant problems with rating and placement of securities, the portfolio

---

[25] Extract from: 'PEH AG, 2002/03 Annual Report', page 4: 'Chairman's Report on the Financial Year 2002/03'.

securitization alternative was abolished. Moreover, it generally takes too much time to place the notes on the market, whereas PEH needed a relatively fast solution.

That left only the sale of a significant portion of PEH's assets as a viable option. This would reduce the unfunded commitments by more than 80% to CHF59 million, and repayments from the retained portfolio of funds were expected to finance the 20% remaining undrawn portion. Secondly, the Swiss Life loan amounting to CHF325 million would be repaid completely, and there would be no more leverage and hence a debt-free balance sheet. Thirdly, the transaction would have little execution risk and would allow PEH to shake off its legacy.

4.4.4.2 Portfolio sell-off

After a review of the different solutions available at that time, PEH finally sold most of its positions to Credit Suisse First Boston (CSFB). CSFB bought a portfolio for a total unadjusted fair value of CHF616 million as of March 2003 for CHF305 million. It corresponds to a 50% discount of its more recent fair value 'which compares favorably with current secondary sales of private equity portfolios'.[26] The transaction resulted in additional write-downs of CHF311 million on top of CHF400 million for the rest of PEH's portfolio. PEH suffered write-downs of CHF711 million that were 85% of the total expenses and represented 15% of the total investment's book value.

Finally, PEH managed to negotiate an 'earn-out' feature that allowed 'PEH shareholders to benefit from upside on sold investments'.[27] Under the earn-out agreement PEH was entitled to a share in the net distributions from the portfolio after CSFB had received priority distributions equal to a set multiple of the sum of aggregate fair values plus the remaining undrawn commitments as of 31 March 2003.

Box 4.3: Earn-out

Earn-out agreements are provisions sometimes written into the terms of a transaction that the vendors will receive further payments if the business sold achieves specified performance levels. They are common for companies in high-growth, high-tech where valuations are extremely difficult to agree on, or in service industries where a great deal of the value of a business is tied up with the people working in it. Earn-outs allow sellers of stakes in private equity funds to benefit from a future upside. Under an earn-out agreement the seller is usually entitled to a share in the net distributions from the portfolio after the buyer had received priority distributions equal to a set multiple of the sum of aggregate fair values plus the remaining undrawn commitments as of the date of the sell transaction.

Say, a seller of a stake in a private equity fund is asking €2 million based on the projected cash flows, but the buyer is willing to pay only €1 million based on a discount on the fund's NAV. An earn-out provision structures the deal so that the seller receives more than the buyer's offer only if distributions are above an agreed threshold. The buyer of a large part of PEH's buyout portfolio, CSFB Strategic

---

[26] Extract from: 'PEH AG, 2002/03 Annual Report', page 5: 'Chairman's Report on the Financial Year 2002/03'.
[27] See 'Repositioning of PEH and annual results 2002/2003', Press and Investor Meeting, 27 May 2003 in Zürich.

Partners II LP (the 'CSFB Fund'), agreed in 2003 to pay an incremental purchase price to PEH if and when certain earn-out thresholds on the sold portfolio would be reached. For example, for one sub-portfolio PEH will receive 50% of all distributions once the CSFB Fund has received a multiple of 1.15 of the portfolio's aggregated NAV plus its undrawn commitments as of 31 March 2003, 75% once a multiple of 1.3 and 100% of all distributions once a multiple of 1.5 has been returned to the CSFB Fund.[28]

The CSFB Fund is contractually obliged to give notice as soon as this threshold is reached.[29] However, PEH does not account for the value, if any, of the stream of the future earn-out payments on its balance sheet and therefore does not include it in the published NAV per share. This is because sellers usually do not have sufficient information about the remaining investments sold in order to attribute a value to the earn-out.

On the other hand, the sell-off left PEH's retained portfolio in a weaker state, as it became increasingly unbalanced and unevenly spread over the vintage years. PEH's retained portfolio started to mature since almost no investments or new commitments were made from 2001 to 2004 except for follow-on funds on a very selective basis. Despite PEH's depressing state, Wiegers (2003) still found a funny side in the company's annual meeting in August 2003, where its Dutch chairman Marinus Keijzer gave the introductory presentation. 'It sounded like an abdication moderated by Rudy Carell' and apparently briefly lifted the spirits of PEH's otherwise very unhappy shareholders.[30] Besides, the annual meeting aimed at putting a final stroke under PEH's recent past. Since then the company's financial situation has seemed 'healthy' and the investment process started again.

4.5 DEFINITION AND ANALYSIS OF RATIOS

Ratio analysis allows relationships to be expressed between accounting numbers and their trends over time and the establishment of values and evaluating risks. It is a quantitative technique for comparing a firm on a relative basis to other firms or to the market in general. Specifically for analyzing the risks of private equity funds investment programs, the over-commitment ratio (OCR), the adjusted current ratio (ACR), the outstanding commitment level (OCL) and the investment level (IL) are of relevance. Changes in these ratios can help to interpret in which direction the program is going.

---

[28] See http://www.peh.ch/pdf/peh_praesentation_030527_d.pdf [accessed 11 March 2007].

[29] See http://www.huginonline.is/plsql/try/pressreleases [accessed 11 March 2007]: 'As of December 31, 2006 the Fair Value of the Earn-Out shown on the Balance Sheet amounts to EUR 54.905 million. A first payment under the Earn-Out right has been received from the CSFB Fund on January 4, 2007 in the amount of EUR 2.912 million. The total income from the Earn-Out shown in the Profit & Loss Statement up to December 31, 2006 amounts to EUR 57.817 million (September 30, 2006: EUR 48.873 million). It can be expected that Private Equity Holding will regularly receive payments from the Earn-Out in the future. The ultimate value of the Earn-Out, however, cannnot be assessed prior to June 30, 2010.'

[30] Unfortunately the irony is likely to escape most non-German speakers unfamiliar with this popular show master. Over many years the late Rudy Carell was an icon of German entertainment. As he himself said, when he came to Germany the first time he only spoke English, but because the German language has been acquiring more and more English words, 'my German is now fluent'. The 'Rudy Carell accent' of German-speaking Dutch is proverbial.

Box 4.4: Adjusted current ratio

In the context of an over-commitment strategy, monitoring and managing liquidity is of key importance. The CR is the standard tool to analyze a firm's capacity to finance its short-term liabilities by its short-term resources:

$$CR = \frac{\text{current assets}}{\text{current liabilities}}$$

The CR is a measure of a firm's ability to survive over the near term, by being able to meet obligations with available funds. A CR of 100% means that even without doing any business it could theoretically survive for one year. A low CR is a signal that the available liquidity would be insufficient. However, over the long term a high CR could also be an indication for an inefficient use of the firm's resources. In any case, it is obviously highly risky to over-commit for CR below 100%. But it still gives an incomplete picture as it ignores the undrawn commitments.

For the analysis of a private equity funds investment program the CR is of limited explanatory power, as it ignores the off-balance sheet items:

- In the short term, a fund-of-funds will have to pay a part of its current outstanding commitment, which can be considered as a short-term liability (% × undrawn commitment).
- Also the percentage of the distributions that will be received by the fund-of-funds can be taken into consideration (% × paid in).

These items are reflected in the ACR:

$$ACR = \frac{\text{current assets} + \% \times \text{paid in}}{\text{current liabilities} + \% \times \text{undrawn commitment}}$$

The projected amount of distributions as a percentage of the current paid in depends on the maturity of the portfolio and on the cumulative distribution to paid-in capital (DPI). This figure, and the percentage of the undrawn commitments to be disbursed in the short term based on the current cumulative outstanding commitment, can be determined based on the analysis of historical data (see **Appendix 4A**).

4.5.1 Comparison of Private Equity Holding and Castle Private Equity

One ready explanation for PEH's problems was that it was suffering the 'perfect storm' when the dotcom bubble finally burst. While this is certainly part of the overall picture, it has to be highlighted that a comparable listed Swiss private equity fund-of-funds, Castle Private Equity (CPE), with a similar history and operating in the same environment was able to 'ride out the storm'.

The other thing the failures we shall examine have in common is their apparently puzzling nature. Although something has clearly gone wrong, it is hard to see what; rather, it seems that fortune – evenly balanced between both sides at the outset – has turned against one side and favored the other [. . .] Competent professionals have failed in their task, for reasons that are not immediately apparent.

Cohen and Gooch (1991)

Even if it suffered from the 2001 stock market downturn, CPE managed to maintain a strong balance sheet and to some degree avoid any major troubles. It therefore makes sense, when comparing CPE's and PEH's key financial figures, to look for clues that explain success in one and near failure in the other.

4.5.1.1   Different approaches to valuations

CPE did its IPO in September 1997, i.e. 6 months after PEH. Since inception CPE used 'fair values' in its financial statements and based its investment policy and commitment management on this measure. The valuation methodologies related to accounting matter, as management at the end of the day would be kept accountable for them and the results. However, at least at the time of the PEH case such valuation methodologies gave a poor approximation of a fund's fair value. To some degree, this may have created a false sense of security and could even have misled PEH's management. Regarding the valuations of its investments in funds, PEH's 2000/2001 annual report gives the following explanation:

The fair value of a fund investment is the stake of that fund's net capital owned by the Group. A fund's net capital or net asset value (NAV) reflects the paid-in capital plus/minus the retained earnings/accumulated deficit. The investments entered into by the funds are generally valued in accordance with the EVCA guidelines [. . .] The fair values of the fund investments are based upon the last reported NAV of the fund investments plus contributions and minus distributions through March 31, 2001.

This description of the valuation approach gives no details on its actual implementation. If we take this explanation at face value, we see the following issues:

- The time lag between the valuation conducted by fund managers and the LP receiving reports and aggregating all valuations can be significant. The general partners are allowed between 60 and 90 days for quarterly reporting and for the USA between 45 and 90 days time lag for reporting accounting and performance data is typical.[31]
- Firstly, during those 45 to 90 days, the NAV can go down as almost certainly happened during the months preceding PEH's crisis. Secondly, contributions were kept at cost and, particularly in a situation where there were repayments, this is likely to have led to a significant overstatement of the NAV.
- This approach could even be considered as conservative in a growth environment where valuations follow the market with a significant time lag, but during the rapid downward

---

[31] See Meyer and Mathonet (2005).

movement this method failed to give a timely warning signal that could have alerted management and forced it to rethink its strategy.

- The explanation suggests that valuation for accounting purposes was rather a mechanical exercise and that the NAVs reported by fund managers were accepted without reviews or adjustments. There are no indications that investment managers provided updates on the value development of the portfolio companies managed by the funds.

Box 4.5:   Outstanding commitment level

Comparing the outstanding commitment to the total commitment gives information on the maturity of the portfolio. The OCL is defined as:

$$OCL = \frac{outstanding\ commitments}{total\ commitments}$$

Assuming that there is no change in the investment and commitment strategies, the current OCL can be indicative for the capital drawn over the following financial year. It is important to maintain a reasonable OCL over time as it represents a future liability.

The analysis of PEH and CPE suggests that the OCL be kept at about 30%.[32] For example, since 2000 CPE maintained an OCL around 29%. The OCL depends on the strategy of the fund but should be kept stable over time. Ratios are inter-related and need to be analyzed as a whole. For example, a CR slightly below 100% does not appear as problematic for a low and stable OCL as in cases where the OCL was 50%.

CPE was following a slightly different approach, as described in its 2001 annual report:

Private equity investments for which market quotations are not readily available are valued at their fair values as determined in good faith by the Board of Directors in consultation with the investment manager. In this respect, investments in other investment companies (fund investments) which are not publicly traded are normally valued at the underlying net asset value as advised by the managers or administrators of these investment companies, unless the Board of Directors are aware of good reasons why such a valuation would not be the most appropriate indicator of fair value. In estimating the fair value of fund investments, the Board of Directors considers all appropriate and applicable factors relevant to their value, including but not limited to the following:

- Reference to the investment vehicle's reporting information;
- Reference to transaction prices;
- Result of operational and environmental assessment.

All fair valuations may differ significantly from values that would have been used had ready markets existed, and the differences could be material. The valuation of the investments is done on a regular basis but at least quarterly.

---

[32] Also the 2001 PricewaterhouseCoopers MoneyTree Survey (US Report) gives as industry average for the ratio of outstanding commitment to total commitments of 30%.

Again we have no insights into the details on CPE's implementation of this approach. In theory, this procedure should have drawn management's attention to the deteriorating situation earlier, as valuations were reviewed against benchmarks and apparently also non-quantitative criteria were taken into account. It is unclear to what degree this has really been a factor, but the case highlights the potential dangers of an incomplete valuation model.

Compared to PEH, CPE had a more conservative bias when valuing its portfolio of private equity funds. Here rapidly declining valuations were indeed an early warning signal and when in 2002 CPE had its first real losses, the situation was probably not as bad as it could have been had more commitments been made the previous year. This does not necessarily mean that they had a better understanding of the market, but during the sharp downward correction in the market, CPE's 'fair values' were more conservative and in a declining market closer to the truth than PEH's. Strategic decisions undertaken by CPE's management were consequently based on what we believe were at that time more realistic forecasts.[33]

4.5.1.2 Different stage orientation

While originally CPE aimed to focus on the growth sectors of the future, i.e. worldwide, venture capital investments with special attention to the new technologies, telecommunications and life sciences, quite early on, the buyout segment had a higher weight. Whether this was a strategic decision based on a realistic assessment of the market's prospects, or because proposals for buyout fund investments were more attractive than those for VC, or whether high-quality VC funds became more difficult to assess is unclear. In any case, since 2000 over 90% of the new commitments were made to buyouts and special situation partnerships. Therefore, the portfolio generally moved toward more traditional activities such as manufacturing, retail and distributions and to some extent away from communications and IT-related investments.

Box 4.6: Investment level

As explained before, the amount committed to a fund will not be invested right away. The over-commitment strategy aims to assure a full investment level:

$$IL = \frac{\text{investment at book value}}{\text{shareholders' equity} + \text{long-term debt}}$$

An IL moving away from 100% suggests that the fund-of-funds be under- or over-invested. Ideally, the IL should be kept at 100% with the lowest OCR possible. However, the IL is effectively controlled by the OCR, albeit with a significant delay. Due to the time lags inherent in commitments to funds, the management requires long-term planning and cannot be steered through short-term interventions.

However, when the VC market collapsed and dried up, CPE's buyout funds continued to generate positive cash flows and hence allowed managers to make commitments

---

[33] See CPE annual reports.

as new opportunities were created in the distressed assets and restructuring area. These repayments came particularly from mature partnerships of early 1990s vintages and underline the importance of vintage diversification. In 2001, VC investments suffered substantial write-downs but above all CPE experienced a fall in the fair-value reserve and therefore slowed down its investment activity during that year. Nevertheless, there were strong repayments from investments[34] and as a result CPE maintained a positive cash flow and a strong balance sheet with its highest net profit since inception in 2004. From 2001 onwards, CPE took various measures to optimize the management of the portfolio and improved its monitoring. Possibly learning from its 'close shave', CPE is said to have intensified the dialog with the general partners to ensure that reported valuations were accurate.

Hence, for instance in 2001, despite huge profits the investments and commitments were reduced to a very low level because of the significant overall net loss.[35] This should be compared to PEH in 2001, where first significant write-downs were not considered as the signs of a structural crisis. Here management remained optimistic and even bet on a market upswing and accelerated investing, as they believed that the market fall was a great opportunity to access funds at a bargain. Rösch (2000) reports that PEH's management was still confident in 2000 and believed that coming IPOs would be of higher quality and terms and conditions more reasonable. The 'outlook section' in PEH's 1999/00 annual report declares that despite 'the downturn in technology stocks, we feel that the venture field still has the greatest potential and will therefore continue to overweight early stage funds focusing in the technology sector'.

4.5.2   Other factors

One could argue that because of its later stage orientation and the associated closeness to public markets, CPE was more exposed to 'quantifiable risk' whereas PEH with its early stage VC focus had a far higher exposure to 'non-quantifiable uncertainty'. The differentiation between 'risk' and 'uncertainty' is critical when discussing the management of VC-focused fund investment programs and is an important theme that we will need to tackle throughout this book.

The famous quip (though perhaps apocryphally) attributed to John Maynard Keynes that 'the market can stay irrational longer than you can stay solvent' also held for PEH as the fall in the tech markets continued for years rather than weeks. PEH followed an aggressive strategy without, as it turned out, having the liquidity to do so. Certainly the characteristics of VC funds contributed to the crisis, but PEH's near failure was more the consequence of a flawed liquidity management that triggered the 'fire sale' rather than a case of allocating too much to venture capital. Compared to PEH, CPE's balance sheet remained sound in spite of high capital outflows for new investments. It is partly the efficient vintage year diversification that resulted in stable cash flows, including during the difficult times.

The question remains how one can form an integrated picture of PEH's and CPE's development and how the resulting insights can be turned into a system for the management of a private equity fund investment programs. See Table 4.2.

Assuming that these ratios are interdependent, one may suspect that significant changes over time are also indicative for increased risks. One approach to analyzing and managing several dimensions in parallel could be along the lines of the balanced scorecard

---

[34] Write-down that was largely covered by the high level of distributions that year.

[35] Based on the net unrealized gain (loss) from fair value valuation of investments credited to equity.

Table 4.2   Ratio development

Year		ACR	OCR	OCL	IL
1997	PEH	60%	246%	78%	86%
	CPE	279%	130%	89%	15%
1998	PEH	270%	144%	63%	49%
	CPE	138%	166%	54%	68%
1999	PEH	211%	166%	49%	70%
	CPE	129%	137%	34%	61%
2000	PEH	70%	202%	40%	104%
	CPE	140%	133%	29%	61%
2001	PEH	124%	152%	33%	111%
	CPE	197%	144%	29%	82%
2002	PEH	113%	124%	13%	149%
	CPE	115%	172%	29%	109%
2003	PEH	235%	113%	8%	144%
	CPE	121%	169%	28%	98%

methodology.[36] A balanced scorecard allows the management of the important performance metrics that drive success. Instead of using such a sophisticated technique, we just linked the ACR, OCR, OCL and IL very simplistically by tracking their changes over time and aggregating them into an average percentage change. Nevertheless, this coarse technique already visualizes the main differences in the historical development of the two investment companies (Figure 4.5).

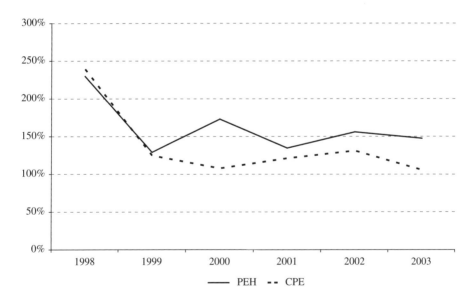

Figure 4.5   Percentage changes of ratios (aggregated)

---

[36] Developed by Harvard Business School's Robert Kaplan and David Norton in 1992.

The picture becomes even clearer if we compare the four ratios' difference between the minimum and the maximum change for PEH and CPE. Here Figure 4.6 suggests that during the critical market period for PEH the ratios were more 'out of sync' than those of CPE.

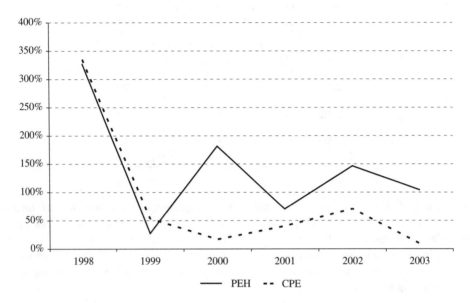

Figure 4.6   Difference between max and min percentage change of ratios (aggregated)

In 2002 and 2003, CPE over-committed more aggressively than PEH. However, the private equity market environment had certainly changed and, moreover, at that time PEH was lacking resources and thus would have been unable to follow CPE's strategy.

4.6   LESSONS AND EPILOGUE

While diversification is seen as the primary risk management tool for private equity funds-of-funds, PEH demonstrates that this can often be of little relevance and liquidity issues can be of much higher importance. Apparently, overly high over-commitment ratios characterize the early phase of a private equity funds investment program. When PEH was set up in 1997 in a favorable context with improving market conditions, its 'aggressive' over-commitment strategy paid out handsomely. Over the long term, however, high over-commitment ratios are unsustainable and need to come down to a level in line with the average returns that characterize the asset class. PEH was not wrong in aggressively over-committing during its early years, but it slipped up when it should have slowed down its investment pace to get into 'cruising speed'. Where PEH stumbled, therefore, was the moment when it had to adjust its strategy and decelerate its investment pace. Moreover, during the years 2000 and 2001 management appears to have entirely misjudged the medium prospects of the market.

While wide ranges for over-commitment ratios have been documented – and also this study can serve as guidance – it should be highlighted that in practice no manager should rely solely on observing ratios only. Instead, a disciplined cash flow projection and planning process should be followed, where over-commitment ratios should be tracked as a plausibility check and early warning system.

Projecting cash flows in private equity and notably in venture capital is easier said than done. They are notoriously hard to forecast with any degree of reliability. In this context Grundt (2003) interviewed Thomas Staubli from Partners Group in Zug, Switzerland. According to the interviewee, the precise projections of cash flows have a significant impact on the overall return of a fund-of-funds. At Partners Group more than one-third of staff are involved in forecasting cash flows. Only large institutions with significant know-how are able to properly do this and the interviewee believed that this was a competitive advantage. Blindly relying on mathematical models, however, is a recipe for disaster as they can only estimate the exposure to liquidity risk. Therefore, reliance on such models should be limited and other methods should be used in parallel. Planning should also take a range of scenarios into consideration and contingencies such as liquidity lines should be put in place.[37]

As a second-line stock in the SWX, PEH's debacle never had an impact on the financial system but the fallout in the aftermath went beyond it. An article in the *Neue Züricher Zeitung* on the expected collapse alerted a member of Basel's governing council, Daniel Goepfert, who in 2003 requested an official inquiry into the city's pension fund management. The article pointed out that with 9.3% of PEH's capital, Basel city's pension fund was the largest shareholder and that such a stake was 'recklessly high'; it suggested that the pension fund's management was generally too aggressively invested in equity and wantonly negligent in its investment policy regarding PEH, as this second-line stock caused a disproportionately high part of the portfolio's losses. By and large the commission's final report on this matter in December 2004 shared this assessment. Interestingly, the report found that still in March 2002 the pension fund's management remained optimistic and believed that share prices would go up again soon – another indication that PEH's former management was not alone in its assessment of the market.

In the case of PEH, it was the strong backers Swiss Life and implicitly CSFB – that traditionally has cooperated closely with Swiss Life – who could provide additional capital and were the key to PEH's rescue. Despite a restructured portfolio and an upward trend in the venture market worldwide, PEH realized a consolidated net loss of CHF13 million and CHF33 million in March 2004 and 2005, respectively, essentially because of write-downs. Nevertheless, the comprehensive net loss decreased by 70% to CHF15 million at the end of the 2004–2005 financial year compared to the prior period 2003–2004. PEH was starting to see the benefits of its restructuring as the portfolio cash flow was positive for the first time in its history. Commitments, investments and shareholders' equity continued to decrease since significant exits occurred, whereas only restrictive follow-on fund investments were undertaken. Improvements suggest that PEH, now under new management, had 'turned the tide' and avoided collapse.

---

[37] For an in-depth discussion on liquidity planning for a private equity fund investment program please refer to Meyer and Mathonet (2005).

Appendix 4A   Adjusted Current Ratio Methodology

The Thomson Financial's VentureXpert database gives both the cumulative PICC (Paid In to Committed Capital) and the cumulative DPI (Distribution to Paid In) since inception. The cumulative $PICC_N$ for year N is defined as:

$$PICC_N = \frac{\sum \text{paid in}_N}{\sum \text{committed capital}_N}$$

Analysis of this statistic supports the simplified assumption that yearly, 25% of the undrawn commitments will be called. The cumulative DPI_N for year N is defined as:

$$DPI_N = \frac{\sum \text{distributions}_N}{\sum \text{paid in}_N}$$

By comparing DPI_{N+1} with DPI_N we can calculate the distributions as a percentage of the committed capital in year $N+1$. Unlike in the case of the undrawn commitments, percentages for distributions differ significantly over a fund's lifetime. Analysis of the quarterly data from all European private equity funds between 1987 and 2004 gives the pattern for the average fund (Table 4.3).

Table 4.3   Distribution pattern

Year	Percentage of distribution	Cumulative distributions
1	1%	1%
2	4%	5%
3	8%	13%
4	12%	25%
5	11%	36%
6	16%	52%
7	17%	69%
8	16%	85%

Part II
The Economics of Private Equity Funds

5
Venture Capital Fund Fair Value

In April 2001, the International Accounting Standards Board (IASB) disseminated a comprehensive platform of International Financial Reporting Standards (IFRS). The standards, which became effective 1 January 2005, apply to all listed companies in the European Union and stress the importance of reporting assets and liabilities on an entity's balance sheet at 'fair value', defined as 'the amount for which an asset could be exchanged between knowledgeable, willing parties in an arm's length transaction'. Fair value stands now as the prevailing valuation principle and is addressing the needs of a growing number of investors. While this valuation principle was clearly aimed at investments in more liquid entities such as public companies or private companies with viable business models and predictable revenue streams, it has created a difficult situation for the VC industry, where companies commonly generate little or no revenue and face sustained periods of uncertainty.

5.1 VALUATION GUIDELINES

In March 2005, the most recent set of valuation guidelines produced by the Association Française des Investisseurs en Capital (AFIC), the British Venture Capital Association (BVCA) and the European Private Equity and Venture Capital Association (EVCA) were published following previous sets in 2003, 2001, 1993 and 1991. These new International Private Equity and Venture Capital Valuation Guidelines (IPEV guidelines)[1] aim to increase the practical applicability of the IFRS to private equity. They were the result of increasing importance and acceptance of this asset class during the last decade, combined with the internationalization of the industry, the clear increase in the quality and availability of information, new applicable laws, regulations and accounting standards.

However, it has to be highlighted that the IPEV guidelines do not relate to funds but to their investee companies. In the past, limited partners in funds have reported the value of their fund interests using the net asset value (NAV) as reported by the general partner. The NAV is also often referred to as a fund's 'residual value' and defined as the value of all investments remaining in the portfolio minus any long-term liabilities and net of fees and carried interest as of a specific date.[2] As methodologies for determining company values differ considerably across general partners, from using investment cost as a proxy for current value to marking investments up to the price of the most recent financing round, auditors will no longer accept NAV as the partnership fair value without significant checks and tests involving verification of the individual portfolio company values. Moreover, as Kinsch and

---

[1] Available on www.privateequityvaluation.com [accessed 9 May 2006].
[2] See Blaydon *et al.* (2003) or Reyes (2003). In practice we have observed that the NAV is occasionally not reported directly, but needs to be calculated based on information additionally provided.

Petit-Jouvet (2006) pointed out, this simultaneously makes valuation a much more proactive exercise than it was prior to the revision, when its conservative value principle mainly consisted of reacting to events.

Box 5.1: The J Curve

The title of our book calls for at least a brief description of the (in-)famous 'J Curve' – also referred to as 'hockey stick'. The European Venture Capital and Private Equity Association (EVCA) defines the J Curve as the 'curve generated by plotting the returns generated by a private equity fund against time (from inception to termination). The common practice of paying the management fee and start-up costs out of the first drawdowns does not produce an equivalent book value. As a result, a private equity fund will initially show a negative return. When the first realisations are made, the fund returns start to rise quite steeply. After about three to five years the interim IRR will give a reasonable indication of the definitive IRR. This period is generally shorter for buyout funds than for early stage and expansion funds.'

The 'classical' fund performance J Curve is mainly caused by the fact that valuation policies followed by the industry and the uncertainty inherent in private equity investments allow revaluing upwards promising investments quite late in a fund's lifetime. As a result, private equity funds tend to demonstrate an apparent decline in value during the early years of existence – the so-called 'valley of tears' – before beginning to show the expected positive returns in later years of the fund's life.

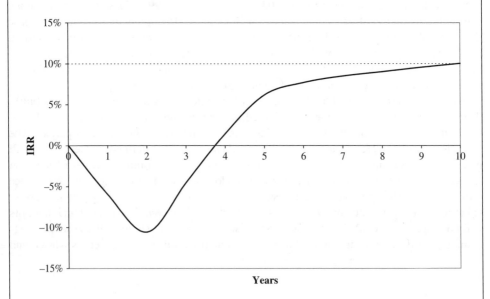

Figure 5.1 'Classical' fund performance J Curve

Some time ago,[3] we were musing whether the introduction of the new international private equity and venture capital valuation guidelines in 2005 would drive the J Curve 'to extinction' as a truly fair value for funds should not show a conservative bias. The reality was, as per Mathonet and Monjanel (2006), that the J Curve for young funds is not removed but, based on their estimations, only reduced to maintain a gap that decreases continuously up to the fifth or sixth fund's anniversary when, on average, the interim IRR becomes a reasonably reliable estimator of the final performance.

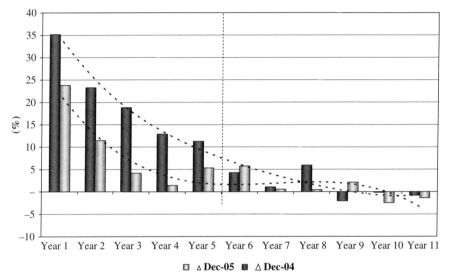

□ Δ Dec-05 ■ Δ Dec-04

Figure 5.2   Old vs. new J Curve (gap between the EIF portfolio's final IRR projections and interim IRRs as of December 2005 vs. December 2004)
Source: Mathonet and Monjanel (2006) and EIF.

But other J Curves can also be observed in private equity funds: the cash flow J Curve and the NAV J Curve. The cash flow J Curve is a representation of the evolution of the net cash flows from the limited partners to the fund, which are first increasingly negative during the early years of existence before making a U-turn to become positive in later years of the fund's life. This is explained by the fact that, in standard private equity fund structures, commitments are drawn down as needed, i.e. 'just-in-time', mostly to make investments in recently identified companies and that when realizations are made, after having successfully developed these companies, they are distributed as soon as practical.

Finally the NAV J Curve is a representation of the evolution of the NAV versus the NPI, which first decreases during the early years of existence before improving in later years of the fund's life. Like in the case of the performance J Curve, this is explained by the valuation policies followed by the industry and the uncertainty inherent in private

---

[3] See Meyer and Mathonet (2005).

Box 5.1: (Continued)

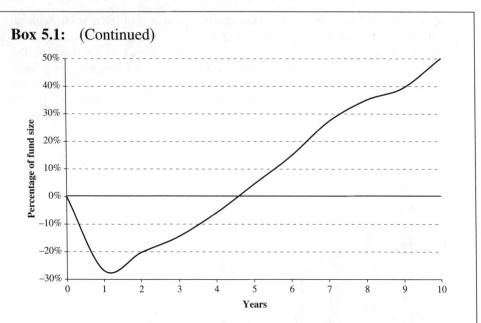

Figure 5.3   Fund cash flows J Curve

equity investments that allow revaluing upwards promising investments only after, on average, having been able to write down or off poorly performing investments.

Lemons mature faster than pearls

Proverb in Venture Capital

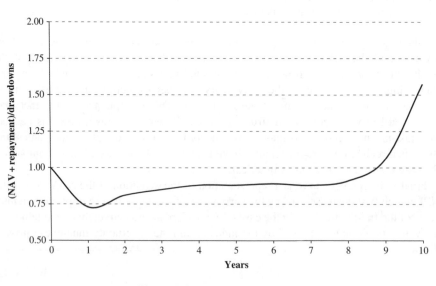

Figure 5.4   Fund NAV J Curve

VC funds are highly difficult to value. The negative impact of the J Curve, the workload associated with validations and a range of conceptual questions may even belong to the main obstacles to attracting institutional investors to venture capital. The experience of producing the first set of accounts under the IPEV guidelines for its private equity fund investments suggests that the practical and methodological problems related to the valuation of VC funds are often under-estimated.[4]

- Despite the introduction of IPEV guidelines, currently established practices for VC fund valuation approaches do not remove the J Curve for young funds.
- Uncertainty remains about the validations to be conducted by limited partners. A look-through for young VC funds with valuation reviews for start-ups creates a high workload, is of limited usefulness and is conceptually doubtful.

This, together with the J Curve, effectively creates barriers for investors considering an entry into the venture market. Additional problem areas are:

- The current practices for VC fund valuation cannot fully capture the risks to which limited partners are typically exposed.
- The J Curve not only has a conservative bias, but can lead to the misinterpretation that 'it is just the J Curve' and that a VC fund is doing better than it is in reality.
- The economic reality of, and the real risks inherent to, VC fund investments require valuation models. However, validation and acceptance of such models pose dilemmas.

The structuring of the investments in limited partnerships, which are the predominant form of VC funds, at least in the early years, has more in common with loans than with typical direct investments in equity, and, in fact, there have already repeatedly been proposals to introduce a 'rating' for private equity funds. This chapter's focus is on the practical valuation questions related to VC funds rather than their proper accounting treatment.

5.2 MOTIVATION

The IPEV guidelines have established a convincing framework for the valuation of individual unquoted companies. These valuation guidelines have found broad endorsement and are likely to be widely accepted. However, there is still a high degree of uncertainty and confusion regarding valuation and accounting for limited partnership shares.

In the context of private equity, fair value does give rise to questions and problems. So far EVCA together with PricewaterhouseCoopers has released two discussion papers[5] and there is an ongoing conceptual debate in the auditing industry around the application of the fair value option (choice between 'cost minus impairment' or 'fair value' accounting) to instruments lacking liquid markets. In the absence of market prices, valuations depend on judgment. Estimates can be significantly off the mark and they are also easy to manipulate. The reliability of valuations is the main concern of the auditing profession and creates considerable uncertainty for limited partners who have to draw up IFRS-compliant accounts.

---

[4] See Mathonet and Monjanel (2006).
[5] See EVCA (2005a,b).

Quoting one anonymous industry player, 'a mistake made by a large number is acceptable, not a mistake made by one auditor'. This is probably true and, as a corollary, auditors will most likely reject what is correct but not widely applied. Reliability of valuations has two main drivers:

- The soundness of the valuation model – an ineffective valuation model will skew otherwise accurate input information.
- The quality – precision, consistency, appropriateness – of information and judgment of the input for the valuation model.

The current approaches do not always give the economic reality of a fund investment, cause significant and often superfluous workload, and may even create entry barriers for investors into this important sector of the economy. The arguments brought forward here relate to the mainstream modus operandi for institutional activities in venture capital, i.e. investors that follow a buy-and-hold approach and invest exclusively through fund intermediaries structured as limited partnerships.

5.3   CURRENT PRACTICES

The IPEV guidelines do not address the specifics of private equity funds but of their investee companies. The absence of clarification has made this a debated topic with auditors. The established NAV method for fund valuation has the advantage of simplicity but it has to be kept in mind that this traditional market practice was not developed for addressing the question of a yet emerging fair value regime that would be expected to capture the economic substance of an investment. Consequently, a number of methodologies for limited partners have been under discussion.

- An idea that immediately springs to mind is to use a price recently obtained in the secondaries market. Kinsch and Petit-Jouvet (2006) see this as a theoretically valid approach, although EVCA (2005a) suggests that as such transactions often involve a forced seller this does not meet the primary fair value test in IAS 39R. Moreover, there are a number of practical problems. Only in rare instances do secondary market transactions exist for a given fund and not constitute public information. Moreover, they often cannot be considered relevant because of the time elapsed since the said transaction. Thus, this technique appears appropriate only to specific circumstances or to support other valuation methods.

Box 5.2:   Valuation disputes

Whether the NAV can be seen as the fair value of a private equity fund may appear to be a rather esoteric discussion, but a real-life case illustrates the relevance of the question. Lindroth (2006) reported a legal dispute in 2006 between the Norwegian listed investor Norsk Vest ASA and its management company Norsk Vekst Forvaltning related to a secondary sale worth NKr500 million (€62 million) to HarbourVest.

   In 2005 Norsk Vest asked Norsk Vekst Forvaltning to explore sales option for its private equity portfolio, comprising eight direct investments and its 67% stake in the

Norsk Vekst I buyout fund. Norsk Vekst I was founded in 1998 and quoted at the Oslo stock exchange with Norsk Vekst Forvaltning as the general partner. In August 2005 HarbourVest agreed to acquire six of the direct investments and the firm's stake in Norsk Vest I. For this purpose HarbourVest raised a separate fund, Norsk Vekst Private Equity Secondary LP, to finance the deal. This fund was controlled and partly financed by Norsk Vekst Forvaltning's previous managers. The deal value represented a 20% premium to the price quoted on the stock exchange, therefore apparently a favorable deal.

This secondary sales transaction, however, spurred a shareholder revolt at Norsk Vekst, and the firm's board was ousted at an extraordinary shareholders meeting in September 2005. The newly elected board hired a law firm to explore whether the sales process was rigged. Pareto Securities conducted an independent valuation based on a projection of what the investments would be worth in 12 to 18 months. This valuation approach, in line with our argument that the value of a fund is not just the NAV but rather the NPV of the expected cash flows going in and out of the fund, valued the company 30% higher than the sale to HarbourVest.

Therefore, in Norsk Vekst's opinion this clearly undervalued the assets and even led to allegations that Norsk Vekst Forvaltning acted in the buyer's interest and that only bids were pursued that promised a €10 million commitment to the new Norsk Vekst Forvaltning fund and involved the continuation of the management contract. Consequently, the deal was declared void in October 2005, and Norsk Vekst also revoked its management contract with Norsk Vekst Forvaltning with regard to its remaining direct investments on the grounds of breach of trust. Norsk Vekst Forvaltning's previous managers denied any wrong-doings and, together with HarbourVest, chose to take the case to court with the claim that Norsk Vekst was legally bound to carry out the agreements. Nevertheless, Norsk Vekst won the case (see Norsk Vekst, 2006).

- Another approach is to use the cost minus impairment methodology, as it is rarely possible to obtain sufficient fair value information on the investee fund and hence the range of possible outcomes for fair value cannot be reliably measured. Generally, it should be applied only where no reasonable range of fair value can be estimated through the application of other methodologies.
- Certain practitioners in the limited partners community have developed valuation models consisting of estimating future cash flows from their investments in underlying funds based on several factors including a grading and classification of the partnerships' management teams, discounting these expected cash flows and thus measuring and incorporating the value of undrawn commitments. This group feels that only by reflecting all these factors can a private equity fund's 'real' fair – in the sense of economic – value be determined.

Auditors see model-based approaches as 'conceptually interesting' but generally reject them. According to Kinsch and Petit-Jouvet (2006), the 'current lack of successful back-testing and the analytical resources they require constitute the main obstacles to a broader application of this valuation methodology'. However, at least the first argument is debatable, as also in the case of the IPEV guidelines it is convention and not necessarily economic substance that makes them acceptable under IFRS. Although the IPEV guidelines had been undergoing a rigorous peer review, to our knowledge they have been accepted as reliable without being backed-up. In fact, it is puzzling why back-testing, i.e. the examination of past performance to predict the future value, is thrown into this discussion. One wonder for which asset class – even where it is generally felt that it can be fairly valued – really a comprehensive back-testing for valuations has been conducted. Apparently a back-testing is supposed to validate that a valuation method used at time t is able to forecast the value of an asset at time t+x. In other words, it is based on the assumption that either all what happened in the past will continue to happen in the future as well, or all information relevant for an asset's value at time t+x is available already at time t. Even stock market valuations, which clearly are 'fair', would fail this test, as they after time t continuously react to all new information and events. Instead of being able to predict a price over a longer time period – who could would be better off by keeping this methodology a secret and exploiting it oneself – a valuation at time t can be considered as fair if it reflects the consensus opinion of market participants at that time. This is testable, for example through polls among experts, and our experience (see Figure 16.15) suggests that – with all the caveats associated with the limited sample sizes available for an alternative asset class – that our grading methodology can reflect the current consensus of investors in private equity funds.

Auditors see, for portfolios of private equity funds, the aggregation of underlying funds' NAVs as both the most common and the most appropriate valuation technique under current circumstances. Consequently, this method is broadly used by market participants for valuation of funds-of-funds when referring to the IFRS accounting framework. The general hypothesis underlying the NAV method is that the fair value of investments in a VC fund is represented by the NAV as advised by the fund manager (general partner). This valuation method implicitly assumes that the NAV of a fund can be considered as compliant with fair value accounting requirements if the fair value guidelines have been followed for the portfolio companies.

At the core of the debate is what has to be valued and under which assumptions. The views on what is the object to be valued and what is the purpose of the valuation exercise deviate. It has to be kept in mind that VC fund valuations are derived from portfolio company valuations but that they are not always equivalent. An IPEV-compliant NAV is the fair valuation of the underlying investee companies only. It is a good proxy for the private equity fund's fair value in situations where a portfolio of investee companies exists, where valuations are reliable, where there are no or insignificant undrawn commitments and where the future impact of the fund management is negligible, or under a break-up assumption.

If a limited partner would want to give the fair value of the limited partnership shares, and under the assumption that they will be held over their full contractual lifetime, the NAV aggregation cannot be reconciled with the discounted cash flow on the fund level. These two opposing views make the fair value debate in the context of private equity funds a confusing and debated subject.

5.4   PROBLEM AREAS

5.4.1   The negative impact of the J Curve

Even if portfolio companies are fairly valued, the development of the VC fund's NAV will continue following the J Curve. This happens for two reasons: firstly, even if no write-offs of portfolio companies happen, upward valuations take time. Management fees paid to the fund manager are not reflected in the NAV and result apparently in a 'loss'. Secondly, the J Curve is the result of an incomplete valuation model that is only connected to the investment already done. A major tangible component of a VC fund – the undrawn commitment in relation to the prospective deal flow – is not reflected and an important intangible – the fund manager's value – is left out entirely. Assessing the impact of these components requires a high degree of judgment.

Indeed, practitioners admit that this treatment does not always give the fair value for young VC funds,[6] and therefore auditors occasionally allow keeping such funds at cost. Deciding on whether or not a VC fund is still 'young' cannot be done by looking at its age alone.[7] Judgment is required to some degree, but generally funds would be considered as 'young' when having no or an insignificant number of portfolio companies years away from their realization or with significant undrawn commitments. On the other hand, a VC fund would be seen as 'mature' in cases where a sizeable portfolio exists, portfolio company valuations are reliable, and the fund manager impact on undrawn commitments is insignificant compared with the NAV.

If one interprets the objective of a valuation method as being to capture the economic substance of an investment, the NAV method currently in use for VC funds can be problematic. It does not always capture the economic reality from the viewpoint of a limited partner of an investment into a VC fund, as some risks are exaggerated while others are left out entirely. Risk models particularly need to reflect the economic substance of an investment. In other words, if an investment is 'good', then it should not show an accounting loss, while if there is an accounting loss, readers of the accounts should draw the conclusion that an investment is 'bad'. To base risk strategies on a fund's NAV rather than on its economic reality leads to short-term thinking. A valuation approach that is truly 'fair' should not follow the J Curve, but interim valuations should move randomly around the 'true' value with a decreasing error as the VC fund is approaching maturity.

5.4.2 The high workload associated with valuation reviews

Documentation of the fair value measurement methodology and the disclosure of the associated methods are crucial. Auditors require a number of checks to address consistency with IAS 39 valuation principles and guidelines used by the general partners in the calculation of the NAV, the quality of the valuation reporting, or the timeliness of the VC funds' valuation. It is indisputable that auditors should ask for relevant validations, but they should not ask for irrelevant and highly expensive checks.

For example, one of the most common features of venture capital investing – and more pronounced than in later stage private equity – is staged financing. In situations of high uncertainty, making new financing dependent on the achievement of defined milestones helps align interests and provide incentives to entrepreneurs to perform. Starting with a high number of start-ups and quickly pulling the plug where milestones are not met is integral to the venture capital business model. Accounting for this as a loss of the fund's value, or even as impairment, does not always reflect economic reality. Moreover, in such a situation a 'look through' approach, where start-ups are assessed individually, is questionable, as valuations need to take the fund manager's financing strategy into consideration.

---

[6] See, for example, EVCA (2005b).
[7] In the approach described in Mathonet and Monjanel (2006) this was restricted to funds not older than one year. How to measure a possible impairment is another question.

In a situation of high uncertainty auditors want limited partners to thoroughly check valuations provided by general partners and document the reviews undertaken.[8] But for investors with a high number of investments in VC funds the associated work can be considerable. In any case under uncertainty, even unlimited effort cannot render valuations more reliable, and it is neither practical nor meaningful for a limited partner to check or second-guess how a general partner assigned a fair valuation to these start-ups. Even where having access to all relevant information, with broad sector and regional expertise, and facing no resource constraints, a limited partner would still need to take a high degree of responsibility and justify a revised valuation.

A practical problem is that in the majority of cases limited partners do not have access to the insights that would allow them to make material adjustments to portfolio valuations. It appears conceptually questionable for investors in VC funds to review valuations. While general partners regularly interact with the management teams of their portfolio companies and receive frequent detailed reports on company progress, limited partners rarely even receive revenue or earnings numbers, let alone company financial statements or forecasts. In addition, limited partners typically lack the necessary expertise to value companies across a broad range of industries and regions, while considering the complex financial structures surrounding individual investments. They do not perform a due diligence on investee companies, do not monitor them and have less information than a VC fund's management and/or its auditors. This approach does not appear to be meaningful for venture capital as an appraisal-based asset class and most limited partners would feel uncomfortable taking responsibility for adjustments.

5.4.3   Entry barriers for new investors in venture capital

Is the J Curve of relevance? It depends – if you are an established player in the industry it may not matter too much. Experienced investors are familiar with the phenomenon and factor it into their considerations. Moreover, re-flows stemming from mature funds compensate for downward value adjustments for young funds. However, new investors are concerned about the J Curve. For investors considering setting up a VC fund investment program the J Curve forms one significant entry barrier as portfolios of young funds follow a steeper and more prolonged J Curve.

An analysis conducted by us on larger diversified VC fund portfolios showed that historically the maximum impact of the J Curve was 40% unrealized value loss when the undrawn commitments are not taken into consideration and 22% when undrawn commitments are factored in. If you compare the unrealized loss in value against the overall amount of resources dedicated to venture capital, the J Curve impact was never higher than 14%. One may argue whether this is then really an issue, but for pension trustees it is more than just a question of psychology. This, in combination with a number of conceptual problems and the workload associated with this exercise, could make those institutional investors who are subject to regulatory capital requirements question their activities in venture capital.

---

[8] See Kinsch and Petit-Jouvet (2006).

5.4.4   Current valuation techniques do not capture risk

Valuations and the associated risk measures need to reflect realistic assumptions in line with the investor's intention and his ability to hold an investment until maturity. One could argue that implicitly underlying a NAV-based valuation is the assumption of a break-up, as future management fees and the use of undrawn commitments are not considered. If there is no intention to sell, investors are not exposed to the ups and downs of the underlying portfolio and what happens to interim valuations is a matter of indifference.

VC funds are not just portfolios of unquoted assets, but as primary investments they are 'blind pools', where funding is committed to a specialist manager who will go out, identify and build investee companies. A fund portfolio valuation (expressed by the NAV) is only one input relevant for a fund share valuation and the impact and relevance of this input changes over time. In the beginning of a VC fund's lifetime, there is even no portfolio at all and the fund share valuation depends entirely on the fund manager's history and on judgment. There is simply no, or no material, NAV and the undrawn capital, i.e. the sum of all open and not drawn obligations to fund start-ups, is not captured in the NAV. Notably the NAV ignores the fund manager's role in growing start-ups or, unfortunately not all too seldom, destroying capital. A fund portfolio valuation is meaningful as a proxy for the fund share valuation only for mature funds.

Studies on the risk profiles of private equity and venture capital demonstrate that the risks of investing in a diversified fund-of-funds portfolio are much lower than usually perceived.[9] An investor who does not have the intention to sell is not exposed to the intermediate changes of investee companies' valuations. As economically a fund is different from a pool of direct investments, looking at changes in interim valuations of investee companies may exaggerate risks as it introduces an artificial volatility that is in contradiction to the view taken in the study, which takes the perspective of a buy-and-hold investor. As a measure of risk, the authors used the standard deviation around the average return, because it is not possible to measure the risk of VC funds as the volatility of a time series. While these results led to a reduced risk weighting for venture capital under CAD III (the European Union directive to implement the Basel II Accord in the EU designed to reflect specific European economic objectives), the corresponding accounting treatment remains unchanged and takes a different point of view.

5.4.5   The J Curve creates a false sense of security

'It is the J Curve' is an expression somehow equivalent to the accounting malpractice of 'taking a big bath'. Later on 'spectacular gains' give short-term oriented (or forgetful) investors the impression that high returns are typical for VC funds, while all the bad news is history. If in accounting terms a good fund looks like a bad one, there will be an inclination not to take action even if experts judge a fund a troubled case.[10]

Our experience with the development of NAVs for a portfolio of more than 200 VC funds revealed no clear differences between 'good' and 'bad' funds during the first four to five years. The major relevant information was found in non-quantitative indicators.

---

[9] See EVCA (2004).
[10] The philosophical question aside, whether in an illiquid market one can do something about it.

5.4.6   Models can be abused

According to the fair value guidelines, the 'objective is to estimate the exchange price at which hypothetical Market Participants would agree to transact'. Despite the notions of 'market participants', for venture capital fair transactions that lead to observable prices occur too seldom.

Limited partners hold shares in VC funds as financial instruments. The fair value of these fund shares depends not only on the current portfolio valuations but also on expected future cash flows that are not necessarily limited to investee companies within this portfolio. Indeed, in practice such valuations are often done with the help of cash flow libraries for comparable VC funds.

In principle a model-based valuation approach relies on financial data provided by a VC fund's general partner, market statistics, and on judgment in the form of assumptions and predictions. Some auditors are challenging the marking-to-market for the 'more esoteric items', as it is in reality a marking-to-model approach.[11] To address fair value under IFRS there is a problem when trying to value financial instruments where no market value is available – as is the case for VC funds – and where valuation models therefore need to be used.[12] At the heart of the argument is that marking-to-model can produce very different results when quite small changes are made to the underlying assumptions and predictions. How audit concerns can be addressed still needs to be seen, but these arguments put forward appear to be shared by many in the profession and pose a series of dilemmas for the venture capital industry.

5.5   CONCEPTUAL QUESTIONS

VC funds themselves are long-term and illiquid assets for which no market prices exist. One could argue that VC funds are always marked-to-model as the NAV is just a very simplistic model. It leaves out too much information and therefore may represent an occasionally highly distorted view of the economic substance of an investment in a VC fund.

Values derived by marking-to-model are certainly not observations. Indeed, the value of any long-term and illiquid asset is unobservable – only prices can be known. Assuming that the concept of 'fairness' in valuations is implying a kind of 'market consensus', then for an alternative asset like venture capital by definition there will be little consensus, and an expert will come to an appraisal-based valuation that will usually not be shared by the majority of other market players as they lack the specific insights or experience and cannot understand the assumptions. Therefore, the 'fair value' of a young VC fund is an artificial construct that does not 'exist' in reality and consequently cannot be tested.

5.6   CAN ONE DO WITHOUT JUDGMENT?

Usage of more sophisticated models for valuing VC funds for accounting purposes is not documented. For VC funds the reporting entities are the fund managers themselves. Such

---

[11] See Ernst and Young (2005) and Bruce (2005).
[12] Ernst & Young (2005) expresses its reservations with the subjective assessment and the associated calculations underlying such models: 'In all these cases, "fair values" will be determined by hypothesising what a market price would be if there were a market, very often based on management assumptions about the future and using a valuation model. We consider that it is inappropriate to refer to such calculated values as "fair value".'

reported valuations – that are marked-to-model as mentioned – are definitely not free from bias. Limited partners know – or should know – what are the good and what are the bad funds in their portfolio. They could theoretically mitigate biases and make these valuations more consistent; for example, through a 'rating' for the funds, if so permitted. To our knowledge, for accounting purposes this is not current market practice, as it requires a high degree of judgment. However, one can mislead by withholding judgment as much as one can by giving wrong judgment. Currently, if it is early days, readers of accounts are regularly told that this is the 'J Curve' and it is 'too early to tell' – basically saying, 'forget our accounting figures'. Whether the new valuation guidelines will change this is yet to be seen, but certainly comments and disclaimers in financial statements do not increase institutions' confidence in such investments.

For alternative assets in general the quality of the fund managers is key and consequently should be reflected in valuations. To pretend after two to three years of monitoring not to have any idea whether a fund manager is good or bad could even be misleading. Hopefully, all investors will have an idea on this before committing to any fund. It is certainly misleading to say 'too early to tell' if you know that a fund manager is inept, or to hide that for the bad performing funds there is still a contractual obligation to 'throw good money after bad'. Also, the readers of accounts should be told that only second-tier funds were invested in, in situations where the top teams were inaccessible. In alternative assets expert judgment is required, at the end of the day 'mainstream institutions' often delegate this task as they lack the necessary in-house expertise. A non-specialist reader of accounts will not know whether the fund manager was conservative or whether the portfolio is not doing well, but the limited partner should know and communicate this. Specialist investors in VC funds should be able and willing to give their views on the economic 'true and fair' value of their assets, which is not possible without some modeling, and it is a fair assumption that most use such models in their day-to-day management.[13]

5.7   IS THERE A PRAGMATIC WAY FORWARD?

Valuing the VC fund's investee companies through a consistently applied set of standards only addresses some problems associated with NAV. This method falls short of arriving at a true fair value as it fails to capture several relevant aspects associated with venture capital fund structure. To address these limitations, a handful of innovative limited partners have begun to model funds. While these models are imperfect and highly dependent on inputs, they generally result in more realistic fund values. For auditors, who look for both consistency and accuracy, this presents a dilemma, as the traditional bottom-up approach is more consistent but the model-based approaches are closer to the economic reality. Given this higher level of accuracy, it would seem appropriate that auditors should accept the latter approaches after first verifying that sound methodology is consistently applied.

An 'as true and fair as possible' view of the financial situation of companies would improve the investors' ability to make informed decisions. One has to accept that there are diminishing returns of time and work spent on valuing start-ups and that in alternative assets there are limits to reliability and verification. As discussed, this poses dilemmas for the accounting treatment.

---

[13] See EVCA (2005b).

Auditors want reliability, but reliability does not exist in the world of venture capital with its high uncertainty. In light of the problems discussed above, the question is whether one nevertheless tries to determine a fair value, or as some auditors advocate,[14] one should restrict the 'fair value' concept to deep market assets. A clear downside of using a model-based approach is that it is difficult to understand and that it can only be as good as the underlying assumptions. As models are to some degree 'black boxes', the potential for abuse is very high.[15] A practical approach will be a trade-off between sophistication and credibility.

Models cannot be fully avoided, and – as there are a number of structures to facilitate investing in venture capital – a 'one size fits all' approach should not be imposed. Limited partners need to choose the valuation technique best suited to their specific situation and modus operandi. For example, the specific characteristics between VC funds, buyout funds, emerging market private equity funds, young and old funds merit different techniques and models.

5.7.1 Differentiate between young and mature VC funds

There should be stronger differentiation between young and mature VC funds and tailored fund valuation approaches for different stages in their lifecycle. As accounting rules should be used to determine the financial circumstances of decisions, we propose for young VC funds a 'fair value' approach similar to credit ratings that may often reflect economic reality better than the net asset value-based valuation technique used traditionally. For mature VC funds, the traditional NAV-based approach should be followed.

This may not be an 'ideal' approach, but in an accounting framework that increasingly moves towards fair value across the board, it is still preferable to a fair value method that for young VC funds gives investors a wrong picture.

5.7.2 Accept different standards for reliability

Due to the private nature of the industry there are limits to data availability, and a fair value option that depends on increased disclosure and reporting requirements for VC funds will be difficult or even impossible to implement. Which creates a dilemma: how reliable can such valuations be? Any long-term asset valuation has by definition a high number of underlying assumptions and a wide range of outcomes, and valuations are generally appraisal-based.

If one takes the precision of valuations as a measure of reliability, there is an inherent conflict between fairness and precision for illiquid assets. To only take into account precise data and to leave out judgment does not reflect the economic substance of a long-term-oriented investment; on the other hand, a fair assessment that incorporates judgment cannot be sufficiently precise. If valuations for assets like VC funds were to be found precise and

---

[14] See, for example, Ernst & Young (2005): 'Perhaps the answer lies in a return to reality and a limitation on the application of the fair value model to those assets and liabilities that have real and determinable market values.'

[15] To back-test models for alternative assets is problematic or even impossible. The samples are too small to gain any credibility – for all cases exceptions can be found, while no statistically significant data can be compiled. Models probably would be more credible if applied by an independent party. This, however, may not always be feasible in the alternative investment industry that relies on judgment based on privileged insights.

reliable by a larger number of market participants, in one way or another real trading would also start – directly[16] or indirectly[17] – and the asset class would cease to be illiquid.

5.7.3   Assure reliability through valuation process reviews

One way out would be to accept, depending on the depth of the market for an asset, different standards regarding reliability. There is no absolute truth in valuation, and any valuation is at least to some degree based on judgment. However, third parties can review the model used, the process leading to a valuation and the consistency in its application.

Although in absence of prices, valuations for illiquid assets are not testable and their reliability cannot therefore be fully assessed, the process leading to valuations can be reviewed and found reliable. The review has to show that all available relevant information is systematically taken into account, and where judgment is applied, that it is structured and reasonable. Readers of such accounts can gain sufficient insights to form their own judgment from comments on the model review, clarification that the model takes significant expert judgment into account and explanations on how the model is regularly recalibrated.

---

[16] Publicly quoted private equity does not contradict the argument. Normally these vehicles are not 'blind pools' but have built up a significant portfolio. Secondaries are occasionally described as the 'advent of liquidity', but constraints normally surrounding such transactions make prices paid diverge from fair values. Moreover, there are too few secondary transactions and negotiated prices are usually kept confidential, so this is not a practical means to routinely value VC funds.
[17] For example through certificates.

6

Model-Based Approach
to VC Fund Valuation

The techniques of physics hardly ever produce more than the most approximate truth in finance, because 'true' financial value is itself a suspect notion. In physics, a model is right when it correctly predicts the future trajectory of planets or the existence and properties of new particles, such as Gell-Mann's Omega Minus. In finance, you cannot easily prove a model right by such observations. Data are scarce and more importantly, markets are arenas of action and reaction, dialectics of thesis, antithesis, and synthesis [. . .] Models are only models, not the thing in itself. We cannot, therefore, expect them to be truly right. Models are better regarded as a collection of parallel thought universes you can explore.

Derman (2004)

The quote is out of Emanuel Derman's autobiography *My Life as a Quant*. Derman was one of the first physicists to move to Wall Street and became managing director and head of the renowned quantitative strategies group at Goldman, Sachs & Co. His observation refers to efficient public markets, but the same issues hold even more in the inefficient and opaque private equity market. If we assume that the purpose of a VC fund's valuation is to determine its economic value, then we are faced with two issues:

- Firstly, despite the notions of fair market value in the context of VC investments, the valuations are based on guidelines that refer to methods with a set of variables and a set of logical and quantitative relationships between them – in other words, these valuations are to a large degree model-based.
- Secondly, the limited partnership agreement is a financial contract and its value is derived from the value of the underlying portfolio companies. According to this financial contract the limited partner has given up the right to sell the shares in the fund or the underlying portfolio. Consequently, when valuing the VC fund this has to be done under the assumption that the limited partner will hold the fund in accordance with the contract over its full lifetime.

We refer to valuations in a number of contexts, and it does not make the subject easier that various parties have differing expectations regarding what constitutes 'value'.

6.1 WHY MODEL?

'Fair value' in the context of accounting is, as we discussed above, an artificial construct that cannot in most situations be observed and so therefore cannot be tested for an illiquid asset like a private equity fund. Here the test for 'fair value' is essentially a check for compliance with the international valuation guidelines – or better, looking for absence of material violations of these guidelines.

Furthermore, valuations are used for determining a price for an acquisition. For this purpose a number of techniques – often techniques that are not acceptable under international valuation guidelines – are used. Ultimately, the price for which an investment in a venture-backed unquoted company is undertaken is a matter of supply and demand, negotiation skills and bargaining power, rather than of sophisticated financial analysis.

Finally, valuations take the form of forecasts. In fact, the most commonly accepted valuation methodology – the discounted cash flows (DCF) method – is based on a number of projected scenarios. If one can forecast an asset's cash flows and the risk related to them with reasonable precision one can also determine its economic value. However, it has to be pointed out that the reverse does not necessarily hold true: assets like gold certainly have a value and a price for which they get exchanged, but there is no cash flow stream that stems out of gold. Also take as example pieces of art that have no theoretical value, produce no cash flows, dividend yields or price–earnings ratios to help collectors to assign a fair value. Nevertheless, prices for an artist's work get established, for example through auctions, and set the benchmark for all future valuations. Despite the notions of fair value, venture capital – like real estate, art or antiques – is an appraised asset class, valued not by the consensus of many market players but by a few expert specialists who evaluate each investment based on their views of the investment's earnings potential and/or comparisons with other investments. To project cash flows for VC funds is a difficult exercise, which relies to a large degree on expertise and judgment.[1]

6.1.1 Modeling simplification

As we will discuss in this chapter, in the context of private equity, models can only to a very limited degree be driven by precise, reliable and complete statistical data. To allow drawing conclusions for management, to a large part we have to make explicit assumptions that are known to be 'heroically' simplistic but describe the economics sufficiently well to implement computer simulations that illustrate the behavior of a portfolio of private equity funds over time and its reaction to changing variables. What is included or left out of the model needs to depend on the approach to the management of a private equity funds portfolio.

While it would certainly be interesting to track the ups and downs of the portfolio valuations on a daily basis, this information is largely irrelevant for the typical limited partner that has the intention to hold the investment until its maturity and cannot trade on this information. Consequently, we see for such an investor the modeling to be mainly targeted at two questions:

- Assuming that it is to be held over its full lifetime, what is the private equity fund portfolio's economic value?
- What cash flows are stemming out of this portfolio? The asset class illiquidity and the statistical cash flow patterns make the second question of high relevance, as the PEH case demonstrates, where the inability to cater for a significant scenario change brought the company close to a collapse.

---

[1] A number of techniques are discussed in Meyer and Mathonet (2005).

Regarding the first point, in the context of the fair value exercise for accounting purposes auditors have reservations regarding model-based techniques as there is a perceived lack of successful back-testing. This argument is based on the implicit requirement postulated by auditors that valuations are predictions. It is certainly true that a DCF-based valuation is trying to predict cash flows, and a reliable prediction is therefore also an acceptable valuation. On the other hand and as discussed above, valuations should not be confused with predictions. Over longer time periods even prices for publicly quoted shares would fail this test, as they are continuously adapting to new information and unexpected changes in the environment.

When trying to value a VC fund ex ante when it is a 'blind pool' without portfolio companies or when it is in its early years and the portfolio is insignificant compared with the undrawn commitments, comparisons against historically realized returns form at least a reference point. Even if the valuation model is 'correct', due to the long timeframe and to the poor data quality, parameters have wide ranges that make results imprecise and not accepted by consensus. Moreover, the uncertainty of the VC market regularly leads to boom and bust, and investors tend to be either hopelessly optimistic or profoundly pessimistic of its prospects.

6.1.2 Model limitations

The auditing profession's concerns regarding model-based valuation of private equity funds appear to come from two main directions. Firstly, conventions are sticky. While a simple-to-understand, albeit not always correct method, i.e. the NAV aggregation approach, is widely used, and only few limited partners so far have systematically worked towards well-documented models. These models can be complex and difficult for auditors to check. Secondly, models can be 'massaged' to camouflage the limited partner's portfolio of funds' true situation, not only through higher, but also through lower valuations. The potential for abuse is very high, and quite correctly in an unregulated industry few would blindly trust model-based valuations.

The other important use of models in the context of the management of a private equity funds investment program is the commitment management. For this purpose indeed the model ideally should produce a prediction, which for venture capital due to the inherent uncertainty can only be possible over short timeframes and with limited reliability. Indeed, in this context modeling has a number of downsides. Typically the available data sets are too small to give the results any statistical significance and credibility. It is probably best to use a set of models like a pilot uses instruments in an airplane. No one of these instruments is giving the full picture, and all of them may fail or be entirely useless under certain circumstances. Rather than trying to forecast, they measure where the plane is and in what direction it is heading. A pilot is using several instruments together, sometimes as a check, sometimes because nothing better is at hand, but always with caution and as input to his own judgment. Model results can only be provisional and managers need to look for signals that indicate a gap between the stable model and the fluid situation.

6.2 THE PRIVATE EQUITY DATA MARKET

A major challenge for modeling facing both practitioners in private equity and academics is how to obtain good data on this industry. In the USA, private equity funds are exempt from the reporting requirements of the Securities Acts of 1933 and 1934 and the Investment Company Act of 1940. Although the literature intensively covers traditional asset classes, research on the private equity industry as a whole remains quite limited. Empirical research is still emerging but is hampered by limited data availability. It is felt that one actually knows very little about how and why the venture capital industry works.[2] As Bivell (2006) observed, historically 'accuracy' and 'venture capital statistics' have 'not been terms often associated'. Particularly in recent years there was a public outcry for 'transparency', and not only players in the industry started requiring certain disclosures. Particularly policy-makers, supported by academics, see an urgent need to gather more data in order to make rational and well-grounded policy decisions. The question of data availability is closely linked to discussions on transparency in the USA around the Freedom of Information Act (FOIA) and about making information available that venture capitalists perceive proprietary and hold very close to their chest.

However, there are also a number of practical difficulties and complications associated with producing high-quality data in private equity, for example related to inconsistent definitions of key concepts between countries and data gatherers that go beyond the scope of this discussion. We reflect on the economics of the market and very simplistically aim to shed some light on the trade-offs and constraints that affect the data quality. The objective is to gain a better understanding of private equity data limitations, but the purpose is not to discuss the pros and cons of specific data providers but the economics of the data market. It has to be highlighted that the private equity data industry does not stand idle. There are new entrants and types of service, regional coverage and quality of data in the widest sense are continuously changing, albeit not necessarily always improving.

6.2.1   Players in the private equity data market

Data on private equity investments is provided either directly by the general partners or indirectly by their investors – the limited partners – to data service providers (Figure 6.1). Generally there is reluctance in the private equity industry to make investment data available to the public. Some information in more or less aggregated form that gives a broad indication of market developments may be seen as desirable, as it attracts investors to the asset class, but detailed data on specific funds cause worries – not only for their managers but also for their investors. It should also not be overlooked that regular reporting creates additional work with possibly little benefit for the providers of data.

Figure 6.1   Private equity data market's information flow

Data service providers see this primarily as a business opportunity, as there is a clear gap between supply and demand for information on the private equity industry. Consequently, they push for higher disclosure standards.

---

[2] See Ginsberg (2002) or Beauchamp (2006).

Ideally we should have a system of performance measuring and reporting that is equal in quality and public disclosure to that of, say, managed equity funds, the names and performance of which are published regularly in major newspapers. The data consumer wants nothing less and I think that one day the industry will need to provide it.

Bivell (2006)

The main users of private equity data are institutional investors, governments, private equity practitioners, other industry professionals such as service providers, entrepreneurs and capital seekers, academics and the media.

Simplistically, the interests of the various parties involved could be summarized as follows: while relying on external data for investment decisions, general partners and limited partners would prefer not to give out their own data, data service providers want to sell data, academics like to analyze data and investors want to make money with the help of data.

6.2.2 Data providers

The data are largely self-reported by the venture capitalists or the portfolio companies in which they invest. Data service providers also receive much of their data from limited partners. These providers support the accuracy of their data, although it cannot be verified.[3] They describe this business as a 'win–win' proposition, as in the words of Private Equity Online (2004), the increased transparency would 'help to unlock potential increases in allocations to the asset class'. However, there are limited incentives to do so as they can easily freeride on information provided by others. While participants are usually being offered data services, such as tracking performance of others for benchmarking, for free or at a preferred rate, reporting data to the service providers also comes at a cost comparable to such savings in fees.

Why do general partners voluntarily provide information? To some degree there is peer pressure. For example, members of the various venture capital associations – predominantly general partners – are encouraged to report their financial figures. Also, general partners can be requested by their investors, particularly public or semi-public institutions, to be a 'good corporate citizen' and participate in surveys. Voluntary participation can also signal quality. According to Private Equity Spotlight (2005), a growing number of fund managers are sharing data with Private Equity Intelligence (PEI) on a voluntary basis, as they want potential investors to have access to the latest and most accurate figures of their funds. PEI claims that the 'best private equity firms will gain from a new "Gold Standard" in performance monitoring'.[4]

For limited partners the motivation is slightly different. Data service providers like Cambridge Associates are advisors to institutional investors and mainly collect data from their own clients.[5] Other players like PEI have been using public disclosure laws to extract information on private equity funds with the intention to resell this data to subscribers.[6]

---

[3] See Beauchamp (2006).
[4] See Private Equity Online (2004).
[5] Cambridge Associates claims to provide 'unbiased information and advice on financial and investment issues to endowed nonprofit institutions and private clients'.
[6] See Tricks (2005).

6.2.2.1   Freedom of Information Act

Under the FOIA documents and information in the custody of public bodies are open to public inspection or copying, subject to certain exemptions. This may include information held by those authorities in their capacity as investors in private equity funds.

Proponents of the FOIA argue that use of public money should be completely transparent and that pensioners should get full visibility on where their retirement funds are being invested. Opponents disagree and suggest that most pensioners would not be able to understand the complexities underlying the data, such as the J Curve effect. Such data are often seen as trade secrets therefore with legal risk related to disclosure. In the USA, where the debate was launched, fund managers have made it a point to avoid certain public funds. For example, Sequoia Capital made headlines some years ago. It initially allowed two universities into one of its funds, but changed its mind and excluded them to avoid any chance of FOIA-related publicity. But it is not only general partners but also the other limited partners of the affected funds who occasionally react negatively to disclosure. MacFadyen (2005) reported that the UK version of FOIA caused similar debates and quoted a private equity partner at SJ Berwin, Simon Witney: 'The new rules have blown a hole in the open relationship between fund managers and their investors. As a result, some funds have decided not to seek public authority money.'

In recent years, a shaky consensus has emerged that disclosure of partnerships in which public pensions have an investment, fund-level performance data or basic historic information such as commitments, contributions, distributions or unrealized values at fund level is acceptable. Representative for the current state of the debate is the California bill, sponsored by the University of California and CalPERS and signed by California governor Arnold Schwarzenegger, that codifies disclosure requirements, but also exempts certain items, for example due diligence material, quarterly and annual fund financial statements, capital call and distribution notices, or fund government agreements.[7] Also outside the USA comparable legislation is being adopted.

Generally exempt from disclosure under FOIA is information supplied in confidence to the public body by a third party and information dealing with commercial interest, i.e. does public interest in keeping the information confidential outweigh the public interest in its disclosure? Both general partners and limited partners are concerned about the risk that information on individual portfolio companies would have to be made publicly available under FOIA. But even data service providers do not pursue transparency on this level: 'We hope that it is clear that PEI has never, and will never, ask for portfolio company information to be disclosed.'[8] It is now generally accepted in the USA that fund-level information can be disclosed, where portfolio company-level information is exempt.

Some funds, however, feel that the only way to absolutely protect themselves against disclosure of sensitive information is to exclude investors subject to FOIA requirements. Where this is not feasible, Hamilton and Walton-Jones (2005) list a number of possible tactics such general partners could employ, for example to minimize the sensitive information and to ensure that documents which have been disclosed and are no longer being used are returned. General partners should also check the public authority disclosure processes. In the USA, general partners have been known to employ agents to request information from public

---

[7] See MacFadyen (2005).
[8] See Private Equity Spotlight (2005).

authorities to test how easy it is to obtain sensitive information. US legislation defines that public authorities who receive requests for information are required to notify the information provider when a request has been made or if they intend to disclose such information. In other legislations the limited partnership agreement should provide that limited partners are required to notify general partners if any request for information is received. The general rule is to avoid physical handover of information. Instead it is recommended to increase spoken communication or to prohibit investors from taking hard copy information away from briefings. Although password protection may not prevent the information from being subject to disclosure, it is suggested to use encrypted and password-protected websites for making data on funds accessible to limited partners.

6.2.3   Data service providers

For private equity there are no rules comparable to those of the stock exchange commission for enhancing transparency. Whereas in public markets everybody is obliged to provide a standard level of disclosure – with essentially the same costs and benefits for all participants – in private equity there is no regulatory body. All data is collected primarily through private equity and venture capital associations or through commercial institutions.[9]

6.2.3.1   Reporting format/standards

To increase the response rate, a reporting format has to be simple and self-explanatory. Data on private equity funds is often on paper and faxed to several data providers at the same time. To reduce workload and overcome reluctance to provide data, some data service providers follow a 'give us what you have' approach, with a set format with regards to data submission. Consequently, formats and level of detail are rather similar between various databases. On top of the work associated with the exercise, limited partners need to clear with the general partners that they are giving away the information. With this additional instance in the reporting chain, the time lag increases.

From the limited partners' point of view private equity is increasingly becoming an international industry, and data service providers need to have this reach. Local services are of varying quality. There are national databases that offer higher-quality information, but in some countries the private equity industry is too small to make commercial services viable, and therefore they are not covered at all. Variability in the quality of publicly available data may be caused, for example, by competitive pressures between data service providers, precedents that encourage the acceptance of incomplete data or by lack of experienced data gatherers and underestimating the task.

6.2.3.2   Private equity and venture capital associations

A number of private equity and venture capital associations undertake surveys, sometimes on their own or in conjunction with another organization such as a publisher or an accounting firm. For example, EVCA has had a longstanding partnership with PricewaterhouseCoopers. EVCA surveys have covered private equity firms that are not members and compile data

---

[9] In some cases governments also undertake private equity surveys. They can essentially force private equity firms to provide information, but not being subject to commercial pressures can create problems regarding quality, for example timeliness regarding dissemination of data.

from a large number of countries. Bivell (2006) rates the level of methodological disclosure in EVCA surveys as consistently very high. Although such associations are often able to provide data where a commercial service is not viable, they are perceived as not sufficiently independent.

6.2.3.3 Commercial services

Investors as well as researchers primarily rely on data provided by a handful of commercial services. Arguably, for limited partners Cambridge Associates, Private Equity Intelligence or Venture Economics from Thomson Financial are the main sources of private equity data.[10] Cambridge Associates appears to have wider usage among US-based investors, whereas VentureXpert is probably more widely used in Europe. Summary investment and valuation statistics of these services are often cited in the popular press and by policy-makers.

- **Thomson Financial (Thomson)** provides profiles of firms backed by venture capital and buyout funds through its VentureXpert (formerly known as the Venture Intelligence) database. Thomson admits that the data published is the result of a census of a large but still limited number of funds and considering that there is no commonly accepted authority or standard regulating the reporting activities, the data published could not be totally reliable.[11] According to Kaplan et al. (2002) Venture Economics claims to collect its data primarily from the general partners and is the official database partner of the National Venture Association. Based on our discussions with Thomson, in Europe limited partners provide half of VentureXpert data. EVCA encourages its members to participate: therefore, and also because the general partners receive benchmark data in return, their response rate is said to be high. VentureXpert does not provide its customers access to the cash flows themselves, but only aggregated measures such as average IRR or multiples. Grabenwarter and Weidig (2005) pointed out that Thomson actively tries to complete the data retrospectively, i.e. ask existing fund management firms for so-far unreported data on their earlier funds. This may lead to a bias, as unsuccessful VC firms are likely to have dropped out of the market and their underperforming funds are therefore not part of the sample.[12] Even considering VentureXpert's drawbacks – which are representative for the problems providers of private equity data incur – it is still the industry standard for benchmarking, and it is currently seen as the most accurate historical data source available for venture capital. The data is generally considered accurate enough for benchmarking purposes by the vast majority of the industry. Nevertheless, those relying on VentureXpert for modeling purposes should be aware of its shortcomings.

---

[10] See Kaplan et al. (2002).

[11] See: '2002 Investment Benchmark Report', Thomson Venture Economics.

[12] However, with an increasing proportion of data being reported by limited partners, survivorship and reporting biases should decrease. According to Grabenwarter and Weidig (2005), VentureXpert covers about 2500 funds (1700 USA and 800 Europe, representing between 70% and 80% for recent vintage years, although the coverage is significantly lower before 1990). Fraser-Sampson (2007) believe that more than for other classes of private equity, figures for European venture are very inaccurate. This is mainly because of what they include, not because of the individual return data. Firstly, many 'venture capital' funds are in reality university seed funds, local development funds, etc. It is suggested that just half of the European funds shown covered in VentureXpert would be eligible for investment by institutional investors, either because they are too small or they are not managed by independent, professional venture capital firms. In addition, there are many funds that are wrongly classified as 'venture' but which are in fact buyouts or something similar.

- **VentureOne** operates the VentureSource database that is said to provide more detailed profiles compared with VentureXpert, including information on directors and business profiles. For the USA, Kaplan *et al.* (2002) assess VentureSource's accuracy and detail of information as superior with data generally more reliable, more complete and less biased than VentureXpert data. However, its coverage does not extend as far back in time as VentureXpert and only includes venture-backed firms. VentureSource restricts subscriptions to limited partners in private equity funds and corporations making direct investments. VentureOne claims to collect its data primarily from the companies themselves, although it also surveys VC funds.[13]

- Like VentureOne, also **Sand Hill Econometrics**, which was launched in 2001, provides data on the level of individual venture-backed companies. It covers companies that are privately held, organized as C corporations and have sold securities to outside investors. According to Hwang *et al.* (2005), Sand Hill Econometrics reported then 50,734 funding events, which included the contemporaneous valuations of 9,092 private equity firms disclosed 19,208 times starting in January 1989. Using existing data from Thomson and VentureOne as a starting point, Sand Hill has developed a proprietary database system and methodology for evaluating private equity performance and releases the 'Sand Hill Econometrics Index of Venture'. The data is disaggregated in four sectors: information technology, retail, health and 'other industries'. To address intermittent pricing, essentially to get from an occasional price to a monthly price series, Sand Hill uses an interpolation method and for missing data – either missing valuations for known valuation events or for companies of unknown status – uses econometric methods to impute values. Price interpolation and correction for selection bias allows producing what Sand Hill claims to be an unbiased, continuous index of value for the universe of venture companies.

- **Cambridge Associates** operates a proprietary 'Cambridge Associates Non-Marketable Alternative Assets Database' with data primarily collected from their clients. Consequently, more limited partners than general partners are said to report to Cambridge Associates. Also, general partners contribute to the database, often in the context of their fundraising process and apparently because they hope that they will appear on the radar screen of Cambridge Associates' clients. At the time of writing this book Cambridge Associates is the second of the two largest private equity databases on funds that covered, as of 2004, 2100 funds with cash flow data.[14] Cambridge Associates mainly operates as an advisor gatekeeper and not a professional data provider as such. According to Grabenwarter and Weidig (2005), it often takes over the back-office functionality of fund investors, thus collecting data directly from financial data and not via questionnaires. The database covers 80% of existing US funds, but Europe is less significant due to Cambridge Associates' later arrival in this market. Dinneen (2004) claimed that Cambridge Associates' benchmark statistics is increasingly covering Western Europe and also emerging markets.

- **Private Equity Intelligence** is a relative newcomer to the industry. It made headlines when it used FOIA open-records laws in Massachusetts, Texas and elsewhere to collect data on state agencies' holdings in more than 1500 private equity funds to launch its service. Hancock (2004) reported that PEI's Mark O'Hare has *'peppered hundreds of state and city pension pools with requests for venture-capital data, which he sells to investors*

---

[13] See Kaplan *et al.* (2002).
[14] See Grabenwarter and Weidig (2005).

through his company, Private Equity Intelligence'. According to Beauchamp (2006), for approximately 800 out of 2800 funds PEI had the underlying cash flows, whereas Venture Economics for undisclosed reasons does not provide this any more. Its 'Performance Analyst' database gives individual fund data, e.g. fund-level data regarding returns, IRRs, cumulative IRRs, percentage called, percentage distributed or unrealized values.

Other publishers covering the private equity industry, such as Dow Jones or Incisive Financial Publishing, also collect data for this purpose. As they operate on a commercial basis they have to provide a minimum level of quality, but as the commercial success of the service depends on the size of the market, publishers do not cover all segments and geographies.

Data services' coverage, focus, quality, etc. can have significant differences, and the statements made above can only be seen as a 'snapshot' of continuously changing market conditions. Therefore, definite statements are not possible, but investors have simply no choice but to work with these data – although with a (large) pinch of salt. There are diminishing returns to transparency and quality of financial data in venture capital, as valuations are largely appraisal-based and do not constitute a transaction price. This is for a number of reasons, but also because limited partnership shares are not (or only rarely) traded in venture capital. With few investors as recipients of financial reporting and this reporting being largely inconsequential, spending too much time and diligence on achieving high quality is probably not worth the effort.

6.2.4   Users of data

The main users of data services are institutional investors in private equity, who are interested in funds rather than in individual start-ups. Detailed data on a large number of small start-ups can be meaningless as these companies are not tradable or even not accessible at all. However, different user groups have different requirements. Simplistically, one could differentiate between 'primary' and 'secondary' users of data services.

- PEI identifies the primary users of their data service: 'PEI provides information products and services to private equity and venture capital firms, fund-of-funds, investors and advisors'.[15] This group of users generally creates wealth through the investments based on the analysis of data and continuously need such information for monitoring purposes.
- We define as secondary users journalists, policy-makers or academics that aim to profit from the analyses, which are very often of a one-off nature.

Primary users are again general partners and limited partners, who are also the providers of data and caught in a dilemma. They face a trade-off between the costs of reporting own data and a potential loss of competitive advantage caused by disclosing them on one side and the benefits of accessible information for investment purposes on the other. Investors do not have to prove their findings to academic peers, but they need to generate investment success, which is easier to achieve when operating in secrecy. This user group is interested in transparency, but not necessarily at a level comparable to that in public markets.

---

[15] See http://www.preqin.com [accessed 25 August 2006].

There is more transparency in business, so it is increasingly difficult to find a hidden jewel.

KKR's Henry Kravis

Secondary users ask for the rigor and disclosure levels of listed equities – which is easy to understand, as they aim to maximize the data quality they receive for the price charged and do not perceive the trade-offs. Usually this is the group that appears most vocal regarding transparency and access to data. Academics want full disclosure of data with high reliability, but are likely to be less interested in timeliness. Policy-makers rely on academics as they usually appear to be less biased.

Many of the academic presenters at the conference lamented that good data is extremely difficult to find and that the lack of it has hampered their efforts to discover what, exactly, venture capitalists do.

Ginsberg (2002)

Essentially there is a trade-off between the costs associated with high data quality and the resulting benefits, which depends on the intended use of data. The various user groups weight their priorities differently. Academics have high standards regarding data precision and detail. While they and the policy-makers who rely on their research are interested in a complete set of data, they are usually unable or unwilling to pay the 'true costs' for this exercise. For investors, however, incomplete, inaccurate but timely and proprietary information has more value than detailed and highly accurate but outdated data available to the public. In other words, you do not need 'perfect information' to make money, and, in fact, reflecting on the economics of the VC data market provides some insights into why the situation is not as bad as it seems at first glance.

6.2.5 Quality of data

Essentially the ideal set of data should be complete, correct and timely. Private equity data quality suffers in all these dimensions:

- Private equity data are likely to have gaps, as market participants are not all known. Not everybody participates in surveys and previous contributors often drop out. Therefore it is difficult to assess how complete the picture of the market is. This may even be a requirement of the data providers to preserve some degree of confidentiality of their data.
- Data are also expected to be error-prone, as, in fact, relatively few parties work with the data. Funds and portfolio companies are usually not accessible for investment purposes anyway and therefore there is only a limited degree of peer review as a check and balance.
- Data can be stale, as they are often only updated after significant events. Moreover, reporting of financial statements can be delayed. For the USA, a 45–90 days time lag for reporting accounting and performance data had been described as typical.[16] Our own experience for European private equity data suggests an average delay of around 60 days between the end of the relevant quarter and receiving reports from the fund managers.

---

[16] See Maginn and Dyra (2000).

However, variations can be quite pronounced. Sometimes reports are already received within less than one week. For more than 700 reports observed during 2005, 30% were received within less than 45 days, 25% between 45 and 60 days, 33% between 60 and 90 days, and for 12% more than 90 days passed before financial statements were received.

Databases are not without bias and noise. Kaplan *et al.* (2002) suggested that for example VentureXpert and VentureSource understate capital committed, but provide relatively unbiased measures of the amount of financing. Measures were generally found to be noisy. For VentureXpert Beauchamp (2006) suspected that there could be selection bias caused by under-performing funds withholding negative information that systematically skews average return calculations upwards.

6.2.6   The economics of the VC data market

The main reasons why limited partners are interested in improved information is that it, according to Private Equity Online (2004), 'will help investors to make improved decisions and to monitor their portfolios better'. One could add that for some limited partners, e.g. funds-of-funds, research findings based on the analysis of this information help to attract new investors and to retain them. However, the higher the workload to produce these figures and to assure their quality, the lower the number of those who engage in this exercise and vice versa.

6.2.6.1   What level of transparency?

Data service providers engage in this exercise to make profits. They can maximize their financial gains through a combination of maximizing the number of subscribers and the fees they pay and minimizing the associated costs related to the collection of the data. The number of subscribers and the subscription fees that one can charge them depend on the quality of data. On the other hand, the quality of data is associated with costs proportional to the number of reporting entities and the depth of information requested. General partners have limited incentive to provide data to data service providers, as they can free-ride on data already given by others for benchmarking purposes. Usually they only provide data on the limited partners' request or to appear on the radar screen of potential investors. Limited partners negotiate reporting formats and can exercise pressure on fund managers to provide data to data service providers. Essentially thus the community of limited partners sets the transparency standards in the industry. In fact, there can be situations where limited partners and general partners agree and no data will be disclosed at all, e.g. in situations where limited partners want to have a privileged relationship with a high-quality fund manager and again can 'free-ride' on published macro statistics. Therefore we can simplistically reduce the information deficiency problem to a limited partner – data service provider relationship model.

Ideally from the viewpoint of a data service provider, one limited partner with data on all funds 'hands over' its entire database and the service provider sells it on, but of course then the limited partner would rather do the selling himself. In fact, the larger the limited partner the more information is given incrementally to the market. Under the assumption that everybody has the same access to the published information, such a limited partner might provide more data than is received in return from the other participants.

6.2.6.2   Limited partner workarounds

Many institutional investors in the sector create and maintain their own databases on industry statistics. They have privileged access to data on the funds they have invested in and are not constrained by the standard format and detail of publicly available industry data. They can therefore develop their own methodologies, and their reporting formats can go beyond what is required under EVCA reporting guidelines and even include portfolio company information. The quality of internal data is generally better, but biased by the institution's investment style.

On the other hand, such institutions receive many PPMs with quite detailed information, meet many teams at conferences and could therefore 'fill the gaps'. Being able to sift through external low-quality data and to link them with internal high-quality data to produce research or to run proprietary models often gives funds-of-funds the edge when acquiring mandates.

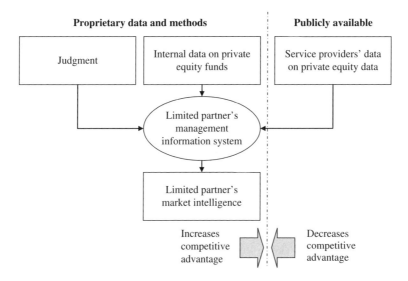

Figure 6.2   Limited partner's management information system

A limited partner's MIS (management information system, i.e. the application of people, technologies and procedures – collectively, the information system – to business problems) builds on external and internal data and on the judgment its users apply to the application (see Figure 6.2). As external data is publicly available, mainly internal data and the enrichment model that blends both with the limited partner's judgment drive the competitive advantage the MIS generates. Investment managers are trained to work with poor-quality data and their hunches do not have to stand the test of an academic peer review, whereas academics shun judgment. Whether models are academically appealing or 'elegant' from a theoretical viewpoint also does not overly bother investment managers.

The firm's portfolio database, designed and built from scratch, comprises detailed information on the private equity funds that Partners Group has invested in, on the more than 3,000 portfolio companies owned by these funds and on 'literally hundreds of thousands underlying cash flows,' as Wietlisbach puts it. 'It's the backbone of our entire fund marketing and investment process,' he says.

Borel (2005)

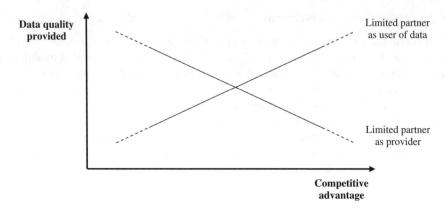

Figure 6.3   Equilibrium 'model' of the VC data market

The higher the data quality, the higher the costs involved. There are diminishing returns of scale, as one can also work with imperfect information and few data users will be willing to pay the price for perfect information (Figure 6.3). As real-time trading is in practice not feasible, there is no investment strategy in private equity that builds on accurate and timely information. Therefore, the benefits of increasing data quality are quickly diminishing. With increasing volume of own data, the MIS becomes more valuable and limited partners will be less interested in external data.

Researchers occasionally combine data from various services such as VentureXpert or Cambridge Associates, as this helps them to close the gaps in their view of the private equity market.[17] External data are never as timely as internal data (own models can estimate NAV, cash flows are known and not accessible externally).[18] For private equity databases, Beauchamp (2006) suggests that merging data from various sources reduces the selection bias.

---

[17] Compatibility of presentation in databases is a technical complication that to some degree can lead to distortion or loss of information (for further information see, for example, Ueda and Hirukawa, 2006). Take industries codes that are classified in more and some in less detail in different databases such as Cambridge Associates or VentureXpert. VentureXpert uses its own proprietary industry classification system VEIC (Venture Economics Industry Code). On a private equity fund level Cambridge Associates differentiates nine industry codes, whereas in VentureXpert eleven industry codes appear in the application menu to query for funds. The definitions are also slightly different: a single industry in one database may comprise more than one industry in the latter and vice versa. A fund labeled as 'Consumer/Retail & Services' in Cambridge Associates finds possible equivalents in VentureXpert under 'Consumer Related' (VEIC 7000), 'Business Services' (VEIC 9300) or – for the undecided – 'Others' (VEIC 9900). Internet-focused funds (VEIC 2800) in VentureXpert could be mapped to 'Communications' or to 'Software' or to 'Others' in Cambridge Associates. It is clear that this could make comparisons diffuse. Two funds with different industry codes in VentureXpert, for example 'Communications and Media' (VEIC 1000) and 'Computer Hardware' (VEIC 2100), may best both be mapped to 'Communications' in Cambridge Associates that has a broader definition. However, this makes any analysis across these databases more coarsely grained. Finally, there is no regulator that sets or confirms the allocations to specific codes. This is mainly based on the fund managers' self-declaration and often subject to 'style drifts' – in other words, an for example originally Internet-focused VC fund over time may well build a portfolio of companies from other industries.

[18] One could take the Global Positioning System (GPS) as a technical analogy. Its accuracy has been so good that the USA feared rogue states could use it for precision guidance of their missiles and therefore decided to just offer a degraded level to unauthorized users. Whereas standard users can determine their position within 100° m of truth, horizontal, 95% of the time, users that are authorized for the full precise positioning service can achieve 20° m accuracy. In January 1996, however, the Russians completed their full constellation of 24 operating satellites in the GLObal NAvigation Satellite System (GLONASS), a system almost exactly the same as GPS. With suitable hardware now even unauthorized users could then combine GLONASS and GPS data to achieve the quality level of the precise positioning service.

In practice investors do not appear to really need to have the full picture of the market, but only a high 'local resolution' where it is relevant for their specific activities. With a reasonable portfolio size, investors have access to high-quality information in the area they are active in and therefore is likely to concern them most. They just need external data on funds to get the big picture and not to miss out on trends. For co-investment activities, limited partners find information on portfolio companies within their own data. For these needs the sample size of private equity funds covered may then be more important than the level of detail provided. In this context limited partners mainly use external information for the calibration of internal data, for picking up deviations from the market and for benchmarking how they are doing compared with the market.

6.2.6.3 Protecting competitive advantage

The trade-off is between information that is kept proprietary and information that is shared with others. Ideally, a user of data would be able to get access to all information others have without disclosing own data.

General partners and limited partners do not want to provide information that benefits other investors at their expense. They accept transparency only to a degree where others cannot create a competitive advantage. Therefore, no party will provide data of higher quality than one is expected to receive from the data service provider, as this would create advantages for others and disadvantages for oneself. Parties that do not need data, or are not put under pressure from their investors to participate in surveys, are unlikely to voluntarily provide information.

The data quality provided by limited partners would therefore be just the minimum that makes internal models feasible. If data service providers request too much information, limited partners and general partners will not provide data. On the other hand, if data quality is too poor, few clients will subscribe to the service. Also, for the data service provider the minimum level of data quality acceptable for the limited partners is likely to achieve the highest participation with the lowest cost.

6.2.7 Conclusion

Lack of private equity data and its deficiencies in quality have been lamented within and outside the industry and repeatedly even provoked calls for regulatory action. A heavy-handed approach of regulators or policy-makers could, however, be counterproductive in the private equity industry that to a large degree depends on light-touch supervisory oversight and consequently sees self-regulation as a viable basis for its continuing development.

Taking 'private' out of private equity and trying to introduce public market-like transparency standards would just temporarily shift the demarcation line between standard and alternative asset classes. As the discussions around the US FOIA and the negative reaction of highly successful fund managers like those from Sequoia Capital show, the emergence of a 'confidential equity' asset class would be the likely outcome, as a significant population of institutional investors exist that are not under regulatory supervision. According to Forbes magazine's 2006 rankings of the world's richest people, in that year the number of billionaires around the world rose by 102 to a record 793, and their combined wealth grew 18% to $2.6 trillion. The industry would come full circle, with mainly high net worth individuals, endowments and family officers investing in inefficient market segments to the public.

Secondly, the quality problem related to publicly available private equity data remains to a large degree misunderstood and in practice is of less concern to the established players in this market. In fact, for experienced investors who can merge information from various sources and apply judgment to their interpretation, the coarse data rather offers opportunities to build up a sustainable competitive advantage. With a continuously evolving private equity industry and the lack of data, it is impossible to 'prove' a model. However, for in-house purposes limited partners are likely to view this more pragmatically in the tradition of Deng Xiaoping, who found that it 'doesn't matter if a cat is black or white, so long as it catches mice'.[19] The value of the limited partner's MIS is a function of the quality, completeness and relevance of external data, the quality and completeness of internal data, and the approach to enrich the data. The associated costs depend on the price for the data service subscription – which is of secondary relevance and the same to all subscribers – and the required effort to achieve quality and completeness of internal data for enriching the MIS.

---

[19] It is a fair assumption that for the limited partners the Arab proverb 'the dream of a cat is filled with mice' holds.

7
Private Equity Fund Valuation Approaches

As we discussed in previous chapters, when talking about the fair value of private equity funds we need to differentiate between determining the economic value of limited partnership shares under the assumption that they will be held over their full contractual lifetime and a valuation for the portfolio of companies that primarily aims to assure the timeliness of the reported NAVs and the compliance with the International Private Equity and Venture Capital Valuation (IPEV) guidelines.[1]

7.1 DETERMINING THE ECONOMIC VALUE OF A PRIVATE EQUITY FUND

In the 'NAV aggregation' approach typically followed for accounting purposes, the fund is not modeled in a traditional sense. Rather, the estimated current value of individual companies is determined 'bottom-up' and aggregated to arrive at what is assumed to be the fund's value. IFRS and the IPEV guidelines for this type of company-level valuation include using quoted prices for similar assets, earnings multiples and industry valuation benchmarks, but many of these methods are simply not applicable to most venture capital companies, and they still only provide guidance for valuing in a 'fire sale' scenario.[2] As a result, the NAV can represent a fund's fair value just in certain situations. This approach ignores the impact of the undrawn commitments and thus only makes the assumption that the limited partner is not liquidity constrained – as the Private Equity Holding case demonstrates (see Chapter 4), a possibly dangerous simplification.

Also in other respects a solely NAV-based valuation technique fails to reflect the risks of private equity funds entirely. For example, we would expect that the valuation of a young fund's portfolio – with still years before exit – would be less certain, show greater variability and accordingly more risk than a mature fund's NAV, where the portfolio has already been developed over some years, companies are relatively close to their IPO or trade sale, and where some consensus on transaction prices is emerging.

To work around the NAV's limitations some limited partners have developed models for determining the economic value of a private equity fund. Examples for techniques used in practice are based on a so-called 'modified bottom-up' and on a 'modified comparable' approach.

---

[1] Available on www.privateequityvaluation.com [accessed 9 May 2006].

[2] For entities with profits or positive cash flows, the fair market value should be based upon multiples (price/earnings, price/cash flows, etc.) based upon comparable companies or sub-sector averages. The valuations obtained should be discounted to take account of the illiquidity of the investment. It is recommended that the discount be at least 25%. Although IPEV guidelines and the valuation techniques mentioned by IAS 39 could be compatible, the use of the conservative value as a fair market value and the illiquidity discount can create differences.

7.1.1 Modified bottom-up approach

A fund can be modeled 'bottom-up' by analyzing its main value drivers in detail and aggregating these individual components to a big picture. Here an investor must first obtain information on the quality of the fund managers, the legal structure of the partnership and the current portfolio holdings. Next, exit projections for the underlying portfolio companies, including exit multiples and timing, are determined, resulting in company-level cash flow streams. The cash flow streams are then combined and filtered through the partnership structure to arrive at a series of net cash flows, which represent the cash flows the limited partner can expect to receive. These cash flows must then be discounted, typically by the target rate of return or the cost of capital, to arrive at a present value for the fund.

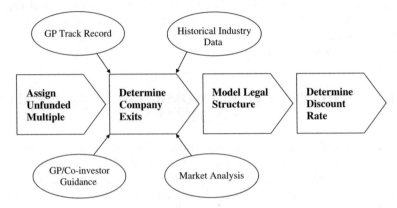

Figure 7.1   Modified bottom-up approach – overview
Source: Cogent.

However, limited partners may have difficulty determining exit scenarios for individual companies, especially in cases where even the general partner is unable to provide meaningful guidance. Furthermore, even if a limited partner was able to project accurate portfolio company exit values on a consistent basis, institutions with large portfolios would have to conduct extensive due diligence on potentially thousands of companies every quarter, which may not be feasible from a resource perspective. This high workload calls for practical solutions, such as for example the 'modified bottom-up approach' developed by Cogent Partners,[3] an international investment bank specializing in transactions of private equity secondary assets, private equity research and the investment of alternative assets. Their model depends on a variety of inputs including historical data, fund manager guidance and broad venture capital secondary market insight. According to Cogent, the model has the following characteristics that distinguish it from other approaches:

- It incorporates fund-related metrics and structural elements including undrawn commitment and partnership terms.
- It achieves a high degree of accuracy when specific company data is available.

---

[3] We would like to thank Bill Farrell, Brenlen Jinkens and Colin McGrady of Cogent Partners for the feedback on our model, the helpful discussions, and their explanations and material they provided us with on their approach.

- It provides transparency regarding actual fair value and discount rates due to proprietary knowledge of the secondary market.

In Cogent's model, both fund- and company-level inputs drive the valuation of a private equity fund. This methodology includes the following steps:

- Acquire fund manager track record, partnership terms and information regarding current holdings.
- Determine expected unfunded multiple, i.e. the amount the general partner is expected to generate on the undrawn capital.
- Develop expected multiples and exit timing for individual companies.
- Filter the expected company and unfunded capital proceeds through the partnership structure to determine final limited partner cash flows.
- Discount at the appropriate rate to determine a present value.

In order to begin an analysis, Cogent first obtains fund documents including the private placement memorandum, limited partnership agreement and financial statements. These documents provide relevant information regarding the general partner's track record, the legal structure of the partnership and the current portfolio holdings.

After obtaining this information, Cogent assigns an appropriate unfunded multiple. This is achieved by benchmarking a general partner's past funds against VentureXpert return data for funds of similar vintage years. After assigning each fund to a quartile, the results for all funds are weighted by commitment size to arrive at a total firm quartile. This result is translated into an appropriate range of likely unfunded multiples based on historical VentureXpert return data.[4] A subjective component allows for adjustments to be made based on the current investment environment, absolute strength of past returns and other considerations.

After assigning the unfunded multiple, Cogent determines expected exit multiples and timing projections for individual portfolio companies. In the case of an immature fund, where little or no information on companies is available, the base case exit multiple is equal to the unfunded multiple while the exit timing is equal to the average holding period for similar investments in the manager's realized track record. Since specific company holding periods cannot be reasonably estimated, exits are projected to occur over several quarters based on a normalized distribution of exit timings for previously realized investments. In the absence of a meaningful track record, exit multiple and timing assumptions can be estimated using historical data by deal type (early, balanced, late stage venture) and region (North America, Europe, other). As the portfolio matures, and as information on the companies becomes more readily available, the exit multiple and timing assumptions are refined to reflect better information. This is generally based on a combination of general partner guidance, co-investor insight and market analysis. All public investments are valued using a mark-to-market analysis, removing the effect of general partner discounts.

The expected return on unfunded capital and exit assumptions for individual companies are then combined with estimated future capital calls, resulting in a projected gross cash flow stream. The gross cash flows are then adjusted based on the partnership's legal structure, taking future management fees and the distribution waterfall (which we will discuss in detail in the following chapter) into account to arrive at a net cash flow stream for the fund. Once

---

[4] Based on discussions with Cogent, the final multiples generally range between 1.0× and 3.0×.

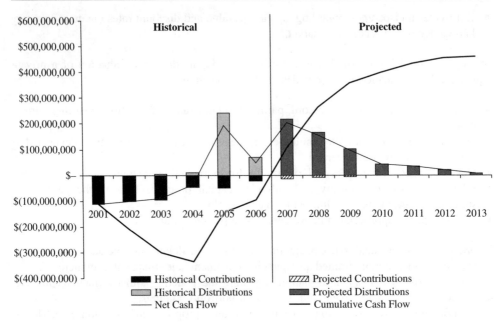

Figure 7.2   Modified bottom-up approach – projected cashflows
Source: Cogent.

the projected net cash flows are determined, the present value is calculated by discounting the net cash flows at an appropriate discount rate.

7.1.2   Modified comparable approach

In Meyer and Mathonet (2005) we have described in detail another option for valuing a fund, the GEM (Grading-based Economic Model) which could be seen as a 'modified comparable approach' as the principle valuation techniques used are multiples and a DCF. The expected performance grading is the major parameter of a relative valuation technique, where the value of a private equity fund is determined by benchmarking it to the observed values of similar or comparable funds. To apply this 'relative valuation' technique we need to obtain benchmark data for private equity funds and identify the best comparable peer group. The selected benchmark data is scaled to the commitment size of the fund to be valued, and the grading controls for any qualitative differences between the funds that might affect the value. The GEM does not rely on the projection of individual portfolio company exit values but rather on a high-level evaluation of the overall private equity fund and on information on the past performance of comparable funds. This technique is based on the assumption that the comparable funds' historical performance is representative and that the grading allows identifying these comparables. The expected performance grade (P-grade) is a ranking of a fund within its peer group that incorporates the following:

- A qualitative scoring which we will discuss in more detail later on (see Table 11.1).
- A quantitative scoring.

- A method to combine these two scores by weighting them according to the fund's 'internal age'.
- A review of the combination and, if necessary, an adjustment to arrive at the fund's grade.

Box 7.1:   Expected performance grades

The **expected performance grades** try to classify all funds into specific unambiguous classes where all members share similar characteristics. They are assigned based on the evaluation of both quantitative and qualitative criteria. In essence this system is based on general considerations and on experience, and not on mathematical modeling. It cannot be regarded as precise, and it also clearly relies on the judgment of the evaluators.

As the private equity industry obviously 'thinks' in term of 'top-quartile' funds, the quartile statistics form the basis for an intuitively simple grading scale. Normally, the industry participants define as peer group the funds with the same vintage year, geographical focus and the same stage focus. Due to scarcity of and lack of reliability in data on the private equity market, finer grades do not appear meaningful. Under the assumption that the fund's ranking does not change within its peer group and that it maintains its current quartile position within its peer group, its return is expected to fall into the respective quartile of the benchmark. That leads to the definition of the expected performance grades as in Table 7.1.

Table 7.1   Expected performance grades description

Expected performance grade	Description
P-A	At the time of the grading the fund's rank falls into the first quartile of the peer group.
P-B	At the time of the grading the fund's rank falls into the second quartile of the peer group.
P-C	At the time of the grading the fund's rank falls into the third quartile of the peer group.
P-D	At the time of the grading the fund's rank falls into the fourth quartile of the peer group.

The grading is based on the assumption that all investors are treated pari passu and relates to the assessment of the fund, not to the structuring of the investment. For example, secondary transactions are sometimes closed at a steep discount to the NAV. This, however, does not affect the fund's grade. A fund with a low expected performance grade of P-D does not receive a better grade because the investment was done under favorable conditions. Indeed, once the purchase price has been paid, it becomes a sunk cost and it is only the intrinsic quality of the fund that will support the future cash flows.

It has to be kept in mind that a fund with the highest ex ante grade of P-A may also fail and that funds with the lowest grading of P-D can well turn out to be spectacular winners. Moreover, just doing P-A graded funds should not be confused

---

Box 7.1: (Continued)

with selectivity. An ex ante P-A grading states that the proposal is closely complying with prevailing best market practices for funds, but does not address the question whether there are better funds around.

The expected performance grading could be seen as a proxy for a private equity fund's NPV and thus as tool to value it at a given point in time. The grading measures the perception of value and of risk, rather than predicting them. The GEM is projecting cash flows under the assumption that private equity funds' past behaviour will continue in the future and that the expected performance grades were correctly assigned – which can be heroic assumptions, indeed.

The comparables underlying the multiples are modified by filtering out benchmark data in line with a so-called 'expected performance grade' that is based on a grading system similar to the credit ratings of bonds and takes quantitative and qualitative criteria into account. Like Cogent's approach, the GEM allows for the valuation of other fund-related metrics such as undrawn capital, general partner quality and capital constraints. The GEM aims to forecast the terminal value of a private equity fund. The steps of this methodology include the following:

- Translate the limited partner's due diligence into a qualitative score.
- Determine a peer group of comparable funds and benchmark the private equity fund to determine a quantitative score.
- Combine quantitative and qualitative scores into an expected performance grade to rank the private equity fund within its peer group.
- Review expected performance grade.
- Estimate likely investment returns using the peer group's benchmarking data.
- Translate these investment returns into cash flow forecasts based on a library of historical cash flows or on a model for private equity funds. Discount these cash flow forecasts using an appropriate rate to arrive at the fund's NPV.

Box 7.2: Operational status grades

The expected performance grades are complemented by the **operational status grades**. The operational status grades capture information that is conceptually close to event risk. These events – unless a mitigating action follows within the short to medium timeframe – are expected to have a negative impact on a private equity fund's performance. The operational status grading methodology aims to identify these events and to form a judgment on its severity. In essence the grades have two functions: one is to alert in cases where 'red flag' events could have such an adverse impact that they need to be addressed right away, and the other is diagnosis, i.e. forming a judgment on the degree of the potential impact resulting in a priority setting for the monitoring corrective actions.

Events related to operational status grades can be the symptom of, as well as the reason for, underperformance. For example, tensions within a team are not necessarily the cause of a private equity fund's under-performance. It could well be that the team understands the status of its portfolio far better than the limited partners and do anticipate the private equity fund's failure.

Assessment of the severity of the event's impact is of course highly subjective. As there are all kinds of events possible, no exhaustive list can be given. Accumulation of such events is also a sign that a private equity fund is running off course and a sub-standard performance is to be expected. As these operational status grades can be indicative of a possible impairment, they should always be reflected in an updated expected performance grade and, therefore, tied into the fund's valuation. We also suggest four grading classes for the operational status grade depending on the severity of the operational issue (Table 7.2).

Table 7.2   Operational status grades description

Operational status grade	Description
Neutral	No adverse signals or information so far.
Problems	Presence of signals or information that – if no appropriate measures are quickly put in place – would be atypical for a first-quartile fund. Absence of signals or information that would be inconsistent with an expected second-quartile performance.
Failure likely	Presence of signals or information that – if no appropriate measures are quickly put in place – would be atypical for an above-average fund. Absence of signals or information that would be inconsistent with an expected third-quartile performance.
Failure happened	Events that – if no appropriate measures are quickly put in place – will result in a sub-standard performance or even in a failure or collapse of the private equity fund.

The grading system draws upon analogies from established rating techniques for credit risk. It aims to make the valuation process as neutral as possible and allow that two independent parties following this methodology arrive at broadly the same assessment. The grading system cannot eliminate the need for judgment, but aims to incorporate it in the process where it is best suitable.

7.1.2.1 Determine qualitative score

The qualitative scoring evaluates several criteria related to the quality of the private equity fund. Despite the frequent claims of 'we are investing in top-quartile funds only', investment proposals are rarely clear-cut and in fact usually there are shades of gray which the qualitative scoring aims to capture. It is a systematic evaluation of due diligence results to overcome the usual biases of investment managers. The purpose of the qualitative scoring is to benchmark the fund against best practices for the private equity market. Dimensions assessed are management team skills, management team stability, management team motivation, conflicts of interest, structuring and costs, and validation through other investors.

7.1.2.2 Determine quantitative score

The quantitative score is calculated by benchmarking a fund's interim IRR against its peer group to arrive at a linear quantitative score between 1 and 4, with 1 being the highest and 4 being the lowest. This method is relatively straightforward but could benefit from the inclusion of additional performance measures. While IRR is used universally in the evaluation of private equity fund performance, it is highly dependent on both the NAV calculation and cash flow timing.[5]

To determine the peer group for a private equity fund, a data service provider such as Thomson Financial is used to identify all funds with the same vintage year, stage and geographical focus as the fund to be modeled. The formation of a peer group for a fund allows a limited partner to see how a particular fund is performing relative to other funds at a specific point in time. The fund's performance is compared, usually on an IRR basis, against this peer group and a quartile ranking is assigned. While this method is relatively straightforward, a few potential issues, namely the quality of the data source used for comparison and the specificity of the peer group, must be considered.

In addition to the questionable accuracy of publicly accessible private equity data, another potential area of concern is the non-specific nature of the peer group. For example, VC firms are primarily focused on high-tech industries. Assuming that they are all expected to have similar growth patterns regardless of industry or regional focus fails to take into account specific investment strategies. Historical data does not necessarily justify this lack of specificity and, as a result, a fund focused on a specific industry or region could be penalized or elevated based on which funds are included in its peer group. However, it is admittedly difficult to perform consistent benchmarking involving industry or region. Private equity databases are limited in the number of industries or regions for which data is available, and often the industries that are available have extremely small sample sizes. Therefore, while more accuracy in peer group determination may be present in groups with large samples, the general lack of sufficient data would most likely render an industry or region-based ranking system unreliable and inconsistent.

7.1.2.3 Combine the two scores

The expected performance grade categorizes a private equity fund as P-A, P-B, P-C or P-D graded and ranks it within its peer group. Once the quantitative and qualitative scores have been calculated, they are weighted through a linear combination of the fund's internal age. When the fund is new, the performance grade is fully weighted toward the qualitative score. As the internal age approaches 1, which is equivalent to the fund having

---

[5] This leads to some concerns regarding the consistency of the measure as general partners follow different valuation policies and large early cash flows often have a disproportionate impact on IRR. As a result, the quantitative score could also consider other measures including total-value-to-paid-in (TVPI) and distributions-to-paid-in (DPI). Both ratios remove the impact of cash flow timing, and NAV is not considered in DPI. However, DPI is not particularly useful in the early life of a fund, as it will likely be zero in most cases. This limitation could be over-come by taking a weighted average between DPI and TVPI based on a fund's paid-in percentage, with TVPI having more of an impact in the early life of a fund and DPI being more heavily weighted in the later stages. This result could then be combined with the IRR, perhaps with an equal weighting for IRR and the DPI/TVPI weighted average, to help mitigate the effects of the NAV calculation and cash flow timing.

distributed the majority of its value, the performance grade becomes more heavily weighted toward the quantitative score. The total score is then reviewed and can be adjusted if necessary.

While being relatively straightforward, the formula for internal age incorporates the NAV. As previously discussed, the NAV may be an inaccurate representation of the current status of the fund's investments. In addition, the NAV is included in the denominator of the calculation of internal age in order to illustrate the potential total distributions of a given fund. This can also be inaccurate, since the NAV is not necessarily an indication of future distributions from the fund. Finally, it is another modeling simplification that the internal age implicitly assumes that uncertainty decreases in a 'straight line'.

Box 7.3:   Internal age

A private equity's internal age is defined as a combination of the 'drawdown age' and the 'repayment age' (see Meyer & Weidig, 2003). The fund cash outflows are relatively clearly defined in the limited partnership agreement with a pre-agreed maximum and should thus evolve between 0 up to the fund size.[6] In formula and using a scale from 0 to 1, the 'drawdown age' can be written as:

$$0 \leq \frac{\sum_{t=0}^{i} DD_t}{\sum_{t=0}^{L} DD_t} \leq 1,$$

where DD_t is the drawdown during the period $t-1$ until t, i is the interim time and L is the fund lifetime. The total cash inflows will only be known at the end of the fund's life. One approach would consist in estimating based on general market statistics (average total repayments) or any other estimator of total repayment. For simplicity, the third component of the interim IRR, the NAV plus the undrawn, can be used as a proxy. In formula and using a scale from 0 to 1, the 'repayment age' can be written as:

$$0 \leq \frac{\sum_{t=0}^{i} RP_t}{\sum_{t=0}^{i} RP_t + NAV_i + Undrawn_i} \leq 1,$$

where RP_t is the repayment during the period $t-1$ until t.

Then, by combining what we have called the 'drawdown age' and the 'repayment age', we get an estimator of the fund's internal age. Finally, to make it easier to use, it is divided by 2 in order to have the internal age ranging from 0 to 1.

---

[6] However, to be fully accurate, it should be taken into account that the total fund size is not always fully drawn down and that some structure allows to drawdown more than the fund size (e.g. reinvestment of the management fees).

7.1.2.4   Review expected performance grade

The last step in the calculation of a fund's expected performance grade is the review and adjustment of the grade. The grade can be adjusted based on such qualitative factors as diversification of a fund's portfolio or its operational status grade (O-grade). While these are all valid reasons, there is room for bias and, to some degree, abuse, since this is a purely subjective adjustment that can significantly change the projected performance of a fund vis-à-vis the GEM. Introducing quality controls into this process would allow it to become less subjective and more automatic. Such quality controls could take a number of 'red-flag' criteria into consideration, for example:

- Is the fund's portfolio over-diversified, i.e. are there too many portfolio companies per fund manager?
- Is the fund taking too much exposure to too few portfolio companies, sectors, etc.?
- Is the fund's remaining liquidity insufficient to support the portfolio companies?
- Is the quality of portfolio companies doubtful?

Funds meeting certain criteria could be upgraded while others could be downgraded. Such a system of checks, not dissimilar to the qualitative scoring method, would remove some of the potential bias and ensure the integrity of the scoring system.

7.1.2.5   Estimate likely investment returns

After the relative position of a private equity fund within a peer group has been estimated and a grade determined, the expected IRR of the fund is calculated. This is done by taking into account the fund's current grade, its past cash flows, its internal age and the probability that it will end in a particular quartile. Without going into the details of the model (see Figure 7.3), for an ex-ante P-A graded fund we assume that the probability to end in each quartile is the same, i.e. 25%.

One could argue that such weightings are too conservative. While one should certainly not expect a P-A graded fund to always have first-quartile performance, neither would one expect such a fund to end its life in the fourth quartile one-quarter of the time when the investment is made. Likewise, though one might expect fourth-quartile performance from a P-D graded fund, we observed that such fund turned out to be more successful then assumed at the time the investment was made. However, as long as the fund grades are updated on a regular basis, thus allowing funds that are performing better or worse than previously expected to move between quartile probabilities, these conservative assumptions will most likely be acceptable.

7.1.2.6   Forecasting cash flows

Forecasting cash flows for any alternative asset class is a challenge and requires significant effort and experience. Typically practioners need to utilize a number of complementary approaches. Simplistically we differentiate between techniques for estimates, projections and scenarios:

- The estimates method is based on relatively concrete near-term cash flow data. It relies on detailed information on individual funds, ideally obtained from the fund manager, reflecting the manager's own perceptions regarding the current portfolio and market

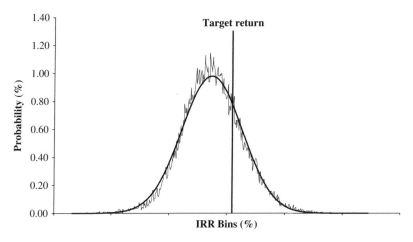

Figure 7.3   Monte Carlo estimation of the likely investment returns

conditions. Capital call and distribution notices that have been received are also taken into account. Additionally, as the estimate method is purely forward-looking, no historical data is taken into account, and the resulting estimates will consider the current economic and market environments. The problem with the estimates method is the limited partner's ability to obtain the information needed on a consistent and regular basis. The task of collecting expected cash flow data from numerous fund managers over a large venture portfolio and integrating it into a model on a quarterly basis is tedious.

- The projections method uses a library of historical cash flows. Given a fund's current performance, the fund is compared to similar funds in the library. Then the cash flows from the comparable funds are aggregated to forecast the future cash flows for the target fund. The method assumes that past patterns in venture capital cash flows will repeat themselves. The primary advantage of the method is that once a suitable cash flow library has been developed, forecasted cash flows can be obtained with little difficulty. The main disadvantage of this method is the assumption that historical cash flows have any predictive power in relation to current cash flows.[7]

- Scenarios allow managers to understand the different ways in which future events could unfold. A scenario should not be confused with a forecast of what will happen, but it is, according to the Forecasting Dictionary, 'a story about what happened in the future'.[8] A well-documented scenario tool for alternative assets is the Yale model[9] developed by Takahashi and Alexander (2001) of the Yale University Investments Office. The inputs to the model are the interim IRR, the fund age, the NAV, a growth factor (the expected

---

[7] This is questionable given the history of different vintage years in venture capital. For instance, many 1997 and 1998 vintage funds were fully invested within two years, and they subsequently distributed the majority of their capital at the height of the venture bubble. This clearly represents a more condensed timeframe than would typically be expected. Similarly, many funds investing in the post-bubble era waited significantly longer than would normally be expected to invest their capital, hoping for the market to recover. The timing of cash flows for these funds was correspondingly stretched. In order to alleviate this problem, a cash flow library must robustly cover at least a full economic cycle.

[8] See http://www.forecastingprinciples.com/, [accessed 25 November 2006].

[9] A detailed description of their model is given in Chapter 10.

fund IRR) and a 'bow factor' that tries to capture the current divestment environment for the target fund. The model generates a cash flow scenario for the remainder of the life of the target fund that is consistent with these input parameters and the dynamics of a private equity fund. The main problems with the Yale model are that it has no predictive power, has limited parameters and is entirely based on historical averages. As a result, it is useless for short- and mid-term cash flow forecasting. However, over long-term horizons, this relatively coarse model is acceptable simply because it is unlikely that any better forecasts could be made. Therefore, it seems unnecessary to use significant resources in an effort to make a long-term forecast more accurate, when additional accuracy may be unobtainable.

The estimates method is reasonably accurate in the near-term. Likewise, projections would be more suitable for mid-term forecasting, whereas scenarios have their main strength in long-term planning. Combining the various techniques can mitigate for their respective weaknesses, but operating them in practice can pose a significant challenge as it requires powerful IT support for the management information system. The various forecasts for the private equity fund are then discounted at a suitable rate and combined randomly through a Monte Carlo simulation to determine the fund's net present value.

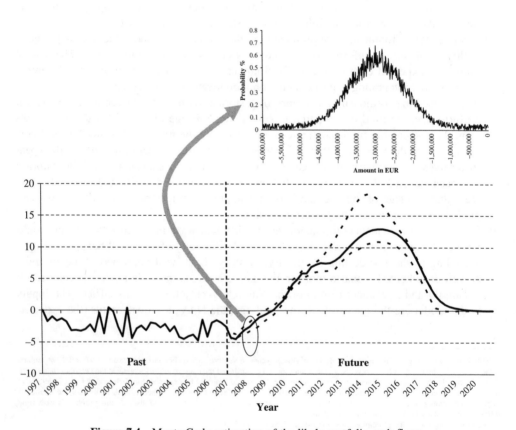

Figure 7.4   Monte Carlo estimation of the likely portfolio cash flows

7.1.2.7   Practical issues

Certainly the grading system cannot fully eliminate subjective elements or biases. Practices for venture capital will often deviate significantly from those followed in the buyout sector. Moreover, because market practices are in continuous flux, they have to be systematically monitored and reviewed by a panel of experts. If necessary, the qualitative scoring methodology has to be updated. Often this assessment has to be based on anecdotal evidence rather than on 'provable' facts. On the other hand, the approach is to a large degree based on common sense: for example most investors would have difficulties believing that inexperienced teams systematically perform better than experienced ones.

When applying the grading to more exotic private equity funds, e.g. in emerging markets, it is repeatedly suggested to define a different grading scale.[10] Theory would suggest that a comparable private equity fund is similar to the one being analyzed in terms of fundamentals. Therefore, for valuation purposes a different grading scale could certainly be meaningful in situations where another benchmark data provider offers better quality data for this specific market, which however is rarely the case. In absence of such data there is no reason why a private equity fund cannot be compared with another in very different markets, if the two are reasonably close in their characteristics.

Another item for debate is the question of conservative bias in assigning grades. In our daily work we often hear statements like 'I prudently assign an expected performance grade of P-B to this investment proposal' – an understandable reaction in an environment of high uncertainty. However, to be able to make proper investment decisions and to apply the appropriate monitoring during a fund's lifetime, assessments need to be as unbiased as possible. Otherwise there is a danger of deluding oneself or even misrepresenting one's value-added. When giving assessments a conservative bias, one essentially sets one's own benchmark, as no external party is able to understand the degree of conservatism being applied and could not measure a value-added. If an investment turns out better than the manager predicted, was it because his monitoring improved the situation or because he set his hurdle so low that the investment took care of itself? Or was the investment actually better than announced, but turned sour because the manager did not properly monitor it? It is certainly good investment management to have a conservative bias in decision-making, but the assessment from an expert has to be as free from biases as possible to allow the decision-maker to form an opinion. In other words, the questions of 'what is it worth?' and 'is it worth it?' have to be tackled separately.

7.1.3   High-level comparison of modified bottom-up approach and GEM

The modified bottom-up technique and the GEM approach private equity fund valuation from slightly different perspectives. Whereas Cogent uses the modified bottom-up technique for valuation to derive a private equity fund rating, the GEM uses the grading as input to value a private equity fund. While both tackle the problem of valuing funds differently, both methods address the concerns associated with the determination of fair value (see Table 7.3).

When discussing the long-term accuracy of both approaches, one has to keep in mind that any valuation relates to an asset with a remaining lifetime of usually several years in a

---

[10] However, a decision-maker who has the choice between two funds with grades related to different benchmarks needs to understand the characteristics of both or needs to be provided with a mapping between the two grading scales, which is usually not possible.

Table 7.3   Comparison of modified bottom-up technique and GEM

	Workload	Addresses NAV issues	Short-term accuracy	Long-term accuracy	Application
Modified bottom-up technique	High	Yes	High	More reliable than NAV	Focused
GEM	Moderate	Yes	Moderate	More reliable than NAV	Broad

highly uncertain environment – how accurate could any technique be under such conditions? However, here both approaches give definitely a more realistic picture than the traditional NAV-based fund valuation. In many ways the modified bottom-up approach appears to be the more satisfying approach, particularly for more mature portfolios. On the other hand, the associated workload to monitor a portfolio of funds and to measure the risks through aggregating – largely appraisal-based – valuations of individual companies can be uneconomically high.

In venture capital, where risk is very high even on a fund level and where there is little consensus on the portfolio companies' valuations, it does not make sense to spend too much time on detailed analysis. Moreover, for young funds it often cannot be assumed that portfolio companies are independent entities.[11] Here it is – in theory and in practice – more meaningful to view the fund's entire portfolio as one entity.

The GEM leads to valuations in all circumstances. A combination of the due diligence completed at the time of investment, readily available historical data and a moderate level of attention to the fund's current performance is all that is required to project the future fund cash flows and determine a present value. However, this approach also has limitations, as the GEM is fairly inaccurate when attempting to determine short-term cash flows. Additionally, the GEM, like other models based on comparables, fails to take into account the specific partnership structure. It can therefore only approximate the future cash flows that will be received by limited partners and so is more meaningful for younger funds where these factors matter less.

Consequently, the modified bottom-up technique and GEM could be seen as complementary and therefore combinable in practice. The main practical application of the GEM could be:

- To model the private equity funds portfolio structure and the associated risk–return trade-off.
- To simplify the cash flow forecasting process by initializing the projections for a larger number of funds, and then limiting the in-depth analysis to the value drivers of the private equity fund portfolio.

Moreover, the GEM can be used as a plausibility check and as an impairment test for funds in the context of accounting valuations.

---

[11] See Inderst and Muennich (2003).

7.2 ACCOUNTING VALUATION OF A FUND'S PORTFOLIO OF INVESTEE COMPANIES

The IPEV guidelines took effect for all reporting periods since January 2005. Mathonet and Monjanel (2006) presented the results of a survey on the subsequent adoption and accurate application of the IPEV guidelines conducted on more than 200 private equity funds in the European Investment Fund's (EIF) portfolio for the annual closing in December 2005.

7.2.1 Surveyed portfolio of private equity funds

As of 31 December 2005, the EIF had committed just above €3.1 billion to 217 private equity funds.[12] This portfolio was, with an average age of approximately 4.5 years, relatively young and in terms of vintage year spread well diversified and significantly invested in all vintages since 1997. Geographically it was also well diversified, being invested in all the European countries (see Figure 7.5). However, compared with other institutional investment programs it could be described as over-exposed to venture capital with an allocation of more than 40% in early stage and approximately 30% in expansion and balanced funds (see Figure 7.6).

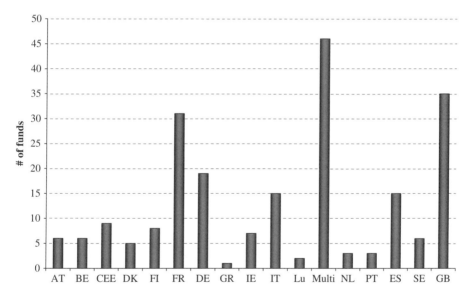

Figure 7.5 Portfolio by geographical focus (multi: funds investing substantially in more than one country)

Source: Mathonet and Monjanel (2006) & EIF.

---

[12] EIF's portfolio is financed by the following sources: EIF's own resources, capital from the European Investment Bank, the European Commission and the German Federal Ministry of Economics and Technology.

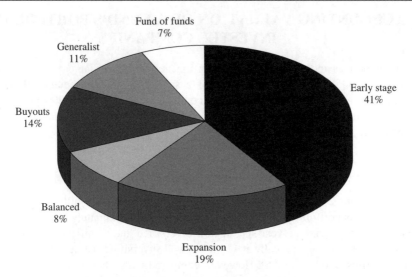

Figure 7.6   Portfolio by stage focus
Source: Mathonet and Monjanel (2006) & EIF.

7.2.2   Assessing compliance with IPEV guidelines

In June 2005, the EIF asked the funds in its portfolio to confirm that, as from 30 June 2005, they would comply with the new IPEV guidelines and report accordingly going forward. The funds' responses were classified as follows:

- **Class I** – funds that intended to adopt the IPEV guidelines and calculate Net Asset Values ('NAVs') that can be considered as a fair value in line with IAS 39 rules.[13]
- **Class II** – funds that did not intend to adopt the IPEV guidelines, but where minimum valuation requirements would be respected (e.g. old AFIC, BVCA and EVCA valuation guidelines) or where the NAVs would be produced under standards that can be considered as a fair value in line with IAS 39 rules.
- **Class III** – funds that did not intend to adopt the IPEV guidelines, and where minimum valuation requirements that could have been considered as a fair value in line with IAS 39, would not be respected.

Eighty percent of the funds indicated that they would adopt the new IPEV guidelines (see Figure 7.7). These results clearly show a very large market acceptance and intention to comply with these guidelines. The reasons given for non-compliance (i.e. Category II and III) do not raise concerns about this conclusion mainly because they were not related to the IPEV guidelines per se: as fund specificities (e.g. too small fund size or its liquidation status), cost implications (i.e. increased audit fees or administrative costs), the compliance with the limited partnership agreement – which only requires compliance

---

[13] The IAS 39 deals with the recognition and measurement of financial instruments and therefore of private equity fund investments. The International Accounting Standards Board has amended the IAS 39 in 2004 to be applied for annual periods beginning on or after 1 January 2005.

with older guidelines – the obligation to comply with local GAAPs, the GP's prefer-ence to report conservative valuations or not being decided on the intention to comply or not.

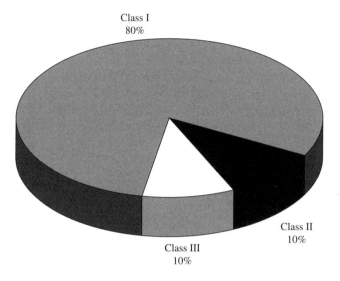

Figure 7.7   Intention to comply with the new IPEV guidelines
Source: Mathonet and Monjanel (2006) & EIF.

7.2.3   Assessing the degree of compliance

For its first year-end closing under the fair value regime, the valuation process for all funds in the portfolio was monitored. The objective was to verify whether or not the fund was in compliance with IAS 39. This review was conducted:

- For Class I funds, by assessing the compliance of the fund manager's valuation process with the new IPEV guidelines (and, therefore, its implied compliance with the IAS 39).
- For Class II and III funds, by estimating deviations of the fund manager's valuation process with the new IPEV guidelines and assessing its compliance with IAS 39.
- For all funds, by performing several spot checks to verify the accurate use of the fund manager's valuation process.

Within the portfolio, 91% of the funds have been assessed as IAS 39 compliant; mostly due to ex ante acceptance (80%) and accurate applications (almost 100%) of the new IPEV guidelines (see Class I in Figure 7.8). Almost all the funds that intended to adopt the new IPEV guidelines or chose to adhere to minimum valuation requirements (Class II) were found to be IAS compliant. Some funds that were not ex ante deemed to be compliant were also found to be compliant.

7.2.4   The impact of the new IPEV guidelines on valuations

As very few of the funds had reported simultaneously under the old and the new guidelines, it was not possible to accurately measure the impact of the new IPEV guidelines on valuations.

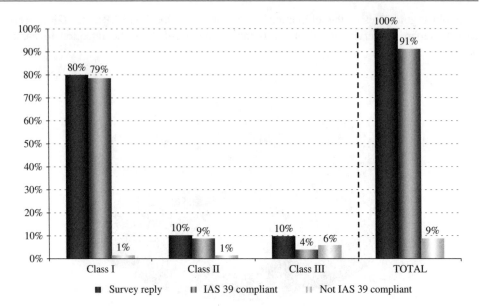

Figure 7.8   Compliance with the IAS 39 vs. the intention to comply with the new IPEV guidelines
Source: Mathonet and Monjanel (2006) & EIF.

Nevertheless, an attempt to isolate this impact was undertaken, which led to some preliminary indications.

Firstly, as of December 2005 and 2004, the quarterly and 'last 12 months' changes of the portfolio's average interim IRR[14] were calculated.[15] As these changes depend not only on the valuations of the NAV but also of distributions, one can assume that the fluctuations due to the market and distributions were similar for 2004 and for 2005. In 2004 the average interim IRR improved by more than 5 percentage points, while in 2005 it improved by more than 10 percentage points. Under the assumptions made, these results suggest that the average interim IRR of the portfolio as a whole has increased by almost 5 percentage points following the introduction of the new IPEV guidelines (see Figure 7.9). However, knowing that the 2005 distributions were more than 100% higher than in 2004, there are strong indications of good market conditions in 2005 and, therefore, the impact of the IPEV guidelines may have been less important.

As illustrated by Figure 7.6, the analysed portfolio was highly exposed to venture capital, while market participants normally tend to invest rather in buyout funds. Therefore, to better understand the impact of the new IPEV guidelines on the private equity market, we have also estimated the potential impact by stage focus. For buyout funds the potential impact was above 13 percentage points (see Figure 7.10), while venture capital valuations were much less impacted by the new guidelines with only a 3 percentage points change in performance (see Figure 7.11). An examination of the 2005 distributions confirms this conclusion; for buyouts funds, they were only 82% higher than in 2004, while for venture capital, they were 175% higher.

---

[14] The arithmetic mean of the interim internal rates of return of the funds in the portfolio since their respective inception.
[15] Impact of new signatures has been neutralized, so that only changes in IRRs are taken into account.

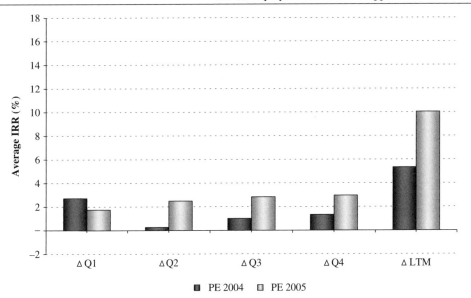

Figure 7.9 Comparison of the 2005 vs. 2004 returns for the entire portfolio – Quarterly and LTM (last 12 months) pooled interim IRR changes (Dec 2005 and 2004)
Source: Mathonet and Monjanel (2006) & EIF.

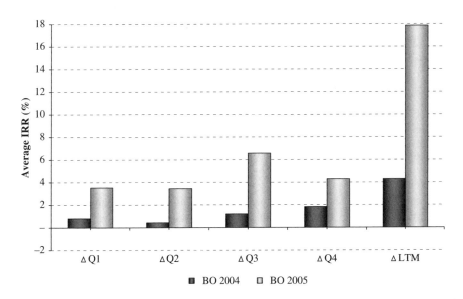

Figure 7.10 Comparison of the 2005 vs. 2004 return for buyout portfolio – Quarterly and LTM (last 12 months) pooled interim IRR changes (Dec 2005 and 2004)
Source: Mathonet and Monjanel (2006) & EIF.

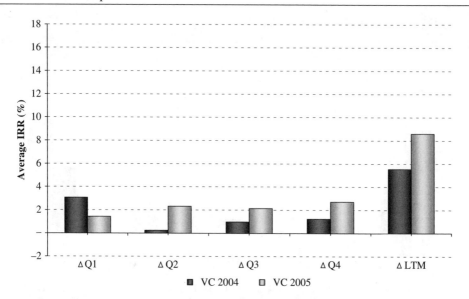

Figure 7.11 Comparison of the 2005 vs. 2004 return for venture capital portfolio – Quarterly and LTM (last 12 months) pooled interim IRR changes (Dec 2005 and 2004)
Source: Mathonet and Monjanel (2006) & EIF.

Certainly this over-performance could also have come from better market conditions in 2005 than in 2004. Therefore, also the horizon IRR[16] on a quarterly and yearly basis of the buyout and venture capital portfolios was calculated and those figures were compared against relevant market indexes, the DJ Euro Stoxx 50 for buyout and the DJ Stoxx 600 Tech for venture capital. Assuming that the private equity market is perfectly correlated with the relevant public markets,[17] these results suggest that for buyout funds the impact of the introduction of the IPEV guidelines was around 25 percentage points (see Figure 7.12) while for venture capital, this did not appear to have an impact (see Figure 7.13). However, assuming, as many do, that private equity is more risky than public equity (i.e. beta>1), the impact of the guidelines on buyout funds may have been less important.

This analysis also gives preliminary indication of a higher correlation between public indexes and reported fund valuations. Indeed during 2005, the horizon IRRs of the buyout and venture capital portfolios have been relatively well correlated with respectively the DJ Euro Stoxx 50 and the DJ Stoxx 600 Tech index (see Figures 7.12 and 7.13). This is further evidenced by the fact that when the same analysis was performed on the 2004 figures, the correlations were not similar. However, the limited number of observations and the interference of the new IPEV guidelines did not allow us to draw any final conclusions.

---

[16] The horizon IRRs are calculated using the fund's net asset value at the beginning of the period as an initial cash outflow and the residual value at the end of the period as the terminal cash flow. The IRR is calculated using those values plus any cash actually received into or paid by the fund from or to investors in the defined time period (i.e. horizon).

[17] There is a series of papers analyzing the correlation of private equity with public equity. A more detailed discussion on this topic can be found in chapter 17 of Meyer and Mathonet (2005).

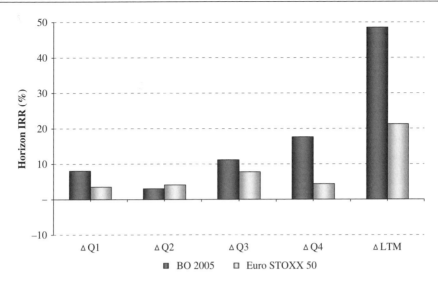

Figure 7.12 Comparison of buyout portfolio against stock market. Quarterly and LTM (last 12 months) horizon IRR changes (Dec 2005 and 2004)
Source: Mathonet and Monjanel (2006), EIF & Bloomberg.

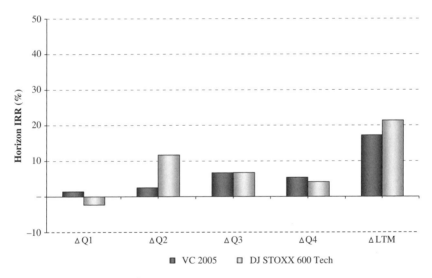

Figure 7.13 Comparison of venture capital portfolio against stock market. Quarterly and LTM (last 12 months) horizon IRR changes (Dec 2005 and 2004)
Source: Mathonet and Monjanel (2006), EIF & Bloomberg.

7.2.5   The implications for limited partners

Though the new IPEV guidelines have found broad endorsement and, as illustrated above by the 91% compliance within the surveyed portfolio, have been widely accepted and apparently accurately used, there is still some uncertainty and confusion regarding valuation and accounting for limited partnership shares.

7.2.5.1   J Curve

Current fund valuation techniques are giving a too pessimistic picture initially and occasionally a too optimistic picture later on. The J Curve phenomenon itself is an indication that traditional techniques fail at least for young funds. Despite the introduction of the new IPEV guidelines, the J Curve is not removed, but based on the survey, only reduced. As an indication of the remaining gap (see Figure 7.14), we have compared the final IRR projections produced by the GEM and the interim performance of the funds that report under the IPEV guidelines before and after the introduction of the new IPEV guidelines (i.e. as of December 2004 and 2005). To assess the J Curve effect, we have shown the data by age (year 1 being all the funds younger than one year, year 2 younger than two years and so on).

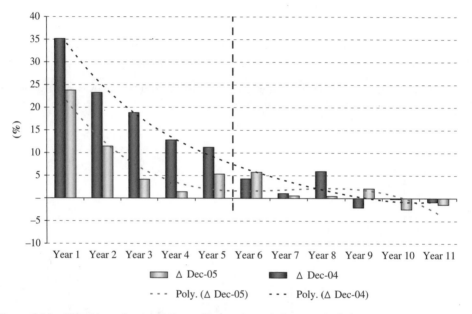

Figure 7.14 The old vs. the new J Curve (lines polynomially smoothed) (gap between GEM's final IRR projections and interim IRRs)
Source: Mathonet and Monjanel (2006) & EIF.

Both curves show very similar results. The gap for the first and second years and even the third year for 2004 data is very large (more than 10%), due of course, to the time needed to show 'fair' upward valuations and to the common practice of paying set-up costs and management fees out of the first drawdowns without producing an equivalent investment in portfolio. This clearly questions the relevance of the NAV for 'young' funds and explains why some practitioners prefer keeping such funds at cost (minus impairment, if applicable). Knowing the time needed to put the capital to work and to have reliable information to show 'fair' upward or downward valuations, keeping young funds (as a rule of thumb for two years, at least) at cost would be a more meaningful approach. Indeed, as previous studies or for example Burgel (2000) have shown, this gap decreases continuously up to the fifth or even sixth year where, on average, the interim IRR starts to become a reliable estimator of the final performance. However, some auditors, based on the one year 'grace period'[18] mentioned in the new IPEV guidelines, argued that NAVs should be used for all funds older than one year.

The difference between these two curves could also be seen as an estimate of the impact of the introduction of the new IPEV guidelines. The average difference between the 2004 and the 2005 J Curve is 5.3 percentage points, suggesting that the introduction of the new IPEV guidelines could allow showing earlier 'fair values'. However, as the market fluctuations are not isolated in this analysis, final conclusions cannot be drawn. Notably, one could argue that the good exit market conditions prevailing at the time of the survey could have decreased the magnitude of the J Curve effect.

7.2.6 Model valuation process

The model valuation process described below was followed by the EIF for its 2005 year-end closing. Its objective was to verify the compliance with IAS 39 of the latest private equity funds' valuation as reported by fund managers at year-end closing. These valuations form the input for the aggregated NAV method to determine a private equity funds' portfolio valuation. The only exception at the time of the study was related to quoted investments, which under IAS 39 have to be re-valued at available market bid prices while, under the IPEV guidelines, under certain circumstances a 'marketability discount' could then be applied. Limited partners are required to challenge valuations provided by the fund managers. This was done based on several monitoring activities, as illustrated in Figure 7.15.

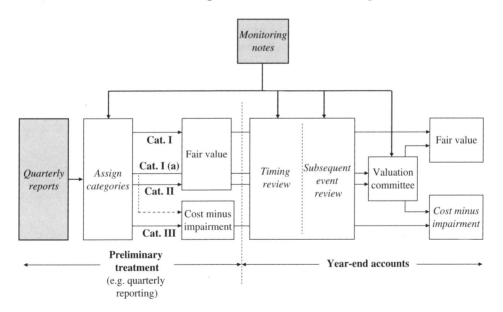

Figure 7.15   IFRS valuation process overview
Source: Mathonet and Monjanel (2006) & EIF.

---

[18] 'For some period of time after the initial Investment, the Price of Recent Investment methodology is likely to be the most appropriate indication of Fair Value. This period of time will depend on the specific circumstances of the case, but should not generally exceed a period of one year.' From the new IPEV guidelines.

Other approaches to valuation reviews are documented (see Box 7.5), but experience shows that no effort can change the fact that limited partners need to rely on the fund managers to conduct the valuations, and that the review itself can just detect lack of formal compliance with prevailing valuation guidelines.

Box 7.4: Valuation committee

For limited partners that need to fairly value their investments in private equity funds, what role could a valuation committee take and what would be its responsibility? To reflect on this question it is useful to take a look at private equity in the context of open-ended mutual funds where investors can come and go on a daily basis. At least in theory, mutual funds can also hold unquoted investments, for example in venture capital. Usually such funds must be able to constantly sell or redeem shares at a daily price that reflects the value of the securities owned by the fund, and the 'fair value pricing' must be based on a consistent and reasonable basis.

In the mutual fund industry the ultimate responsibility for valuations, pricing and liquidity lies squarely with the directors who need to devise policies and procedures and have to ensure that they are carried out. In some institutions the board handles such responsibilities, whereas others use a valuation committee. The SEC allows the board to delegate its day-to-day responsibilities to a valuation committee and/or the investment adviser, who may have their own valuation committee. However, the ultimate responsibility and liability remains with the fund's board of directors. The 'Valuation Committee is responsible for establishing and monitoring policies and procedures reasonably designed to ensure that each fund/portfolio is valued appropriately, objectively and timely, reflecting current market conditions. The Committee's primary responsibilities include:

- Assisting in defining the director reporting policies and procedures
- Defining valuation policies and procedures for the funds
- Monitoring and managing these policies and procedures
- Dealing with valuation anomalies as they arise
- Reviewing, testing and selecting vendors to assist in the valuation process
- Reviewing policies with the full Board and reporting on the success of the valuation procedures.'[19]

In situations where the board chooses to delegate its responsibility, it must approve pricing procedures, which the valuation committee or investment adviser must use in its valuation of the fund's investments in which market quotations are not 'readily available'. For the US market the SEC requires mutual funds to determine and report the fair value of their investments – meaning value in current sale – in restricted shares and other illiquid equity claims such as private equity. Under the Investment Company Act, fair value reporting is a 'certification standard' that presumes investors rely on the value representations of the fund board and its auditors. According to

---

[19] Quoted from MPI (undated).

Smith *et al.* (2000), the SEC apparently expected valuation committees to do more than approve the computation of fair value and thus to engage in some activities that normally would be the responsibility of an auditor. The SEC implied that, unless the valuation committee regularly challenges the valuation conclusions of fund managers, it is not performing its function. This SEC policy may have caused mutual funds to retreat from investing in private equity. Smith *et al.* (2000) contrast this certification standard with a transparency-based approach that simply requires that a fund disclose its holdings and describe them in terms of acquisition dates, original cost, restrictions on the holdings and other possibly relevant information, and then allow the market to determine value. In the case of publicly quoted private equity, investors or analysts would then demand more information, and funds that withhold information are certain to be perceived negatively and as a result trade at a discount.

From the viewpoint of a limited partner that invests in the typical unlisted private equity funds, however, the market's price-setting mechanism does not exist and thus provides no way out, which brings the valuation committee back to a certification role. According to Smith *et al.* (2000), by 'emphasizing certification over transparency, the ASRs[20] rely on the court system instead of the market to discipline fund boards. However, [...] the only cases likely to be heard are those where the SEC can demonstrate that the board's valuation procedures have been deficient. In such cases, the court is in the position of arbiter of fair value, a responsibility for which it often is not qualified.'

According to Kinsch and Petit-Jouvet (2006), some limited partners use valuation models aimed at capturing directly the fair value of the underlying investments of their partnerships: 'These models apply a "look-through" approach consisting in analysing and challenging the partnerships' fair values of all the significant underlying investee company positions and thus obtaining a consistent and reliable fair value at the level of the fund of fund [...] In the medium term however, with the increasing application of the Guidelines throughout the industry and the expected issuance of similar guidelines by non-European associations, less adjustments to the NAVs of the underlying partnerships should be required.' From this and also from informal communication with auditors we conclude that it is indeed expected that the limited partners 'certify' the individual portfolio companies' fair value and conduct adjustments where deemed necessary. As discussed in previous chapters, this creates a lot of work but is also conceptually questionable. At least for venture capital it is a fair assumption that most directors would feel highly uncomfortable taking responsibility for signing off on valuation committee decisions; where usually no independent sources for valuations exist, a 'true' fair value is unobservable and thus cannot be verified.

Consequently, rather than aiming at a true 'certification' for the fair value of funds held, we see a limited partner valuation committee's role in applying best business judgment appropriate to the circumstances. To a larger degree than for listed securities this judgment needs to be simply trusted. For this purpose, the valuation committee needs to underpin its judgment with clear policies and procedures and document their consistent application. Mutual Fund Governance Consulting[21] recommends a five-step

---

[20] Accounting Series Release.

Box 7.4: (Continued)

process that forms a mesh of policy and procedure by which it can be assured that valuations are consistently and fairly applied. This process can be taken as a template of a limited partner's valuation committee, where it would comprise understanding applicable guidelines, setting policy and procedures, isolating exceptions, deciding on treatment and recording rationale as required.

Understand applicable guidelines
The valuation committee's first job is to be thoroughly familiar with the IPEV guidelines, the relevant sections of IFRS and other applicable regulations, and the limitations of valuation approaches in private equity. Working closely with associations such as EVCA, private equity advisors and accountants is the best way to accomplish this.

Set policy and procedures
To a large degree, the IPEV guidelines have set the methodology for valuing private equity assets and are likely to lead to standardization and some degree of consistency across funds. The valuation committee has to assure that procedures for monitoring the proper application of the IPEV guidelines by the private equity funds and the limited partner's review process are put in place. Secondly, the valuation committee has to ensure that these procedures are followed. Here an institution's compliance and audit functions can assist in carefully watching that the system is working.

Isolate exceptions
In most situations a limited partner will not be able to value venture funded investments independently from a private equity fund's managers. Consequently, a limited partner to a large degree has to rely on the IPEV guidelines being correctly applied for the reported Figures. Reviews of valuations can only detect clear deviations from IPEV guidelines, but due to the information asymmetries, because valuation in private equity largely remains art rather than science and simply because of the workload, the compliance cannot be confirmed to the degree many auditors would wish for.

   The greatest potential for inconsistencies is usually in distressed funds, where fund managers may start to become 'creative' to put the status of their portfolio into a better light,[22] or for early stage investments, where obviously there will be the widest deviation of opinions on valuations. Consequently, the valuation committee needs to base its judgment mainly on the feedback on monitoring these funds (see Table 7.4 for an example of a standardized monitoring note, particularly comments in context with operational status grades and expected performance grades).

   The monitoring notes address 'triggers', i.e. events that require the limited partner's investment managers to notify the valuation committee of the possible impact on valuations. By specifying triggers, the valuation committee is placing the responsibility

---

[21] See MPI (undated).
[22] See for example Kaneyuki (2003).

on its investment managers to pro-actively inform them of potential valuation problems.

Deciding on treatment
Impairment triggers are reflected in the operational status grades O-C and O-D, which could indicate a situation of distress and where reported valuation figures may not be reliable to be considered as fair value. In such cases the accounting treatment under IFRS would be cost minus impairment. Based on this information the valuation committee decides whether a private equity fund has to be seen as impaired or not, and has to determine the amount of the impairment.

Furthermore, the limited partner could try to get an alternative valuation from reliable sources, i.e. in situations where several funds in the limited partner's portfolio have invested in the same portfolio company. A check of a sizeable portfolio of private equity funds demonstrated that of more than 2800 investee companies around 350 (13%) where held by several funds, which limits the application of this solution. Alternatively, and as apparently, suggested by Kinsch and Petit-Jouvet (2006), limited partners can try to value portfolio companies themselves. In practice, an approach where limited partners independently value venture funded portfolio companies appears only defendable in the case of so-called co-investments, i.e. the syndication of a financing round between a private equity fund and one or more of its limited partners. In this case the limited partner needs to monitor the directly held portfolio company as well, and therefore has the same access to information as the fund itself. Here the limited partner's valuation can certainly overwrite the fund's valuation for the same portfolio company, but such valuations are also subject to audits and require very detailed documentation. Moreover, co-investments are still usually only done in exceptions.

Record rationale as required
It has to be recognized that private equity valuations cannot be an exact science and often require a certain degree of discretion. The valuation committee is responsible for signing off on reported valuations or for determining the impairment of investments for which market quotations are not readily available. The presumption is that the directors act in good faith if they consider all facts that are reasonably available to them at the time and have acted with appropriate care and attention. Generally, the best evidence for this is to have a well-documented valuation process in place, to ensure that compliance and audit personnel attest that it works, to rely whenever practical on third-party experts and, above all, to have sufficient documentation on recorded values, methodology applied and resulting accounting treatment.

A last interesting point is whether valuation reviews in private equity should address the question of whether to investing institution itself still has sufficient liquidity to respond to the fund's capital calls. The liquidity issue is quite complicated from a valuation committee's point of view because it touches other investment decisions. However, as the PEH case demonstrates, a limited partner can only maintain valuations if defaulting as an investor or fire sales can be avoided.

Box 7.4: (Continued)

Table 7.4 Monitoring feedback form

Monitoring action	Visit, phone call, etc.
Monitoring action date	DD-MM-YYYY
Processed by	Name of investment manager
Processing date	DD-MM-YYYY (if different from monitoring date)
Valuation guidelines	Information into which valuation guideline category fund falls
Summary findings	Based on investment manager's judgment
	• Operational status grade (before/after).
	• Expected performance grade (before after).
Valuation compliant with stated guidelines	That is, no exception found
Further monitoring to be issued	Yes (in case follow-up required or specific case) or no
If breach of contractual terms involvement of legal services required?	Yes or no

Findings

Operational status

- Awareness of deviation from strategy.
- Conflict of interest detected.
- Defaulting LPs.
- Team events/changes/key-man event.

Other relevant events

- For example, new limited partners.

Valuation events

- Significant changes in valuation.
- New write-offs since last report.
- Major portfolio events/new exits since last report.

Valuation guideline compliance

- Valuation in line with relevant valuation guidelines.
- Guidelines inconsistently/wrongly applied.
- Valuation deemed to be doubtful.

Contractual compliance

- Awareness of breach of contractual terms (investment guidelines, terms and conditions).

Other significant events	That is, issues related to compliance with private equity valuation standards

7.2.6.1   Collecting quarterly reports as basis for valuation

Where funds do not report NAVs at fair value in line with the IPEV guidelines or IAS 39, limited partners could discuss with the fund managers the possibility of obtaining fair values. All future limited partnership agreements should foresee reporting under the applicable valuation guidelines.

7.2.6.2   Compare against monitoring notes

As limited partners do not generally have direct access to portfolio companies, they cannot independently come up with valuations that could be seen as reliable. Valuation reviews depend on the continuous monitoring implemented, where events that put the timeliness and reliability of reported valuations into question are systematically captured. We suggest documentation in the form of one standardized monitoring template as the basis for applying the described valuation review. The monitoring template has to capture events relevant for valuation, such as:

- 'Flash reviews' of regular financial reporting received from funds.
- Monitoring visits.
- Any significant information with potential valuation impact.
- Subsequent events.

The monitoring template covers a review of the valuation guidelines applied by the fund with the objective to assess as far as feasible whether or not the fund follows fair value compliant guidelines. This will be done by assessing the process applied by the fund manager, and by having this evidenced by spot checks of a couple of portfolio companies.

As part of the full annual review, the investment managers also assign, based on their judgment, an expected performance grade (P-grade) and an operational grade (O-grade) to each fund and express a view on any operational issues that are likely to have an impact on the reliability of valuations obtained from the fund (e.g. poor reporting quality and other factors which could be indicative of impairment, etc.). The operational status grades relate to events during the lifetime of a fund that were unknown pre-investment, but are considered to potentially have an impact on the fund's expected final return. Typically such events have an adverse rather than a positive effect.

Box 7.5:   Valuation reviews

Another example for a documented approach to valuation reviews is the Ohio Bureau of Workers' Compensation (OBWC) that retained Chicago advisory Ennis Knupp + Associates to formally review the valuations of all its 68 private equity funds.[23] Allegedly this exercise was prompted by 'Coingate', the nickname for the Thomas Noe investment scandal in Ohio. The OBWC invested hundreds of millions of dollars in high-risk or unconventional investment vehicles run by people closely connected to the Ohio Republican Party. One of these vehicles was a rare coin investment fund,

---

[23] See Primack (2005) and Ennis Knupp & Associates (2005).

Box 7.5: (Continued)

where later $10 million to $12 million worth of rare coins went missing and only $13 million of the original $50 million invested could be accounted for. The 'Coingate' scandal was a wake-up call for OBWC, which realized that its reporting, infrastructure and data maintenance was 'woefully inadequate and archaic'.[24]

Ennis Knupp + Associates asked each general partner to submit a 'valuation certification', in which the partnership manager was asked to fill in the blanks in the sentence to attest to the value of OBWC's holdings in the partnership: 'We certify that the Ohio Bureau of Worker' Compensation (Bureau) is invested in (name of partnership). The Bureau's proportion of the partnership assets as of March 31, 2005 was (percentage), and the market value of such assets as of that date was (dollar amount).'

Ennis Knupp + Associates examined additional information submitted by the managers. Furthermore, the advisor held phone conversations with most general partners in order to authenticate the partner's valuation methodologies and to determine whether or not the valuations were accurate. The final report included current valuations for each general partnership and write-ups capturing the substance of the telephone interviews and the verbal rationale the general partner provided to Ennis Knupp + Associates for the valuation of individual portfolio companies. Finally, the report states:

On the basis of this examination, and of our conversations with the general partners, Ennis Knupp + Associates believes the values shown [...] fairly and accurately reflect the fair market value of the Bureau's investment holdings in these partnerships on the date of the valuation.

However, the experience showed some limitations of such an approach. A number of general partners did not respond and – based on the report – apparently no corrections were done on reported values. Thus, even engaging an external advisor did not prevent OBWC from reporting numbers for some funds that were called 'wildly inaccurate'.[25]

7.2.6.3 Assign categories for preliminary treatment

Following the analysis performed above, the funds are classified accordingly:

- **Category I** – funds that have adopted the IPEV guidelines and calculated NAVs that can be considered as a fair value in line with IAS 39 rules.
- **Category II** – funds that have not adopted the IPEV guidelines, but where minimum valuation requirements that can be considered as fair value in line with IAS 39 have been respected (i.e. old AFIC, BVCA and EVCA valuation guidelines) or where the NAVs are produced under standards that can be considered as a fair value in line with IAS 39 rules.

---

[24] Quoted from Red Herring (2006).
[25] Quoted from Red Herring (2006).

- **Category III** – funds that have not adopted the IPEV guidelines, and where minimum valuation requirements have not been respected. In case of funds that cannot clearly show compliance with IAS 39, Categories I and II funds could be reclassified as Category III.

Category I funds with operational status grade worse than O-B will be labelled as Category I(a) for preliminary treatment. For Categories I and II, unrealized gains resulting from the fair value measurement go through Net Equity and unrealized losses will be assessed for impairment so as to determine if they need to go through the P/L accounts rather than through Net Equity.

7.2.6.4 Preliminary treatment

To draw up the first accounts and for quarterly reporting to mandators who require fair value compliant valuations, the preliminary treatment is as follows:

- Acknowledge NAV as fair value for Category I and II (unless operational status worse than O-B for more than three months).
- Determine impairment for Category III funds and Category I(a) funds based on operational status grade.

7.2.6.5 Timing review

The timing review is required to bridge the interval between funds' valuation date (typically 30th September) and the limited partner's year end (31st December).

7.2.6.6 Subsequent Event Review

The Subsequent Event Review (SER) is required to bridge the time interval between the limited partner's year end and final closing of accounts. Timing review and SER can be done in one step as year-end review. This requires contacting the funds.

To deal with timing differences between the limited partners' reporting date and the date when the NAV of the underlying investments are determined in accordance with IAS 39, the NAV will be determined based on the NAV as per the latest available reporting adjusted for changes in the fair value identified through the monitoring procedures performed on the underlying fund (drawdowns and repayments) or the re-valuation of NAVs on events known to the limited partner in course of the monitoring activities. Valuation-relevant events are to be documented in monitoring notes.

Publicly quoted investee companies will be re-valued based on latest quoted price (bid) as at valuation date. Private equity funds denoted in foreign currencies will be re-valued using the foreign exchange rates as at valuation date.

7.2.6.7 Valuation committee

The valuation committee comprises the limited partner's key executives. Based on the documentation provided (financial reporting received from private equity funds and monitoring notes) the valuation committee has to give its sign-off to acknowledge each private equity fund's unrealized gain for:

- Category I(a) funds, i.e. funds that allegedly comply with fair value guidelines, but where the private equity fund's operational status casts doubt on the consistency in applying the guidelines.
- Category II funds, i.e. in situations where there is no change vs. the old industry guidelines (such as those from EVCA before the introduction of the IPEV guidelines), but valuations provided by private equity funds can be seen as reliant and monitoring information is deemed to be sufficient.

Alternatively, the valuation committee may decide to assign the respective fund to Category III. This will involve detailed documentation of decisions taken and judgments made in a sign-off form.

7.2.6.8   *Private equity fund impairment measurement procedure*

Categories I and II with unrealized losses have to be assessed for impairment so as to determine if they need to go through the P/L accounts rather than through Net Equity. The decline in value is estimated as significant and prolonged and, therefore, will be seen as an impairment, only when funds are graded P-D, i.e. the worse performance grade. In the case of funds graded P-A, P-B or P-C, the decline in value is not significant and prolonged, as supported by market statistics.

Furthermore, when funds are put into Category III, i.e. where valuations provided by the fund managers cannot be considered as fair value, they need to be accounted for at cost minus impairment under IFRS. For such private equity funds it needs to be checked whether there are indications for impairment, and, if necessary, its amount needs to be determined. The treatment of young funds is cost minus impairment. Impairment triggers are reflected in operational status grades O-C and O-D and performance grades P-C and P-D. The amount of impairment can be estimated based either on a valuation model, such as the GEM or, more simplistically, based on an impairment matrix. The inputs to this matrix are the expected performance grade and the operational status grade. As there is insufficient information to accurately assess the impairment, decreases in value are, in practice and in conformity with relevant industry valuation guidelines, assessed in tranches of 25% of the net paid out (or cost).

7.3   CONCLUSION

In this chapter we have discussed three valuation techniques for private equity funds. The modified bottom-up approach and the GEM, while following different approaches, should – at least in theory – lead to comparable results. The third technique reflects current accounting practices, but is an incomplete valuation model that is taking, as described in previous chapters, another and not necessarily realistic perspective and therefore will not always reflect the economic reality of the entire investment into a private equity fund.

8

Distribution Waterfall

The distribution waterfall sets out how distributions from a private equity fund will be split and in which priority they will be paid out, i.e. what amount must be distributed to the limited partners before the fund managers receive carried interest.

The problem is that over the years, so many layers have been added to the equation that often it is extremely difficult for anybody to understand or even model the waterfall. Some newer GPs (who can tend to have fewer financial staff) might not even understand their own waterfall, let alone their LPs.

CPEE (2004)

8.1 INTRODUCTION

The timing and manner in which a private equity fund makes distributions to its partners are provided for in the partnership agreement. These provisions are commonly referred to as 'the waterfall' and are often the most complex parts of the agreement. This is, as we will see in this chapter, not straightforward. Moreover, a private equity fund's economics is basically driven by the distribution waterfall mainly comprising return of capital, preferred return or 'hurdle', general partner catch-up and general partner carried interest. As it is confusing to explain one term without referring to the others, already at this point short definitions based on the EVCA glossary are given:[1]

- **Carried interest** is '*a bonus entitlement accruing to an investment fund's management company or individual members of the fund management team. Carried interest (typically up to 20% of the profits of the fund) becomes payable once the investors have achieved repayment of their original investment in the fund plus a defined hurdle rate.*'
- **Hurdle** rate is the '*IRR that private equity fund managers must return to their investors before they can receive carried interest*'. The term 'preferred return' is often used as equivalent.
- A **claw back clause** requires '*the general partners in an investment fund to return capital to the limited partners to the extent that the general partner has received more than its agreed profit split. The claw back ensures that, if an investment fund exits from strong performers early in its life and weaker performers are left at the end, the limited partners get back their capital contributions, expenses and any preferred return promised in the partnership agreement.*'

---

[1] Available from http://www.evca.com/html/PE_industry/glossary.asp [accessed 30 March 2007].

The carried interest allocation to the individual fund managers also sheds some light on a private equity firm's decision-making process. As a generalization, in firms where the carried interest is divided unevenly, decision-making will be less consensus-driven than in firms where the carry is divided evenly. In this context, Fleischer (2005) found that internal 'GP compensation practices are an even bigger mystery than GP-LP practices'. Many firms appear to adjust carried interest shares according to the involvement of each individual in a particular deal. Often management fees are paid to a separate company owned by senior members of the management team and are thus also unequally allocated to the individuals. Likewise, vesting schedules and divisions of clawback liabilities can be markedly different and are likely to have an impact on the fund management team's decision-making process and internal governance.

Incentive structures will always have an effect, sometimes even unintended ones. They affect motivation and attitude, sense of responsibility, accountability, purpose and priorities. Experience has shown that consistent superior performance is based on a true alignment with investors' interests. Limited partners need to understand a fund's economics as this has a significant impact on the behavioral drivers of the fund managers' performance. For this purpose it is necessary to consider a whole range of scenarios in response to the incentive structure. The design of terms and conditions is one of the few opportunities where limited partners can anticipate and manage risk. Consequently much attention is put on this question, although the exact value of terms and conditions is difficult to work out.[2]

Another reason why the waterfall is of relevance is the subsequent event review in the context of the fair value process. To cater for timing differences between the limited partner's reporting date and the date when the NAV of the underlying investments are determined in accordance with IAS 39, it may be necessary to adjust the NAV reported by the fund manager. As the NAV reported to the limited partner is a net figure, this re-valuation requires several steps:

- The starting point for the calculation is the fund's last reported gross NAV (net of fees but not of carried interest). This gross NAV is mainly the sum of the unquoted and quoted portfolio companies' values.
- This gross NAV figure is updated based on monitoring procedures performed on the underlying fund, i.e. adding all drawdowns and subtracting all repayments.
- Publicly quoted portfolio companies need to be re-valued based on the latest quoted price as at valuation date.
- The entire portfolio needs to be re-valued based on the latest foreign exchange rates as at valuation date.

As we will see, it is not always possible to determine the gross NAV if one knows only the NAV reported to the limited partners. In some situations, both values are required to conduct the subsequent event review. For example Tredegar Corporation (2002) states that the 'fair value of ownership interests in private venture capital funds is based on our estimate of our distributable share of fund net assets using the general partners' estimate of fair value of securities held by the funds and fund formulas for allocating profits, losses and distributions'. In other words, particularly the carried interest due to the fund's general partner has to be stripped out.

---

[2] See Rouvinez (2005).

To put it in more mathematical terms, the function that maps the gross NAV onto the net NAV is not information-preserving. In situations where there is a 100% catch-up, several different gross NAV values – representing the underlying portfolio's value – will result in the same net NAV due to the fund's limited partners (Figure 8.1).

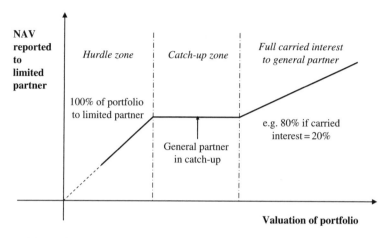

Figure 8.1   Impact of catch-up on NAV attributed to limited partner

8.1.1   Terms and conditions

According to Axelrad and Wright (2001), parties generally select terms from among a small number of paradigms that are well known within the industry and, as Bell (2005) observed, fund terms 'have shown remarkable stability across the broader market cycles'. Fund agreement provisions, such as management fees, carried interest allocations, investment limitations, transfers, withdrawals, indemnification or the handling of conflicts of interest, tend to look quite similar between different fund agreements.

Two opposing forces lead to this quasi-equilibrium. Firstly, limited supply of 'top funds' in combination with strong investor demand results in over-subscriptions. Under these circumstances investors who try to push for better terms shut themselves out. Such 'difficult' investors will immediately be replaced by limited partners who accept either market terms or even unfavorable conditions. Secondly, particularly buyout firms aim for larger fund sizes and therefore often propose attractive terms to capture almost every conceivable source of investor. Moreover, private equity firms are interested in building up and maintaining a good working relationship with their investors to build on and institutionalize their capital base. Offering unfavorable terms or over-charging their limited partners could work in specific market situations but may backfire when raising future funds in another phase of the cycle when conditions are difficult, capital is scarce or, particularly, when their last fund's performance is weaker.

As a generalization, both fund managers and their investors have sufficient negotiation power to reject 'off market' terms sought by the other side, but not so much leverage as to move the market in one direction or the other. Focus of this chapter is the impact of key terms related to the hurdle rate and the preferred return respectively, the general partner's catch-up, the amount and payout structure of the carried interest, and clawback clauses.

8.1.2 General partner investment in fund

General partners typically invest a significant amount of capital – typically about 1% of the total fund size – in their funds that is normally treated in the same way as that contributed by the limited partners. There are a number of reasons for this, for example tax. General partners contribute a meaningful amount of capital to ensure their status as a partner of the fund for income tax reasons. This allows receiving in-kind distributions of portfolio securities on a tax-free basis and paying tax on the general partner's allocated share of the fund's recognized profits at reduced capital gain rates. Fleischer (2005) sees this as largely an artefact of tax history. He considers it insignificant in comparison to the carried interest, with generally a negligible effect on incentives.

This, however, under-estimates the importance of putting 'skin into the game' to help align the interests between fund managers and their investors. Gilson (2003) interprets this investment as a substitute for the operation of a reputation market among venture capitalists and to insure that new fund managers have a direct share of the downside. To achieve this, not the absolute amount is relevant, but what share of the fund managers' personal wealth is at stake. For established, successful and increasingly wealthy fund managers this investment becomes certainly less and less relevant, putting the proper alignment into question.

The question remains whether fund managers should pay management fees on these commitments or whether there should be a fee waiver mechanism. This fee waiver could be seen as a way to subsidize the fund managers' commitment through the management fee and put up less of their own net worth. On the other hand, in the USA it is a tax-efficient method for the managers to commit to the fund, since capital gains are taxed at a lower rate than fees. CPEE (2004) reported that the industry consensus is in favor of a waiver mechanism, but only to the degree that it does not lower the general partner's upfront commitment on a tax-adjusted basis, or in other words the general partner's commitment should be grossed up to take into account tax effects of the fee waiver mechanism.

In the following examples we have, for simplification purposes, always ignored the general partner's own investment in the fund that has the same pay-off as that of the other limited partners anyway.

8.1.3 Management fees

The purpose of a private equity fund's management fees is to cover the basic costs of running and administering the fund. These costs comprise mainly the salaries for investment managers and back-office personnel, expenses related to the development of investments, travel and even entertainment expenses, and office expenses such as rent, furnishing, utilities or supplies. Almost all funds are structured in such a way that the general partner or one of its affiliates receives the management fee. The limited partnership usually absorbs directly the fees paid for professional advisory services, insurance premiums and partnership taxes. According to CPEE (2004), the most common structure seen in the market is one in which after the fifth year, the management fee starts to decline. They are typically paid in quarterly, semi-annual or annual instalments and predominantly at the beginning of the period.

Management fees are paid throughout the contractual lifetime of the fund. They are nearly always calculated as a percentage – typically between 1% and 2.5% depending on the fund size and on the resources required to implement its strategy – of capital the limited partners commit to the fund, but are generally tapering off after the investment period or when a successor fund is formed. Fees may also be reduced after a key person event or when the limited partners vote the termination of the investment period earlier than originally foreseen. While the management fees need to cover many expenses arising from actual investment work, including reasonable salaries from the investment managers at least during the five-year investment period, they are not intended to remain their primary source of income and their main incentive. Instead, limited partners prefer to have the fund managers' compensation come through the carried interest.

While the management fee's calculation is relatively simple and fairly objective, there are controversies surrounding the finer details. Firstly, it is difficult to set a single standardized percentage because of differences between funds and their investment approaches. Emerging fund management teams require a lot of money to start their first small fund, whereas established teams operate several and larger vehicles that already provide a reliable income stream. On the one hand, a low percentage can bring the smaller funds to the verge of being unviable and where the managers need to borrow to cover expenses. On the other hand, for many established private equity firms even a low percentage results in a comfortable salary, but is an insufficient incentive for fund managers to build the portfolio companies.

Occasionally other ideas are discussed, like giving the investors a choice, such as a 2% management fee with ordinary carried interest or an annual budget plus a higher carry. Theoretically this may be a great idea for investors who dislike fees on committed capital and believe that fund managers should put their money where their mouth is. As Toll (2001) pointed out, this may certainly be interesting for wealthy senior partner, but usually will not be feasible for juniors who depend on management fees. Larger funds that keep the percentage-based fees approach can offer much better compensation packages and thus find it easier to compete for junior talent.

Secondly, what items are to be paid by the management fees? In the 1980s, according to Gompers and Lerner (1999a), it was common particularly for buyout funds to earn fees for providing investment banking-like services in putting together a transaction, such as an IPO or M&A. The general partners in addition typically received the full carried interest over and above any transaction fee income they took. As they continued to receive their annual management fee in full, these transaction fees provided a significant additional revenue stream. Some of these fees turned out to be quite large, notably in transactions funded by the pioneer in this industry, KKR.

This is heavily contested between fund managers and their investors, but during the 1990s the pendulum swung back and limited partners won the right to share in such fee income and to make this activity less rewarding for the funds. The main motive behind this was the wish to discourage fund managers from participating in activities that come at the detriment to increasing the value of portfolio companies. Consequently, transaction fees are typically applied as a reduction to the future management fees. The most commonly applied split for this so-called 'offset' is 50/50, although it is also argued that 100% should be offset or that the split should be 80/20, mimicking the typical carried interest. Among those fees that are usually offset against the annual management fees are:

- **Investment banking fees and origination fees**, where the private equity firm charges portfolio companies to compensate for efforts in finding, conducting the due diligence, negotiating and structuring the investment. Based on CPEE (2004), many limited partners accept that these fees were not offset, as this constitutes money that would need to be paid by the portfolio company to someone else (i.e. an investment bank) if it did not go to the fund. However, limited partners should be vigilant that this does not give improper incentives to maximize transaction fee income.

- **Break-up fees**, where the acquisition agreement that precedes the actual investment contains a provision that commits the prospective investee company to pay a fee that compensates the fund for lost time and expense if the transaction is not consummated.
- **Monitoring fees**, that require the portfolio company to pay for the time fund managers spend in board meetings and their other efforts intended to improve the company's performance. Fund managers argue that working with the portfolio company provides it with a real service and should be compensated as such. Limited partners, however, do not usually agree. They believe that the fund's raison d'être is to build value in the portfolio company. For this the fund managers should therefore be compensated through the carried interest only.
- **Consulting fees**, where funds charge portfolio companies for the extra time and effort required for specific projects.

Also, in cases where the private equity firm is managing several funds, the general partner's management expenses should be shared on a pro-rata basis with the other funds. Paying management fees for successor funds should not start until they begin their investment activity. The clear resolution of these issues in the partnership agreement prevents disputes with the fund's investors and avoids misunderstandings and allegations that the fund managers have engaged in suspect transactions. Ancillary fees are more relevant in the context of buyout funds, where the portfolio companies are cash generators. For venture capital they are much less common, because portfolio companies are usually cash burning and charging them fees could threaten their survival.

Box 8.1:   Affiliates' arms-length services

Another area for limited partners to watch for is the provision of affiliates' services. This is an issue which is not uncommon, for example in the Japanese VC industry that in several ways has followed a different path from the US model. In Japan many VC firms are captives of larger financial groups that often have consulting companies as affiliates. Allegedly, the VC firms 'encourage' the portfolio companies to buy these services, but the consulting fees are not netted against management fees of the VC funds. One interviewee mentioned a VC firm that charges its portfolio companies $600 000 p.a. for such backing. 'If they put in $2 million, they make a profit, even if the start-up goes bust and the LPs' investment is lost.'[3]

In any case, investors in private equity funds remain concerned that fees are excessive, and, as reported by CPEE (2004), there are renewed discussions on how to structure management fees. One alternative to the percentage of committed capital model currently in use is to base the fees on a reimbursement of expenses in order to prevent the management fees from becoming excessive. This model has appeared in the hedge fund world, but so far it is not common in the private equity industry. The reimbursement model may be a move toward

---

[3] Quoted from Meyer (2006b).

more transparency, especially in situations where private equity firms are earning fees from multiple funds under management. Another solution for limited partners is to ask for a budget during the initial negotiations in order to set the fee percentage. This budget concept is widely seen as making most sense economically, but its implementation can be mechanically complex. Consequently, the simple percentage-based model has still not gone out of favor and essentially the fee structure is again dictated by supply and demand in the market.

8.1.4   Profit and loss

Agreeing on a formula for dividing profits is relatively straightforward, but how is the profit figure determined? Among the typical partnership operating costs are:[4]

- Non-investment-related interest expense.
- Cost of vehicle set-up and creation.
- Legal and accounting fees.
- Annual audit fees.
- Custody and escrow fees and expenses.
- Cost of errors and omissions.
- Directors and officers insurance policy.
- Cost of equipment and services used in communicating with custodian or other agents.
- Fees and travel expenses of managers.
- Sales charges to selling and placement agents.
- Brokerage commissions.
- Government fees and taxes.
- Tax return preparation.
- Administrative fees.
- Shareholder servicing fees.
- Advertising expenses.

Normally, deal-specific expenses are allocated to the respective transaction while organization expenses and non-specific deal expenses are allocated on a pro-rata basis.[5] The fund managers are typically required to return an amount equal to one of the following to the limited partners before they can participate in fund profits:

- All the capital that limited partners have committed to the fund.
- All the capital drawn down by the fund.
- A portion of the capital that limited partners have contributed to the limited partnership, relative to realized investments.

Returning all the capital that limited partners have committed to the fund first is for the fund managers certainly the most unfavorable option, and is common for European VC funds and in a difficult fundraising environment where investors have the upper hand in the negotiations.

Profit and loss for the fund can either be aggregated or the general partner can be allowed to take a share of the profit on each individual investment. As the general partner typically

---

[4] See Worthington *et al.* (2001).
[5] See CPEE (2004).

commits only little capital to the fund, participating in every investment's profit can be problematic. In this case the general partner could make profits on successful investments with little exposure to unsuccessful transactions. As the limited partners thus take the bulk of capital risk, this approach significantly weakens the alignment of interests.

As an example (see Table 8.1), consider a fund that makes two investments A and B of €10 million each. Investment A is successful and generates a €10 million profit, whereas investment B is a complete write-off. In aggregate the fund has invested €20 million and has generated neither a profit nor a loss. However, if the general partner was allowed to take 20% on each individual transaction's profit, this would result in €2 million carried interest for the fund managers.

Table 8.1 Example for net profit and loss for limited partners

	Individual		Aggregate
	Investment A	Investment B	
Investment	€10 million	€10 million	€20 million
Profit/loss	€10 million	(€10 million)	€0 million
Carried interest	(€2 million)	€0 million	(€2 million)
Net profit for limited partners	€8 million	(€10 million)	(€2 million)

Based on Toll (2001), VC funds moved toward aggregation of profits and losses in the late 1970s and early 1980s, most buyout funds adopted the approach a decade later and, not surprisingly, the aggregation method – i.e. where carried interest is only paid on the profits of the entire portfolio – is now the standard.

Nevertheless, also under the aggregation method there can be different approaches for determining the timing of carried interest payments. As an example, consider a fund with a size of €200 million that makes an initial €10 million investment in a company that is sold several months later for €110 million. One approach would be that the general partner does not receive carried interest until the fund has returned the total committed capital to the limited partners. In this case the entire €110 million goes to the limited partners. Another option is to subject distributions to a NAV test requiring that the value of the fund's portfolio is sufficiently greater, say by 25%, than the capital invested at the time. In the example this would clearly be the case. The limited partners would receive their original capital of €10 million plus their share of the profits and, assuming 20% carried interest, the general partner gets:

$$(\text{€110 million} - (\text{€10 million} + \text{€2.5 million})) \times 20\% = \text{€19.5 million}$$

Also, the re-investment of capital has to be taken into consideration. Ideally the full capital commitment to a fund should be put to work and be invested in portfolio companies at least once. As management fees and expenses need to be taken into account, this is not feasible without re-investments. Some funds even permit re-investment in excess of 100% of capital and the recall of distributions for this purpose. Generally, limited partnership agreements only foresee the re-investment of capital returns but not of profits and only allow this during the investment period. Occasionally separate provisions are put in place for re-investment of 'quick turns' on investments and for loans and bridge investments over between 12 and 18 months. On the other hand, the effect of re-investment may be to further delay the receipt of carried interest by the general partner and to put the limited partners' commitment at risk longer. This would also result in an increased base for management fee calculation after the investment period.

8.1.5 Carried interest

Management fees are paid regardless of the fund's performance and therefore fail to provide an incentive to work hard. Excessive and quasi-guaranteed management fees stimulate tentative and risk-averse behavior such as following the herd. Certainly in the case of under-performance limited partners could remove the fund manager, but for such a long-term-oriented asset class under-performance is problematic to identify early, and the removal would often be a too drastic step with often unforeseeable consequences. Reputation provides a significant performance incentive, as the managers need to raise follow-on fund. However, some individuals are more talented than others, and tracking the involvement of each individual manager is difficult.

Consequently, the carried interest, i.e. the percentage of the profit that goes to the fund managers, is the most powerful incentive to create value. The most common carried interest split is 80/20 and gives the fund managers a share in the fund's net profits that is disproportionate to their capital committed and is essential to attracting talented managers.[6]

A crude example of a 20% carried interest on a €50 million investment may give an idea of how lucrative it can be for the fund managers to have big wins. Assume that the investors get their original €50 million and the fund achieved a multiple of three on the investment, which is over a timeframe of, say, four to five years certainly good but by no means exceptional. In this situation (and ignoring the hurdle rate) the fund managers would walk away with:

$$(\text{€150 million} - \text{€50 million}) \times 20\% = \text{€20 million}$$

Provided that the fund is successful the fund managers can indeed receive their greatest return through their carried interest.

Toll (2001) explains that the standard carried interest figure may have its roots in the oil and gas business, where taking 20% of the profit has long been the rule for companies engaged in exploratory drilling. Several early VC firms chose the 20% rate, which established it as a market practice. However, different rules usually apply for in-house corporate VC funds, where the carried interest is often less than 20%. Moreover, a small number of mainly US 'elite' private equity firms require a 'premium carry'. According to a survey conducted by Private Equity Analyst in 2001, Sevin Rosen, Draper Fisher Jurvetson, Greylock or Hummer Winblad charged 25%, whereas firms like Accel Partners, Benchmark Capital or Sequoia Capital even managed to negotiate a 30% carried interest. All of them are VC firms, but also buyout firms like Bain Capital took 30%, albeit after a 15% preferred return.

---

[6] In principle the carried interest granted to the fund managers gives a payout profile very similar to those of a free call option. To ensure that the manager gets adequate compensation both in terms of management fee and performance-based fee, Rouvinez (2005) suggested valuing it at the fund's inception and monitoring during its lifetime. In the 1980s, it was common for funds to take down capital under a fixed schedule, but this practice is not followed any more. Instead, limited partners need to provide capital on a 'just-in-time' basis after the fund has given an advance notice of five to 60 days before the capital call.

Ripplewood Holdings, another buyout firm, gave investors the choice of paying a traditional 20% carried interest after an 8% preferred return, or a 30% carried interest after a 20% preferred return. Occasionally the carried interest split is contingent upon performance, e.g. 20% unless IRR to the limited partners exceeds 25%, in which case it becomes 30%.

Fund managers argue, according to Kaplan (1999), that a higher share in the profit helps to retain and attract new talent and that top performers should be rewarded adequately. Frequently the conviction is stated that 'it is better to invest with a strong team and have mediocre terms, than to invest with a mediocre team and have strong terms'.[7] Carried interest is not a zero sum game where the limited partner's gain or loss is exactly balanced by the losses or gains of the general partner. Many believe that 'elite' VC funds consistently outperform the typical fund to justify the carry of 30% rather than 20%. This line of argument suggests that the cake get larger if fund managers are more highly motivated.

On the other hand, investors worry that this sends the wrong message and that other private equity firms would feel compelled to match this. Also, trying to signal (non-existing) quality by demanding 'premium carry' could be one of the undesirable consequences of this trend. At the end of the day it comes down to supply and demand. As a manager becomes more successful, investors have less leverage to negotiate terms. The 'proven performers' tend to be over-subscribed. Their apparently lower risk or higher expected returns translates into a higher price.

8.1.6 Vesting

An important item for investors to check during the due diligence is how the carried interest is allocated among management team and what are the vesting provisions? Vesting is the process of granting full ownership of conferred rights such as stock options and warrants, which then become vested rights. Rights which have not yet been vested may not be sold or traded and can be forfeited. This question also ties into the key person provisions and has the objective of keeping the fund managers focused on the fund during its entire term and rewarding superior performance.

For establishing a vesting schedule several objectives should be kept in mind:[8]

- The schedule should create an incentive for the fund managers to continue with the firm until all of the work on the fund's portfolio is complete.
- However, often particularly the best performing individuals quickly move on to subsequent fund-raisings. The vesting has to ensure that a departed fund manager is not unduly compensated for work done by others after he left.
- There should be sufficient carried interest for replacements and new hires that gives proper incentives to the remaining team to successfully continue the operations of the fund.

Vesting can be pro-rata over the investment period or over the entire term of the fund or something in between, such as determining the vesting percentage on an annual basis. A schedule also does not necessarily have to follow a straight line, as the example in Table 8.2 shows.

---

[7] Quoted from Toll (2001).
[8] See also Tegeler & Poindexter (2007).

Table 8.2 Example for vesting schedule for general partner removal without cause

Period	percentage share of carried interest
Prior to the first investment date	0%
On or after the first investment date and prior to the first anniversary of the initial closing date	20%
On or after the first anniversary of the initial closing date and prior to the second anniversary of the initial closing date	30%
...	...
On the xth anniversary of the initial closing date (termination of investment period)	75%
...	...
On the yth anniversary of the termination of the investment period	100%

The vesting schedule should correspond to the fund's investment strategy and align interests between fund managers and limited partners.

- If the strategy depends mainly on sourcing and structuring the transaction during the investment period and less on nurturing portfolio companies over long periods of time, most of the carried interest should vest during the fund's investment period. This is likely to be appropriate for buyout, mezzanine or co-investment funds, where entry conditions, deal structuring and financial engineering are arguably most important. The arrangement chosen also depends on how the carried interest is split. If the carried interest is paid on individual deals the vesting should also correspondingly be 'deal-by-deal'.
- For venture capital, on the other hand, building a company and engineering a profitable exit pose the main challenge which is probably better reflected in a straight line vesting over the fund's entire lifetime.
- Some funds may add value and require significant work rather in later years. For example early stage VC funds initially start with a larger portfolio and subsequently back few 'winners' in their portfolio which they have to nurture over many years and then need to work hard on generating a profitable exit. Here it would be more meaningful to have a 'back-loaded' scheme where most of the carried interest vests in the later years of the fund.

Vesting is only foreseen for persons that are named as carried interest recipients and only until they withdraw. For participants in fundraising, senior professionals and for participants in realizing exits there is often an accelerated vesting. Vesting can also be delayed until carried interest recipients meet defined requirements. One way of delayed vesting is a 'cliff' to define the threshold date when the vesting starts. The motivation behind this is to reward longer engagement with the fund and to reduce the cost of providing benefits to professionals who leave after a short period. Specific vesting clauses can cater for termination on disability or death, termination without cause or good reason. Usually forfeiture provisions are put in place to address termination for cause or the violation of non-compete agreements with the fund. Post-withdrawal clauses assure that only an interest is retained in deals done prior to withdrawal, and where recipients have interests in different deals it has to be determined how to allocate subsequent losses on other deals. Such provisions aim to assure that departing carried interest recipients do not do better on deals in which they have an interest than they would have based on the entire portfolio.

8.1.7 Main drivers of distribution waterfall

While carried interest allocations determine the basic economics for the partners, the distribution provisions govern the timing and content of payments in respect of the carried interest. While fund terms are by and large stable, the significant exception to this general rule appears to be the set of fund agreement provisions governing the timing and apportionment among the partners and how to operate distributions. Axelrad and Wright (2001) found that based upon their experience, the number of alternative distribution arrangements in common use seems to be increasing. This multiplicity of approaches arises because no single mechanic can satisfy all the economic goals of both the general and limited partners. Often one party's gain in the arrangement is the other party's loss. As a consequence, negotiations over such distribution arrangements for capital and carried interest can be difficult and time consuming. Often this process results in the method that has the fewest disadvantages for all parties in light of their respective situations. The main distribution arrangements are:

- **'Fund-as-a-whole':** under this arrangement, no distributions are made to the general partner until the limited partners have received distributions equal to the amount of their capital contributions. Thereafter, distributions are made to the limited and to the general partner according to the agreed carried interest split. This arrangement provides limited partners with the greatest percentage of early distributions and reduces clawback risk, too. It greatly reduces the possibility that the general partner will receive more than its agreed-upon percentage of the fund's cumulative net profits. Currently fund-as-a-whole is market standard for funds-of-funds and for funds in Europe, particularly for VC funds.[9] It does, however, has timing disadvantages for the general partner and thus creates perverse incentives. With a **general partner catch-up** all limited partner capital contributions are returned prior to the general partner receiving any distributions. Once the limited partner's capital contributions are returned, however, the general partner participates in a higher share of succeeding distributions until it has received aggregate distributions equal to the agreed carried interest split of the total distributions made by the fund since inception. Thereafter, distributions are made to the limited and to the general partner according to the agreed carried interest split.
- The other extreme is the **'deal-by-deal'** distribution methodology that currently is the standard across the Atlantic.[10] According Warburton (2006), in the US all LBO funds and the majority of the VC funds follow this approach. Here carried interest distributions are made following the return of capital contributions attributable to individual realised investments. However, investments that have been written off or written down and fund expenses and management fees allocated to such deals need to be recovered first. From the viewpoint of the fund managers the 'deal-by-deal' has a major advantage, as it allows them to receive carried interest distributions sooner. It therefore provides a, in

---

[9] In cases where VC funds experienced large losses and are far under water switching back to calculating the carried interest on a deal-by-deal basis may be a meaningful restructuring that gives new incentives to the fund managers.
[10] Alternatively fund formation layers call the two approaches, according to Thomson (2006), 'back end loaded' or 'front end loaded', respectively.

the words of Axelrad and Wright (2001), 'perverse incentive' to the fund manager to realise successful deals early and to delay the recognition of unsuccessful deals and write-downs of unprofitable investments. As a result, the 'deal-by-deal' methodology creates a clear possibility of over-distributions to the general partner and thus requires a clawback provision.[11]

These two arrangements are most relevant in practice, although – mainly in the context of deal-by-deal carried interest – other variants like 'split distributions' or 'NAV tests' are in use as well:

- **Split distributions:** here each amount available for distribution is divided into separate 'return of capital' and 'profit' components. Return of capital amounts are distributed to the limited partners, while profit amounts are distributed according to the agreed carried interest split to the limited partners and to the general partner.

    For example, assume that an investment that was acquired for €100 million is realized for €150 million. €100 million would then be the return of capital amount and €50 million the profit amount. The limited partners would receive the full €100 million of the capital, whereas the €50 million of return would be split 80/20% and distributed to the limited and general partners accordingly. This helps the general partner to benefit earlier from distributions related to profitable investments.

- **NAV test:** under this arrangement, the general partner participates in the carried interest of each distribution only to the extent that, immediately following the distribution, the NAV of the fund equals or exceeds a set threshold. There are various forms of NAV tests in place. Typically the cushion of the combined NAV of the fund and the escrow has to exceed between 110% and 125% of the limited partners' unreturned capital contributions.[12] This reduces the likelihood of a clawback by increasing the amount of subsequent losses that would have to be incurred before the general partner had received over-distributions.

    This, however, causes another technical complication as the general partner is typically given discretion to value the fund's portfolio but may have an incentive to inflate the NAV. For VC funds a relatively common safeguard is the use of a valuation committee that reviews and approves the valuations prepared by the general partner. It is typically made up of independent limited partners selected by the general partner, but also third-party appraisers are used in situations where a dispute arises between the general partner and the valuation committee. Against this background it will be interesting to observe what impact the switch to a fair value regime in venture capital will have. While 'fair' theoretically implies lack of bias, it is difficult to see how limited partners could not have a preference for more conservative valuation approaches.

These distribution arrangements also give to the general partner some possibility of rebalancing the distributions along the agreed split at every distribution in order to reduce

---

[11] For the subsequent event review in the context of determining the fair value of the fund, the view is taken that the fund is discontinued and broken up. Under this assumption is makes no difference for the calculation whether the treatment is fund-as-a-whole or deal-by-deal.

[12] See CPEE (2004) and Friedman (2005). That, however, raises the question of the valuation guidelines and whether the write-downs and write-ups of investments should be done on the portfolio or on a deal-by-deal basis. Following the portfolio approach could encourage fund managers to be aggressive on write-ups. Also, the switch toward a fair value regime in private equity may create problems, as under this approach theoretically there should be no conservative bias in valuations.

the likelihood of a clawback scenario from the limited partners. They usually come in combination with provisions such as hurdle rates, clawbacks and escrows. Fund managers may time the recognition of income, gains and losses so that a greater carried interest is realized for earlier periods. This 'gaming' can be mitigated through two main approaches that are used in various combinations. Firstly, the preferred return to the limited partners before any carried interest is paid to the general partner. Secondly, a so-called 'clawback' provision can be put in place that requires the general partner to put over-distributions back into the partnership.

Occasionally distributions are treated differently depending on whether they are in cash or as distributions in kind. For example, cash distributions could be made 100% to the limited partners until they have received distributions equal to the amount of their capital contributions. However, also distributions-in-kind is a widely accepted mechanism. Here general partners distribute returns to their limited partners in the form of listed securities as opposed to cash. This happens usually when a fund's portfolio company achieves an Initial Public Offering (IPO) or when trade sales are completed as share-based transactions. Distributions-in-kind are of higher importance during periods of high IPO activity.

In the context of distributions-in-kind, the timing of paying out carried interest becomes an important item for the fund managers as they would not want to miss out on the appreciation of any distributed stocks that might perform especially well once a portfolio company goes public. Delayed distributions to the general partner mean that participating in early distributions-in-kind is not possible. On the other hand, accelerating distributions to investors reduces the amount of preferred return due to limited partners and increases the IRR of the fund.

Therefore, for distributions-in-kind other methods such as the split distribution could make more sense. There are several possible reasons for treating cash and distributions-in-kind differently. For example, the general partner may like to participate in share distributions as investment opportunity. Also non-tax-exempt investors may prefer this method because it encourages the general partner to make in-kind distributions rather than selling securities at the fund level and triggering recognition of taxable gain. Depending on whether the general partner can already participate in the distribution, the mechanism can also reduce the perverse incentive to distribute under-performing securities in kind.

8.2 BASIC WATERFALL MODEL

Most partnership agreements foresee that the hurdle rate and the catch-up are defined on the basis of the IRR, in other words as compound interest. In this case the preferred return calculation could be defined as 'amount as is equal to interest at an annual rate of 8% (compounded annually) on the daily amount of the partnership share'. The IRR is the discount rate that gives a NPV equal to zero:

$$\sum_{n=1}^{L} \frac{C_n}{(1+\text{IRR})^{t_n}} = 0$$

where C_n is the cash flow at time t_n and L the lifetime. The interim IRR is a rough but widely used estimation of IRR performance and forms the basis of most published comparative performance statistics. For active funds, the interim IRR is computed by taking the NAV as the last cash flow at time T,

$$\sum_{n=1}^{T<L} \frac{C_n}{(1+\text{IIRR})^{t_n}} + \frac{\text{NAV}_T}{(1+\text{IIRR})^T} = 0$$

Let a_x be the amount required as the residual value of a fund's portfolio to give an IRR of $x\%$ before splitting it up according to the waterfall,

$$\sum_{n=1}^{T<L} \frac{C_n}{(1+x)^{t_n}} + \frac{a_x}{(1+x)^T} = 0$$

This gives for a_x:

$$a_x = - \sum_{n=1}^{T<L} C_n (1+x)^{T-t_n}$$

See Figure 8.2.

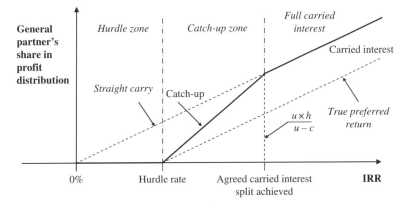

Figure 8.2   Components of the distribution waterfall

As a simplified example for the basic waterfall, we assume that the limited partners contribute €100 million in the first year to fund an investment, an 8% hurdle rate, a full catch-up, an 80/20 carry split and that the investment is sold by the fund in the second year for €200 million. In this case the sales proceeds are distributed as in Table 8.3.

Note that simply directly splitting the profit of €100 million (the difference of €200 million sales proceeds minus €100 million purchase price) on an 80/20% basis would have given the same result. The reason for this is that the fund's return is above the catch-up zone and therefore the hurdle is 'extinguished' and does not make any difference.

Let c be the carried interest due to the general partner, h the hurdle rate and u the catch-up (with $u > c$). The payout of the portfolio value of a attributable to general and limited partners is given in Table 8.4.

Table 8.3 Example for basic waterfall

	Limited partners	General partner	Total
Original contributions	(€100 million)		(€100 million)
	Sale of investment for €200 million		
Return of capital	€100 million		€100 million
Preferred return for limited partners	€8 million		€8 million
Catch-up for general partner		€2 million	€2 million
80/20% split of residual amount	€72 million	€18 million	€90 million
Closing balance	€80 million	€20 million	€100 million

Table 8.4 Payout formulas

	IRR range	Distribution key for:	
		Limited partners	General partner
Hurdle zone	IRR $\leq h$	a	0
Catch-up zone	$h \leq \text{IRR} < \frac{u \times h}{u-c}$	$h + (a - a_h) \times (1 - u)$	$u \times (a - a_h)$
Full carried interest	$\frac{u \times h}{u-c} \leq \text{IRR}$	$a \times (1 - c)$	$a \times c$

A number of partnership agreements foresee that the hurdle rate and the catch-up are applied as an annual interest, often compounded annually. Here the preferred return calculation could be defined like a 'return of 8% (compounded rate) per annum with respect to all unreturned capital contributions made on the partnership shares in excess of the nominal value of such partnership shares'. As an example, assume for a fund drawdowns of $C_1 = €30$ million in year 1 and $C_2 = €10$ million in year 2, a hurdle of 8%, a 100% catch-up and an 80/20% carried interest split. In case the fund realizes both investments in the third year for €100 million, how should the proceeds be distributed? Firstly, to cover the original costs €40 million will go to the limited partners as return of capital. The preferred return to be paid under this arrangement is the 8% interest on these drawdowns, i.e.

$$(€30 \text{ million} \times (1.08)^2 + €10 \text{ million} \times 1.08) - €40 \text{ million} = €5.8 \text{ million}$$

We know that of the €100 million, €40 million has to go to the limited partner as return of capital immediately. Moreover, with €100 million the fund's return should be well beyond the catch-up zone in any case. Therefore one knows that of this €100 million, (€100 million − €40 million) × 80% + €40 million = €88 million will finally be distributed to the limited partners and the remaining €12 million is for the general partner. With a full catch-up and as the hurdle amounts to €5.8 million, one can easily work backwards and arrive at €1.4 million that goes to the general partner next. This results in the distribution waterfall given in Table 8.5 for this scenario.

However, how does one determine the amount to be caught up and the residual amount to be split up as carried interest for $u < 100$ %? The waterfall can be generalized as in Table 8.6.

Table 8.5   Example waterfall

	Limited partners	General partner	Total
Original contributions	(€40 million)		(€40 million)
	Sale of investment for €100 million		
Return of capital	€40 million		€40 million
Preferred return for limited partners	€5.8 million		€5.8 million
Catch-up for general partner		€1.4 million	€1.4 million
80/20% split of residual amount	€42.2 million	€10.6 million	€52.8 million
Closing balance	€48 million	€12 million	€60 million

Table 8.6   Generalized waterfall

	Limited partners	General partner	Total
Original contributions	(d)		(d)
	Sale of investment for amount a		
Return of capital	d		d
Preferred return for limited partners	$a_h - d$		$a_h - d$
Catch-up for general partner	$(1-u) \times x$	$u \times x$	x
80/20% split of residual amount	$(1-c) \times y$	$c \times y$	y
Closing balance	$(1-c) \times (a-d)$	$c \times (a-d)$	$a-d$

To answer the question, we have to determine x and y. One can see from the 'Total' column immediately that

$$x + y = a - d - (a_h - d) = a - a_h$$

To achieve the agreed carried interest split after the catch-up zone,

$$u \times x + c \times y = c \times (a - d)$$

has to hold. Solving the equations gives

$$x = \frac{c \times (a_h - d)}{u - c}$$

and

$$y = a - d - \frac{u \times (a_h - d)}{u - c}$$

Note that for

$$a \leq d + \frac{u \times (a_h - d)}{u - c}$$

the fund is still in the catch-up zone, meaning that any amount in excess of a_h will be split according to the catch-up key between limited partners and general partner. In case of a 100% catch-up the full amount goes to the general partner.

Example I
We assume a hurdle rate of 8% with a 100% catch-up. What is the residual value required in year 3 to give an IRR sufficient to meet this hurdle rate?

$$a_{8\%} = \left(\text{€}30 \text{ million} \times (1+0.08)^{3-1} + \text{€}10 \text{ million} \times (1+0.08)^{3-2} \right) = \text{€}45.8 \text{ million}$$

The amount to be caught up is

$$\frac{100\% \times (\text{€}45.8 \text{ million} - \text{€}40 \text{ million})}{100\% - 20\%} - \text{€}45.8 \text{ million}$$

$$+ \text{€}40 \text{ million} = \text{€}1.4 \text{ million}$$

A residual NAV of €100 million in year 3 would be distributed as follows:

(1) The limited partners receive €40 million as return of capital.
(2) The limited partners receive €45.8 million − €40 million = €5.8 million as preferred return.
(3) The general partner receives €1.4 million as catch-up.
(4) The remaining amount of €52.8 million is split. The limited partners receive €52.8 million × 80% = €42.2 million and €52.8 million × 20% = €10.6 million goes to the general partner.

The distribution waterfall for this example is given in Table 8.7.

Table 8.7   Example I waterfall

	Limited partners	General partner	Total
Original contributions	(€40 million)		(€40 million)
	Sale of investment for €100 million		
Return of capital	€40 million		€40 million
Preferred return for limited partners	€5.8 million		€5.8 million
Catch-up for general partner		€1.4 million	€1.4 million
80/20% split of residual amount	€42.2 million	€10.6 million	€52.8 million
Closing balance	€48 million	€12 million	€60 million

As a next example we look at the same fund with a different hurdle rate and a catch-up of less than 100%.

Example II

Again, assume drawdowns of $C_1 = €30$ million in year 1 and $C_2 = €10$ million in year 2, a hurdle rate of 10% and a catch-up of 50%. What is the residual value required in year 3 to give an IRR sufficient to meet the hurdle rate of 10%?

$$a_{10\%} = \left(€30 \text{ million} \times (1+0.1)^{3-1} + €10 \text{ million} \times (1+0.1)^{3-2} \right) = €47.3 \text{ million}$$

The amount to be caught up is:

$$\frac{50\% \times (€47.3 \text{ million} - €40 \text{ million})}{50\% - 20\%} - €47.3 \text{ million} + €40 \text{ million}$$

$$= €4.9 \text{ million}$$

The residual amount to be split up according to the agreed carried interest split is:

$$€100 \text{ million} - €40 \text{ million} - 50\% \times \frac{€47.3 \text{ million} - €40 \text{ million}}{50\% - 20\%} = €47.8 \text{ million}$$

The distribution waterfall for this example is given in Table 8.8.

Table 8.8   Example II waterfall

	Limited partners	General partner	Total
Original contributions	(€40 million)		(€40 million)
	Sale of investment for €100 million		
Return of capital	€40 million		€40 million
Preferred return for limited partners	€7.3 million		€7.3 million
50% catch-up	€2.45 million	€2.45 million	€4.9 million
80/20% split of residual amount	€38.3 million	€9.6 million	€47.9 million
Closing balance	€48 million	€12 million	€60 million

8.2.1   Preferred return and hurdle rate

The preferred return is the IRR that a private equity fund must achieve before the managers may receive an interest in the proceeds of the fund.[13] The addition of this provision generally has the effect of further subordinating the general partner's right to receive distributions, and is intended to align the interests of the general and limited partners by giving the fund managers an additional incentive to outperform a traditional investment benchmark. Fund managers cannot take a share in the distributions until the limited partners have received

---

[13] CPEE (2004) interprets the preferred return as the limited partners' downside protection only, not as any sort of incentive for the fund managers.

aggregate distributions equal to the sum of their capital contributions and a typically 6–10% return thereon.

For this contractual term only the fund's ultimate performance matters. The preferred return does not offer the limited partners the power to place the fund in default if it is not paid. From an investor perspective, it protects the return on investment in case of low return and gives the manager the incentive to achieve returns above this threshold. It is a standard term for buyout funds worldwide, at it ensures that the limited partners receive at least as much as they would have made on a safer investment. The term 'preferred return' is often used interchangeably with the slightly different 'hurdle rate' (see below).

Preferred returns are often tied to a spread over risk-free returns. According to CPEE (2004) the market rate seems to be 8%, but preferred returns are much more common in buyout funds than in VC funds where most investors are not entirely concerned with the rate. In their view increasing it to, say, 10% would not make a huge difference since in the real world the actual result is more like either 20% or −20%. As explained in more detail below, for a number of reasons in the USA usually VC funds – unlike buyout funds – do not give their limited partners a preferred return or hurdle rate. Theoretically, by failing to use this contractual term, VC funds reward both superior and mediocre performance, as all profits are divided according to the agreed carried interest split.

Box 8.2: 'Hard' hurdle rate

With a 'true' preferred return, also called a 'hard' hurdle rate, gains realized from the fund's investments are allocated as follows:

- First, 100% to the limited partners until they have received back their initial contribution of capital.
- Second, 100% to the limited partners until they have received an amount equal to the preferential return rate (typically 8%), compounded annually, on their initial contribution of capital.
- Thereafter the gains are distributed according to the carried interest split, i.e. usually 80% to the limited partners and 20% to the general partner.

This arrangement is also sometimes called a 'floor', because the general partner receives no carried interest until reaching the 8% return (see Fleischer, 2005). The annual compounding of the preferential return rate is what makes it an important contractual term.

Most agreements, however, are not organized to provide a true preferred return, but a hurdle rate. In this case, once a fund has returned the initial capital plus the, say, 8% return, it has cleared the hurdle and thus becomes entitled to take the full carried interest. To achieve this objective, the agreement includes a catch-up provision. Once the hurdle is cleared, profits are then allocated disproportionately to the general partner until it catches up to the point where it would have been had it received its carried interest on the entire profit.

More importantly, perhaps, clearing the hurdle rate does not mean that the contract term was irrelevant. The significance of the preferred return term is more than distributional; it changes incentives.

Fleischer (2005)

CPEE (2004) found that the 'hard' hurdle rate is more the norm in Europe, whereas in the USA the prevailing market terms are for a 'soft' hurdle rate.

Box 8.3:   'Soft' hurdle rate

With a 'soft' hurdle rate, gains realized from the fund's investments are allocated differently compared to the 'true' preferred return:

- First, 100% to the limited partners until they have received back their initial contribution of capital.
- Second, 100% to the limited partners until they have received an amount equal to the preferential return rate (typically 8%), compounded annually, on their initial contribution of capital.
- Third, typically 100% to the general partner until having 'caught up' with the agreed carried interest split, i.e. having received the usual 20% of the amount in excess of the initial investment.
- Thereafter the gains are distributed according to the carried interest split, i.e. usually 80% to the limited partners and 20% to the general partner.

In contrast to the 'true' preferred return, the significance of the hurdle rate vanishes after it is cleared and unless the fund's return falls below the hurdle again in subsequent years.

8.2.1.1 Option character and screening of fund manager

The preferred return gives the limited partnership agreement an option-like character. Once a fund has made a number of profitable exits, the preferred return no longer matters or serves as an incentive. The fund managers as holders of the carried interest, like the holder of a call option, enjoy the possibility of theoretically unlimited upside gain. If the fund loses value, the fund managers – apart from their personal wealth invested in it – have neither gain nor loss, just like when an option holder declines to exercise an option.

This option-like character is a main argument against preferred returns for VC funds. Venture capitalists have to be willing to take large but informed investment risks, but a preferred return can lead, according to Toll (2001) and Covitz and Liang (2002), to a number of undesirable situations:

- The requirement of preferred return might cause a team to invest too cautiously from day one and pursue investments that have limited downside, but also limited upside.
- Large losses early on in a fund's life could put it so far under water that it even discourages the fund managers who would then either be inclined to quit the game altogether, to pay

little attention beyond the minimum needed to justify acceptance of the management fee or to take exaggerated risks to get a chance to be back in the carry.
- Probably worse, fund managers might 'swing for the fences' and become overly aggressive with subsequent investments to get back into the zone where they could receive carried interest.

Limited partners could mitigate this by volunteering to re-price the preferred return. This would be similar to public company compensation committees that often re-price stock options when they are deep out-of-the-money, and it would lead to similar problems. Particularly in the case of VC funds, where the implied cost of capital is different than in debt-based structures, the hurdle can give sub-optimal incentives. Indeed, according to Toll (2001) and CPEE (2004), for example in the case of mezzanine funds where there is less volatility, the preferred return is argued for more fervently. Here doing away with it entirely would create a moral hazard, as fund managers could then receive carried interest for pursuing a low-risk, low-return strategy.

In the context of VC funds the role of the preferred return may rather be to screen out bad venture capitalists. Indeed, Covitz and Liang (2002) found that preferred returns are more common at young firms, thus supporting this screening hypothesis. However, at least in the USA partnership agreements for VC funds usually do not provide for a preferred return.

8.2.1.2   Preferred return for VC funds

In the context of the US private equity market Fleischer (2005) investigated the 'mystery of the missing preferred return'. While managers of buyout funds generally offer their investors an 8% preferred return before they take a share of the profits for themselves, this is usually not the case for venture capitalists. VC funds usually take their cut from the nominal profits right away. Based on his discussions with venture capitalists, most practitioners claimed not to use a preferred return, and a study showed that only 35% of VC fund agreements included this feature as opposed to 90% of buyout funds. This could be seen as evidence that compensation practices in venture capital do not properly align incentives, as the missing preferred return suggests that venture capitalists may take a share of the gains even if their funds perform poorly compared with others. The disparity between buyouts and VC funds appears striking, as their contracts to determine fund organization and compensation are otherwise very similar, and it may be caused by the venture capitalists' bargaining power. However, bargaining positions are continuously changing and are better at explaining the amount of compensation than the form of compensation. Fleischer (2005) came to the conclusion that bargaining power, boardroom culture, cognitive biases, camouflaged compensation or accounting rules do not offer a satisfactory explanation for the missing preferred return in VC funds.

Certainly, 'stickiness' of contract terms can be a barrier between the status quo and a more efficient contract, but his basic point is that it is primarily the US tax law that makes it rational for venture capitalists to not use a preferred return. VC funds are encouraged to adopt a compensation structure that, although misaligning incentives, maximizes after-tax income for all parties. This is achieved by not recognizing the receipt of a profits interest in a partnership as compensation, by treating management fees as ordinary income, and by treating distributions from the carried interest as capital gain. Eliminating the preferred return increases the present value of the carried interest.[14]

Additionally, Fleischer (2005) saw institutional differences between VC funds and buyout funds that explain this phenomenon. The preferred return is more important as an incentive to properly screen the deal flow. Without it, buyout fund managers could pursue a low-risk, low-return strategy, for example by being inactive or by choosing companies that have little potential to generate large returns. A preferred return forces managers to make riskier investments to generate a return in line with the investor's targets. In the case of VC funds, however, investments are always risky, and the high-risk, high-reward strategy makes it meaningless to bother about preferred returns.

Box 8.4: Hurdle rate distortion

High hurdles can tempt the fund managers to focus on clearing the hurdle rather than maximizing returns for the limited partners. In other words, there could be a so-called 'hurdle rate distortion', as illustrated by the following example.[15] Assume that fund managers have the choice between three different strategies for a hurdle rate of 8%, full catch-up and 20% carried interest:

- A low-risk, low-return strategy that achieves €107 after one year on €100 investment. In this case, the fund's performance will be 7% and the limited partners would receive €7 whereas the fund managers always walk away empty-handed.
- A medium-risk, medium-return strategy with an 80% chance of achieving €115 and a 20% chance of getting back €105 after one year. In this case, the fund's performance will be 13% and limited partners would receive:

$$80\% \times €15 \times 80\% + 20\% \times €5 \times 100\% = €10.6$$

whereas the fund managers' expected pay-off would be:

$$80\% \times €15 \times 20\% + 20\% \times €5 \times 0\% = €2.4$$

- A high-risk, high-return strategy with a 20% chance of getting back €155 and an 80% chance of achieving €105 after one year. In this case, the fund's performance will be 15% and limited partners would receive:

$$20\% \times €55 \times 80\% + 80\% \times €5 \times 100\% = €12.8$$

whereas the fund managers' expected pay-off would be:

$$20\% \times €55 \times 20\% + 80\% \times €5 \times 0\% = €2.2$$

---

[14] Fleischer (2005) argued that the tax law should stay the same, as the implicit subsidy given to venture capital would be beneficial from an economic growth perspective.
[15] The example is based on Fleischer (2005).

Box 8.4: (Continued)

In this example fund managers would be inclined to go for the medium-risk, medium-return strategy to the detriment of their investors. However, the scenarios are certainly artificial and unlikely to be of relevance in practice. Firstly, the medium-risk, medium-return scenario's pay-off distribution function is upward sloping, i.e. the chance of generating a higher return is larger than the probability of achieving a low return. A downward-sloping distribution function is likely to be more realistic. Secondly, even the most sophisticated fund managers are unlikely to have such detailed insights into the expected return profiles to deliberately trade-off their preferences against limited partner objectives.

Whether a preferred return makes sense or not ultimately depends on the importance of deal flow relative to deal harvesting. In cases where deal flow incentives are relevant, e.g. in the case of buyout or mezzanine funds, the fund managers should not be rewarded for investments that do not return at least the investor's cost of capital. Setting a hurdle achieves this objective, whereas a straight carried interest creates an incentive to go for low-risk, low-return investments. For VC funds, however, deal harvesting is clearly more relevant, and with the hurdle incentives they are even distorted when the option on the carried interest is 'out-of-the-money'. Here a straight carried interest is more efficient than a preferred return in providing the proper incentives to the fund managers.

Ray Maxwell – considered to be a founding father of private equity in the UK – explains that the preferred return was introduced when the European private equity market was in its infancy. He sees it as more confusing than useful and believes that it has passed its 'sell-by date'.[16] He argues that a preferred return is not a genuine hurdle rate, because it does not stay in place throughout the life of the fund. By giving preference to the limited partners, carried interest may fail to properly motivate the fund managers.

Capital in € million	Increments in € million	Carried interest in %	Carried interest in € million	Accumulated in € million	Accumulative carried interest in %
500	0	0			
625	125	10	12.50	12.50	10.0
750	125	15	18.75	31.25	12.5
875	125	20	25.00	56.25	15.0
1000	125	25	31.25	87.50	17.5
1125	125	30	37.50	125.00	20.0
1250	125	35	43.75	168.75	22.5
1375	125	40	50.00	218.75	25.0
1500	125	45	56.25	275.00	27.5

Source: Magnolia China (quoted from Kuan et al., 2007)

---

[16] See Maxwell (2003).

As an alternative he proposed a model that builds on a flexible carried interest schedule – in essence, the greater the multiple, the higher the carried interest – and believes that this aligns the interests better than the classical preferred return. Maxwell introduced for the Magnolia China Energy and Media Fund a mechanism he describes as 'performance based carried interest' which rewards the achievement of performance milestones at regular intervals with incremental increases in the level of carried interest.

Kuan *et al.* (2007) describe the mechanics of this approach: if the fund's capital for example doubles in size from €500 million to €1 billion the accumulative carried interest of 17.5% is triggered. Should the fund size treble, this increases to 27.5%.

8.2.2   Catch-up

Whether it is a 'soft' hurdle or the 'floor', i.e. the 'hard' hurdle, can significantly modify the economic value of the stated carried interest percentage. With a 100% catch-up the hurdle will have no ultimate effect on the carried interest if the fund clearly exceeds its target IRR and does not terminate with returns still in the catch-up zone.

The typical catch-up seen in the US market is around 70–80%. CPEE (2004) found that there was general agreement in the industry that the general partner should be caught up to 100% and not 50/50 or 80/20 once the limited partners are provided with their preferred return.

Example
Weaver (2003) referred to a case with a 10% hurdle rate, a 60% catch-up and a 20% carried interest. Here the catch-up zone ends, when

$$\text{IRR} = \frac{60\% \times 10\%}{60\% - 20\%} = \frac{6\%}{40\%} = 15\%$$

That means, after the fund has reached a 15% return, further cash flows will be split according to the 80/20% carried interest split, and the hurdle rate as well as catch-up do not have to be taken further into account.

Additionally, this particular limited partnership agreement foresaw that the general partner's share of the carried interest increased to 25% once the IRR passed a threshold of 25%. This arrangement protected the limited partners on the downside through the higher hurdle and through the deferral of the catch-up. In return, the general partner would have been able to take more of the upside in the case of outstanding performance.

In instances where there is a 'floor' and therefore no catch-up has been agreed, the carried interest only applies to those net profits that exceed the hurdle. Axelrad and Wright (2001) suggest that this feature is strongly resisted by private equity fund managers and more common for hedge funds or real estate private equity funds.[17]

---

[17] See Weaver (2003).

8.3   IMPACT OF CARRIED INTEREST DISTRIBUTION APPROACHES

There are different methodologies for making carried interest distributions that can lead to varying needs and uses of a clawback mechanism. At one end of the spectrum is the already mentioned fund-as-a-whole distribution methodology, that had historically been followed in the USA before the 'deal-by-deal' distribution methodology became more widely used.

8.3.1   Fund-as-a-whole

Under a fund-as-a-whole approach, fund managers must often wait for several years before reaping the fruits of their labors. That the fund-as-a-whole approach emerged as the standard for European funds is seen by Gold (2006) as due to 'entrenched investor expectations'.

8.3.1.1   Full-fund-back approach

The full-fund-back concept as a variant of the fund-as-a-whole approach goes even one step further. Grabenwarter and Weidig (2005) explained that especially in the European markets concerns regarding over-distributions produced this different concept of carried interest distributions. Following the full-fund-back approach not only all drawn money but an amount equivalent to the full committed capital plus, where applicable, preferred return on drawn capital has to be paid to limited partners prior to any carry entitlement of the general partner. The clear advantage for the investors is that there is no over-distribution scenario for carried interest to the general partner and hence there is no credit risk for the limited partners on the general partner. However, it may lead to over-distributions to limited partners that can require specific clawback provisions.

The full-fund-back concept could be seen as the extreme outcome of a highly advantageous negotiation position of investors in private equity funds in Europe from 2000 onwards and caused by the difficult fundraising environment since the collapse of the technology markets. Grabenwarter and Weidig (2005) suggest that most fund managers are unable to present historical instances of where a distribution of carried interest on a full-fund-back basis would have made a difference to them and that those rare cases where it mattered relied on one or two lucky winners rather than a systematic pattern of success. However, that raises the question why limited partners then have a preference for the full-fund-back method? It is argued that this clause becomes relevant in situations where things between limited partners and fund managers go wrong, i.e. when limited partners have to remove a fund manager, when the fund management teams fall apart or when fundraising for a successor fund fails. 'In these scenarios, the last thing a LP would like to deal with is the question of how to recover overpaid money from the GP.'[18]

Box 8.5:   Full-fund-back impact

If the partners' earnings from the investment of distributed assets are taken into account, the order in which partners receive distributions can have a substantial effect

---

[18] Quoted from Grabenwarter and Weidig (2005).

on their respective benefits from participating in the fund. We take a look at two examples to demonstrate the impact of the 'full-fund-back' approach.

- In the first example a fund returns four times on total contributed capital of €100 million. Assume that the limited partners contribute €25 million to the fund at the beginning of years one through four and that distributions of €80 million are made to the partners at the end of years six through ten.
- In the second example again a fund returns four times on total contributed capital of €100 million, but – unlike in the first case – not all contributions are in the beginning and all distributions are at the end of the fund's life. Instead there is one repayment in year three followed by other years with capital calls before years follow with repayments only.

In both examples, the hurdle is calculated on the net cash flows, or, as defined in a real-life limited partnership agreement, the hurdle shall be 'such amount as is, at the relevant date, equal to interest at an annual rate of 8% (compounded annually) on the amount by which:

(a) the aggregate cumulative amounts paid to the Fund by Partners (being LPs and GPs) exceed
(b) the aggregate cumulative amounts received by Partners from the Fund.'

For both examples the partners receive the same aggregate amount regardless of which distribution scheme (full-fund-back hurdle and fund-as-a-whole hurdle) – in the first example approximately €346 million goes to the limited partners and €54 million to the general partner, and in the second example €342 million goes to the limited partners and €58 million to the general partner.

Both examples show, however, that the distribution cascade can be different between a full-fund-back hurdle and a full-fund-back hurdle, depending on the cash-flow pattern. In situations where repayments follow the disbursement with no change in 'direction' of the cash flow there is no difference. In our experience that is the standard situation anyway.

However, should – as in the second example – some high repayments occur quite quickly in the life of the fund, then the IRRs – depending on the methodology full full-fund-back and full-fund-back hurdle – will be different for the partners. But regardless of which method is chosen, there is no difference in the total amounts received at the end. The full-fund-back hurdle in case of high and quick repayment delays the cash flows to the general partner but has no impact on the amount.

In the first example the net cash flows and the compounded hurdle result in an amount of €31.97 million in year seven that needs to be repaid to the limited partners first before the general partner can take a share in the profits. The hurdle rate of 8% is applied to the net cash flow and the hurdle reserve of the preceding period as it is compounded.

In the second example, the overall methodology remains the same. The hurdle is calculated on the net cash flows. In one case, however, the amount to pass the hurdle is

---

Box 8.5:   (Continued)

repaid when the first repayment – which exceeds the disbursement– appears, whereas in the full-fund-back hurdle this amount is put in 'reserves', i.e. not being accrued as the repayment exceeds the disbursements. As long as the net cash-flows remain positive, the hurdle is 'extinguished'. As illustrated above, the hurdle reserve will start growing again in year five when the net cash flows fall below zero. Clearly for the general partner under a full-fund-back hurdle, the carried interest payment is postponed in favour of the limited partners. Based on our experience, however, these quick 'reverse' cash flows occur quite rarely in practice (see Table 8.12 and 8.13).

8.3.1.2   Fund-as-a-whole concerns

Unfortunately, under the fund-as-a-whole approach fund managers often have to wait several years before receiving rewards for their efforts. Indeed, psychologists say that deferred gratification – the ability to wait for the things you want – is critical to life success.

Although such restrictive rules on the distribution of carried interest were originally designed to give the right incentives, the long waiting times can be highly demotivating to fund managers and make it difficult for firms to recruit and retain the best talent. 'How much?' is not really the issue but 'how soon?' seems to be increasingly up for negotiation and the mechanism for carried interest distribution is typically one of the most intensively discussed topics. In fact, according to CPEE (2004), some general partners have even offered to take a lower carried interest if they can have it on a deal-by-deal basis instead of on an aggregating methodology.

Another aspect is that the fund-as-a-whole concept may not always be the right motivational tool for the fund managers. Certainly, for venture capital to a large degree the fund's success is a team effort, and here the fund-as-a-whole carried interest offers the type of reward that is probably best in line with the success of the team as a whole. For buyouts, however, this approach does not recognize that individual contributions vary from transaction to transaction and thus is not always the best incentive for individuals to excel on their own deals. Furthermore, a fund-as-a-whole carried interest may give the appropriate incentives to the senior partners in the team. But the long delays before the fund's first distribution of carried interest can be too heavy a burden for younger fund managers who are often still in the process of founding a family or buying real estate.

Also, investors have begun to become sympathetic to these arguments, as a motivated and highly incentivized management team should lead to a highly performing fund. Moreover, there is the increasing threat from the hedge fund industry where fund managers are rewarded with annual bonuses and hedge fund firms are beginning to lure disenchanted private equity professionals into their industry. Indeed, private equity fund managers can only look with envy at these practices and would love to build in yearly compensation as opposed to having to wait more than five years for the fruits of their labor. As the fundraising climate changes the pendulum may swing back in favor of the fund management teams and strengthen their negotiation position. Consequently, according to Gold (2006), a small number of European managers, especially those raising larger funds, have persuaded investors to accept the deal-by-deal carried interest structure familiar to their US counterparts. To some degree this may also reflect the growing internationalization of the asset class, where US institutions want to see arrangements in European funds they are familiar with.

8.3.2 Deal-by-deal

A contrasting approach is the deal-by-deal concept. Here carried interest is payable in accordance with the performance of each separate investment, but it is subject to losses on realized investments having been recouped. Clearly, fund managers have a preference for distributions to be made on a deal-by-deal basis, as this puts hard cash in their hands much sooner than the fund-as-a-whole model. In the words of a US-based fund formation lawyer, the 'name of the game is liquidity – you want your managers to be cultivating exists, not being patient money managers. The plainer it is that there's tangible reward for a liquidity event, the better.'[19] The drawback to this method is the need for clawback provisions in the event of overall under-performance and the issues that come with enforcing such provisions, a subject we discuss below in more detail.

As an example for an over-distribution consider a scenario where limited partners contribute in the first year €100 million to fund investment A and B with €50 million each. See Table 8.9.

Table 8.9 Example for over-distribution – year 1

	Limited partners		General partner	Total
	Investment A	Investment B		
Original contributions	(€50 million)	(€50 million)		(€100 million)
	Acquisition of investment A and B			
Closing balance	(€50 million)	(€50 million)		(€100 million)

Investment A is sold in the second year for €90 million. The profits of €40 million for this investment are distributed to limited and general partners in line with the agreed 80/20% split. See Table 8.10.

Table 8.10 Example continued – year 2

	Limited partners		General partner	Total
	Investment A	Investment B		
Opening balance	(€50 million)	(€50 million)	€0 million	(€100 million)
	Sale of investment A for €90 million			
Return of capital	€50 million			€50 million
80/20% split of residual amount	€32 million		€8 million	€40 million
Closing balance	€32 million	(€50 million)	€8 million	(€10 million)

Then in the third year, investment B fails and is written off entirely. See Table 8.11.

---

[19] Quoted from Thomson (2006).

Table 8.11   Example continued – year 3

	Limited partners		General partner	Total
	Investment A	Investment B		
Opening balance	€32 million	(€50 million)	€8 million	(€10 million)
		Total write-off of investment B		
Return of capital 80/20% split of residual amount		€0 million		€0 million
Closing balance	€32 million	(€50 million)	€8 million	(€10 million)
Sub-total		(€18 million)	€8 million	(€10 million)
Clawback		€8 million	(€8 million)	€0 million
Loss on capital		(€10 million)	€0 million	(€10 million)

The fund overall made a loss of €10 million, and without the clawback the general partner would have received €8 million of carried interest and the limited partners a loss of €18 million.

Tegeler & Poindexter (2007) point to other complexities and possible tensions created by a deal-by-deal approach and the associated potential clawback. As an example they considered a situation where the carried interest of an investment A is split among the members of the fund manager's team A and carry from investment B is split among members of team B. When investment A is sold for €100 million gain with €20 million of carried interest, team A theoretically would receive €20 million. But in situations where investment B was previously sold at a loss a portion of the €100 million gain from investment A would have to be used to restore the loss to the limited partners, and as a result less than the €20 million carry would go to team A.

Another issue around the deal-by-deal approach is the need to define the frequency and scope of valuations for the portfolio companies. CPEE (2004) suggests that general partners tend to be extremely conservative on valuations to try to head off the clawback issue.

8.3.3   Considerations and possible solutions

Most of the problems with the fund-as-a-whole concept could be resolved, with a deal-by-deal carried interest in combination with a suitable escrow arrangement. However, many limited partners used to the strong investor protection under the typical European fund terms appear to consider this a step too far.

Also under several legislations[20] the fund-as-a-whole approach is a more efficient solution. Until the carried interest is to be distributed there is an advantage in allocating all gains to investors while proceeds of realizations are paid out to them. Otherwise the fund managers as recipients of the carried interest will be liable to tax on these gains. With a deal-by-deal carried interest this advantage will be lost. Warburton (2006) pointed out that one of the

---

[20] For example the UK, see Bygrave *et al.* (1999).

Table 8.12 Example 1: Compounded interest vs. full-fund-back comparison (8% hurdle) – no difference

	Year 1	Year 2	Year 3	Year 4	Year 5	Year 6	Year 7	Year 8	Year 9	Year 10	Total
Drawdown	−25.00	−25.00	−25.00	−25.00							−100.00
Repayment						80.00	80.00	80.00	80.00	80.00	400.00
Compounded interest											
Acc. net cash flow	−25.00	−50.00	−75.00	−100.00	−100.00	−20.00	60.00	140.00	220.00	300.00	
Hurdle	0.00	−2.00	−4.16	−6.33	−8.51	−8.68	−2.29	4.62	11.57	18.53	
Sum (1)	−25.00	−52.00	−79.16	−106.33	−108.51	−28.68	57.71	144.62	231.57	318.53	
Compound hurdle	0.00	−2.00	−6.16	−12.49	−21.00	−29.68	−31.97	N/A	N/A	N/A	
Capital repayment						80.0	20.0				
Hurdle							31.97				
LP carried interest							22.42	64.00	64.00	64.00	
LP total						80.0	74.39	64.00	64.00	64.00	346.39
GP carried interest							5.61	16.00	16.00	16.00	53.61
Full-fund-back, compounded hurdle											
Compounded hurdle	−100.0	−102.00	−106.16	−112.49	−121.00	−129.68	−51.97	0.00	0.00	0.00	
Capital repayment						80.00	20.00				
Hurdle							31.97				
LP carried interest							22.42	64.00	64.00	64.00	
LP total						80.00	74.39	64.00	64.00	64.00	346.39
GP carried interest							5.61	16.00	16.00	16.00	53.61

Table 8.13 Example 2: Compounded interest vs. full-fund-back comparison (8% hurdle) – difference

	Year 1	Year 2	Year 3	Year 4	Year 5	Year 6	Year 7	Year 8	Year 9	Year 10	Total
Drawdown	−25.00	−25.00		−25.00	−25.00						−100.00
Repayment			80.00			20.00	10.00	80.00	80.00	130.00	400.00
Compounded interest											
Acc. net cash flow	−25.00	−50.00	30.00	5.00	−20.00	0.00	10.00	90.00	170.00	300.00	
Hurdle	0.00	−2.00	−4.16	0.00	0.00	−1.55	−0.12	0.00	0.00	0.00	
Sum (1)	−25.00	−52.00	25.84	7.07	−19.43	−1.55	9.88	90.79	177.26	314.18	
Compound hurdle	0.00	−2.00	−6.16	0.00	0.00	−1.55	−1.68	0.00	0.00	0.00	
Capital repayment			50.00			20.00	10.00	20.00			
Hurdle	0.00	0.00	6.16	0.00	0.00		0.00	1.68			
LP carried interest			19.07					46.66	64.00	104.00	
LP total			75.23			20.00	10.00	68.34	64.00	104.00	341.57
GP carried interest			4.77				00.00	11.66	16.00	26.00	58.43
Full-fund-back, compounded hurdle											
Compounded hurdle	−100.00	−102.00	−106.16	−100.00	−100.00	−101.55	−81.68	−73.84	0.00	0.00	
Hurdle reserve			−6.16				−1.68				
Capital repayment			80.00			20.00					
Hurdle							7.84				
LP carried interest							1.73	64.00	64.00	104.00	
LP total			80.00			20.00	9.57	64.00	64.00	104.00	341.57
GP carried interest								0.43	16.00	26.00	58.43

high-profile European funds to adopt the deal-by-deal approach has only a 10% carried interest. To tackle the issues he discussed two possible solutions:

- One approach is to use a fund-as-a-whole carried interest, but to allocate the distributions to individual fund managers on a flexible basis, e.g. by way of an annual or deal-by-deal allocation. Arrangements can be implemented in a way that closely mimics the individual returns that would result from a deal-by-deal carried interest. This can result in better incentives for individual members of the fund management team while retaining the tax advantages of a fund-as-a-whole carried interest.
- An alternative is to retain the fund-as-a-whole model in principle, but to build into it a small element of deal-by-deal carried interest. This is a compromise solution that may be more readily accepted by investors than an unfamiliar deal-by-deal model while giving a similar degree of investor protection to the pure fund-as-a-whole approach. The distribution waterfall under this arrangement is the same as for a normal fund-as-a-whole carried interest, except that the repayment of capital contributions and the payment of the preferred return to investors are subject to an 'interim carried interest'. The interim carried interest delivers a small carried interest calculated on the basis of the investment that is being realized. The fund-as-a-whole carried interest distributions are then reduced by the amount of all interim distributions that have been made so that the overall carried interest remains the same.

There are distinct positions between those who want the carried interest paid sooner rather than later in a fund's life cycle and those who desire the reverse. Thomson (2006) reported that Graphite Capital in 2003 offered the option of either deal-by-deal or fund-as-a-whole carried interest. Shifting distributions to the limited partners to the front end and distributing carried interest to the general partner later can significantly increase the limited partner's IRR. CPEE (2004) raises the question whether this can create an incentive for the limited partners to chase IRR at the expense of return on investment.

At the end of the day it again comes down to supply and demand. Thomson (2006) suggested that, for example, Asian private equity firms will need longer track records before they can make deal-by-deal carried interest a campaigning issue when raising funds. Also, the Asian limited partners usually refuse to back funds featuring deal-by-deal carried interest, although sometimes they do but as a compromise put stricter clawbacks in place than US groups would normally accept.

8.4 CLAWBACK

'Clawback' provisions in private equity fund partnership agreements aim to protect the economic split agreed between the general partner and the limited partner. The clawback provision is sometimes called a 'give-back' or a 'look-back', because it requires a partnership to undergo a final accounting of all its capital distributions at the end of a fund's lifetime. General partners should not receive profits in excess of the agreed carried interest percentage, and limited partners should receive at least the preferred return.

Allegedly such provisions are seldom utilized, but nevertheless they pose a legal right to recover from parties – typically at the end of the fund's life – any distributions already made to such parties.[21] When talking about clawbacks we usually mean 'general partner clawbacks', i.e. corrective payments to prevent a windfall to the fund managers. Nevertheless, situations are also thinkable where limited partners have received more than their agreed percentage of carried interest. Consequently, some partnership agreements address the question of the so-called 'limited partner clawback' as well – a subject that we will discuss as well.

During a fund's life some investments may be exited earlier and distributions can already be made to a general partner. However, this may be followed by years of losses, e.g. caused by failures of portfolio companies or through lack of exit opportunities during prolonged economic downturns. This may mean that the general partner receives more than the intended carried interest based on the overall performance of the fund.

In any event, irrespective of what the future holds for private equity fund formation, one thing is certain – clawback provisions will no longer be negotiated with a mindset that they will never come into play in the real world.

Small (2002)

Clawback provisions are a relatively new phenomenon and have arguably been taken more seriously since the VC market downturn after 2000. Before that the clawback scenario had existed more in theory than in practice. According to industry experts, many of the vintage 1998 and 1999 VC funds, the ones most vulnerable to early success and subsequent failure, did not have terms sufficient to mitigate potential clawback problems.[22] Aragon (2003) quotes an insider: 'We've never had a clawback issue [but] they're looking for that across the board.'

Nevertheless, during that time some fund managers had taken steps to settle potential clawback issues through arrangements, for example, involving a reduction of future management fees. Capital Eyes (2002) also mentioned a VC fund that admitted to its investors a possible over-allocation of carry, and proposed a 'fix' going forward. The fund, which at that time was about four years old, offered to not pay itself any carry until an amount equal to total drawn-down capital was distributed to its limited partners. Such pro-active approaches were seen as a positive step to maintain good investor relations, particularly with a view to future fundraising. In fact, CPEE (2004) noted that meanwhile general partners see stopping carried interest payments on a go-forward basis as a more palatable compromise. It may avoid actually getting to the clawback point and is preferable to taking money out of the fund managers' pockets.

Under clawback provisions at a minimum, fund managers that received carried interest on the early successes have to give back payments in excess of 20% of cumulative profits. Some agreements go further and require that not only carried interest in excess of the initial capital investment but also a preferred return have to be returned. See Table 8.14.

The fund has an early success and realizes investment A for €110 million with a profit of €30 million. We assumed no hurdle rate. See Table 8.15.

---

[21] Whether management fees and comparable fund operational expenses are taken into account in the determination of net profits and in the calculation of excess distributions is subject to negotiation.
[22] See Capital Eyes (2002).

Table 8.14 Example for over-distribution – year 1

	Limited partners		General partner	Total
	Investment A	Investment B		
Original contributions	(€80 million)	(€20 million)		(€100 million)
	Acquisition of investment A and B			
Closing balance	(€80 million)	(€20 million)		(€100 million)

Table 8.15 Example continued – year 2

	Limited partners		General partner	Total
	Investment A	Investment B		
Opening balance	(€80 million)	(€20 million)	€0 million	(€100 million)
	Sale of investment A for €110 million			
Return of capital	€80 million			€80 million
80/20% split of residual amount	€24 million		€6 million	€30 million
Closing balance	€24 million	(€20 million)	€8 million	€10 million

Then in the third year, investment B fails and is written off entirely. At the time of liquidation the fund managers have to give back part of the full carried interest of €6 million they received previously:

$$\text{€6 million} - [(\text{€110 million} - \text{€100 million}) \times 20\%] = \text{€4 million}$$

See Table 8.16.

Table 8.16 Example continued – year 3

	Limited partners		General partner	Total
	Investment A	Investment B		
Opening balance	€24 million	(€20 million)	€6 million	€110 million
	Total write-off of investment B			
Return of capital		€0 million		€0 million
80/20% split of residual amount				
Closing balance	€24 million	(€20 million)	€6 million	€110 million
Sub-total	€4 million		€6 million	€110 million
Clawback	€4 million		(€4 million)	
Return above capital	€8 million		€2 million	€10 million

This clawback aims to guarantee a minimum return to the limited partners in any profitable situation. Without this clawback, a preferred return accomplishes this objective if the fund has failures before successes but not vice versa.

8.4.1 Controversy

Clawbacks and the practicalities surrounding them are a subject of discussion among fund managers and their investors. Fleischer (2005) sees partnership provisions related to allocation, distribution and clawback difficult to draft as they can influence the fund management's behavior in unforeseeable ways. For a number of reasons investors in private equity funds do not like to see clawbacks. Firstly, the excess distributions received amount to an interest-free loan to the general partner. Also, it may be easy to insert a clawback provision into the fund agreement but how clawback liabilities will be satisfied and with which methods to secure their repayment are logistically far from simple. Several years later the clawback may be difficult to collect from the fund managers, or some of these individuals may no even longer work for the firm.

An alternative to the clawback could be a distribution mechanism where general partners cannot receive carried interest before the end of the fund's life. General partners should recognize that they are long-term investors and should be compensated accordingly and only after having proven that they have generated the promised high returns. But fund managers oppose it, as current compensation is an important incentive for the investing professionals. They argue that clawbacks, if necessary in combination with a preferred return, offer sufficient protection.

8.4.2 Protection of investors

A clawback provision is a promise to repay over-distributions, but such promise is only as good as the creditworthiness of the general partner. This is normally a limited liability vehicle with no assets other than its interest in the fund. In partnership agreements of many funds the clawback only binds the general partner. As the general partner usually distributes the carried interest immediately to its owners, enforcing the clawback requires the cooperation of these owners. In other words, the value of the clawback provision rather depends on the creditworthiness of these individuals.

Box 8.6: Nightmare clawback scenario

Allegedly a nightmare clawback scenario materialized in the case of a VC firm of undetermined identity. Capital Eyes (2002) admitted that details of this story were vague, and it may well be an urban legend, but the scenario itself is not far-fetched. Apparently this fund had an early exit leading to a very high interim IRR and with the proceeds of the transaction being distributed in kind, i.e. as shares, as opposed to cash. VC firms usually base the value of an in-kind distribution on the share price at the time of the distribution. According to the rumor, the shares subsequently became worthless, as did most of the fund's remaining portfolio companies, and the fund's final IRR turned out to be negative. In this situation the fund managers owed their limited partners a huge clawback, but simply did not have the money, as the full value of their received carried interest had evaporated, and they also did not have the necessary personal wealth to make good on the clawback. One version of this story had the fund managers being forced to declare personal bankruptcy.

The statement that 'clawbacks are worthless' is not uncommon. There can be situations where limited partners are unable to receive the clawbacks they are owed. Enforcing them allegedly leads to years of litigation without getting any cash back.[23] CPEE (2004) gave an example of a 1995 vintage fund maturing presently keeping one company alive in order to extend the life of the fund and avoid paying out the clawback. Therefore such provisions may be toothless and not fully protect the investors, as they would not want to chase the recipients of carried interest for excess distributions. To give the clawback teeth, the recipients of carried interest often have to give guarantees where they are jointly or severally liable for each other and can find themselves paying for the defaults of others. CPEE (2004) found that many US firms have put such guarantees in place since 2001, but before the end of these vintages it will not be clear whether they will really be effective.

Under a 'several' liability, recipients of carried interest are liable only for their individual share of the clawback. Under this arrangement investors will not receive the entire required clawback payment unless each guarantor is able to pay his or her part. To give more comfort to their investors, fund managers need to put themselves at correspondingly greater risk. Under the more stringent 'joint-and-several' liability, each individual is guaranteeing the full obligation even though they may have received only a small portion of the over-distribution. 'On a joint-and-several basis, if there are four partners, and two go bankrupt and one flees to Panama City, the fourth must pay the entire clawback.'[24] The several liability is commonly used in the buyout market and can also be negotiated for by the stronger private equity firms.[25] Joint-and-several is apparently often found in the case of VC funds. This may be because VC funds are likely to be in a weaker negotiation position or because VC investing is more of a team effort compared with buyouts.

According to CPEE (2004), a hybrid form of 'joint and several to a cap' is also in use. Under this scheme, the individual is never liable for repaying more than he or she has received. For example, two fund managers A and B were paid €100 each as carried interest and under the clawback both have to pay back three-quarters of this amount. In the case where B defaults, fund manager A would only have to repay €100 instead of the full €150 comprising his €75 and fund manager B's €75.

Tax issues pose another practical complication. When the general partner or the fund managers as individuals have to pay their clawback obligation, they typically incur a capital loss. However, under most income tax rules individuals cannot carry back capital losses, i.e. such losses cannot be offset against prior year capital gains, which were taxed at that time. Therefore the general partner may offer only a clawback net of taxes and net of tax liabilities due on sale of securities distributed in kind. Usually the partnership agreement's provision and the associated guarantees will be based on an assumed tax rate and set out that the amount of the clawback obligation never exceeds the excess of (1) total distributions received by the general partner over (2) total taxes paid or payable thereon.[26] When excluded from the clawback the potential tax forms a cost that is completely unrelated to the ultimate net profitability of the fund but needs to be borne by the limited partners. Where the clawback includes tax distributions, the general partner may be required to

---

[23] See Toll (2001).
[24] Quoted from Capital Eyes (2002).
[25] See Toll (2001) and CPEE (2004).
[26] See Warburton (2006) and Friedman (2005).

pay that cost out of their own pocket. Another option is to exclude only a portion of tax distributions from the clawback and thereby require all partners to share some of the potential downside.[27]

Box 8.7:   Clawback insurance

Insurers have begun to offer a so-called 'clawback insurance' to increase the portability of partnership shares by protecting their buyer against the potential clawback liability.[28] An example for the application of this insurance is a limited partner who is in the process of selling its interest in the fund to a third party.

When pricing the secondary deal a potential buyer has to factor in the clawback liability it must assume, but this reduces the price the selling limited partner can achieve for his stake in the fund. As usually the seller would not want to offer an indemnity for the clawback liability, insurance provides an alternative way of covering obligations relating to distributions made to the selling party prior to the date of sale.

8.4.3   Escrow

Limited partners aim to minimize the risk that the general partner lacks liquid assets and the clawback right would be unenforceable. The simplest and, from the viewpoint of the limited partner, the most desirable solution is that the general partner does not receive carried interest until all committed capital has been repaid to investors. But, as discussed before, that can take several years before the fund's team sees any gains and it could demotivate the individuals. An accepted compromise for securing the clawback obligation is to put a fixed percentage – according to Friedman (2005) typical percentages are 25%, 30% or 50% – of their carried interest proceeds into an escrow account as a buffer against potential clawback liability.

From a limited partner's perspective the ideal escrow would contain assets that are at least sufficient to cover the fund managers' maximum potential clawback obligation. Any excess assets could then be disbursed without risk. However, provisions protecting against remote contingencies and therefore requiring unreasonably large amounts are likely to be resisted – possibly one of the reasons why escrow is, according to CPEE (2004), more common in the buyout world than for VC funds. In any case fund managers tend to dislike escrows, as they want to spend the cash or invest as they please. Additionally, there is the opportunity cost of having large amounts of cash sitting idle in escrow and the complexity of administrating this.

For example, who controls the escrow account? Most often, the general partner has exclusive rights to manage the investment of escrowed assets. Cash deposited in a segregated reserve account should be invested in cash-equivalent-type investments, which tend to yield low returns. There are also restrictions such as a prohibition on investment in tangible property or non-marketable securities. Usually, and unless the escrowed assets are used to satisfy the clawback, all gains and losses resulting from their investment are solely for the

---

[27] See Axelrad & Wright (2001).
[28] See for example Continental Casualty Company, http://www.cnapro.com/html/popup/TFI_Products.html [accessed 22 November 2006].

general partner's account. This motivates the general partner to manage the escrowed assets well, rather than seeing them as just owned by the fund or the limited partners.

Also it is hoped that this reduces 'perverse incentives' compared with a situation where the general partner shared to a lesser extent in early fund distributions or was unable to manage escrow account assets as it saw fit.[29] Moreover, escrowing delays the fund managers receiving the carried interest distributions, depending on the timeframe for release or the threshold valuation, i.e. NAV test, that the fund's remaining portfolio must equal or exceed prior to the release of the escrowed funds.

8.4.4   Timing

Rather than clawing back just once at the end of the fund's life, alternatively the general partner could be required to make payments from time to time – typically annually – back into the fund to satisfy potential obligations. This approach is sometimes referred to as a 'true-up' made during the life of the fund and has the benefit of avoiding a major readjustment at the end of the fund while accelerating distributions to investors. The amount to be put back is the equivalent of the clawback the fund managers would have to return if the fund was to be terminated at the true-up date. General partners may prefer a true-up as it circumvents the need to chase people.

A hybrid approach of utilizing a fair value test with respect to carried interest distributions would be another alternative. In this case distributions would be made to all partners pro rata based on capital contributions unless the sum of the fund's distributions to its limited partners plus the fair market value of its portfolio equals or exceeds an agreed-upon percentage of the limited partners' aggregate capital contributions.[30] In the case of VC funds this can be problematic, as interim numbers for returns and the resulting carried interest will be highly unreliable. Also the lack of consistent valuation methodologies across funds renders this approach not always an acceptable substitute for a clawback provision. As a result, limited partners are likely to set the threshold for a residual fair market value test at a too high level.

Finally, interim clawback could also be based simply on realized transactions. In this case the carried interest instead of going into the escrow would be paid to the limited partners. Under this 'cushioning provision' the general partner would not get additional distributions until the clawback is complete. In any case, the administration of periodic clawbacks incurs costs, which again may pose a problem for smaller funds. Often they are light on financial staff and simply are not prepared to implement such an approach.

8.4.5   Limited partner clawback

In recent years, particularly in LBO funds, it is increasingly common for private equity fund sponsors to include in the fund documentation a so-called limited partner clawback.[31] This provision allows the general partner to recall certain funds distributed to the investors.[32]

---

[29] See Fleischer (2005).
[30] See Small (2002).
[31] The global law firm Debevoise & Plimpton's international counsel Geoffrey Kittredge had surveyed his firm's database of roughly 1200 limited partnership agreements and other public sources to analyze the terms. He found that 35% of the first-time funds' and 34% of the successor funds' agreements had a limited partner clawback provision.
[32] In fact, the limited partner clawback is a misnomer because it is usually drafted as a clawback from all partners.

8.4.5.1 Protection against legal claims

This provision is mainly designed to protect the general partner from legal claims and liabilities that may arise from investment and business activities associated with the partnership. It requires investors to return some portion of distributions received to satisfy the fund's obligations related to indemnification, i.e. the legal exemption from the penalties or liabilities incurred by any course of action. Usually general partners are indemnified unless they engage in fraud or wilful misconduct. Limited partners should pay attention to this type of clawback, as they commit to pay for any legal judgment imposed upon the limited partnership or the general partner. The limited partner clawback can also relate to taxes, although the majority of investors are likely to be tax-exempt. The limited partner clawback is usually applicable only to the fund's profits, i.e. distributions received by the limited partner in excess of its return of capital. As with the general partner clawback, the ultimate goal is to protect the economic split agreed between the parties.

Warburton (2006) described a possible situation for a limited partner clawback. In his scenario a fund disposes its last investment in its portfolio and distributes the proceeds to the limited partners but has not yet been dissolved. Subsequently, the exited portfolio company's purchaser alleges a breach or representations and warranties in the sales agreement, a securities fraud claim or another claim. Even if the claim is without merit, legal costs quickly mount. The fund may not have sufficient assets to defend the claim or indemnify the general partner if the general partner has to defend the claim or incurs a liability on behalf of the fund. If the claim had occurred at an earlier time when the fund still had assets, the investors would have borne 80% of the loss and the general partner 20% because profits would have been reduced by the amount of the loss. In the described scenario the general partner would have borne more than its share of the fund's losses, and the limited partners would have received a windfall. However, the limited partner clawback indemnifies the general partner against losses.

8.4.5.2 Full-fund-back scenario

Under a full-fund-back approach, also known as 'super fund-as-a-whole', there can be over-distributions to the limited partners in the case where the full amount of committed capital is not drawn down over the life of a fund. Limited partners – not unlike the fund managers that often feel uncomfortable with the general partner clawback – could certainly debate the validity of such a scenario. After all, the fund manager's general partner went out raising their vehicle, claiming that there was a market and based on this the limited partners put their capital at risk and were also blocked from allocating it to other funds.

As an example, consider a fund with a full committed capital of €200 million. For a drawdown of €100 million two investments A and B are acquired for €50 million each. See Table 8.17.

After the first year investment A is realized for €200 million. For simplification we assume no catch-up, and under a full-fund-back the entire proceeds are distributed to the limited partners. See Table 8.18.

After the second year investment B is written off and the fund is terminated because of lack of deal flow – a scenario that is not too far-fetched and happened in comparable forms after the burst of the dotcom bubble with funds focusing on Internet businesses. Assuming a hurdle of 8%, the amount to be returned to the limited partners before the hurdle is cleared

Table 8.17   Example for limited partner clawback – year 1

	Limited partners		General partner	Total
	Investment A	Investment B		
Original contributions	(€50 million)	(€50 million)		(€100 million)
	Acquisition of investment A and B			
Closing balance	(€50 million)	(€50 million)		(€100 million)

Table 8.18   Example continued – year 2

	Limited partners		General partner	Total
	Investment A	Investment B		
Opening balance	(€50 million)	(€50 million)	€0 million	(€100 million)
	Sale of investment A for €200 million			
Return of capital	€50 million			€50 million
Full-fund-back	€150 million		€0 million	€150 million
Closing balance	€150 million	(€50 million)	€0 million	€100 million

Table 8.19   Example continued – year 3

	Limited partners		General partner	Total
	Investment A	Investment B		
Opening balance	€150 million	(€50 million)	€0 million	€100 million
	Total write-off of investment B			
Return of capital		€0 million		€0 million
Closing balance	€150 million	(€50 million)	€0 million	€100 million
Sub-total		€100 million	€0 million	€100 million
Clawback to achieve 80/20 split		(€20 million)	€20 million	
Return above capital		€80 million	€20 million	€100 million

is now €108 million. This clearly has been achieved and the fund managers should receive their share in the carried interest. See Table 8.19.

Mechanisms that have a higher probability of resulting in over-distributions to limited partners could be seen as less problematic than those that lead to a higher probability of over-distributions to the general partner. Grabenwarter and Weidig (2005) argued that it is more affordable for the general partner to accept credit risk on the limited partner, most of which are institutional investors with significant financial resources, than the other way round. Moreover, mechanisms like split distributions (see above) or of continuous rebalancing of distributions between limited and general partners can help avoid clawback situations for both parties. Nevertheless, there are scenarios where there remains a residual risk of over-distributions to the limited partners.

Grabenwarter and Weidig (2005) describe a more creative mechanism for the full-fund-back approach that avoids clawback obligations and provides adequate protection to the general partner in the case of over-distributions. Here over-distributions to limited partners can only occur in the case where not all the commitments to a fund are drawn. As this can only amount to a portion of the undrawn commitments, the general partner may simply make an equalization drawdown from the undrawn commitments to balance the distributions according to the agreed profit split and thus avoid any clawback obligation on either side. As the general partner draws from an existing commitment, a limited partner's non-compliance with this equalization drawdown would immediately make it defaulting limited partner, with all the consequences defined for such a scenario. This is seen as a more powerful protection against credit risk than any clawback obligation can possibly offer, as it is immediately enforceable by virtue of the fund's legal documentation.

8.4.5.3 Limitations

Frequently, investors negotiate for clauses that set limitations on the time and percentage of the limited partner clawback. They want to know that distributions received by them are not subject to being clawed back after a set period of time. Amounts that could be subject to the limited partner clawback typically cannot exceed the capital committed by the investors, or may also be limited to a percentage of the net distributions. Unlike the general partner clawback the limited partner clawback, is virtually never secured or guaranteed, even though some limited partners invest in the fund through a special purpose vehicle. Note that in cases where a fund is still in the catch-up zone on termination and where no limited partner clawback provison was negotiated, fund managers will receive less than 20% carried interest although the hurdle has been passed and should be extinguished.

The limited partner clawback does not stop here, but may also be an issue for some limited partners themselves, i.e. the funds-of-funds. Since the liability of their investors is generally limited to their subscriptions, funds-of-funds may wish to consider establishing a limited partner clawback of their own. Bogner et al. (undated) recommend that funds-of-funds at the very least should establish internal mechanisms to manage their clawback exposure vis-à-vis their own limited partner.

9

Break-even Analysis

Management fees, carried interest, hurdles, catch-ups, etc. are provisions that aim to create real economic incentives for fund managers to achieve significant capital gains. These provisions and how they are put into relation vary from fund to fund. Though not all the features of the structure impact the cost of holding a private equity position, some do and therefore, it is worth analyzing this aspect and to determine their value or costs. For example, an important part of due diligence on a private equity fund is to assess the impact of variations on these provisions and to assure that fund managers receive an adequate compensation in terms of management fee as well as a proper incentive. Moreover, a limited partner should track the influence of these provisions over the fund's lifetime to monitor for potential risks in situations where the fund managers' incentives are deteriorating.

The cost of investing in private equity is also significant. Whilst it might well be that returns on average are sufficient to offset these costs, it is bound to deter some investors.
Lane Clark & Peacock Actuaries

9.1 OBJECTIVE OF BREAK-EVEN ANALYSIS

The main objective of the break-even analysis is to estimate the portfolio gross performance required to cover the cost of the structure and allow the investors to 'break even'. This analysis can be performed for both the IRR and the multiple. Below, we only present our approach using the IRR.

A break-even can be calculated either at the level of the capital or of a pre-defined target rate of return. More formally, a '**capital break-even IRR**' can be defined as the portfolio gross IRR at which an investment into the fund produces neither a gain nor a loss, or at which the investor's net IRR is equal to 0%. In other words, calculating this break-even allows estimating how well the portfolio has to perform before the LPs start to make nominal profits on the capital invested.

Furthermore, a '**target rate break-even IRR**' can be defined as the portfolio gross IRR at which an investment into the fund produces a gain for the LPs equal to a pre-defined target rate of return. In other words, calculating this break-even allows estimating what portfolio performance is needed before an LP begins to earn a return equal to a pre-defined target. This target can be, for example, the program return objective but also the hurdle rate in order to assess how high the portfolio's performance needs to be before the GP begins to earn his carried interest. As we will discuss in the following, such information can prove valuable in order to assess the adequacy of GP's incentive structure.

9.2 METHODOLOGY

The basis for the break-even analysis is the Yale model developed by Takahashi and Alexander (2001) for the standard limited partnership structure. As discussed previously, this financial model has no predictive power but only models the cash flow patterns representative of private equity funds. To do so the model assumes that the underlying assets (i.e. the portfolio companies) will have a pre-defined average growth rate, and that historical growth rate, patterns of capital contributions and distributions are representative of the future. Of course, these assumptions can be relaxed, and scenarios and sensitivity analyses are possible. Furthermore, as the private equity sub-asset classes (buyouts, venture capital, mezzanine, etc.) show significant cash flow pattern differences, it is recommended to use different parameters for each of them.

As such, the Yale model does not allow calculating directly a break-even IRR and requires some modifications. The key ones relate to the fact that the model does not split the drawdowns into the amount invested and the costs of the structure (set-up costs and management fees) but considers that 100% is invested and that the distribution does not take into account the waterfall.

The modified model uses the inputs and outputs listed in Table 9.1 to model the private equity funds cash flow patterns.

Table 9.1 Modified Yale model – inputs and outputs

Inputs	Description	Outputs	Description
$RC_{(t)}$	Rate of contribution during the period t (%)	$C_{(t)}$	Capital contribution during the period t ($)
CC	Capital commitment ($)	$RD_{(t)}$	Rate of distribution during the period t (%)
SC	Set-up costs ($)	$D_{(t)}$	Distribution during the period t ($)
$MF_{(t)}$	Management fees during the period t ($)	$NAV_{(t)}$	Net Asset Value at the end of the period t ($)
N	Number of periods	$PIC_{(t)}$	Sum of the paid-in capital ($) or $$PIC_{(t)} = \sum_{0}^{t-1} C_{(t)}$$
B	Factor describing changes in the rate of distribution over time	$INV_{(t)}$	Amount invested in portfolio companies during the period t ($)
IRR_p	Portfolio gross internal rate of return (%)	IRR_i	Investors' net internal rate of return (%)

The following description does not incorporate all the elements or specificities that can impact the cost of the structure. For example, fee offsets have not been considered, and for simplicity, we rather concentrate on the key aspects. However, in a more advanced approach it is possible to model their impact on the management fees and on the portfolio performance. Likewise, we just look to only one management fee calculation method.

9.2.1   Step 1: capital contributions

The first step is to be able to estimate the capital contributions $(C_{(t)})$ or drawdowns. These contributions are normally concentrated during the investment period and especially in its first years, reaching around 60–70% after four to five years (see Figure 9.1). The model estimates the capital contributions by multiplying the rate of contribution $(RC_{(t)})$ by the remaining capital commitment, or the initial capital commitment minus the sum of the paid-in capital $(CC-PIC_{(t)})$:

$$C_{(t)} = RC_{(t)} \left(CC - PIC_{(t)} \right) \quad \text{with} \quad PIC_{(t)} = \sum_{0}^{t-1} C_{(t)}$$

The rate of contribution, which is the percentage of the remaining capital commitment expected to be drawn during the current period, can be estimated based on historical data, either from own databases or from an external provider such as the Thomson Financial. In practice, Takahashi and Alexander (2001) suggest using as input: 25% contribution rate in year one, 33.3% in year two and 50% in all subsequent years. As said before, since the private equity sub-asset classes show significant differences, it is recommended to use different rates of contribution for each of them.

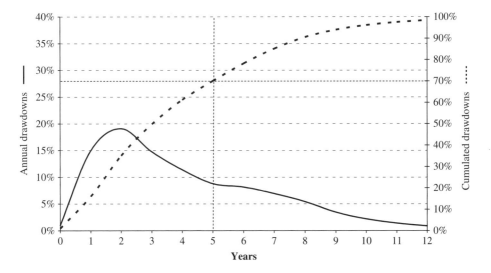

Figure 9.1   Annual and cumulated capital contributions as percentage of fund size

9.2.2   Step 2: use of the contributions

The second step is to determine the use of these contributions or drawdowns $(C_{(t)})$. The first drawdown is normally used to cover the set-up costs (SC), the first call of the management fees $(MF_{(t)})$, which will be called periodically during the whole fund's life and the first investments $(INV_{(t)})$ (see Figure 9.2). Based on the assumptions that the set-up costs are paid at the beginning of the fund's lifetime (i.e. when $t = 0$), $C_{(0)} = SC$. For

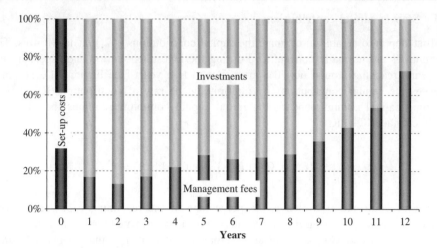

Figure 9.2   Annual contributions split between set-up costs, management fees and investments

simplicity, it is assumed that all the other cash flows occur at the end of the considered period.

$$\text{INV}_{(t)} = C_{(t)} - \text{MF}_{(t)}$$

In the market, we do observe different calculation methods for the management fees. For example, a common one is: a fixed percentage (MFR) of the total fund size during the investment period and of the 'managed capital'[1] during the disinvestment period:

$$\text{MF}_{(t)} = \text{MFR} \times \text{CC} \quad \text{during the investment period}$$

$$\text{MF}_{(t)} = \text{MFR} \times \left(\text{NAV}_{(t-1)\text{at cost}} + \left(\text{CC} - \text{PIC}_{(t)}\right)\right) \quad \text{during the disinvestment period}$$

9.2.3   Step 3: net asset value

The next step is to model the NAV (see Figure 9.3). To do so the model makes the assumption that the investments ($\text{INV}_{(t)}$) have a pre-defined average growth rate (IRR_p). The NAV is here assumed to be a function of this growth rate, the NAV at the end of the previous period and all the cash flows of the considered period. A NAV at cost is also calculated in other to calculate the management fees (see step 2).

$$\text{NAV}_{(t)} = \left[\text{NAV}_{(t-1)} \times \left(1 + \text{IRR}_p\right)\right] + \text{INV}_{(t)} - D_{(t)}$$

$$\text{NAV}_{(t)\text{at cost}} = \text{NAV}_{(t-1)\text{at cost}} + \text{INV}_{(t)} - D_{(t)\text{at cost}}$$

---

[1] The managed capital is defined as the total fund size minus the cost of the transactions exited or fully written off. It can also be calculated as the investments still in the portfolio at cost plus the undrawn commitment (or the fund size minus the sum of the paid-in capital).

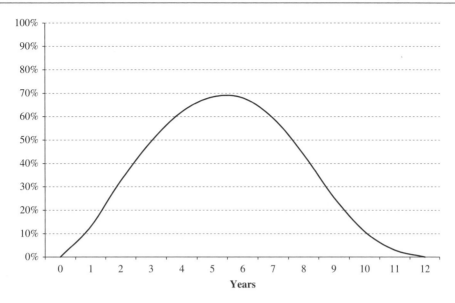

Figure 9.3   Net asset value as percentage of fund size

9.2.4   Step 4: distributions

The fourth step is to estimate the cash distributed from the realizations of the investments (see Figure 9.5). Recognizing that distributions vary with the age of the funds, Takahashi and Alexander (2001) have defined the distribution formula based on a rate of distribution ($RD_{(t)}$) (see Figure 9.4). As time passes, realizations do increase up to the fund maturity where the distribution rate reaches 100%. Despite this high distribution rate, the nominal amounts remain small when the fund gets closer to its maturity. A so-called 'bow factor' (B) controls for the speed of distribution: the higher the factor, the slower the initial increase and the faster the later acceleration (see Figure 9.6). This factor can be estimated based on historical data, either from own databases or from external providers such as Thomson Financial. In practice, it is suggested to use a factor of two.

$$RD_{(t)} = \left({}^{t}/_{N} \right)^{B}$$

The distribution is then calculated based on the rate of distribution, the NAV and the portfolio average growth rate (IRR_{p}). A distribution at cost is also produced in order to calculate the NAV at cost and the management fees (see step 2 and 3).

$$D_{(t)} = RD_{(t)} \times \left[NAV_{(t-1)} \times \left(1 + IRR_{p} \right) \right]$$

$$D_{(t)\text{at cost}} = RD_{(t)} \times NAV_{(t-1)\text{at cost}}$$

As said before, as the private equity sub-asset classes show significant differences, it is recommended to use different rates of contribution for each of them. Indeed, at constant contribution rate and IRR_{p}, the longer the holding period the larger the total

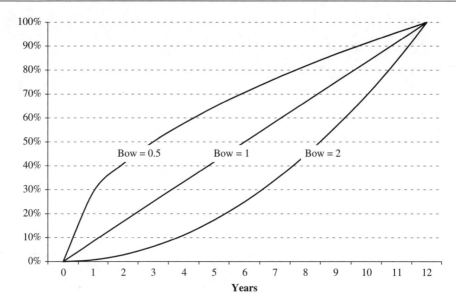

Figure 9.4   Rate of distribution

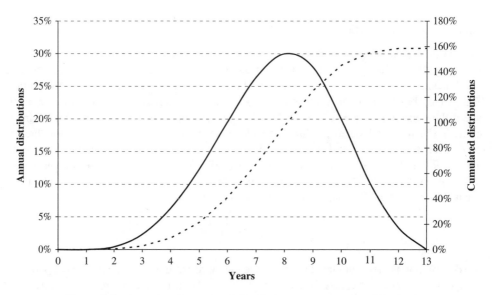

Figure 9.5   Annual and cumulated distributions as percentage of fund size

distribution will be. Figure 9.6 illustrates the significant impact, for the different speeds of distribution.

9.2.5   Step 5: distribution waterfall

The distributions $(D_{(t)})$ generated in step 4 are then split between the various parties (see Figure 9.7). An example of a possible waterfall is:

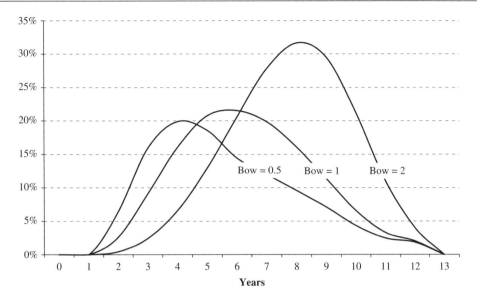

Figure 9.6 Annual distributions by bow rates as percentage of fund size

(1) LPs' capital repayment up to total capital commitment.
(2) Hurdle rate payment.
(3) Catch-up payment.
(4) Carry distribution, i.e. 80% to LPs and 20% to GP.
(5) Claw-back from LPs for the over-repayment of capital (if applicable).

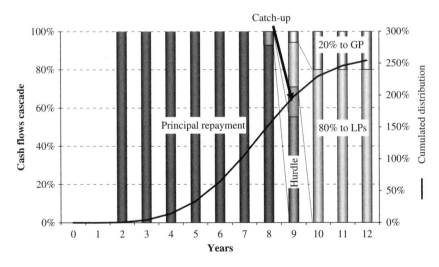

Figure 9.7 Distribution waterfall as percentage of fund size

9.2.6 Step 6: break-even IRRs

Using the cash flows generated by steps 1 and 5, the LPs' cash flows (see Figure 9.8) and, therefore, their net internal rate of return (IRR$_i$) can be calculated. Then, by iterations and by changing the IRR$_p$, the capital and target rate break-even IRRs can be calculated (see Figure 9.9):

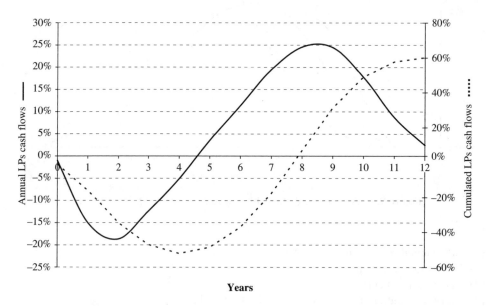

Figure 9.8   Annual and cumulated LPs' cash flows as percentage of fund size

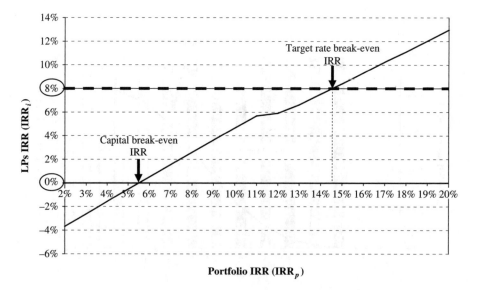

Figure 9.9   Capital and target rate break-even IRRs

- The capital break-even, which is the IRR_p where

$$\sum_{t=0}^{N} C_{(t)} = \sum_{t=0}^{N} D_{(t)}$$

- the target rate break-even IRR (IRR_T), which is the IRR_p where

$$\sum_{t=0}^{N} \frac{C_{(t)}}{(1+\text{IRR}_T)^t} - \sum_{t=0}^{N} \frac{D_{(t)}}{(1+\text{IRR}_T)^t} = 0$$

Since 2002, we have estimated for all the transactions we have analyzed (i.e. predominantly EU funds, see Figures 7.5 and 7.6) the capital break-even IRR. Based on these, we came to the following ranges:

Below 6%	Low, i.e. the structure is 'cheap'
6%–8%	Medium
Above 8%	High, i.e. the structure is expensive

9.3   SCENARIOS AND SENSITIVITY ANALYSIS

Though it is assumed in the model that historical patterns are representative of the future, the prospective investment environments may differ significantly from historical ones. Therefore, these assumptions should be relaxed and scenario analysis using different historical time periods to parameterize the model should be performed.

The break-even IRR approach can also be used to perform a sensitivity analysis or, in other words, to assess the impact of changing the fund structure. For example, as already mentioned, the decision on the length of the investment period has an impact on the cost of the structure. Following the analysis of the quality of the deal flow, one could conclude that the probability of extending the investment period is high. Indeed, many funds are structured with the possibility of extending by one year the initial four years of the investment period. But as management fees are normally more important during the investment period than after, such a decision will, with a 'standard' VC fund structure, increase the cost of the structure by more than 20%.[2]

In Table 9.2 we have calculated, for illustration purposes, the impact of changing some of the fund structure compared with our 'standard' venture capital fund.

---

[2] To simulate a standard venture capital fund structure, we have used 1% incorporation costs, a five-year investment period and a fund's lifetime of 12 years and management fees of 2.5% of the fund size during the investment period and 2.5% on the managed capital, thereafter.

Table 9.2   Break-even sensitivity analysis

Scenario	Break-even IRR	Δ vs. standard VC fund
Standard VC fund	7.20%	—
+1% Mgt fees	10.59%	+ 47%
−1% Mgt fees	4.17%	− 42%
+0.5% Mgt fees	8.87%	+ 23%
−0.5% Mgt fees	5.55%	− 23%
+1 year fund's lifetime	6.94%	− 4%
−1 year fund's lifetime	7.53%	+ 5%
+1 year inv. period	8.74%	+ 21%
−1 year inv. period	6.01%	− 17%
+0.5% incorp. costs	7.41%	+ 3%
−0.5% incorp. costs	7.00%	− 3%

9.4   ADDITIONAL ANALYSIS

The break-even IRR analysis can also be a useful tool to analyze some other aspects of a transaction. Some examples of these potential add-ons are presented below; many others exist.

9.4.1   Incentive scheme analysis

The tool used to calculate the break-even IRRs can also be used to analyze the GP's incentive scheme. Examples of such analyses are the 'hurdle rate inflexion point', which is the assessment of the portfolio gross performance (IRR_p) required for the GP to be 'in-the-carry'.

   Using the same approach as the target rate break-even IRR, it is possible to estimate the 'hurdle rate inflexion point', i.e. the IRR_p required for the GP to be in-the-carry. This can be done by setting the target rate equal to the hurdle rate. As once beyond this point the GP will be in-the-carry, this is valuable information to assess the feasibility for the GP to participate in the upside. With a 'standard' venture capital fund structure, this inflexion point is estimated to be around 12%.

9.4.2   Analysis of the wealth transferred

As is often said in the private equity industry, 'the GP has to eat sandwiches with the management fees and caviar with the carry. But one should also make sure that these sandwiches are not filled with caviar.' Indeed, in some structures, the likelihood that the GP receives a carried interest and its amount, which should remain the main upside incentive, can become immaterial compared with the quasi-certain management fees and, therefore, lose its effectiveness.

   The data obtained via the break-even IRR analysis allow us to estimate the wealth transferred (see Figure 9.10) from the LPs to the GP by calculating for various IRR_p the distributions to the LPs and to the GP (i.e. management fees, catch-up and carried interest). Using a 'standard' venture capital fund structure, before the hurdle rate inflexion point the wealth transferred from the LPs to the GP remains constant in absolute terms but decreases in relative terms up to a level of around 20%. After, when the GP catches up and gets a share in the carried interest, this transfer increases continuously in absolute terms with the constant increase of the carry and reaches in relative terms a level close to 24%.

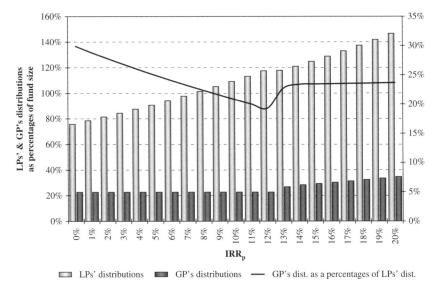

Figure 9.10   Wealth transfer between LPs and GP

9.4.3   IRR distributions

Though the Yale model has no predictive power, it can be complemented by some portfolio performance probability distributions to allow projections. For example, based on the analysis performed by Cochrane (2005),[3] it is possible to generate via a Monte Carlo simulation a probability distribution associated with the IRR_p. Such an analysis is also possible by using directly the net IRR data from the Thomson Financial's VentureXpert database.

There are a number of techniques in use to assess the impact of variations in fund structures. For instance, Gompers and Lerner (1999a) observed that the carried interest has the character of a call option that entitles the fund managers to a certain share of the increase in value of the underlying fund. Schmidt and Wahrenburg (2003) used this approach to analyze 122 private placement memoranda and 46 partnership agreements for European VC funds. Based on a binomial model, they calculated the option value for different capital gains scenarios and changing hurdle rates.[4] Also, other researchers have developed simulations or formulas to calculate this value.[5]

The break-even analysis was described here in a simplified form that offers flexibility to cover more complex structures as well. It is meant to be a starting point for developing more sophisticated tools to value and track the limited partners' and the fund managers' interests in a fund.

---

[3] Cochrane (2005) used the VentureOne database, which includes over 15 000 valuations in over 7000 companies where a new financing round or IPO happened.
[4] Their analysis suggested that the ex ante mean value of the carried interest option is about 15.30% of the total invested fund capital, and that there was a 92% concentration of the carry option value at 15.22% median.
[5] See, for example, Rouvinez (2005).

10
Track Record Analysis

Institutions think track record and private equity experience are by far the most important elements of a general partner's experience.

AltAssets (2002a)

In principle, a track record analysis is the assessment of the past achievements of a person or an organization. In the context of private equity, track record analysis is normally the analysis of the past financial performance of a private equity management house and as such forms part of the due diligence process. But it can go beyond that, and, for example, can be expanded to other types of achievements such as non-financial objectives or indirect financial benefits.

What has to be noticed is its orientation toward the **past**. The track record analysis will say little about the present and even less about the future. It aims to establish a link with the **present** proposal, i.e. the management team and its industry and deal experience. Are the team members responsible for the track record still there; are those responsible for the successes fairly remunerated; and is there a proper succession planning? Regarding the **future**, Costabile (2006) sees it as important that a fund's espoused strategy matches its management team's history. With the track record analysis we look at a quite narrow and apparently very technical aspect of the due diligence, which may give the impression that we consider this a purely quantitative, mechanical and – as one is tempted to say – pseudo-scientific exercise that more or less automatically leads to a 'yes' or 'no' as investment decision. This calls for some comments on the due diligence exercise in general.

10.1 DUE DILIGENCE

Due diligence is a requirement for prudent investors as well as the basis for better investment decision. Due diligence is a huge subject that has been covered in a number of publications in great detail. For further readings, we for example refer to the relevant chapters in Meyer and Mathonet (2005) or – the highly readable – Fraser-Sampson (2007). We neither see due diligence as bureaucratically 'ticking the box' nor can it be a purely artistic undertaking. There are two main purposes why investors do this: firstly, to cover the downside risk of an investment. This is an aspect that most investors have no problems understanding, and it is simply a question of, well, diligence. There are a number of good hints and recipes how to go about this.

10.1.1 Performance persistence

Several studies undertaken concluded that in private equity fund managers show some degree of persistence in returns and, therefore, suggested that past success be a good predictor for future performance.[1] Certainly one would expect that professional fund managers who have worked together to build companies could apply their experience to new funds and stand a better chance of success.

> *If your first fund was top quartile, there is a 45% chance your next fund will also be top 25% and a 73% chance it will be top half. A new fund management team has a 16% chance of being in the top quartile [. . .] Success in private equity is persistent.*
>
> Conor Kehoe, Partner, McKinsey & Co.

Simplistically, the typical argument of private equity advisors or funds-of-funds goes along the lines, 'performance is persistent, therefore you must invest in teams that historically delivered "top-quartile" returns. Of course, the problem is that such funds are oversubscribed, but we can give you access to them.' This view of the industry is intuitively convincing and would make things very simple. However, taking a closer look does not fully support this view.

Box 10.1:   'Experts' vs. 'tourists'

Figure 10.1 is taken out of a publicly quoted private equity fund-of-funds' investment prospect and representative for the typical arguments of the industry players. It is based on performance data from Thomson Financial (on behalf of EVCA) and is adding as a comment that selecting the 'top funds' is key. While the investment in the average private equity fund would just generate an IRR of 11.9% p.a., funds performing in the top quartile show significantly higher returns.

While not expressed directly, the implicit message is that this manager has access to the 'top-quartile' funds and that therefore the average return figure should be easy to beat. This line of argument is reflecting the conventional wisdom – or rather the myth – that there is an inner circle of 'experts' who have privileged access to the consistent value creators while the 'tourists', i.e. the inexperienced newcomers, will find it an insurmountable obstacle to identify and get admitted to this exclusive club and therefore are bound to leave the industry after having been disappointed by dismal returns.

We do not dismiss this argument entirely, but can 75% of limited partners really be considered as such tourists? This should not be misunderstood as an attempt to promulgate the private equity industry's equivalent of the efficient market theory. The private equity market is not efficient, and good research and proper due diligence will significantly improve the selection of fund proposals. However, that the private equity industry is not efficient does not mean that it is not competitive. Most investors base their views of this market on long-term industry statistics that also cover periods where probably only 'experts' were active in the market. Such statistics, however, covers mainly funds where investors after a rigorous due diligence committed to because they were convinced that these funds would deliver a 'top' performance.

---

[1] See von Braun (2000), Tierney and Folkerts-Landau (2001), Scardino (2004), Kaplan and Schoar (2005) or Rouvinez (2005).

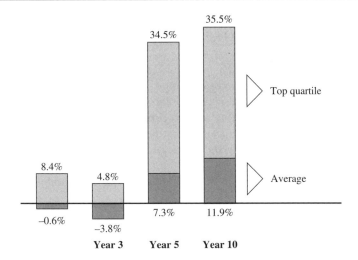

Figure 10.1 Private equity average returns (net IRR p.a.) from 1993–2003 as of 31 December 2003

   We therefore take another point of view, namely that the majority of investors are 'experts' and follow comparable methods for their due diligence. Consequently, also in private equity the average return figure will be hard to beat. We have occasionally been challenged for following an apparently over-conservative approach. We concede that this may have a cautious bias, but when asked to choose between the alternatives of a market composed of '75% tourists' or '100% experts', we believe that '80–90% percent experts' is probably closer to reality under ordinary market conditions.

   In reality, the big gap between top and bottom performers can also to a certain degree be explained by randomness (see Box 10.2). The research firm Asset Alternatives studied 182 venture capital firms that had raised at least two funds.[2] The authors found that only 5% of the firms performed in the top quartile between 50% and 75% of the time and only 3% of the firms did more than 75% of the time. That means that only 8% of all firms[3] performed in the top quartile more than half of the time. 'If, in fact, there was a tendency for the same firms to perform in the top quartile, we would expect larger percentages as both the 50% and 75% levels.' They conclude that past performance has been a fairly bad indicator of a successor fund's future performance.

   Furthermore, the peer groups cannot be compared from one vintage year to another. Private equity firms raise funds in irregular intervals, and therefore the firms that raised the funds that comprised the previous peer group may not be out looking for investors at

[2] See Pease (2000).
[3] Likewise Scardino (2004) identified a group of 60 out of 522 (11%) private equity firms from around the world and across different fund types that have managed to deliver such sustained good performance.

the same time again. In other words, the peer group compositions will not remain constant. Consequently, the persistence claim is even more difficult to verify.

> *It is vital to look further than the pure numbers. Returns are still important factors to consider and we still look for groups that have produced, and are likely to continue to produce, above average realised returns. But when we look at those returns, we need to have an understanding of who produced them and in what kind of environment they were produced. I would add, though, that all things being equal, GPs who have been consistently successful in the past will attract richer opportunities in the future.*
>
> Judith Elsea, Knightsbridge (AltAssets, 2003)

In private equity, there is a wide divergence between top and bottom performers and to focus on the best or the 'top-quartile' managers is a common advice. Unfortunately, this is easier said than done, and the hint to focus on top funds is probably as helpful as the observation that to become rich one needs to earn a lot of money.

Box 10.2: Spread

Many observers of the private equity market point to the fact that the range of historical outcomes is wider for private equity than it is for other asset classes. Statements like this are quite typical: 'In fact, over a decade, the spread between a top quartile bond fund's perfomance [sic] and a third quartile fund is only about 1%. For shares the spread in returns rises to about 3%. But get this, depending on which piece of research you accept, the spread between top quartile and third quartile private equity performance sits somewhere between 15% and 22%. Massive Implication? If you can't get your money into a top-performing private equity fund you're better off staying out of the asset class. It's all about access.'[4]

According to an analysis done by Otterlei and Barrington (2003), selecting a mutual fund that provides the median return would result in a return only 4.8% less than the top-quartile mutual fund. However, for private equity funds the difference between a top-quartile return and a median return can be two or three times as much. It is certainly true that picking the wrong private equity fund is likely to have a strong adverse impact on returns. But can we draw the conclusion from this observation, as many do, that in private equity fund managers add significant value and that skills are the main explanation for the large observed spread, i.e. the range between the best and the worst managers?

Firstly, taking mutual funds as a reference point is comparing apples against oranges. Mutual fund managers usually have to track an index, and one should not expect such a large spread in such a situation in the first place. Assuming that we build a portfolio by selecting funds randomly, the probability of observing a large range of outcomes for returns is influenced by two factors:

---

[4] Quoted from http://www.carriedinterest.com/ [accessed 22 November 2006].

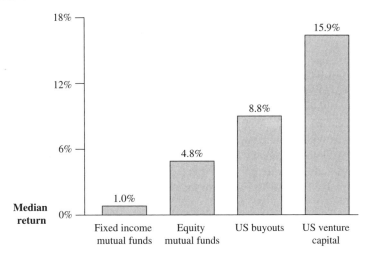

Figure 10.2   Spread between top and bottom performers
Source: Otterlei and Barrington 2003.

(1) The variance of the distribution of achievable multiples for each fund. The higher the variance, the higher the probability of observing a large range of outcomes. This in turn depends on three factors: (a) the average variance of the underlying portfolio companies, (b) their average covariance and (c) the diversification, i.e. the number of companies in the fund's portfolio.[5]

(2) The size of the population of funds observed. The larger this population, the higher the probability of observing a large spread between the best and the worst fund managers.

Irrespective of the fund managers' skills, a wide spread between the highest and the lowest return figures is likely to be observed if the asset class is volatile enough, preferably positively correlated, if the funds' portfolios are little diversified and if the observed population of funds is large. Based on an in-house analysis we found that VC funds on average hold between 13 and 14 portfolio companies, and, taking the riskiness of venture funded start-ups into account, it cannot come as a surprise that in this case the spread is as large as it is. On the other hand, the observable population of mutual fund managers is much larger that in private equity, which theoretically should result in a significant spread here as well.

We ran a simple Monte Carlo simulation to investigate the relative impact of (a) diversification and (b) observable population on the expected observable

---

[5] The variance of an equally weighted portfolio can be expressed as:

$$\sigma_P^2 = \frac{1}{n}\overline{\sigma}^2 + \frac{n-1}{n}\overline{\text{cov}}$$

where $\overline{\sigma}^2$ is the average variance of individual stock returns, $\overline{\text{cov}}$ is the average covariance between all pairs of stock returns and n is the number of stocks in the portfolio.

Box 10.2:   (Continued)

performance range between the best and the worst managers for randomly selected funds (see Appendix 10A). The results of our simulations show that the large spread of outcomes observed in the funds' realized returns might – at least in part – be explained by purely statistical effects. In fact, what is actually surprising is that the range between the top and the worst managers is not even larger considering the volatility of the underlying companies and the results of the simulation. Paradoxically, this may even be an argument for skill and against randomness, as the stronger the effect of randomness, the larger the expected spread. But still this observation could easily be explained in another way: the fact that the simple average multiples of real direct investments and real VC funds do not match is not surprising. To have a match, we would need to use capital-weighted averages. The most likely explanation for the decrease in average multiple is that the companies with the highest multiples were also the smallest ones. This would also explain the small spread in real fund performances when compared with our simulation. Therefore, the observed spread in the real fund data set could still be consistent with randomness.[6]

We are not suggesting that in private equity the fund managers' skills are not highly important. However, the results also support our hypothesis that actually the majority of published data on investment returns in private equity relate to skilled fund managers. Consequently, unlike many in this industry believe, it remains a challenge to consistently pick above-average fund managers and the recipe to 'go for the top quartile' is over-simplistic.

Lastly, even if the claim was true, for a track record analysis it would be of little use as private equity firms need to raise new funds when the old funds are still just in their fourth or fifth year, and therefore they and their peer group are far from being fully realized. Before a reliable comparison within a peer group is feasible, in private equity, the ship has sailed (or sunk) already. That experience is important and that skillful fund managers can repeat successes is certainly plausible, but based on the research available no final conclusion on the persistence of performance can be drawn yet.

10.1.2   Gathering and evaluating the data

To a large degree the due diligence is based on historical data and starts by gathering all the required data. Obviously, as the objective is to compare the performance of the funds against their peer group, both funds and benchmark data need to be evaluated. Ideally, the data needed to measure the past performance and the related return measures (see Box 10.4) is provided in a standard format to make comparisons between different proposals easier. Often information is a bit more than covered by the industry standard reporting.[7]

---

[6] Clearly the simulation could be refined as well. We ran each simulation for equally weighted portfolios. Adding a little bit more randomness in the simulation by allowing for varying weights is likely to result in an additional increase of the expected range. We also note that the simulation process (random picking of portfolio companies across vintage years, industries and regions regardless of correlations) is not consistent with reality. But rather than providing an explanation for the low observed range in real funds, this means that by ignoring correlations our simulation is likely to understate the expected range.

[7] See, for example, the EVCA Reporting Guidelines or the International Private Equity and Venture Capital Valuation Guidelines.

Box 10.3: Questionnaires

Apparently nothing makes an investor less popular than asking fund managers to fill out a questionnaire, and industry practitioners often feel quite strongly about this or any other forms of checklist. According to Byworth (2005), 'virtually everyone interviewed did the telephone version of rolling their eyes at the mention of due diligence questionnaires [...] One experienced investor stated that many groups simply don't have the staff to fill out 20–30 questionnaires, and that such activity represented a poor use of the general partner's time, which after all is paid to make and dispose of investments profitably, not engage in pointless administration.'

We may be biased, as in Meyer and Mathonet (2005) we have proposed an – admittedly exhaustive – questionnaire ourselves, but we beg to differ. It is not only the private equity firms who get showered with questionnaires. It is also the prospective investors in funds who get peppered with proposals and have the task of properly evaluating them. Some of these investment proposals may be of interest in principle, and at least before better ones are found, they certainly merit a closer look. The assessment of fund proposals on a standalone basis can be highly misleading, and we see it as critical to do as many comparisons as possible. To find the occasional gem you simply need to evaluate many proposals. Even if the evaluation does not result in a commitment, it is an important part of a private equity fund investment program's research process, as it can provide up-to-date information on the market. However, data gathering and formatting for an in-depth analysis can easily overwhelm a research team. Well-designed questionnaires can therefore be a useful tool to help split what is necessary but routine and often overly time-consuming – for example, data gathering – from what is important and cannot be standardized, namely analysis and judgment.

Certainly the etiquette needs to be respected. For example, it will not promote a hopeful investor's case if he asks the fund managers of an oversubscribed fund to 'fill out the attached questionnaire, please'. On the other hand, in cases where a private equity firm approaches the investor, it does not appear too much to request saving the prospective limited partner some time and formats the requested information in a way that allows the due diligence team to put things into the right perspective. At the end of the day, a general partner knows, or should know, their own proposal best. Speeding up the evaluation process is in the interests of both parties. Finally, questionnaires to be filled out by the general partner should focus on the essentials, whereas limited partners may have additional points covered in in-house checklists.

10.1.3 The perils of charisma

There is a general belief that success in private equity is not due to luck but based on skills, and the assessment of the fund management team tends to dominate the due diligence. Investors need to get a good understanding of the dynamics in the team and the team members' ability to work together in order to understand if the team is cohesive and complementary or rather the addition of independent stars. To illustrate this, let's just imagine an improvised band comprising Neil Young, Madonna and Vanessa Mae, all of them gifted artists, but what would they play? Even if the members of the band are slightly more complementary, it will take them significant time to practice and to find the right arrangement, assuming their egos and their rivalry allow them do so.

An important part of a thorough due diligence is reference checks, calling for example the portfolio companies, previous colleagues or investors. Such reference calls may be seen as 'gossips' but they are, as Russel (2006) stated, relevant data points that pierce the 'united front' of the fund management team.

> *However, we increasingly use our network for informal reference checks, which can often be an even greater source of 'off the cuff' information on internal issues. These are otherwise extremely difficult to research. For example, we try to identify and speak to recent leavers. They can give you the real view on the internal office politics, who the real decision-makers are, how due diligence is really carried out, whether the stated strategy is really perceived as such at analyst level and how it actually gets implemented. This type of interview provides additional insights as to how a team really functions and should be an essential part of the overall due diligence process.*
>
> Jeremy Golding, Founder and Managing Partner, Golding Capital Partners
> (AltAssets, 2002)

With CEOs of portfolio companies the investor can get more details on the sourcing of the deal, how competitive was the process, how 'hands-on' is the fund team, what was its value added, what are the future performance expectations or what are the exit plans. With co-investors, one can get more details on the rationale behind the co-investment decision, the perception of the fund manager's past performance, the style of cooperation, the comparison of type of value-adding approach or the view on the deal's future development.

Due diligences are often stretching over weeks, during which you may get to like the team. Fund managers in private equity tend to be great salespeople. Furthermore, they also get to genuinely like you. You have several millions in your pocket for them and you may, contrary to others, have 'understood' how brilliant they are and how well their still unrealized portfolio will perform. Fund managers are often bright and charismatic, and a common pitfall for inexperienced investors is to succumb to their charm and make investment decisions based on mutual sympathies.

> *One example was of a fund set up by a number of individuals who had worked at other high quality firms. The superficial due diligence on these individuals resulted in positive reference checks from their prior firms. But when we really dug in and got the true, off the record evaluation, it turned out that several of these individuals had been pushed out of their firm and the actual reference check came out quite negative. When we did the attribution analysis, a lot of their track record also melted away. It became very clear that these guys were not the stars they made themselves out to be.*
>
> Clint Harris, Managing Partner, Grove Street Advisors (AltAssets, 2002)

There are many 'war stories' from industry practitioners giving the impression that due diligence is some kind of detective work, going along the lines of 'I did the extra phone call' or 'I talked to this guy and found that out – ha!'. However, the real danger is being too shallow and believing that 'it is the team only'. Reference calls, etc. can only demonstrate the presence of issues, but they do not really answer the question of how strong the investment proposal is.

10.1.4 Improving investment decisions – luck or skills?

As Fraser-Sampson (2007) stated, if 'you have a standard due diligence checklist which you dutifully and meticulously follow in each case (or, even worse, a standard questionnaire which you expect the investee to complete) then you are completely missing the point' (see Box 10.3). Arriving at a better investment decision requires more than ticking the box. Many investors give the impression that they, with strict discipline, apply stringent cut-off criteria to filter out the top quartile – no, the top decile! – funds. The reality is likely to be different, as in private equity usually investment decisions have to be made despite various issues. Assuming that the major points related to downside protection are adequately covered and that there are no skeletons in the closet, the second major purpose of the due diligence is to assess the upside potential of an investment. This, however, is a far more difficult and important exercise, as it aims to lead to a superior investment decision. Here a track record analysis can be a useful tool.

Before explaining its use, we need to become clear about what we cannot and do not try to achieve with a track record analysis. Firstly, it is not an attempt to 'blind with science and quantity' and do many different analyses to achieve certainty where, as we elaborate on in subsequent chapters, certainty is out of reach in principle. It also should not primarily be seen as an exercise to challenge audited valuations or to recalculate the historical cash flows for checking whether the stated IRR is correct. Finally, to base decisions purely on IRR performance is superficial. The idea is not to equate future with past performance or try to prove or disprove that a fund is top quartile, because 'we exclusively invest in top-quartile teams'. The track record analysis aims to get a better understanding of how the fund management team worked in the past, how they compared against their peers, what were the drivers of their performance or what differentiates their approach from others. It could be seen as a pattern recognition tool with the objective of rather understanding than just measuring, although benchmarking forms an important part of the purely 'technical' work to be done.

Looking at the track record of private equity managers we always ask: what is it about that GP that has enabled them to outperform in the past and what gives us confidence that they will be able to continue outperforming?

John Greenwood and Stuart Waught, TD Capital (AltAssets, 2003)

The main question we would like to answer is whether a fund management team's success was due to luck or to skills, as skills are more likely to be repeatable (although also luck sometimes appears to be persistent, albeit with mostly the wrong people – life is not always fair). Track record analysis is based on comparisons; therefore we need to look at benchmarking next. The objective of benchmarking is to judge on the quality of the past performance and whether the drivers for success in previous funds are applicable for the future, taking changes in the market into account.

Sadly most investors seem to fail to recognise that the aim of due diligence is to help them make better decisions, and prefer to see it as a means of covering their backs in advance should anything go wrong with the investment in the future.

Fraser-Sampson (2007)

Finally, the track record analysis is a tool that can help us to decide between several apparently equally acceptable investment proposals.[8]

10.2   BENCHMARKING

The basic approach is to compare the fund's return measures against its peer group. The most intuitive and classical one is the group of funds that have a similar risk profile. These funds are effectively the competitors of the fund to be benchmarked. But several other benchmarks are used in practice. We describe below the most common ones.

Box 10.4:   Return measures

Venture capital associations and the Association for Investment Management and Research (AIMR)[9] deem the IRR,[10] which is a cash-weighted rate of return, to be the most appropriate return measure for venture capital and private equity funds. AIMR recognizes that when a management contract calls for a series of investments, spread out over time at the discretion of the manager, time-weighted rate of return-based performance measurement and evaluation are not appropriate.

The **IRR** is a cash flow-based return measure, which considers the residual value or NAV of the partnership's holdings as a final cash-inflow. Mathematically it is expressed as:

$$\sum_{t=0}^{T} \frac{D_{(t)}}{\left(1+\text{IRR}_{(T)}\right)^t} + \frac{\text{NAV}_{(T)}}{\left(1+\text{IRR}_{(T)}\right)^T} - \sum_{t=0}^{T} \frac{C_{(t)}}{\left(1+\text{IRR}_{(T)}\right)^t} = 0$$

where $D_{(t)}$ is the fund distribution during the period t, $\text{NAV}_{(T)}$ is the NAV of the fund at the end of period T, $C_{(t)}$ is the capital contribution or drawdown during the period t and IRR_T is the investors' net interim internal rate of return at time $t = T$.

The IRR is not the only measure used in the industry. It assumes re-investment at the same conditions and only measures the efficiency of the capital invested but fails to conclude on its effectiveness. For example an annual IRR of 100 percent would clearly be a highly efficient private equity investment but if the capital invested was only exposed during let say one month, an investment of €100 will only generate €5,5 of additional capital, leaving the investor with cash and still far from industry like target returns. Therefore, other performance measures are commonly used:

---

[8] Also the due diligence should not be confused with the private equity fund grading we have described previously. The grading is a valuation tool and indeed meant to be as much tick-box as possible. Its importance for investment decision-making is, as we will discuss in the next chapters, more in the context of portfolio management.

[9] See Geltner and Ling (2000): in 1993, AIMR proposed performance measurement guidelines that recommended a time-weighted approach. After investors and fund managers expressed concerns, a special sub-committee of private equity industry investors and experts appointed by AIMR studied the applicability of time-weighted returns to the private equity industry. They recommended that fund managers and intermediaries present their private equity performance results on the cash-weighted IRR basis.

[10] Note that as database providers are focusing on net return to the limited partners, it is the fund's net IRR and not the gross that has to be benchmarked.

- The **multiple** or the total value to paid-in ratio (TVPI):

$$\text{TVPI}_{(T)} = \frac{\sum\limits_{t=0}^{T} D_{(t)} + \text{NAV}_{(T)}}{\sum\limits_{t=0}^{T} C_{(t)}}$$

- The **distribution** to paid-in ratio (DPI), which is a measure of the cumulative investment returned relative to invested capital:

$$\text{DPI}_{(T)} = \frac{\sum\limits_{t=0}^{T} D_{(t)}}{\sum\limits_{t=0}^{T} C_{(t)}}$$

- The **residual value to paid-in** (RVPI), which is a measure of how much of the investors' invested capital is still tied up in the equity of the fund:

$$\text{RVPI}_{(T)} = \frac{\text{NAV}_{(T)}}{\sum\limits_{t=0}^{T} C_{(t)}}$$

These ratios are measures of net returns to invested capital without taking the time value of money into account, contrary to the IRR. While the TVPI covers the global performance, the DPI focuses on the realized one and the RVPI the unrealized one, helping to assess the importance of the still uncertain return. Therefore, a good track record analysis should contain all these return measures.

10.2.1 Classical relative benchmark

The basic approach defines success on the quartile position in the benchmark. This is done by comparison against funds that are subject to the same market conditions to assure that we are comparing apples with apples. It is common practice to do comparisons against a vintage, geographic and fund-type specific benchmark, often referred to as 'peer group cohort' (e.g. 1995 European buyout funds). The interim performance of the fund is compared against its benchmark and the results are expressed in terms of quartile.

In some cases, however, there are simply not enough funds to obtain a meaningful 'peer group cohort' (e.g. in the case of emerging markets). As the industry is private, the data providers mostly rely on voluntary participation and, as a result, certain markets are not effectively covered. In these cases, more general or alternative benchmarks can be used.

When a representative 'peer group cohort' is not available, the simplest method is to extend the peer universe to the most similar funds. For example, if the number of 1995 European early stage funds are not sufficient, the universe of the 1995 European VC funds can be used as an alternative benchmark or the universe of the 1994–96 European early stage funds.[11] A wine analogy to this would be that if you want to assess a white Château Smith Haut Lafitte vintage 2000[12] and if you do not have any other white Pessac-Leognan vintage 2000 wine to compare with, you could use other vintage 2000 white wines from the nearest Bordeaux regions or a white Pessac-Leognan vintage 1999 or 2001[13] as substitutes but obviously not a Burgundy white wine.

Box 10.5:   Other influences on track record

A number of governments have instituted publicly supported insurance schemes against investment failures. For example in France financial institutions investing in VC funds targeting small- and medium-sized enterprises may obtain guarantees against loan default or failure of a company in which the institution has taken a financial stake. La Société française pour l'assurance du capital-risque des petites et moyennes entreprises (Sofaris) generally only guarantee 50 percent of the funding, but there are exceptions, such as a guarantee of as much as 70 percent for some biotech investments. The premium to be paid for a Sofaris guarantee is much lower than for a normal insurance, the difference being provided by the Ministry of Finances.

Ignoring this support of public institutions can lead to a wrong interpretation of the performance figures. For example, we have seen a VC fund showing the best DPI ratio[14] of its peer group (0.37x vs. a maximum of 0.15x for the peer group), which may be interpreted as a very good indicator of the team's ability to generate exits.

In reality, all of these distributions were related to the guarantee calls they made for defaulting deals. In other words, all of these deals were write-offs but a public guarantee scheme stepped in and reimbursed the fund's losses. Therefore, the right interpretation of this high DPI ratio was that the team may have good financial engineering skills as they arranged a downside protections via the public guarantee scheme, but that there is no indication that the team has the skills to build companies.

Practically, the track record analysis has to exclude from the fund's cash flows all the impact of the public supports and by recalculating the performance measures net of the impact of these mechanisms. In our example, the adjusted DPI ratio was 0.0x and not 0.37x, resulting in a quite different interpretation of this team's ability to generate profitable exits.

Figure 10.3 shows one example of a benchmarking. The fund starts as a fourth-quartile fund and moves after several quarters into the first-quartile area to peak with a 25% IRR. Then, it goes down into the second quartile and ends its life at the limit between the first and second quartiles.

---

[11] Indeed, what happened during the night of 31 December that makes a December 1995 fund so different from a January 1996 fund? One could have the same question with regard to the time limitations for yogurt, for example. What does exactly happen at midnight that makes an up to then still eatable yogurt improper for consumption?

[12] As for funds, the best way to taste a wine is to meet on-site its producer. We thank Mrs and Mr Cathiard for having given us the opportunity to taste their amazing white Château Smith Haut Lafitte vintage 2000 on the terrace of their superb Chartreuse in their estate.

[13] Although for wines the vintage year may be a more important differentiator than for VC funds, which for two consecutive vintage years have normally eight common years of activities.

[14] See Box 10.4 for further explanations on the DPI ratio.

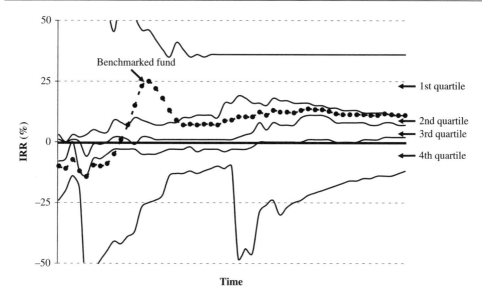

Figure 10.3   Individual fund benchmarking – quartile evolution since inception within the peer group

The quartile is a quantitative relative measure. A top performer in a dismal vintage year may barely return the invested money, while in some spectacular vintage years even fourth-quartile funds have returned double-digit returns (see Figure 10.4). At least initially a quartile position has little predictive power, and does not reflect any qualitative assessment.

A top quartile fund by definition belongs to the 25% best funds in its peer group, which erroneously leads to the conclusion that only 25% of the funds may legitimately be qualified

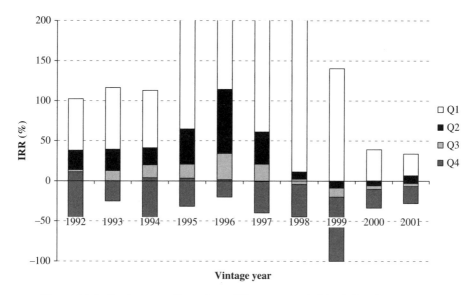

Figure 10.4   Performance dispersion – US venture capital funds by vintage years
Source: Thomson Financial (VentureXpert database)

as such. The fact is that many more funds in the market are being labeled 'top quartile'. One reason is that except for the 25% ratio itself, nothing else in this definition is cast in stone. Whether 'best performance' refers to total value or internal rate of return, net or gross, realized or not, is open to interpretation, as is the question of who are the 'peers'. Again, as stated before, several return measures, each with their advantages and disadvantages, exist. As a fund can have a different quartile position depending on the return measure used, it is, therefore, good practice to benchmark the fund using these various measures and then to use judgment.

Private equity funds do not have a track record, but only its management team may have one. Therefore, the analysis of a team's track record requires analyzing the funds that have been or are under their management. The presentation of an aggregated historical track record over several fund generations provides a good indication but can be misleading, when some funds are not relevant to assess the current investment opportunity. For example, part of the historical track record can be attributed to team members who have left or are going to leave the management company, or some older funds may have followed strategies significantly different from the current one. This requires a methodology to aggregate the funds's individual analysis, such as the one described in Box 10.6. An alternative to the aggregation would be to split the fund performance into its various subcomponents or strategies that then can also be benchmarked.

The main criteria to take into account for the relevance factors are:

- The full or partial attribution to the current team members.
- The similarity of the market conditions and strategies.
- The predictive power of the interim performance.

Box 10.6:   Aggregation methodology

One possible aggregation methodology is to weight the performance of each fund and of their benchmark by their total commitment:

$$\text{IRR}_{P,T} = \frac{1}{\sum\limits_{i=1}^{N} \text{CC}_i} \sum_{i=1}^{N} \text{CC}_i \times \text{IRR}_i,$$

where CC_i is the total commitment made to fund i and $\text{IRR}_{i,T}$ is the IRR of fund i at the end of time period T and N is the number of funds under management. In this analysis, the IRR can be replaced by another performance measure (TVPI, DPI or RVPI).

Our suggestion is to weight by both the total commitment and by a relevance factor ranging from zero (fund not relevant at all), for example, for funds that have been managed only by retired or departed team members, to one (fund fully relevant). An example of such aggregation is presented in Table 10.1.

$$\text{IRR}_{P,T}^{*} = \frac{1}{\sum\limits_{i=1}^{N} \text{CC}_i} \sum_{i=1}^{N} \text{CC}_i * \text{RF}_i * \text{IRR}_i,$$

where RF_i is the relevance factor for fund i.

Table 10.1   Team benchmarking

Fund data						
	VC fund 1	VC fund 2	VC fund 3			
Relevance factor	0.75	1.00	0.50			
Vintage year	**1994**	**1998**	**2002**	**Combined**	**Commit. weighted**	**Relevence factor**
Commitment	47.1	120.6	330.0	497.7	497.7	497.7
Paid in	47.1	120.6	246.0	413.7	413.7	413.7
	100%	100%	75%	83%	83%	83%
Undrawn	0.0	0.0	84.0	84.0	84.0	84.0
Distributed	175.5	14.1	5.4	195.0	195.0	195.0
Net Asset Value	17.8	69.1	194.3	281.2	281.2	281.2
Total Value	193.3	83.2	199.7	476.2	476.2	476.2
Net TVPI	4.1	0.7	0.8	1.2	1.1	1.1
Net DVPI	3.7	0.1	0.0	0.5	0.4	0.5
Net IRR	28%	−7%	−8%	**12.9%**	**−4.2%**	**−3.6%**
Benchmark position				ALL VC **Q1**	**Q2**	**Q3**
				ALL PE **Q1**	**Q3**	**Q4**

Benchmark data						
ALL VC	**1994**	**1998**	**2002**	**Combined**	**Commit. weighted**	**Relevence factor**
Upper quartile	15.8%	1.5%	−1.2%	**1.1%**	1.1%	1.7%
Median	2.8%	−0.9%	−6.0%	−3.9%	**−3.9%**	**−3.1%**
Lower quartile	−2.3%	−7.6%	−11.8%	−9.9%	**−9.9%**	**−9.2%**
ALL PE	**1994**	**1998**	**2002**	**Combined**	**Commit. weighted**	**Relevence factor**
Upper quartile	23.7%	4.3%	2.0%	**4.6%**	3.9%	5.3%
Median	14.6%	0.0%	−2.0%	0.1%	−0.4%	0.6%
Lower quartile	2.0%	−2.0%	−5.4%	−3.9%	**−4.1%**	**−3.3%**

10.2.2   Public market equivalent

It is not uncommon to see as the stated objective of a private equity fund investment a program to 'beat public equity' performance. This implicitly implies that the success or the lack of it of a program will be estimated based on its outperformance or not versus some public indices, often small caps. However, annual returns of quoted companies cannot be compared directly with private equity returns because they are computed on a totally different basis. Quoted company returns are time-weighted yearly returns, while private equity returns are cash-weighted multi-period returns.

The goal of the public market equivalent methodology is to calculate a private equity-equivalent public index return, which can then be compared with the private equity return. The methodology described in Cheung *et al.* (2003) is based on the estimation of a public market equivalent terminal value, which substitutes the NAV in the interim IRR calculation. This terminal value is constructed by buying and selling the index using the fund's cash flows schedule.[15] Once estimated, the NAV is replaced by this terminal value and the private equity equivalent public index return is calculated.

10.2.3   Absolute benchmarks

In some cases, even extended peer group or public market equivalent benchmarks cannot be designed, such as in the case of some emerging markets. For these cases, investors are left only with absolute benchmarks. As private equity is often perceived as an absolute return asset class, it may be meaningful to use absolute return targets to evaluate performance.

The first and most 'simple' one is to compare the fund performance against the private equity investment program target rate of return (see Box 10.7). During the Internet bubble, it was not uncommon to have target rates of return of 30% or even more. Obviously, we do not believe such high return targets are meaningful, as they were temporary and unsustainable levels.

Box 10.7:   Cost of capital vs. return expectations

The cost of capital, occasionally also referred to as return requirement, depends on the risk, and hence primarily on the use of the funding, not the source. There have been numerous papers written concerning the cost of capital of private equity assets – or in the CAPM context, the beta – with nearly as many answers. Based on these results, one might expect the consensus beta for private equity to be in the 1.5 to 2.0 range (see Meyer and Mathonet, 2005), leading to a cost of capital in the 10–15% range. Because there is no reliable private equity data and because of the pronounced market cycles, it does not make sense to be too precise regarding return requirements and in the market the announced return expectations are often quite different anyway.

Some institutions define their return objective in absolute terms ('in excess of 15%') or in relative terms compared with benchmarks ('5% above public markets') or peer group universes ('top quartile'). Having said this, if two institutional investors in private equity funds come up with different return requirements for the same targeted investment area, they most probably would have difficulty explaining how their respective investment approaches meet their own objective but not the other. What would you do differently if your return objective were 13% as opposed to 5% above public market? What limited partners implicitly say is 'we are confident that our approach can meet this return objective. If we weren't we would not invest in this asset class.'

Return targets and return expectations are often used interchangeably, which calls for some clarification. The return target is the threshold below which an investor will not pursue the investment, whereas the expected return is the return that the investor believes they will earn on a given asset. This leads to the following simple and common investment decision rule: 'Only invest if the expected return is higher than the targeted one'. How can investments in funds contribute to a return target? For conventional asset classes such as loans this is relatively straightforward, as simplistically the return

---

[15] The fact that the fund's cash flow schedule is used explains why only the terminal value has to be changed for the calculation of the public market equivalent IRR.

target is a major input in the pricing mechanism. For private equity funds an efficient pricing mechanism does not exist, and consequently there is no approach to manage returns on an individual fund level. On the level of a portfolio of funds levers like selectivity, balance between buyouts and venture capital or diversification would allow managing toward broad return ranges, e.g. 5% brackets.

Some publications refer to markedly different – usually much higher – return expectation of investors than the 'fair' cost of capital or the returns observed in reality. For example, in the late 1990s, early 2000s return expectations for the VC asset class were, as we know now, highly unrealistic and caused the amount of money going into venture funds to balloon.

Published return expectations are usually based on surveys such as the Astoria LP Survey or the Coller Capital's Global Private Equity Barometer. For instance, the Astoria LP Survey uses a questionnaire for investors' private equity return forecasts as in Table 10.2.[16]

Table 10.2   Extract from Astoria LP Survey questionnaire

Please respond by filling out your expected return (%IRR) in the following questions:

	Domestic	International	We have different %IRR by specific regions
Venture	. . .	. . .	. . .
Buyout fund	. . .	. . .	. . .
Distressed	. . .	. . .	. . .
Other (secondary, distressed)	. . .	. . .	. . .

If you have different expected return by world regions, please respond below:

	North America	Europe	Asia
Venture	. . .	. . .	. . .
Buyout	. . .	. . .	. . .
Other	. . .	. . .	. . .

If your expected return is based on 'market index plus alpha' with 'volatility tolerance', please give specific evaluation method below:

. . .

Figure 10.5 gives an example for the results of such a limited partner survey. Here both buyout and VC fund returns show a similar apex in the return expectation curve, peaking at 20%. Interestingly, in this case the limited partners tended to expect higher returns from venture funds than buyout funds.

In the summer 2006 survey conducted by Franklin Park, respondents were asked to provide their return expectations for top-quartile private equity funds formed in the current year. Knowing that most or all investors target these funds, the results of this survey are a good indicator of expectations for the industry returns.

---

[16] We thank Hal Morimoto from Astoria Consulting for providing us for this questionnaire.

Box 10.7:   (Continued)

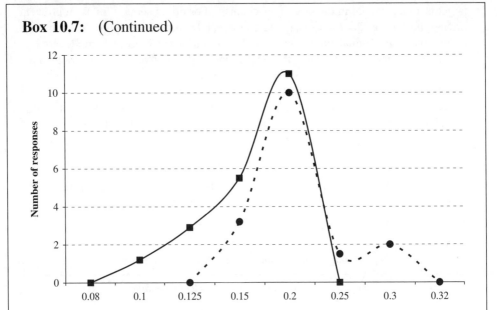

Figure 10.5   Return expectation for private equity funds (net IRR)
Source: Astoria LP Survey, 2006.

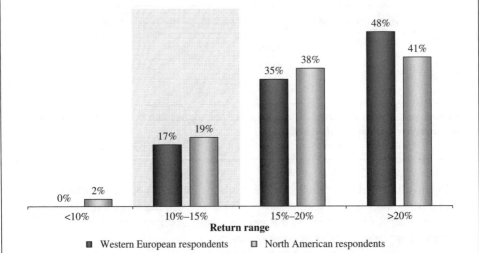

Figure 10.6   Annual return expectations by survey participant's geography
Source: Franklin Park Survey, 2006.[17]

---

[17] Available on http://www.altassets.com/Knowledgebank/Surveys/2006/nz9390.php [accessed 24 July 2007].

For both North America and Western Europe more than 75% of the respondents were expecting returns above 15% and more than 40% returns above 20%.

Another example is the Coller Capital's Global Private Equity Barometer, a twice-yearly survey from the secondaries market player Coller Capital that asks limited partners for their satisfaction with their returns over the previous year and for their forecast for medium-term returns for the private equity asset class. In any case, investors in private equity funds cannot passively buy the market, as no index exists that could be invested in let alone be tracked. Therefore, these surveys can only be a consensus opinion and are to a large degree driven by sentiments.

Another often-used absolute benchmark is a target expressed as a premium over public equity, e.g. 300 to 500 basis points over public equity. This benchmark is hybrid, being both a relative (public index)[18] and an absolute one (premium). Its use is justified by the fact that often the private equity allocation is obtained at the detriment of public equity, which is thus perceived as an opportunity cost with some investors also requiring a premium for the lack of liquidity.

Finally, the performance can be measured against the absolute historical returns of the historical peer universe, i.e. the 'peer group cohort' for all the vintage years or the mature ones (see Figure 10.7). Note how comparatively unstable the statistics is and that, being 'static', this benchmark is normally outperformed during bull markets and under-performed during bearish periods.

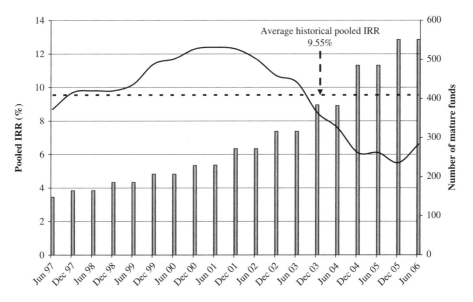

Figure 10.7 Mature European VC funds – pooled IRR
Source: Thomson Financial (VentureXpert database).

---

[18] Many believe that private equity funds are correlated with public equity. Assuming this is true, a public equity index will then be a relative benchmark.

10.2.4 Prospective performance analysis

One limitation of benchmarking is that interim performance measures are based on the NAV with all its uncertainty related to the valuation of private equity investments. The prospective performance analysis tries to solve this issue by estimating the final performance of the unrealized investments. One may argue whether this is really part of the track record analysis, which, as stated above, is the assessment of the past achievements, but such projections can serve as a plausibility check and can also be benchmarked, for example against the historical performance of its peer group.

Practically, this can be done by estimating for each unrealized investment the total expected investment, the exit timing and the anticipated valuation at exit. This considers, for example, the EBITDA at entry, the current EBITDA to project the expected EBITDA at exit, the EBITDA multiple at entry to project the expected multiple at exit and the resulting importance of the potential positive or negative arbitrage. Not unlike techniques for secondary pricing, one takes for each unrealized investment (or at least the most material ones) a low, a base and a high case scenario for both the timing and the importance of each cash flows, that, with estimated probabilities, can generate a distribution of the expected returns (see Figure 10.8).

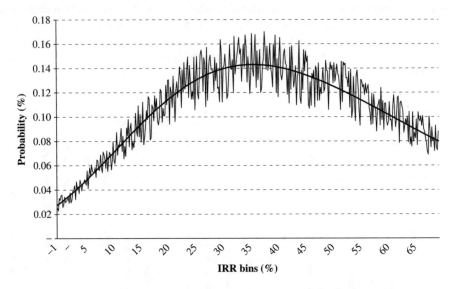

Figure 10.8 Prospective performance – return distribution

10.3   TRACK RECORD ANALYSIS TOOLS

The definition of insanity is continuing to do the same thing and expecting a different result.

John Arquilla (defence analyst, Naval Postgraduate School, Annapolis)

One should not be 'naïve' about the performance figures. Indeed, if it can be due to the good management of the fund and to its noteworthy interventions in its underlying companies, we may be tempted to explain performance by the skills of the management team. However, it may also be the result of pure luck or a favorable market cycle.

We already discussed benchmarking at the fund level against its peer group. Below, we go deeper at the deal level, by deal vintage, deal type, etc. and focus on forward-looking indicators (i.e. past performance that is most representative of what the 'likely' future will be). Understanding how and why a manager achieved superior performance with its previous funds and whether the conditions for such success are likely to be met again in the future is crucial to the investment decision, not the top quartile label per se. Therefore a track record analysis has to be much more than a simple comparison between an interim performance figure and some market statistics.

We do a lot of assessments of a fund's track record, but we break it down and analyse each individual deal that has been made. You can really judge a fund's track record by analysing each individual deal in detail and double-check all our findings with numerous reference calls.
Christopher Bodtker, Lombard Odier Darier Hentsch & Cie (AltAssets, 2003)

10.3.1 Portfolio gross performance stripping

This analysis tries to identify the sub-strategies that have been the most or the least successful in the past. This type of analysis allows highlighting potential risky or promising areas and then to concentrate the due diligence resources on these zones, helping to better understand the reasons for under or over-performance of certain deals or strategies. Practically, the analysis is done by calculating for each sub-group of investments, the IRR based on the cash flows between the fund and the companies of this sub-group and their residual value.

By stripping the portfolio gross performance (Figure 10.9), it is possible to better understand how the value was created, where it came from and how sustainable it is. The performance can be analyzed, for example, by geography, sector, stage focus, team members or by role in the deal (lead, co-lead or followers). Based on this, it may be possible to link some successful deals (or unsuccessful ones) to specific persons or strategies and to verify that the current funds foresee following (or not) the strategies that have proven or not to be successful in the past and will be managed (or not) by the most successful managers. This also helps to understand who within the team is a key person. However, in private equity it is the team and not the individuals that are important. One should avoid investing only based on a 'one man' historical performance but always based on the overall quality, cohesion and stability of a team. This being said, stripping the performance by team members is highly informative, as it allows us to identify and check that key persons are still there, that the split between team members of the ownership of the management company and of the fund economics does reflect their expected added-value and that the limited partner will negotiate an adequate key persons provision.

We examine the track record of each firm and the track record of the people. We find out who was responsible for past performance, positive and negative, who originated the deals and who exactly created the value to date.
Graham McDonald, Bank of Scotland (AltAssets, 2006)

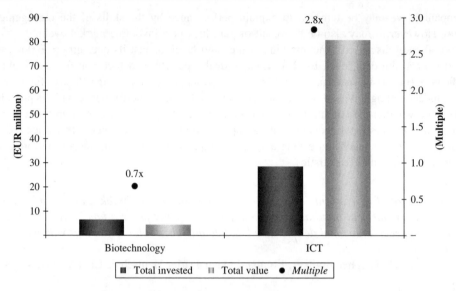

Figure 10.9   Portfolio gross performance stripping

The consistency of the investment strategy of the new fund with the previous ones is also of relevance. Track record, as well as strategies, can easily be manipulated by general partners. It is not uncommon to see a fund manager constructing a track record just from his successful transactions while failing to mention investments that faltered. All arbitrary segmentation of one's track record ('we don't do that any more') should be treated with caution. It is also quite common to see successful teams raising larger successor's funds, leading to a drift of the strategy toward larger transactions. Here the team may often lack the necessary skillset and experience. Moreover, such in larger transactions deal flow is less proprietary and auction-like situations are more common

> *We are very alert to funds in which we have seen style drift. There are two reasons for this. The first is that the fund manager may not have the experience necessary to execute a new strategy or investment style. The second – and possibly most important – is that the necessary deal flow in the new area will be missing.*
>
> Tom Thompson, Director, Private Equity Group, WestAM (AltAssets, 2003)

10.3.2 Performance dispersion (profit and losses)

This analysis for both realized and unrealized investments or separately, compares the number of companies, amount invested and value created against the achieved multiple. This analysis allows us to better assess whether performance is concentrated in few deals or rather in several, suggesting more repeatability of performance.

Furthermore, this also allows assessing the risk diversification within the portfolio. The **Herfindahl index** can be used in the context of a private equity fund to get a feel for whether its performance is concentrated in few companies. For instance, a high performance in combination with a low concentration can indicate a more robust, i.e. less risky, investment strategy, but may also be a signal for managers' skills rather than luck.

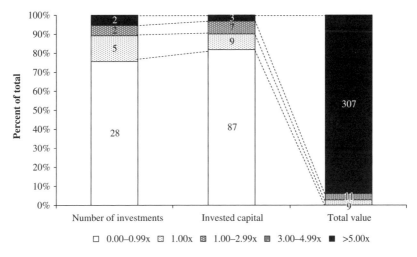

Figure 10.10   Performance dispersion – realized investments

Box 10.8:   Herfindahl index

In economics, the Herfindahl index is a measure of the size of firms in relationship to the industry and an indicator of the amount of competition among them. It is defined as the sum of the squares of the market shares of each individual firm:

$$H = \sum_{i=0}^{N} w \times t_i^2$$

where H is the Herfindahl index and wt_i is the weight of the ith constituent of the index and N is the number of constituents.

As such, it can range from 0 to 10 000%, moving from a very large amount of very small firms to a single monopolistic producer. Decreases in the Herfindahl index generally indicate a loss of pricing power and an increase in competition, whereas increases imply the opposite.

In order to get a feel for the meaning of the index, it is often useful to look at the inverse of the index (i.e. $10,000/H$). This can be interpreted as the number of equally sized firms that operate in this market. Example: Five companies that have a market share of 20% each lead to an index value of $2000 = 5 \times 20^2$. Dividing 10 000 by 2 000 gives the original result of 5.

For the assessment of early stage VC funds we found approaches like looking at the realized track record, and the analysis of 'winners dependence' and 'backing the winners' particularly helpful. To illustrate these tools, we look at two real life cases, both European based firms that raised their first VC funds – in our examples called 'fund A' for the first and 'fund B' for the second firm – during the late 1990s. Their funds benefited from the 'bubble period' and achieved high double digit performance and even temporarily triple digit

IRRs. Based on this stellar performance both firms managed to quickly raise oversubscribed successor funds.

10.3.3   Realized track record

Through focusing only on the realized portfolio we can work around the limitations of the NAV. In the realized track record analysis, one looks at the performance and holding periods for each realized investment, which allows us to assess the dispersion of the performance and therefore its consistency. Practically, the analysis is done by using a bubble chart figuring three values: the holding period, the gross multiple and its costs displayed as the size of the bubble marker.

As illustrated in figure 10.11, though both of these teams had a clearly top quartile performance, fund A shows a much more consistent performance, while fund B has clearly one outlier, suggesting a performance more based on luck than skills.

This analysis can be refined by adding the type of exit to the chart. This allows better understanding and assessing the ability of the team to generate good exit opportunities through various routes. Bar charts (see Figure 10.12) showing the split by exit route of the realized investments (by number and by value) are also helpful to assess the team's dependency on one or more exit routes. Looking at our two real cases, it appears that fund B was highly dependent on the IPO environment while fund A, during the same favorable market conditions, also generated substantial value through trade sales, appearing, therefore, less dependent for the future on the IPO market conditions.

10.3.4   Winners dependence analysis

This analysis tries to estimate how much the best transaction moved the performance of a fund. Practically, the analysis is done by excluding from all the deals the best ones (either in terms of absolute gains or in terms of IRRs). Then the IRR or multiples are recalculated and compared with the initial ones. In doing so, one tries to answer the following questions: is that due again to a couple of highly profitable deals or does the overall portfolio contribute to the good performance of the fund? This will then give indications of *luck* when the performance figures are materially impacted by the exclusion of the best deal or *skill* when performance figures remain roughly the same, no matter whether the best deals are taken into consideration or not. As illustrated by Figure 10.13, fund A's performance was much less dependent on its best deal than fund B, suggesting a more skilled team and/or a less risky strategy.

Basically, we may expect from buyout funds that the performance figures' variability remains quite constant even after excluding the top winners. Nonetheless, for venture funds there are usually a couple of companies that are responsible for the success of the fund.

10.3.5   Backing the winners analysis

This analysis tries to estimate how efficiently the capital available to the fund manager was invested. This is particularly important for venture capital funds where companies are stage-financed and where the ability to identify as early as possible potentially successful investments is almost as important as the ability to make good initial investment decisions.

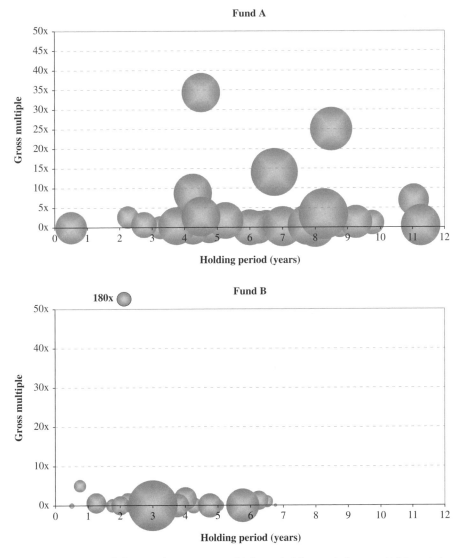

Figure 10.11   Portfolio overview – gross multiple vs. holding period vs. capital invested

Indeed, as soon as the best performers are identified both capital and management resources can be concentrated on these, resulting in higher final fund performances.

Practically, the analysis is done by calculating by ranges of increasing performance (e.g. below 1.5x, between 1.5x and 3x and above 3.0x), the total and average capital invested. This will then give an indication of *skills*, when the fund manager was able to identify early the successful investments and put more capital or average capital to work in these successful deals or *luck*, when best performers were not identified early leading to the allocation of too much capital to the less successful investments.

In our examples, while both funds did allocate the majority of their capital to the poorly performing companies (fund A: $^{32.9}/_{53.7} = 61\%$ and fund B: $^{82.5}/_{90.6} = 91\%$), fund A was

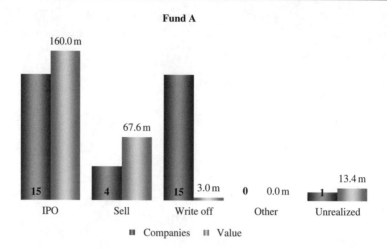

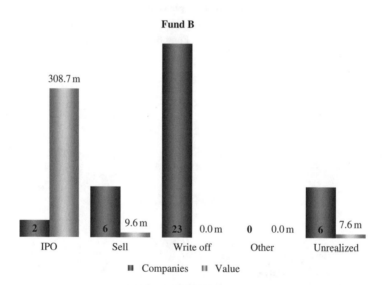

Figure 10.12   Realized value by exit type vs. unrealized value

significantly better as its allocation to the poorly performing companies was a third lower than that of fund B and as, contrary to fund B, its average allocation per portfolio companies was higher for the best performer (fund A: 2.1 vs. 1.4 and fund B: 1.7 vs. 2.4), suggesting an ability to identify success. See Figure 10.14.

To sum up, fund B's performance depended on one deal only, whereas fund A delivered a more consistent performance. Moreover, the team appeared to be better in identifying and backing fund A's emerging winners, suggesting a closer involvement with the portfolio companies. All these factors support that fund A's success was more based on skills, whereas fund B appeared to have simply hit the 'jackpot'.

The comparison shows that, firstly, a proper understanding of the drivers of past returns is far more important than the quartile itself. It is a fair assumption that it is not the 'quartile

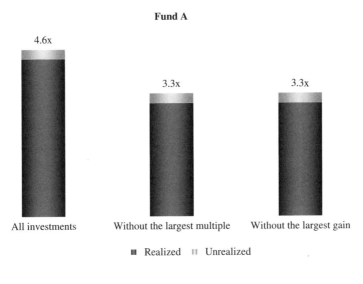

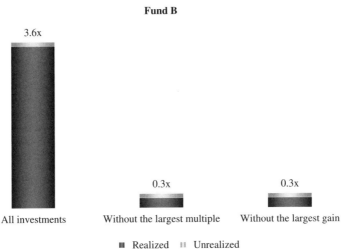

Figure 10.13   Winners dependence analysis

position' in the benchmark that is persistent in future funds, but that a management team can repeatedly apply superior skills. Secondly, it demonstrates that when evaluating a fund 'in isolation' most analysts will have difficulties coming to a proper judgment. It is rather the comparison of several proposals in parallel that raises the questions and leads to insights that help to differentiate between skills and luck.

The first firm that managed fund A is still in business and meanwhile a well-established private equity 'brand' having raised several successor funds since then. The second firm that managed fund B, however, fared less well and at the time of writing this book is lingering more in obscurity. In its successor fund they did not manage to repeat their luck and without another big winner delivered a very poor performance.

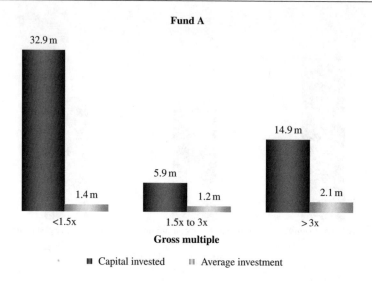

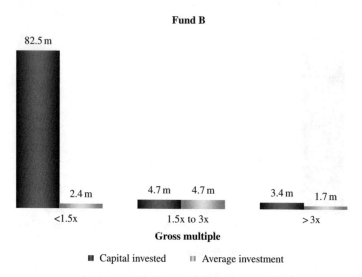

Figure 10.14   Backing the winners analysis

10.3.6   Value creation analysis

The value creation analysis looks at drivers like debt reduction, revenue expansion, EBITDA expansion or market 'arbitrage' to better understand the fund managers' overall approach, i.e. whether it is more financial engineering-based, opportunistic or more hands-on in growing a company. This analysis applies to both the realized and unrealized investments. It is admittedly less relevant for early stage VC funds, as their portfolio companies are simply not in a position to create growth in non-existing EBITDA or to obtain leverage with offering assets as collateral.

With financial engineering skills commoditised and the opportunity for multiple expansion generally limited, the remaining major driver of private equity returns is the fundamental profits growth of the portfolio companies.

John Hartz, Managing Partner, Inflexion (AltAssets, 2002)

Practically, the analysis tries to split the value between its key components: the EBITDA growth, which can be further split into the organic versus the acquisition growth or the sales growth versus the evolution of margins, the debt reduction and the multiple arbitrage or expansion. See Figure 10.15.

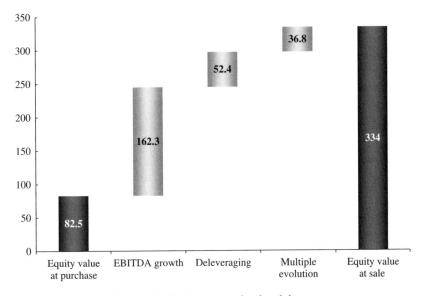

Figure 10.15   Value creation breakdown

10.3.7   Deal structuring analysis

This analysis tries to estimate the portion of the value created that is due to the use of leverage. The basic principle is to partly finance the acquisition through debt and to amortize it based on the free cash flows generated by the deal. The leverage level has to be cautious so as to provide enough headroom for growth and operational improvement.

Practically, the analysis is done by looking at some key indicators: the debt/equity or debt/EBITDA (on-going) ratios, the terms of any leveraged recap, as well as the downside protection. All these indicators are then useful to estimate how 'aggressive' or how risky the deal structuring was and its potential impact on the future fund performance. During bullish markets, the use of leverage will boost performance, but during bearish markets may lead the fund performance deep into the 'valley of tears'. See Figure 10.16.

10.3.8   Multiple arbitrage analysis

This analysis tries to estimate the portion of the value created that is due to the multiple 'arbitrage' done. In the context of private equity, this refers to an investment in a firm where

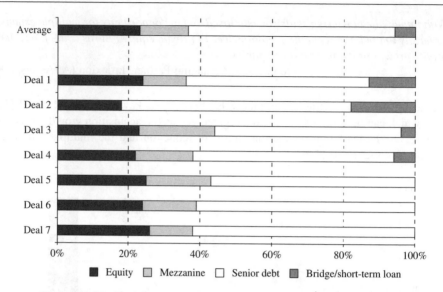

Figure 10.16   Deal financing split between the various sources of funding

by standard multiples (earnings/price, book/price), the price paid is far cheaper than industry averages. To assess whether the team was able to buy 'cheap' and sell high or at the higher industry average price, one should look at the entry price as a multiple of, for example, EBIT or EBITDA, the deal pricing evolution and the comparison with the market.

Though this analysis may help to assess team skills and whether the deal flow is proprietary, one should also take into account that markets evolve and that unexploited niches may become overcrowded markets, drying up the sources of arbitrage opportunities.

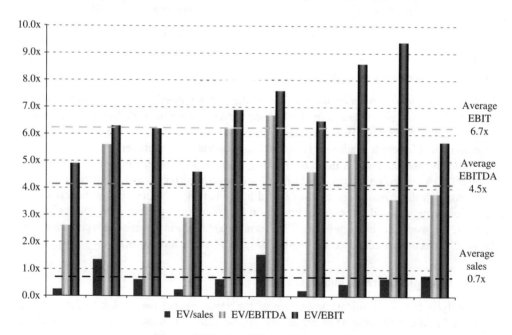

Figure 10.17   Portfolio multiple analysis

10.3.9   Added-value analysis

A private equity fund can have achieved a high IRR and a good multiple thanks to successful exits whereas it did not intervene at all in the management of the company. Therefore the track record analysis should go beyond the pure quantification and check with the portfolio companies how the fund management team really helped them, for example through contributions to the definition of the strategic positioning and branding, the improvements brought to the organization, the procedures and the financial reporting systems, the optimization of the financial efficiency through the restructuring of the balance sheet or structured funding strategies, the support provided for add-on acquisitions, or the enhancement provided to the distribution. Charting such as Figure 10.18 helps us to visualize the importance of the value added by the team and to identify areas of weakness. It is obvious that the broader the areas where the team added value, the more likely it is that its good performance is due to skills rather than luck.

So, in a decade when 'rational caution' is more likely to prevail than 'irrational exuberance', being able to demonstrate that you can add value and help your investee companies generate earnings growth will be a key skill for private equity firms. Sounds like 'added value' is becoming a critical success factor rather than a cliché.

John Hartz, Managing Partner, Inflexion (AltAssets, 2002)

Company	Team enhance-ment	Stratery & branding	Operational & organizational improvements	Financial efficiency	Add-on acquisitions
Company 1	X	X			X
Company 2	X			X	X
Company 3	X	X		X	X
Company 4	X	X			
Company 5	X	X		X	
Company 6	X	X			

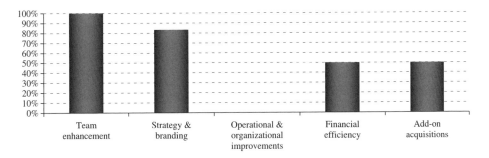

Figure 10.18   Value creation analysis

10.4   LIMITATIONS

We have been presenting analytical techniques that – based on our experience – are applicable to all kinds of private equity funds. The key limitation of any track record analysis is related to the fact that it focuses on the past and, therefore, to some degree 'outdated' information, while the objective is to assess the future. Hard data is more than five years' old and you have to assess how a team will do over the next ten years mainly based on these. Therefore, there is almost always a huge amount of judgment involved in the evaluation of a team's track record. On top of that, this analysis is limited by the uncertainty related to the valuation of the interim results. The analysis of the recent activities has by nature of the industry to be done on interim figures with normally a significant portion of the portfolio unrealized.

Emerging managers, strategies or markets are difficult or impossible to analyze, as there are little reliable data available. Here, we have to differentiate between first-time teams and first-time funds: an investment is qualified as a first-time team when its investment professionals have never managed together private equity investments. It is qualified as a first-time fund when its investment professionals have already managed private equity investments together and when they are raising independently a fund for the first time.

> They [the endowments and foundations] managed it by investing with groups before they gained their excellent track records. So they would work with a relatively small team, write a relatively small cheque, but over time they would increase their exposure if those groups performed well. If you walk into a Kleiner Perkins, a Greylock or a Matrix, you find that those with the highest allocations are the long-term, loyal investors.
>
> Clint Harris, Managing Partner, Grove Street Advisors (AltAssets, 2002)

With a **first-time fund**, the team has already a track record, which can be analyzed. The main issue you are going to have is to get information from the old team's firm to verify the track record that is being presented and check that it is the complete track record for those managers. Another issue is to identify the added value that has been provided by the old firm that is not available any more for the current fund.

> The largest proportion of new funds in Italy are managed by new teams anyway, teams that have typically worked together but in other professional fields, just not in investment.
> Giuseppe Campanella, Chief Executive Officer, State Street Global Investments
> (AltAssets, 2006a)

With a **first-time team**, the team itself, by definition, has no track record but the individuals or several of them jointly may have one. It is usually not too difficult to get information on people's track records because the industry is pretty transparent. The individuals can provide access to the companies that they invested in previously. But the main issue limited partner face is track record validation.

Box 10.9: Attribution letter

Institutional investors are often reluctant to back emerging fund management teams, but funds managed by such teams have increasingly become a relevant part of many institutions' allocation. In fact, Lerner *et al.* (2004) believe that the US endowments may enjoy superior returns in private equity, because their early involvement gave them a 'seat at the table' or a 'first-mover's advantage' with the superior fund manager's that allows them to continue investing in subsequent funds of private equity firms that are closed to new investors. Emerging fund managers have room to accept allocations and may also be willing to grant more favorable terms and conditions. Moreover, there are also under-researched niches, such as turnarounds, with small middle-market firms with little competition that are attractive but where no or too little data exist. However, gaining access to information and being able to verify it for evaluating a track record is a challenge when doing due diligence.

In any case, few institutions are willing to invest in teams without investment experience. The minimum requirement is a track record of successful private equity transactions attributable to the individual fund managers, who usually gained this experience while working for a more established firm. However, particularly VC investing is a team effort and it is difficult to sort out the responsibility for individual transactions, which can make this a very contentious issue. Consequently, it has become more common for private equity professionals to negotiate a so-called 'attribution letter' when leaving a firm. This document can be very detailed and aims to highlight the individual's contribution to investments and their carrying value at the time of the professional's departure. Attribution letters describe the specific roles that an individual had in sourcing an investment, undertaking the due diligence, negotiating the purchase price, overseeing the investment and serving on the company's Board of Directors, or directing the exit of an investment.

Certainly fund managers will be inclined to construct a track record by highlighting their successful deals while leaving poorly performing investments out. However, a professional's former firm has no reason to hide transactions that have not gone well, and in fact would be better off if it can clearly identify transactions that under-performed and were the responsibility of someone who is no longer with the firm. Therefore, one aspect of attribution letters that is most beneficial to an investor doing due diligence is that they tend to eliminate this 'cherry picking'.

10.5 CONCLUSION

To sum up, the track record helps to understand how the fund managers worked in the past and whether their successes were based on skills or on luck. The track record analysis is subject to interpretation, where mainly comparisons, pattern recognition, experience and judgment make the difference.

As we said in the introduction, the track record analysis forms part of the due diligence process and as such there is more in it than only to estimate whether a team has skills or not. Indeed, this analysis can also help to capture valuable information to improve the fund's organizational and managerial structure. For example, the assessment of the past and expected future carry earned from previous funds, and therefore of the team's wealth, helps to assess the adequacy of the team's investment in the current fund. Another example is the analysis of the performance by attribution to specific team members, which provides useful information to assess the fairness of the financials of the management company (ownership, salaries and carry) or to negotiate an adequate key persons provision.

Finally, the track record analysis also offers an opportunity for getting to know people better and sets the theme for future monitoring activities. For example, it can highlight areas where the team's performance has been weaker or more risky, which therefore, could require a more intense monitoring. Furthermore, as the monitoring process is about identifying problems and developing a plan to address them, the re-updating of the track record analysis can be a very useful tool.

There are diminishing returns on the detail of the analysis and it definitely cannot give certainty about the future. That raises the question how limited partners can manage under uncertainty, a subject that we tackle in the next chapters.

APPENDIX 10A   PERFORMANCE SPREAD BETWEEN BEST AND WORST MANAGER

For analysing the performance spread between the best and the worst managers for randomly selected private equity funds we used the same data as in Weidig and Mathonet (2004), covering 5141 US portfolio companies. Their multiples are very volatile, with a mean multiple of 6.2 and a standard deviation of 53.8, and ranging from a miserable 0 to a staggering 3310. The model aimed to simulate the expected performance ranges of equally weighted portfolios of randomly selected portfolio companies:

- Select n companies randomly and average their performance.
- Repeat the process as many times as there are managers.
- Store the multiples of the worst and the best manager.

For every fund we calculated the gross and the net performance. The net performance was calculated by subtracting 20% of the fund multiple in excess of 1 for the gross multiples above 1.5 to account for the carried interest to the fund managers, and then subtracting 0.2 from the fund multiple to account for the management fees. We ran the simulation for the following scenarios:

- A number of equally weighted investments per fund of (1) 40 portfolio companies and (2) 13 portfolio companies.
- A population of (a) 80 fund, (b) 800 funds and (c) 8000 funds.

As expected, the results in Table 10.3 support that the expected spread between the top and the worst managers is influenced by (a) the average diversification level of funds and (b) the size of the fund population.

The results also demonstrate that diversification has a larger impact on spreads than the size of the population. If we reduce the diversification level by roughly 3 from 40 to 13 portfolio companies for a population of 800 funds, this yields an increase in the spread by a factor of 2.6. Conversely, for a diversification level of 13 portfolio companies, increasing the number of funds from 80 to 800 managers yields an increase by about the same factor.

Table 10.3   Performance spread – simulated US funds

Observable population of funds		Number of equally weighted investments per fund			
		40 companies		13 companies	
		Gross	Net	Gross	Net
80 funds	Worst multiple	1.9	1.5	0.9	0.7
	Best multiple	56.6	45.3	88.6	70.9
	Spread	**54.7**	**43.8**	**87.7**	**70.2**
800 funds	Worst multiple	1.4	1.2	0.5	0.3
	Best multiple	93.4	74.8	240.9	192.7
	Spread	**92.0**	**73.6**	**240.4**	**192.4**
8000 funds	Worst multiple	1.1	0.9	0.3	0.1
	Best multiple	110.0	88.0	278.3	222.7
	Spread	**108.9**	**87.1**	**278.0**	**222.6**

Table 10.4 compares the simulation against real data. The first column gives the real data for 5141 US portfolio companies, the second column real data for 802 US venture capital funds, and the third column gives the simulated data for a similar population of funds with 13 underlying investments.

Table 10.4   Comparison between observed US companies and funds with simulated funds

	Observed US companies	Observed US VC funds	Simulated funds with 13 portfolio companies
Population	5141	802	800
Average multiple	6.2	2.3	5.0
Worst multiple	0.0	0.0	0.3
Best multiple	3309.7	28.0	192.7

Note: fund multiples are net multiples

Indeed, the spread between the top and the worst managers observed for real VC funds is large (28.0). But this pales in comparison with the spread given by the simulation (192.4). According to the simulation, the probability of observing a spread of at least 28 for a population of 800 funds with a diversification level of 13 companies is 100%. For comparison purposes, the probability of observing a spread of at least 28 for a population of 80 funds with a diversification level of 13 companies is 67%. Interestingly, we also note that the mean multiple of real funds (2.3) is lower than the mean multiple of simulated funds (5.0).

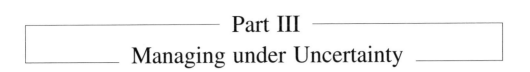

Part III
Managing under Uncertainty

11

Grading and Fitness Landscapes

If you can look into the seeds of time
And say which grain will grow and which will not,
Speak then to me . . .

Shakespeare, The Tragedy of Macbeth, Act 1, Scene 3

It is usually said that investors deal with risk whereas managers face uncertainty, but for venture capitalists the line is blurred as they are investors as well as managers. Limited partners commit to a VC fund that is a blind pool which the fund manager is free to manage at its own discretion, provided its actions are in accordance with the fund's investment prospectus and with any shareholder agreement.[1] Portfolio companies usually do not exist and often even the technologies their business models are based on are usually still in the R&D stage. Technical innovation renders statistical data obsolete and incomparable. During the seed and start-up phases, the portfolio companies are not viable. Valuation changes are to a large degree driven by the venture capital backer's financing strategy, portfolio companies are years away from an exit and have far too many 'moving parts' that have a significant impact on their valuations. Not even a range of possible future outcomes can often be determined, and attempts to quantify uncertainty will generally not work. See Figure 11.1.

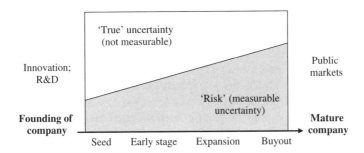

Figure 11.1 Development of exposure to 'true' uncertainty and risk

Later stage private equity is arguably closer to public markets. Here portfolio companies are mature and operate in the same environment as publicly quoted companies. Public market data can serve as a reasonable proxy for valuing and for assessing the risks of non-quoted but mature companies. Although private equity funds are blind pools, sometimes the

---

[1] On agreeing to invest in a blind pool, the investor loses almost all control over its funds, and can only recover control where there are serious issues of dishonesty, gross negligence or gross incompetence.

companies targeted for future investments are already identified when the general partners go out fundraising. So despite information falling short of public market data precision, with some justification it is fair to speak about 'risk' in the sense of 'quantifiable uncertainty' when looking at later stage private equity.

Box 11.1: Uncertainty

In his 1921 work *Risk, Uncertainty, and Profit*, Frank Knight established the distinction between 'risk' and 'uncertainty'. He interprets 'risk' as referring to situations where the decision-maker can assign mathematical probabilities to the randomness which he is faced with. He contrasts this with 'uncertainty', i.e. situations where specific mathematical probabilities cannot express this randomness.

> *By 'uncertain' knowledge, let me explain, I do not mean merely to distinguish what is known for certain from what is only probable. The game of roulette is not subject, in this sense, to uncertainty [. . .] The sense in which I am using the term is that in which the prospect of a European war is uncertain, or the price of copper and the rate of interest twenty years hence [. . .] About these matters there is no scientific basis on which to form any calculable probability whatever. We simply do not know.*
>
> John Maynard Keynes

Nonetheless, many economists dispute this distinction and there is a long-running 'risk versus uncertainty' debate that goes beyond the scope of this book. In efficient markets there is little differentiation between risk and uncertainty, as uncertainty is practically the same for all participants. In private markets, however, decision-makers usually face situations that are unique and unprecedented, and where alternatives are not really known or understood. Information is hard to get hold of, and the quality of data is generally very poor. Especially in venture capital with fast-moving technological changes, newly evolving business models, short boom-to-bust-periods and long investment periods it is highly difficult, or even impossible, to systematically collect data that allows establishing patterns with any statistical significance. In these situations, mathematical probability assignments usually cannot be made.

Nevertheless, there are significant 'assessable' or even measurable factors in private equity, and much more is known about events and their chances than typically perceived. Therefore we believe that a clearer differentiation between risk and uncertainty can be a useful tool for the management of a private equity investment program. Experts can put lessons learned into a new or changed context and extrapolate from their experiences. While a precise quantification is – except in very specific situations – nearly impossible, experts can associate experiences and opinions on various dimensions with categories for return expectations. For this purpose we developed a qualitative scoring methodology as part of a private equity fund grading system (see Meyer and Mathonet, 2005).

In venture capital, on the other hand, exceptions appear to be the rule and the search for certainty is fruitless. As Robert Rubin, Treasury Secretary under President Clinton in his memoirs *In an Uncertain World* observed, a 'process of weighting odds in a world without absolute or provable certainties' rather has to consider alternatives, try to understand possibilities, make the best judgment possible and try to raise chances for success.

In this chapter we interpret the VC market as a complex adaptive system that, in the definition of Stacey (1996), consists 'of a number of components, or agents, that interact with each other according to sets of rules that require them to examine and respond to each other's behaviour in order to improve their behaviour and thus the behaviour of the system they comprise'. We use parallels to biological evolution to explain its dynamics, as we believe that this analogy provides a good map for the environment limited investors in VC funds are operating in.

Schumpeter argued that economic development was characterized by 'spontaneous and discontinuous change' that 'forever alters and displaces the equilibrium state previously existing'. Economic evolution refers to 'the changes in the economic process brought about by innovation'. Many uncertain factors interact and trigger discontinuous change. New technologies (e.g. personal computers), new markets (e.g. global readership targeted by Amazon), products or services (e.g. eBay, Skype) or innovative means of production (e.g. open source software development, Wikipedia) can temporarily introduce volatility across the economy. Sea changes in social attitudes and behavior (e.g. environmental concerns, the rise of 'green' products), the opening of former closed economies (e.g. China) or the global integration of product, service, capital and labor markets increase these effects. Such disruptive changes are in fact the main sources of opportunities for venture capital.

11.1   FITNESS LANDSCAPES

Although it is neither safe nor certain, there are proper management tools for risky environments. Scenarios for possible outcomes can be identified, probabilities can be assigned and managers can determine the costs for risk mitigation or transfer. In venture capital we are dealing with true uncertainty rather than risk. In other words, we have either no or no reliable up-to-date statistics that could form the basis for 'precise' decision-making. In a networked environment like the VC market uncertainty is especially unsettling since its origins and effects are connected in a non-linear manner.

> *Venture capital firms are, in essence, a portfolio of strategy experiments. Their portfolios contain a variety of investments with a spread of risk, relatedness, and time horizon. Venture capital portfolios will often have more than one investment in the same industry segment, in essence trying a variety of Business Plans and betting that at least one will find a high-fitness peak. The position of venture capitalists is somewhere between the market's broad coverage of the fitness landscape and the narrow coverage of most single companies.*

Beinhocker (2006)

This uncertainty sets limits to effective planning and thus makes managing in such an environment a more improvizational skill than control. For investors this raises the question of how to approach the design and management of a portfolio of VC funds. As uncertainty cannot be eliminated, it is preferable to acknowledge its presence and draw the appropriate conclusions.

11.1.1   VC market as an evolutionary system

According to Hovhannisian (2001), most of the economic theorizing, be it implicitly or explicitly, is based on allegories and allusions taken from other fields of science, or from real-life situations. She as well as a number of researchers, such as Chen (2003) or Beinhocker (2006), to name a few, draw parallels between organizations, markets and economies and nature itself. In nature species are dealing with cataclysmic events, like asteroids, diseases, earthquakes and volcanoes, and tectonic shifts. In venture capital one observes:

- 'Asteroids' like the personal computer or the Internet.
- 'Diseases' like the viral spread of applications such as Google, Hotmail or eBay.
- Local 'earthquakes' and 'volcanoes' like I-mode in Japan.
- 'Tectonic shifts' like the growth of life-science product for an ageing society and a growing world population.

Whereas in nature evolution enables species to avoid the adverse effects of environmental changes, one could argue that in venture capital it works the other way round. Here evolution aims to increase an investor's chances of 'being hit by an asteroid', i.e. capturing the wealth creation associated with disruptive events.

Evolution caused by mutations is nature's robust way of dealing with such events and striving to prosper in an uncertain environment. Consequently, economic systems are viewed as intrinsically evolutionary where the simple recipe for creating novelty, knowledge and growth is differentiation, selection and amplification.

> *Evolution is a general-purpose and highly powerful recipe for finding innovative solutions to complex problems. It is a learning algorithm that adapts to changing environments and accumulates knowledge over time. It is the formula responsible for all the order, complexity, and diversity of the natural world.*
>
> Beinhocker (2006)

Also we use metaphors from evolution theory to explain portfolio strategy consideration for a private equity fund investment program and suggest design portfolios of funds as an evolutionary system. Evolution is a model, and certainly the parallel to biology only holds up to a point. For example, biological evolution is mainly driven by random changes to the genetic material. To some degree these so-called mutations could be interpreted as 'real options' to be exercised in the case of a changing eco-system. In the world of finance, however, rules in the form of fund structures, terms and conditions, etc. do not emerge just randomly, they are usually engineered.

11.1.2   VC firms' genetic code

Nevertheless, nobody has full knowledge of the market and its future, so market participants always look for improvements and experiment. Newly emerging fund managers need to 'mutate' by introducing new strategies and 'rules' for managing their funds to differentiate themselves from the mainstream and offer a unique selling point to prospective investors. Without change in the private equity market such 'mutations' usually will not work out, unless the fund managers are simply lucky. Highly successful new 'rules' will be rare, few may work out 'big', but the majority of mutations fail. What is a successful rule quickly becomes best practice. As a consequence the set of rules undergoes an evolutionary process, with the bottom-performing rules being eliminated and new rules engineered to fill their place. Particularly in the volatile VC market there is more randomness in what rules will work out.

In evolutionary biology the set of all possible genotypes – the specific genetic make-up of an individual in the form of DNA[2] – their degree of similarity and their related fitness values is called a 'fitness landscape'. Such fitness landscapes, also called 'adaptive landscapes', use 'height' and 'distance' to visualize the fitness, i.e. the reproductive success, and the relationship between genotypes. 'Height' describes the fitness of a genotype, whereas 'distance' indicates how similar or different they are. Since the 1930s, biologists have pictured nature as a fitness landscape with a series of hills and valleys of different heights and depths and they describe fitness as the ability to successfully search such landscapes to survive and compete.[3] Species adapt through a process similar to 'hill climbing', where mutations from one generation to the next generation result in a move within the landscape. Natural selection and survival of the fittest will push a population of species toward a peak on a fitness landscape. The fitness landscape allegory has stirred up the interest of economists in recent years.

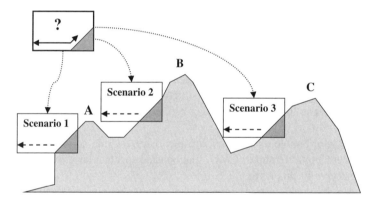

Figure 11.2   Navigating a fitness landscape

Figure 11.2 illustrates the problems of searching in a fitness landscape when decision makers can only oversee a limited area. In scenario 1 the low-risk strategy of moving to the right/upwards brings the species closer to the local optimum A, whereas making the risky long jump lands it in a 'death valley'. In scenario 2 the low-risk strategy brings the species closer to the global maximum B, whereas the risky long jump into the unknown to the left, while not ending in a disaster, does not improve the situation but sets the species on its way to the local maximum A. Only in scenario 3 does the high-risk strategy pay off: while the low-risk strategy would bring the species to the local maximum C, the long jump sets it on course to reach the global maximum B through subsequent smaller steps with lower risk.

---

[2] DNA (deoxyribonucleic acid) contains the genetic instructions for the biological development of a cellular form of life or a virus.
[3] The idea was first introduced in 1932 by Sewall Wright, an American geneticist known for his influential work on evolutionary theory.

Fitness landscapes associated with evolutionary systems tend to be roughly correlated, so there is neither a completely random 'zigzag' nor one symmetrical single peak. Neither are they static, but change over time. Uncertainty relates to how the landscape is structured – one can see neither the hills nor the valleys – and where, how and how quickly it is changing. When significant changes happen, well-adapted species are more likely to lose than to gain. For mutations that are not well adapted anyway, however, one can assume that the change in the environment does not worsen their chance more than for well-adapted species but it may occasionally improve their position.

11.1.3   Does this allegory hold?

To what degree does this allegory hold? Can we really observe an evolution in the VC market? Private equity in general is a very long-term-oriented asset class and general partners and limited partners enter in relationships every three to four years. Changes in private equity fund market and market practices are more like tectonic shifts – they happen, but too slowly to be understood as such. Therefore, and because we are lacking consistent data, we usually find it very difficult to recognize whether any 'evolution' is taking place. There is an element of 'creeping normalcy', e.g. major change can be accepted as normality if it happens slowly, in unnoticed increments. To stay within our analogy of fitness landscapes, Diamond (2005) has coined the term 'landscape amnesia' for situations where changes to an environment take a long time to occur and therefore fail to be perceived. The closer investors monitor and are involved in a market, the less they may be even aware of the speed of change going on.

When taking a long-term perspective we see indications for evolutionary processes at work. The industry is experimenting with structures, terms and conditions – not always successfully, but what is 'best practice' today can well be outdated tomorrow.

- Examples for 'tech bubble extinctions' are incubators, or the so-called 'Tech Keiretsus' like the Internet Capital Group or CMGI that boasted spectacular growth during the 1990s but did not survive in this form.
- Recently, deal-by-deal carried interest has been becoming increasingly popular. Particularly in venture capital, limited partners perceive this distribution approach as sub-optimal, but over-subscribed top funds have been successfully arguing for it as indispensable for attracting investment management talent in competition from the hedge fund industry.
- Another example is the contractual lifetime of VC funds. While limited partners would like this to be as short as possible, fund managers prefer 'patient' money. A contractual lifetime of typically ten years with one or two one-year extensions has emerged as a standard, but during the late 1990s VC funds came to the market that offered a contractual lifetime of four to six years – mainly trying to differentiate themselves in the competition for institutional investors but arguably also reflecting the perceived pace of innovation during the 'New Economy'.

The current limited partnership structure and the VC market's dynamics have apparent parallels with biology organisms and are well adapted to cope with uncertainty as well as with the current pace of innovation. The lifetime of funds allows them to profit from frequency of revolutionary innovations observed over the last decades; essentially this also implies a bet that the pace of innovation continues. VC firms pass on their DNA in the form of strategy, expertise and experience to the successor funds. Markets change very quickly, but the need to regularly fundraise forces fund managers as well as their investors to adapt this 'genetic code' to each other's needs and requirements – the description of fundraising as a 'mating ritual' is not far-fetched. The spawning of new funds into emerging teams occupies attractive market niches. This dynamics is well suited for dealing with discontinuities that require constant exploration and generating options.

However, that raises the question of what happens when innovation slows down. As the theoretical biologist and complex systems researcher Stuart Kauffman pointed out, the vast majority of species that have ever lived on this planet are now extinct. Ecosystems in general are fragile and are faced at regular intervals with mass extinctions. There is no guarantee that the market economics remain favorable to VC funds in their current form.

11.1.4   Extinctions in VC markets

We know very little about how private equity fund investment programs that are managed in-house evolve. However, the development of the private equity fund-of-funds market may be indicative. This market broadly falls into two categories. One comprises established players like HarbourVest, Pantheon, Adam Street Partners or Horsley Bridge Partners that operate as limited partnerships and raise funds like a traditional private equity firm. The second category is multi-product asset managers and investment banks that on and off enter the market by offering specialist funds-of-funds to exploit their existing client base's interest in private equity.

AltAssets (2003a) predicted in March 2003 a shake-out and that around 40% of the private equity funds-of-funds would struggle to survive over the medium term. At that time, a number of industry insiders saw the market as well past its peak. For example, Swiss fund-of-funds Adveq's Bruno Raschle stated that the 'rise in the attractiveness of the capital markets was just delaying the shake-out by two or three years so when it comes, it will be more brutal and take a lot longer', and another expert added that these 'things take time, they tend to die a slow lingering death'.[4]

Weak funds-of-funds without brand name, with only recent vintages and relationships with equally weak general partners are most vulnerable. They may be able to attract some capital, but they are usually then unable to access the proven performers among the general partners. This in turn makes attracting further funding more difficult, turning into a vicious circle. A shake-out may come in various more or less overt forms, such as being faced with falling management fees, shifting into other asset management areas, merging with another fund-of-funds, or large asset management groups and investment banks buying up smaller funds-of-funds to increase their exposure to private equity. Probably extinction would be too strong a word. It is more consolidation that describes this development. In such contracting markets, which players are more likely to survive?

It is not just the financial aspects that matter to investors. Funds-of-funds will continue to succeed where they serve a purpose for investors, such as outsourcing the selection of funds and monitoring their activities, or providing value-added services such as liquidity planning on top of their investment services. There are economies of scale and advantages of getting large, such as slack resources to bridge market downturns or to switch strategies, increased visibility and brand identity, and access to larger-scale deals. But there are also limits to

---

[4] Both quoted from Allchorne (2004a).

growth, as venture capital is 'oversupply of ideas for undersupply of money'. In addition to the mega generalist, fund-of-funds groups with niche strategies emerge. €50 million to €100 million fund-of-funds focusing on a specific niche could be more than sufficient if the strategy is very specialized.[5] Differentiation and specialization are sound survival strategies but do not always work. For example, it is documented that in recent years several attempts to launch technology-focused VC funds-of-funds failed.

Critical mass is perceived to be a problem. On the question of what was the minimum amount of capital needed to run a global fund-of-funds, HarbourVest's George Anson responded: 'My guess is €1bn if you want to be able to offer globally diversified longevity and for the clients to feel you're going to be around. You wonder how the small groups will survive.'[6] The established funds-of-funds have grown in step with the mega-buyouts, have built this critical mass, have been in the market for decades and have vintage year diversified portfolios, and even during market downturns they are reported to earn long-term returns superior to public equities.

Booms, however, often follow extinctions. Despite predictions of a consolidation and a shake-out the industry remained stable and the market was even set to grow further. So in 2006 it was reported that private equity funds-of-funds were becoming increasingly popular, and that it would even be a good time to start one.[7] Again, a typical behavior of evolutionary environments is that new entrants immediately replace extinct species. As the program manager is unlikely to always only pick the best funds and thus generate the highest possible performance, to, in the words of Dequech (1999), 'fare no worse, generally, than others' would be a more realistic objective. Depending on the private equity fund program's investors this could mean doing better than other private equity managers, doing better than other asset classes, generating better performance most of the time, etc. or simply having a good relationship with the investors. Private equity fund investment programs primarily survive if their investors continue backing them. However, this is not necessarily achieved only through high returns. In an interview Guy Kawasaki (the CEO of Garage Technology Ventures, a venture capital investment bank for high-technology companies) responded to the question of what criteria make a VC firm a first tier, second tier or third tier: '*Either the egos of the partners or the VC's PR firm decides that it's a first-tier firm.*'[8]

Managers of a private equity fund investment program need to understand that they are essentially in an arms race against other managers with a similar capacity for evolutionary improvement. According to Dawkins (2000), evolution 'has equipped our brains with a subjective consciousness of risk and improbability suitable for creatures with a lifetime of less than a century'. But arms races are run in evolutionary time, rather than on the short time horizon most investors perceive to be relevant.

11.2 GRADING-BASED EVALUATION OF PRIVATE EQUITY FUNDS

Uncertainty does not mean that we cannot put venture capital funds into certain categories. The grading methodology that we discussed in previous chapters does this, but four grading

---

[5] See Sormani (2003b).
[6] Quoted from Sormani (2005d).
[7] See Avery (2006).
[8] See Forbes (2004).

classes is admittedly a coarse classification. The expected performance grading is a tool for the evaluation of private equity funds[9], and ex ante it is based on a score for a number of mainly qualitative dimensions (see Table 11.1).

Table 11.1 Qualitative scores

Score	Description
1	In the dimension assessed the fund's characteristics are in line with mainstream characteristics (=P(A) for internal age=0).
2	In the dimension assessed the fund's characteristics are in line with mainstream characteristics (=P(B) for internal age=0).
3	In the dimension assessed the fund's characteristics show some deviation from mainstream characteristics or are to be considered as weak points. Too many of such weaknesses in other dimensions would make it unlikely that the fund finds (additional) investors (=P(C) for internal age=0).
4	In the dimension assessed the fund's characteristics show a clear deviation from mainstream characteristics or are seen to be a considerable weakness. Unless compensated by strengths in other dimensions, it makes it unlikely that the fund finds (additional) investors (=P(D) for internal age=0).

In the fleeting environment that characterizes the VC market it would be preposterous to claim that the qualitative score has any significant predictive power. Instead of attempting to forecast success, the grading just aims for the identification of weaknesses. However, it provides two pieces of interesting information. Firstly, it gives the qualitative input for assigning a fair value to a fund. Secondly, the qualitative score can be seen as a measure of how well a fund is adapted to the prevailing VC 'ecosystem'. Mainstream as a definition is only temporary, and the scoring method is certainly not static. Its dimensions and the weight of the dimensions within the total grading can change over time with the evolution of the private equity market. What is the mainstream today may not be best practice tomorrow.

Box 11.2: 'Elite' funds

A few transactions such as Yahoo, eBay or Google made up the vast majority of the US VC industry gains since 1996. Apparently a relatively small group of eight or ten US 'elite' firms occupies an extraordinary position in the VC market. Ward (2005) put the hypothesis forward that these elite firms, like Kleiner Perkins Caulfield & Byers, Sequoia, Benchmark or Draper Fisher Jurvetson, are 'White Holes'™ – Fraser-Sampson (2007) uses the term 'Golden Circle' – and that they attract 'mega deals' like Google due to their track record. On average there is less than one 'mega deal' per VC fund generation and elite firms are highly likely to monopolize these deals.

As these venture capitalists come with exceptional judgment and experience and possess a long track record of successfully building companies, entrepreneurs often go to great lengths and initially accept very unattractive conditions just to get their

---

[9] See Meyer and Mathonet (2005).

Box 11.2:   (Continued)

backing. The stronger negotiation position of this elite, their widespread network and their superior access to capital markets translates into an increased probability of success in combination with a very high pay-off. As a consequence, while funds managed by these firms continue to outperform, the rest of the VC industry could be likely to under-perform. To underline the point, Ward (2005) remarked that 'the' example for success of the European VC industry, Mangrove's Skype transaction, still with Draper Fisher Jurvetson, involved a 'Golden Circle' fund. Unfortunately, for the average investor such elite VC firms limit assets under management. They are extremely restrictive regarding new limited partners or even do not accept them at all. Swensen (2005) stated that 'the inability to access the venture elite drives the final nail in the coffin of prospective venture – investor aspirations'. Indeed, many investors who are new to the asset class perceive access to this elite as an insurmountable obstacle.

To stay with our analogy of fitness landscape, the elite VC firms occupy a privileged position in the private equity market landscape that allows them to exploit their position. But how sustainable are these positions? While 'Golden Circle' funds so far were mainly a US phenomenon, technology is becoming increasingly global, and even the elite firms cannot be everywhere. The scalability of their funds is limited, management talent is difficult to pass on to the next generation and generally few firms in the venture world manage to tackle the succession issues.

At the end of the day all empires decline and fall. Take, for example, American Research & Development that back in the 1970s had a reputation comparable to that of Kleiner Perkins and the like today. According to Stein (2002), inner turmoil and management squabbles made many of its young, ambitious professionals abandon this firm and start their own VC outfits. So Greylock rose from American Research & Development's ashes and this firm that 'should still be an industry leader is now a mere footnote'. To quote Gary Bridge, managing director of Horsley Bridge Partners, firms 'break up, people get together who were in separate firms. It'll happen, and it'll happen again.'

Industry experts characterize the VC business as one of the last great crafts. Education and talent is certainly important, but business acumen and judgment are different challenges. It takes a long time to learn how to be good at VC investing, and the necessary skills are difficult to pass on. Succession planning alone does not guarantee that new recruits acquire the 'ingredients' that made the senior partners successful.

Firm that has certainly managed succession well is Kleiner Perkins. Formed in 1972, it is regarded as one of the world's most prestigious VC groups. Over more than three decades this firm has created a pre-eminent franchise that has not been impaired by the departures of Eugene Kleiner, Tom Perkins and Frank Caulfield. But Kleiner Perkins may be an exception as even the best firms suffer from not mentoring and training people. Lucy Marcus, founder of Marcus Venture Consulting, found that '[s]ome of today's top firms may lose their leadership positions while [up-and-coming] funds nip at their heals to take those top spots'.[10]

---

[10] Quoted from Stein (2002).

Indeed, newcomers also have the potential to either occupy new privileged positions in the VC market landscape or even to break into this elite. One well-documented example is Benchmark Capital that was formed in 1995 to invest in technology start-ups and is now almost a household name in technology circles. Stross (2000) has written the story of this new elite firm's first four years where it increased each of its partners' personal net worth by some $350 million. Benchmark achieved spectacular successes such as eBay, which after an initial investment of $6.7 million made in 1997 appreciated in value to an incredible $4 billion just two years later.[11] Apparently, Benchmark's partners, the 'eBoys', regarded established firms like Kleiner Perkins as 'some blue-blood, monied club' and as their arch-rivals.

And, who knows, probably the industry will see in future years other elite VC funds emerging outside the USA, possibly in China, India or Europe. Mangrove may be an example that 'navigation' within the VC industry landscape is not only an abstraction. Institutional investors planning to enter the VC market can conclude that elite funds are often just a temporary phenomenon. They do not pose an impregnable fortress but just temporarily occupy a privileged position in a shifting landscape. With patience all institutional investors can overcome the access problems.

It has to be highlighted that sometimes these best practices are just based on anecdotal evidence as they reflect actual perceptions and mainstream relates to the perception of risk. Whether these risks will materialize is irrelevant, as the perceptions and the resulting best practices reflect the aggregate experiences of the market. As an example, many institutional investors would usually not be willing to commit to the typical first-time funds. Typically such funds market themselves as specialists, in other words, they try to operate in an 'ecological niche' and are less adapted to the general environment. Moreover, these fledgling fund management teams usually lack the resources to switch strategy or to ride out a longer market downturn. With being less adapted and less adaptable, the first-time fund depends on things going according to plan – which often is not the case, and therefore the pessimistic view that such funds may suffer a higher mortality is understandable.

11.2.1   Can we predict success?

We have developed our grading approach for private equity funds as a tool for systematic portfolio management.[12] Our experience with this approach leads us to believe that it does a decent job as an early warning instrument for 'trouble brewing' and that the grading is doing quite well in capturing consensus opinion on a fund of other experienced limited partners in the market. But we have to admit that we are continuously humbled by our inability to forecast success for new investment proposals.[13]

We take one of the greatest success stories in recent history of European venture capital as an example to illustrate the point: Skype, founded in 2003 with a €20 million investment that in 2005 eventually was bought by eBay for a staggering €3.5 billion, to be paid in two

---

[11] Admittedly they also had some failures like WebVan under their belt.

[12] Simplistically we just talk about grading, although ex ante this strictly speaking only relates to a qualitative score.

[13] As Ormerod (2005) pointed out in his analysis of failure and extinctions, once a set of very elementary errors have been avoided, there is almost nothing to be gained by further experience in terms of enhancing the prospects for survival.

instalments. To quote Davies (2005), 'Skype hasn't just been a success for a few big name or late-stage investors. It has validated Europe's seed and early-stage investment model. This grand claim lies on the shoulders of a small Luxembourg-based investment boutique, founded in 2000 at the height of the internet boom.'

Mangrove Capital Partners started operations with its first fund New Tech Venture Capital Fund (NTVC I) in 2000, well before we developed and introduced the grading for VC funds. No one would accuse us of arguing with perfect hindsight, as we admit that based on our technique NTVC I clearly would have received a low expected performance grade, and most investors would have taken this as a clear sign not to commit. We would have based a low expected performance grade on the following arguments (and we believe that most advisors and gatekeepers would have told their institutional investors the same):

- All partners came from a major accounting firm, where they were responsible for the private equity practice. Although they apparently had some own successful VC investments, by today's standards this would not be considered a sufficient track record. Investors typically shy away from first-time teams anyway, and exceptions are usually only made if the team has gained 'real' investment practice together in a respected VC firm.
- Also Mangrove's location – Luxembourg – does not strike one as ideal for seed and early stage investments that require hands-on involvement and close proximity to their VC backers. Where is the deal flow? Luxembourg is not exactly Silicon Valley![14]

In fact, one could say that Mangrove came to the market with perfect timing and teams with comparable characteristics would have found it very difficult if not impossible to raise such a fund during recent years. Nevertheless, at that time the founders were able to tap into their local network, and Mangrove was able to close their first fund easily. Apparently it was not even necessary to look for other institutions outside Luxembourg to get going. The Mangrove partners also learned their trade quickly, and based on the interviews we conducted with the fund's investors, not to a small degree Skype's success can be credited to them. This start-up was initially not all too promising and it was more its creators Niklas Zennström and Janus Friis – serial entrepreneurs who already had the peer-to-peer music sharing company Kazaa under their belt – who were worth the gamble.

Clearly our fund grading technique would have 'failed' to forecast success in the case of Mangrove's NTVC I. However, this calls for some comments. Statistics does not apply to individuals. Take ratings as an example. Even if a bond has only a 'single B' rating – highly risky 'junk' – often such bonds do not default. They in fact can pay a handsome profit and therefore many institutions invest in so-called 'high-yield portfolios' (a more digestible term for junk bonds). In other words, statistics describes the characteristics of populations. Making assumptions about individuals from data on populations is only reasonable when variations within the population is small – this is clearly not the case for VC funds.

We analyzed NTVC I in the context of a portfolio of VC funds with similar characteristics, mainly first-time teams doing seed investments (the funds your gatekeeper will warn you and strongly advise you not to invest in). Indeed, the entire portfolio's projected return profile is very low and thus supports our grading methodology and the perceptions it is based on so

---

[14] Skype was initially registered in the Bahamas but was relocated to Luxembourg. The company is run out of London and the development was done in Estonia's capital, Tallinn. This is an example that geography is becoming increasingly fuzzy and difficult to manage as a private equity fund investment program's portfolio diversification dimension.

far. Regularly, funds that have received a low expected performance grade ex ante indeed 'flop'. However, there are also some other 'home-runs' like Mangrove in this portfolio, which makes us believe that this is not just a freak event and therefore requires a closer look. Based on the consensus expertise it is built on, the grading appears to be reasonable proxy for probability of a 'hit'. Our model assumes that lower graded funds have a reduced probability of making such a hit, but in reality this probability is definitely not zero.

Moreover, the pay-off of such a hit might be as high for a P-C graded fund as it is for a P-A graded fund – for example, because other VC funds may start to invest in its portfolio companies and add value as well. In the case of Skype part of its success is certainly also explained by its follow-on financers Bessemer Venture Partners, Draper Fisher Jurvetson and Index Ventures, that most probably were instrumental in the transaction with eBay. Nevertheless, meanwhile Mangrove is referred to as a 'very secretive fund'[15] – in the world of private equity, the ultimate badge of honor and respect.

11.2.2   Why not invest only in P-A graded funds?

What does the grading measure, since apparently limited partners invest in funds that are graded less than P-A, i.e. that have a lower perceived probability of a 'hit'? A mixed agenda of 'strategic objectives' or portfolio diversification in the widest sense may be an explanation. It could also be that the limited partner is getting compensated for the fund's lower perceived quality through a real option – an angle that will be explored in more detail later on.

11.2.2.1   Limited partner perspective

The picture will be incomplete without acknowledging also that limited partners fall into different categories. The limited partner in question may lack experience or may be unable to access funds of better quality. Not only experienced long-term oriented institutions invest in private equity, but there are also 'tourists' who get attracted into this market by some spectacular success stories. There are limited partners looking for co-investment opportunities and limited partners that commit already in the first closing. There are also public institutions that aim to support an emerging VC industry and are therefore also more likely to back VC funds that are not entirely in line with the mainstream.

Some limited partners are weak from a financial point of view and thus less desirable for general partners. Such weakness can have several dimensions. What is most relevant from the viewpoint of a fund manager is the lack of financial strength – that is not having 'deep pockets', a higher probability of becoming a defaulting investor or of not committing to the follow-on fund.[16] But also from an institutional viewpoint limited partners can be weak, e.g. when they are newcomers without experience there is a clear danger that they become disappointed and withdraw in due course. Institutions that do not really need private equity from a portfolio management perspective may decide to change their strategy and give up their engagement. In any case, it is difficult for fund managers to establish a good relationship with a limited partner that is undergoing a high staff turnover.

---

[15] See http://www.thealarmcock.com/euro/archives/2006/05/mangroves_ searching_for_better.html [accessed 27 July 2006].
[16] In recent years, often high net worth individuals fell into this category, as with the bursting of the dotcom bubble their personal wealth also evaporated.

How can a limited partner become 'strong'? Certainly patience is a virtue, and being continuously around even during market downturns sends a signal to fund managers that this investor can be relied on. Another signal can be hiring individuals who are well known and personally committed to the asset class.

11.2.2.2   Objectives of limited partners

What are the objectives of a private equity fund investment program? The answer appears to be obvious – generating growth in the form of high returns. It is widely discussed how to get access to 'top-quartile' funds, but one should not be mistaken. Private equity is a highly competitive industry and being able to prosper in such a fluid and cyclical environment is a challenge. How many investors are able to pick year after year exclusively top-quartile funds? The stellar return figures and the extraordinary amounts of carried interest apparently all investment managers in private equity take home often blind us.[17] It is clear that people are more likely to boast about their extraordinary accomplishments than run-of-the-mill funds when discussing their average returns in public, but this resembles us reading the Monday morning headlines of people cracking the jackpot. In other words, this is not the normal situation.

We can therefore assume that high returns or, in other words, growth is just one objective for the manager of a private equity fund investment program. The other one is survival, and when threatened, the need for survival will dominate the desire for growth. According to Beinhocker (2006), generating a competitive return to one's investors is not an objective in and on itself. Rather, *it is a fundamental constraint that must be met in order to the objective of survival and replication (or enduring and growing)*.[18] Likewise and when reading the headlines of the financial papers, once private equity firms have become 'too big to fail' other objectives like publicity and prestige of the individual fund managers appears to take priority.

11.2.2.3   General partner perspective

Generally one would expect that the teaming of strong limited partners with strong fund managers will produce the best results, as this is a professional relationship and long-term oriented. Nevertheless, in both directions, terms and conditions are usually very stringent and it is difficult for any side to get more favorable terms and conditions.

There is a trade-off between maximizing the perceived chances of having a 'hit', for example picking a first-quartile fund, and maximizing the pay-off after having selected a winner. Stronger fund managers usually will not grant more favorable economic terms to one of their limited partners. On the contrary, some 'proven performers' even manage to charge a higher carried interest. On the other hand, proposals which are perceived to be more risky, for example first-time funds, often offer 'special deals' to their initial backers.

---

[17] To draw a parallel to the stock market: Foster and Kaplan (2001) analyzed performance data stretching back 40 years for 1000 US companies. As a group, the long-term survivors in the S&P 500 under-performed the average and the longer companies had been in the database, the worse they did.

[18] This is reminiscent of the suggestion put forward by the evolutionary theorist Richard Dawkins, that living organisms exist for the benefit of DNA rather than the other way around. His argument runs that the *messages that DNA molecules contain are all but eternal when seen against the time scale of individual lifetimes. [. . .] Each individual organism should be seen as a temporary vehicle, in which DNA messages spend a tiny fraction of their geological lifetimes.* See Dawkins (2000).

Box 11.3: 'Special deals'

A conversation with an investment manager from a large and experienced institutional investor in private equity sheds some light on the ability to negotiate favorable terms and conditions. This investor negotiated with an institutional quality European buyout fund with a fund size of around €250 million. The fund managers were very interested in getting a limited partner of such high quality 'on board'. Nevertheless, they were only willing to offer a relatively modest reduction in carried interest from 20% to 18%. To benefit from this reduced carry a limited partner had to be a cornerstone investor, i.e. be in the first closing and commit at least €20 million.

But in most of the cases and for bigger investment this institutional investor found it difficult to influence the funds' economics. Because of pari passu or 'most favored nation' clauses, special deals on management fees or carried interest are usually not possible, although on other issues, for example co-investment rights or reporting, changes can be negotiated. If an investor manages to obtain a reduction or favored treatment, this is not always communicated to other limited partners.

In the case in question the general partner either offered the carry reduction or it was already negotiated by another cornerstone investor. The clause was made transparent to all investors in the limited partnership agreement, and the limited partner basically piggybacked on this part of the deal. According to the investment manager, this happens in most cases. There can be exceptions, like situations where a previous captive fund is spun-out, and where the original mother company is likely to retain economic advantages, such as getting part of the carried interest.

A stronger limited partner is in a good position to negotiate better terms and conditions – often outside usual market practice – such as privileged co-investment rights. If we assume that 'weakness' is associated with higher perceived probability of failure, it is questionable whether these favorable conditions can be a full compensation or even result in a premium.[19]

Also quite common is the situation where a weak limited partner invests in a weak fund, for example because the investor can find no better proposal and the fund manager is happy to get funded at all. This can be mutually beneficial as even weak funds often become successful and as a result help to put an investor who tries to enter the VC market onto the map. Both parties learn and this may result in a long-term relationship. However, the combination of weak general and limited partner – not only nature is cruel – will be unlikely to survive: firstly, the fund most probably will not attract other investors and, secondly, as it is more likely to generate a sub-standard return it puts the future of the limited partner's investment program into jeopardy.

The question remains why a strong fund manager should accept a weak investor as limited partner? At the end of the day it often comes down to years of 'begging and pleading' or through building indirectly a relationship, for example through co-investing in portfolio companies.

---

[19] For the purpose of this discussion we ignore socially responsible investing.

11.2.2.4 Pairing of general partners and limited partners

Nature's solution for bridging longer distances in the fitness landscape is – sex. Without stretching this analogy too far, engaging in a relationship between strong parents can increase the off-spring's (i.e. the follow-on fund's) chances in the future significantly. During the lifetime of a fund the interests of general and limited partners are so closely aligned that the fund can be seen as one entity combining positive and negative characteristics – i.e. the 'genetic code' – of fund managers and investors.

To some degree it is not far-fetched to describe the relationship between the limited partner and the fund manager as a 'pairing' that goes beyond the actual fund. For the institutional investor, searching for suitable funds is very cost-intensive, and due diligence, structuring and subsequent monitoring are quite expensive. One should also not under-estimate the emotional element and the bureaucratic obstacles the investment managers working for larger institutions face. Proposing new fund managers will usually result in more scrutiny and critical questions than simply committing to follow-on funds. Presenting and defending the investment into any alternative asset in front of a conservative financial institution's investment committee can take a significant mental toll and experience – experienced investment manager usually would not want to repeat it too often. For the fund manager the certification effect brought about by a reputable institution carries a high value, as it clearly eases the current and future fundraisings, and can give access to deep pockets in case something goes off course during the fund's lifetime. The costs of switching relationships are significant, as in such an opaque market fund managers that lose key investors can also be perceived as 'lemons'.

A number of studies discuss the relationship between managers of VC funds and their investors in general.[20] Fund managers as well as their investors have an interest in maintaining a relationship over the longer term.[21] Investors want to build long-term relationships in emerging top funds as they expect access to such teams to become more difficult in future years. Byworth (2005) emphasizes the importance of informal communication and limited partners need to monitor.[22] For example, the attendance at annual investor or advisory board meetings is critical. A limited partner can exercise more influence on the fund manager and ask for a more favorable treatment or changes in future funds. Over a longer time period the limited partner gets better knowledge and insights relevant for re-investment decisions.

'Strategic investor relationships are the cornerstone of a successful private equity firm over the long term.'[23] Private equity firms prefer investors that are consistently in the market, long term in their approach and likely to participate in subsequent funds.

- Lerner and Schoar (2002) presented the theory that fund managers screen for deep-pocket investors: those that have a low likelihood of facing a liquidity shock that could lead to default or to withdrawing from the asset class.
- Associated with such 'deep-pocket investors' is often a certification effect as such institutions' reputation helps the fund managers in attracting additional investors. As VC aims

---

[20] For example, Byworth (2005), Fruchbom (2005), Gompers and Lerner (2001), Lerner and Schoar (2002).

[21] See Byworth (2005): 'A manager of a multi-billion euro fund admitted that he enjoyed working with certain of his investors far more than others, and intimated that, regardless of their actual importance to the firm in terms of their commitment size, they might receive preferential treatment or advance information. Another mentioned that he used some of his investor base as trusted parties to bounce ideas off, giving them a greater ability to influence the firm and the way it operates.'

[22] Meyer and Mathonet (2005).

[23] Fruchbom (2005).

to build industry champions, foreign limited partners also provide important international contacts for products or exits.[24]

- According to Fruchbom (2005), VC firms are looking for support in a wider sense, i.e. engagement with the firm over the long term. Consequently, endowments and foundations belong to the most desired group of limited partners. Being long-term oriented leads to a better understanding of market terms and conditions and allegedly to fairer negotiations between fund managers and investors, a stronger alignment of their interests, and efficient communication and constructive trouble-shooting throughout the relationship.[25]

Based on this, one can also draw conclusions regarding how to get access to the 'Golden Circle' of top-funds: back them when they are still first-time funds and do not belong to the circle yet.

We have found the answer to our quest: Wealth is knowledge and its origin is evolution.
Beinhocker (2006)

Observing the dynamics of the venture capital industry the idea springs to mind that we are dealing with an 'ecosystem'. Indeed, nature itself with evolution has found a mechanism that allows species to successfully cope and even grow under uncertainty.

11.3 GRADING AS PORTFOLIO MANAGEMENT TOOL

Because of a structural lack of empirical data, the approach is to take analogies from established tried and tested rating approaches. Occasionally the grading task is confused with doing a track record analysis, but in fact the grading is used mainly for two purposes: as the valuation methodology we discussed previously and as a portfolio management tool.

Too many investors and consultants tend to define 'good funds' based on past performance. These markets are developing so quickly and have come along so far since the early 1990s that past performance is not a reliable indicator.
Pat Dinnen, Managing Director of Siguler Guff (see EMPEA, 2005)

The grading measures deviations from market best practices. Here we assume that deviations relate to type of specialization, market focus or structure, but management teams are generally competent and experienced. When assigning an expected performance grade the viewpoint of an investor is taken who invests under the same terms and conditions as all the other limited partners. In other words, special conditions can help to make the deal more attractive but do not change the grade as representative for the value in the eyes of its beholder. The expected performance grade measures what is or could be known to all potential investors and should not reflect individual hunches. In addition to its use as input into a valuation model, the

---

[24] Rice *et al.* (1997).
[25] Lerner *et al.* (2004) establish a link between institutions' approaches to private equity investing and their investment success. They particularly point to endowments as examples for successful investors in VC funds. According to Fruchbom (2005) 'one respondent to our poll noted: "Endowments tend to understand the asset class, have a long-term perspective and recognise the importance of driving returns through operational value-add." '

expected performance grading is a measure for the distance of the move within a fitness landscape.

Grading measures perception of risks, but should not be misunderstood as the 'tyranny of the normal'. A high expected performance grade suggests that private equity experts perceive this as being well adapted to the current industry landscape. This would be a 'small step' for exploring the landscape. A low expected performance stands for a high degree of deviation, in other words, for a big jump to a more distant point on the terrain that, however, carries increased costs, as there is significant danger of falling into a deep valley.

In a stable private equity market environment the landscape would be imagined as smooth, with neighboring positions correlated. Here the best solution is to commit to a P-A graded fund that has a high fit with the current landscape of the private equity funds market. In a disruptive or emerging private equity market environment the neighboring positions in the landscape would be completely uncorrelated. Committing to a P-A graded fund could be just as dangerous and lead as much to unpredictable results as significant deviations from market standards.

The reality is an intermediate case, with the VC environment swinging between the extremes. Current market practices infer some knowledge about future ones, but cannot determine them unequivocally. The practical response to this dilemma is a core – satellite portfolio approach – which we discuss in more detail later – where the core represents small steps and the satellite long jumps when searching the private equity landscape.

In the context of the management of a portfolio of private equity funds, databases such as VentureXperts differentiate peer groups such as early stage VC, mezzanine financing or buyouts. It is of course not meaningful to assume that one best market practice model is applicable to all of them. Based on our experiences this appears to be one of the major misunderstandings and in fact it is quite the opposite. Like equally successful species, for example lions and elephants that co-exist in an ecosystem, there can be several mainstream approaches, with no meaningful differentiation possible. As benchmark data is historical, it is impossible to find an exactly identical private equity fund to the one to be valued. The choice of a suitable peer group could be compared to the famous US Supreme Court judge's description of pornography: you can't define it precisely, but you know it when you see it. One has to apply common sense.

Box 11.4:   Peer groups

Formally, the grading is only defined together with a clearly identified benchmark population. When thinking about how to define a peer group and what we can and what we cannot achieve with a grading, it helps to look at a real-life example for navigating under uncertainty – recruitment for jobs. How can you say that one candidate is better or worse for a job? Firstly, it depends on the job description. A candidate with a PhD in avionics may have excellent qualifications, but it may well be that he or she would not be suitable for working as a surgeon. Likewise, a superb surgeon – even 'risk adjusted' – most likely will not be the dream candidate for designing the new super-jumbo.

Candidates are typically screened based on their CVs. When doing this, we have an ideal profile in mind. Usually it is required that applicants have relevant experience, but often they can have too much of it and be too senior for the position. In other words, it is not the skills and experiences in themselves that are of relevance, but the best fit with the profile that makes a candidate attractive.

Life itself and how we navigate its vicissitudes is probably the best example for what we can achieve through the grading. For job applicants it is a 'survival instinct' to stick to certain conventions, even though we personally question or reject them. There are many examples where college drop-outs become rich and famous, but nevertheless most recruiters place a lot of importance on the candidate's education. Meeting the formal requirements increases the chance of getting a job interview, like we observe for VC funds where a high expected performance grade is representative for the chance that the fund will find a critical mass of limited partners to start its activities.

However, compliance with conventions and job descriptions does not mean that a new employee will turn out to be successful and become the next chief executive. They may be capable of doing their job, but success in the sense of outperforming your peers and making a career takes more than an MBA.[26]

The grading approach is admittedly a coarse technique with little differentiation. Nevertheless, in an environment of such extreme uncertainty as the VC market, it does not pay to be too sophisticated, as adding new factors also adds another source for error and inaccuracy. In a complex market environment this cost of adding a source of error can quickly overshoot the benefit of having a more detailed model. In an environment where information is not existent, costly or obsolete, one can only expect to make decisions that are 'good enough' rather than optimal.

Essentially the expected performance grade is a measure for 'fitness' within the private equity landscape at a given time. The institutional quality mainstream funds are seen as 'best adapted' to this environment and niche funds could be interpreted as 'mutations'. These mutations may be less well adapted to the current – or better to the currently known – environment, but they may be better adjusted to possible future market environments or to the niche markets ignored by or unknown to mainstream investors.

11.4   VC MARKET DYNAMICS – POWER LAWS

In nature, evolution allows life to prosper and to continue despite more or less regular cataclysmic events. Probably for venture capital the avoidance or mitigation of 'catastrophes' is less of relevance, but we argue that its structures and approaches are geared toward capturing the cataclysmic events in the form of 'golden opportunities'. Certainly venture capital covers a wide range, and there are not only 'home-runs' like Google or Skype. The majority of new products are not revolutionary, but many venture capitalists consistently create good companies and profitable exits. Nevertheless, without these occasional 'home-runs' venture capital would be a rather unexciting niche of the financial markets.

---

[26] As Livingston (1971) found, in his classic work 'The Myth of the Well-Educated Manager', '[m]anagers are not taught in formal education programs what they most need to know to build successful careers in management'. Drawing the parallel to private equity investing, we conclude that with a structured grading approach we can screen funds for their fitness within their peer group, but we cannot predict their success.

Like evolution, innovation is also gradual as well as doing sprints and there are both small and large innovations. Over long periods of time there are more small innovations than large ones. There is a relationship between gradual and revolutionary innovation. Over time a large number of minor innovations create the foundation of later profound discoveries. These breakthroughs tend to spur bursts of minor, less significant innovations. Thus, like water behind a dam, the random trickle of discoveries builds up over time. Schumpeter suggested that the entrepreneurs play the role of dam breakers, unleashing a flood of innovation into the market place. Another explanation could be the nature of technology itself that is not developed in isolation. It is not only cumulative but also accelerating and thus allows for a greater pay-off from the next discovery. Some products also have 'viral' and network effects. The greater the number of people who use them, the more useful they become and the more people want to use them.[27]

Mayfield (2004) Stated that perhaps 'no other market exhibits as much inter-dependence as venture capital'. It is neither predictable nor regular, with change not arriving gradually in a way that allows adjusting, but with sudden discontinuities where markets undergo a 'regime switching' from low to high volatility.[28] Such discontinuities can have a profound impact, reshape the entire business landscape and create not only risk but also the opportunities venture capitalists need. In any case, the question is how often will such 'dam breaks' happen that lead to the venture capital home-runs?

Complex adaptive systems show signature patterns like oscillations and punctuated equilibria. Another important signature characteristic of complex adaptive systems is so-called 'power laws'. A power law implies that small occurrences are common, whereas large instances are extremely rare, but they can occur at any time and for no particular reason. For example, there are few large earthquakes but many small ones. Some market phenomena are better described by power laws than the traditional Gaussian distribution. Research shows that in complex systems like the VC market, where interdependence prevents equilibrium, such power laws can be observed. In fact the distribution of innovation 'size' appears to conform to power law distribution. Power distributions appear in numerous biological, physical, economic and other contexts. They are scale-free, i.e. the shape of the distribution remains the same regardless of scaling the analyzed variable.

Venture rules of thumb acknowledge the power law indirectly: such as there is only room for three players in the market and you really only want to own #1 or #2.

                                                                    Mayfield (2004)

The VC market is a closely coupled system, where changes of one group of participants can set off chain reactions of other market players, who are either cooperating or competing. As a result of this close coupling, the VC market is a highly non-linear system. Simplistically, non-linear systems show a behavior that is not just the sum of their parts or their multiples.

---

[27] For this the Internet is probably the most dramatic recent example. It goes back to research funded since the early 1960s by the ARPA (Advanced Research Projects Agency), later known as DARPA (Defense Advanced Research Projects Agency). Despite impressive achievements like ARPANET already in 1969, this research went on more or less in obscurity and mainly academics were interested in it. Only after a number of other factors, such as the wide distribution of the personal computer or cheaper telephony came together, did the usage of the Internet make it into the mass market and explode during the 1990s.

[28] Beinhocker (2006) refers to research undertaken on this subject. Several models suggest that markets form a kind of evolving ecosystem, with patterns of cyclicality, bursts, oscillations completely generated by the dynamics of the interacting agents. Lipowski (2005) has demonstrated that extinction spasms can be caused by the internal dynamics of evolution itself, without a major external event.

Therefore, their behavior is often difficult or impossible to predict and they can even behave chaotically. In such a system one is faced with conflicting constraints and it is impossible to search for the optimal solution. Many locally optimal compromise solutions exist in the large space of possible solutions. The question is, should we search for better solutions within a given fitness landscape?

11.5   SEARCHING LANDSCAPES

According to Bakman (2005), search is any action undertaken to enlarge the knowledge base, to increase the strategic options and to lead to organizational change. The search for knowledge and opportunities is a fundamental concept in explanations for economic evolution. See Table 11.2.

Table 11.2   Principle search modes[29]

	Exploitative search	Explorative search
Objective	To exploit existing knowledge	To explore new knowledge
Mode of development	Incremental	Radical/disruptive
Long-run influence on strategic option set	Decreasing	Increasing
The impact on existing competences	Utilizes and modifies existing competences	Develops new competences and may render existing competences obsolete
Strategic horizon	Short-term	Long-term

   The conceptual distinction between exploration and exploitation has been used as an analytical construct in a wide range of management research areas, including strategic management.

11.5.1   Exploitative search

In a smooth fitness landscape neighboring positions are correlated. Exploitative search aimed at short-term results and improvements is the safe strategy to incrementally adapt to a static or slowly changing environment. In private equity terms, the focus is optimal and maximal exploitation of commercial possibilities inherent in existing competencies, industries and technologies. Change is incremental and associated with the use and development of things already known. Such incremental change accounts for a large part of growth in productivity.

   Burgelman (2002) argues that exploiting existing business opportunities allows us to remain adaptive over some range of environmental variation and over a certain time horizon. But the strategic change resulting out of exploitative search will, in the long run, be lower than the change of environment. Therefore, a sustained long-term development requires the constant introduction of new technologies, products and services.

---

[29] See Bakman (2005).

11.5.2   Explorative search

Explorative search can be compared to the long jumps within a volatile and rugged fitness landscape where neighboring positions are uncorrelated. In such an environment a small step is just as dangerous and can lead as much to unpredictable results as a long jump. Hostile environments and the strategic dependency on the environment increase searching. Here search processes are more ad hoc and improvizational. However, long jumps lead to new knowledge necessary for competing in emerging markets.

Explorative search is typical for the early stages of the technological lifecycle and means experimentation requiring speed and flexibility. It also often makes existing competences obsolete and leads to the development of new technological paradigms. The aim of the explorative search is generating a strategic options menu to protect against environmental shifts and to reduce the likelihood of failure. While long jumps may generate superior paybacks they are expensive. Most become failed experiments and land in the bottom of an even lower valley of the fitness landscape and die out.

Adaptive systems that engage in exploration to the exclusion of exploitation are likely to find that they suffer the costs of experimentation without gaining many of its benefits. They inhibit too many underdeveloped new ideas and too little distinctive competence. Conversely, systems that engage in exploitation to the exclusion of exploration are likely to find themselves trapped in suboptimal stable equilibria.

March (1991)

The reality of course is an intermediate case, where despite an element of uncertainty the knowledge about the current position infers some knowledge about the neighboring ones. Successful search strategies have to balance exploitation and exploration as well as short-term and long-term orientation. Too little exploration results in a stasis where resources get slowly depleted and the system will not be able to keep up with the pace of change in its environment. Too much exploration, however, is highly expensive and results in a chaotic state without any direction where the majority of experiments fail.

Also the short term and the long term pose a dilemma, as the future is not known anyway and only scenarios exist. Short-term developments that deviate from the expected long term may also be signals that other scenarios are evolving. The short term therefore cannot be ignored entirely, but likewise it is dangerous to pursue any opportunity that comes up. This opportunity can be signal for changes in the environment as well as 'noise' that is not representative and mostly leads to failure.

11.6   CONCLUSION

What has been said so far may appear to be of little relevance to individual private equity funds. Indeed, we mainly take the perspective of the manager of a portfolio of private equity funds, some of which show a more explorative and others a more exploitative behavior. The management of such a portfolio could be compared to the foraging behavior of bees that coordinate their activities and engage in concurrent search. The bulk of the bees are exploiting existing sources of nectar that are likely to be exhausted sooner or later, while a few scout bees take real flyers and search quite far. This strategy will inevitably have costly and unsuccessful searches, but it will also have a greater likelihood of finding new and better sources without getting stuck in a depleted area. Concurrent search activities simply increase the chances of discovering peaks in the fitness landscape.

When taking the long-term perspective managers of a private equity fund investment program understand that top VC teams can also go into decline and that therefore the search for the future rising stars is important to achieve sustainability. Venture capital operates in an unpredictable environment and uncertainty is the only thing to be sure of.[30] The selection of VC funds today builds the future opportunities. These choices and the associated options cannot be based on firm predictions but aim to anticipate and form the future. The need to act without being able to understand what the future holds is the challenge when managing under extreme uncertainty. Rather than being a forecasting tool for the success of VC funds, the grading is a method for searching within the fitness landscape of the VC market. It measures the distance and the cost of search activities.

Power laws exist, but they offer no magic formula for superior returns. Complex adaptive systems are complicated, fast-changing and unpredictable, and competitive advantages tend to be short-lived, which makes it difficult to get rich in any competitive evolutionary environment. It requires continuous search for improvements to grow and to survive. Evolution is a search algorithm that automatically strikes the right balance between exploration and exploitation. In the words of Beinhocker (2006), evolution says 'I will try lots of things and see what works and do more of what works and less of what doesn't'. The approach is to differentiate, select, amplify and repeat this continuously.

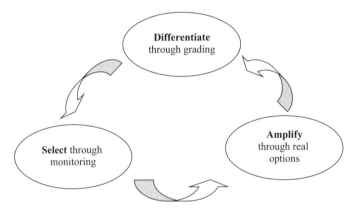

Figure 11.3 Evolution as a search algorithm

A way of amplifying as well as dealing with uncertainty is the use of real options (Figure 11.3). Having flexibility is a survival strategy and flexibility is basically a collection of real options. In situations of extreme uncertainty, it is meaningful to be flexible and bet on many horses, which certainly comes at a significant price. 'Betting on many horses' establishes a link to 'Nature's strategy' of evolution that, with mutations and the associated trial-and-error, is using a comparable mechanism for creating real options. We will explore real options in further detail in the next chapter.

---

[30] And certainly also, not to forget, death, taxes and management fees.

12
Private Equity Funds and Real Options

Co-written with Paulina Junni

Regardless of how deep investors 'dig' in their due diligence process, they still face huge uncertainty when making a commitment to a private equity fund. The due diligence and the limited partnership agreement are normally set against the background of an 'all-or-nothing' decision and therefore do not properly recognize the value of learning more before a full decision is made. One cannot avoid uncertainty, and many investment professionals delude themselves regarding their ability to predict the success of private equity funds, but limited partners can prepare to be able to control for the different emerging outcomes. In the previous chapter we have described evolution as nature's way of navigating within a fitness landscape. The real options concept applies financial option theory to real-life investments. It recognizes the value of deferring investment decisions and of learning over time. The real option methodology is particularly useful when there is a high degree of uncertainty, some managerial flexibility, and not all the information is known ex ante.

> *The value of changing resources and hence changing position in this landscape requires an evaluation of the cost of change against the future unknown reward. This is what option theory does; it puts a value on the investment in the capability to change the position in the landscape contingent on the environmental outcome.*
>
> Kogut and Kulatilaka (1994)

Investment decisions are rarely of a 'take it or leave it' type, and flexibility, i.e. opportunities to make decisions over the life of the investment that affect its outcome, is valuable. Because traditional valuation approaches such as the Net Present Value (NPV) ignore flexibility, real options have become powerful tools in strategic and financial analysis. A detailed explanation of real option theory goes beyond the scope of this book, and we limit our discussion to those that are of relevance to limited partners.[1] A real option can be defined as the right, but not the obligation, to take an action at a pre-determined cost, for a predetermined period of time. Comparable to mutations in biological evolution, real options are costly on one side but have a value in situations where changes are unpredictable.

When considering real options we take a different view on ex post decisions. Obviously, the so-called 'strike price', i.e. the price to exercise the option, decreases its value. On the other hand, the high volatility of the underlying asset makes the option more valuable – in

---

[1] For a practitioner's guide to real options we refer to Copeland and Antikarov (2003).

other words, the option will have value only when there is uncertainty as to the possible outcomes of the initial investment. Moreover, the higher the uncertainty the higher is its value. Also, a prolongation of the time to an option's expiration is of additional value to an investor. Finally, the correct cost of capital with flexibility will be different than assuming the same for every period, which is the case for other financial valuation tools such as NPV. The real options value can be estimated by calculating the NPV of an investment using decision trees and adjusting the discount rate if necessary. Other approaches exist. However, in practice the parameters needed are often very difficult to get. For illustration, the classical real options presented in financial books are:

- The **option to defer** the start of a project or make phased investments, which helps to reduce the uncertainty of an investment.
- The **option to expand** or **to extend** the life of a project through which investors can benefit from an emerging upside.
- The **option to contract** or **to abandon**, which can serve to protect investors from the downside of an investment.

Generally options to expand, extend or defer the start of a project can be classified as **call options**, whereas options to abandon, contract or switch between different modes of operation are seen as **put options**. Some real options, for example to abandon, are inherent in the investment decision, but others can be created in their own turn.

The upside potential of options means that value increases with uncertainty, and it is occasionally argued that even failed projects have a value, as an investor actually gains some knowledge in the process. This knowledge could be seen as an option created that is not used at that time but can be used in future. In some contexts such arguments certainly have merit, but it is also important to recognize that pointing to real options everywhere can be misused as cosmetics for over-optimism or to justify poor investments. Again, the dotcom period at the end of the 1990s can serve as a warning, as at that time real options were often the argument to support unsustainably high valuations of Internet stocks. For our discussion, the real options framework's relevance lies less in its potential use as a valuation technique but mainly as the strategic decision-making tool and mindset it provides for limited partners.

While venture capitalists always face high uncertainty with regard to the prospects of the companies they want to invest in, with a maturing portfolio they learn about the quality of their investments. Essentially exercising real options, venture capitalists typically stage their investments in the portfolio companies. This instalment feature gives the venture capitalist flexibility, for example with a right to abandon, i.e. to write off the investment, if certain milestones are not met. This approach, however, is not, or at least not fully, replicated by the investors in VC funds, although they are faced with a comparable degree of uncertainty. While some of the terms and conditions in the limited partnership agreement can be viewed as having a positive real option value, these are relatively few and most of them are implicit rather than explicitly stated in the contract and, normally, cannot be exercise by a single limited partner but require a collective decision-making. One explanation could be that limited partners are typically quite conservative in their approach to investing, and generally, in finance, real option is a comparatively new paradigm with a potential rarely fully realized. Closer to home as an explanation is that real options in the context of private equity funds are of a more indirect nature and difficult to manage systematically.

Box 12.1: Limited partner real option to defer

The option to defer an investment decision in a fund, which allows reducing the uncertainty, is perhaps the most classical textbook real option. The typical example in the financial literature illustrating the value of an option to defer is a mining company that has undeveloped reserves that it can choose to develop at a time of its choosing – presumably when the price of the commodity is high.

The commitment to a private equity fund is an investment into a 'blind pool', i.e. there are no portfolio companies in the portfolio yet, only a business case and a vague investment strategy. Moreover, in the case of a first-time team, investors have little insight into the team's quality either. The simplest deferral option is to wait until a better investment proposal becomes available, but in many situations it is difficult to find striking differences between one 'blind pool' and another. Alternatively, the right to be accepted after the first closing of the fundraising period allows the prospective investor to reduce the uncertainty before taking the decision to invest. For instance, the quality of the fund's existing limited partners is a positive signal about the team's quality and also allows 'free-riding' on their due diligence. Furthermore, one can gain a better idea about the number and quality of deals currently sourced by the team. The earlier limited partners generally sell this option to defer for a so-called equalization fee: investors who become limited partners later have to make up their contributions as if they had invested at the time of the first closing. These equalization fees are a pre-financing charge and normally based on Treasury interest rates and on the fund's cash flows that occurred before the last closing. They are then distributed to the earlier limited partners in the proportions defined by the previous closing before the new investors joined. On the other hand, limited partners who make a commitment for the second closing will carry a higher risk of not getting their desired ticket in the fund.

Another example for an option to defer is the general idea of putting a small ticket into a first-time team fund and – based on the occasionally 'heroic' assumption that the fund managers can repeat their success – a much larger one in the follow-on funds when the performance is proven. This thought is expressed by Sven Berthold from WEGAsupport GmbH (see AltAssets, 2005): 'For our first-time commitments we allocated between €2–5m per fund – that was not our target allocation, it was part of our plan to use a long-term view on building the portfolio. We chose smaller tickets at the beginning to really get to know the managers. We are now reaching the stage where the first funds we invested in are coming back to market and we have to decide how much money we want to allocate to each of the funds.'

Usually institutional investors have an aversion to first-time teams, but the implicit right to invest in the follow-on fund is of significant value. Private equity is a relationship-driven industry where the investment in previously successful funds is often 'on invitation only' and restricted to those investors who have originally backed the firm. Certainly there are mechanisms to get into such funds nevertheless, e.g. to beg and plead with the fund managers or to acquire a stake in one of their funds through a secondary transaction in the rare situation where other limited partners are willing to sell. However, entering into a relationship early on is one of the best ways to get a 'seat at the table' among evolving superior private equity firms that are otherwise

---

Box 12.1:   (Continued)

inaccessible: 'We think in the mid to long-term we need exposure in Asia. To date though we have only done one investment in the region. The team is very strong and well positioned so we took a small allocation to get our foot in the door. The fund we have chosen is highly sought after and should expectations hold up it might be difficult to get into the team's third fund if you have not been in the second one.'[2]

12.1   AGENCY PROBLEMS AND CONTRACTING

There is an extensive literature on principal–agent relationships that addresses the problems arising from asymmetric information and conflicting interests among contracting parties. The principal, who assigns the agent with a task and subsequently rewards him, does not have as much information as the agent about his type and the level of effort he puts into his work. This asymmetry of information creates the risk that the agent might shirk from his work or take excessive risks.[3] Second, the goals of the principal and agent do not always coincide, thus creating conflicting interests. One source for conflict of interests is the difference in incentives of the investors and fund manager. Furthermore, the fund managers may enjoy some non-monetary benefits or 'perks' like building a reputation and gaining experience in certain asset classes.

A common prescription to remedy these agency problems is to perform an extensive due diligence and to design a contract that aligns the interests of the principal and agent. Indeed, because both limited partners and fund managers are capable of acting opportunistically, the limited partnership agreement is specifically designed to mitigate these risks by assigning these parties control rights, cash flow rights and decision rights. These rights are based on signals or events like the fund's performance, changes in the management team and market conditions.

Through a series of covenants and investment restrictions the limited partnership agreements aim to strike a careful balance between sufficient incentives for the fund management team to ensure they work hard for the benefit of the whole partnership while putting constraints on the team's behavior to assure an acceptable level of risk. Limited partnership agreements usually foresee termination clauses 'for no fault' and 'for cause', that define conditions for the removal of the general partner and the fund termination. 'For cause' terminations are typically triggered by gross negligence, material breach of the limited partnership agreement, bankruptcy of the general partner or felony convictions of a key principal. 'Key person provisions' relate to those individuals who are believed to contribute in a substantive way to the investment success and that are the main reason why the limited partner committed to a fund. Such an individual withdrawing or failing to play an active role in management constitutes a 'key person event' that automatically leads to the suspension of the investment period or even the termination of the fund unless a specified percentage of limited partners vote to continue. Alternatively, a key person event can have no consequences unless the

---

[2] See Sven Berthold from WEGAsupport GmbH (AltAssets, 2005).
[3] See, for example, Akerlof (1970).

limited partners vote otherwise. Although useful in designing incentive schemes, agency theory has limitations as it assumes that complete contracts, i.e. those that take every future event into consideration, exist. It also does not take the costs of writing a contract into account.

12.1.1   Incomplete contracting

Incomplete contracting theory, on the other hand, argues – as the name indicates – that it is virtually impossible to write a complete contract. Firstly, people are assumed to be constrained by so-called 'bounded rationality', in other words they cannot think about all eventualities, negotiate plans and write them down in such a way as to cover all the possible future states of the world. Although some relatively common situations or problems might be included fairly easily in contracts, the more uncertainty there is about future states of the world the larger the chances that contracts will be incomplete. Secondly, to assure the agreed-upon rights and obligations are respected between the principal and the agent, a contract must be designed that specifies the terms and conditions in such a way that it is legally enforceable.

Are complete contracts really desirable? Each additional clause regarding a possible outcome would increase the complexity of the contract and thus the costs of writing it. As more clauses are included to restrict the agent's scope of action, he also loses some flexibility to respond to new information. Bernheim and Whinston (1997) argue that some 'strategic ambiguity' is preferable in situations characterized by high information asymmetries, and complete contracts would induce the agent to divert his efforts and attention from important areas that are less easily measured or verified. We conclude that, particularly for VC funds operating under high uncertainty and in a very opaque environment, having too many covenants that limit the fund manager's flexibility might actually be detrimental.

12.1.2   Renegotiation and real options

While the general partner cannot make material changes to the limited partnership agreement without the limited partners' approvals, on the other hand a single investor cannot either alter the terms and conditions without the other parties' approval. Any renegotiation of contracts can be costly as well. Furthermore, in collective decision-making processes such as between the fund managers and a limited partner, the party that initiates a change bears most of the costs while the other limited partners also enjoy the benefits. This so-called 'free-rider' problem would make it likely that changes are only made when incentives are large, i.e. when the situation is so problematic that the limited partner is forced to take action or when the situation is extremely promising to maximize benefits. These transaction costs will assure that contracts will usually be incomplete to some extent, leaving either party vulnerable to ex post opportunistic bargaining by the party who has more bargaining power. The transaction cost perspective takes a rather negative view on the incompleteness of contracts, and mainly tries to find solutions to minimize the threat of renegotiation – for instance, by trying to make contracts 'renegotiation proof', or by including real options in the contracts. This does not take into account the possibility that there might be situations when incompleteness is actually beneficial, especially when the future looks very uncertain.

Since ex post opportunistic bargaining is a threat in the GP–LP relationship, the allocation of decision-making rights becomes important in steering renegotiations. A simple majority is typically sufficient for making minor changes to the limited partnership agreement, whereas questions that materially impact the position of the limited partners usually require a qualified majority vote, typically 75%. For example, if the limited partners want to remove the general partners without cause, it usually requires a 75% qualified majority vote, whereas a removal for cause requires a simple majority vote. The rest of the changes could be described as 'implicit' real options, because they often involve renegotiation with the rest of the parties, and in order to make changes proposals must be accepted with either a simple or qualified majority.

12.2   CHANGES IN LIMITED PARTNERSHIP AGREEMENTS

Contracts between limited and general partners have mainly been researched as static, one-time events. We took a dynamic perspective on the relationship between investors and fund managers, by exploring changes in limited partnership agreements as well as the monitoring of the funds.[4] The main interest of the study was to find out the most common changes in limited partnership agreements, and in which contexts these changes have been made. We aimed to explore the governance tools limited partners use to mitigate the problems of uncertainty and asymmetric information ex post, as more information is made available about the situation of the fund and the actions of its managers. We found that the separation of ex ante contracting and ex post monitoring does not seem fully applicable in the context of the private equity fund and limited partner relationship. A significant part of the investment contracts were altered after funds had already started their operation, thus supporting the incomplete contracting theory.

Because monitoring is costly, it has been argued that the principal is motivated to monitor the agent more frequently in situations of high information asymmetries, and when there is more uncertainty about the future. The value of monitoring increases with the agency costs, and additional information becomes more valuable to investors who want to evaluate whether they want to increase or reduce their exposure to a project or not.[5] Thus options to expand should be particularly valuable for limited partners, since their investments are precisely characterized by high agency costs and uncertainty about the future.

12.2.1   Main findings

In summary, funds that were characterized by larger information asymmetries were also monitored more, i.e. first-time funds received higher attention than funds with a proven

---

[4] For this analysis we researched data on the changes made in 156 limited partnership agreements, between the years 2002–2006 from a European leading public fund-of-funds investor. Initially nearly 700 monitoring reports were included in the sample, but later reports that were not considered relevant for this study were deleted, i.e. more or less routine decisions that were not considered to have any material effect on the terms and conditions of the investors and the general partners. We have to point to a number of limitations and biases of the study. The data is based on private equity investments in Europe and therefore reflects practices prevailing in this market, and thus it should not be generalized beyond this context. For example, the US and European VC markets differ markedly; the US market is more mature and has been characterized as more GP-friendly than the European VC market (see Schmidt and Wahrenburg, 2003 or Grabenwarter and Weidig, 2005). Moreover, the data reflects modus operandi of one specific fund-of-funds, whose investment strategy as a public sector investor is likely to differ from that of other institutions. On the other hand, in most of the funds monitored other experienced limited partners, sometimes even US-based institutions, were present, and therefore we believe that these findings give a fair picture of prevailing market practices.

[5] See Gompers (1995).

track record. Older funds – in the sense of being closer to the end of their contractual lifetime – were monitored less, as were funds performing in line with expectations. The monitoring intensity increased for younger funds and for funds that were in a distressed situation.

Apparently, most of the limited partners' protection from the downside of the fund stemmed solely from contingency clauses that transfer some control to them in case of extremely poorly fund performance, or in case of a key person event. Here the control rights are transferred to the investors, who get to decide how or whether to continue the fund. In the sample analyzed only ten such incidents occurred in the period 2002–2006, and in a third of cases the situation was resolved relatively quickly with the limited partners preferring to keep the old management team and transferring control back to them. This is explained by the fact that it can be both time-consuming and costly to remove the general partner and to find a new one. Furthermore, the old fund management team has gained substantial knowledge about managing the portfolio and thus may be better suited, albeit after restructuring of their incentives, to manage it than a replacement team. Only in very few and problematic cases do limited partners use this option to completely restructure the fund and change, among others, its management team, incentive structure and investment focus. Essentially, limited partners mainly make changes to reduce their exposure, often through canceling commitments and decreasing management fees, to funds that are performing badly, but give more leeway for funds that are considered neither promising nor very problematic.

Box 12.2:   Limited partner real option to abandon or to contract

The possibility for the limited partners to wind up the fund in a situation where the fund is not performing well is an option to abandon or to contract. We found that the most used option was the option to abandon a fund, although this was nearly always before a fund had started its operations and mainly due to difficulties in the fundraising process. Abandoning a fund after it has begun its operations is far from simple and subject to restrictions spelled out in the limited partnership agreement. The so-called 'key person clause' allows limited partners to wind up the fund in a situation where key members of the team have left for any reason and their departure severely impairs the prospects of the fund. This and other 'good leaver' scenarios require, depending on the specific situation, a qualified or simple majority among the limited partners for abandoning a fund.

Theoretically, as Litvak (2004) argues, limited partners also have the option to abandon simply by defaulting, in which case the exercise price of the option is the default penalty that should be weighted against the undrawn commitments that can be saved. The threat of capital withdrawal, Litvak (2004) concluded, is a useful contractual tool to reduce agency costs between investors and low-quality venture capitalists. Although her reasoning appeals to the real options logic, she does not address the intangible costs a default can have on the investors. Indeed, Fleischer (2004) criticized Litvak's paper for ignoring the 'reputational' penalty venture capital investors suffer when they exercise this walk-away right, i.e. not being allowed to invest in other

---

Box 12.2: (Continued)

venture capital funds. In practice, the repercussions of becoming a defaulting investor go beyond the penalties described in the limited partnership agreement. Fleischer (2004) argued that the reputation cost varies depending on the clientele of the fund. Pension funds, university endowments and other repeat players care deeply about their reputations, while some individuals and corporate investors might be indifferent. The private equity market has been described as relying heavily on informal relationships and the reputation of its participants. Repeatedly defaulting damages a limited partner's reputation as a reliable investor and is likely to hamper future attempts to participate in funds that are highly sought after. The negative consequences for investors that aim to stay longer in the relatively informal and close-knit private equity market can by far outweigh the potential savings achieved through defaulting. We found five cases of defaulting limited partners in the study, and in four out of these cases other limited partners defaulted when the fund was doing poorly. In other words, the option to abandon a fund is rarely used by limited partners, at least in the European context and so far never by the investors covered in our study.

12.2.2 Changes related to promising funds

We found that funds that were viewed as extremely promising were left alone with a minimum monitoring level. Limited partners actually made fewer waivers of investment covenants, and increased their exposure less to these funds. It seems like investors take on funds that are performing well – summed up as 'if it works don't touch it'. Alternative explanations could be that promising funds simply do not need to ask for waivers in covenants or that managers of very successful funds have less need to justify their actions as their investors trust them.

Although one would expect that investors try to reduce their exposure to a distressed fund by selling their shares to other investors or third parties on the secondary market, significantly more secondary transactions were done for funds that seemed promising. This option does not seem to be used in order to protect investors from the downside. On the other hand, some limited partners reserved pre-emptive rights to buy shares in secondary transactions and indeed increased their commitments to promising funds this way.

12.2.3 Changes related to problematic funds

We also observed that the option to contract, i.e. to reduce the investment in the fund, was not used more often in problematic situations, as one might have predicted. In fact, many attempts to change the terms and conditions were triggered on the general partners' initiative. Fewer changes in the overall management were found for problematic funds, as compared to the promising and neutral ones. These changes were mainly related to the management teams or their incentives. More specifically, limited partners mostly restricted the fund managers' scope of action for distressed funds, and did not waive covenants that concern the fund's overall management or investment strategy. Fund managers who requested investors to prolong the investment period or the life of distressed funds were turned down more often than others.

12.2.4   Other observations

We found that limited partners granted more waivers of covenants for funds that were neither promising nor particularly problematic, i.e. considered 'neutral'. One explanation is that they found it more worthwhile to try to influence such funds to improve or even become rising stars. Generally, more changes were made for larger funds, especially if they involve a large limited partner commitment. This is not too surprising as it makes more sense economically than trying to put pressure on smaller funds. Apparently, limited partners also did not monitor funds more that had an early stage or high tech industry focus. On the contrary, such funds were monitored less. This could be because most institutional investors have little knowledge about high tech companies and for this type of funds prefer to give managers more liberty.

We observed more changes in terms and conditions of funds that were incorporated in times of growth in the VC market. An interpretation, and in line with arguments brought forward by Gompers and Lerner (1999a), is that an increased demand for venture capital gives fund managers more bargaining power, which they use to reduce the number of covenants in the limited partnership agreements. Subsequently, limited partners may want to remedy this later by making changes. On the other hand, limited partners more frequently monitored funds that were raised when there was less demand for venture capital. One possibility is that investors were particularly wary of the performance of these funds, as the year of incorporation did not look promising compared with others. Another explanation could be that the funds that were raised when the VC market was less 'hot' had less bargaining power then, and investors increased their monitoring to gain as much influence over the fund as possible.

Also, Seeteboun (2006) challenged the common assumption in principal–agent models that the parties' conduct during the operation is derived only from the context of the contract. Her model-based analysis suggested that stronger managers, i.e. those with a better reputation, have a higher probability of making less of an effort. Therefore, investors may try to introduce more restrictive covenants into the partnership agreement, but are also less likely to be successful in their negotiations and have less power to enforce them. Seeteboun (2006) concludes that limited partnership agreements are to some degree inefficient. While its goal is to prevent and resolve conflicts of interest, severe conflicts cannot be addressed. Where the fund managers have the upper hand – which would make a restrictive partnership agreement necessary – investors will be unable to negotiate rigid covenants.

The uncertainty associated with investing in VC funds, and the risk of opportunistic behavior from the general partner, can be major obstacles for investors interested in this asset class. Although the limited partnership agreement, which spells out the terms and conditions of the GP–LP relationship and is the main governance mechanism of the relationship, specifically aims to mitigate some agency problems, it does not address the role of uncertainty sufficiently.

Our results suggest that investors did not try, or were unable, to take advantage of their funds' emerging upside. There are situations where limited partners pay little or nothing for higher flexibility. For example, in exchange for a higher contribution cornerstone investors have more bargaining power, can enjoy more friendly contractual terms and can influence the management of the fund. Cornerstone investments are of relevance in difficult fundraising times or, more generally, among investors in first-time funds. According to Byworth (2005), a common refrain from general partners and placement agents alike is the request for more institutions to participate in the first closing – in the words of one venture capitalist: 'a good first closing moves the herd'. In such situations, limited partners should make use of real option-like covenants in the limited partnership agreement ex ante, as later on general partners are usually not willing to grant their investors this flexibility, particularly as any contractual changes during a fund's lifetime inevitably bring in the other limited partners as well – collective decision-making can be both controversial and subject to delays.[6]

12.3   BRAIDING

Gilson (2003) argues that the VC market uses two contracting nodes – the fund's limited partnership agreement and the portfolio company investment contract. The structures of the two contracts are intertwined, each operating to provide an implicit term that supports the other, and thereby increasing the contractual efficiency of both. This so-called 'braiding' of the two relationships facilitates the resolution of problems internal to each. Gilson saw the braiding to be particularly apparent with respect to the role of exit and of the reputation market (see Table 12.1).

> *It's all too easy to identify the things that might go wrong with an investment [. . .] It's far more difficult to identify what might be possible.*
> Sequoia Capital's Michael Moritz (quoted from *Business Week*, 2003)

Having worked for an institutional investor that has been backing many first-time funds over the years, we have two observations. Quite often such funds confirm conventional wisdom, and it becomes clear after a few years that they are nearly certain to turn out as failures. Due to the typically small fund size, restructurings are usually not a feasible route to take, and limited partners are faced with the question of how to cut losses and to get out of these problem cases without becoming a defaulting investor. However, also a first-time fund often turns out to be far better than expected and then the limited partner regrets not having committed more to it. A limited partner has problems applying the staged financing approach followed by the venture capitalists.

Generally, the staging of investments followed by venture capitalist is interpreted as an option to abandon, but this view is one-sided. Another interpretation would be that a stage-wise approach aims to maximize a venture capitalist's pay-off – ideally one would put all the resources available on the one 'winner' in the portfolio only. In the highly uncertain environment of early stage technology financing it is simply not possible, therefore financing stages are related to events that reveal important information and thereby reduce the uncertainty. By staging their investments venture capitalists can select which portfolio companies to further invest in, as new information about their performance becomes available, thus not only limiting the downside but capturing upside potential as well. In other words, with increasing knowledge on the portfolio companies, fund managers put the scarce resources behind an ever-shrinking list of emerging winners.

This mechanism is not, or at least not efficiently, replicated in the usual limited partnership agreement. This is less of an issue for later stage private equity funds, that as we argued in

---

[6] See Schmidt and Wahrenburg (2003).

Meyer and Mathonet (2005), have characteristics of debt and equity. For example, for buyout funds the limited partnership agreement is more like a loan and thus a reasonably close match with the usual financing modus operandi of leverage through debt. Financing is not staged, and the maturity structure on the portfolio company level is similar to that of the limited partnership agreement. Also, Gompers (1995) argued that staged financing should occur less often for non-high-tech firms because here information asymmetries are not as important as in the case of high-tech firms. As they usually lack the expertise, initially limited partners cannot evaluate the technology risk. Only after some time does a portfolio company's technology risk vanish, and the limited partner only needs to evaluate the business risk, which he is equipped to do.

Table 12.1 Braiding of limited partner – fund manager – entrepreneur contracts (see Gilson, 2003)

	Fund manager entrepreneur	Limited partner general partner	Braiding of contracting modes
Control	Control through monitoring (if not able to act, diminished incentive to monitor)	General partner high level of control; dependence on fund managers' skills and experience to overcome uncertainty and information asymmetry associated with early stage, high technology portfolio companies	Limited control effectively reduces incentive to monitor
Compensation	Option-like compensation; excessive risk-taking requires monitoring	Option-like compensation; excessive risk-taking requires monitoring	Compensation mainly tied to GP selection
Exit	Entrepreneur gets control back if successful	Mandatory liquidation after fixed term	Mandatory distribution of realized investments
Reliance on explicit contract	Reputation market	Reputation market	Need to raise successor fund

However, for VC funds that braiding is incomplete and the resulting mismatch makes the limited partnership structure less efficient than in the case of later stage private equity. Venture capitalists tend to invest or to require follow-on funding for their investee companies when asset prices are low. Assuming that the limited partner invests – as suggested by Kogelman (1999) – undrawn commitments primarily in publicly quoted equity, drawdowns for VC funds could happen when stock markets are down as well. Here the limited partner is likely to be forced to liquidate stock positions under unfavorable conditions.

Let us take a look at the problem of incomplete braiding with a highly simplified example. Under the usual modus operandi a limited partner commits an amount without being able to walk away from this commitment without becoming a defaulting investor. Here we define 'success' as performance in the first or second quartiles and 'failure' as performance in the third or fourth quartiles. For a one-off investment of €100 we could expect that on average

€50 back 'succeeding' and €50 back 'failing' VC funds. How could we improve on this? Assume that we have an option to commit first an amount X to a VC fund and decide at a later point in time whether to continue and invest an additional amount Y or not, with $X + Y = €100$. See Figure 12.1.

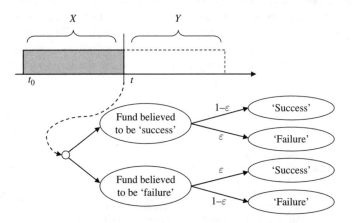

Figure 12.1   Staged investment approach

ε is the probability of error with which a decision-maker at time t gives the wrong prediction for future 'success' or 'failure'. We would expect that over time and with more information on the fund the probability of error should be decreasing. Based on the simplifying assumption that initially investors have just a 50% chance of picking a winner, we take $\varepsilon = 0.5$ at t_0. In this example, we assume that first an amount $X = €50$ is invested and that by t the probability of error has declined to 0.3. See Table 12.2.

Table 12.2   Impact of increased knowledge on potential success or failure

	Expected pay-off	
	'Failure'	'Success'
Fund believed to be 'success'	$\varepsilon \times (X + Y)$	$(1 - \varepsilon) \times (X + Y)$
Fund believed to be 'failure'	$(1 - \varepsilon) \times X$	$\varepsilon \times X$

Figure 12.2 shows the distribution of the results and demonstrates that a higher percentage of funding is backing 'succeeding' VC funds under a staged approach, but the total amount invested declines. Assuming that in half of cases the option to top-up will not be executed, in this example just €75 would be invested on average with a staged approach in total – suggesting a more efficient use of capital.

For a limited partner such a staged financing would be of relevance, particularly on the portfolio of funds level. It is not just about 'rescuing' capital from a likely 'failure', but also being able to allocate it to a better deal, if available. There is clearly a trade-off: the longer a limited partner can observe, the lower the probability of misjudging a fund's prospects,

Expected pay-off for 100 EUR invested

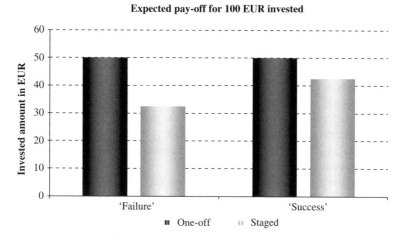

Figure 12.2   Improved pay-off profile through staged approach

but also the amount X, i.e. the price to be paid to wait that long, is becoming higher. The question is, how much time does the limited partner need to significantly reduce his uncertainty? If this takes too long, the real option has little value.

Box 12.3:   Limited partner real option to extend or to expand

Private equity funds have a contractually set limited life, typically 10 years. Yet contractual agreements often offer the possibility to extend the life of the partnership by one or more years. For instance, the life of a partnership can be predetermined as 10 years plus two one-year extensions. This contract feature creates de facto an option to extend for the shared benefit of the general and the limited partners. For instance, let us consider a venture capital fund raised in 1993 with a life limited to 10 years plus two one-year extensions. In 2003, public equity indices were depressed and valuations for venture capital investments low. Without an option to extend the partnership's life, the portfolio would have to be liquidated. Given the difficult environment, portfolio companies would probably be exited with difficulty and at low multiples. However, by exercising the two options to extend the fund's life by one year each, the fund could have been liquidated up to 2005 in a much more favorable environment. The management fee is typically reduced when the life of the fund is prolonged, in order to keep the fund managers focused on the financial performance rather than on the fixed management fee.

Another option to extend as well as to expand is to allow the general partner to re-invest parts of the proceeds in follow-on investments. This can be meaningful in order to keep the fund's share in a company, or to invest more in a promising company, but limited partners retain the right to refuse this in case they find it excessively risky or simply unviable.

Box 12.3:   (Continued)

Investors can increase their exposure to a good fund management team by participating in a follow-on fund. Lerner and Schoar (2002) argued that general partners
screen for investors with long time horizon because it reduces substantially their cost-
of-capital associated with regular fundraising. Likewise, limited partners could already
foresee terms and conditions for re-investment in subsequent funds managed by the
same general partner. Finally, an option to expand is the limited partner's pre-emption
right to buy shares before any third party, in case an investor wants to sell shares of
the fund in a secondary transaction.

Clauses featuring an option to expand one's investment over time would prove
extremely valuable, but limited partnership agreements usually only allow for sub-
optimal solutions.

Certainly for a limited partner such a real option would be the 'financially correct' answer
to deal with a high uncertainty situation and would be, at least in theory, highly valuable:

- It allows the limited partner to observe a fund manager and to monitor how the portfolio
  companies develop.
- In the context of an over-commitment strategy, it allows a limited partner not to execute
  the option if the liquidity is insufficient to honor the resulting increase in capital calls.
  Moreover, it could be used for managing foreign exchange risks as the usual hedging
  products would be too uneconomical for VC funds with their long lifetime and volatile
  cash flow.
- The option for an investment in a next stage could be sold on to another limited partner
  in a better liquidity position.

Also for the VC funds there are advantages, as there could be additional resources to protect
against dilution. Moreover, it could be a mitigant to keep fund managers still interested in
situations where the on-going first fund is quite small and where they would otherwise be
tempted to dedicate more efforts to their second larger fund. While theoretically the limited
partner's case for a stage-wise financing approach may be strong, in practice there are a
number of significant problems that prevent its full-scale application:

- The time period to form an opinion and where a staged approach would have a significant
  impact is quite short for a VC fund, and consequently dramatically reducing the probability
  of error will not be possible.
- Implicitly a real option approach acknowledges that there are different limited partner
  classes, e.g. strong ones in a good negotiation position that come in first and weaker
  limited partners that for example come in the second closing, etc. Different treatments
  may lead to tensions and even disputes between the various limited partners. Generally, it
  will become more difficult to align the interests between all parties – the general partner,
  the limited partner and the other limited partners.
- Finally, limited partners still need to rely on the fund managers' expertise and have to
  show patience. Stage-wise financing by limited partners is likely to lead to interference,

second guessing the fund managers and possibly 'creative' behavior by the fund managers in return.

For any real option there is a 'band' where the existence, or exercising, of the real option becomes detrimental to other critical success factors. For these reasons, stage-wise financing cannot be fully replicated by the limited partners and therefore for VC funds the braiding will remain incomplete with only sub-optimal solutions feasible. This incomplete braiding provides another partial explanation for the occasionally disappointing returns of portfolios of VC funds.

12.4 SUMMARY

To manage uncertainty systematically, limited partners need to develop the ability to respond flexibly to new insights on the funds in their portfolio. When taking a closer look at limited partnership agreements one sees options everywhere. The upside potential arising from uncertainty, and the possibility to learn about the investment and take action after receiving more information, should be taken into account by investors in private equity funds. While many of the real options are of a more indirect nature and impossible to value precisely, investors should not give them up for free: also in this asset class rationality is increasing.

Box 12.4:   Public scheme option to expand

There are also government schemes that essentially offer real options to limited partners. These policy instruments typically aim to promote a fledgling domestic VC industry through compensating investors for taking increased uncertainty through an option to expand. Upside leverage with indirect state support is becoming increasingly widespread in the advanced market economies.[7] This asymmetric risk assumption and uneven distribution of preferences aims at improving the rate of return for private sector investors and making investments in VC funds more attractive to them.

One example where such a scheme was applied is Israel. Kenney *et al.* (2004) considered this the 'most successful case of the export of Silicon Valley-style venture capital practice'. Israel's Yozma program, where the government played an important role in encouraging the growth of venture capital, has received wide attention. Yozma was modeled after the US SBIC scheme and set up by the Israeli government in 1993 to create the infrastructure for a domestic venture capital market. Gilson (2003) believed that, compared with public VC programs elsewhere in the world, Yozma came *'closer to getting the incentive structure right'*.

Yozma received $100 million of public funding to attract private funds for over $150 million. It invested $8 million in each of ten funds that were all required to raise another $10 million to $12 million from 'a significant foreign partner', presumably

---

[7] See Karsai (2004).

Box 12.4: (Continued)

an overseas venture capital firm. The scheme provided a buyout option for these private sector participants, thereby rewarding high investment performance. The private investors had a call option on Yozma's investment at cost plus (i) a nominal interest rate and (ii) 7% of the future profits from portfolio company investments in which the fund was then invested. The return that the government could enjoy from these funds was capped, with the remainder flowing to the private investors.

Yozma also retained $20 million to invest itself. The involvement of overseas venture capitalists is an interesting policy avenue as it may have removed the perception of government interference. Moreover, the scheme provided no guarantee against losses, and, unlike other programs, private investors and the fund's managers bore their share of the downside risk. Yozma did not get involved in selecting the portfolio companies but left this task exclusively to the fund managers who bore the investment's risk and return. While investments in funds were passive, those funds' managers and other investors were highly incentivized. Gilson (2003) identifies this as a critical aspect of the structure, as it tracked the US pattern of interposing a highly incentivized intermediary between passive investors and the portfolio company.

Yozma's performance was consistent with this more highly incentivized investment structure. The program helped to create ten private VC firms and is credited for jump-starting a vibrant VC market. Yozma is interesting because its structure served to leverage the returns, and therefore the incentives, of the intermediary instead of dampening them. It consequently also increased the investors' incentive to monitor the portfolio companies carefully. Certainly other factors – for example that Yozma's activities fell into the technology hype period – contributed to the Israeli success, and it is questionable whether comparable structures can yield such quick results elsewhere. Nevertheless, the main features of the program – namely the alignment of interests and involving foreign investors, thus creating 'knowledge spillovers' building on international best practices while mitigating political influence on investment selection – make this structure a blue print for government intervention in this sector.

In the face of the huge uncertainty that is characteristic particularly of VC funds, real options would be highly valuable. Here limited partners should always try to negotiate clauses in the limited partnership agreement that aim to take advantage of the steep learning curve occurring throughout the fund's life. An example for a simple real option would be the right to invest in follow-on funds under pre-determined conditions, such as a minimum 'ticket size' or percentage share.

In fact, introducing real option thinking makes things less rigid. The possibility to move downhill, to make mistakes, and to learn from the mistakes made, the possibility to observe factors that are not a part of the firm's own production recipe, but are nevertheless known, at least partly by the firm, the possibility to utilize the options created in the process of the past search, it all gives a firm a chance to move towards further oriented, but likely superior positions on the technology landscape with more ease than prescribed in the literature.

Hovhannisian (2001)

There is also a psychological advantage for institutional investors as such predetermined clauses make reaction to new situations easier to implement. Likewise, fund managers are likely to feel less exposed if limited partners execute such an option. If faced with otherwise identical investment proposals – we take a VC fund's expected performance grade as proxy for its NPV – limited partners should give preference to the one that offers the higher flexibility and carries the highest level of uncertainty.

Finally, for private equity funds, real option-like clauses are not easy to manage. To some degree limited partners need to understand the quality of the portfolio companies as well as the fund managers – in other words, a skill set comparable to that of a venture capitalist is required to take full advantage of this flexibility. Moreover, this could lead to detrimental selection effects. Assume that a 'strong' investor manages to get his 'uncertainty' taking compensated by concessions in the form of real options. This clearly carries the danger that usually strict selection standards slip. Instead, these standards should be upheld and only uncertainty regarding the market should be taken. In the following chapters we take a closer look at some real options available to limited partners: co-investments and side funds.

13
Co-investing

For institutions the most relevant approaches to investing in private equity are through fund-of-funds specialists as intermediaries or through similarly structured dedicated in-house private equity investment programs. Usually institutions seek intermediation through the limited partnership structure (see Figure 13.1, scenario A) as few have the experience and especially the incentive structures that would allow them to invest directly in unquoted companies (see Figure 13.1, scenario B). A special case is a co-investment strategy, where a limited partner invests directly into a company that is backed by the private equity funds where they participate (see Figure 13.1, scenario C).[1] Some limited partners generally ask for co-investment opportunities or even rights, but co-investing is not an identical process to fund investing.

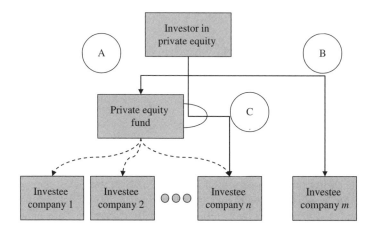

Figure 13.1 Relevant approaches to investing in private equity

Co-investment is the syndication of a financing round between a private equity fund and one or more of its limited partners. Theoretically, this brings complementary capabilities together where funds lacking the financial resources team up with limited partners that usually lack knowledge of technologies and sectors and do not have the industry-specific network.

---

[1] There is little published research on co-investment strategies available. This analysis relies mainly on interviews conducted by the authors and on investor interviews published by AltAssets over a period of five years (see References).

[M]any of the more sophisticated LPs in VC funds will now demand co-investment rights [. . .] This, clearly, deepens the VC's relationship with any such LP and illustrates the web of financial relationships that an entrepreneur enters when dealing with the VC industry.

Pearce and Barnes (2006)

The main difference to direct investing is how it is sourced. Opportunities are generally deals a fund manager has pre-screened, structured, priced and is expected to invest in. Moreover, the fund is generally organizing the co-investment for the limited partner, who needs a significant number of primary fund commitments to generate a meaningful co-investment deal flow.

13.1   MOTIVATION

Limited partners view co-investments primarily as a way of enhancing their overall returns as they do not have to pay a management fee or carried interest on their investment in the private company. The private equity market environment has a strong influence on the types and industries co-investment opportunities stem from. Co-investment opportunities emerge especially in periods where deal flow for larger investments is good but fundraising is difficult. In this situation, and also when funds do not wish to be over-exposed to one particularly large deal, they are likely to turn to their limited partners and propose a co-investment.

Periods of rapid growth of fund sizes – such as in the late 1990s – allow fund managers to finance particularly good deals themselves. Such periods often also result in less favorable terms and conditions for their investors, and as a consequence limited partners become more sensitive to the growth in fees and thus increasingly interested in co-investing.

13.1.1   Relevance

13.1.1.1   Later stage investments

At first glance co-investing appears to be relevant mainly for later stage private equity funds. Indeed, for large-scale investments the limited partners' savings can be considerable. FAZ (2006) reported that for the €11 billion buyout fund Permira IV a number of limited partners with co-investment agreements were interested in matching Permira's investment. For Permira such additional capacity increased its 'bite size' to make large-scale deals, as under industry standard terms and conditions it otherwise could not put more than 10% of fund size or €1.1 billion into one single investment. The large buyout funds Bain Capital LLC and Blackstone Group have even been raising co-investment funds in tandem with their funds.[2] Tracy (2006) presumed that they tried to further their fund sizes without alarming their limited partners, who want to keep the mammoth funds being raised somehow in check.

---

[2] Bain Capital structured previous co-investment programs as separate funds of approximately a quarter of the main fund's size. For the co-investment fund they charged 20% carried interest and annual management fees on dollars invested not committed (see Bushrod, 2004). For some of their funds Bain Capital did not require that investors to the co-investment fund were also committed to the main fund. The term 'co-investment fund' may be slightly misleading as it followed investments in main fund and did not require investor involvement. In other words, it could be seen as just a price discrimination tool.

13.1.1.2   Early stage investments

Nevertheless, the impression that co-investments are only a buyout phenomenon is mistaken. Although opportunities are likely to be more in later stage transactions than those in early stage, co-investment strategies are not restricted to mature companies. In fact, limited partners pursue this activity across the range of stages including start-ups, although some voice reluctance to co-invest in deals outside their area of expertise.[3] To some degree, co-investments may even be of higher relevance for smaller private equity funds. Such funds see many deals that they consider to be attractive, but often lack the capital to pursue these opportunities up to the exit and, therefore, would get diluted. Here limited partners can use co-investments as a tool to assist the fund managers in the execution of transactions. Smaller funds are reported to offer good proposals to their limited partners, whereas larger funds have enough money to do almost any deal they wish without offering co-investments.

13.1.1.3   Specialist players

Funds-of-funds often leverage their co-investment capabilities and offer dedicated co-investment funds on a customized, as well as a co-mingled basis for investors.[4] There are also specialized independently managed co-investment funds.

Box 13.1:   Specialized co-investment funds

One example for a specialized independently managed co-investment fund is Parallel Ventures Managers (formerly affiliated to AXA) that focuses on private equity funds in Europe and claims to have a unique deal-capturing mechanism built on 10-year contractual co-investment agreements with a number of European buyout managers.[5]

Another player following a comparable approach is Glenalta Capital that provides private equity co-investment origination and execution services. This team comprises former senior investment professionals of GE Equity Europe who established and developed GE Equity's European private equity co-investment program between 1995 and 2002.[6]

13.1.2   Co-investment approach

There is no set model for co-investments. According to Bushrod (2004), most co-investment arrangements are informal, rarely written down and not included as part of the fund documentation. The technical term 'promote' is used to encompass both carried interest and

---

[3] For example, Wim Borgdorff, NIB Capital (AltAssets, 2002b,c) excluded co-investments in emerging markets.
[4] See for example http://www.fortwashington.com/privateequity/directcoinvestments.asp [accessed 9 October 2006].
[5] See www.parallelprivateequity.com [accessed 9 October 2006]. According to Hutchings (2002), Parallel Ventures Managers had generated a gross return of 51% p.a. or its investors. In addition to the investment from its own staff, the firm has just four investors in its funds. Between 1998 and 2002 Parallel Ventures Managers invested €1.1 billion and in each of these past years the annual returns had beaten the firm's target of 20%, net of fees of 2%.
[6] See http://www.glenalta.com/. [accessed 9 October 2006].

annual management fees on co-investments.[7] However, generally fund managers charge little or no fees for access to co-investment opportunities and claim no carried interest but just transaction fees without set-off.[8] To be able to go this 'no fee, no carried interest' route the limited partner needs to be, as Young and Meek (2001) point out, an existing investor in the private equity firm it invests alongside and have a good relationship with it and/or be able to offer expertise in a particular field. Most industry practitioners believe that such rights should be a value-added offered by the fund manager to the limited partners to maintain a good long-term relationship.

13.1.2.1 Expected advantages

The lead-investing general partner should have a strong and relevant track record in the dimensions relevant for the portfolio company's success: geographic, industry and sector focus, transaction type and size and value creation strategy. In addition to avoiding the double layer of management fees and the access to transactions of top-tier private equity firms, co-investing potentially offers the limited partner a number of additional advantages.

- **Targeted investment tool:** commitments to private equity funds are a relatively 'blunt' allocation tool. Moreover, funds regularly experience so-called 'style drifts' over their lifetime. Co-investments allow building up a targeted allocation to specific investments.
- **Better management of portfolio diversification:** co-investments can enhance the return profile of a fund investment program and can mitigate its over-diversification or over-exposure. Co-investments provide flexibility to capitalize on industry-specific and country-specific opportunities as they arise. They may also be an answer to side-fund issues, where funds experience liquidity problems, or can be a meaningful strategy with a first-time team, as a tool to assist the fund managers in the execution of transactions.
- **Dual level of review for investments:** the institutional investor can leave the difficult work of deal sourcing and assessment to the experienced industry experts. Even if limited partners still need to do some due diligence, they can save significant time as the main part of the screening is happening through the fund managers and also the time-consuming monitoring is left to a large degree to them.
- **Improved monitoring:** the development of a co-investment activity gives, as an indirect benefit, an improved monitoring of the funds and a further reduction of the information asymmetry between fund managers and their investors. It can help staff to better understand the investment processes and environment, allowing better fund selections and re-investment decisions. The information co-investors receive is quite important because it gives an idea about how the fund managers operate and often goes beyond the standard reporting the limited partners usually receive.
- **Establishing relationships to 'invitation-only' funds:** according to Kreutzer (2006), for limited partners that face problems getting access to top funds co-investments form an important part of a strategy that helps to 'land slots in a handful of sought-after funds'.

---

[7] HarbourVest's George Anson stated in Bushrod (2004) that one out of ten deals they saw had some sort of promote. Their policy was never to pay fees up-front and to require a back-end share profit such as 2.5 times capital plus a 15% IRR before the fund manager can have promote.
[8] Also funds-of-funds often do not charge carried interest or a special fee for co-investments, although there are exceptions. For example, Standard Life or HarbourVest are reported to take carried interest on co-investments (see Young and Meek, 2001).

Moreover, the limited partner can benefit from the investment skills of those top funds even if not yet invested in them.

In any case, experience suggests that the interest in such transactions has to be regularly communicated and when actively working with fund managers they will come with opportunities.[9]

13.1.2.2   Scaling

Portfolio strategies typically include a reserve of between 10% and 20% to be allocated to co-investments. One example for a limited partnership agreement stipulates that no less than 50% can be invested in funds and no more than 50% in co-investments. 'We have, however, found that a 65 per cent fund investments and a 35 per cent co-investments split is more realistic.'[10] Other institutions do not appear to have a specific allocation and tend to do co-investments on an opportunistic basis.

Also for a portfolio of directly held investee companies diversification by vintage years, geography, industry, etc. is important. Consequently, a private equity investment program requires a critical mass for being able to pursue co-investments. There is clearly a 'sweet spot' for the sizing of co-investments:

- The general partner has to keep a meaningful stake in a co-investment to give the co-investing limited partners confidence that an adequate amount of time and energy is spent on the transaction going forward. Essentially, if the limited partners' stake in a portfolio company is getting too high, the incentives for the fund managers might become diluted.
- To some degree the success of a co-investment strategy also depends on the other limited partners with similar co-investment rights, as there is usually no exclusivity for the allocation of deals. If another limited partner is strong in direct investments, it could theoretically become problematic to make use of co-investment opportunities.

For smaller limited partners the fact that a – occasionally too high – minimum amount is required for co-investments can cause problems. In such situations, the opportunity may have to be passed on because the amount co-invested would sometimes almost match the amount that this small institution originally committed to a fund. One way of overcoming this is to approach other investors and do the co-investment alongside them.

13.2   CO-INVESTMENT RISK AND REWARDS

For their risk and reward profile co-investments are between a direct investment and a normal partnership. One co-investment is more risky than investing in a private equity partnership with a downside comparable to those of direct investments – while in a fund's portfolio a failed investment can go under, also co-investments result in more losers – and require significant staff time and legal expenses. It is definitely not a panacea for higher returns in the asset class and, in fact, is often seen as quite difficult to execute. Co-investing is

---

[9] See Jens Bisgaard-Frantzen, ATP Private Equity Managers (AltAssets, 2002b) or Bushrod (2004).

[10] See Giuseppe Campanella, Mediolanum State Street (AltAssets, 2003a).

clearly not for the risk-averse or inexperienced private equity investor. However, a number of institutional investors see this as a key element of their investment strategy.

Institutions that are new to the asset class would do well to steer clear of co-investments – even some of the more established players struggle with them, unsure whether to manage them as limited partnership investments or direct investments.

Young and Meek (2001)

Co-investing theoretically provides maximization of the fund investment's upside as it allows increasing the exposure to the best-performing portfolio companies. For investments in small funds a co-investment also improves the downside protection as it mitigates the dilution of the fund's shareholding when available resources are insufficient for follow-on investing.[11]

13.2.1 Limited partner perspective

Because a limited partner builds up additional exposure to certain companies, industries or geographies, risks can increase very specifically with regard to individual portfolio companies. If too few co-investments are undertaken, there is also the danger of holding an under-diversified portfolio of directly held investments.

Co-investing requires a different skill set than fund investing as institutions need to have a much greater insight into individual deals. If they are unable to form a view on individual investments they can only save management fees and carried interest but will not be able to significantly improve the return profile of their portfolio of funds. In cases of substantial co-investments limited partners often only participate on the condition of gaining either a full board representation or an observer status, depending on the situation. It should be considered that when investment decisions are taken outside a formal partnership structure there is exposure to fiduciary risk. If things go wrong at the investment level, limited partners may be exposed to legal and public relations liabilities.[12]

While the ultimate investments in the fund are unknown at the time of commitment to a private equity fund, for co-investments the limited partner is not faced with a 'blind pool' anymore and has an opportunity to assess the strength of the individual company. Limited partners can target more mature companies under less uncertainty with a proven upside potential and thus amplify a well-performing fund's overall returns.

It is said that fund managers seek limited partners who undertake co-investments as such investors are seen as being able to assist in future investments. Particularly in situations where a portfolio company or a prospective investment is too large for a private equity fund to invest in on its own accord, additional resources from deep-pocket limited partners can make a difference. Allegedly, often limited partners willing to co-invest are even preferred by the general partners when funds are over-subscribed.

---

[11] As selling portfolio companies to other private equity funds is increasingly becoming an alternative exit route, such transactions may even take place within a limited partner's portfolio of funds. Here it can be meaningful for the limited partner to keep a stake in a portfolio company to avoid paying premiums and multiple transaction costs. Co-investment rights can also be sold off to other funds in the limited partner's portfolio.

[12] See Sweeney and Taylor (2002).

13.2.2 Fund manager perspective

From the viewpoint of a fund manager, co-investing limited partners offer some degree of downside protection. Particularly for small funds it avoids dilution of their shareholding when they cannot follow on. This may increase their expected carry and also sometimes management fees, which could prove helpful for making them viable. Co-investing limited partners can be less problematic than syndicating with other venture capitalists as there is less potential for conflict over who leads the deal. Co-investments can be seen as a way of increasing a fund's capital under management and thus its likelihood to deliver a high performance, therefore, facilitating the firm establishment of teams and the follow-on raising of a larger fund. But for a fund manager co-investments can also come at a risk. If disputes over an investment arise, it can affect the relationship with the limited partner and negatively affect future fundraisings.

Another factor is that fund managers and the other non-co-investing limited partners limit their upside. Therefore, established teams that have an investment strategy supporting a stronger deal flow tend to simply raise larger funds and not further pursue co-investments.

13.2.3 Experiences with co-investment programs

A well-designed co-investment strategy can add considerable benefit to a private equity investment program, but there is less transparency and little performance data available on this type of investment. According to Young and Meek (2001), none of the usual private equity research providers, such as EVCA, conduct analysis of co-investment performance. Consequently, opinions are quite mixed. Some investors are enthusiastic and report that on 'average, we have had significantly better returns on co-investments than fund investments, but that is because we have been involved in very good ones',[13] while other institutions experienced 'very poor' results and do not co-invest any longer.[14]

13.3 POTENTIAL ISSUES RELATED TO CO-INVESTMENTS

A number of institutional investors remain skeptical. One criticism is that a properly set up co-investment program can lead to a fully fledged direct investment team that can then essentially start to compete with the funds to which the limited partner is committing.

13.3.1 Second-guessing fund managers

Institutions feel that they would rather back the best teams than compete with them and that the people in their own organization have the necessary time or skills to invest directly in companies. Some practitioners see co-investments as more appropriate on the larger buyouts where there is scope for passive co-investors. Adding value and making a meaningful impact on an early stage company and helping it develop is not an activity large institutional investors feel best suited to and comfortable with. Second-guessing experienced venture capitalists at the direct investment stage can be problematic. Should a VC fund have a position left in a round of financing, they may be better off getting in other experienced

---

[13] See Hans van Swaay, Pictet & Cie (AltAssets, 2003a).
[14] See Peter Hielscher, Gerling Insurance (AltAssets, 2003a).

venture capitalists or strategic investors. Such syndication of investments between funds may increase the chances of success and is seen as an alternative to co-investments and a way of creating better returns overall. This view boils down to 'the limited partner's skill set is in selecting funds and direct investments or co-investments should be the fund managers'job'.

13.3.2 Cherry-picking

Critics of co-investing argue that private equity firms are likely to cherry-pick which deals they send out to institutions. The suspicion is, to quote one industry insider, that 'if the investment prospect they were bringing to you was so great, then they would find a way to put more money into it themselves'. In several respects the co-investment opportunities may not represent the best deals, for example the ones that the fund managers view as being more risky.

In the extreme, fund managers may look for co-investors just to offload marginal or even under-performing investments from their portfolio. However, such a strategy is likely to backfire, as limited partners that got their fingers burned this way would most probably not commit to the private equity firm's next fund. Therefore it is not surprising that Hans van Swaay from Pictet & Cie reported on a different experience: 'Good buy-out funds, when they allow you to co-invest, will offer you some great opportunities. It's the theory that if you're inviting someone round for dinner, you make your favourite dish, you don't experiment on your guests.'[15]

Varying opinions and experiences on the subject of cherry-picking may to some degree be explained by the individual limited partner's characteristics. Small investors tend not to see that many opportunities, and those they do see may not be of the best quality.[16] Fund managers appear to prefer to put their best deals in front of their largest investors. This makes sense, particularly for larger deals that a fund would be unable to finance alone. Moreover, according to Friedman (2005), it is acceptable to present co-investment opportunities exclusively to certain parties that provide some strategic importance to the fund or the portfolio company.

It is critical that a co-investment is undertaken on the same terms for all investors, so that fund managers cannot structure the deal to benefit themselves and disadvantage the co-investing limited partners. Limited partners have to be vigilant and monitor the fund managers. When pursuing a co-investment strategy it is necessary that the co-investing limited partner reviews opportunities on a case-by-case basis and does an own due diligence. Selectivity is key, and co-investments should only be pursued if there is a clearly identified potential to outperform the overall portfolio.

13.3.3 Conflicts of interest

Grabenwarter and Weidig (2005) see in co-investment rights a source for conflicts of interest with fellow limited partners. Co-investing limited partners are likely to give preference to their specific investments even if this is detrimental to the entire fund's performance.[17] Also,

---

[15] Quoted from AltAssets (2003a).

[16] See Daniel Keller, LUMA Capital (AltAssets, 2003a).

[17] Another aspect is problems associated with failing co-investments. One fund manager reported one case where it became a 'very complicated situation' when one company with several co-investing limited partners went bankrupt and led to disagreements between the parties involved.

the fund managers may be inclined to spend more time on particular portfolio companies if they receive additional management fees, carried interest, or if the co-investing limited partner is of 'strategic importance' for them.

There is a wide consensus that investors should focus solely on committing to the very best funds, but could be a tendency toward investing in funds that might give co-investment rights. In situations where limited partners are inclined to commit to a fund simply to gain co-investment rights, another source for conflict of interest is perceived.[18] However, this does not imply that limited partners could not be compensated through co-investment rights for a higher perceived risk.

13.4   IMPLEMENTATION ISSUES

Although at first glance it appears to be highly attractive not to pay fees or carried interest on one's co-investments, institutions should not be mistaken in assuming that this is a free lunch. In fact, to seriously pursue this activity they need a dedicated team and are therefore likely to incur significant expenses.

13.4.1   Speed of execution

Funding for co-investments can be seen as 'stand-by money' being able to do larger deals, and is usually required at short notice. Consequently, the efficient execution of the process is critical. The due diligence and decision has to be quick – rather a matter of days than the drawn-out process for primary fund investments – according to Young and Meek (2001), for the due diligence three days is the average.

> *Say a guy in mid-west America gets a call saying, 'We've got a deal, the paperwork's all in Dusseldorf, and you have to do your diligence, and commit 21 days from now.'*
>
> Jonny Maxwell from Standard Life Investments (see AltAssets, 2002a)

In an interview conducted by the authors, an anonymous fund manager complained that actually very few limited partners exercised their co-investment rights. Although deals are regularly presented to these institutions, they usually do not react. It appeared to the fund manager that these limited partners changed their policies and lost interest in this strategy. While he believed that an inner circle of limited partners, particularly those with an industry network, could be of great value, for the typical corporate, pension fund or insurance institution the reaction time is too long. Even if they want they usually cannot deliver, as their co-investments do not form part of a systematic strategy but are rather of an ad-hoc nature. Even if larger institutional investors have the financial resources to co-invest, execution can be difficult in practice because of the control procedures that their organizations put in place.

To provide comfort to fund managers regarding the capability to deliver, institutions that seriously pursue a co-investment strategy require an adequately staffed team dedicated to such opportunities, with industry sector knowledge and the capability to conduct a due diligence quickly.

---

[18] According to Young and Meek (2001), funds-of-funds with co-investment activities have a conflict of interest issue, too. Because of the increased share in the carried interest they can find co-investments more lucrative than the investments in funds. This is seen as less of an issue if the fund-of-funds offers a separate co-investment vehicle.

13.4.2   Team set-up

Co-investments could be seen as a hybrid between investing directly in private companies and investing in private equity funds. Whether they are closer to direct or fund investing is debatable. Some argue that the skills and time needed to do co-investments are not so different from those required for fund investments, and that direct investment activities are often the result of the knowledge gained investing through and alongside limited partnerships. Often it is the same people making fund and co-investments. But they are generally not experts in direct investing and basically passively use the due diligence done by the fund manager who originated the deal and make the investment decision on that basis.

13.4.2.1   Investment process

The investment process for co-investments is more or less identical to that usually followed by venture capitalists. Co-investing limited partners need to be involved in every step rather than entering it at a late stage after all the negotiations have happened. They have to complete an extensive due diligence, ideally independently from the sponsoring fund manager. This includes, for example, meetings with management, detailed financial projections, market and industry analysis, and a review of the legal, accounting and regulatory issues. After closing the deal, the co-investments have to be actively monitored on an ongoing basis including, when appropriate, representation on the board of directors. Being closely involved with portfolio companies, often even replacing management, requires the right culture and approach. Writing off an individual investment is very different from being invested into a fund's diversified portfolio. Many institutions are ill-equipped to do that and, unless they are willing to put the right structures in place, should rather stay out of co-investing.

The majority of practioners believe piggy-backing on the fund managers is insufficient and that co-investments require direct investment skills and experience, as deals are arguably less standardized and structured differently than limited partnership agreements.[19] This combination with a more hands-on monitoring can be a very time-intensive activity that has to be supported by a much higher staffing level. Knowledge of the business that is being looked at is crucial. Without people who have done a deal themselves before, institutions have to rely on the managers of the funds where they are limited partners, which will not always be desirable. Finally, in situations where funds become distressed, the limited partners will have to be able to generate profitable exits independently from the fund managers.

13.4.2.2   Required skill-set

Having a pool of professionals with the skills to make direct and co-investments in portfolio companies mitigates this dependency and the associated risks. Selecting fund managers who will build a portfolio of investments is a very different business from making a single large 'bet' alongside them and trying to add value to underlying portfolio companies.

We came to the conclusion that you cannot make fund and direct investments successfully with a small team.

Peter Hielscher from Gerling Insurance (see AltAssets, 2003a)

---

[19] That is for example negotiating tag and drag along rights, voting arrangements or rights of first refusal.

Consequently, there is a consensus that a successful co-investment program requires a dedicated and independent team with direct investment experience. Fund investments and co-investments should be kept separately with resources dedicated to each area. Sometimes institutions even set up an own co-investment fund. Such a set-up allows the institutions to be pro-active, respond much more quickly to a call from a fund manager, and avoid conflicts of interests between the two activities.

13.4.2.3   Incentive structures

Hiring people with this kind of background is usually not easy and requires the right incentive structures, for example being able to take a slice of the deal or to receive carried interest. However, there is the danger that such experts will not stick around for too long. According to the Chairman and Chief Executive of Parallel Ventures (see below), Paul Whitney, the 'difficulty with this is that people with direct investment experience are not going to stay in-house because they can earn far more money elsewhere'.[20]

13.5   PORTFOLIO MANAGEMENT

Co-investing is potentially a powerful portfolio management tool that, for example, gives the limited partner implicitly an option to keep on holding portfolio companies even if the fund itself has already been fully liquidated.

13.5.1   Managing portfolio composition

If a limited partner follows the policy to co-invest only in portfolio companies that are profitable already or would reach profitability soon, this would mitigate the exposure to cash-burning start-ups. Also it may be difficult, for example, to find funds that specifically target, say, 'eco-innovation', but it is very likely that a number of funds have one or another company from this sector in their portfolio. Co-investing allows the limited partner to fill such target allocations in his portfolio. In the context of a private equity investment program co-investments often form part of a limited partner's over-commitment strategy, as they allow capital to be put quickly to work, do not imply an obligation to answer to a capital call and thus allow adjustments in the overall commitment level.

In situations where side funds would be a possible solution to support a portfolio of still promising investee companies, but where the fund manager is perceived to be weak or problematic in the widest sense, co-investments can be a meaningful step toward decoupling good portfolio companies from the fund's lifetime restrictions and gradually increasing the limited partner's control over the portfolio. A limited partner that had negotiated strong co-investment rights can cherry-pick even if the entire portfolio does not do well.

Apparently most institutions would not pursue investments in private equity funds with the objective of securing co-investment opportunities. For example, Ivan Vercoutere from LGT Capital Partners stated that they would 'only co-invest if there are the right opportunities available and we will only do it alongside top quartile fund managers'.[21] Intuitively it makes sense to require that every fund investment as well as every co-investment has to stand on

---

[20] Quoted from Young and Meek (2001).
[21] Quoted from AltAssets (2001).

its own two feet and limited partners are certainly well advised to base their decision on whether to proceed with a co-investment also on their trust in, and the relationship with, the private equity firm.

An institution should clearly not invest in a fund because it is able to offer co-investment opportunities when there is a better fund in the market that does not offer co-investment opportunities. However, when pursuing niche activities, e.g. investments in first-time funds, a limited partner is often able to negotiate a preferential relationship with fund managers. The option to co-invest can be a meaningful compensation for the value-added brought by the limited partner.

13.5.2   Link to other strategies

13.5.2.1   Creating relationships

There can be synergies between an institution's fund investment side and the co-investment arm. Co-investments could be seen as more than just financial investments. The knowledge gained from the co-investment activity allows the limited partner to have a closer relationship and exchange of information with the fund management teams they back, and to become a more valuable investor that goes beyond simply providing capital. Therefore, some limited partners even prefer to do a large number of smaller co-investments.[22] The closer relationship also allows the limited partner to assess far more clearly whether or not to invest in future funds that a private equity firm raises.

Experience gained from screening and doing such deals can reduce the information asymmetry between general and limited partners and lead to improvements in the limited partner's selection capability, especially in the case of secondary transactions, where direct investment skills can be important. Essentially, such an investment strategy comprises the selection of high-quality fund managers for a defined investment strategy combined with purchasing fund interests in the secondary market. Around that core of commitments the portfolio of co-investments is built.

13.5.2.2   Link to secondary activities

Doing secondary transactions into exceptional funds that had already closed has similarities with co-investments. Both involve close contact with, and cooperation of, the general partner, as they rely on the general partner's consent to get access to crucial proprietary portfolio company information. Secondaries are predominantly initiated by a limited partner, but for co-investments the impulse is generally given by the general partner.

> *Part of our strategy on the secondaries side is to leverage off the other two parts of our business. We use our fund of funds knowledge and expertise to do a top down analysis of the portfolios that we are looking at. We also leverage the co-investment area to look at the specific portfolio companies that we are considering acquiring.*
>
> David Andryc and Steve Wesson, Auda Group (see AltAssets, 2002b)

While co-investments take place for single assets, secondaries relate to a portfolio of assets. In both situations, the investment is not into a 'blind pool' like in the case of

---

[22] See Giuseppe Campanella, State Street Global Investments (AltAssets, 2006a).

primary investing but into known companies with earlier positive cash flows. An important difference is that secondary fund investments are self-liquidating while co-investments are not necessarily so.

13.5.3   Leveraging international network

To some degree an institution's portfolio of private equity funds could be seen as a network. Indeed, some investors interpret their portfolio as 'an anchor to international strategy'[23] that allows them to break into foreign private equity markets through its co-investment opportunities. Some limited partners also perceive a potential to add value to the funds, for example through tapping into their trans-Atlantic network.[24]

Likewise there can be a situation where private equity funds find deals that would be too small or too early for them, but may be an interesting opportunity to one of their smaller limited partners. This, however, requires that the limited partner has a full direct investment capability, i.e. being able to conduct a full due diligence, deal structuring, follow-up monitoring, etc. and, most of all, exiting the deal. Occasionally limited partners feel that co-investment proposals could be better executed in association with one of their other private equity relationships. They can make referrals to these managers, thus helping them with deal origination. For example, AlpInvest is pursuing such 'reversed co-investment initiatives'. If opportunities fall outside their investment strategy, AlpInvest seeks out an appropriate general partner to take on the lead-investor role and assumes a co-investor position.[25]

13.6   CONCLUSION

Co-investments cover a wide range. On one side limited partners follow a passive and nearly automatic approach and entirely rely on the fund managers. The other extreme are limited partners who operate nearly like a direct investor and where co-investments could be better described as syndication. Limited partners need to ensure that co-investment agreements entered into by funds are governed by full disclosure and transparency, and that equal access to co-investment is proposed to all investors. For practical reasons this may be qualified by inviting only substantial investors.

Opinions on co-investments are divided, and there are many who doubt that limited partners can properly implement such a strategy. Such concerns are clearly justified, but on the other hand a co-investing limited partner is in principle in no worse position than another venture capital firm that invests in later rounds. Moreover, the limited partner can – as discussed here – be in a privileged negotiation position and has potentially access to a strong and internationally diversified deal-flow. The caveat is that co-investments are not simple, and to do them successfully one has to follow a modus operandi that bears only marginal differences compared to that of a VC firm.

Even if not co-investing, limited partners need to ensure that all investors are informed who is co-investing directly into investee companies. Also, arrangements must ensure that funds are not subsidizing the co-investor and that co-investors bear their share of expenses. Lastly, co-investment arrangements must not be detrimental to a fund's own investment rights.

---

[23] See Pierre Fortier, Caisse de dépôt et placement du Québec (AltAssets, 2006a).
[24] See Marc der Kinderen, 747 Capital (AltAssets, 2003a).
[25] See http://www.alpinvest.com/investment_activities/co-investments/investment_strategy.htm [accessed 9 October 2006].

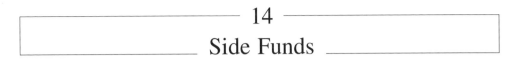

14

Side Funds

Co-written with Gauthier Monjanel

The average life of an LBO fund is about 10 years. How can the LBO fund of funds charge a 2% annual fixed fee and 10% of the profits for the one-time selection process and then do nothing but just sit on the board of their portfolio companies? What a sinecure! What a business!

Biggs (2006)

Following the burst of the Internet bubble, side funds – or similar structures – became quite popular as one solution to provide additional funding to VC funds faced with a difficult exit environment, which had forced them to support their still cash-burning investee companies over a longer than expected period. Moreover, the slowdown of the general economic growth had a negative impact on the revenue growth of most of them, further increasing their cash burn rates and postponing their cash break-even point.

In this chapter, we describe the different types of side funds and similar structures that we have come across in recent years and analyze their pros and cons and the specific context in which they were created. In many ways, side funds are largely improvised responses to specific problems and therefore, admittedly, we can only present a few cases without claiming completeness.

14.1 'CLASSICAL' SIDE FUNDS

Side funds (or annex funds or top-up funds) (see Figure 14.1) are investment vehicles designed to increase the follow-on investment capabilities of an original private equity fund with whom the side fund will invest in parallel. Generally, side funds are launched some years after the creation of the original fund and are managed by the same fund manager but often under different terms and conditions. Investors joining a side fund are normally the original fund's limited partners but can also be new ones. However, though the mechanism is apparently straightforward, there is no pre-defined structure and the motivation to establish a side fund can differ depending on the circumstances. The only common characteristic is that the investee companies of side funds will always be a part of the portfolio of the original funds, as described below.

14.1.1 'Raison d'être'

A side fund is said to be in most cases linked to higher than planned cash needs of the investee companies, a wrong assessment of the market conditions, a failed investment strategy or

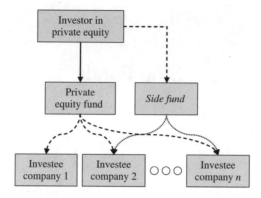

Figure 14.1   Side fund

its flawed implementation. The side funds we have come across were established with the following objectives:

- To secure and further support the development of some investee companies with a real opportunity to become commercially successful.
- To enable the restructuring of companies that would otherwise have to be completely written off, with a view to selling the participation at cost or at slightly better conditions.
- To complement the investment capacity of a fund which, facing a higher than expected deal flow or an increase in the size of the targeted companies, has not sufficient resources to establish a sufficiently diversified portfolio.

In addition to that, when a general partner is not able to raise a follow-on fund, a side fund can be used to prolong the investment period of the current fund and, as a (from the fund managers' point of view) welcome consequence, also the management fees of the original fund. In such case, the side fund mostly serves the interest of the general partner rather than that of the limited partners. Here, side funds could be seen as a temporary solution to fundraise 'through the back door'. But this is not without risks for the limited partners as they could eventually end 'throwing good money after bad'. Finally, given what is mentioned above and in particular the issue of the uncertainty related to the capital needs of the highly cash-burning investee companies, side funds are generally more common in the early stage venture capital. However, also later stage private equity funds are known to have set up comparable vehicles (see **Box 14.1**).

Box 14.1:   UC Stand-By Facility

Side funds are not necessarily restricted to venture capital. In early 2007 Unison Capital, a pioneer of private equity investment in Japan, announced the set-up of a side fund-like vehicle, the 'UC Stand-By Facility'. Unison's website prominently features Charles Darwin's quote that it *'is not the strongest of the species that survives, nor the most intelligent, but the ones most responsive to change'*. In line with this view – it resonates our description of the private equity market as a fitness landscape – this stand-by facility was neither an improvised nor a defensive vehicle, but rather aimed

---

to give an additional boost to emerging opportunities. Following on from 'Unison Capital Partners L.P.', the 38 billion yen (EUR 230m) investment fund, which included both international and domestic institutional investors, Unison in 2004 successfully closed UCP II with a total commitment of 75 billion yen (EUR 450m) primarily for investments in corporate buy-outs in Japan. The stand-by facility had a tentative commitment of 60 billion yen (EUR 360m).[1] The objective of the stand-by facility was to make co-investments in transactions where UCPII makes investments. This vehicle aims to enable UCPII to autonomously target larger investments where a company's value exceeds 100 billion yen (EUR 600m). Unison perceived the opportunity for such a vehicle as potential investments considered by UCPII include a growing number of large deals that also created an urgent need to establish a means of capitalizing on these investment opportunities. With the UC Stand-By Facility Unison expected to capture such opportunities with even greater speed and flexibility.

A quick word on the Japanese private equity industry: Still in 2004 Japan was Asia's largest private equity market with over US$ 7bn invested, more than three times than in Asia's second largest market, Australia. Despite its size, Japan's private equity industry has never developed on a par with the United States and in recent years has been increasingly overshadowed by China and India. Nevertheless, the acquisition of Nippon Chōki Shin'yō Ginkō (Long-Term Credit Bank of Japan) by the US buyout fund Ripplewood in 2000 and its rebirth and IPO as Shinsei – making it the most profitable private equity deal in history – created a lot of interest in Japanese private equity opportunities among foreign investors. Whereas initially foreign players like Ripplewood or Lonestar dominated the restructuring scene and were often perceived as 'hagetaka' (vultures) already since 1997 increasingly 'quieter' and significantly smaller domestic funds were described as *'far more effective'* than foreign buyout firms.[2] The successes of Advantage Partners, MKS and Unison (the 'big three' according to Snow, 2006) brought in foreign investor who gave them a big push: meanwhile these firms are quickly joining the group of the oversubscribed elite of 'institutional quality' firms – demonstrating how rapidly alternative asset markets are developing and how important the backing of emerging managers is for getting access to the 'golden circle'.

To illustrate the use and structure of side funds, let us have a look at two different 'real-life' examples. Both side funds have been created at the same time, shortly after the burst of the dotcom bubble. During that period many technology fund managers had invested large amounts of money in investments which suddenly saw their short exit (or refinancing) horizon prospects disappear while still having high cash burn rates. After having first tried to reduce these high cash burn rates, many funds had still insufficient follow-on reserves to continue supporting all their investee companies, often also including the potential 'stars' in their portfolio. Especially as, at that time, most of the main follow-on contributors decided to stop deploying capital in the VC market. In the two cases described below, the limited partners' motivation was to protect either a good return or to improve the current bad interim performance of a fund.

---

[1] Press release 23 January 2007, Available on http://www.unisoncap.com/en/press/nr_list_en.php [accessed 20 June 2007].
[2] See Meyer (2006b).

- Our first example is a VC fund which had deployed its capital very quickly, in only a couple of years just before the peak of the bubble. The initial funding of the 30 companies in the portfolio was completed in only a year and a half, i.e. much shorter than the 'classical' four to five years investment period. As most of these investments were start-ups, the portfolio was in general still quite immature. The fund had at the beginning benefited from very favorable market conditions for both IPOs and M&A, which resulted already in significant repayments to the investors (55% of the fund). However, after mid-2000 this fund, as most other VC funds, had been affected by the market downturn that led to the closing of the exit window. Despite having some reserves to cope with follow-on funding requirements (around 25% of the fund size), due to the difficulties of attracting follow-on investors and the reduced expected performance of the investees, the fund tried to increase its investment capacity in order to preserve ultimately its profitability.
- Our second example is a VC fund launched three years before the peak but, in contrast to our first example, that could not take advantage of the then still favorable market conditions. The fund had invested €50 million out of €54 million in 40 companies. The team still had enough investment capacity to be able to manage the existing portfolio passively, i.e. only protecting the current performance by providing the minimum financial support to the very best opportunities (five companies). By creating a side fund, the team was hoping to gain again a momentum for managing the portfolio, capitalizing on two factors: the fund would use additional financing to secure and optimize the development of a higher number of investee companies with a real opportunity to become commercial successes. Furthermore, this allowed to restructuring a number of companies with a view to selling the participation at cost or at slightly better conditions. These companies otherwise would have been completely written off.

When faced with such proposal for a limited partner the major issue is, however, to assess the pros and cons of the side fund versus a new fund or other alternatives.

14.1.2 Structuring

Limited partners are faced with two difficult decisions: whether to allow the fund managers to set-up the side fund and whether to invest in the side fund. Firstly, a rejection can have a negative financial impact, the fund being at risk of being diluted in the follow-on rounds or writing off companies simply for a lack of funding. Secondly, when one or several of the existing limited partners do not participate, it creates unavoidable conflicts of interest between the non-participating and the participating limited partners. It is getting even more difficult when new investors are accepted to replace the non-participating limited partners. Here tensions between the non-participating, the participating and the new limited partners are to be expected. As generally the incentives structure of both funds are structured in the same way in terms of cash flow cascade, various limited partners have different interests in the two structures and theoretically could exercise pressure on the fund manager to focus on one of the two structures that will benefit them most. Furthermore, such a situation also creates possible valuation issues.

Grabenwarter and Weidig (2005) give a list mitigants which can eliminate or at least reduce most of these potential conflicts. They recommend that limited partners exercise a greater degree of control of the fund and its side fund by following the development of the side funds, and by monitoring the deployment of the capital and the possible valuation issues. In terms of incentives, the main issue is to keep the team focused and financially interested by the original fund while simultaneously giving the team proper incentive for managing the side fund. Indeed, although a side fund normally has a small size compared with the original fund (10–20%), there is a real danger that the team will focus its efforts on the side fund to get some carried interest (as the original fund is typically out of the carry) and to get a better track record by cherry-picking the best performers for the side fund. To solve these issues, Grabenwarter and Weidig (2005) put some solutions for this issue forward, first not to have any management fees on the side fund but above all to reduce the carried interest in this fund so that the fund managers keep focused on the original fund. Another alternative is to link the carry of the side fund to the original one, as it was the case in our two examples. For illustration, Table 14.1 below discloses the terms observed for the original versus the side fund. It has to be noted that in our two examples both original funds had similar terms and conditions at that time.

Table 14.1   Example of terms and conditions for an original fund and its side fund

	Summary terms	
	Orginal fund	Side fund
Set-up costs	Maximum 1% of total commitments	Maximum 1% of total commitments
Management fee	2%	None
Fee offset	Yes	Yes
Hurdle rate	5% p.a. (IRR)	5% p.a. (IRR)
Catch-up	Yes	Yes
Carried Interest	20%	15%, subordinated to the payment of the drawn down capital and hurdle of both original and side funds
Claw-back	No	Yes
Re-investments	Not allowed	Not allowed
Key-man	Yes	Yes & extended
Equalization premium	Yes, 4% p.a.	Not applicable

While it can be argued that side funds can be beneficial, there are generally numerous drawbacks. In our two examples, the situation after some years showed that the final results are not always positive. In our first example (see Figure 14.2), where the general partner had as primary objective to protect the original fund's performance from deteriorating, the late launch of the side fund did not avoid the deterioration induced by the market downturn. After a significant drop, the original fund slightly improved its performance to finally deliver a relatively acceptable performance (5%) whereas the side fund was clearly in negative territory (−15%).

In our second example (see Figure 14.3), where the general partner originally aimed to enhance the performance of the portfolio, the original fund was unable to exit the negative territory (−5%) whereas the side fund was with 40% a clear top performer.

But beyond these mixed experiences, side funds should be considered in the context of the following trade-offs:

- Either fund managers are very conservative and keep large reserves for follow-on (as can often be the case in the biotech sector), which for the limited partners may translate into

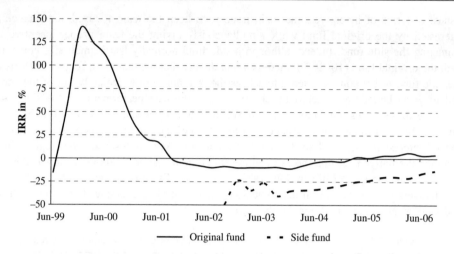

Figure 14.2   IRR evolution: original vs. side fund – First example

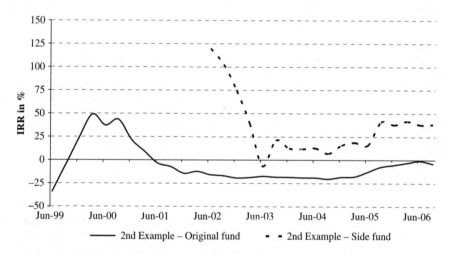

Figure 14.3   IRR evolution: original vs. side fund – second example

an 'inefficient' use of capital with a large undrawn and a high impact of the management fees on the structure and finally on the net IRR.

- Or the fund managers are very aggressive and keep low reserves for investment by maximizing the use of resources with the risk of liquidity shortage and their need to then raise new capital. The issue here is that limited partnerss will certainly question their competence and will be reluctant to invest in the side fund.
- The answer to this dilemma probably lies within a good communication throughout the fund's life between the fund managers and their investors on the foreseen follow-on reserves strategy to be applied.

14.2 SIDE FUNDS – SIMILAR STRUCTURES

14.2.1 Re-investment of proceeds

From a market practice point of view, side funds have been used frequently during the difficult years immediately after the dot-com bubble, but given their drawbacks are now more rarely seen. One common structure that gives more flexibility to the fund managers is the re-investment of proceeds (see Figure 14.4).

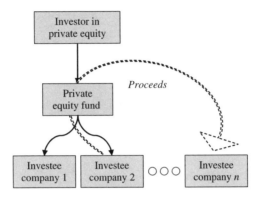

Figure 14.4   Re-investment of proceeds

Re-investment of proceeds or distributions is the possibility granted to a fund manager to re-invest proceeds from an exited investment in new investee companies. Instead of distributing directly the proceeds to the limited partners, the fund manager is then permitted during the investment period to keep the money in the structure for new investment. There is of course a time and a size constraint (generally not more than the total commitment can be invested in portfolio companies).

14.2.1.1 A win–win situation?

The objective of the re-investment of proceeds is that at least 100% of capital commitments are invested in investee companies at least once.[3] Some funds even permit re-investment in excess of 100% of capital up to a fixed percentage to be agreed with the limited partners. The re-investment is most similar to a side fund, which is agreed ex post but can also be agreed in the original LPA. As noticed by Fraser-Sampson (2006b), the practice in the USA is to invest up to 120% of the committed capital in companies whereas in Europe with the typical structure, which foresees no re-investment, the fund will normally invest only 75% of the fund size.

Table 14.2 shows the comparison of three structures: without re-investment (1), with 100% (2) and with 120% of capital re-investment (3). For this example, we assumed a fund size of €100 million, €25 million as management fees and a '3×' final average gross multiple. For simplification, the carried interest is assumed to be paid as soon as the commitment has been repaid (€100 million) on a 20%/80% basis.

---

[3] Without re-investment less than 100% of the commitment is invested in companies as part of them is drawn to notably cover the set-up costs and the management fees.

Table 14.2 Impact of re-investments of distributions on the fund economics

		Structure		
		1	2	3
Fund size	a	100	100	100
Re-investment of proceeds		No	Yes	Yes
% of committed capital invested in companies	b	75%	100%	120%
Management fees – % invested in companies	c	33%	25%	21%
Proceeds on invested companies (gross multiple 3x)	$d = 3 \times a \times b$	225	300	360
Multiple after management fees (before carry)	d/a	2.25	3	3.6
Simplified carry for the LPs (no hurdle)	$(d-a) \times 80\%$	100	160	208
Simplified carry for the GPs (no hurdle)	$(d-a) \times 20\%$	25	40	52

As illustrated by our simplified example, differences can be quite significant: in all our scenarios it is clearly a win–win situation as the relative percentage of management fees to the capital invested in companies is always lower with the re-investment and in case of a successful fund the carried interest can be twice as high for all parties.

14.2.1.2 IRR vs. carried interest

Under the 'classical' re-investment clauses, the fund manager is entitled to re-invest the proceeds received from any exits which occur during the investment period. There can be two alternatives, either the fund can re-invest only the reflow of capital, or it can re-invest both the capital and the profit made. In practice, either the fund manager finds an opportunity and re-invests directly the proceeds or they are distributed to the limited partners but become recallable. Generally the re-investment of 'quick turns' on investments and of bridge loans (12–18 months) can be re-invested without any limits. The re-investment clearly then has an impact on IRR as though the – non-recallable – final repayments will be further delayed, in terms of multiple and carried interests, there is a clear incentive for this structure.

14.2.1.3 Active tool?

The reason that venture capital is more risky is partly due to the 'home run' model of VC portfolios.

Hatch and Wainwright (2003)

In some cases, limited partners can actively use the re-investments of proceeds as a management tool. For example when backing a first time team, limited partners may decide to request special conditions to mitigate the risk associated with investing in these teams. This is the case for one of our funds, which invests in middle market companies in Italy. Launched in 2001 by a team with little experience in private equity (mostly M&A background), limited partners decided not to allow re-investment of proceeds. However, five years later, the fund's performance was really encouraging and given the strong deal-flow, the fund's investors decided to review their position. The fund was then allowed to recall its repayments and for one more year to re-invest this money. As limited partners by then strongly believed in this team, they aimed to increase the fund's return through this measure. It is a way for the top-up or the staged investment which will be analyzed later in this chapter to increase its exposure to a first-time team which has shown its ability to generate returns.

Despite all these advantages, the re-investment of proceeds applies by definition only to the existing investors, which is not the case for the next structure that we will discuss: the top-up fund.

A cynic might say that the Americans are motivated by carry while the Europeans concentrate on getting to the next fund quickly, to maximise management fee income

Fraser-Sampson (2006b)

14.2.2 Top-up funds

The top-up fund is a pool of capital which either brought by the existing investors or new investors add some months or years after the first closing to the original fund. It could be seen as the re-opening of the fundraising to investors.

The difference between a top-up fund and a side fund is that the launch of the top-up fund is done much earlier in the life of the original fund. It is clearly an active management tool used to leverage good market conditions (with a higher deal flow) or to compensate for a lack of diversification in case where original fund invested in larger investee companies than expected.

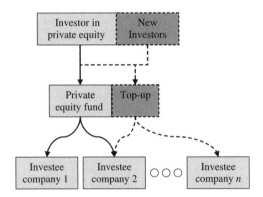

Figure 14.5   Top-up fund

A top-up fund (Figure 14.5) is generally opened in priority to the existing limited partners but it also accepts to new investors that could now be attracted by a successful team. The clear advantage is, as for the re-investment, that it is generally a win–win situation as illustrated by the following real case.

In this example an expansion/buyout fund was launched in 2005 with a fund size of €100 million. Due to bad market conditions this closing was short of the original target size of €150 to €200 million. Its initial target was to build a portfolio of approximately 20–25 companies with an expected average ticket size of three to six million euros. After one year and a half, the team had invested in three companies and deployed already 30% of the commitments. Due to its smaller than anticipated size, the fund then became sub-optimal in terms of investment strategy, team composition and size. The team decided to re-open, with the approval of its existing limited partners its fundraising by way of a top-up fund, with a target of an additional €50 million, bringing the fund size back to its original target. For the existing limited partners, such top-up was interesting as it could improve the fund's portfolio diversification, which, based on the first investments, would have resulted in only five to ten deals. Furthermore, this was an opportunity to increase their exposure towards a fund that already made some promising investments and therefore provided more certainty regarding its expected performance. Looking at the terms and conditions, neither were management fees back-dated nor did the new entrants need to pay equalization fees for the past year. The only issue was the condition of entry for the new investors, as one investment had been re-valued slightly upward.

In summary, the main advantages of a top-up are to increase the exposure towards a team that has begun to show promise. Indeed, after one to two years, the uncertainties surrounding a team (deal flow, investment strategy, team stability) are potentially reduced and investors are more willing to invest, especially for the teams which have a limited track record.

In Table 14.3, we compare the main terms and conditions of the different structures we have been through.

Table 14.3 Comparison of terms and conditions between the different structures

Terms and conditions	Side funds	Re-investments of proceeds	Top-up
Management fees	Generally no	No – free of any fees	Yes, aligned to the main vehicle terms
Carried interest	Yes but subordinated the main vehicle performance	Yes	Yes
Duration	Liquidated on the same date as the main vehicle	Liquidated on the same date as the main vehicle	Liquidated on the same date as the main vehicle
Fund size (as % of main vehicle)	15–20%	20–25%	No limits but generally up to 50%
New investors	No	No	Yes

14.3 LPS STRUCTURE OR HOW TO INCREASE FLEXIBILTY

All the structures we have observed and described above were introduced by GPs. But could the limited partners put real option like structures in place to increase the flexibility, such as the ability to top-up its investment within a team when the uncertainty is reduced?

14.3.1 Conditional commitment

Commitments are conditional when limited partners commit for a global amount that is structured in tranches that get confirmed when some pre-agreed conditions are met. In most cases these conditions are linked to a minimum fund size.

As we discussed previously, there is no risk-adjusted pricing mechanism for primary investment in private equity funds. It is therefore difficult for investors targeting emerging teams to get an adequate reward for the high uncertainty related to such investments. This often results in sub-optimal funds, with the fund size often too small, the team often underpaid or understaffed, and the strategy often unproven. Nevertheless, at fundraising, some solutions or improvements may exist to address these issues. Indeed, for many venture capital proposals we receive, we often observe a huge gap between the minimum fund size and its target size. While for many teams the first closing is a way to raise the attention of potential investors, these investors are often not willing to be among the first ones.

- They want to see brand names in the list of investors, which would then confirm the outcome of their due diligence.
- Because a sub-optimal fund size is likely to make it difficult for the team to implement its investment strategy.
- As during the fundraising period the team focuses mainly on attracting investors, there is to some degree a negative impact on the investment activity.

Anyhow, although entering at a later stage has some advantages, it also has a cost, through the equalization fees and the potential negotiation issues on terms and conditions. Indeed, by entering at the second closing, the negotiation power is much limited as discussions have already taken place with the investors in previous closing. In this case a minimum commitment at the first closing is certainly an advantage.

In order not to be excluded in case of successful fundraising and to solve some of the issues described above of not being at the first closing, a possibility for limited partners is to consider a conditional commitment, i.e. commiting for a maximum amount with a maximum percentage of the fund size. For example, you commit for €50 million with a maximum of 10% of the fund size. Should the fund make a first closing at €100 million then your investment at first closing is limited to €10 million. Another possibility is to commit for 100% of the investment only if the fund raises the minimum fund size the investors would consider as sufficient to deploy the strategy.

Conditional commitments are increasingly used by investors and are also quite welcomed by the emerging fund managers, which are facing problems to have a first closing. To cope with this problem, teams have introduced preferential terms, such as an increased carried interest for first movers.

14.3.2   Limited partners' staged investment

Behind this conditional commitment concept, the idea for the LPs is to push the market toward a structure which first could provide more flexibility and secondly increase the upside. See Figure 14.6.

Direct investments work as an amplifier of trends, they increase the negative effects during a downturn. They also need a different set of skills and, compared to a VC fund, a fund-of-funds can't really add value to an investment.

André P. Jaeggi, Managing Director, Adveq, quoted from Cowley (2002)

To amplify the good performance of a fund, the idea would be – as for a direct investment – to have some tools available to increase or to stage its exposure toward a fund and its portfolio in case of good performance. One example of this, which is described in detail in Chapter 13, is to negotiate some co-investment opportunities or rights to increase its stake toward some specific investee companies. Most of the large investors try, to the extent

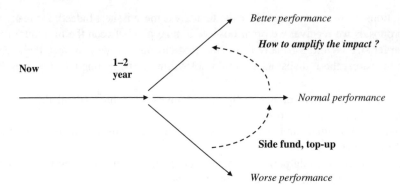

Figure 14.6   Limited partners' staged investment

possible, to negotiate such rights. But this has one main disadvantage as it requires that the limited partner has direct investment skills.

Theoretically, the limited partner could negotiate and put in place a staged investment approach. This would result in committing upfront a certain amount and keeping in reserves a follow-on commitment which would be 'called' within a certain timeframe following the development of the fund and/or at the limited partner's discretion. See Figure 14.7.

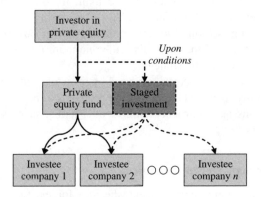

Figure 14.7   Side fund for staged investment

Such an approach undoubtedly raises a certain number of practical issues.

14.3.2.1   How?

The first one is based on the negotiation power between investors and fund managers. Such a structure would most likely be implemented in the context of emerging teams which are more willing to accept increased fund size after a certain period. The idea is to test during some years the investments strategy of the team and in case of reasonable success to increase its investment in the fund. The investors, having negotiated this staged investment, would then see their interest held in the fund increased by their new commitment. But contrary to co-investments, it is here not a question how of picking the investee companies which could outperform but increasing its global investment in the fund, in other words as a pre-agreed right to top-up. Terms and conditions should not deviate from the original ones. The purpose is not to modify the incentive structure but to give more 'firepower' to a team which has convinced its investors.

14.3.2.2   When?

On the timing issue, the stage investment should be negotiated with a foreseen time frame – the investors would have the ability to increase their investment after a specific period to be agreed with the fund managers, which should not go beyond the investment period. It is difficult to envisage a too long period as by increasing their investment the staged investors are diluting the other investors. But a two to three years timeframe seems reasonable, leaving sufficient time to check if the investment strategy works while still having a relatively young portfolio, i.e. without too significant upward valuation. Indeed, one of the key structuring issues apart from the dilution question is the valuation issues. As new money enters into the fund, the portfolio valuation could be a real problem and has clearly to be settled up-front, either by considering that at the time of the new investment no investee company will have been re-valued (up or down) or by using an independent valuation agent with some clear guidelines like the IPEV (International Private Equity and Venture Capital) to fix the price.

14.3.2.3   Who?

This staged investment approach is likely to be granted just to the investors who take the higher risk, i.e. the biggest investors. Indeed this staged investment cannot be proposed to all investors as it could then jeopardize the success of the first closing. If all the investors postpone part of their investment, it is then impossible for the team to have a decent pot of money to properly manage the fund. The purpose is for the team to have enough money without the staged investment to deploy its strategy. It is also true that given the structure of the staged fund, the limited partner must have high negotiation power, staged investment will then be easier to implement in the case of a first-time fund.

> *We suggest that large and successful VC funds use seed investment activity as a form of 'market intelligence' to identify and track exciting (and above all 'disruptive') new technologies and emerging new industries. Given the scale of these established and predominantly US funds, first round seed investments represent trivial costs with substantial potential (but invariably highly uncertain) pay-offs. Seed investment is a 'numbers game' and a well respected VC fund with a large portfolio of options has a distinct advantage.*
> Dimov and Murray (2006)

Again, the main purpose of staged investment is to reinforce a successful strategy. It has the following advantages:

- For the fund managers there is more 'oxygen' as their first funds have a tight budget. With this, they will not have to go back early in the market to raise a follow-on fund with the difficulties of showing a proper track record and with a sub-optimal fund that was most likely not yet able to show the full potential of its strategy. The staged investment will be here to give extra months to facilitate the process.

- For the limited partners it is a flexible way to increase their exposure in a promising team once they have become familiar with the team, can assess the portfolio and the uncertainty is reduced to an acceptable degree.

But there are the following practical issues:

- The increased commitment coming from the staged investment should be introduced during the investment period. But at this point in time the portfolio is still in its J Curve. It is then difficult to assess the value of the portfolio. That is why this structure is helpful to invest with a reduced uncertainty only on the team's deal flow quality and investment strategy but not on the team's ability to add value to its investee company and on its exit strategy.
- The portfolios are likely to show success after the end of the investment period. Staged investment could be perceived basically as co-investing on an entire portfolio.

14.4 CONCLUSION

The side fund structures already developed in the market tend to be passive. Most of them have been initiated by the general partner and not by the fund's investors. They therefore always require consensus among all the parties present in a fund. Historically, side funds have been a reaction to market downturns or to distressed funds. However, the cyclicality of the market and the usual institutions' lack of appetite to back emerging teams should raise the question of how additional incentivize could be given to investors.

Conceptually we see side funds close to co-investments, and indeed the lines are blurred. Theoretically any limited partner that has negotiated co-investment rights could create a 'virtual' side fund by simply always exercising these rights and by proportionately topping up the fund's investments into portfolio companies. Rather than cherry-picking companies – requiring that the limited partner has a direct investment capability – side funds could thus be interpreted as a further bet on a fund management team. In fact, we suggest a hierarchy of active management of a private equity investment programme:

- Investors only take a passive role as limited partners in funds:
- In addition to being limited partners in funds, investors use side funds;
- Investors selectively co-invest alongside funds in individual portfolio companies;
- Investors directly source, invest in and manage portfolio companies.

Like co-investments, side funds offer characteristics of real options but have a number of drawbacks and are not yet well developed as solutions for staged investments. Nevertheless, limited partners should take a closer look at such investments, more regularly envisage them in the limited partnership agreement and make them part of their strategy for investments in VC funds.

15
Limited Partner Decision-Making Fallacies

It is impossible to completely rationalize behavior under uncertainty. Under such circumstances the investment decision-making process cannot be entirely formalized or objective and it will certainly be influenced by subjective opinions and 'gut feel'. Uncertainty, however, does not imply complete ignorance but more that a decision-maker would have to take so many variables into account that it becomes unmanageable. In such situations heuristics, i.e. 'rules of thumb', are required to save the time involved in analyzing a large amount of information and make affairs manageable, as no alternative would be workable. For example, Swensen (2000) pointed out that many 'investors simply allocate among the asset classes popular at the time in proportions similar to those of other investors, creating uncontroversial portfolios that may or may not address institutional needs'. Imitation and adherence to conventions can be a substitute for reason, the latter being unable to operate for lack of data.

15.1 DECISION-MAKING WITH POOR DATA

Humans are used to instant decision-making based on data that are incomplete, ambiguous and often conflicting. The more data we have, the more likely we are to drown in it, and therefore we naturally cling to ideas and conventions that have worked before. Thus when an environment is perceived as being inscrutable, managers tend to rely on experience and intuition. Humans are good at pattern recognition, converting an unknown and uncertain situation into a more structured and manageable model of their world. This, however, leads to common errors and biases and it is important to understand the fallacies of decision-making under uncertainty. Complementary teams can look at a situation from different angles. This may to some degree reduce errors and raise the probability that at least one team member will spot warning signals earlier. But it does not eliminate the biases and may even lead to others, like group think where camaraderie and cohesion goes too far. Investors in the private equity market often confuse random chance with cause and effect, draw big conclusions from very small and biased samples, or base their decisions on data that is easily available as opposed to searching for data that is really needed for a good decision.

Associated with a long-term oriented asset class such as private equity is the problem of selective memory. Instead of remembering the past accurately, decision-makers will recall those events that suit their needs and preserve their self-image. When funds eventually turn sour, decision-makers claim – often with full justification – that the problems were caused by their predecessors. The difficulties associated with interpreting the J Curve phenomenon illustrate the point. On the one hand there is the tendency to panic when – often meaningless – interim returns are highly negative. Occasionally this results in an over-reaction and the demise of the institution's private equity activities. Likewise, decision-makers become complacent about the J Curve and lull themselves into the belief that 'it will always turn out well'. Just because many funds eventually give good returns, it does not mean that all funds recover and in fact some need the limited partner's attention.

Related to selective memory is representativeness, which is a mental shortcut that causes people to give too much weight to recent events and too little weight to evidence from the more distant past. For VC funds, stock market booms and busts drive interim valuations up and down, but these interim valuations do not systematically bear a relationship to the fund's economic value.

> *Of course, though, people with long-term stakes don't always act wisely. Often they still prefer short-term goals, and often again they do things that are foolish in both the short term and the long term.*
>
> Diamond (2005)

Two thousand years ago, Aesop in one of his fables noted that the rabbit runs faster than the fox because the rabbit is running for his life, while the fox is only running for his dinner.

Limited partners tend to be less patient than general partners, not only because they are more risk-averse but also because they have more alternatives, such as hedge funds. Instead of putting such valuations into perspective and comparing them against appropriate benchmarks, decision-makers are tempted to over-react. The mushrooming of commitments to VC funds at the end of the 1990s is one example, and the 'fire-sale' of these portfolios and the associated boom of secondary players is another. Also herding demonstrates how lessons of the past are forgotten.

15.2   HERDING AS A RESPONSE TO UNCERTAINTY

Looking back at the dotcom bubble during the late 1990s one is tempted to dismiss this as a period of exceptional folly that is unrepresentative and therefore should not be taken into account when thinking about future scenarios. But one should not be mistaken. Any market environment with uncertainty, imperfect information and irreversible decision-making will regularly generate herding, bubbles and frenzies.

> *But don't make the mistake of thinking that this was an era of unrepeatable strategic madness. Behavioral economics tells us that the mistakes made in the late 1990s were exactly the sorts of errors our brains are programmed to make – and will probably make again.*
>
> Roxburgh (2003)

Devenow and Welch (1996) define herding as a behavior pattern that 'can lead to systematic erroneous (i.e. sub-optimal relative to the best aggregate choice) decision making by entire populations' and presented two polar views on this subject. Non-rational herding is driven by investor psychology, with agents behaving like lemmings, foregoing rational analysis and with less crazy investors being able to profit handsomely. The rational view on herding acknowledges that information difficulties or incentive issues can distort optimal decision-making. Between these two extremes are decision-makers who are near rational and are economizing on information processing or information acquisition costs by using 'rules of thumb'.

15.2.1   Betting on every horse

The literature has emphasized that asymmetric information is at the root of these apparently irrational market reactions. Usually there are so many technological innovations that it is simply too costly to try to understand them all and so most venture capitalists remain relatively uninformed even about the technologies in which they invest. Under uncertainty the safe strategy is, in the words of Beinhocker (1997), to 'bet on every horse'. As we have argued in the discussion on power laws, over time a large number of minor innovations create the foundation of later profound discoveries. For example, during the 1990s progress in telecommunication, the wide distribution of personal computers in households and maturing computer networking techniques converged and created a virtually infinite multitude of potential business and technical opportunities with interdependencies that were impossible to assess. In this situation there were simply too many horses to bet on.

15.2.2   Imitate and turn to experts

As a consequence of betting on many horses there is even less knowledge on what one is betting on. Everybody believes everybody else has better information and the reliance on the opinion of others is increasing. Therefore, independent decision-making across all market participants is a fiction. For example, M&A and IPOs come in waves that appear to be more amplified than possible waves in underlying fundamentals. In interviews conducted by Devenow and Welch (1996), 'many influential market participants continuously emphasize that their decisions are highly influenced by other market participants'. Herding requires a coordination mechanism, which in venture capital is mainly observing what other venture capitalists are doing or turning to opinion-makers, who allegedly know more about this subject.

> *Firms do not choose courses of action in isolation: they monitor each other, and make inferences about the uncertain situation they face by noting the success or failure of others' strategies. When this leads to diversity – to firms selecting different strategies and coming to occupy different 'niches' – a stable market structure can result. But, if firms imitate, each choosing the same strategy, disastrous 'crowding' occurs.*
>
> MacKenzie (2003)

Mimetic behavior is rational if there are other participants, who are thought to be better informed. It is no coincidence that excesses during bubble periods are often associated with persons, from the Scottish economist John Law to Wall Street's Henry Blodget, who when the party is over turn into scapegoats.[1] As a consequence, uninformed investors follow the supposedly informed market participants and adopt a 'collective rule of thumb', i.e. a shared convention that conforms to the average opinion and that may to some degree be arbitrary but is followed at least in part because others are following it.

---

[1] Henry Blodget was an Internet analyst for Merrill Lynch in the late 1990s and early 2000s securities. In his research he was highly optimistic regarding dotcom stocks, arguing that 75% of all Internet companies were destined for failure but adding that investors would find the long-term winners from the remaining 25% (see Gasparino, 2005). This is an interesting parallel to the VC industry's argument that you have to be in the top-quartile funds to be profitable. In other words, he admitted that most companies were over-valued but saw the sector as under-valued. Essentially, Blodget described a return distribution curve that is skewed to the right, i.e. with many under-performers, but few extreme winners.

15.2.3   Protect one's reputation

Initially, technical innovations usually draw skepticism from the established industry experts. Sticking to conventions is a defensive behavior as it is the safest course of action. At the end of the day, imitation and hiding in the crowd belong to the proven and strongest survival techniques among all species.

> *Failing conventionally is the route to go; as a group, lemmings may have a rotten image, but no individual lemming has ever received bad press.*
>
> Warren Buffett in his 'Letter from the Chairman',
> Berkshire Hathaway Annual Report, 1984

Even if this strategy eventually fails, following it protects one's reputation and minimizes 'regret' – at least everybody made the same mistake. Succeeding unconventionally may certainly be more 'heroic', but under uncertainty there are serious doubts about the chances of success. As a result, even the top VC funds will be biased toward following the crowd, but also sub-standard VC funds can then make good decisions, which poses a challenge for conducting a track record analysis.

15.2.4   Creating reality

Schumpeter argued that the entrepreneur does not project all the relevant aspects of the existing situation into the future, but instead creates a new future. In this context the apparently irrational herding can become a self-fulfilling prophecy. As an example, New York University's Stern School of Business Finance Professor Aswath Damodaran published a number of valuations for Amazon and occasionally saw the company as significantly over-valued. In his words, 'Amazon cannot have Wal-Mart's (WMT) growth and Ann Taylor's (ANN) margins'.[2] Damodaran saw its share as worth $34 in 2000 when it was trading at $84. Nevertheless, the publicity around Amazon's market capitalization may have contributed to the network effects and thus have even created a reality.

Box 15.1:   Are investors in VC funds rational?

Could the VC industry itself be prone to herding behavior and are investors in VC funds irrational? This question may not be exactly welcome among venture capitalists and their lobbyists, but it is a valid one.

   To shed some light on the dotcom bubble of the late 1990s, Boucher (2003) used a model for analyzing 'technology shocks' in the shape of new firms. The main model-ing assumptions were that only part of these firms would be viable, that the uncertainty related to their identification and to their viability was decreasing over time. Despite the model's simplifications, its assumptions also describe the VC industry's dynamics and thus the results are also of relevance to investors in VC funds. The author found uncertainty and incomplete information to be the determining factors in the forming

---

[2] Quoted from Hough (2003).

of bubbles, which emerge even though market participants have a perfect knowledge of the impact of the shock and the date on which it occurs.

According to the press, the spectacular growth of the private equity asset class is primarily due to a widely held belief among investors that it has exhibited high performance in the past. Despite the fact that private equity funds represent a major class of financial assets, Phalippou and Gottschalg (2006) found that a comprehensive account of the historic performance of such funds is still missing. They conducted an analysis that was based on a sample of 852 funds – mainly buyouts – out of a population of at least 1579 funds raised between 1980 and 1993. These authors also referred to a related study for the same time period done in 2005 with a sample of 639 funds. Covering more than a decade of private equity investing, both studies are not only based on a surprisingly small sample size but also demonstrate the staleness of reliable data available on funds. Although it is therefore unclear to what degree these findings are of relevance for the current investment environment, they are not too encouraging:

- Phalippou and Gottschalg (2006) concluded that the stunning growth in the amount allocated to this asset class cannot be attributed to genuinely high past performance of private equity funds.
- After correcting for sample bias and overstated accounting values, these authors found that mature private equity funds under-perform the S&P 500 by 3.8% p.a.
- In fact, the documented performance was so low that one may be led to think that certain investors might have mispriced this asset class.

Phalippou and Gottschalg (2006) put forward a number of explanations for these puzzling findings. The venture capitalists' learning may play an important role in performance, and indeed Kaplan and Schoar (2005) found that experienced funds and US funds offer significantly higher performance. There may also be a real option value associated with participating in inexperienced and hence poorly performing funds, as the limited partners tacitly obtain the right to participate in future more profitable funds. As it is very difficult if not impossible to get access to the 'proven performers' later on, this option carries a value that is not reflected in the statistics.[3] Moreover, skills and learning are also relevant for the limited partners, as the results of Lerner (2005) suggest.

There are also side benefits of investing in private equity funds, and limited partners may not only invest to maximize investment returns. Instead, they may follow dual objectives, such as increasing the likelihood that the funds will purchase services – e.g. consulting or underwriting securities for debt or equity issues – that the limited partner's corporate parent has to offer. Also, public institutions that for example aim to promote innovation or employment may distort the picture.

VC fund home-runs like Google or Skype are likely to have a significant halo effect, where investors attribute too much weight to the performance of such highly successful but very rare transactions. In addition, they may be willing to pay a 'lottery premium', i.e. sacrifice the average return for a chance to earn a huge although remote

---

[3] See also Meyer and Mathonet, 2005.

Box 15.1: (Continued)

return. In a 2001 Senate Budget Committee hearing, US Federal Reserve Chairman Alan Greenspan offered as explanation for the dotcom mania the not quite rational impulse that drives millions of people to buy lottery tickets. Internet stocks will either be worthless or worth 'some huge number'. Also, asset classes like VC funds show comparably skewed return distributions. According to the 'lottery premium' hypothesis, the bigger this pay off, the higher the premium investors are willing to pay for a chance at winning.

The private equity funds industry caters exclusively for 'sophisticated' investors and thus so far has avoided regulation. Phalippou and Gottschalg (2006) suggest that because apparently sophisticated investors are misled by current reporting practices, then regulation from authorities such as the SEC may be warranted. This argument, however, overlooks that this market cannot be seen as an index, but that its frontiers are blurred and moving. Firstly, there are continuously 'style drifts' where VC funds shift toward later stages when early stage investing becomes too difficult and buyouts consider technology-oriented start-ups when a stock market boom is under way. Secondly, you cannot passively invest in private equity funds. The art market may serve as an example. Many people produce art but the fact that your and my paintings do not fetch any price does not imply that an artist cannot make a living out of this activity and even become rich and famous. Limited partners require experience, good research and management, and to some degree it may also be an art that can be mastered, as continuously successful players in this market demonstrate.

15.2.5 VC industry as 'crisis hunter'

We conclude that it may be tempting to dismiss bubbles as aberrations because people tend to forget past experiences, but to some degree they may be an integral part of the VC industry's business model. Technological innovation creates information asymmetries and uncertainty. It regularly leads to smaller or larger market bubbles that create the opportunities venture capitalists need to generate extraordinary returns. Portfolios of VC funds are likely to often lose a small quantity of money, but are expected to make money in the long run because of these occasional spurts. It is rather the long draughts with their disappointing returns between such 'cataclysmic events' that could be seen as unrepresentative for the VC business model.

> *Our assumption of irregularly timed major events implies that companies in turbulent environments will likely face extended periods of relative calm punctuated by intensive bursts of activity, rather than a uniform onslaught of shocks or once-in-a-lifetime cataclysmic events.*
>
> Sull and Escobari (2005)

It is often heard that it is only very small numbers of transactions such as Yahoo or eBay that made up the vast majority of the exceptional gains in the US VC market between 1996 and 2000 and that depending on the benchmark, the US VC market's return between 2000 and 2005 becomes negative when stripping out Google. Taleb (2005) pointed out that rare events are not fairly valued and suggests that technology investments may have a bad press, but there is a small albeit significant possibility of extraordinary gains. These infrequent 'golden opportunities' skew the distributions, and therefore they are frequently removed from statistics as outliers, apparently making a case against venture capital. However, venture capitalists can operate as crisis hunters, losing money frequently but in small amounts, and making money rarely but in large amounts.

Active waiting is an important strategy under uncertainty. It aims to anticipate shocks by carefully monitoring the emerging situation and actively probing the future by purchasing real options on possible futures. Sull and Escobari (2005) suggest that slack resources be built up during times of relative calm that can be deployed in times of turbulences. In venture capital, however, the opportunities arise when the market becomes volatile and periods of calm are more difficult to sustain. Nevertheless, the limited partners' goodwill also needs to be considered as a slack resource, and sometimes VC firms return funds to their investors when there are no opportunities, thus working on good relationships.

Box 15.2: Active waiting

Sevin Rosen, a highly respected 25-year-old VC firm in the USA, provides an example for active waiting. It was about to close its tenth fund and had received commitments from investors for $250 to $300 million when it decided to abort that process. Sevin Rosen believed that the 'venture environment has changed so that overall returns for the entire industry are way too low and even the upper-quartile returns have dropped to insufficient levels'.[4] This decision appeared to be motivated mainly by uncertainty on how the VC market would develop, but did not mean that the firm stopped its activities. Sevin Rosen could rethink its strategy while protecting its strong reputation and being able to continue investing commitments it raised in earlier funds. This 'sitting on the sidelines' is a risk that a VC firm with a strong reputation can afford to take. As an industry insider pointed out, if Sevin Rosen changes its mind and decides to raise a new fund, there would be many institutions ready to commit quickly.

Real option theory states that the higher the uncertainty, the higher is the value of waiting. Options to wait arise from the earlier investments made. Also limited partners can use active waiting strategies, for example by taking smaller stakes in private equity funds when either the prospects for the entire market or a specific firm are unclear. Retaining the relationship allows scaling up of commitments in future funds to be raised by the same firm. Not committing to a fund at all may backfire when the market turns around and access to the 'top-quartile' funds becomes difficult. As one venture capitalist during a 2006 conference complained about institutional investors, 'they did not respond to phone calls in 2001, now they come back and want even more'.

15.3 DECISION-MAKING BIASES

Investors in private equity funds have to make their decisions in situations that preclude reliance on fixed rules and compel to rely on their intuition. They need to judge probabilities

---

[4] Quoted from Helft (2006).

and assign values to outcomes. Intuitions play a crucial role in most of these decisions and lead to biases, i.e. systematic errors of judgment. Decision-making in private equity is highly consensus-driven, as in such an uncertain environment all available information should be put on the table for evaluation and discussion. This is certainly a very powerful instrument for screening proposals ex ante, but once the investment has been done there is a clear danger of 'group think', i.e. the pressure to agree with others in team-based cultures as they often, for example, impute hostile motives to critics or question their competence.

People need rules of thumb for decision-making when facing complex problems or incomplete information. In psychology such rules are 'hard-coded' by evolutionary processes and work well under most circumstances, but in certain cases lead to systematic biases and thus to flawed decisions. Much of the work of discovering heuristics in human decision-makers goes back to the Nobel Prize winners Amos Tversky and Daniel Kahneman, who originated prospect theory to explain irrational human economic choices.[5] Prospect theory suggests that the way a person subjectively frames a transaction in their mind will determine the utility they receive or expect. Investors use subjective weighted probabilities rather than 'objective' probabilities and behave as if they regard extremely improbable events as impossible and extremely probable events as certain. It goes beyond the scope of this book to discuss this in detail, and we can just point to some typical biases observed when looking at the VC market.

15.3.1   Mental accounting

Mental accounting, i.e. creating new categories of spending such as 'strategic investment', is an often observed fallacy. Here spending is less scrutinized because of the way it is categorized but represents real costs – something apparently quite common in institutional investing, where often just an immaterial part of the assets are allocated to venture capital because they are considered to be 'loose change' but cannot make any difference.

Box 15.3:   Mental accounting

One case for mental accounting is illustrated by comparing the returns for two private equity fund models. Industry benchmarks represent just the fund data, but do not reflect how the limited partner invests the undrawn commitment. Example 1 shows a VC fund with an IRR of 15%, while example 2 only has an IRR of 12%.

Comparing the two investments on this basis overlooks the fact that from the viewpoint of a limited partner the return of the undrawn commitment is also of relevance. If we assume the same Treasury return of 3% in both cases, in the case of example 1 the limited partner would receive a return of 8.4% for the entire commitment comprising drawn and undrawn. The commitment to the VC fund in the second example, however, would yield 9.3%. In example 2 more money has been put to work more quickly. Considering the total return of investments is one way of avoiding the negative aspects of mental accounting.

---

[5] In the original formulation the term 'prospect' referred to a lottery.

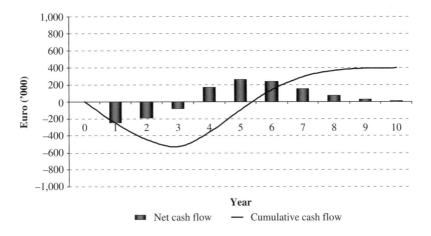

Figure 15.1   Example 1

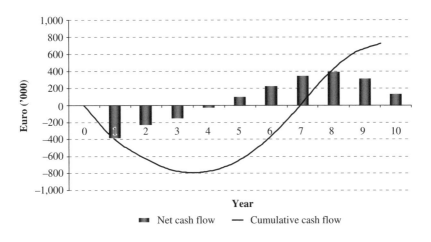

Figure 15.2   Example 2

Another form of mental accounting is 'framing', i.e. how a reference point, often a meaningless benchmark, can affect a decision. Investors in private equity funds may have a biased view of performance, for example because they look at multiples rather than a profitability index. As Phalippou and Gottschalg (2006) reported, in 'our conversations with LPs, we note that a recurrent argument is that they are satisfied with past performance because they "doubled" their money, i.e. obtained a multiple of two [. . .] In our dataset, we find an average fund duration of 75 months, i.e. 6.25 years. The stock-market portfolio has returned on average 1% per month from 1980 to 2003, which means that over 6.25 years an investor would have more than doubled her/his money ($\times 2.1$) which is significantly higher than $\times 1.8$.'

15.3.2 Anchoring

The term used in psychology to describe the common human tendency to rely too heavily on one trait or piece of information when making decisions is called 'anchoring'. One example for anchoring investors in private equity funds are faced with is the focus on past performance record. As we discussed before, there are practical problems in establishing a link between good past performance and future performance. By citing their track record, a VC fund management team anchors the notion of future top-quartile performance in the prospective limited partner's mind.

A related fallacy example is the 'price implies quality' bias. People are likely to perceive more expensive beers as better tasting than inexpensive ones. Behavioral researchers conducted experiments where the higher price was assigned to the normally cheaper beer brand. This signaling led many participants in these experiments to perceive that beer as tasting better than the beer that is normally relatively expensive. In venture capital we see comparable mechanisms. For example, there is a group of self-declared elite funds that charge a 30% carried interest. It can be suspected that such signaling of apparent quality influences investors in VC funds. Even if such an investment were to be lagging in the future, limited partners may hold on to it not only because they paid a hefty price, but also because it was so difficult to get into such a star fund in the first place. It can be suspected that limited partners will be far more lenient and patient with a 'top team' than they would be with a first-time fund. At the end of the day most researchers preach that 'top-quartile performance is sticky' and will be repeated.

Box 15.4:   Institutional quality funds

The buzzword 'institutional quality fund' can illustrate framing and anchoring. The majority of the broader studies report the cash-on-cash performance of private equity funds either below or not much different from stock market investments. As Gottschalg (2007) observed, some of the studies that do report substantial outperformance look at smaller samples from a historically better performing sub-segment of the private equity market only, e.g. investments made by funds that were selected by a sophisticated limited partner. Indeed, particularly venture capitalists, where average performance is often disappointing, counter such unwelcome statistics with the concept of 'institutional quality'. For illustration, Dinneen (2004) defined institutional quality in the context of emerging market private equity funds. The criteria – somehow comparable to those reflected in our qualitative scoring methodology – mainly relate to:

- The **identity and the characteristics** of the other limited partners: the fund must include amongst its limited partners at least some 'qualified' third-party institutional investors and/or family foundations. 'Captive' bank funds without third-party investors would therefore be excluded. Also, funds with only the 'friends and family' of the fund managers as investors would not be considered as institutional quality, unless the friends and family were qualified limited partners. Funds denominated only in a local currency that is not freely available to non-local limited partners would be excluded as well.

- The **percentage of the equity** contributed by other 'qualified limited partners' vs. that contributed by International Finance Institutions (IFI) as public investors: although not always the case, the percentage of the total capital provided by qualified limited partners should generally be at least 50%.
- The **fund size** relative to timeframe and region: for example, a $25 million fund in 1992 might qualify, but not in 2000, or a $25 million fund in country X might be considered, but not one in country Y.
- The **verifiable track record**: verifiable data, especially regarding performance, is seen as essential. Unless the fund can provide audited financial statements, for each year since inception, it will be excluded as its track record cannot be verified.

The 'institutional quality argument' is very difficult to refute as there is no generally accepted definition of which funds belong in and which funds fall out of this category. At the end of the day, this can just be a grand way of referring to funds managed by established private equity groups without having a specific meaning. The term to some degree is even a tautology, as it refers to groups that were successful with their funds in the past, and it is anchored in the investors' minds that success is likely to be repeated. On the other hand, investors may pay a price for their peace of mind, as the institutional quality private equity groups can often 'dictate' their terms and the fund's structure – particularly high management fees or increased carried interest – can deviate from what limited partners would perceive as 'ideal'. Cynically speaking, the 'institutional quality funds' mainly offer their investors protection against reputational risk.

15.3.3 Endorsement effect

Related to anchoring is the 'endorsement effect'. In situations where respected private equity funds-of-funds – like Adams Street Partners, AlpInvest Partners, HarbourVest Partners, Pantheon or Horsley Bridge Partners – are present, less experienced investors will tend to trust these limited partners' judgment. As Zheng *et al.* (2006) observed, linkages with high-status players could confer status to the focal firm and generate an endorsement effect. Also in our qualitative scoring we use as input into the expected performance grading, we take the fund's other limited partners into consideration. However, in the extreme, when faced with uncertainty and incomplete information about a fund management team, investors may rely too heavily on this piece of information when making their decision. In fact, reliance on the due diligence conducted by other parties and their decision-making can be 'dangerous to your financial health'. Firstly, such parties may pursue non-financial 'strategic' objectives, may have negotiated undisclosed 'special deals' with the fund managers, may want to invest in the fund as a 'gamble' to explore a market, or they may have simply made a wrong investment decision – caveat emptor!

15.3.4 Status quo bias

Limited partners can be tempted to extrapolate hopes and engage in confirmation bias, i.e. treating information that supports what they want to believe, more favorably. Once investments are made, decision-makers often show a tendency to seek out opinions and facts that support the own hypotheses and to selectively recall only those facts and experiences that reinforce these assumptions. Such evidence is quickly accepted while contradictory evidence is subjected to rigorous evaluation and almost certain rejection. When private equity funds do not perform as expected, limited partners may feel reluctant to turn away from their original decision and face the fact that they will incur a loss. Rather, they are likely to stick with the status quo in the hope that the fund will eventually turn around.

In real life there exist tremendous amounts of inertia in individual decision-making. This 'status quo bias' is to some degree explained by loss aversion, because the disadvantages of changing the current situation loom larger than the advantages. People are more concerned about the risk of loss than they are excited by the prospect of gain. In fact, many institutional investors have a culture of avoidance of mistakes rather than taking action. For private equity the problem is that the status quo is not always wrong, caution and conservatism can be strategic assets, and patience is definitely a virtue. Investors are continuously told that they have to be patient and that the development of a fund's value always follows the J Curve. Here it is a challenge for a limited partner to understand where patience ends and inertia sets in, particularly when the fund's other limited partners also take a passive role.

In this context we recall a discussion we had with one investment manager who – in our opinion – tended more toward inertia. When confronted with the poor performance figures for a number of relatively mature funds, he did not appear to be overly concerned. He stated that he spoke to an acquaintance at another fund-of-funds who told him not to worry about the write-downs, because 'particularly the bad funds later on turned out to be the star performers!' While this may occasionally happen, this statement is quite difficult to accept as a rule, and in many cases it is rather the restructuring of a fund that can stop the value destruction or even result in additional returns.

15.3.5 Regret

Connected to loss aversion is regret that makes people often unable to distinguish between a bad decision and a bad outcome. Regret can describe not only the dislike for an action, but also, probably more importantly for limited partners, regret of inaction. One example would be not committing to a fund that subsequently turns out to be a star performer.

Box 15.5:   Regret

Despite Mangrove's impressive results and experience, allegedly it was not easy to raise their second fund, as many investors believed that Skype was a fluke and Mangrove would not be able to repeat this success. *Real Deals* reported in its 6 October 2005 issue that since 'the sale, Mangrove has been busy with its own shareholders, explaining what the deal means for the small outfit. The firm is in the middle of raising its second fund with a modest target of €100 m. It has so far raised €50 m, but, as a testament to the gruelling environment for raising a venture fund in Europe, it is struggling to raise the remainder, despite Skype's success.' This could be interpreted as an example for regret, where investors with hindsight observe that they could have taken a different decision in the past with a better outcome. By any objective criterion Mangrove II should be a very promising proposal: an excellent track record generated by an experienced and respected team embedded in a network with the

---

internationally leading VC firms – for European venture capital this is as good as it gets. But psychologically many potential investors may have seen the following likely outcomes: Skype was the best exit of a European start-up ever and that Mangrove II (or any other VC fund in Europe) could top this would be highly unlikely. Because European high-tech early stage financing is notoriously difficult, Mangrove II may even generate a negative return. It is difficult to make oneself free of Mangrove I when making a decision on Mangrove II. Regret is such a powerful negative emotion that the prospect of its future experience may lead to an apparently non-rational decision. Also, Lerner (2005) reported that he hears frequently from investors that they considered investing in a specific fund, but they 'decided that their success must be a fluke'.

Another factor driving loss aversion is inability to ignore the sunk costs of poor investments that causes decision-makers to fail to evaluate a situation such as this on its own merits. Examples in the context of private equity fund investments are distressed funds or tail-end situations, i.e. funds approaching the end of their contractual lifetime with little return potential left. Here the initial investment is unlikely to be recovered, but limited partners could extract more value out of these situations if they were willing to accept the costs as sunk. In Meyer and Mathonet (2005) we described the case of a distressed fund where limited partners set back the 'clock' and gave the fund manager new incentives to do their best for the remaining portfolio companies.

15.3.6   Home bias

It is often observed that investors tend to overweight the allocation to their home market or region. Such an approach is quite logical. Firstly, the local market does not normally carry currency risk and, therefore, is less risky. Secondly, proximity allow us to decrease the uncertainty thanks to a lower information asymmetry – investors usually know their own markets better – and to have a more efficient monitoring of the investments.

> *The portfolio construction varies according to our clients' needs. So our European investors tend to have around 60:40 US to Europe, whereas our US clients tend to have around 75:25 US to Europe. Our Asian clients have some Asian exposure and then around 50:50 US to Europe exposure and our Gulf clients roughly the same.*
> Wayne Harber, Managing Director, Hamilton Lane

Indeed, the so-called 'home bias', a common tendency to invest mainly within one's own country, is explained by investors putting too much emphasis on information close at hand. Even though they know that diversification is good for their portfolio, a large majority of both US and European institutions appear to invest far too heavily in funds in their home countries.

15.3.7   Over-optimism

People also tend to see the future through 'rose-colored glasses'. There is a demonstrated systematic tendency to be over-optimistic about the outcome of planned actions. Related to optimism is over-confidence, i.e. believing that an outcome is more certain than facts would suggest. The more pioneering and unfamiliar the market is, the more managers are likely to be over-confident in their judgment of uncertain events and their ability at picking winners. In an opaque environment some market players certainly have better insights than others. Decision-makers will evaluate just the data available and often assume that others may be less well informed than they are. Here it is also difficult to avoid 'superstitious reasoning', i.e. confusing random chance with cause and effect, and over-reacting to chance events. As for innovation, by definition, there is no long-term statistics available, and decision-makers often reason by false analogy like 'this is the new Internet'. Particularly in the context of track record analysis there is a danger of superstitious reasoning as one is very much tempted to extrapolate from past performance as an indicator of future performance. That a first-time fund looks like Mangrove does not necessarily imply that it will create another Skype.

Optimism bias arises in relation to estimates of costs and benefits and duration of tasks and leads to under-estimating the likelihood of bad outcomes over which decision-makers have no control.[6] Given human optimism, the risk of getting pessimistic scenarios wrong is probably more prevalent than misjudging the upside. Sanditov *et al.* (2001) argue that over-optimism 'based on mutual illusions makes the system vulnerable to two-sided "high-tech" bubbles, and may be one of the reasons behind "dot-com" crash'. To mitigate for optimism bias it is, for example, recommended to add 20–25% more downside to the most pessimistic scenarios. However, in venture capital such rules of thumb will usually not be of any help, as this asset class is not about protecting one's downside. Based on a quantitative analysis an investor would find few grounds for accepting the assumption in a VC fund prospectus that it would return a targeted 20% IRR. In fact, Butler (2006) found that even LBOs tend to yield particularly poor return profiles and quotes one banker who stated that if 'you were to base your decisions on what the computer says, you would never do it'.

Regardless of how rigorously one conducts the financial or commercial due diligence, in venture capital financial risks cannot be measured with a meaningful precision. In contrast, limited partners of private equity funds base their decision on the hope that each one will turn out be a great investment. One could argue that this uncertainty to a large degree stimulates venture capital. Not knowing that success is unlikely helps us to embark on journeys that lead to new discoveries. As only a few start-ups will succeed, it requires great optimism to launch a new business. Take as an example the aviation engineer Igor Sikorsky, who was told by several aeronautical engineers that, according to the laws of aerodynamics, the helicopter could not fly. His response was that according 'to the laws of aerodynamics, the bumblebee can't fly either. But the bumblebee doesn't know anything about the laws of aerodynamics, so it goes ahead and flies anyway.'

15.4   CONCLUSION

Irrational (or let's better say, not fully rational) behavior to some degree may even be part of the 'VC business model'. We tend to get blinded by examples like Google and are tempted to believe that a private equity funds investment program is just looking for top-quartile funds. While one can mitigate to some degree such biases, for example by becoming aware

---

[6] Other researchers, like Bent Flyvbjerg, pointed out that what appears to be optimism bias could rather be a strategic misrepresentation. For example, when political pressures are high, costs may deliberately be under-estimated and benefits over-estimated in order to get the investment approved.

of them, they cannot be eliminated. Their greatest danger is that they give limited partners a wrong picture of a private equity fund investment program and deflect from those areas that can be better managed. Generally in life there are many more opportunities to play 'small gambles' than large ones.

While a satisfying quantitative method appears to be out of reach, we nevertheless can draw upon the allegories we developed in previous chapters to come up with such 'rules of thumb' as a rational approach for portfolio construction. 'Rational behavior' is here defined in the sense of Dequech (1999), who suggested that in addition to being based on knowledge it also be *'the most adequate, in the light of the available knowledge, to the achievement of some end, even if it turns out to be unsuccessful ex-post'*.[7]

---

[7] Underlined by authors.

Part IV
Managing Portfolios of Private Equity Funds

16
Portfolio Construction Principles

> Because investment management involves as much art as science, qualitative decisions
> play an extremely important role in portfolio decisions.
>
> Yale Endowment Annual Report, 2004

When comparing publications on private equity to those on more conventional asset classes, it is baffling how few books touch upon the subject of portfolio management for a private equity funds investment program. The goal of the portfolio construction is to combine assets that behave in fundamentally different fashion to optimize the risk–return relationship and to meet the manager's objectives. But the idiosyncrasies of private equity mean that standard design tools are difficult to apply and that trade-offs are inevitable. In this chapter we first discuss why modern portfolio theory does not offer the right tools to tackle this question and introduce broad concepts underlying the portfolio construction for private equity.

The key issue is diversification, and we present results on studies of the risk profile of diversified portfolios of private equity funds.[1] Rather than basing the portfolio construction on correlations, we feel that in practice it is more relevant to achieve a defined degree of independence between sub-portfolios. Diversification not only has benefits but also disadvantages that motivate some 'rules of thumb'. Finally, we return to our evolutionary model of the private equity market and derive another set of rules of thumb to steer exploitation and exploration within a 'fitness landscape'. There are challenges at all steps, and, frustrating though it is, there is no optimum solution, but it all boils down to building a structured and disciplined investment process.

16.1 PRIVATE EQUITY AND MODERN PORTFOLIO THEORY

Institutional investors' asset allocation decisions are made based on the concepts of modern portfolio theory (MPT). The basic concepts of MPT were described by Harry Markowitz in his seminal paper 'Portfolio selection' that appeared in the 1952 *Journal of Finance*. Thirty-eight years later, he shared a Nobel Prize with Merton Miller and William Sharpe for what has become a broad theory for portfolio management. The MPT assumes that investors seek to achieve the highest return with the least risk and, for simplification, that they pay no taxes or transaction fees. To apply MPT, investors should be able to evaluate returns, risk – as measured by the standard deviation of returns – and correlations for all considered assets to determine an efficient asset allocation. Models based on MPT may be adequate for the universe of publicly traded instruments but rely on parameters that are instable, unreliable or even

---

[1] We thank Gabriel Robet for his help in updating our previous study (see Weidig and Mathonet (2004)).

unavailable in private equity. The apparently low volatility and correlation with public market assets makes private equity look very attractive in the typical portfolio optimizer model.

> *To say that private equity is less volatile and thus less risky is a bit like saying that the weather does not change much when you stay inside and rarely look out of the window.*
> *Economist (2004b)*

Assuming that return expectations are above publicly quoted assets and that the investor is not constrained by liquidity needs, the optimizer would allocate all the money to the highest return per unit of risk asset class in order to generate the highest value added for the portfolio. This is often countered by forcing ad hoc constraints on the modeling results to make the asset allocation more palatable, which defeats the purpose of the whole exercise.[2]

16.1.1   Fitting private equity into the requirements for MPT

There are great difficulties fitting private equity into the requirements for MPT because of both the challenges presented by private equity data and other model assumptions; i.e. investors exclusively hold publicly traded liquid financial assets and act as though security prices are unchanged by their own trades in those securities. All investors have to have the same information, interpret it in the same manner, and have the same time horizon. Private equity fails to meet this critical MPT assumptions.

- Only the funds that invest in a private company generally have access to the company's financial data, and only limited partners who invest in a given fund have access to that information. The market for private equity is inefficient; valuations are unreliable and infrequent, holdings are illiquid, and there are relatively few buyers and sellers. In the large universe of publicly traded financial assets, typically one relies on six months' time series with daily data to estimate correlation coefficients. In contrast, private equity valuations are infrequent and more likely to be estimates than actual transactions that establish a fair market price. Therefore it is not possible to measure risk as the volatility of a time series and the subsequent interpretation of correlation as a measure of dependence can be misleading.
- The long investment period of between 10 to 12 years and the illiquidity of ownership stakes in private equity funds are difficult to reconcile with the assumption that all investors have the same time horizon. As capital calls are spread out over time at the discretion of the manager the standard measure of return is the IRR – a commitment-weighted measure of return and not the classical time-weighted measure of return used for most other assets classes. Some authors even advocate that for long-term investors with illiquid assets and a fixed time horizon, using alternative measures of return and risk such as expected terminal wealth and terminal wealth standard deviation rather than expected annual return and times series standard deviation is more appropriate.[3]

It is not just a problem of data availability or quality. Even if we can obtain reliable indicators, standard correlation-based asset allocation techniques will probably yield misleading results

---

[2] See Winograd (2002).

[3] See, for example, Brands and Gallagher (2003). In general, the terminal wealth can be defined as the investment value at the end of the holding period. In the context of private equity, it is to be understood as the fund multiple. Weidig and Mathonet (2004) used the standard deviation around the average return when analyzing the risk profile of diversified portfolios of private equity funds.

when dealing with highly non-normal returns like private equity fund returns. Correlation is the heart of modern portfolio theory, where it measures dependence between financial assets under the assumption of multivariate normally distributed returns.[4] However, empirical evidence shows that the distribution of private equity fund returns is highly non-normal.[5] It exhibits a relatively high probability of large gains – i.e. positive skewness – and extreme outcomes – i.e. excess kurtosis. Kat (2002) shows that if the joint distribution is not normal, correlation is not a good measure for the dependence structure between variables involved.[6] In the framework of VC funds these shortcomings are likely to be exacerbated to the point of making correlation-based portfolio diversification meaningless.

Box 16.1: Skewness and kurtosis

Skewness is a parameter that describes asymmetry in a random variable's probability distribution. Both probability density functions in Figure 16.1.1 have the same mean and standard deviation, but the one on the left is positively skewed, i.e. the right tail is the longest and the mass of the distribution is concentrated on the left, while the one on the right is negatively skewed, i.e. the left tail is the longest and the mass of the distribution is concentrated on the right. The skewness for symmetric distributions – such as the normal distribution is zero.

μ   μ

Figure 16.1 Skewness

The skewness of a distribution is calculated as:

$$skewness = \frac{\sum_{i=1}^{n}(x_i - \bar{x})^3}{n}}{\sigma^3}$$

Kurtosis is a measure of whether the data are peaked or flat relative to a normal distribution. Higher kurtosis means more of the variance is due to infrequent extreme deviations, as opposed to frequent small deviations. Normal distributions have a kurtosis of three. Leptokurtosis (kurtosis greater than three) is associated with distributions that are simultaneously peaked and have fat tails. Platykurtosis (kurtosis lower than three) is associated with distributions that are simultaneously less peaked and have thinner tails. High kurtosis means having 'fat tails', i.e. the payoff of winners

---

[4] It is not enough that each variable is normally distributed, but one must also verify that their joint distribution is normal.

[5] We are more likely to encounter symmetrical return distributions where there is equilibrium between supply and demand and many market participants push prices in one or the other direction. Therefore it is not surprising that for private equity return distributions are asymmetric.

[6] The danger for the risk manager is that correlations might appear to increase dramatically during extreme events. For example, correlation between hedge fund returns and stock market returns tends to be higher in down than in up markets. Some practitioners argue that this is also the case in private equity.

Box 16.1: (Continued)

and the losses associated with losers tend to be more extreme. It is therefore of interest for investors who believe that they can pick winners.

Both probability density functions in Figure 16.2 have the same mean and standard deviation, but the distribution on the left is platykurtic while the one on the right is leptokurtic.

Figure 16.2   Kurtosis

The kurtosis of a distribution is calculated as:

$$kurtosis = \frac{\sum_{i=1}^{n} (x_i - \bar{x})^4}{n}$$

$$\frac{}{\sigma^4}$$

16.1.2   Private equity fund risk

It is meaningless to ask if a risk metric captures risk. Instead, ask if it is useful.

Holton (2004)

For an investor in private equity funds interim changes in their NAVs are more or less irrelevant. Volatility fails as a proxy for risk because, as Bernstein (1996) pointed out, the risk inherent in an asset has meaning only when it is related to the investor's liabilities. Variability should be studied in reference to some benchmark or some minimum rate of return that the investor has to exceed. As Fraser-Sampson (2006a) suggested, investors in funds should be concerned only about what he called capital risk and return risk.

Box 16.2:   Return risk and capital risk

Return risk is the probability that the portfolio of private equity investments will not achieve a set target rate of return:

$$P\left(IRR_{P,T}\right) \leq IRR^*$$

where $IRR_{P,T}$ is the interim internal rate of return of the portfolio P at the end of time period T and IRR^* is the target IRR at the end of time period T.

Capital risk is the probability that the portfolio of private equity investments yields a return of less than 0%, thus leading to some loss of the original nominal capital:

$$P\left(IRR_{P,T}\right) \leq 0\%$$

If I am taking a train to travel to a very important meeting that will begin promptly at a stated time and which I cannot possibly miss, then do I really care about how quickly or slowly the train will travel at any time during its journey? No. All I care about is that the train should arrive on time at the end of the journey.

Fraser-Sampson (2006a)

Both measures are an expression of shortfall risk, i.e. denoting the risk that a specified minimum return (target return, threshold return, minimum acceptable return) may not be earned by a financial investment. In fact, capital risk is just a specific case for return risk where the target rate is set as zero.

16.1.3   Private equity fund exposure

A problem one is facing in practice when constructing a portfolio of private equity funds and monitoring its allocation is what 'exposure' to look at. Firstly, should it be defined on the fund or on the fund's portfolio company level? Secondly, which components of a fund should be taken into consideration – the NAV, the undrawn commitments, the repayments or all commitments?

16.1.3.1   *Exposure on portfolio company level*

Measuring exposure at the underlying portfolio company level takes the view that the fund is mainly characterized by the value of the cash already invested, i.e. its portfolio. Assuming that the commitments not yet drawn are not exposed to the market risk, it is then only the capital invested that is exposed to the systematic risk. Only when the drawn capital is invested will the valuation start to fluctuate with the market. Measuring exposure at this level theoretically allows the limited partner to monitor better for potential style drifts away from the initially declared investment strategy.

However, directly managing diversification of a portfolio of private equity funds on the portfolio company level is not practical as this is outside the limited partner's control. Nevertheless, an investor who has embedded private equity investments into a portfolio of publicly listed securities could manage exposure through trading these quoted investments. Although at first glance a convincing approach, there are practical problems: for start-ups, industry sector codes are difficult to assign, they are often missing and managing a portfolio based on such unreliable data is cumbersome and requires a high workload. There are also conceptual problems: undrawn commitments are not reflected and funds have different remaining lifetimes. For example, fund A may either be at the end of its lifetime or facing a 'liquidity squeeze' whereas fund B could still be in its investment period with significant undrawn capital. Even if they hold stakes in the same company, fund A will be subjected more to the prevailing market conditions than fund B. In fact, you can be in the same investment, but this does not mean that you are exposed to the same risks. As an example: a distressed company may offer excellent opportunities to a turnaround specialist, but not to a VC fund. Looking at exposure at the portfolio company level only neglects the fund manager style and strategy as a risk measure.

It is not correct to assume that each portfolio company within the same portfolio will follow their own independent 'random walk'. The evolution of each company can have an impact on the others, for example in the case of venture capital, where financial and managerial resources are gradually concentrated on the most promising companies, leaving the other investee companies in the fund's portfolio with reduced chances of success.

16.1.3.2 Exposure on fund level

When looking at a portfolio's exposure at the fund level one takes the view that a fund's risk and return profile is mainly determined by its manager and the declared investment strategy. This approach is comparable to the style diversification for hedge funds-of-funds, and its main benefit is that it is easier to measure exposure at the fund level than at the underlying portfolio company level. Also, the style and the specific strategy of the manager is taken into account as a relevant diversification dimension. Another rationale is that funds are initially blind pools, and at closing date its manager's declared investment strategy is the best guess for the future exposure.

On the other hand, this is a relatively crude way of characterizing a fund. Markets, strategies, teams and portfolios evolve, this approach leaves the possibility for 'style drift' and the true fund exposure will regularly deviate somewhat from the manager's initial strategy, which anyway often allows for some flexibility or has broad focuses (e.g. multi-country). Because of the private equity fund's illiquidity there is very little the limited partner could do about it. One could argue that, in a large portfolio, this risk of style drift is to some degree diversified away, but when there are 'trendy strategies', which is often the case, this is probably not true any more and unexpected concentrations may emerge.

16.1.3.3 Exposure measures on fund level

To measure the exposure of a portfolio of private equity funds, limited partners normally use one or several of the following measures: the commitment, the NAV plus the undrawn, the NPI plus the undrawn or finally only the NAV.

- Measuring the portfolio's exposure **by commitments** is obviously easy to apply, as exposure remains the same from the initial commitment till the full liquidation. However, when fund exposures are weighted on a commitment basis, they keep a high weight even if close to expiry and if all the committed capital has been repaid. To some degree, this issue can be addressed through the adoption of vintage year as one of the risk dimensions or by analyzing the exposure by fundraising cycle.
- The self-liquidating limited partnership has, contrary to the other asset classes, an important specificity, which is that the exposure changes continuously even without any buy or sell transaction, as capital is drawn as needed and as exited investments are normally distributed directly to the investors. When the exposure is analyzed by fundraising cycle, investors make the assumption that the portfolio will be replenished at each cycle, maintaining its exposure and diversification.

- Another approach is to measure the portfolio's exposure by the **NAV plus the undrawn**. When investors use this approach, they take the view that the fund is characterized for the amounts already drawn by the value of the investments still in the portfolio and for the undrawn by its manager and its declared investment strategy.[7] ·
- Some argue that as the undrawn is only exposed to specific risk and not to the market risk, the portfolio's exposure could be measured **only by the NAV**. As the cash has not been drawn and invested, it does not appear to be exposed to the market risk, while the NAV reflects the portfolio companies and is exposed to both the market and the fund's specific risks. Therefore, in a diversified portfolio, there is no need to take them into account for the current exposure but only to measure how the exposure will evolve and steer the portfolio accordingly.

However, the management of diversification based on the NAV is not without problems. Firstly, the real financial exposure should be equal to the economic or present value, which the NAV in many situations is failing to address. Moreover, it could stimulate a counter-productive behavior, i.e. reducing the allocation to the funds that have shown the highest value increases. As an example, we look at two funds A and B and assume that the investor committed €10 million to both of them and there are no undrawn commitments left. Fund A's NAV has grown to €100 million while fund B is a 'lemon' with its NAV fallen to €1 million. Based on the pure numbers, the limited partner would conclude that he is overexposed to fund A's industry sector and should allocate more to that of fund B – which at least based on historical experience would be slightly questionable.

When managing illiquid assets like private equity funds, the age structure of the portfolio has to be taken into account. In its usual definition, private equity fund exposure varies over time. See Figure 16.3.

To some degree this resembles the situation of the age pyramid of a human population. It is not possible to change the composition of an age group later, except through immigration

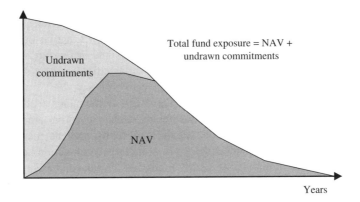

Figure 16.3   Development of exposure over time

---

[7] Such an approach would be in line with the Basel II treatment of exposure. Under Basel II, the measure of a private equity fund exposure is the value presented in the financial statements, i.e. normally its NAV, plus the total amount recorded off-balance sheet, i.e. its undrawn.

(secondary buys may be the equivalent from the limited partner perspective): 50% men and
50% women may be OK, but it is definitely not a healthy balance if the population only
comprises women over the age of 90 and men under the age of 10.

- To avoid this problem, diversification in private equity could be managed, as suggested
  before, on a **commitment basis** or alternatively by the **NPI plus the undrawn**. When
  investors use this NPI plus the undrawn approach to measure the portfolio's exposure,
  they take the view that a fund's risk–return profile is mainly driven by its manager and
  its declared investment strategy, but this time taking into account the age of the investment, through the importance of the repayments. This solves the valuation issues associated with the estimation of the NAV. However, ignoring the valuation gives an overly
  strong weight to highly written down positions, while financially they pose a minimal
  exposure.

As for the exposure level, we believe that there is no right answer and that exposure
should be measured by several of these alternatives. When the program just started or for
investors with limited staffing, looking at commitments may be more suitable. Later, when
the committed capital gets invested and a fund's value is influenced by market fluctuations,
an approach based on the NAV starts to make more sense.[8] Finally, and as a compromise
solution, which combines convenience without deviating too much from the financial reality,
exposure could be measured by commitment per fundraising period or vintage year. Within
a sufficiently diversified portfolio, and knowing that all positions are self-liquidating, such
an approach will systematically converge toward the target allocation as defined by the
investor.

16.1.4 How much to allocate to a private equity funds investment program?

Many financial institutions give guidelines for private equity allocations in the neighborhood
of 5–10%, although purely nominal allocations below 5% are not atypical for institutional
investors in general but cannot possibly make any difference to overall portfolio returns.
Several critics, notably Fraser-Sampson (2006a), point to the fact that historically the aggregate of alternative assets – including private equity funds and hedge funds – had less than
1% of UK pension plans: '[. . .] investors have adopted an attitude of "let's just do it a little
bit and then it doesn't really matter", setting an allocation of, say, 2%'.

   Nevertheless some institutions, notably US university endowments such as Yale, invest
a significant portion of their assets in private equity. Such investors are able to pay the
large minimum investments and endure the long illiquidity that prevents many other types of
investors from participating. Allocations above 10% are largely a function of the institution's
ability to access a sufficient number of quality funds and the financial ability to have locked
up a high proportion of capital in such an illiquid asset (Table 16.1). Another major factor
that has to be taken into account is the limited scalability, because only an allocation up to a
certain point is possible without depressing returns. Particularly venture capital is seen more
as a 'talent pool' than an asset class, with too much investment 'stripping' this pool.

---

[8] Especially in the case of buyout funds that are usually quicker fully invested and where valuation is less of an issue.

Table 16.1 Publicly announced changes in allocations to private equity by major US institutional investors in 2002 and 2003 (see Hatch and Wainwright, 2003)

		2002	2003	2007
CalPERS	State pension	6%		7%
CalSTRS	State pension	5%		8%
Colorado PERA	State pension	11%	8%	
Yale	Endowment	25%	18%	
Stanford	Endowment	17%	10%	

According to Ian Barnes from the multi-manager fund company Russell, in 'order to come up with an allocation it is not greatly scientific, often it's pragmatic'.[9] Indeed, the typical institutional approaches to private equity asset allocation are not satisfying. Often institutions seek allocation to private equity in proportion similar to those of other investors. Swensen (2000) is highly critical of this approach, as by 'relying on the decisions of others to drive portfolio choices, investors fail to consider the function of particular asset classes in a portfolio designed to meet specific goals'. Others follow rules of thumb. For example, Grabenwarter and Weidig (2005) suggest that 'institutional investors with the appropriate long-term investment horizon who have concluded that private equity exposure improves their risk-adjusted portfolio return should be able to invest from 5 to 15 per cent of their assets in private equity. [. . .] A quantitative analysis in the style of Markowitz might tilt the balance between a smaller share of between 5 per cent and 10 per cent, or a share of between 10 per cent and 15 per cent.'

The decisive constraint, however, is the institution's need for liquidity. Private equity is clearly mainly a 'cash asset' where the maturity of the investment program – i.e. whether it is net cash absorbing or generating – is the main driver of the asset allocation. This, in fact, differentiates self-liquidating funds-of-funds with limited lifetime and evergreen funds-of-funds.[10] A self-liquidating fund-of-funds mimics the structure of the limited partnership typical for private equity funds. Investors commit for a certain amount for an investment period over five to six years during which the capital will be called. The private equity funds invested in start to return after three to four years, and as a consequence, without over-commitment, the fund-of-funds' investment level usually does not achieve more than 60–70% of the original commitment level. Evergreen structures, on the other hand, have no time limitations, distributions from private equity funds can be re-invested, over-commitments more 'smoothed' and a lower level of commitments is sufficient to achieve high exposure that gets preserved over the long term. Additionally, having staggered vintages can mitigate the illiquidity and long time horizon of the investments and can generate a steadier stream of cash flows. Large institutions that manage an in-house private equity investment program implicitly follow a long-term-oriented evergreen approach. Repayments from funds are interlocked with new investments and thus difficult to manage with precision. Therefore, the institution sets a minimum and maximum size for the program. If the value of the portfolio falls below a minimum threshold additional funding will be injected, whereas if it gets

---

[9] Quoted from Sormani (2003a).
[10] See Matter (2005).

above a maximum threshold distributions from the funds will not be re-invested into the program.[11] See Figure 16.4.

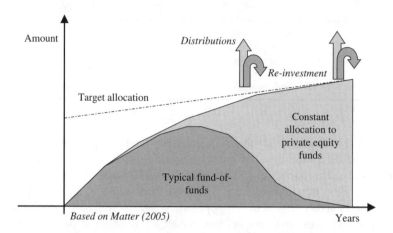

Figure 16.4 Approaching target allocation

An alternative, albeit highly simplified, model based on the institution's regular liquidity needs offers insights relevant for systematically tackling the question of allocation to private equity funds. Essentially, two factors constrain the maximum allocation to private equity within the portfolio. Firstly, there are diminishing returns to scale as there is a limited number of high-quality private equity funds in the market. Beyond a certain threshold of capital to be put to work the private equity portfolio's returns start to deteriorate and within a 'Multi Asset Class Investment Strategy', as discussed by Fraser-Sampson (2006b), forces the allocation to other alternative asset classes. Secondly, the liquidity needs or – at a later stage – the liquidity generated by the portfolio private equity funds determine its weight in the asset allocation. For illustration we look at two asset classes:

- Standard assets with medium growth potential but high liquidity (through regular interest or dividend payments or a liquid secondary market; Figure 16.5).

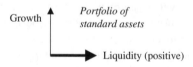

Figure 16.5 Standard assets: medium growth with high liquidity

- A private equity funds investment program with higher growth potential, but where the liquidity profile is undergoing changes depending on the maturity of the portfolio of funds. Simplistically we look at two stages. Initially there is a negative liquidity stream

---

[11] External program managers offer only specifically structured products. For example, we spoke to a private equity firm that has been managing such an evergreen fund-of-funds mandate on behalf of an insurance company, with the constraint to give back 7% of initial investment to the insurer p.a. and the rest can be committed again.

as the program needs to be funded and distributions need to be re-invested to get really invested in private equity (Figure 16.6). For this purpose institutional investors need long-term excess capital, as slack resources, that is not needed for supporting their other activities and does not have to be returned to shareholders.

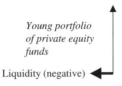

Figure 16.6   Young portfolio of private equity funds: high growth but requiring funding

- A mature portfolio of private equity funds, however, will generate a steady stream of cash distributions that either do not need or, because of the program's limited scalability, cannot to be re-invested (Figure 16.7).

Figure 16.7   Old portfolio of private equity funds: high growth with low positive liquidity

Under very simplified assumptions we can translate the problem of allocation to private equity funds into a linear program,[12] i.e. maximize allocation to private equity (or in other words, maximize growth for the entire portfolio of all assets) given a set liquidity constraint. See Figure 16.8.

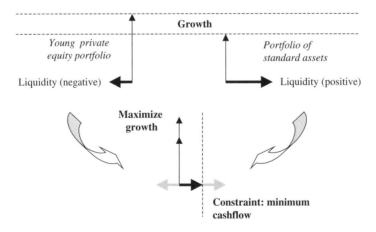

Figure 16.8   Determining the allocation to private equity funds

---

[12] Linear programming is a mathematical technique used to obtain an optimum solution in resource allocation problems, such as production planning.

The constraint essentially depends on the institution's regular liquidity needs to support their on-going business. These considerations lead to the following conclusions:

- An investor with high regular liquidity needs and no excess capital is not well placed to launch a private equity program.
- The lower the on-going liquidity needs and the more excess capital, the more an investor can allocate to private equity.
- The more mature a private equity program and therefore the more liquidity it yields, the more an institution can allocate to private equity.

Under the assumption that a non-financial institution can generate more growth with its core business than out of its portfolio of assets, it is – unless it is a corporate VC – questionable to invest in private equity. Assets are only required to provide liquidity for this company's operations, and any excess capital should be returned to shareholders.

Investments in private equity funds are therefore mostly of interest for institutions with long-term liabilities, such as insurers or pension funds. As endowments or family offices are less constrained by regulatory requirements cases, with up to 30% of the assets allocated to this activity documented. As they have long-term 'excess capital' that they do not have to return, for example, to shareholders in the form of dividends, for them private equity's illiquidity does not matter.

16.1.5   Other issues

It is usually argued that a specific liquidity management for the private equity funds investment program does not really matter for most institutional investors, as they are awash with cash anyway. If the allocation to private equity funds is in the typical area of 1–2% that is certainly true. But moving toward a substantial allocation to private equity puts the question of over-commitments, the projection of cash flows and the management of the associated back onto agenda. Therefore another important subject in the context of the risks and returns of a portfolio of private equity funds is over-commitments, a subject we have already discussed in the context of the case study presented in Chapter 4.

16.2   CREATING A PORTFOLIO OF PRIVATE EQUITY FUNDS

Limited partners have little control over the success of their investments in VC funds, but they can control the process of creating, selecting and amplifying experiments to increase their odds of success. They have to build into their strategy more flexibility and options to allow for scaling up or for retrenching as uncertainties are resolved. Limited partners can create real options on a portfolio basis, for example by experimenting with emerging teams, or on an individual fund level through negotiating special terms and conditions. For a portfolio of private equity funds diversification comes at a price and limited partners can even be over-diversified. On the other hand, if a limited partner systematically negotiated real option-like components in the partnership agreements, this can well compensate for the costs of diversification and carry a significant value.

For private equity funds investment program portfolios are usually constructed either bottom-up or top-down. The bottom-up approach puts emphasis on screening investment opportunities for the best managers. The quality of the fund management team is the overriding criteria, much more important than sector or geographical diversification. The starting point of a bottom-up approach is the identification of suitable investments, followed by an intensive analysis and due diligence in order to rank the funds by their attractiveness. A top-down approach could be described as strategy research-based, i.e. where the investor focuses on strategies and the determination of allocation ranges. The top-down approach gives priority to the choice of sectors, countries, fund styles or trends as opposed to individual fund selection. It could be argued that investors who follow a top-down approach put a stronger emphasis on the asset allocation and the diversification of their portfolio.

While appearing to be each other's opposite, the bottom-up or top-down approaches are complementary. In fact, neither top-down nor bottom-up can be 'purely' implemented. Even if investors have a desired portfolio composition it may well be that no opportunities come up that would fit the allocation or, even more likely – especially for newcomers to the industry – that they are not accessible. When selecting fund managers bottom-up, investors also look for their portfolios not to become overly concentrated – although some do not shy away from going to the extreme: as Horsley Bridge's Managing Director Kathryn Abbott phrased it during one conference: if 'the best 25% of all GPs are all in Poland, we put all our money into Poland'.

The mainstream is something 'in between'. Bottom-up and top-down are usually used in tandem, starting with bottom-up with increasing optimization top-down in what is called a mixed approach (see Figure 16.9). For the start-up phases of an investment program, one of the main objectives is to put capital as quickly as possible to work in the best available teams in order to minimize idle liquidity. As young programs cannot count on an established relationships, the available universe of investment opportunities is restricted to a limited number of accessible 'wish list' teams. This makes a top-down approach difficult to implement, as allocation targets would make little sense. After a sizeable portfolio (and also relationships) have been built, a top-down approach starts to become important as

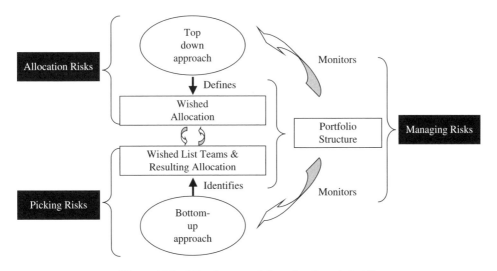

Figure 16.9   Mixed approach (see also Jaeggi, 2005)

concentration can create unrewarded risks and also as a lack of exposure to wished segments of the market can increase the likelihood of not meeting the program objectives.

In a bottom-up approach, investors makes a 'market mapping', where all teams are ranked by their attractiveness (see Figure 16.10).

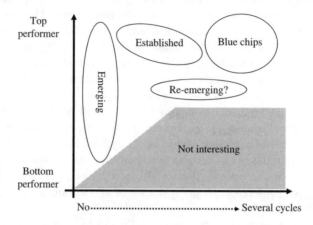

Figure 16.10   Market mapping

Attractive teams are normally the ones that have been able to generate top performance during several market cycles and that are the most likely to continue to do so in the future. One way to classify the teams is to rank them based on their track record (from bottom to top performer) and the length of their joint experience (from no to during several market cycles joint experience). This suggests the following classification:

- **Blue chips team**: teams that have been able to generate top-quartile performance for all their funds through at least two business cycles (i.e. more than three funds).
- **Established team**: teams that have been able to generate a top-quartile performance for most of their funds (i.e. some funds may not be first quartile) through at least two business cycles (i.e. more than three funds).
- **Emerging team**: teams with limited joint history but with the characteristics to become at least an established team.
- **Re-emerging team**: previously blue chips or established teams that have been through a restructuring following recent poor performance or some significant operational issues and have regained the potential to re-emerge as established or blue chips.
- **Not interesting**: all the teams not included in the other categories.

Finally, this has to be complemented by a qualitative review in order to confirm the classification or amend it. For example, a blue chip team can be reclassified as established due to some succession issues. This approach is simple and robust as it depends solely on ranking. Once the 'wish list' has been compiled, a 'virtual portfolio' can be projected based on the expected next fundraisings, commitments and probabilities of signature. Then, in a mixed approach, risk concentrations can be identified by comparing this virtual portfolio with the strategic allocation, as defined by the top-down approach. Finally, the risk profile of this virtual portfolio can be evaluated based on historic data.

16.3   THE RISK PROFILE OF PRIVATE EQUITY ASSETS

So far we always stressed the high non-measurable uncertainty related to individual private equity fund investments, particularly in the case of venture capital, and discussed the techniques to properly manage these investments. However, for diversified portfolios characteristics become more measurable, and in this context it is fair to say that we are dealing with risk, which motivates taking a closer look at the relationship between diversification and the resulting risk profile of portfolios of private equity funds.

16.3.1   Private equity funds

Private equity funds sub-asset classes do show some quite different risk profiles. Looking at the main ones, i.e. buyouts and venture capital in the United States and Europe (see Figure 16.11 and Table 16.2),[13] interesting observations can be made:

- Considering only the average multiple, US VC funds (2.4x) have historically clearly outperformed all the other sub-asset classes (returns around 1.6x).
- This US VC funds outperformance has been obtained under much higher risk level, as evidenced by the standard deviation above $3.0\times$ compared with levels below 2.0x for European VC and below $1.0\times$ for European and US buyout funds. Other risk measures, such as the skewness or the kurtosis, further demonstrate the higher risk level of VC funds both in the USA and Europe.
- Looking at the return-to-risk ratio (see Box 16.3), buyout funds in the USA and Europe appear then to offer much better risk profiles than VC funds in the USA and Europe.
- The probability of loss tells us that four out of ten European VC funds, three out of ten US VC funds, and around two out of ten US and European buyout funds will show a loss. The average losses given a loss are quite similar for all sub-asset classes, around 30%.
- There have been very few total losses in all the funds included in the Thomson Financial's VentureXpert database (only a few US VC funds). This comes notably from the fact that distributions also include equalization fees, which cannot be considered as a repayment from the fund or some small distributions or immaterial exits from some of the investments made. Therefore, we have also looked at the probability of losing more than 80% of the capital initially invested, which to some degree can be assimilated to a total loss and found that for all sub-asset classes around 1% of the funds do lose more than 80% of the capital initially invested.
- Standard deviation is not all bad for this type of asymmetric distributions and cannot alone be a reliable measure of risk. We have, therefore, considered other indicators such as the expected multiple in bottom and top deciles, probability of a multiple above a certain threshold, semi-deviation and the Sortino ratio (see Box 16.4). While the standard deviation is much higher for US VC funds, this is no longer the case when looking at the semi-deviation below a multiple of one. The gap between buyout funds and VC funds is much narrower and the highest figure is now observed for European VC funds.

---

[13] These figures have been produced with the same approach as the one followed by Weidig and Mathonet (2004) but with updated data. We also used the Thomson Financial's VentureXpert database and dropped all funds raised before 1987 and the ones younger than five years, i.e. funds up to vintage year 2001. The risk profile was produced based on a Monte Carlo simulation with 10 000 runs with a realistic selection (i.e. each vintage year has the same probability of being drawn), allowing for multiple draws.

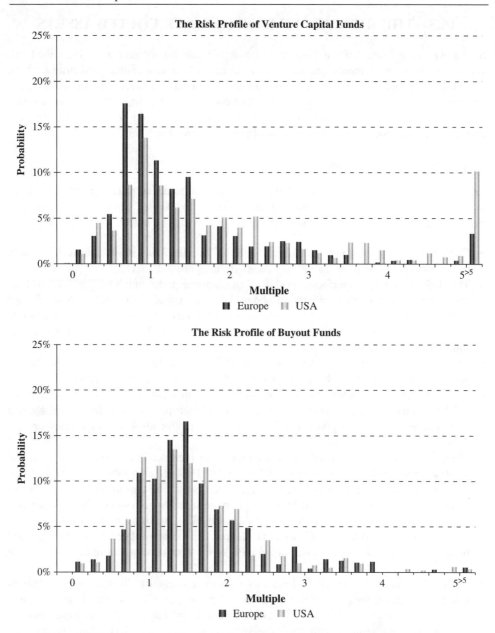

Figure 16.11   The risk profile of venture capital and buyout funds – USA vs. Europe
Source: Thomson Financial (VentureXpert database) and our own simulations.

- Looking at the downside, we do not see large differences between the various sub-asset classes. The expected multiples in bottom deciles are similar in the USA and in Europe VC and buyout funds. The main differences come from the upside. There is a much higher probability of reaching a multiple above 3× in the US VC funds (22%) than for all other sub-markets (below 10%). The expected multiple in top deciles is also much higher in the US VC funds (9.5×) than in European VC funds (5.4×) and buyout funds (around 3.4×).

Box 16.3:   Return-to-risk ratio

The return-to-risk ratio we have used is similar to a Sharpe ratio, which is a measure of risk-adjusted performance of the asset. The ratio is calculated as:

$$S = \frac{\frac{1}{N} \sum_{i=1}^{N} (R_i - 1)}{\sigma}$$

where R is the fund return or multiple, the return on a benchmark is set to 1, $\frac{1}{N} \sum_{i=1}^{N} (R_i - 1)$ is the expected average excess return, and σ is the standard deviation of the excess return.

In conclusion, there is between sub-markets a big discrepancy in the upside combined with relatively similar downsides. These differences are well evidenced by the Sortino ratio, which shows that US VC funds have been historically much better than the other sub-markets. Finally, knowing that the Sortino ratio depends on the hypothesis that the future will be similar to the past and that our statistical data are representative of the market, on a threshold level, which we chose to set at 1 and that investors may have different return–risk preferences, these quite general conclusions have to be challenged and adapted to each investor's objectives and expectations.

Box 16.4:   Sortino ratio

Frank Sortino's ratio is a measure of a risk-adjusted return of an investment asset. It is an extension of the Sharpe ratio. While the Sharpe ratio takes into account any volatility in return of an asset, the Sortino ratio differentiates volatility due to up and down movements. The up movements are considered desirable and not accounted for in the volatility. Here, the ratio is calculated as:

$$S = \frac{\frac{1}{N} \sum_{i=1}^{N} (R_i - 1)}{\sigma_d}$$

where R is the fund return or multiple, the return on a benchmark is set to 1, $\frac{1}{N} \sum_{i=1}^{N} (R_i - 1)$ is the expected average excess return, and σ_d is the downside volatility or semi-deviation below 1, i.e. the downside volatility is computed using the standard deviation formula, keeping only the contribution of negative excess returns.

Table 16.2   The risk profile of venture capital and buyout funds – USA vs. Europe

	Buyout		VC	
	Europe	USA	Europe	USA
Average multiple	1.6	1.5	1.6	2.4
Median multiple	1.5	1.4	1.1	1.5
Standard deviation	0.8	0.8	1.9	3.1
Skewness	1.4	1.9	6.0	4.0
Kurtosis	3.4	7.3	50.1	21.4
Probability of a loss	16%	22%	38%	30%
Average loss given a loss	−31%	−27%	−32%	−32%
Probability of total loss	0%	0%	0%	0%
Expected multiple in bottom decile	0.5	0.5	0.4	0.4
Expected multiple in top decile	3.4	3.3	5.4	9.5
Probability of a multiple above 3	6%	5%	8%	22%
Probability of a multiple above 2	22%	21%	20%	37%
Return-to-risk ratio	0.8	0.7	0.3	0.5
Semi-deviation below a multiple of 1	0.16	0.16	0.24	0.22
Sortino ratio	3.8	3.3	2.5	6.6

Source: Thomson Financial (VentureXpert database) and our own simulations.

Looking at the private equity 'efficient frontier' (see Figure 16.12) is also very informative on the very different risk profiles of these sub-markets. The US market looks more like what we expect as a positive correlation between long-term returns and long-term risk level on a rather straight line. Within the US market, clear differences emerge between three groups: (1) seed and early stage funds with high long-term returns and risk levels; (2) balanced, later stage and buyouts with lower long-term returns and risk levels; and (3) mezzanine with the lowest long-term returns and risk levels.

In Europe such a relationship does not seem to exist. The relationship between realized multiple and standard deviation is almost flat, even slightly negative. We do not find the same groupings as in the USA and balanced, later stage and buyouts show quite different risk profiles. Contrary to what was expected, buyout funds have both a higher realized multiple and a lower standard deviation than early stage funds. Finally, all segments of the European market – with probably the exception of buyouts – seem to have a less favorable risk–return profile than US ones. However, some people believe that these results may come from a lower 'quality' of the data in the European database.[14]

But of course these historic data are not necessarily a good guide to future performance. This is also the case for all other asset classes, but for private equity the time horizon that needs to be covered is extremely long and therefore any precision of the forecast is out of reach in principle. The past will most certainly not be the future in private equity, but to some degree the available statistics can be sufficient for defining the 'laws of gravity' of the long-term development for this asset class. It is clearly not a good idea to base one's long-term forecasts on optimistic scenarios that rarely or never materialized in the past.

---

[14] Mowbray Capital (2005) believed that more than for other classes of private equity, figures for European venture are very inaccurate. This is mainly because of what they include, not because of the individual return data. Firstly, many 'venture capital' funds in reality appear to be university seed funds, local development funds, etc. It is suggested that just half of the European funds shown covered in VentureXpert would be eligible for investment by institutional investors, either because they are too small or they are not managed by independent, professional VC firms. In addition, there are many funds that are wrongly classified as 'venture' but which are in fact buyouts or something similar.

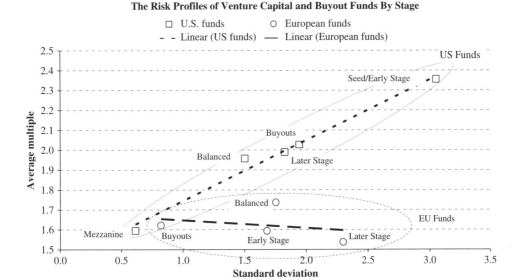

Figure 16.12   The private equity funds 'efficient frontier' in the USA and Europe
Source: Thomson Financial (VentureXpert database) and our own simulations.

We are amazed when we hear practitioners claim that history and statistics are worthless, and that past performance tells us nothing about how a hedge fund will perform in the future. Surprisingly or not, the same people usually select the funds that had the best historical returns, regardless of their strategy.

                                                                    Lhabitant (2004)

While most or all investors look at historical performance figures to decide on their allocations, only few dare to base their investment decision on their future expectations. This behavior can be compared to driving a car through the rear-mirrors, but is not untypical. Some investors argued that changes in the culture and maturity of private equity markets are so slow that past information of investments and exits can be used for evaluating also the potential deal flow in the future.

A mature but crowded market segment may see its average return decrease due to an increasing competition for deals. It may also see its return becoming more volatile due to the use of more aggressive structuring or leverage. On the other side, historically inexistent or poorly performing markets may develop further and deliver higher and more constant returns.

Box 16.5:   Risk-adjusted pricing

Especially for VC funds there is no set formula that automatically strikes the proper balance of risk and return. Why is that so? It is well understood that there can be

Box 16.5: (Continued)

no excess return without incurring risks. In fact, often there is the expectation that this works in reverse, too, and in return for taking the risk an investor would get automatically rewarded. This, however, requires a risk-adjusted pricing mechanism that is inefficient for early stage VC investing and does not exist for a limited partner taking a primary position in a VC fund. In a nutshell, risk-adjusted pricing means that the higher the risk, the higher the premium required by the investor.

After adjustment for risk, the overwhelming majority of venture capital fails to produce acceptable risk-adjusted returns.

Swensen (2005)

In principle, a risk adjusted pricing mechanism for a VC fund could either be implemented by the venture capitalists themselves or by their limited partners:

- As venture capitalists are best positioned to project valuations and to evaluate the risks associated with entrepreneurial companies, usually it is expected that they are also fully taking care about the pricing for their investments. Limited partners would monitor or define incentive structures – e.g., as discussed in one previous chapter, set an appropriate hurdle rate – that the venture capitalists select investments that are in line with the agreed risk profile.
- Alternatively the limited partners could theoretically require a discount on their stake in a fund that reflects their assessment of the risk.

From the limited partner perspective, both mechanisms are not fully applicable to VC funds.

VC investments in portfolio companies

Risk-adjusted pricing requires the quantification of risks to determine the premium to reach the risk-adjusted return targeted by the investor. For venture capitalists it is difficult to value early stage investments in the first place, as data for calibrating are weak or non-existent, and the typical approach is to use 'rules of the thumb' to capture the various risk categories as in Table 16.3.

Table 16.3   Targeted annual returns for VC investments

Stage	Bygrave *et al.* (1999)	White (1999)	Frey (1998)
Seed	80%	Not less than 40%	
Start-up	60%		40% to 80%
First stage	50%	30% to 50%	
Second stage	40%		
Third/late stage	30%	20% to 30%	25% to 50%
Bridge/pre-IPO	25%		

Valuations are usually based on a discounted cash flow (DCF) analysis (or need to be reconcilable with a DCF), where the targeted annual return is used as a discount rate to reflect the venture capitalist's level of risk-taking. There is a link between valuations, target returns and percentage ownership and there are a number of techniques to determine the percentage ownership the investor will require to achieve his target return. One example, according to White (1999) is the 'Hockey Stick' formula:

$$\text{percentage investor ownership} = \frac{\text{initial investment} \times \text{targeted multiple}}{\text{projected valuation}}$$

The percentage ownership determines the ratio between the investor's expected return on investment and the market valuation for the company as whole. For investors in venture capital the typical projection period is between three and five years.

Table 16.4 Examples of different multiples resulting from return requirements

Multiple	3 years	4 years	5 years
3 times	44%	32%	25%
4 times	59%	41%	32%
5 times	71%	50%	38%
10 times	115%	78%	58%

For a venture capital-funded company in its first stage it is projected that after four years it would achieve a market valuation of €1.5 million. A return requirement of 50% annual return would be reasonable (see Table 16.3). This translates into a multiple of five times (see Figure 16.13).

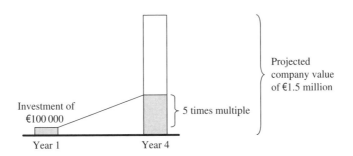

Figure 16.13 Investor ownership based on 'Hockey Stick'.

Therefore, the investor would require at minimum 33% ownership of the company for a €100 000 investment to achieve this target return. Ultimately, this is a matter of negotiations, but what is the venture capitalist's gain to some degree is also

Box 16.5: (Continued)

the entrepreneur's loss. Should the company's projected market value just be €500 000, the venture capitalist would need 100% of the ownership – here at the latest the entrepreneur would walk away from the deal.

Let's take another look at this relationship between ownership stake in a portfolio company and the multiples the venture capitalists demand to compensate for the risk they perceived. Assume that the projected portfolio company's value would just be one million euros after 5 years. For a second stage investment with an annual return target in the range of 40% (see Table 16.3) this would still leave the entrepreneur with about half of his company. For a start-up the annual return target would be about 60% translating into a target multiple of 10, leaving the entrepreneur nothing of his own company, and for a seed stage investment with an annual target of 80%, the entrepreneur in fact has to pay to make it a meaningful investment for the venture capitalist.

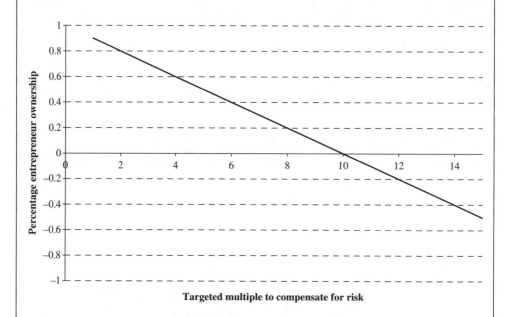

Figure 16.14   Relationship risk and entrepreneur ownership

Note that here the entrepreneur can control mainly two variables for funding: the targeted returns decrease with the maturity of the company. Consequently, the entrepreneur could try to reduce his funding needs through, say, two rounds within the four years interval with the second round at a lower risk level. Alternatively, the entrepreneur may give away more of his ownership, but as discussed, for high-risk investments in the seed and early stages there are clear limits.

Particularly in the early stage and high-tech area the discount rates targeted to compensate for the 'true' risks go beyond what is meaningful from the entrepreneur's point of view. This also sheds light on the importance of business angels and the 'three Fs' – friends, family and fools – in funding this kind of activity. This group of investors is often less risk-averse and less interested in being fully compensated for the risk taken.

VC investments in funds

The venture capitalist's target returns are a function of their own investors' return requirements. As we discussed before, the increased risks perceived by the VC funds' limited partners cannot be – or at least not fully – passed on to the entrepreneurs through increasing the return requirements.

The typical limited partnership structure does not allow for risk-adjusted pricing.[15] All primary positions are bought at par (i.e. without premium or discount) and there is no pre-defined coupon payment but only an uncertain performance and a pre-defined cost structure.

'Institutional size' funds usually charge around 1% management fees, while for small funds fees in the area of 2.5% are common. Occasionally newcomers to the VC industry see potential for savings in such 'excessive' fees and try to negotiate them downwards. However, it is overlooked that for small funds, which are not atypical for the specialist early stage technology sector, 2.5% rather marks the lower end of what is feasible. In fact, according to Murray and Marriott (1998), between 4% and 5% of the commitment size would be required to cover such funds' operating costs. We had discussions with managers of very small – i.e. between $10 and $20 million of commitments – early stage funds. When questioning the feasibility of these vehicles, the response was that the fund managers basically lived from their personal savings – the interviewees admittedly were well off – and hoped to be able to raise larger funds in the foreseeable future.

Situations where the price system does not work in matching supply and demand are not uncommon. In such situations other mechanisms will take its place. One possibility is queues or line-ups that were a familiar sight in the controlled economy of the former Soviet Union. In the case of weaker VC fund proposals, two mechanisms compensate for the lower demand.

- Firstly, the lower demand leads to decreased fund sizes and associated with this to proportionately higher management fees. This essentially results in a premium for lower quality: the administrative costs of the funds were not in line with the total level of finances available, particularly as a substantial proportion would not be allocated to the targeted portfolio firms but paid to the management. Therefore, such fees would be unacceptable to the vast majority of institutional investors.
- As a second consequence the probability that a weak VC fund finds the critical mass of limited partners and can close to start the operation is decreasing in line with the lower quality.

---

[15] To some degree leverage provided by government VC promotion programs could bridge this gap.

Box 16.5: (Continued)

Our analysis of more than 200 VC fund proposals between 1997 and 2006 (see Figure 16.15) supports this view. While P-A graded proposals – i.e. funds of institutional quality – are nearly certain to start their operation, 30% of P-D graded funds – i.e. with strong deviations from best market practices or clear weaknesses – did not manage to close, and these commitments eventually needed to be canceled.

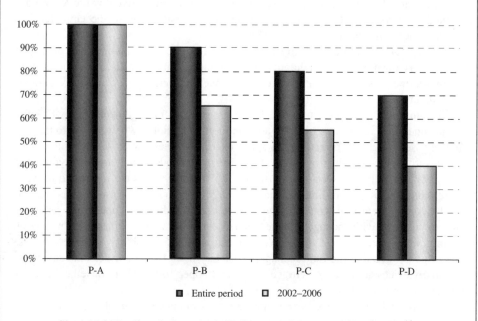

| Entire period | 2002–2006 |

Figure 16.15   Cancelation rate dependent on VC funds' ex ante grading[16]

When we analyzed proposals after mid-2002, we found that market standards became stricter and the probability that a VC fund with ex ante grade of P-D had to be

---

[16] We introduced a systematic grading for all VC fund proposals in 2003. To do the analysis above and take out the element of hindsight we had to base the grading for VC funds proposed before 2003 on a simplified 'quick scoring'. The 'quick scoring' is based on the technique described in Meyer and Mathonet (2005) but takes only those elements into account that could have been observed ex ante:

• Stage focus: from 5 for seed to 0 for buyout.
• Fund size: from 5 for < €40 milion to 1 for > €100 million.
• Geographical focus: based on ranking given by EVCA survey.
• First time team: 5 for yes, 1 for no.
• Assessment of co-investor quality.
• Ex ante label as 'strategic' in the widest sense: 10 for yes, 1 for no.

The 'quick scoring' gives a maximum score of 30 points that is translated into P-A to P-D (the higher the score for the operation, the lower the expected performance grade). For those funds that were canceled, data on fund size and the co-investors quality usually were missing. Here the assessment was mainly based on the stage focus.

canceled went up to 60%. Moreover, our experience suggests a link between the ex ante assessment and the 'troubled cases' in the portfolio. VC funds with low operational status grades over a longer time are also likely to under-perform, as in many cases the operational troubles are a symptom rather than the cause of poor financial performance – when it becomes unlikely that team members will ever receive carried interest, the alignment of interests falls apart and leads to tensions within the team, with the fund's investee companies and with its investors.

However, our findings cannot be considered as significant and have to be taken with a grain of salt, as there were simply fewer 'weak' proposals than VC funds of institutional quality in our sample. Further collection of data may provide additional insights, but the absence of statistically significant sample sizes is a problem inherent in alternative assets. In any case, also these findings support our view that available industry statistics by and large represents a majority of private equity funds – including some high-quality niche investments – that passed the rigorous selection process of experienced investors.

Furthermore, investors may have different access to a market and these profiles may not represent that of the market a specific investor can invest in. Therefore, for some investors not having access to the best teams, established markets may fail to deliver the often – but wrongly – expected guaranteed top return.

On the other side, when an investor has exceptional access, picking, structuring and monitoring skills, some emerging or poorly performing markets, though having an unattractive average risk profile, may still offer few but interesting investment opportunities in what is called their 'fat tail'.

16.3.2 Portfolio of private equity funds

But it is important to remember that we are never looking at an opportunity in isolation but always in the context of our total portfolio construction.

Greg Uebele, Assistant Investment Officer: Private Equity, OPERS

Investors rarely invest only in one private equity fund but rather construct portfolios of such funds. As for private equity funds, for portfolios of private equity funds or funds-of-funds, sub-asset classes also show quite different risk profiles. Looking at the main ones, i.e. portfolios of buyouts and venture capital funds in the United States and Europe (see Figures 16.16, 16.17 and Table 16.5), the following observations can be made:

- As expected, for all sub-markets, the average returns remain unchanged[17] between funds and funds-of-funds and the standard deviation, skewness and kurtosis all decrease. However, our simulations do not account for program size and diseconomies of scale, which in reality should impact and decrease the average returns.

---

[17] Due to the selection process (realistic selection, multiple draws allowed), the average return is not exactly the same, though statistically they should be. However, the differences observed are minor.

- As for funds, US VC outperformance has been obtained also under higher risk level, as evidenced by the standard deviation around $1.0\times$ compared to $0.6\times$ for European VC and below $0.5\times$ for European and US buyouts. Other risk measures, such as the skewness or the kurtosis, also further demonstrates the higher risk of VC, both in the USA and Europe.
- The return-to-risk and Sortino ratios naturally always improve with diversification, as they simply compare the mean return (stable) to a risk measure (always decreasing). Based on these ratios, buyouts in the USA and Europe appear to offer better risk profiles than VC.
- The probability of loss tells us that one out of ten portfolios of EU VC funds, less than one out of ten portfolios of US VC funds, and close to zero out of ten portfolios of US and European buyout funds will show a loss. The average losses given a loss are around 12% for VC and 3% for buyouts. The probability of total loss is apparently remote for all portfolio of funds, as the probability of losing more than 40% of the capital invested is also equal to zero for all sub-markets.
- Standard deviation is probably now a much better indicator of risk as distributions are much less asymmetric. We have, still, considered other indicators such as the expected multiple in bottom and top deciles, probability of a multiple above a certain threshold, semi-deviation and the Sortino ratio. As for funds, looking at the semi standard deviation below a multiple of one, the gap between buyouts and VC is much narrower and is higher for VC, with the maximum observed for European VC.
- Looking at the downside, we do not see large differences between the various sub-asset classes. The expected multiple in bottom deciles is similar in all sub-markets. The average loss given a loss is a bit higher for VC (around 12%) than for buyouts (around 3%). For VC there is a lower probability of suffering a loss in the USA (5%) than in Europe (11%) and for buyouts in general the probability is very low (close to 0%). As for funds, the main differences come from the upside. There is a much higher probability (higher than for funds) of reaching a multiple above 3 in the US VC (30%), than for all other sub-markets (below 3%). The expected multiple in top deciles is also much higher in the US VC ($4.6\times$) than in the other sub-markets (below $3.0\times$). It is interesting to note that because of higher average returns for US funds, the probability for a diversified portfolio of US funds, of reaching a multiple above 3 increases with diversification, while for the other sub-markets – because of lower average returns – it is the opposite.

In conclusion, between sub-markets there is some discrepancy in the upside combined with relatively similar downside. Diversification is beneficial to all segments as it decreases the level of risk taken by investors. However, it also 'normalizes' the risk profile and limits the upside potential. One exception to that have been portfolios of US VC funds, which look more promising, but this is thanks to their historically high average returns. Finally, as for funds, these quite general conclusions have also to be challenged and adapted to each investor's objectives and expectations. For example, we know that though the future is never equal to the past, these conclusions depend on the hypothesis that such future will be similar to the past. We are also aware of the limitations of the statistical data used, which due to their limited history and sample size are not totally representative of the market. And finally, we know that investors may have different return–risk preferences, and that this should impact their respective portfolio construction.

The Risk Profile of European Venture Capital Investment Vehicles

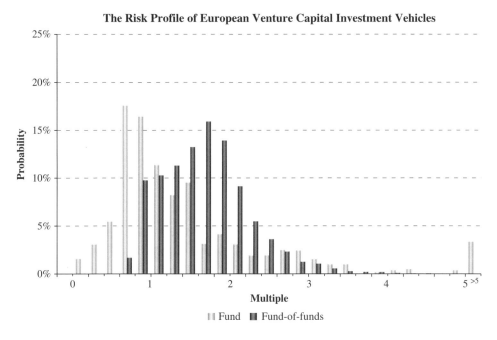

⫴ Fund   ▮ Fund-of-funds

The Risk Profile of U.S. Venture Capital Investment Vehicles

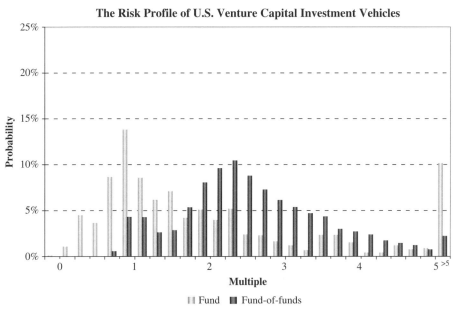

⫴ Fund   ▮ Fund-of-funds

Figure 16.16   The risk profile of venture capital investments (EU vs. US)
Source: Thomson Financial (VentureXpert database) and our own simulations.

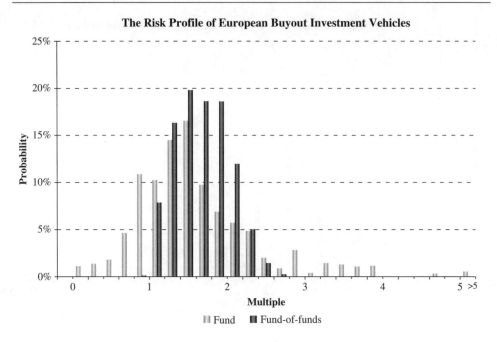

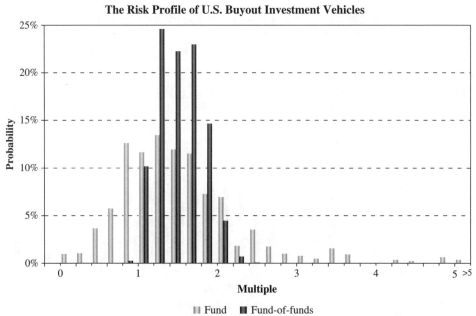

Figure 16.17 The risk profile of buyout investments (EU vs. US)

Source: Thomson Financial (VentureXpert database) and our own simulations.

Table 16.5 The risk profile of venture capital and buyout investments (USA vs. Europe)

	Buyout				VC			
	Europe		USA		Europe		USA	
	Fund	FoFs	Fund	FoFs	Fund	FoFs	Fund	FoFs
Average multiple	1.6	1.7	1.5	1.5	1.6	1.7	2.4	2.6
Median multiple	1.5	1.7	1.4	1.5	1.1	1.6	1.5	2.4
Standard deviation	0.8	0.3	0.8	0.3	1.9	0.6	3.1	1.0
Skewness	1.4	0.2	1.9	0.2	6.0	0.8	4.0	0.7
Kurtosis	3.4	−0.6	7.3	−0.7	50.1	1.3	21.4	0.8
Probability of a loss	16%	0%	22%	0%	38%	11%	30%	5%
Average loss given a loss	−31%	−3%	−27%	−3%	−32%	−12%	−32%	−11%
Probability of total loss	0%	0%	0%	0%	0%	0%	0%	0%
Expected multiple in bottom decile	0.5	1.2	0.5	1.1	0.4	0.9	0.4	1.0
Expected multiple in top decile	3.4	2.28	3.3	2.0	5.4	2.8	9.5	4.6
Probability of a multiple above 3	6%	0%	5%	0%	8%	2%	22%	30%
Probability of a multiple above 2	22%	19%	21%	5%	20%	24%	37%	72%
Return-to-risk ratio	0.8	2.0	0.7	2.0	0.3	1.2	0.5	1.6
Semi-deviation below a multiple of 1	0.16	0.00	0.16	0.00	0.24	0.05	0.22	0.03
Sortino ratio	3.8	669.0	3.3	240.2	2.5	14.7	6.6	56.0

Source: Thomson Financial (VentureXpert database) and our own simulations.

16.3.3 Further remarks

A lot of people are running around with an exact number of partnerships you should have in a portfolio to make it diversified [. . .] There is no such number.

Dynamics' Managing Director Christophe Rouvinez (see Granito, 2006)

Despite what has been said so far about the various limitations, we can say at least something about a diversified portfolio of private equity funds. This has admittedly more the character of a 'back of the envelope' calculation, but it is an important starting point for reflections on how to construct a portfolio.

Many institutional investors aim to invest in approximately the same number of funds somewhat independently of the size of the institution's assets. They expect benefits from diversification without having overwhelming monitoring responsibilities from investing in too many funds or having to compromise on fund manager quality.

Empirical evidence suggests that 20 to 30 funds are sufficient to eliminate most of the specific risk. Assume you look at a portfolio of ten funds invested in 40 investee companies each and at another portfolio of 40 funds invested in ten investee companies each. Two questions spring to mind: firstly, both portfolios have invested in 400 investee companies. Don't they have the same level of diversification? Secondly, according to rules of thumb, diversification benefits level off after 20 positions of whatever is to be diversified. Isn't a portfolio of 400 investee companies far beyond this point?

Most private equity partnerships have relatively concentrated strategies and therefore are to us more like companies than portfolios.

Sweeney *et al.* (2001)

One answer to these questions is that for VC funds you cannot assume that the failures of portfolio companies are just subject to statistics. In fact, venture capitalists run a milestone approach where, in the extreme, they are happy even if there was just one winner left in their portfolio. On the other hand, we can assume that the returns of funds to some degree follow a statistical process, and that therefore a portfolio of 40 funds has a different risk profile from a portfolio of ten funds.

The simulation results presented here need to be taken with a 'pinch of salt', as the modeling assumptions are simplistic if not to some degree unrealistic. How can you implement a random pick among a population of private equity funds? Neither are they all known nor are they all accessible. Moreover, can they really be seen as independent, or how can we assure that they are as independent as possible? We turn to this question in the next section.

16.4 RISK DIMENSIONS

Stacking a portfolio with too many similar funds will lead to a regression of the mean. Because figures on correlation are unreliable, unstable or not available at all, portfolio construction rather aims to assure a high degree of independence between the funds. Investors see the stage focus, the vintage year, the broad industry sector (e.g. ICT, life science, generalists), the geographical region (e.g. USA, Asia, Western Europe, Eastern Europe, emerging markets), the currency and the agent or counterparty concentration, i.e. the exposure to a specific fund manager, as the main dimensions of private equity portfolio diversification.[18] Some are specific to private equity, such as the stage focus and the vintage year; others are also applicable for standard asset classes, such as the industry sector, the geography, the currency or the agent concentration. In principle, for each dimension, the higher the resolution, the more we will be able to differentiate funds, but definitions can only be very fuzzy. For example, the investment focus is mainly based on the self-declaration of the managers, and drifts in strategy are common. Does 'geography' relate to the fund or to the portfolio companies? Probably the fund's location is the 'best guess', but some are operating in several countries. How relevant is it anyway for venture capital, where technology is increasingly becoming global? Does the stage focus relate to the stage of the portfolio company at the time of commitment or its current state? A seed investment five years later may already be in its pre-IPO stage. Does the currency definition relate to commitments, the fund's currency or the portfolio companies' currencies? For all these questions certainly rules can be drawn up, but it can become quite complex and we also have to ask ourselves the question of how we can manage this. In reality, for most of these dimensions, only a 'low resolution' will be practical.

16.4.1 Stage focus

Spreading investments across companies at various stages of maturity also leads to a staggered pace of realizations and thus less dependence upon market conditions at particular points in time. Furthermore, as illustrated before, the risk profile of a private equity investment appears to be significantly different depending on its stage focus. Thomson Financial uses two main categories split into nine sub-categories (see Table 16.6).

Table 16.6 Stage focus categories

Venture	Buyouts and other private equity
Seed stage	Mezzanine stage
Early stage	Buyouts
Balance stage	Generalist
Later stage	Other private equity
	Funds-of-funds[19]

Source: Thomson Financial.

As an extension to this, investors also often take into account the investment size as another dimension. For example, Thomson Financial[20] defines venture and buyout funds sizes as:

---

[18] Standard & Poor's conducts ratings for structured notes backed by a portfolio of private equity funds. The basis of the rating is the analysis of a portfolio of private equity funds' diversification level in a multidimensional fashion. The following dimensions signal how diversified a portfolio is: number of fund managers or general partners and number of funds or limited partnerships, vintage years and calendar years, type of private equity funds or strategies, industry or sector, geography and single investment exposure. In Standard & Poor's opinion, mainly the portfolio diversification provides downside protection to the holders of the rated notes (see Erturk *et al.*, 2001).

[19] With regard to funds-of-funds, we recommend looking at the stage allocation of the funds in their portfolio rather than considering them as one position.

[20] These classifications were the ones used in 2006. Considering the very large funds raised in the market, it is to be expected that these ranges should move up.

Table 16.7 Investment sizes by stage focus categories

Size	Venture	Buyouts and other Private equity
Small	0–25 $mill	0–250 $mill
Medium	25–50 $mill	250–500 $mill
Large	50–100 $mill	500–1000 $mill
Mega	100 $mill+	1000 $mill+

Source: Thomson Financial.

Finally, a problem that is often ignored is that portfolio companies grow over the portfolio build-up. Indeed, seed investments are expected to germinate and allow the business to start. After these early stages, these investments, when successful, will expand and develop during their later stages to end up, finally and hopefully, in fruitful exits. This implies that after several years, the risk profile of a fund will change with the evolution of its portfolio companies. To take this into account, investors can either adjust the stage focus of their funds with the evolution of their portfolio companies or, more simply, take the vintage year as one of the diversification dimensions.

16.4.2   Vintage year

In standard private equity funds, the total capital available gets invested mostly during the investment period, i.e. the first three to five years of the fund's lifetime, but also afterwards, in a more targeted manner, to follow on the most successful investments. The distributions of capital to limited partners are done as soon as investments get exited, mostly during the divestment period, i.e. the remaining fund's lifetime. Therefore, for private equity funds commitments should be made over the full course of the economic cycle and should not be concentrated in any one year to reduce the risk of getting in or out at the wrong time.

> *Time diversification is also a critical component of any well-balanced portfolio. Investments, especially venture capital investments which follow a more pronounced cycle, need to be staged such that the weight of money in any given period does not overwhelm that of other periods to the detriment of portfolio return.*
>
> Frank Brenninkmeyer, Principal, Performance Equity Management

Whether vintage year should be defined as the year of the first closing, the year of the final closing, or the year of the first capital draw poses a, albeit minor, complication. In our practice we tend to rely on the funds' vintage years reported in the Thomson Financial's VentureXpert database, which complies with the EVCA's definition, i.e. 'the year of fund formation and first drawdown of capital'.

> *Analyzing the different fund raising and return cycles over the last 20 years makes one thing very clear: the perfect timing in an asset class which requires long-term commitment and does not offer daily liquidity is rather impossible.*
>
> Maximilian Brönner, LGT Capital Partners

One issue that investors can encounter in their effort to get an adequate vintage year diversification is when too many current general partner relationships come back to market in the same year. Obviously a trade-off between fund manager quality and vintage year diversification has then to be made. However, this issue has to be put into perspective. Assuming funds with the same investment and divestment patterns (e.g. four years investment period and six years divestment period), funds raised in two consecutive years will have three common years of investment period (75%, i.e. years two, three and four of the oldest fund and years two, three and four of the youngest one) and five of divestment (83%) and should therefore have quite similar time exposure to the market.

16.4.3 Industry sector

Spreading investments across managers with skills in different industry sectors protects against a sector going out of favor (e.g. Internet in 2000) or against cyclical industries. In practice, investors have to rely on the fund managers' declared industry focus – often in line with the definitions and categories of the industry, such as in the Thomson Financial's VentureXpert database or as used by EVCA. Figure 16.18 gives an indication of the European market sector breakdown.

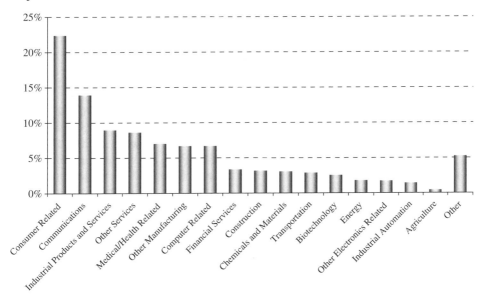

Figure 16.18   Sector distribution of investments per year
Source: EVCA Yearbooks (2002–2006).

For buyout funds, opportunities are available in many industries mostly from the 'old economy'. These funds often have a generalist focus, which in itself will already give some industry diversification. For venture capital funds, however, opportunities tend to be more concentrated in fewer industries, i.e. the ones that are likely to have significant technology breakthroughs.

With respect to sector diversification, we believe that a portfolio composed largely of 'generalists' will have ample diversification with respect to sector, and that therefore it is unnecessary to have a high number of relationships that are sector specific.
Frank Brenninkmeyer, Principal, Performance Equity Management

16.4.4   Geography and currencies

The private equity industry has traditionally been very nationalistically fragmented. Funds have been raised, investments have been made and exits have been achieved primarily domestically. Since the mid-1990s the private equity market has increasingly internationalized. This trend has been especially pronounced in the growth of cross-border capital commitments done by funds. Heikkilä (2004) found that there are 'surprisingly few papers' on how investors create their portfolios of private equity funds and that assessing benefits of geographical diversification of a private equity portfolio was extremely hard. Consequently, many of the investors told us that their geographical diversification principles are based on rules of thumb rather than on systematic analysis. They usually do not consider diversification at country level, but rather between areas like Northern Europe versus the UK, or even Europe versus the USA. In fact, interviewees in Heikkilä (2004) appeared to be more careful in diversifying their portfolios across investment stages – specifically venture capital versus buyouts – than across geographical areas. Some of the interviewees claimed that rather than spending too much time calculating potential benefits of geographical diversification, the more relevant issue is to consider the management teams of the funds.

16.4.5   Agent concentration

The number of general partners, with their specific management 'style' or strategy and their specialized expertise in a particular segment of the market, is one of the key dimensions to consider when building a portfolio. Maintaining a relationship with the same general partner extending over several funds reduces the need for screening and pre-investment due diligence work and thus saves the investors time and money. However, during the normally ten plus two years lifetime of a fund, it is quite likely that a fund management team will go through a crisis situation, such as tensions among the team members, the departure of a key person, or the spin-out of part of the team. Having several general partners mitigates the potential over-reliance upon few key investment professionals.

16.4.6   'Naïve' diversification

Despite the wide acceptance of MPT, most managers of private equity fund investment programmes follow simplistic diversification approaches. Even for hedge funds-of-funds, where one would expect that quantitative models play a strong role, Lhabitant and Learned (2002) not all too long ago found that techniques were not sophisticated at all: 'A recent survey [. . .] of Swiss hedge fund investors and fund of hedge funds managers confirms our intuition. It appears that most participants do not use a quantitative approach for their asset allocation strategy. Many respondents even admitted to having no asset allocation strategy at all!' Naïve diversification is appealingly simple and normally results in reasonably diversified portfolios.

The naïve diversification (also called $1/N$ heuristics) may be less rigorous than traditional portfolio models, but it is nevertheless valuable to the prudent investor, as it can avoid extreme concentrations by managing the relevant risk dimensions. MPT is seldom applied to the full degree anyway, and naïve diversification in practice usually results in reasonably diversified portfolios that are surprisingly close to some points on the efficient frontier. In fact, Kempf and Memmel (2003) state that when data and forecasts are not reliable, equal weighting is the theoretically optimal solution.[21] Under a pure naïve diversification approach, one decreases the expected variance of a portfolio simply by increasing the number of funds in the portfolio. Sometimes, when investors have not identified that the funds in a portfolio are highly correlated, this can give a false sense of security and the belief that the portfolio is well diversified when in reality it may still be overly concentrated. For example two funds, even if focusing on different industries but raised in the same year and exposed to the same economic cycles throughout their life, should exhibit more dependence than two funds raised in different stages of the business cycle. Therefore the portfolio construction process should aim to assure a high degree of independence between the funds, for example by trying to maximize the 'distance' between funds (see Box 16.6). In other words, a VC fund A raised in year 2000 with focus on life sciences is likely to have less dependencies with a buyout fund B raised in 2003 than with another VC fund raised in 2001 with focus on biotechnology.

Box 16.6: Cluster analysis

Cluster analysis is a technique that is used to classify objects into relatively homogenous groups that share some common trait. In the basic setting of naïve diversification, there is no or too little information that allows differentiation between assets. But private equity funds can relatively clearly be classified based on their different vintage years, geographical regions, industry sectors or fund management teams. We can take as common trait the similarity between private equity funds and apply cluster analysis to the management of diversification and construction and monitoring of a portfolio of funds. We can express the concept of dissimilarity between two funds by distance between points in an N-dimensional space, and in order to do so, we must agree on a distance measure. The distance measure will determine how the similarity of two elements is calculated and influences the clustering as some elements may be close to one another according to one distance and further away according to another. The distance should be small for very similar funds and large for very different funds. It has to fulfill four properties (see Lhabitant, 2004):

- Identity: $d(i, i) = 0$ for all i.
- Non-negativity: $d(i, j) \geq 0$ for all i and j.
- Symmetry: $d(i, j) = d(j, i)$ for all i and j.
- Triangle inequality: $d(i, j) \leq d(j, k) + d(j, k)$ for all i, j, k.

There are several methods to calculate the distance between two points. The most important ones are:

---

[21] Even for publicly traded assets, DeMiguel *et al.* (2004) show that, due to estimation errors in estimating the inputs to the optimizing models, naïve diversification has a better out-of-sample Sharpe ratio than optimal asset allocation models. They tested static naïve diversification against several models of optimal asset allocation and showed that the optimising models have a higher Sharpe ratio in-sample, but the $1/N$ rule has a higher Sharpe ratio out-of-sample: the gain from optimal diversification relative to naïve diversification is typically smaller than the loss arising from the error in estimating the inputs to the optimizing models.

Box 16.6: (Continued)

- *Euclidean distance*: the geometric distance between two objects in the *N*-dimensional space (also called 'as the crow flies' or 2-norm distance):

$$d(x, y) = \sqrt{\sum_{i=1}^{N}(x_i - y_i)^2}$$

- *Manhattan distance*: the average distance across dimensions. In this measure, the effect of single large differences is dampened as they are not squared (also called 'taxicab' distance or 1-norm distance):

$$d(x, y) = \sum_{i=1}^{N}|x_i - y_i|$$

- Both the Manhattan and the Euclidean distance can be regarded as special cases of the *Minkowski distance*:

$$d(x, y) = \sqrt[a]{\sum_{i=1}^{N}|x_i - y_i|^a}$$

The Minkowski distance is a generalized metric distance. When a = 1 it becomes the Manhattan distance and when a = 2 it becomes the Euclidean distance.

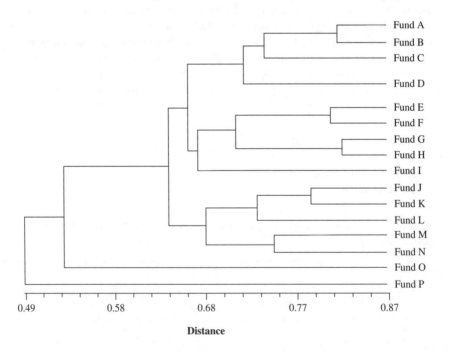

Figure 16.19 Example for dendrogram

To classify funds we used a so-called agglomerative clustering algorithm as a simple and effective way to classify data: the algorithm starts with every data point being its own cluster, finds the 'most similar' pair of clusters, and then merges smaller clusters into bigger clusters incrementally until all funds end up in the same cluster. For this purpose we used the complete linkage procedure, where the distance between two clusters is determined by the distance between the two furthest objects in the different clusters. The result can be shown in the form of a hierarchical tree called a dendrogram.

If we cut the tree when the dissimilarity between any two clusters exceeds a given threshold, we are left with M clusters. Two funds in the same cluster are expected to be completely correlated, and two funds in different clusters are expected to be completely independent. Therefore the choice of a particular threshold depends on how much we want to stress the portfolio: at the lowest threshold, all funds are assumed to be independent, while at the highest threshold, all funds are taken to be completely correlated. For a detailed discussion of cluster analysis in the context of managing funds-of-hedge-funds, we refer to Lhabitant (2004).

It is nevertheless possible to refine this approach. Brands and Gallagher (2003) found for actively managed equity funds-of-funds that better than a naïve random pick one should rather follow investment strategies that ensure equal representation across investment styles. Practically, investors have to identify the main risk dimensions and define the wished split and ranges between these dimensions. To take one simplified example and assuming only two dimensions (e.g. vintage year and stage focus), a four-year investment program could be composed of:

- An expected split of 25% committed to each vintage year within a range of ±10%.
- An expected allocation of 60% to buyouts and 40% to venture capital within a range of ±10%.

There are practical obstacles to naïve diversification. Limited partners cannot freely decide on the stakes they want to take in funds, as fund managers may have a preference for larger ticket investors, so the fund sizes will have an impact on what is feasible. Moreover, too large stakes in a small fund can trigger a consolidation of the fund in the limited partner's accounts, something most will try to avoid under any circumstances. To some degree, investing always the same ticket size implicitly over-weights investments in the smaller funds.

Naïve diversification also relates to the vintage year diversification. Limited partners should avoid timing the market but rather follow an investment strategy where a constant amount is allocated to commitments in funds at regular intervals, regardless of what direction the market is moving. Thus, as more fund management teams seek investors, limited partners can be more selective, whereas when fewer private equity funds operate in the market they are faced with less price competition. This assures that limited partners are not caught in an over-exposure in part of a cycle. Fund managers have the tendency to be cyclical and to shift their strategies anyway. If the limited partner adds cyclicality, it, to quote a practitioner, 'becomes a mess'.

17

Portfolio Construction Rules of Thumb

Based on the points discussed so far, how does this translate into an investment strategy and how does one construct a portfolio of private equity funds? We cannot make crystal-ball predictions about the future and thus have no answer for what would be the 'optimum' portfolio composition. For financial managers this may be difficult to swallow, as they generally have an aversion to ambiguity. With traditional asset classes, risk is quantifiable and for this reason may also be perceived to be lower. It is certainly a good idea to try to plan as well as possible and to have contingencies. But for VC funds it is simply not possible to specify ex ante all the possible states that might influence the actions and, as we discussed already, the claims of various industry experts that they have the ability to forecast which funds are going to be winners has to be taken with a huge pinch of salt. Furthermore, and as Generalfeldmarschall Helmuth, Graf von Moltke observed, '[n]o plan survives contact with the enemy'.[1]

Therefore, a portfolio of VC funds should rather provide flexibility for a future that is inherently uncertain and allow, within the constraints given by an illiquid asset class, adjustments over time. The strategies followed for such portfolios must be robust, i.e. perform well under several scenarios. The strategy essentially has to build on creating options and keeping them open as long as possible. These options have to be relatively cheap to continuously allow exploration in various directions and in parallel. To stay with the military analogy, reconnaissance has to explore not only one but several paths the army could be following. Many smaller bets with a high uncertainty need to be amplified into bigger bets once there is more certainty regarding their outcome.

In this chapter we try to address some of the key questions that should be answered for the portfolio construction:

- How many funds should a portfolio have to be 'properly' diversified?
- What should be the composition of a portfolio in terms of key risk dimensions (e.g. venture capital vs. buyouts or the broad geographical split)?

These questions right away lead to a series of other questions:

- What is the investor's ability to identify and access top teams? Limited access leads to different risk profiles and should lead to different routes to invest in private equity. For example, assuming that an investor sees, due to its limited access to the best US VC managers, its probability to access first-quartile funds reduced by a 50% probability, the risk profile of the accessible market will deviate substantially from that of the overall US VC market and may result in the conclusion that it is not worth investing in this market.

---

[1] This saying has variously been attributed to Napoleon, George Patton or Dwight D. Eisenhower, but it originated with Moltke 'the Elder' who actually said that '[n]o operation plan extends with any certainty beyond the first encounter with the main body of the enemy'.

- What trade-off between risk-taking and profit-seeking is the investor looking for, i.e. what is the investor's 'risk appetite'? The approaches for assessing VC funds do not allow calculating and balancing between the return to be expected from the investments and the risk taken with them.
- Does the investor have other 'strategic' objectives? Having such objectives leads to significantly different portfolios. For example, investment banks may be looking for business opportunities for their corporate finance services. Here the portfolio construction process should find a balance between the benefits and the cost of achieving them. Often this will result in a more diversified portfolio than the one only driven by financial considerations.

For private equity, there is no 'formulaic' or one-size-fits-all type of answer to determine what are the optimum diversification level and the optimum portfolio composition. Therefore, investors should follow a structured thought process to try to tailor their portfolio toward their needs. Below we present what we know and what we think we know – but were unable to find sufficient evidence to be certain about it – or what we do not know and should be further researched.

17.1   WHAT WE KNOW

Don't put all your eggs in one basket

The old proverb 'Do not put all your eggs in one basket', sometimes mis-attributed[2] to the character Sancho Panza in Miguel de Cervantes *Don Quixote*, seems to make sense. Put all your eggs in one venture or fund and a single event can destroy all or most of them.

Like all assets, private equity funds also carry two types of risk: the market or systematic risk and the asset's specific, unsystematic or idiosyncratic risk. While efficient markets do reward the former, which cannot be diversified away, the latter, which can be diversified away, is normally not rewarded. Though the private equity market cannot be qualified as efficient, we know that diversification is a useful tool for investors to manage the risk–return profile of their private equity funds portfolio.

> *How does an investor deal with a high variance situation? If they're fools, they try and pick one or two winners. If they are professionals, they average. You'll notice that the UM portfolio has at least five different VC funds in every complete year from 1996 onward. They are pros.*
>
> Oren (2003)

Don't put eggs in all baskets . . . baskets are expensive and not all baskets are of good quality

In general, diversification should be increased as long as the marginal benefit of adding a new asset to a portfolio exceeds the marginal cost. In private equity, it is common advice

---

[2] As B.J. Herbison has pointed out, this saying was actually introduced in an English translation and is not in the original text (see www.herbison.com, [accessed 9 January, 2007]).

and sense not to put all your eggs in one basket, but does that mean it's always the right strategy?

With increasing diversification, investors reduce the downside risk, but also reduce their chance to earn a very high return mainly because of the increased due diligence and monitoring effort. There are 'adverse' diversification effects and diseconomies of scale. The number of relationships rather than the invested amounts sets the cost base – such as legal expenses, due diligence and monitoring effort – for a portfolio of funds. It also becomes increasingly difficult identifying and getting access to suitable funds, as the number of quality opportunities is limited.

Furthermore, a diversification strategy without taking into account the specificities of the asset class and the objectives of the investor can be quite inefficient. We know that diversification drives return to the mean, which will reduce the chances for the portfolio to perform extremely well (see Figure 17.1).

LPs have recognized that beyond a certain point, the return of any additional diversification is likely to diminish [. . .] To avoid such regression through excess diversification to an undesired mean, a growing number of investors are aggressively cutting back on the number of managers they want to commit money to.

Borel (2004)

For some markets this mean can be above the investor's targeted return, and for some others it can be below. In the first case an 'excessive' diversification will be more acceptable than in the second case, where it will drive the investor to the certainty, irrespective of picking skills, not to meet return objectives. When the targeted market average performance is higher than the investor's target return, a high diversification is more acceptable, as it will drive return above target.

However, an investor can also rationally choose to be under-diversified because the benefits of achieving positive skewness more than compensate the cost of taking on higher diversifiable risk. Indeed, for private equity funds the distributions of returns share characteristics with lotteries: few extraordinary winners will compensate for many small losses. Like in a lottery, where buying all lots guarantees picking the winner but associated costs exceed the total gain, being invested in too many funds assures that the few top performers cannot adequately compensate the many funds with mediocre or sub-standard returns.[3] Therefore, in a lottery as in venture capital, one common strategy is to make few 'bets' under the assumption that luck or selection skills – provided that the targeted funds are accessible – will deliver the winners without having to support all losers.

If you buy many tickets you have a greater chance to win the lottery

As seen above, too much diversification can be detrimental to your portfolio. It is costly and drives return to the mean. However, within the list of initial questions to address before designing a portfolio, one was about the investor's trade-off between risk-taking and profit-seeking. For large investors, having only a relatively small allocation to private equity, the goal is often to get access to top-quartile funds irrespective of the risks.

---

[3] See Waters (2005): 'Yet the big gains are concentrated in a handful of funds, leaving most investors with mediocre returns'.

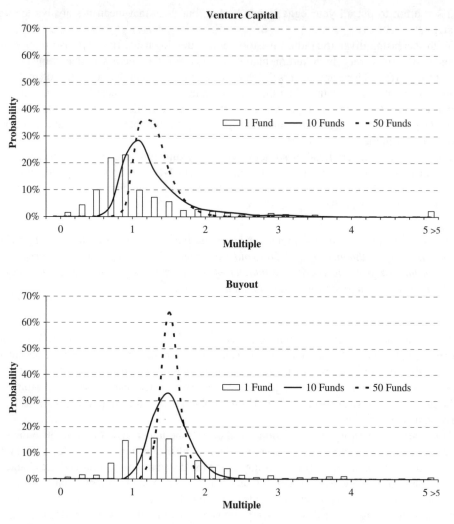

Figure 17.1 Probability distribution of final multiples for a portfolio of European VC and BO funds (random selection)

Yes, in Loto 100 percent of the winners tried their chance, but 99.99 percent of the ones who tried their chance lost their money!!! I'd rather buy the « Française des jeux » . . . and get ten times my money back!

Anonymous quote about the French national lottery « Française des jeux »

To establish long-term relationships with the emerging top-quartile funds, i.e. the future 'golden circle' managers, a certain level of diversification would be necessary. As a back-of-the-envelope calculation and assuming no picking skills and full access to the market, an investor has with one investment a 75% chance not of picking one first-quartile fund, with two investments this probability drop to 56%, with three to 42% and with four to 32%. Practitioners recommend, depending on the stage focus, ranges of two to six investments per year, but every investor will have their own preferences regarding the right level of diversification.

> *In buy-outs, you could probably get away with making two or three commitments per year if your financial analysis was sufficiently good, and still pick upper quartile funds with reasonable regularity. But in venture that just won't work. You really need to be committing to something like six venture capital funds in a year, giving you around 18 in a fundraising cycle. This is because there is a far greater disparity between the top-performing funds and the upper quartile in venture than in buy-outs. Venture capital is an upper decile game and diversification is crucial to managing risk. It is far too dangerous to put your eggs in too few baskets.*
>
> Guy Fraser-Sampson (AltAssets, 2004)

Avoid same eggs in different baskets

Just investing in many teams without considering interdependencies can create a false sense of security, as diversification sets in more slowly when funds are highly correlated. For example, investing in 20 different Internet funds can hardly be seen as a strong diversification.

> *J.P. Morgan's outfit bet big on technology during the bubble – and lost a bundle.*
>
> Economist (2005)

An unbalanced portfolio with few clusters, e.g. with high exposure to early stage investments or specific vintage years, works against diversification benefits. This is also the case when a market is characterized by many 'club deals'.

> *We do not have too many large buy-out managers in our portfolio. Their tendency to do club deals interferes with our portfolio diversification strategy. If you have four or five of the big funds in your portfolio, from a portfolio construction point of view there is not as much diversification as we would like to see.*
>
> SPF Beheer (AltAssets, 2006a)

Don't put all your eggs in one basket . . . and avoid bad eggs

In all markets and for all strategies, investors in private equity have to keep in mind that selectivity is key. Not investing at all looks smart when compared to committing to basket of 'bad eggs'. Many investors argue convincingly that quality by far over-rides the diversification or allocation objectives. This also seems obvious, but in reality, it is often forgotten, especially during hypes or in well-established markets, where the high market performance averages give the wrong impression that all deals will be successful.

> *Even so, if you have the opportunity to associate with an outstanding investment manager, who has a structured approach for leading an industry sector into the future, I believe this opportunity could override any sectoral diversification considerations.*
>
> Raschle (2001)

17.2   WHAT WE THINK WE KNOW OR SIMPLY DON'T KNOW

While there is no formulaic answer to the question of the 'optimum' diversification level of a portfolio of private equity funds, the portfolio composition of other institutional investors can be at least a starting point, especially as at the end of the day the performance of a program will often be assessed against those of other programs. Investors have to monitor their portfolio and the market environment and react to changes, if necessary – according to Hovhannisian (2001) – by copying the moves of the competitors. This should not be misunderstood as a call for blind imitation or for creating an uncontroversial portfolio, but for taking a critical view and for being contrarian.

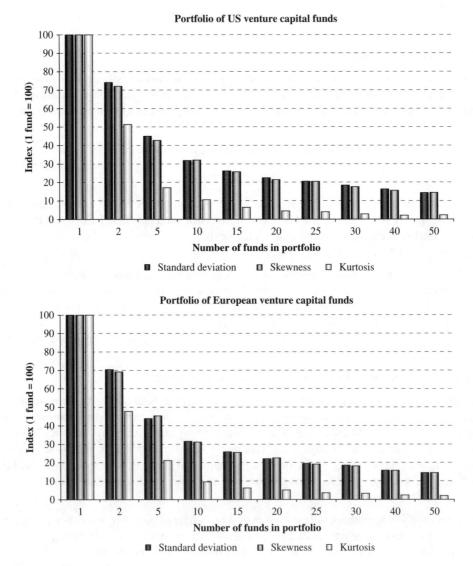

Figure 17.2 Standard deviation, skewness and kurtosis of portfolio of funds with increasing diversification

Diversification decisions were generally influenced by overall portfolio considerations, such as currency exposure, allocation size, and build up, etc. Often, however, decisions were also based on soft factors, including the behavior of other institutions.

Raschle (2001)

The optimum number of funds in a portfolio

Research suggests that, for most assets, sufficient diversification is achieved with 20 positions of whatever one is seeking to diversify.[4] As for the other asset classes, diversification kicks in rapidly for private equity. Figure 17.2 illustrates the situation for European and US venture capital fund portfolios, but the conclusions are similar for buyout funds:

- 80% of the standard deviation is diversified away with a portfolio of 20 – 30 funds.
- Skewness decreases more or less at the same rate as standard deviation.
- 80% of the kurtosis is diversified away with a portfolio of five funds.

Box 17.1:   Desirable and undesirable diversification effects

Our simulation results suggest that there is no need to have more than 20–30 funds in a portfolio and that when investors target the 'fat tail', more than five funds do not appear to make much sense.

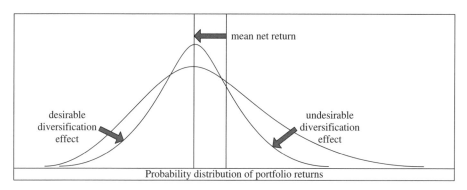

Figure 17.3   Desirable and undesirable effects of diversification

Diversification not only has the desirable effect of increasing an investor's protection against the downside, but it also has a detrimental impact on the portfolio's upside. Therefore, for positively skewed return distributions investors can consciously choose to remain under-diversified. Our simulations have shown that there is a loss of skewness but that it may not be relevant for normal return requirements. However, it is questionable whether investors in VC funds have 'normal' return requirements. For them the 'lottery premium' they may be willing to pay, for the opportunity to participate in rare but extraordinary pay-offs, could be a factor – which would result in a preference for skewness.

---

[4] See Flag Venture Management (2001), Weidig and Mathonet (2004) and Meyer and Mathonet (2005).

Box 17.1:   (Continued)

Over a five-year market cycle, sponsors may wish to spread risk across 25 to 50 partnerships. Fund of funds are an efficient vehicle to achieve this level of diversification.

Allen *et al.* (2001)

Probably the strongest argument against a high diversification of VC funds is the quick 'fading' of their quality. There are simply too few excellent fund management teams within a vintage year peer group. Over-diversification not only leads to a loss in skewness, but also depresses the portfolio's expected return. The fading of quality and the loss of skewness may be more of an issue for venture capital. For buyouts the distribution function looks more symmetrical and there are usually more high-quality teams. Finally, these thoughts only hold for the 'plain vanilla' limited partnership stakes in funds. Real options like co-investment rights – that allow amplifying the impact of extraordinary hits – can justify a higher level of diversification.

The optimum number of funds in an evergreen portfolio

Many programs, including also some funds-of-funds, are structured as evergreen. This structure, compared with the classical self-liquidating fund-of-funds with an often four-year investment period, re-opens the diversification question, as the optimum number of funds cannot be the same for both of them. We have found no study on this question and our own analyses have been inconclusive.

   We know, however, that standard funds are self-liquidating, and therefore that the exposure is decreasing over time. We also know studies concluding that a classical portfolio invested over a period of four years should be composed of probably between 20 to 30 funds, were looking at the terminal wealth, i.e. ignoring what is happening during the portfolio's lifetime. Therefore, in an evergreen program continuous replenishment is needed in order to maintain this 'optimum' exposure.

   As the net duration[5] of a standard fund can be estimated around four years, i.e. not far from the average fundraising frequency, it could be argued that per fundraising cycle an evergreen program should then also invest in between 20 to 30 funds. Assuming a funds' lifetime of ten plus two times a one-year extension, an evergreen program should have around 60–90 funds in a portfolio respectively aged from zero to twelve years, which corresponds to five to eight investments per year.

Portfolio composition in term of key risk dimensions

In the previous chapter, we have seen the key risk dimensions considered in the construction of a private equity portfolio, namely the stage focuses, the industry sectors, the countries and the currencies. For each of them, investors should define their wished

---

[5] The net duration of a fund is the difference between the duration of the fund's repayments (around seven years) and the duration of its drawdown (around three years).

sub-allocations. There are very few studies that tried to assess these sub-allocations. One of them, Grabenwarter and Weidig (2004), attempted to quantify these correlations and found that they typically fluctuate 'substantially and changes dramatically with the period of sampling. Hence the saying: "Lies, volatilities, and correlations".' They studied the correlation within and between market segments[6] and found that 'the correlation within the markets is greatest and around 40 percent, and is small between markets'.

At a very high level we believe that the split between buy-out and venture in a mature portfolio should be approximately 70 per cent buy-out/30 per cent venture capital and growth equity.

Frank Brenninkmeyer, Principal, Performance Equity Management
(AltAssets, 2006a)

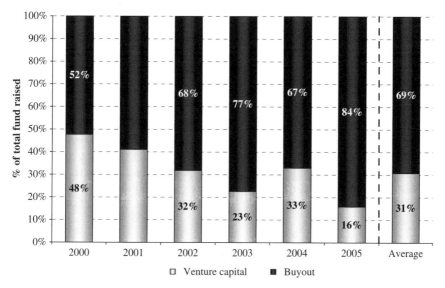

Figure 17.4   Expected allocation of funds raised
Source: EVCA.

But as in practice it is difficult to come up with an optimal allocation, investors tend to look at the market average allocation statistics (see for example Figure 17.4) – the question aside whether correlations can be stable over such long time horizons.

Generally, our portfolio consists of one third venture capital funds and two thirds buy-out funds.

David G. Proctor, Senior Vice President, Wind River Holdings
(AltAssets, 2006a)

---

[6] The analyzed market segments are both from the United States and Europe, and comprise early stage venture capital funds copyright material and mid-market funds composed of late stage venture capital and small to medium-sized buyout investments.

17.3   EXPLOITATION VS. EXPLORATION

We come back to the question of uncertainty that we have discussed in previous chapters, and how the concepts of exploration and exploitation affect the portfolio construction. Diversification management for a private equity portfolio is about managing uncertainty: we do not know the future, but we want to be prepared for different scenarios. In other words, diversification creates choice rather than being a risk mitigant in the MPT sense.

While a vast number of publications deal with the question of how to identify and get access to 'top-quartile' funds or, in other words, to improve the probability of a 'hit', we believe that the importance of this aspect may even be over-estimated. Certainly, statistics clearly demonstrates that if you consistently pick these top performers it would give you the exciting investment returns typically expected from the private equity asset class.

> *Venture capitalists are also very quick to scale up successful enterprises and very ruthless in cutting their losses. Although they tend to focus very hard on the short-term performance of their investments, venture capitalists also use a broad, long-term investment thesis and return targets to provide selection pressures.*
>
> Beinhocker (2006)

However, we remain skeptical regarding the ability to successfully implement an investment strategy that is just based on picking winners. In fact, as relevant as picking the winner is amplifying the pay-off of a 'hit' – or cutting the loss once it becomes clear that a VC fund is a 'dud'. After some time of monitoring, limited partners should become increasingly confident about which VC fund investments are promising and which are not. As in venture capital, one cannot rely on valuations based on quantitative data alone, limited partners require clearly thought through measures of success and a plan for monitoring their portfolio of funds.

17.3.1   Structured exploring

Simplistically, investments in VC funds could be seen as an exploration-oriented strategy, while a bottom-up portfolio design is closer to an exploitation-oriented strategy. However, a bottom-up approach does not necessarily exclude exploration, but the ability to negotiate co-investment arrangements or top-ups with established 'top' fund managers will be limited. A natural bias toward loss aversion causes institutions to systematically under-invest in experimentation. To some degree that works against the long-term oriented need to explore, and therefore the investment process should force a defined degree of experimentation, for example through a core/satellite portfolio approach or through an 'uncertainty budget'.

We see two major 'psychological pitfalls' for investors in VC funds that we also try to address with our grading technique. One is – as discussed already – the tendency to succumb to charisma. Venture capitalists, at least those who are successful in their fundraising, are great salesmen. However, this is not black and white between 'perfect top funds' and those who fail to get off the ground, but there are shades of gray in between. For investors it is a sound survival strategy to distance one-self from the sales pitch and try to identify these shades of gray. The other pitfall is the industry practice of making investment decisions in consensus or even unanimously and, paradoxically, over-analyzing. One can simply do better analysis on established private equity firms than on emerging teams, but as Beinhocker

(2006) pointed out, an evolutionary strategy requires tolerance of people going in different directions at once and experimenting with risky ideas.

17.3.2 Core/satellite portfolio

Funds in the selection process can be split into core and non-core allocations. Core groups are conservative mainstream vehicles – those with established track record. The non-core allocations can be first time funds that have an experienced management team raising a first time fund, or a group that has spun out of a larger institution.

Sormani (2003a)

Behavioral portfolios, such as those reflected in the rules of 'core–satellite', also known as 'hub and spoke', are sensible ways to allocate portfolio assets. This method, based on the behavioral portfolio theory, aims – by constructing portfolios as layered pyramids – to increase risk control, lower costs and add value. A well-diversified core or bottom layer provides downside protection for the portfolio (risk-aversion), while a less diversified satellite or top layers aims for the upside (risk-seeking).[7]

- The core portfolio typically comprises institutional-quality funds that are able to raise large pools of capital and are expected to generate a predictable base return. If there is no change or the pace of change is 'tectonic', such mainstream funds are perceived to be the safe bet. A solid core of high-quality relationships allows limited partners to stay in the game long enough to seize the golden opportunities, but the exclusive reliance on the core leaves them susceptible to long-term decline.
- The satellite portfolio usually comprises niche strategies that fall out of the mainstream (emerging market, new teams, specialist funds, etc.) and could be interpreted as a bet on radical changes. In practice, the line between core and satellite is blurred. The qualitative scoring underlying our grading methodology measures various degrees of deviation from mainstream funds.

This method aims to increase risk control and lower costs. The core–satellite approach is a way of allocating assets to protect and grow wealth and provides the framework for targeting and controlling those areas where an investor believes they are able to better control risks or are willing to take more risk. There is a danger of mental accounting associated with satellite portfolios, as decision-makers may be tempted to treat them as a budget to gamble. In fact, satellite strategies require a higher degree of diligence and monitoring than core relationships. Funds in the satellite portfolio are typically comparatively small, and in regard to their impact on the portfolio would not move the needle. They rather need to be seen as real options that are expensive and would be meaningless if not monitored systematically and exercised when appropriate. Consequently, they need to be complemented by, for example, a co-investment program.[8]

---

[7] See Statman (2002): 'The desire to avoid poverty gives way to the desire for riches. Some investors fill the uppermost layers with the few stocks of an undiversified portfolio like private individuals buy lottery tickets. Neither lottery buying nor undiversified portfolios are consistent with mean–variance portfolio theory but both are consistent with behavioural portfolio theory.'

[8] Conceptually, co-investments could be seen as an exploitation strategy: as discussed previously, in the case of large buyouts they mainly aim at cost savings, whereas for VC funds they are rather to be seen as exercising a real option.

17.3.3 Uncertainty budget

The uncertainty budget is based on the grading for private equity funds and takes the two components of risk and uncertainty into consideration. The P-grade dimension assesses how well a fund is adapted to its peer group within the current private equity market environment and measures the distance and implicitly the cost of the jump within the private equity market fitness landscape. This allows mixing the two choices of an adaptive walk with few random jumps against random jumps over larger distances in the fitness landscape. Extreme jumps, however, will be difficult because other investors also need to be convinced to back a fund. When setting the uncertainty budget for managing the balance between exploitation and exploration, investors need to take into consideration:

- The slack resources available. With a larger reserve buffer a higher degree of exploration is possible. The initial stages of a private equity funds investment program are dominated by a primarily exploitation-oriented bottom-up approach to build up slack resources that enable exploration going forward.
- The anticipated 'volatility' of the private equity market environment: the more disruptive a market environment, the more one needs to spread one's options, whereas in a stable environment exploration can be reduced to the minimum.
- The time horizon for the private equity funds investment program. The more long-term oriented, the higher the value of real options and therefore the higher the degree of exploration that should be undertaken.

Based on the slack resources, a budget is set for each grading class. The investment proposals are ranked according to their estimated real option value and the highest valued are taken. In the example of Table 17.1, Fund 1 is clearly a better investment proposal than Fund 2, and Fund 3 should be given preference over Fund 4. However, whether Fund 2 is worth more than Fund 3 plus its real option value is unclear, and even the rank of Fund 1 compared with Fund 3 cannot be determined. It is a futile exercise trying to quantify the real option value of a fund with any degree of precision.

Table 17.1 Uncertainty budget

		Expected performance grade			
		P-D	P-C	P-B	P-A
Real option value:	High		Fund 3		
	Medium		Fund 4	Fund 2	Fund 1

17.3.4 Balancing exploitation, exploration, growth and survival

Portfolio construction needs to strike a balance between exploitation, which is more reactive and defensive, and exploration, which is pro-active and taking the offensive. Intuitively investors do this, for example it is recommended that especially new entrants to the private equity asset class should play on a diversified basis – a behavior consistent with giving priority to survival first before focusing on growth. Later on, established players find themselves with too many relationships that are detrimental to the growth objective and then, like CalPERS recently began to do so, need to reduce them.

Having built a core portfolio of mid cap, large cap and small cap funds, we now increasingly look for more specialised funds.

Sven Berthold from WEGAsupport GmbH (see AltAssets, 2005)

In a known and stable environment, exploration is not a meaningful strategy. Therefore we would expect to see exploration strategies more in venture capital as it is driven by innovation and change than in later stage private equity investing which is arguably built more on a specific and stable economic environment. Exploration is required for growth but is an expensive strategy for two reasons. Firstly, many experiments pursued in the course of exploration fail. Secondly, if experiments turn out to be successful, resources are required to amplify their impact. Consequently, for a limited partner exploration is only a feasible strategy if there are also sufficient slack resources available to develop the discovered opportunities into a success. Otherwise exploration has to be put aside and the short-term survival of the portfolio has to be assured through exploitation of identified opportunities.

Finance theory suggests that in well-functioning markets there be quick access to capital through investors or lenders. However, the Private Equity Holding case provides an example that critical situations often coincide with, or are even caused by, periods of capital scarcity. In uncertain environments the availability and the cost of capital can be highly restricted, which may be one reason why side funds are mainly observed in the context of VC funds. Here a large cash reserve provides a cushion against unforeseen threats and unanticipated opportunities. This gives an edge to larger private equity groups with alternative sources of financing and can be a disadvantage for small VC funds. It also sheds some light on the importance of reputation and a good relationship with strong limited partners who trust the fund manager and are willing to provide quick support. See Figure 17.5.

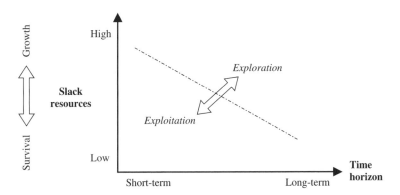

Figure 17.5 Trading off exploitation against exploration

An implication of 'creative destruction' associated with innovation is that all advantages are just temporary. The duration of advantages is difficult to predict ex ante, but due to confidentiality might be better manageable in private equity. Nevertheless, if an opportunity turns out to be successful it may also be fleeting. This will often require more financial resources and excess liquidity 'on call', for example for co-investing in a VC fund. Negotiating real options pre-investment and monitoring the funds will not be of much use unless they can be turned into adjustments of the portfolio. It also requires the ability to absorb failed opportunities. Resources can be understood in the widest sense, for example it may also relate to 'social capital' the manager of the private equity funds investment program has built up with his investors, i.e. to what degree would they be willing to back experiments over a protracted time period despite the associated failures?

The other main dimension to be taken into consideration is the private equity funds investment program's time horizon. A too short-term oriented program, such as the typical fund-of-funds, essentially restricts the kind of real options a limited partner has available. For example, the implicit option inherent in the investment into a newly emerging team only has a 'value' if the investor's program has a time horizon beyond one fund commitment. Otherwise, exploring newly emerging markets or teams will not yield opportunities that could be exploited during the program's lifetime. Instead, limited partners then have to go for the 'best adapted species', usually buyout and the 'golden circle' of VC funds.

For established players exploring may be less important, as for example a well-known private equity investor like HarbourVest would be able to get access to any fund. Such institutions are able to create value through a superior and defensible position. Their net-work of fund relationships makes a market entry for newcomers difficult. One could argue that the private equity funds-of-funds industry is less scalable and thus more competitive than more conventional asset classes such as mutual funds. Having established and proven relationships with well-known private equity funds creates a number of sustainable advan-tages. Competing funds-of-funds cannot imitate the privileged access to 'invitation-only' high-quality funds. When trying to attract new mandates, the private equity funds invest-ment program manager can refer to these relationships and the associated track record. Having other fund proposals as fallback position also helps when negotiating with new fund managers.

17.3.5   Adapting, shaping & insuring

Investors try to address uncertainty mainly through diversification or through improving the quality of prediction. However, the future behaviour of a complex adaptive system like the VC market is sensitive to a myriad of uncertainties. Decision makers then discover – if, as Davies (2002) phrased it, *'they have the courage and integrity to address the issue'* – that they are unable to make meaningful predictions. This creates a dilemma; after all, decisions have to be made, even if uncertainties are high.

Investors are often biased in favor of avoiding mistakes and waiting for uncertainty to diminish, particularly if they do not know better. In fact, doing nothing is one of the most important generic mechanisms for coping with uncertainty, and can be meaningful if the cost of recourse later is small. Investors can also hedge against problems by developing capabilities to cope with plausible events, e.g. through adapting, shaping or insuring.

17.3.5.1   Adapting

Adaptation is an adjustment in structure or approach to improve conditions in relationship to an environment. Adapting to an existing environment is preferable when key sources of value creation are relatively stable. Under these circumstances it makes sense to 'place a bet', i.e. an irreversible commitment usually to institutional quality funds that leaves little room for making adjustments for different contingencies. Adapting does not necessarily exclude exploration. Although the existing and future market structure and conduct is largely taken as a given, under high uncertainty adapting requires speed and agility in recognizing and capturing new opportunities as the market changes. This require monitoring for the latest industry best practices in incorporating them in the investment strategy.

17.3.5.2   Shaping

Investors can avoid foolhardy mistakes by waiting for uncertainty to diminish, but on the other hand high uncertainty offers the greatest chance to shape the outcome to one's advantage. Investors can squander the chance to grab a golden opportunity, and in fact, an aversion to risk is misguided when one can strongly influence the outcome of an investment.

> *Bold decisions give the best promise of success.*
>
> Field Marshall Erwin Rommel

A bold decision up-front can itself determine the outcome of uncertainty in an investor's favor, for example by corner-stoning an emerging team. For limited partners a shaping strategy requires the building up of real options for amplifying or scaling down the degree of investment and continuous monitoring as this decision can be deferred to a point when more information on a fund's evolution becomes available.

As discussed in the context of co-investing for limited partners, a rapid approval process provides the reaction speed to respond quickly when opportunities arise. Under time pressure, when decision-makers have to perform multiple tasks, there can be reluctance to search out relevant data. However, in a volatile environment efficient implementation and monitoring can also be more important than in-depth analysis. As Sull and Escobari (2005) observed, strategies are obvious, can easily be imitated by competitors and rarely spell the difference between success and failure. But sudden-death threats affect all players in an industry and weaken some more than others. Here execution can make the difference, particularly if multiple initiatives are pursued in parallel and uncommitted slack resources need to be deployed or quickly redeployed. For many institutions pursuing private equity funds investment programs this poses a problem, as they are unable to react on a hunch but require in-depth analysis and do not allow the 'just try it' approach. To some degree this is explainable through the fact that investments in private equity funds are, compared with other asset classes, extremely long-term oriented and to a large degree irreversible.

On the other hand, for VC funds we have identified amplification of a 'hit' as a major portfolio management strategy, as committing to a follow-on fund would have too much lead-time: Now is the time that a working fund management team has found a good opportunity, and in five years from now team, incentives and market will be different. To successfully implement a shaping strategy, 'deep pockets' in the sense of slack resources and reactivity are of key importance. As it does not really blend with the usual limited partner culture, the investment process has to provide procedures and guidelines for a short-term plan to quickly evaluate actions and to allow immediate action. A triage allows sorting into three categories: clear winners that are valuable and vital for investment success, clear losers that can be sacrificed without too much cost to just cut the downside and limit the reputational damage, and question marks that require attention.

17.3.5.3   Insuring

The polar ends of choices under uncertainty are 'move now' and reserve the option to move later. In reality there is a middle ground, and no dominant solution exists. Even if the environment is uncertain, shaping is not always possible, for example because the limited partner does not have the expertise to successfully implement a co-investment strategy. Moreover, the elite group of VC fund managers will usually resist any attempt to negotiate special rights for scaling up or down a commitment.

In such instances investors may move in early with a relatively sizeable and inflexible commitment, while finding ways to reduce the downside risks of different scenarios for market evolution. Chakravorti (2003) describes this as taking insurance. A limited partner envisions alternative scenarios for the market and ensures that no matter which of the plausible scenarios occur, the current choice provides insurance against their occurrence.

Insuring is an expensive up-front investment in situations when one cannot afford to fall behind and yet is not in a position to eliminate the substantial uncertainties. The limited partner has to pay an 'insurance premium', for example through a higher degree of diversification than necessary in cases where uncertainty is reduced or shaping would be possible.

17.3.6 Diversification and portfolios as networks

Sull and Escobari (2005) found that successful companies that flourished under uncertainty were more rather than less diversified, which is contrary to conventional wisdom or to our simulation results for 'plain vanilla' – i.e. not considering real options – portfolio of VC funds. Lerner (2005) provided evidence that a decline in the funds' specialization leads to poorer performance, while in nature extreme specialization has been unfavorable to survival. Apparently, private equity firms trade off generating very high returns against consistently delivering competitive returns. They necessarily first manage specialized funds, but then tend to broaden their footprint once they have achieved their first successes. A typical example is starting as an ICT-focused early stage VC fund but subsequently raising life science-oriented vehicle and moving into later stages.

Rather than viewing a portfolio of private equity funds as a 'static' portfolio of assets, it may be looked at as a network that provides intelligence that helps to reduce uncertainty and allows the sharing of risks that increases the likelihood of surviving external shocks. Like in complex biological and social systems, surviving and thriving of this network depends on its ability to generate fast and powerful responses to environmental volatility. It is managed through alignment of incentives and decentralized implementation according to centralized strategies. Priority-setting in this network is centralized at the limited partner level, but decentralized fund managers have high flexibility in achieving the priorities within a set framework of investment guidelines.

Based on our knowledge of published research and our own experience, we see little evidence that makes us believe that the portfolio of limited partnership shares in VC funds itself could consistently generate the returns investors demand from this asset class. While this network itself may not be profitable enough, it, however, provides a flow of real options. These real options help to navigate towards the exploitable positions in the private equity fitness landscape, i.e. generate access to the future 'golden circle' of consistently high performing VC funds, or allow amplifying unforeseen positive developments within the 'ordinary' VC funds. Limited partners need to actively monitor their portfolio to identify 'hits' and exercise their real options.

18

Guidelines, Monitoring and Corrective Actions

For a limited partner the investment process does not end with the selection of a private equity fund and signing the limited partnership agreement. By committing investors engage in relationships that sometimes last more than ten years and regularly extend beyond one fund. The longevity of such relationships requires a thorough approach to codifying objectives and constraints in a framework of investment guidelines, policies and strategies, monitoring the investment programme's conformity with these objectives and constraints, and taking, where necessary, corrective action to assure this conformity.

- There cannot be a disciplined investment process without proper investment guidelines and their development is one of the most important aspects of fiduciary responsibility. Market practices in private equity are in constant flux. Practically, in such an environment a rigid definition of permitted structures and, because of the illiquidity of such assets, a strict adherence to targets is not feasible. If guidelines are too restrictive there is danger that management will always try to get them changed rather than bringing investments in line with the guideline categories.
- Monitoring has many aspects and is not just about verifying conformity with guidelines. Particularly in situations of increased perceived risks, some limited partners are known to have introduced their proprietary reporting formats for monitoring that go beyond the industry standard reporting as for example put in place by EVCA. Often such limited partners complement the 'routine' financial reporting with informal but more or less regular contacts with the fund manager, e.g. through conference calls. As discussed in previous chapters, real option-like situations comprise a significant part of the portfolio of funds' value proposition. Systematically looking for and identifying such opportunities can turn monitoring in a value creating activity.
- There are many ways a limited partner can monitor the investment strategy implementation. As suitable reference data are missing or are not accessible, we developed a specific technique to benchmark portfolio of funds. However, any benchmarking can only be backward looking, and therefore we found it useful to base our assessment of the projected risk profile according to the GEM (see section 7.1.2 in Chapter 7).

In case the portfolio of funds is projected to fail meeting its objectives or to threaten the violation of the constraints set under guidelines or policies, corrective action should be taken, but this causes problems for such an illiquid asset class like private equity.

18.1 INVESTMENT GUIDELINES AS FRAMEWORK

Guidelines need to look beyond types of investments and have to be in line with the venture capital environment's uncertainty. They have to be sufficiently far-sighted and stable for a period that is in line with the long-term orientation of an institution's activities in private equity. The guidelines need to express the expectations of the various stakeholders in a language that accurately reflects their thinking. A general observation is that guidelines often cover a broad range of related subjects – e.g. policy or strategy – that, however, are of a somehow different nature and therefore should rather be dealt with in separate documents.[1] We found it useful to differentiate between the guidelines that define the framework, the policies that set the objectives and restrictions and the strategy that results in an action plan. Investment policies and strategies cannot be static documents but are evolving and need to keep abreast of industry practices.

Box 18.1:   Investment guideline design

> *First, your return to shore was not part of our negotiations nor our agreement, so I must do nothin'. And secondly, you must be a pirate for the Pirate's Code to apply, and you're not. And thirdly, the Code is more what you'd call 'guidelines' than actual rules. Welcome aboard the Black Pearl, Miss Turner.*
>
> Captain Barbossa (*Pirates of the Caribbean – The Curse of the Black Pearl*, 2003)

Why bother about investment guidelines? Regulation does not require that they be put in place. Wikipedia[2] confirms Captain Barbossa's interpretation of guidelines as of only loosely binding nature – 'A guideline is any document that aims to streamline particular processes according to a set routine. By definition, following a guideline is never mandatory (protocol would be a better term for a mandatory procedure)' – but also points out that guidelines 'are an essential part of the larger process of governance'. Investment guidelines come in various forms and names – e.g. several US university endowments and public pension schemes call them 'investment policy statements' – that are not standardized and do not usually specifically cater for the needs of a private equity investment program but target alternative asset investments in general. Nevertheless, these examples may serve as a reference that may help to draft a broad framework for private equity specific guidelines.

- The guidelines have to define roles and responsibilities and identify the broad approach to be followed and any general limitations on the discretion given to the institution's investment managers.

---

[1] Generally, guidelines should not repeat regulatory rules, definitions (e.g. valuation guidelines) or give data from other sources (e.g. benchmark figures), as changes of such information are driven outside the institution. Rather, the reference should be given and rules regarding updates and reviews of such information be established.
[2] Accessed 24 May 2006.

- The investment guidelines can be complemented by a number of other documents. For example, a policy that defines eligibility and exclusion criteria for investments or the institution's valuation procedures.
- The guidelines should discuss trade-offs between various objectives. For example, socially responsible investing cannot be done in all situations without sacrificing investment returns.
- Broad principles should be given, e.g. that investments are made with judgment and care, under circumstances prevailing, which persons of prudence, discretion and intelligence exercise in the management of their own affairs, not for speculation, but for investment, considering the probable safety of their capital as well as the probable income to be derived.
- The guidelines should specify what investments are authorized. For example, investments have to meet eligibility criteria and not violate exclusion criteria as set out in applicable investment policies.
- Usually, institutions active in private equity are buy-and-hold primary investors and mainly do primary commitments to private equity investment vehicles that in turn invest in privately held companies. But guidelines can also give authorization to do secondary sells or acquisitions of private equity funds, private equity funds-of-funds, or publicly listed private equity vehicles as a portfolio management tool or to benefit from market opportunities.
- Often, institutions either do not permit direct investments or just authorize them as co-investments alongside private equity funds. However, sooner or later direct investments are inevitable, for example in cases where fund management teams have disintegrated and left their investors with so-called 'orphans'. Also in the case of publicly quoted securities, private equity funds do so-called distributions 'in kind' where general partners distribute returns to their limited partners in the form of listed securities as opposed to cash. Although such positions may be held just temporarily to avoid losses, they should be liquidated as soon as possible and not be held for speculative purposes, the guidelines should cater for this contingency as well.
- Due to the specific nature of private equity funds, immediate and full investment of assets is not always possible, and in order to maintain a high level of allocation to private equity funds commitments may exceed the institution's available resources. The guidelines should particularly address the question of over-commitments and possible borrowing in case of short-term liquidity needs.
- There can never be absolute certainty on the compliance of private equity funds with the terms of the limited partnership agreement. However, an adequate monitoring system reduces the likelihood of any potential non-compliance, even if it cannot fully eliminate these cases. Guidelines should give an outline of the monitoring system, the intensity of monitoring and how it is documented. Any extraordinary losses, conditions that could reasonably be expected to lead to an extraordinary loss, policy violations or cases of fraud are to be reported immediately to the institution's Board of Directors. It should be acknowledged that in private equity monitoring, feedback from investment managers is judgmental.

Box 18.1: (Continued)

- Particularly in a high-risk asset class, the guidelines should make clear that investment managers acting in accordance with the institution's investment guidelines, policies and procedures and exercising due diligence are relieved of personal responsibility for an individual private equity investment's risk and valuation changes, provided deviations from expectations are reported in a timely fashion.
- The guidelines should also address the question of performance measurement. The implementation of the investment strategy needs to be monitored continuously by comparing the portfolio's interim performance against appropriate benchmarks.
- No guidelines are without exemptions, updates and amendments, but changes in investment schedules cannot be quickly implemented. Therefore, the guidelines should state that any investment held that does not meet a new rule under an updated investment guideline shall be exempted from it. At maturity or liquidation, such monies shall be re-invested only as provided by the prevailing investment guidelines. The institution's Board of Directors should regularly review the guidelines formally to reaffirm their relevancy or revise them as appropriate.

Every investment committee responsible for the management of a private equity fund investment program should develop investment guidelines that are tailored toward its specific needs and constraints. It is clear that in an innovation-driven environment such as venture capital not all possible situations can be addressed.

18.1.1   Trade-offs

Guidelines primarily aim to enable a management process that offers sufficient flexibility for capturing investment opportunities as they may occur, while maintaining prudence and care in the execution of the investment program. One key dilemma is to design restrictions that do not create more risks than they offset. Even apparently modest restrictions can severely hamper the investment manager's ability to meet the set objectives and lead to unintended consequences. Conversely, lack of investment discipline creates significant risks, and generally practitioners believe that adherence to a discipline leads to clear-cut thinking and better investment decision and will ultimately produce higher and more consistent returns. To a certain degree, guidelines are part of expectation management. Investment guidelines are also designed to outline internal controls, i.e. what is the investment manager allowed to do and how and what are the criteria against which he is to be measured and to communicate them to staff, investment managers, auditors, the institution's clients and all other interested parties. Finally, they serve as a review document to guide the ongoing oversight of the investment manager.

18.1.2   Investment policies

Investment policies can be understood as political and management mechanisms put in place to reach explicit goals. Objectives should be precise enough to avoid misunderstandings and to allow setting measurable criteria based on which one can judge whether and to what degree they have been achieved. Moreover, they have to be realistic, and there should be clear priorities in case there are several objectives that could even be conflicting and thus cannot all be achieved in full. Policies are relatively fixed principles that help to develop and sustain an investment program's direction as well as defining the reasons for its existence. There is certainly a 'political' element in investment policies and they may even be established independently from an investment-related rational.

On the other hand, investment policies can also offer protection against political interference in investment decisions, although the dividing line between inappropriate political interference and justified political involvement can be difficult to define. Investment policies are so specific that they cannot be covered generically and therefore should be dealt with outside the investment guidelines. Within the constraints set under the guidelines and policies, the institution's investment managers have to develop and propose the strategies.

18.1.3   Investment strategy

Fraser-Sampson (2006a) defines investment strategy as 'an action plan designed to achieve specific objectives'. It describes how the actual management decisions and actions aim at survival and growth as well as at accomplishing the long-term objectives under the constraints given by investment guidelines and policies. The investment strategy needs to be precise enough to be a meaningful road map for the portfolio construction and the program's implementation, but also requires continued updating to reflect market developments.

The investment strategy may also define specific risk tolerances and should not only document investment goals, but also set a process for implementation, for example establish criteria for the selection of investments. Moreover, the investment strategy should also define the applicable benchmarks, and an effective review procedure to monitor whether the investment is in or out of compliance with the institution's guidelines and policies and whether the implementation is meeting its objectives.

18.2   IMPLEMENTATION OF INVESTMENT POLICIES

Policies are often driven by ethical considerations – e.g. no 'sin'-related investments like arms sales or gambling – and also aim to reduce reputational risk and safeguard non-investment-related interests. Therefore, such policies are often quite detailed, based on case-by-case considerations and undergo frequent updates. In the context of socially responsible investing, typically three methods are applied for screening. Negative screens, positive screens and best-of-sector (or best in class) are approaches to exclude or include companies. These approaches reflect different investment styles, but may also be combined.

Box 18.2:   Socially responsible investing

State pension funds such as the California Public Employees' Retirement System (CalPERS) or the California State Teachers Retirement System (CalSTRS) are important investors in VC funds and also aim to promote good corporate governance standards and use social criteria to guide their investment policies. Related

Box 18.2:   (Continued)

to this, governments have used pension funds to support VC funds as economically targeted investments (ETI) to create local jobs or fund small businesses.
On the other hand, the US Employment Retirement Income Security Act (ERISA)
precludes the sacrifice of financial return for social return. The consideration of
'non-financial' factors in an investment decision might reduce returns, and therefore could be seen as a violation of the fund manager's fiduciary duty. There
is an ongoing discussion on the potential conflict of interests between fiduciary
responsibilities and socially responsible investing or political goals.[3] Having said
this, the assessment of risks related to VC fund investments is conceptually difficult and comes down to perceptions and judgment, where opinions are likely
to diverge.

18.2.1   Negative screens

Negative screens have been applied in the ethical investment sector for decades. Many institutions are not prepared to invest in a range of sectors that are seen as socially undesirable
as they entail unacceptable market, image and/or liability risks. Companies are excluded
based on their involvement in activities that are not in line with the investor's value set. In
the context of private equity typically 'sin' sectors like tobacco and alcohol, gambling and
gambling equipment manufacture or manufacture of weapons and armament are excluded.
In venture capital often proposals related to animal testing or the production of genetically modified organisms have to be excluded. Investment decisions can, for example,
be screened by a body or group of respected professionals such as an independent ethics
advisory board.

18.2.2   Positive screens

Positive screening is targeting companies involved in business activities that are seen to be
inherently beneficial. These are usually companies engaged in activities with positive social
or environmental benefits. In private equity usually investments related to environmental
management (such as renewable energy or ecological innovation) or health care often fall into
this category. Also, companies that promote ethical and responsible product development,
corporate citizenship, governance and ethics, regulatory compliance, and human and labor
rights are targeted through positive screens.

18.2.3   Best-of-sector approach

According to DEH (2001), the best-of-sector approach is a more recent technique applied
by some fund managers. Under this approach the manager identifies social and environmental performance criteria appropriate to each sector, and – for example through a rating

---

[3] See, for example, Emerson (2003) or Stowers (2004).

process – ranks company performance against these benchmarks. Although investment can be across all industry sectors, this approach aims to select the best performing companies and puts strong emphasis on communicating benchmarks as incentive for lifting performance across all companies in each sector.

18.3   MONITORING INVESTMENT RESTRICTIONS

Once an institution has become a limited partner in a private equity fund, it has entered into a long-term – often more than ten years and even beyond the current fund – relationship. How can the limited partner ensure compliance with the guidelines and policies transposed into investment restriction in the limited partnership agreement?

18.3.1   Investment restriction checking

Possible violations of investment restrictions can be detected ex ante before an investment is undertaken by the fund manager – at the time of the capital call – or ex post, i.e. after the investment was done. See Figure 18.1.

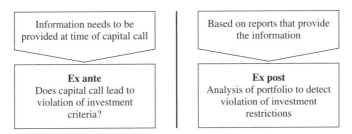

Figure 18.1   Checking restrictions

- At the time of the capital call, the fund manager has to provide all the information relevant for checking investment restrictions.[4] Unfortunately, the availability of information is limited, not only due to the private nature of the industry, but also – in the interest of a fund's investors – to protect the fund manager's negotiation position there is sometimes a reluctance to put detailed information forward.
- Ex post violations can be detected through checking the quarterly report. Monitoring visits undertaken by investment managers would certainly allow the best possible check, but due to resource constraints cannot continuously cover the entire universe of fund investments under management.

---

[4] It should be noted that there is often no contractual power to request additional information to perform checks for compliance with investment policies. In the extreme the limited partner needs to authorize the disbursement without having the full set of information to perform these checks – creating operational risk – or would block the disbursement and get exposed to the risk of becoming a defaulting investor.

Ex post checks do not prevent the violation of investment restrictions; they can only detect them or warn of a possible breach. They can only serve as a fallback, in case the fund manager did not provide the relevant information at the time of the drawdown. It is too late as the event has already happened. After the fact, in the extreme, limited partners that see an investment as incompatible with their policies and feel strongly about this can do nothing except selling off the fund.

Controls on investment restrictions set out in agreements signed between the limited partner and each private equity fund are to be systematically performed and/or formalized. These checks aim at the compliance with investment policies rather than trying to protect against mis-statements or embezzlement, as such things are unlikely to be detected with the information given at the time of the drawdown anyway. When a drawdown occurs during the lifecycle of a fund, the limited partner does not always have the necessary information available in order to verify the investment restrictions and is by consequence unable to fully perform such a control.

In addition to this, the limited partner has to systematically perform these checks when inputting quarterly reports received from the fund managers. However, eligibility criteria as set out in the investment policies often go beyond what is standard in the industry for capital call documentation, and some compliance checks would require information that does not belong to the standard VC industry reporting (e.g. genetically modified organisms); they therefore are generally not accepted by the fund managers and do not form part of the contract.

18.3.2 High-level process description

Essentially, investment restriction monitoring comprises the three steps shown in Figure 18.2.

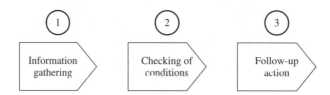

Figure 18.2   Restriction monitoring process

(1) To be able to conduct the required checks, in a first step all the necessary information has to be provided by the fund manager. As mentioned already, in many cases this information is not part of industry standard reporting. As checking is done on the basis of regular reporting and information needs are driven by policies, completeness, timeliness and correctness of data are the main problems.

(2) The information provided is used to check whether conditions as set out in the limited partnership agreements are met or whether investment restrictions are violated. To be able to conduct, for example, limit checks – such as 'not more than x percent of investments outside a specific geographical region' – input data has to be complete and historical portfolio data is required. Moreover, contractual terms have to be interpreted correctly by back-office staff.

(3) Under normal conditions – no violation of investment conditions – the follow-up action would be the continuation of the payment process.

What are the possible sanctions in case of violations, as such behavior would not comply with the commercial approach pursued by the limited partner?

Box 18.3:   Ensuring compliance with investment restrictions

Institutional investors often try to ensure that the investment criteria of the funds explicitly exclude such sectors or insist that funds will seek assurance from their portfolio that, as an example, they will only resort to animal modeling where there is no other generally acceptable alternative solution, and that such modeling will be conducted in strict accordance with applicable regulations. Pre-investment, mainly screening assures that restrictions are respected.

Screening phase
- Avoiding – exclude non-illegible private equity fund (negative screens).
- Targeting – focusing resources to look for private equity fund in certain sectors in line with policy objectives (e.g. country or industry) (positive screens).
- Agreeing with fund manager – specifically following up during due diligence on evidence that makes it plausible that the private equity fund will focus on the policy objectives (no active steering ex post).

Post-investment, the limited partner's monitoring is required to detect and follow-up on violations of restrictions.

Monitoring phase
- Influencing – monitoring the private equity funds development and exercise influence throughout its lifetime so that the fund manager adheres to the policy objectives.
- Opting out – allowing the fund manager to deviate from policy objectives for some portfolio companies but opt out in such cases.

Enforcing compliance with investment restrictions, for example by not allowing the fund manager to deviate from contractually agreed objectives with the threat of taking the case to court, is not too realistic. As this could have a negative financial impact on the other limited partners, an investor threatening litigation to push his investment restrictions through risks getting a reputation of being 'problematic' and locking himself out of future funds. A better way could be providing positive incentives if the fund is managed according to policy objectives, for example by 'guaranteeing' to commit to the follow-on fund. However, we know of no cases where this approach was taken.

Information required for verifying compliance with investment restrictions can be given by the fund manager or be requested. Ex post information is reported regularly by the fund manager in standard reports, or is collected by investment managers in the course of their monitoring activities (with contractual compliance grades). The major safeguard against violations in investment restrictions is the check conducted in the course of its administration activities (processing of capital calls or quarterly report).

18.3.3   Conceptual questions

There is a series of conceptual questions associated with the checking of compliance with investment criteria that make clear that the checking of investment restrictions is not – or at least not just – a 'technical' problem:

- In an unregulated industry definitions of industry sectors, investment stages or geographical focus are notoriously fuzzy or not detailed enough under EVCA definitions.[5]
- Interpretation is subject to misunderstandings, disagreements or even creativity and window-dressing by the fund managers.[6]
- Moreover, the current investment guidelines are ambiguous and are not clear about how the different limits have to be interpreted. Example: in case 25% of a portfolio has moved to the USA after having originally been incorporated in the EU – is a geographical restriction on US investments still respected?
- A violation of investment criteria can happen outside the fund manager's control and without his fault.[7]

Box 18.4:   Exclusion criteria interpretation

Exclusion criteria appear to be straightforward, but in discussions many fund managers pointed out that for practical purposes the boundaries needed further clarification. For instance, 'military' is often subject to debate as theoretically products from the semi-conductor target area might make their way into military use at some point.

The history of id Software's best-selling game 'Doom' may help to illustrate the difficulties in drawing the line in practice. Historically, venture capitalists have been reluctant to invest in games because technology-oriented start-ups generally show a higher return potential than media companies. However, according to James and Walton (2004), the VC industry has been becoming increasingly interested in this space, and famous firms like Kleiner Perkins Caufield & Byers, Sequoia Capital or Draper Fisher Jurvetson did investments in gaming.

id Software is widely recognized for its pioneering use of immersive 3D graphics and networked multiplayer gaming on the PC platform.[8] In the early 1990s, id Software discovered an efficient way to perform rapid side-scrolling graphics on PCs, something

---

[5] For example, 'tobacco' would be under 'consumer' in EVCA's industry sector definition – how to detect a breach? Also, the geographical location of a company is not straightforward: should it be the legal country or the country where most activity is done?

[6] For illustration, one set of investment policies required that investee companies comply with the SME definition and particularly with the restriction on the number of employees. We know of a case where a fund invested in a holding of 20–30 employees which, however, had a majority stake in a +1000 employee company, something that was detected only in the course of an in-depth analysis.

[7] As a theoretical example, where an entrepreneur gets a major defense contract, or decides to move the company seat outside Europe, or merges with a company outside Europe.

[8] See http://en.wikipedia.org/wiki/Id_Software [accessed 14 October 2006]. Interestingly, for id software the traditional ways of funding start-ups – friends, family, business angels or venture capitalists – did not come into play. Essentially, the founders were moonlighting, or to quote one of them, Jay Wilbur: 'We were all working in the computer industry at the time and everyone had a PC of their own. Just pick 'em all up and move them into the same room and you're a start up.'

previously technically only possible on consoles. The founders tried to commercialize their discovery by developing a full-scale carbon copy of the popular 'Super Mario Bros. 3' game for the PC, hoping to license it to Nintendo. However, Nintendo had then no interest in the PC market and turned them down.

Instead, id Software eventually applied its technology to Doom, a 1993 computer game and a landmark title in the 'first-person shooter' genre. Doom was voted, according to GameSpy, by industry insiders to be the #1 game of all time. Initially Doom was distributed as shareware and downloaded by what was believed to be 10 million people within two years. According to estimates, in late 1995 Doom was installed on more computers worldwide than Microsoft's new operating system Windows 95, and allegedly Bill Gates briefly considered buying id Software.[9]

The history of Doom took another turn when the Commandant of the US Marine Corps General Charles C. Krulak entrusted the Marine Corps Modeling and Simulation Management Office (MCMSMO) with the task of developing, exploiting and approving computer-based war games to train US Marines for 'decision making skills, particularly when live training time and opportunities were limited'. It is rumored that MCMSMO unsuccessfully tinkered with an own development, before in 1995 eventually researching off-the-shelf retail video games. Lieutenant Scott Barnett and Sergeant Dan Snyder of the US Marines were looking for a fast-moving and network-able shooter game that they could also modify. According to Lieutenant Barnett, 'Doom was the only game out there that fit the bill'.[10]

MCMSMO adapted the game for training four-man fire teams, comprising team leader, two riflemen and one machine-gunner. The product was 'Marine Doom', which was used to teach concepts such as mutual fire team support, protection of the automatic rifleman, proper sequencing of an attack, ammunition discipline and succession of command. As in real life you are (hopefully) unlikely to battle 'Arachnotrons', Marines and enemy soldiers replaced Doom's original characters. Marine Doom incorporated real-world representations to reflect realistic tactical situations and instead of the 'Chainsaw', the 'BFG9000' or the 'Plasma Gun' players used M16A1 rifles, M249 squad automatic weapons and M67 fragmentation grenades. Missions like rescuing American hostages from an overseas embassy were simulated, and for this purpose digitized embassy floor plans could be incorporated into the training.[11]

What started with a technological breakthrough which allowed moving a harmless game for children to PCs turned into an, in the words of Nuttycombe (1994), 'ultra-violent' game on the 'cutting edge. And the slicing edge. And hacking. And gouging . . .' And finally the game even morphed into an application for the training of fighting personnel.

---

[9] In a press release dated 1 January 1993, id Software had written that they expected Doom to be 'the number one cause of decreased productivity in businesses around the world'. During the mid-1990s the wife of one of this book's authors brought the installation files for Doom II home. Six weeks later, after having battled nearly day and night (and dreaming about) 'Hell Knights', 'Heavy Weapons Dudes', 'Mancubi', 'Revenants', 'Arachnotrons' and 'Pain Elementals' through 30 plus two further secretly accessed levels and after having finally destroyed the 'Arch-Vile', author and wife decided to de-install the game and vowed never to touch it or comparable ones again.

[10] See http://www.wired.com/wired/archive/5.04/ff_doom_pr.html [accessed 14 October 2006].

[11] Today the US military uses 'America's Army' as a training tool. See http://gov.americasarmy.com/projects.php [accessed 14 October 2006].

The basis for checking limits in a fund's underlying portfolio, but updates on this – in accordance with VC industry reporting guidelines – are only reported on a quarterly basis. In between, events can happen in the portfolio that lead to limit breaches, even if the checking was correctly done: a fund manager could commit to invest in different tranches – or through warrants – in a non-US company. At the time of the first drawdown there is no breach, and in the quarterly reports the managers disclose the amounts effectively paid, but at a certain point the limit on non-US is exceeded. Nevertheless, a fund is legally obliged to pay the other tranches.

18.3.4   Statement of assurance

One possible safeguard is a statement of assurance (i.e. a compliance checklist) to be filled in by the fund managers. This might be feasible for future new operations by adding it to the legal documentation, but there is the risk that such obligations are – rightly or wrongly[12] – perceived as highly bureaucratic and that more established fund managers are reluctant to accept the institution as limited partner. A statement of assurance was proposed by institutions in the USA.[13]

Box 18.5:   Drawdown note/disbursement compliance checklist

Name of fund, payment date requested, currency
Total amount called from all investors
Amount called from LP
Split:

- Investment
  - Individual investment restriction (eligibility of investment) with comment if deviation
  - Portfolio-level investment restriction (geographical distribution)
    - Limits respected before (yes/no)
    - Limits respected after (yes/no)
    - If no: comment on deviation

- Management fees
  - For which period?
  - Applicable rate in %
  - Base amount for calculation of the management fees
  - If specific calculation, please specify

- Others (please specify)

Date and signature of authorized person to certify correctness of information

---

[12] One could argue that a typical VC fund in its entire lifetime will make possibly 20–30 drawdowns and that this extra effort should not be too much of a burden.
[13] See the 'Limited Partnership Agreement Project' undertaken by the Tuck School of Business in Dartmouth, July 2004 (http://www.altassets.com/pdfs/TuckLPASurvey.pdf), p. 16: '"A rep [sic] attesting to the compliance with the terms of the lpa before and after a capital call would be useful." Public pension plan ($10-25B assets under mgt)'.

Finally, one may come to the conclusion that strict execution of investments in line with set guidelines can only be done in the case of direct investing, but it is neither suitable nor fully enforceable for an institution that invests through a fund as intermediary. It could make more sense to select funds that meet policy criteria ex ante, define the investor's expectations regarding the management of the fund, and communicate to the fund manager that in case investment restrictions are not respected, the institution may not be willing or permitted to further invest in follow-on vehicles.

18.4 MONITORING STRATEGY IMPLEMENTATION

When investors start to have a sizeable portfolio, it becomes increasingly important to have a fund monitoring process that allows aggregating the assessment of each individual fund to monitor the overall portfolio. Important tools for the monitoring of portfolios of private equity funds and their compliance with an investment strategy are the setting of limits and benchmarking.

18.4.1 Portfolio limits

Results from the monitoring of individual funds can be summarized in the three key indicators of expected performance grade, operational status grade and exposure. Breaking down the portfolio of funds according to these dimensions helps, as we described in Meyer and Mathonet (2005), creating a map for prioritizing the limited partner's monitoring activities.

In the discussion of portfolio construction we have already touched upon the question of how to define exposure for private equity funds and concluded that there is no solution that fits all purposes. When basing limits on the usual definition of exposure – the sum of the private equity funds' NAV plus their undrawn commitments – we are faced with the problem that such an exposure behaves erratically even when everything goes as foreseen and no management action would be required at all. Therefore, for the setting of limits in the context of investment guidelines we propose to set limits on a commitment and ex ante basis and for this purpose use as measure of exposure of a private equity fund its commitment minus repayments. One could certainly criticize that a fund could have paid back its full commitment, and therefore the exposure to it is zero, but there may still be a sizeable NAV left. In the definition we take the view that the risk one is mainly concerned about is to lose the initial commitments, and thus when a fund has fully repaid the limited partner would not worry about it any longer. One could think of different and more sophisticated solutions, but we believe that in most cases defining limits on this basis is sufficient.

18.4.2 Portfolio benchmarking

The benchmarking we discussed in previous chapters related to individual funds, whereas here we discuss benchmarking of portfolios of private equity funds. In the context of an investment strategy benchmarking provides a yardstick to what degree an investment program's objective has been achieved or not. This is important for the sound management of a program as lack of benchmarking leads to poor, i.e. misleading, analysis, and poor analysis leads to poor decision-making.

Box 18.6:   Interim performance of a portfolio of private equity funds

As a portfolio is an aggregation of funds, its performance measures are simply the aggregation of the ones used for the funds (IRR, TVPI, DPI or RVPI) according to one of the following methods.

Simple average: the arithmetic mean of the private equity funds' performance measures:

$$\text{IRR}_{P,T} = \frac{1}{N} \sum_{i=1}^{N} \text{IRR}_{i,T}$$

where $\text{IRR}_{i,T}$ is the IRR of the fund i at the end of time period T and N is the number of funds in the portfolio.

Median: the value appearing halfway in a table ranking funds' performance measures:

$\left(\dfrac{N+1}{2} \right)$ th observation within the ordered list of funds' IRRs

Commitment weighted: the commitment weighted average of the funds' performance measures:

$$\text{IRR}_{P,T} = \frac{1}{\sum\limits_{i=1}^{N} \text{CC}_i} \sum_{i=1}^{N} \text{CC}_i \times \text{IRR}_i$$

where CC_i is the commitment made to fund i.

Pooled: portfolio performance obtained by combining all individual funds' cash flows and residual values together as if they were from one single fund:

$$\sum_{t=0}^{T} \sum_{i=0}^{N} \frac{\text{CF}_{i,t}}{\left(1 + \text{IRR}_{P,T}\right)^i} + \frac{\text{NAV}_{i,T}}{\left(1 + \text{IRR}_{P,T}\right)^T} = 0$$

where $\text{CF}_{i,t}$ is the cash flow at the end of time period t between the fund i and the investor, T is the number of periods, $\text{NAV}_{i,T}$ is the latest NAV of the fund i and $\text{IRR}_{P,T}$ is the interim internal rate of return of the portfolio P at the end of time period T.

Arguably, the pooled measure is giving the 'true' return of the portfolio. However, for practical reasons, it may make sense to also use the others. For example, the simple average can be a good indicator of the selection skills, while the commitment weighted average can be useful to assess the added value of the decision on the size of the commitments to each specific fund.

To benchmark a portfolio of private equity funds we need to compare it against another portfolio of private equity funds, but there are two problems. Firstly, publicly available database providers report too few funds-of-funds to make a comparison meaningful.[14] Secondly, these funds-of-funds implement other investment strategies and have a different portfolio composition and, most of all, usually a different vintage year structure. To get around these problems, we generate synthetic portfolios based on private equity performance data. For this purpose we generate synthetic portfolios with the same allocation to the various sub-asset classes (i.e. vintage year, stage and geographies) as the one to be benchmarked. Such benchmarking allows us to assess the 'picking' skills, i.e. whether the program manager was able to select within the defined allocations the best fund managers. If the portfolio is composed of, say, 40% buyouts and 60% venture capital, all the synthetic portfolios also need to have this 40–60% split.

Box 18.7:   Portfolio of funds benchmarking

The benchmark is constructed as the commitment-weighted average of the benchmark of each individual fund, i.e. the 'peer group cohorts' (i.e. the same vintage, geographic and stage focus):

$$PB_T = \sum_{i=1}^{N} C_i \times FB_{i,T}$$

where PB_T is the portfolio benchmark at the end of time period T, C_i is the commitment to the fund i, N is the number of funds in the portfolio and $FB_{i,T}$ is the benchmark of fund i at the end of time period T. To compare apples with apples the portfolio performance measure that has to be compared against the benchmark is the commitment-weighted portfolio performance. The problem with this approach is that, as it offers only one reference point and not a distribution, it does not allow us to assess the importance of the over- or under-performance.

To do this we need to generate synthetic portfolios of private equity funds similar to the one to be benchmarked. For this purpose we use the Monte Carlo method, a widely used class of computational algorithms for simulating the behavior of various systems. This is done by drawing at each simulation run the same number of funds as in the portfolio out of all the relevant 'peer group cohorts' weighted by the commitment sizes of the funds in the portfolio. For example, for a portfolio composed of eight early stage funds and five later stage funds, the simulation will be drawn for each run, eight funds out of the early stage cohort and five out of the later stage cohort. After weighting the performance of each fund drawn by the relevant commitment size, a portfolio performance is obtained. This is repeated many times so that a distribution can be created, which is then used to benchmark the portfolio. The commitment-weighted IRR of the portfolio is then compared against the synthetic benchmark, which, as for fund benchmarking, can be split into four quartiles (see Figure 18.3).

---

[14] In Thomson Financial's VentureExpert database we found just benchmark data on five funds-of-funds that were from different vintage years. All of these funds-of-funds were US-based.

Box 18.7:   (Continued)

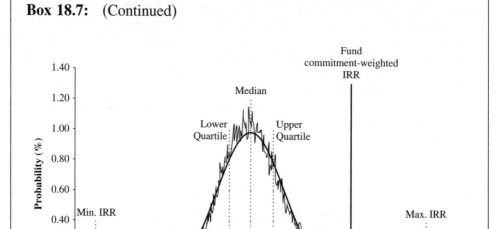

Figure 18.3   Portfolio of funds benchmarking – Monte Carlo simulation

The results obtained from this approach should be taken with care. Indeed, by construction, i.e. the random pick, it is implicitly assumed that the fund manager knows and has access to the entire population of the peer group cohorts, which in reality is not often the case.

The example in Box 18.7 suggests that the investment manager is clearly outperforming the hypothetical peer group of managers following the same investment strategy. However, it gives an incomplete and possibly even misleading picture as this result is based entirely on interim figures and because of the J Curve effect does not fully allow tracking whether the investment program is meeting its long-term objective. To do this, we need to model the portfolio of private equity funds' final expected performance.

Box 18.8:   Final expected performance

As the J Curve has an impact on the interim performance figures and as, before five to six years, a fund's interim performance figures are not on average good estimators of the final performance, these biases need to be eliminated by projecting the portfolio's expected pooled final IRR taking into account the qualitative assessment of the investments. These projections require a modeling technique, like the GEM or the modified bottom-up approach (see Chapter 7).

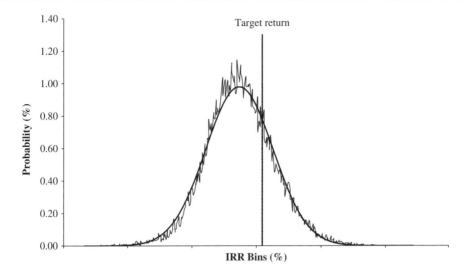

Figure 18.4 Final expected performance – Monte Carlo simulation

The GEM takes historical statistics on mature[15] comparable funds, a qualitative assessment of the funds, the vintage year structure and amounts committed to the funds into consideration to project the range for the portfolio of private equity funds' final expected performance.

The example in Box 18.8 suggests that with a high probability the portfolio of private equity funds' returns will fall short of its set target return. What could be done in such a situation? The interim figures in Box 18.7 suggest that already good funds were picked and that therefore the potential for further improvements of the portfolio's average expected return through higher selectivity is limited. Consequently, only a change in the overall allocation could potentially have a significant impact. One possible avenue would be reducing the level of diversification. While this would, at least in theory, have no impact on the expected returns, it would increase the standard deviation and thus the probability of achieving the target return, but with the price of an increased downside.

18.5 CORRECTIVE ACTIONS

While in conventional asset classes reducing risks means moving money into safer investments, in the context of private equity funds it mostly means monitoring the existing investments to minimize risks taken. Unlike investors in other asset classes, limited partners cannot easily withdraw their commitments or rebalance their portfolios to adhere to limits or manage toward objectives. However, many private equity investors view an active management through secondary transactions, i.e. interests in private equity partnerships purchased

---

[15] i.e. with vintage year older than 5 years.

from the original investors before the expiry of the partnership, as an essential part of their investment strategy.

18.5.1   Rebalancing through secondary sells

According to research from Almeida Capital, the secondary market has grown fivefold since 2002, when it started to take off after the dotcom had burst. At that time, institutions and particularly individual investors who had previously enthusiastically committed to private equity funds acutely felt the liquidity squeeze and could often not afford to meet further capital calls. Brown and Berman (2003) reported that just in the USA then 400 individuals were looking for bailouts and were willing to sell at a discount rather than becoming a defaulting investor. Secondary specialists like Coller Capital or Landmark Partners were even able to close a number of so-called 'walk away deals' where they paid the original investors nothing for the position and in exchange just agreed to cover future capital calls.

Secondaries were probably about 10% of the total private equity market in 2005 and are now seen as an option not just for the desperate but also for those who want to actively manage their portfolios.[16] The main arguments for secondary transactions – i.e. that limited partners should pro-actively exit non-strategic assets and recycle capital for new strategic investments, and that the secondaries market is now a fact of life with most general partners being used to the fact that sometimes limited partners want to sell[17] – may be convincing for the buyers. Although occasionally the existing investor may be under pressure to exit a fund, from an economic point of view the case for selling is far from clear under normal circumstances. Certainly, a simple NPV calculation shows that it can be better to sell an interest in a private equity fund today at a discount instead of waiting until it matures – the more so the longer the time to maturity. However, for a limited partner this raises the question of whether an early exit is not against the main idea of private equity, namely to be patient until the 'pearls' emerge, and by and large institutions are justifiably reluctant to sell. For example, according to Private Equity International (2006), for CalPERS conducting a sale is not an option.

On the other hand, in private equity limited partners are described as generally very ill-informed. Although they (should) monitor their often sizeable portfolios of funds they rarely take advantage of the information they have privileged access to. PREA (2005) pointed out that there 'are buyers in the market who haven't been investors in those funds in five years, don't know the assets well, and are more likely to misprice those funds than investors who have been in the market longer'.

18.5.2   Portfolio segmentation

After having committed to hundreds of private equity funds, larger investors regularly try to simplify the management of their sprawling portfolios.

> *Top of its list of problems to tackle are how better to manage its many GP relationships and how best to gain access to newer, smaller funds without having its small staff blow a gasket.*
> Private Equity International (2006) about CalPERS

---

[16] See Skypala (2007).
[17] See Allchorne (2004b).

In principle, limited partners have to regularly assess their private equity funds under management and do some kind of 'triage' as described in Table 18.1. The relevant factors to take into consideration are the potential of the funds' underlying portfolio companies and the quality of the fund management teams. This requires some pragmatism, as due to the valuation problems in venture capital the assessment of portfolio companies is easier said than done. Also in reality the line between 'good' and 'bad' fund managers will be difficult to draw and naturally the majority of fund managers will fall somehow in the middle.

Table 18.1   Management framework

		Investee companies	
		Good	Bad
Team:	Good	No LP action beyond standard monitoring	New incentive structure
	Bad	Restructure or replace team	Write-off, sell-off or ring fence

Ideally, from an investor's point of view, is a situation where the portfolio of investee companies is doing well and when its fund manager is competent. Theoretically, no further management action beyond continuing the standard monitoring is required. However, a fund manager may have changed the strategy and does not comply any more with the limited partner's investment policies. This is one of the situations where a limited partner may consider a sell-off even if the case for holding the fund until maturity is stronger.

18.5.2.1   Promising portfolio companies but under-performing fund manager

When portfolio companies are promising but the fund manager is under-performing or experiencing operational problems, limited partners could try either to strengthen such a team or to restructure the fund. If it becomes clear that the original investment strategy cannot be successfully implemented and no credible alternative is brought forward, investors can influence the fund manager to reduce management fees or even release limited partners from portions of their commitments.

Box 18.9:   VC fund restructuring case study

This box aims to highlight the different actions taken by one limited partner – Camford Partners, a fund-of-funds focusing on European venture capital – to minimize the downside risk of a non-performing fund, Flashlight Capital.[18]

Camford Partners committed $20 million to Flashlight Capital, a fund raised in 1998 with a trans-Atlantic focus. Flashlight Capital aimed to make investments in technology companies with emphasis on early stage and growth companies targeting the international market. It had a contractual lifetime of five years with termination

---

[18] While this box describes a real-life case, characters, organizations and specific investment details are fictitious.

Box 18.9: (Continued)

foreseen in mid-2003. While this appears to be very short comparatively to the typical private equity limited partnership, such a short investment horizon did not raise eyebrows at the height of the dotcom bubble where the time between start-up and IPO had shrunk to years and even months rather than a decade. Flashlight Capital had a total fund size of $100 million and attracted around 25 investors as limited partners. With the exception of Camford Partners, no investor held more than 5% in the fund.

An extension followed by extensions . . .

Flashlight Capital was hard hit by the worldwide downturn of VC markets, and soon it became clear that it would not be able to generate profitable exits in an environment where IPO markets were essentially closed. Consequently, in early 2003 Flashlight Capital requested an extension of the fund's lifetime until mid-2005. At that time the portfolio comprised ten companies representing approximately a cost of $41 million and a NAV of $13.5 million. The management fee amounted to a flat fee of 2.25% of committed capital, resulting in an annual fee of $2.25 million or some 16.5% on NAV. Camford Partners considered the management fee as excessive compared with the assets managed and together with one other limited partner voted against the extension, but they were not able to get the majority of the investors on their side.

In mid-2004, during a Flashlight Capital annual meeting, an additional loss of investments was announced. By then just six companies were remaining in the portfolio. Their NAV was approximately $11 million compared with costs of $31 million, resulting in a multiple of 0.35. In early 2005 Flashlight Capital requested another extension of one year – at a time when only five companies were left in the portfolio. Costs amounted to approximately $27 million with a NAV of $7 million, implying a multiple of approximately 0.26. For this disappointing performance the total management fee received by Flashlight Capital amounted to almost $15 million for an initial fund size of $100 million. Nevertheless, none of the other limited partners took any action to address this inconsistency, and despite Camford Partners trying to block this move, the extension for another year was confirmed at the annual general meeting. Nevertheless, the controversy around the extension triggered a number of follow-up discussions between Camford Partners and the Flashlight Capital management team.

These discussions gained momentum when an additional extension for another two years was about to be requested. The management fee implied by Flashlight Capital's proposal would have amounted to a total cost for the limited partners of $4.5 million, potentially resulting in a flat fee close to $40 million for a fund valued at less than one-third of its initial investment cost. Camford Partners put a counter-proposal forward: an incentive-based structure consisting of a low flat management fee and a carried interest kicking in on a threshold based on committed capital.

Even at this stage all other limited partners remained passive in the discussions. Therefore, in mid-2005, Camford Partners made a second proposal, which did not contain any further management fee but, as a trade-off, accommodated a slightly lowered hurdle as incentive. During a conference call the limited partner committee achieved a preliminary agreement on the principles of this proposal. However, during the remainder of the year, Flashlight Capital lobbied for different remuneration proposals in order to re-incorporate a fixed fee component and to decrease the hurdles. As this proposal deviated substantially from market standards, Camford Partners consistently rejected them. In between, Camford Partners also had one-to-one conference calls with the other limited partners in order to broker a majority to push through its earlier proposal. Finally, in early 2006 the limited partner committee took the decision and went along with Camford Partners' proposal.

Conclusion

Already in mid-2003 the Flashlight Capital team proposed a first extension of the fund indicating exit scenarios, which clearly did not materialize. It thus became obvious over time that the fund management team was not able to deliver on its promises within the given timeframe. Camford Partners believed at that time that the proposed time horizon would have been sufficient to sell the remaining four portfolio companies, whereas a fire-sale would certainly have led to a nearly total loss of the investment. Therefore, Camford Partners was rather skeptical when the Flashlight Capital team came up with a new proposal for an additional lifetime extension of the fund at the annual general meeting in 2005, but this extension was approved more or less without serious opposition from the other limited partners. These limited partners were clearly experienced investors in private equity, but chose to 'sit on the fence'. There are several possible explanations for their lack of taking action:

- The first explanation is that Camford Partners had simply the highest share in the fund and that probably for this reason the other investors expected it to take the lead.
- Secondly, due to their relatively small stake in the fund, the other investors had too little 'skin in the game' to spend a lot of time with the Flashlight Capital case. While incentives certainly have a strong role in private equity investing, this does not explain why the other investors initially did not support Camford Partners in its proposals.
- Certainly the other limited partners were happy to 'free-ride' on limited Camford Partners' initiative at the end, but a general reluctance of investors in private equity funds to admit to failure – and the resulting inertia to deal with the laggards in their portfolio – appears to give the best explanation.

While the amount recovered by Camford Partners does not appear too much compared to the overall commitment size, the effort gave a strong signaling. Camford Partners took steps, reflecting best market practice, to transform an active investment vehicle into a 'liquidation trust' with a reasonable remuneration structure compared with the funds remaining NAV. The results of this initiative clearly demonstrate the lead role limited partners can play in such situations and underlines the value potential to be achieved through active downside risk management. In this particular case the saving for the investors amounted to some $4 million, of which 20% accrued to Camford Partners – compared with the usual sums in private equity this may not appear to be material, but a penny saved is a penny got.

18.5.2.2   Portfolio companies with poor prospects but competent fund manager

By definition, situations where portfolio companies are not performing according to the investor's expectations – although the fund managers are competent – are quite common in a high-risk market environment. Where the private equity fund's returns have fallen below its hurdle rate, any remaining value extracted after management fees goes entirely to the limited partners, whereas the general partner cannot expect any carried interest. In this situation the fund managers have little incentive to care whether the IRR of an old deal is in the positive area or whether it is generating even a negative return. As the team is the main driver of any future value creation, replacing it cannot be a meaningful approach.

Instead, limited partners could 'recalibrate' the fund and provide a carried interest incentive on old portfolio companies that otherwise would have produced little return.[19]

> *In a certain light, this looks like a form of GP forgiveness. But forgiveness has been known to heal wounds and it may yet be the key to 'maximizing' value in under-nourished corners of LP portfolios.*

Private Equity International (2006)

18.5.2.3   Portfolio companies with poor prospects and under-performing fund manager

The worst case scenario is portfolio companies with poor prospects in combination with an inept fund management team. It certainly makes sense to try and put some pressure on the fund managers, for example to reduce the fund size when the fund is not fully committed yet – which theoretically would also be in the general partner's interest as it increases the likelihood of receiving carried interest. Investors could also ask for a reduction of management fees, and in many situations the general partner will give in, as an investor-friendly behavior can build up goodwill and ease the next fundraising exercise. The simplest management action of a limited partner not happy with a fund manager is not to commit to its follow-on fund. In situations where a fund management team clearly demonstrated that they are not up to the job or that they are not cooperating with their limited partners, this is a straightforward solution. This is also most feared by the fund managers as often the loss of a reputable investor sends a negative signal to the market. Indeed, not only does the team need to go back to the capital market for fundraising, but they are also now faced with a 'handicap'.

On the other hand, fund managers may understand that it is time for changing the industry anyway and therefore refuse such voluntary actions to make the most out of their last 'cash cow'. In situations where teams are not susceptible to suggestions from their investors, going beyond the routine monitoring may not be meaningful as the cost of control has to be reasonable relative to the size of the asset. In the extreme, and if there is an agreement among the limited partners, the fund management team can be terminated 'for good cause'. At the end of the fund's contractual lifetime or after having 'pulled the plug', the limited

---

[19] In Meyer and Mathonet (2005) we have described a real life case where this approach was taken with great success.

partners will be left with a portfolio of directly held companies without a competent team to manage them. What can they do now?

18.5.2.4   Tail-ends

To some degree the problem of the so-called 'tail-ends', – i.e. non-exited portfolio companies either managed by general partners who do not have a strong incentive to care much about the fate of these investments or directly held by the limited partners after the fund management team disintegrated – is a direct by-product of the limited partnership structure. Tail-ends are of relevance for the general partner as well as for the limited partners. The general partner would like to focus on a new fund, although being stuck with portfolio companies that may still have prospects but have drained time and money without showing a return after many years.

> *One thing that's changed over the last year is that there are a large number of tail-end opportunities.*
>
> Hans Swildens, Managing Director of Industry Ventures (see Sheehan, 2005)

Also, limited partners need to be aware of the fact that an increasing maturity of a portfolio also implies a growth of legacy situations, and over time this can become quite 'messy'. Therefore, limited partners as well want to get the fund wrapped up, as they are unwilling to pay more management fees if they are not making money on it.

18.5.2.5   Secondary directs

Historically, the secondary market has largely been driven by the sale of interests in private equity funds, with the limited partners being forced to exit prematurely. Kießlich (2004) suggested that the first secondary private equity transaction took place in 1979 when David Carr bought Watson's stake in a VC fund when Thomas J. Watson had to exit after being appointed as new ambassador to the Soviet Union. However, over recent years also an active market for the sale of directly held portfolio companies has emerged. Here it is rather the general partners that want or are under pressure to sell. In such 'synthetic' secondaries, portfolio companies are packaged up and sold to another manager usually with the backing of a secondary fund specialist. In fact, dedicated secondary direct strategies have only recently become recognized as independent strategies deserving of specialized fund managers. This market is attractive due to its inefficiencies, as demonstrated by the landmark direct secondaries deal when Lucent Technologies Inc. in 2001 sold off its New Ventures Group portfolio. Coller Capital acquired Lucent's corporate venturing portfolio comprising 27 companies for under $100 million and just five months later sold one of these companies (Celiant Corp., a maker of radio power amplifiers) to Andrew Corp. Coller achieved a multiple of 1.6 times and an IRR of 209% on its entire investment in a single exit. On the one hand this inspired great interest in this emerging secondary market for direct portfolios. On the other hand it may give second thoughts to sellers on what value they potentially throw away.

18.5.3   Conclusion

In reality, tail-end portfolios with dozens of firms are, in the words of Brown and Berman (2003), *'devilishly hard to value'*. The due diligence is complex and the risk concentrated in few companies. Consequently, there is only limited, if any, market interest for smaller stakes in single portfolio companies, as the secondary direct specialists are rarely interested in bidding for the 'tiny' positions and 'toxic waste' the limited partners typically want to get rid off. Therefore, in most situations limited partners need to look for in-house solutions such as managing a portfolio of direct investments.

Improving liquidity to improve portfolio management through secondaries or listed products is one of the key issues of the private equity industry. Another more complex avenue to liquidity is securitization, a subject we will discuss in the next chapter.

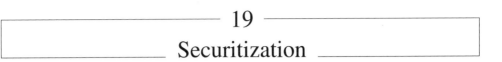

19
Securitization

Co-written with Olivier Amblard

To our knowledge, more than €5 billion of securitization transactions backed by portfolios of investments in private equity funds have been issued to date, i.e. early 2007. Such structured finance transactions, often called collateral fund obligations (CFO), proved over the years to be an efficient portfolio management instrument for a still rather illiquid asset class, as well as an attractive fundraising tool for fund managers. From a distribution's point of view, CFOs have also broadened the potential investor base by opening the asset class to fixed-income investors. This new investors' category in the private equity market now has access to a new underlying asset type, in a format attractive to them, offering low correlation to the other more traditional asset-backed securities (ABS), backed by bonds, loans, etc.

In this chapter, we first give an overview of the securitization techniques and their application to the private equity market. Then we analyze such CFO transactions from the point of view of the main parties involved. We then go through the specificities of the qualitative and quantitative risk analysis performed for modeling such deals. Finally, before describing some existing transactions, we discuss the external rating process and its implications.

19.1 STRUCTURE OF PRIVATE EQUITY CFO

19.1.1 Introduction to securitization techniques

Securitization is the mechanism by which financial assets (e.g. loans, bonds, credit cards receivables, derivatives, investments in hedge funds or private equity funds) are packaged together in a pool which is sold to a special purpose vehicle (SPV). The SPV refinances itself by issuing debt instruments, i.e. the ABS, with various risk profiles, sold to investors with different appetites for risk. Securitization of private equity investments are classified as collateralized debt obligations (CDO), or more specifically as private equity collateralized fund obligations (CFO).[1] Therefore, private equity CFOs simply represent an application and an adaptation of traditional technologies of securitization to portfolios of private equity investments. The structuring process of CFOs is typically as follows (see Figure 19.1):

- A stand-alone SPV bankruptcy-remote is established.
- The SPV gets funding by issuing several tranches of fixed-income notes (senior and mezzanine classes) and a residual equity layer (junior class). The SPV uses the proceeds

---

[1] In the remaining part of this chapter we will use the term 'CFO' to designate CDO backed by investment in private equity funds.

of the notes and the equity to purchase an existing and/or to-be-built portfolio of private equity assets (i.e. the SPV buys some limited partners' interests in private equity funds), which is then available as collateral with a first priority of interest to the investors in the various tranches issued by the SPV.

- The collateral is designed (i.e. portfolio composition by vintage, strategy, geographical exposure, etc.) so that it offers the best risk/reward profile, taking into account not only the specific requirements of the fixed-income/equity investors and the originator, but also the specific risk profile of the private equity assets.
- The service (principal and interest) of the issued notes relies on the cash flows received from the collateral (i.e. the distributions coming from the purchased private equity assets) that follow a specific waterfall reflecting the seniority of the various tranches issued by the SPV.
- The issued senior and mezzanine notes are normally rated by an external agency on the basis of the quality of the purchased or to-be-purchased assets (in accordance with pre-agreed eligibility criteria), the quality of the manager, the soundness of the legal structure and, for each tranche, the level of available credit enhancement (i.e. the level of subordinated notes and equity that will absorb the losses before hitting a specific rated note).

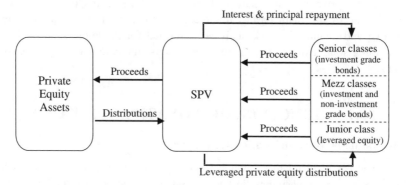

Figure 19.1   Structure of private equity CFOs

In a CFO, distributions from the private equity assets are typically assigned first to the service of the senior notes. Only once the senior investors have been fully repaid, will the mezzanine and then the junior classes be repaid. The same allocation among the different tranches is also applied (although inversely, starting with the most junior tranche) to the losses.

Because of the difference in risk profiles, interest on the senior tranche will be lower than that on the mezzanine tranche. This structure will offer some potential leverage to the junior investors, as the difference between the return generated by the assets and the cost of the senior and mezzanine notes (i.e. the 'excess spread') will be passed on to them.

Table 19.1 provides a simplified example of the allocation of the proceeds received from the private equity assets to repay the principal of the CFO's liabilities at maturity.

Table 19.1 Simplified examples of the allocation of the proceeds

Tranche	Initial investment	Scenario 1	Scenario 2	Scenario 3
		Multiple of 2.20× realized on the private equity assets	Multiple of 1.50× realized on the private equity assets	Multiple of 0.80× realized on the private equity assets
Senior	25	25	25	25
Mezzanine	45	45	45	45
Equity[2]	30	150	80	10
Total	100	220	150	80

For simplification purposes, the service of the interest of the senior and mezzanine classes are not reflected.[3]

In a 'bullish' scenario (scenario 1) the equity investor will therefore benefit from the leverage of its investment (i.e. return of 150 for an initial investment of 30), whereas in a stress scenario (scenario 3) he might be the only one to suffer a loss (i.e. loss of 20, whereas investors in the senior and mezzanine notes are fully reimbursed).

19.1.2 The CFO market

The CDO market developed in the late 1980s but CFOs only came to the market in the late 1990s. The first private equity securitization transaction took place in 1999 when Partners Group closed the Princess Private Equity Holding Limited (Princess) deal to **fund new investments** in private equity funds. Princess was set up as a private equity investment company, established to acquire primary funds and funded by a $700 million zero-coupon convertible bond, with a par value guaranteed at maturity by the re-insurance company Swiss Re. Following Princess, significant transactions put forward to the market have also included transactions originated for **portfolio management purposes** (see Section 19.3). For example, Deutsche Bank, which in 2003 decided to reduce its exposure to the private equity asset class, sold $550 million of ABS through the Silver Leaf transaction backed by investments in 65 existing private equity funds. In some situations, originators have also looked for off-balance-sheet treatment of their private equity assets by selling them to the SPV.

In addition, governmental institutions have also been active in the CFO market in order **to develop or strengthen their local private equity market**. Governments usually see private equity as an efficient tool to promote the development of entrepreneurship and small and medium-size enterprises and as such have offered their guarantee (in various formats) to investors in some CFO transactions targeting local private equity investments. Such transactions include The New Economy Development Fund (TANEO) in Greece or recent fund-of-funds deals in the states of Utah and Michigan, which offered a state guarantee in the form of tax credits to investors.

---

[2] The size of the equity in CFO transactions amounts typically to 25–40% of the structure.
[3] That is, the collections of the private equity assets have only been used to cover the principal of the various tranches and not to serve any interest or coupon payment.

Box 19.1:   Securitization of VC funds

The Greek TANEO program was the most successful European private equity securitization in 2003 with Deutsche Bank, EFG Telesis Finance and NBG International as joint arrangers and allegedly more than seven times over-subscribed. By creating TANEO, the Greek government sought to kick start the country's VC market while avoiding criticism that it is investing 'soft' money in local funds with a poor incentive to achieve strong returns. This scheme was described by Cope (2005) as 'truly innovative', as the required funding was raised in the international debt markets. TANEO – the acronym for The New Economy Development Fund – is a fund-of-funds, incorporated under the laws of the Hellenic Republic as a public sector limited liability company (société anonyme) in May 2001 with Hellenic Republic as its sole shareholder holding €45 million of preference shares. Another €105 million were successfully raised through an issue of notes. The debt notes are listed on the Irish Stock Exchange and have a 10-year life maturing in 2013 with the Greek Treasury guaranteeing the capital and interest on the notes. Moreover, they benefit from a credit rating of 'A' from both Standard & Poor's and Fitch.

Article 28 of Greek Law 2843/2000, which provided for the New Economy Development Fund S.A. creation, set out that the 'purpose of the company is the minority participation in venture capital organisations'. It was planned to invest in between 10 and 12 VC funds operating in the Greek market and focusing on innovative businesses. These funds should invest in limited liability company shares, or in shares, or in convertible bonds of small enterprises, preferably in early development stages, and with actual and registered offices in Greece. TANEO intended to be a minority investor, with up to 50% of each fund's capital and an average investment of €12 million. Despite the government support it operates like a 'normal' limited partner and does not interfere with the investment decisions made by these funds. It is represented in the investment committees without the right to vote but with veto power in cases where decisions to invest would be in breach of TANEO's investment guidelines. The selection of the VC funds is based on commercial criteria. They should be managed by the private sector and fund managers should take investment decisions on a commercial basis.

The Hellenic Republic provides a direct, irrevocable and unconditional guarantee that constitutes state aid[4] and is subject to strict limitations by the European Commission. The Greek government had to ensure that the Treasury's involvement in the structure and operations of TANEO were compatible with the EC Treaty state aid rules. For this purpose the EC has a procedure where it reviews 'notifications' from member states that wish to provide state aid and gives an assessment. In line with this

---

[4] State aid is related to the question of subsidies, where the government offers a monetary grant to lower the price faced by producers or consumers of a good, generally because it is considered to be in the public interest. Opponents of subsidies refer to them also as 'corporate welfare'. The framework for the EC rules on state aid is defined in articles 87–89 of the EC treaty. The rules on state aid concern measures with which the public sector grants aid or other benefits to undertakings, with the form of the aid not being significant. State aid is basically prohibited, and member states themselves cannot assess eligibility for aid, so a prior notification procedure is applied whereby the Commission is invited to adjudicate on the eligibility for aid. Aid granted without prior notification is illegal and in this case the beneficiary can be ordered to pay back the aid received.

procedure, on 23 August 2002, TANEO notified the European Commission, describing its anticipated function and structure. The European Commission indicated certain tests that it would use for guidance on whether to allow the state aid in the structure presented. For example, the business purpose of TANEO had to be making progress toward remedying a market failure in its purpose of capital investment in new technology. The state aid had to be minimized and it had to be demonstrated that without it TANEO would not be able to carry out its purpose: the European Commission agreed that TANEO's business purpose was to make progress toward remedying a market failure, as VC investment in Greece is considerably smaller than in other member states. Therefore, investment in new technology is lower, creating a drag on economic development. Consequently, in September 2002 it was decided that the aid scheme is compatible with the EC treaty.[5] However, it is possible that the European Commission decision could be overturned at some future time and the guarantee deemed to constitute unlawful state aid. As this potentially interferes with the Hellenic Republic's ability to honor its obligation, Fitch analyzed the likelihood of such a ruling but found that the likelihood is sufficiently low to be consistent with its 'A'-rating of the notes.[6]

TANEO's board of directors informed the noteholders in November 2005 about the resignation of the chief executive officer and gave notice of a potential trigger event. They found it 'highly likely, indeed virtually certain, that [. . .] the aggregate amount of funds already invested in Investment Vehicles and all Conditional Outstanding Commitments and Unconditional Outstanding Commitments on the Final Commitment Date will be less than €105 million'.[7] The board found that this was for reasons out of the fund-of-fund's control. In its commentary on this trigger event, Fitch expressed the belief that it would not affect the payments to investors because the notes still benefit from the guarantee.

The noteholder consultation in October 2006 provided some clues on the problems TANEO experienced. The fund-of-fund's investment period ended on 31 December 2005. Until then it managed to commit €38.5 million for investments in VC funds – just a quarter of the entire resources available and approximately one-third of the minimum amount to be reached. The slow growth of the VC market in Greece was given as the reason for this disappointing development. However, the Hellenic Republic voiced the political desire to continue the operation, and the management saw 'indications of increased demand in the market more recently (although these opportunities have not yet been subject to detailed due diligence)'.[8] For this purpose the following proposals were put forward:

- To extend the investment period until 2008 as a help for the company to invest in further VC funds that meet the quality thresholds, thus enabling upside payments to the noteholders.

---

[5] See http://ec.europa.eu/comm/competition/state_aid/register/ii/by_case_nr_n2002_540.html [accessed 27 November 2006].
[6] See Kolotas et al. (2003).
[7] See http://www.investegate.co.uk [accessed 29 November 2006].
[8] See http://www.investegate.co.uk [accessed 29 November 2006].

> **Box 19.1:** (Continued)
>
> - To increase TANEO's maximum participation in VC funds to 70%, as in the present state of the Greek VC market obtaining the remaining 50% of the capital would be too difficult. As this represented a new asset class and many institutional investors were not permitted to invest, the VC fund managers have found it harder to find investors than originally envisaged.
> - To expand the investment activities outside Greece to the Balkan region. However, the underlying funding would predominantly target Greek SMEs.

Since the first Princess deal, a number of CFOs, more or less structured and with different objectives, have been completed. The main ones shown in Figure 19.2 have raised a total amount of more than €5 billion and to some extent it could be argued that they have brought transparency and discipline to the private equity market, as the bonds issued in such deals are publicly traded.

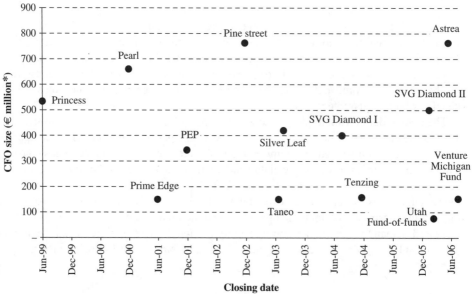

*: Exchange rates as of end of February 2007 have been used.

Figure 19.2   Major CFO transactions

19.2   WHICH PRIVATE EQUITY ASSETS?

While there has been a growing interest in CFOs over the past years, securitization backed by private equity investments remains a niche market. The first obvious reason is that instruments on the **asset side** of CFOs (i.e. private equity assets) and on the **liability side** (i.e. notes) have completely different characteristics. On the one hand, the investment and repayment profiles of private equity investments are unknown and very volatile, while noteholders expect a direct full investment at closing and the timely payment of a coupon until a well-known maturity, and low volatility in the underlying performance of the collateral. Furthermore, a private equity investment manager will target high returns ('risk-taker'), while a debt investor will generally focus on not losing the principal of its investment and making a good return through the coupon payment ('risk-adverse'). As such, and in order to build the apparently 'impossible bridge' between private equity and securitization, not all private equity assets seem to be appropriate for securitization.

• The securitization of an investment in a single private equity fund is not appropriate.

Private equity funds generally make few investments, they do not offer much diversification in terms of industry and geography, and therefore are very dependent on the performance of all underlying companies they have invested in (there is a high 'obligor concentration') and on the performance of its specific fund manager. There can therefore be much volatility in the performance of the fund, which an ABS investor would typically avoid.

• Investments in several private equity funds offer some comfort to debt investors.

The securitization of investments in several private equity funds can bring the necessary diversification among obligors, industry, geography, fund managers that is required by fixed-income investors. It implies that a fund-of-fund manager will be mandated in order to select the various private equity assets and another level of fees would be added in the structure. Usually a minimum of 10 different investments is expected.

• What kind of private equity fund?

All the sub-asset classes of the private equity market could be eligible as collateral to CFOs. However, buyout funds show more stable historical data as they tend to invest in mature companies already generating incomes. As such, for many investors, their risk profile is more suitable for a securitization transaction and existing CFOs have essentially been backed by investments in buyout funds, although often mixed with some exposure to venture capital funds to add some diversification, and to mezzanine funds in order to provide regular payments to the CFO. Private equity assets can be primary investments but also secondaries that would likely bring quicker realizations, leading to the increased liquidity necessary for the timely payment of interest to debt investors.

• Does a co-investment program make sense?

A co-investment program, combined with investments in various private equity funds, can also form part of the collateral of a CFO as it can allow some 'cherry-picking' in order to increase the potential return of the CFO. In addition, it can lower the cost of the structure, as one level of management fees can be substantially reduced.

In the rest of the chapter, we will focus on securitization of investments in various private equity funds, potentially combined with a co-investment program, which is what has been observed in the market so far.

19.3 PARTIES INVOLVED AND THEIR OBJECTIVES

19.3.1 Overview

Many parties are usually involved in setting up a CFO transaction:

- **Originator**: an institution (bank, insurance company, fund manager, governmental institutions, etc.) that either owns a portfolio of private equity investments, or wants to build one.
- **Fund manager**: the originator itself (or a dedicated team of the originator), or a third party mandated by the originator or by other parties to the deal. The fund manager will select the underlying investments and monitor their performance over the life of the CFO transaction.
- **Investors**: CFOs offer fixed-income investors access to an unusual underlying asset class, with potentially higher expected returns, and various risk profiles in a simple and common bond format. Typical investors in senior tranches include banks and insurance companies, mezzanine investors are usually insurance companies and sometimes other fund managers, whereas junior notes are typically bought by hedge funds.
- **Credit enhancer**: in some cases, and because the underlying asset class is still relatively new to the market, CFOs might involve a credit enhancer to provide an insurance 'wrap' and in order to facilitate the placement of the notes (i.e. a credit enhancer will usually be a well-rated insurance company that will guarantee, against a fee, the timely payment of interest and/or the repayment of principal at maturity). In such a case, the risk taken by an investor is the combined risk of the underlying securitized pool defaulting and the credit enhancer defaulting on its obligations.[9]
- **Liquidity provider**: as mentioned above, assets and liabilities of CFOs have different characteristics, especially in terms of repayment profiles. As such, a liquidity provider is often needed in such transactions, in order to ensure that interests will be paid on time to the noteholders. As the liquidity line is used to pay coupons on investment-grade rated notes, the liquidity provider is often a very well rated institution.
- **Administrative services**: in addition to the parties described above, CFOs also involve several administrative services such as trustee, paying agent, depositary, cash manager, etc.
- **Arranger**: usually an investment bank. The arranger is in charge of driving the whole process of setting up the CFO transaction, including the tranching and the negotiation with the rating agencies, spearheading the legal documentation, finding potential investors, etc. Often, the arranger would underwrite the transaction (i.e. will commit to find investors or buy the transaction itself) in order to guarantee a proper execution.
- **Rating agency**: the rating agency will assess a probability for the investor in the potential transaction not to receive timely payment of interest and repayment of principal at legal maturity for each tranche issued by the SPV (i.e. the 'rating' of the tranche).
- **Law firm**: the lawyers will ensure that the structure is sound from a legal and tax point of view and will draft all the documents (such as the offering circular, the investment management agreement, the debenture, etc.) regulating the relationships between the participants.

---

[9] An example of such transaction is the Princess deal mentioned above for which Swiss Re provided, at closing in 1999, a guarantee on the zero-coupon convertible bond. Swiss Re was rated AAA by Standard & Poor's at closing but was subsequently downgraded to AA+ in September 2002 and to AA in the third quarter of 2003. Such downgrades were translated into a downgrade of the zero-coupon bond. In 2006, the bond was converted into ordinary shares and the insurance arrangements with Swiss Re were terminated.

- **Valuation agent**: when the SPV purchases an existing portfolio at the closing of a CFO transaction, a third-party valuation service provider, specialized in the evaluation of private equity assets, will certify the value of the purchased assets.

Below is a more detailed analysis of the three main parties involved in a CFO transaction, i.e. the originator, the fund managers and the investors.

19.3.2   The originator

The originator of a CFO transaction is often a '**seller**' of an existing portfolio of investments in private equity funds or a '**buyer**' of private equity investments (such as a fund manager) looking to set up a new structure.

For the **seller** of an existing portfolio of private equity investments, a CFO transaction allows:

- Getting an attractive alternative to a secondary sale and, in some cases, keeping or generating fees for the management and the administration of the private equity assets: indeed, in a CFO, the originator of the private equity assets could keep the relationship with the general partner of its investment and thus avoid selling its portfolio at a big discount to a secondary player, as the cost of the debt of a CFO is likely to be less expensive. However, setting up a CFO would be more time-consuming than a secondary sale, and as such originators selling their portfolio through a secondary transaction are often time-sensitive, whereas those using a CFO are generally price-sensitive.
- Reducing exposure to selected private equity investments, avoiding concentration risks and, therefore, managing its portfolio: as an alternative to a cash transaction where the private equity assets are sold to the SPV, an originator could also set up a synthetic CFO transaction, where only the risk of the private equity assets is transferred to investors against the payment of a premium (i.e. such transactions would then be very similar to an insurance contract).
- Getting a different risk exposure to the private equity market (more or less leveraged) by re-investing in the CFO: indeed, the originator is often requested by other investors in the capital structure to keep a significant part of the equity component, so as to maintain some alignment of interest with investors and avoid any moral hazard. The seller might therefore leverage its private equity exposure by keeping only the equity piece of the CFO.
- Crystallizing the profit (or losses) of private equity investments through the transfer of the portfolio to the SPV.
- For banks, under certain circumstances, securitizations allow some relief of regulatory capital that can be allocated to other activities.

For the **buyer**, a private equity CFO transaction allows:

- Getting more funding sources: an originator may be interested in achieving an increased level of diversification of funding sources as a CFO, through the use of the tranching techniques, can target a broader base of investors of not only traditional limited partners (high net worth individuals, endowments, etc.) but also ABS investors interested in different risk profiles, hedge funds interested in leveraged private equity or some regulated institutions which cannot invest in traditional private equity assets but will be allowed to do so in CFO transactions.

- Reducing the cost of funding: the CFO transaction also separates the credit quality of the fund manager from the funding, which relies on the quality of the collateralized assets. Where the underlying assets are of high credit quality relative to the originator (or when the institution/fund manager is not rated and cannot achieve any debt raising on the capital markets), a CFO transaction may result in lower cost of funding.

However, for an originator, a private equity CFO transaction is not without some disadvantages. For a seller, the transfer of private equity assets may be difficult and would require the consent of the general partner and a right of first refusal for each limited partner. It implies a lot more disclosure in order for the rating agencies and the fixed-income investors to be comfortable with the structure. The time needed to complete a CFO and its costs are high as it involves many parties such as an arranger, rating agencies or lawyers. The originator will most likely have to deal with additional reporting tasks due to the leveraged structure of the new transaction, which usually involves a complex waterfall with predefined triggers to be met. Finally, the institution will most likely be required to keep part of a leveraged exposure in the equity piece of the transaction, clearly a highly risky investment.

19.3.3   Fund managers

Private equity managers want to increase their revenues, which are, for most of them, strongly dependent on the amount of assets under management. However, the fund manager's fee structure in a CFO often involves an additional layer of subordination to take into account the servicing of the debt, as well as an investment in the equity of the CFO. Typically, the fund manager would be paid as follows:

(1) Senior fees (before servicing of the debt).
(2) Subordinated fees (after servicing of the debt). This level of fees would typically not be paid to the fund manager if the underlying investments have not produced enough cash to repay entirely the noteholders.
(3) Return on the manager's own required investment in the CFO's equity.

Such a fee structure is usually set up to maintain some alignment of interest between the fund manager and the investors. In addition, such structures also put additional pressure on the fund manager, to find some good investments quickly in order to reduce the negative carry created if the CFO is not fully ramped-up[10] at closing, as the debt is running interests to be paid, and the portfolio of assets is not yet fully invested at closing and does not generate returns immediately.

19.3.4   Investors

CFOs, as a specific form of fund-of-funds, often offer a diversified and privileged access to private equity funds, the best of which are traditionally difficult to access, especially with a rather small investment. As such, it provides access to a new underlying asset class for **ABS investors** and offers some leverage to **investors in the equity piece**. The rating of the notes allows fixed-income investors to look at a private equity risk, and create some, although limited, liquidity on the investment.

---

[10] A ramp-up period is a period during which the fund manager of the CFO transaction makes new investments in order to allocate fully the proceeds of the notes and the equity issued.

The tranching of the transaction offers some risk–return flexibility. Fixed-income investors will typically look for a higher yield on this type of transaction compared with other CDO transactions reflecting the still nascent market, the still relative lack of liquidity and the uncertainty on the performance of the underlying assets. As an example, investors in the AAA-rated tranche of SVG Diamond II required a spread of 55 bps over Euribor 6 months, whereas at the same time, spreads on ABS AAA-rated tranches were issued at 14 to 41 bps (see Table 19.3). Tranching and pricing of the SVG Diamond Private Equity II plc transaction (issued in March 2006, with a legal maturity of 18 years) was as in Table 19.2.

With regard to the equity investors, they will look for enhanced returns due to the leveraged structure of a CDO. Table 19.4, which is based on simplified simulations, gives examples on the range of expected equity returns depending on the performance of the private equity assets.

Table 19.2 SVG Diamond Private Equity II plc Transaction – issued in March 2006

Class	Rating	Original principal balance	Interest rate
A-1	AAA	€55 million	E6M + 55 bps
B-1	AA	€76.5 million	E6M + 90 bps
C	A+	$47.8 million	L6M + 210 bps
M-1	BBB	€43 million	6.90%
Pfd Equity	NR	€175 million	EXCESS INT.
A-2	AAA	$71.6 million	L6M + 55 bps
B-2	AA	$40 million	6.06%
M-2	BBB	$20 million	8.41%

Source: S&P.

Table 19.3 ABS spread curves – March 2006

EUR AAA-A	Current	3 m	12 m	Z-score
RMBS	14	14	12	1.0
Cash SME CDO	21	21	19	1.0
Managed CDO	41	41	39	0.8
Auto	14	14	14	−0.3

Source: Deutsche Bank.

Table 19.4 Ranges of expected equity return in a CFO transaction (simplified simulation)

Underlying funds IRR	IRR of the equity investment in the CFO
0%	Negative
5%	0–5%
10%	10–15%
15%	20–25%
20%	30–35%
25%	50–55%

From an ABS investor's point of view, such transactions remain difficult to analyze due to the lack of historical data on the underlying asset class and on the performance of the few existing CFO transactions. However, they are still much easier to assess than straight private equity investments as the rating gives an independent estimation of the risk level and creates a risk-adjusted investment that does not exist for a pure equity investment in a private equity fund. Finally, an investor should also consider the high costs of such deals (in addition to the double fee structure similar to each and every fund-of-fund, a CFO would also bear high structuring costs, for example for the arranger, the rating agency and the legal counsel), which might be deducted up-front from the structure (usually at the equity level).

19.4 MODELING THE TRANSACTION – SIMULATING THE PERFORMANCE OF THE ASSETS

19.4.1 Monte Carlo simulation

In order to simulate the performance of the assets (i.e. the investments in the private equity funds), arrangers often use a Monte Carlo simulation. The model is based on a 'random pick' assumption[11] (i.e. the CFO will be able to invest in the total population of private equity funds that fall under the investment strategy). Under this technique, the performance of the underlying investments is simulated thousands of times. The results of the simulation are used, together with the structural features of the transaction (e.g. waterfall/distribution of proceeds), to generate a tranching of the liabilities of the CFO. A rating is assigned to the different classes of notes, reflecting the probability of default of the issued notes.

The basic steps for modeling private equity CFO transactions using a Monte Carlo simulation are then:

- One or several distributions of IRRs or multiples[12] are defined based on historical data.
- The cash flows based on the resulting IRR/multiples (see Section 19.5.2 on how the IRR/multiples can be transformed into cash flows) are allocated according to a waterfall reflecting the order of priority of payments defined in the terms and conditions of the transaction to produce an outcome of default or no default for that run, i.e. has the relevant tranche fulfilled all its obligations of principal and interest payment (no default) under that run, or not (default)?
- The probability of a default to occur and, for some rating agencies, the magnitude of such default (derived from the waterfall of the cash flows) which would then be used to compute an 'expected loss',[13] is combined with the weighted average life of the respective tranches to provide a rating to the various classes of notes.

The data in Table 19.5 illustrates the expected loss concept for a given tranche in a CFO transaction. The expected loss for this specific tranche is equal to the sum of all the losses under each possible scenario, weighted by the probability of each scenario occuring. In our

---

[11] As already discussed, in some situations, the random pick will have to be challenged. This will especially be the case when the CFO manager has a restricted access to assets.
[12] However, the multiples show no impact of the timing distribution, which is of paramount importance in the CFO's risk analysis, as explained above.
[13] According to Moody's methodology.

Table 19.5 Example of expected losses for a given tranche

Multiple	Probability of this multiple to occur	Loss on the rated note under this scenario
0.00	1%	100%
0.25	9%	70%
0.50	10%	10%
1.00	60%	0%
1.25	30%	0%

example, and assuming, for simplification purposes, that only five scenarios are possible, with the respective probability (derived from the Monte Carlo simulation) and the loss impact on the tranche (derived from the waterfall), the expected loss (EL) would be:

$$EL = 1\% \times 100\% + 9\% \times 70\% + 10\% \times 10\% + 60\% \times 0\% + 30\% \times 0\% = 8.3\%$$

Based on this expected loss, and assuming a weighted average life of 10 years for these notes, a rating of Ba2 can be derived from Moody's expected losses table.

Alternatives to such Monte Carlo simulations exist. The main ones are:

- **A comparison with the public markets performance.**

In the approach taken by Standard & Poor's (2006), instead of assuming a distribution of IRRs, some of the inputs can be derived from the performance of public equity indexes. Under this approach:

- A path of a public equity index (such as S&P 500, etc.) is generated.
- A year from the available pool's vintages is then randomly selected.
- The over-performance of this vintage is then adjusted compared with the performance of the public index.
- A J Curve is computed for this specific vintage.
- Cash flows are then created, passed through the waterfall of the transaction, and then it is checked if the obligations of the rated notes are met under this scenario. This process is repeated thousands of times.

However, some authors[14] argue that the relationship between public and private equity performance is not fully understood and, therefore, some may have difficulty feeling comfortable with such assumptions.

- **The CDO methodology.**

Use a CDO methodology, under which a probability of default would be assigned to each underlying private equity fund, some degree of correlation would be assumed, a default distribution would be generated and its results would be applied to a cash flow waterfall.

---

[14] See, for example, Meyer and Mathonet (2005).

However, individual funds have not been yet officially rated, and such methodology could be difficult to implement practically.

19.4.2   Modeling approaches

Monte Carlo simulations use inputs and parameters based on historical data on the performance of the underlying assets,[15] which are derived from IRR and multiples rather than NAV.[16] In the case of CFOs, one needs to simulate the performance of the underlying private equity funds, the performance of which itself depends on the performance of the underlying companies in which the funds have invested. For private equity CFOs there are two generic approaches (see Figure 19.3) to look at and analyze the performance of the underlying private equity investments:

(1) **'Bottom-up approach'**: one can analyze the performance of the underlying investee companies, analyze the structure of the fund (fee structure, drawdowns, etc.) and derive the performance of the fund. The bottom-up approach aggregates performance and cash flow data at the direct investment level.

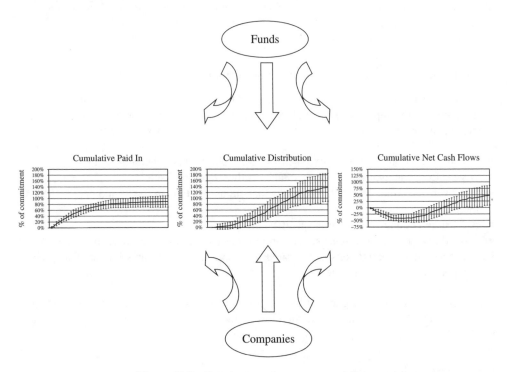

Figure 19.3   Top-down vs. bottom-up modeling

---

[15] It has to be highlighted that the results obtained are based on historical data. As past data are not perfect predictors of the future, investment decisions should not be taken based only on these results, but also, and mainly, based on the expectations of the market evolution.

[16] Indeed, NAV are often booked at cost and marked up or down only if there is a significant outside element.

(2) **'Top-down approach'**: one can look directly at the historical performance of the funds, which would already capture the performance of the underlying investee companies and the structure of the private equity fund. The top-down approach tries to model the performance and the cash flows of the private equity funds directly at the funds level.

In practice we find the top-down approach a good compromise because it is simpler to analyze as the results capture directly the often complex structure (level of fees, drawdowns, etc.) of the private equity funds, the correlation at the investee companies level and the risks related to the fund as whole, including its manager and strategy.

19.4.3   Use of historical data

One way to simulate future flows in a new transaction and to fit the Monte Carlo simulation is to use performance and cash flow data sets of liquidated or quasi-liquidated private equity funds. This methodology may be used only if the data set is reliable, unbiased or is conservatively adjusted and comprehensive or sufficient in statistical terms. The most intuitive approach is to use a group of funds that have a similar risk profile, i.e. with the same style or specialization, also called peer group[17] as we discussed previously in the context of benchmarking.

One of the first tasks of the arranger is then to gather historical data on the performance of private equity funds that are relevant for the envisaged CFO transaction. However, the limited amount of information on the private equity industry, and the fact that the available information is subject to 'survivor bias', makes it difficult to estimate the behavior of investments in such an asset class.[18]

In addition, the private equity market is still a relatively young market with long realization periods and only a few managers have gone through the full investment cycle from fundraising till full liquidation. Also, to some extent, the performance of the private equity market is cyclical. As such, because of the cyclicality and the time lag in realizing private equity investments, the possible under-performance in the venture capital sector since the late 1990s has not been fully reflected yet in the relevant databases.

As mentioned previously, CFOs can cover primary investments in funds, secondary investments and co-investments, the performance of which also needs to be properly simulated.

19.4.3.1   Performance of primary investments

The Monte Carlo simulation is based on a probability law that reflects the performance of the private equity investments. Many practitioners use a normal law to model the performance of private equity funds, usually with stressed parameters to capture the fat tails (i.e. the non-negligible probability that extreme events will occur). We believe that an asymmetric distribution replicating the 'multiples' realized by private equity funds better captures their risk profiles.

The base parameters of the distribution can then be derived and adjusted by the arranger from historical IRRs/multiples data on as many as possible private equity funds obtained from database providers. See Figure 19.4.

---

[17] One should consider the strategy of the funds (VC/buyouts), its geographical coverage, its industry coverage, its vintage, its size, etc.

[18] See Chapter 6 for a more detailed discussion and description of the VC data market.

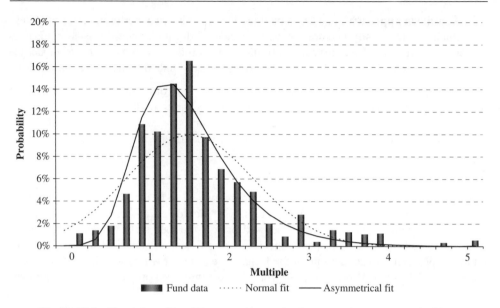

Figure 19.4   The risk profile of European buyout funds – normal vs. asymmetrical law

19.4.3.2   Performance of secondary investments

Secondary transactions can have a positive impact on the timing of the realizations. However, this is a business that is very much dependent on the ability of the manager to assess the right price to the secondary portfolio to be bought (i.e. additional skills are needed from the fund manager). In addition, the fund manager needs to work on higher time pressure as the bid is often competitive and needs to be closed within a stringent deadline.

Based on existing data, and considering that the underlying fund is still a private equity asset, it is difficult to find supporting evidence that secondary investments have fundamentally different risk and return profiles than primary investments and, therefore, we are rather in favor of using the same probability distribution as for the primary transactions. However, the timing of the cash flows would need to be adjusted to reflect the seasoning of the underlying secondary funds.

19.4.3.3   Performance of co-investment

The co-investment program can be simulated as one fund position. Therefore, its performance has to be adjusted for the absence of the 'second layer' of set-up costs, management fees and carried interests.

However, as per secondaries, co-investment requires a specific set of skills from the fund manager, which also needs to be assessed through a qualitative analysis.

19.4.3.4   Correlation

The various types of investments will have an impact on the correlation in the underlying portfolio. The correlation will have opposite effects for the various investors in the CFO, as a junior investor will favor high correlation while senior investors will look for low correlation.

However, this correlation is extremely difficult to measure and, as opposed to other actively traded asset classes, cannot be derived from the market as an 'implied correlation'. Therefore, arrangers will tend to adopt a conservative approach to the correlation as an assumption in their rating models, especially in limiting the scope of the random pick in the Monte Carlo simulation.

19.5 MODELING THE TRANSACTION – STRUCTURAL FEATURES

19.5.1 Investment guidelines

As CFO transactions are usually not fully ramped-up at closing, investors require the fund manager to agree on some investment guidelines up-front in order to ensure that the actual portfolio composition will be in line with the risk they have agreed to underwrite. The key structural features of the investment guidelines generally cover the type of eligible assets, the geographical/industry repartition and the vintage but also the number of fund managers, and the maximum single private equity fund exposure.[19]

19.5.1.1 Type of assets

There is more information available on the LBO market than on other sub-private equity markets, and the information available shows less historical volatility for this segment, making this asset class easier to securitize (e.g. LBOs represent 60–70% of the underlying portfolio in SVG Diamond and Tenzing). However, one should obviously consider also the recent development of the LBO market characterized by an increase in the EBITDA multiple paid and in the level of leverage, and the stretching of the financial covenants that could lead to more volatility in this industry.

19.5.1.2 Geographical repartition

There is also more information available on the US than on the European market, making it more difficult to consider a purely European CFO. However, in order to achieve a proper level of diversification one often sees CFOs referencing a majority of US assets with some European ones as well (for approximately 40% of the portfolio).

19.5.1.3 Industries

CFOs would typically seek some diversification also in terms of industry of the underlying funds (biotechnology, information and technology, etc.). This again explains why buyout funds, which often have a generalist focus, are easier to securitize than VC funds, which usually have a specific focus targeting new technologies on which, by definition, no data exist and where we are dealing more with uncertainty than with risk.

---

[19] These risk dimensions have been discussed in Chapter 16, which describes the portfolio construction. We highlight in this chapter their specificities in the context of a CFO transaction.

19.5.1.4   Vintages

CFOs are typically structured with an investment period of approximately three to five years, allowing the fund manager to also create some diversification in terms of vintages and to limit the exposure to disadvantageous investment cycles. However, the most efficient way of creating such diversification is to allow for a bucket of secondary transactions, which can potentially bring exposure to much younger vintages and offer the CFO a proper time diversification ab initio. As the secondary market is occasionally difficult to access, sometimes CFOs also are allowed to invest in publicly quoted private equity to achieve this diversification.

19.5.1.5   Fund manager concentration

CFOs would also limit the exposure to one specific fund manager in order (notably) to get diversification of management skills as well, and to target a broader scope of investments.

19.5.2   Cash flow management

One of the main challenges in a CFO transaction is to structure, in an efficient manner, the timing of the various cash flows relating to the investments in the private equity assets, the various costs of the transactions and, especially, the servicing of the liabilities of the SPV, such as the timely payment of the coupons and repayment of principal at maturity for each tranche.

In CFOs, timing has a large impact (Figure 19.5) as it refers to:

- The CFO's ramp-up period (i.e. the period during which the CFO will commit its capital to underlying private equity funds if not fully committed at closing).
- The investment period of the underlying funds (i.e. the period, which traditionally lasts four years, during which a private equity fund identifies investments).
- The distribution of realizations (i.e. the disinvestment period of the underlying funds).

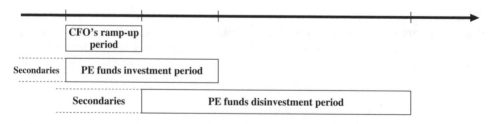

Figure 19.5   Timing of CFO transactions

The timing of drawdowns and distributions from private equity funds can be derived from historical data (see Figures 19.6 and 19.7), and can be stressed to simulate front-loaded and back-loaded scenarios.[20]

---

[20] Front-loaded scenarios stress the performance of the transaction when realizations occur at the beginning of the transaction, whereas back-loaded scenarios do it at the end of the transaction.

In order to take into account these timing mismatches, and in order to offer sufficient flexibility to manage its cash flows in a cost-efficient manner, CFOs are often structured with:

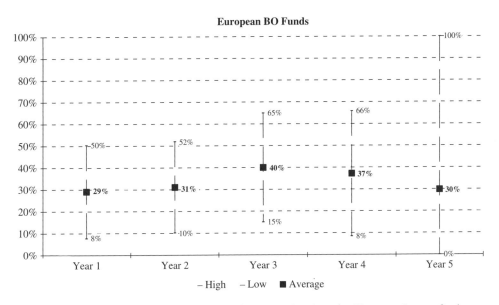

Figure 19.6 Historical drawdown patterns (per cent of undrawn) – European buyout funds
Source: own calculations.

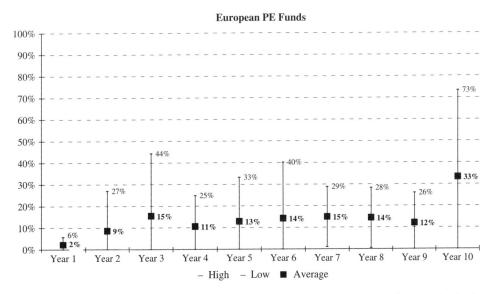

Figure 19.7 Historical repayment patterns (per cent of fund size) – European private equity funds
Source: own calculations.

(1) The issuance of zero-coupon notes

Early CFO transactions, such as the Princess deal, were structured with a zero-coupon note (with potential equity upside) in order to limit the cash flow mismatches between the unpredictable nature of realizations of the assets and the timely interest distribution due to noteholders. However, the more recent transactions have been structured with 'fully fledged' notes offering a timely payment of interest.

(2) The issuance of notes paying semi-annual/annual coupons

In order to limit the liquidity issue, notes can be structured with less frequent coupon payments. Instead of paying quarterly as per the majority of ABS transactions, CFOs tend to pay coupons semi-annually, or even annually.

(3) A full issuance of the capital structure

In such a case, the full amount of notes is issued by the SPV at closing date of the transaction, even if the underlying portfolio is not fully ramped-up. The advantage for the fund manager is that the cash is fully available from day one to make new investments, however, it is under time pressure to find good eligible investments as there can be a significant negative carry.[21] To mitigate this concern partially, in most transactions the proceeds of the notes can be invested in liquid investments, before being used for actual private equity investments in order to limit the negative carry. However, the scope of these liquid investments is usually restricted by the rating that they can bear, as rating agencies and investors want to limit the likelihood of the CFO defaulting on treasury management.

(4) A tap issuance of the notes

In order to avoid the negative carry created by a full issuance of the notes at closing, some structures allow for 'tap' issuances (i.e. delayed issuance of some notes). Usually there is a pre-agreement for these future issuances on the price, the dates and a minimum amount. Such issuances are often structured with a sequential drawdown, starting normally with the equity in order to have some cash available directly with no counterparty risk and to cover all expenses at the beginning of the transaction. In some cases, however, a delayed drawable equity can also be structured, but in that case the equity holder should carry a minimum rating, or provide a guarantee that the undrawn amount of the equity will be paid on demand. If the rating of the equity holder were to be downgraded, an immediate payment of the undrawn equity would be triggered.

(5) A partial repayment of the notes

CFO transactions can also allow a partial repayment of the notes, after a certain period of time (usually after five to seven years), once big realizations occur.

---

[21] The negative carry is created by the fact that the notes bear interest as soon as issued, whereas private equity investments need time to produce some realization.

(6) A revolving loan facility

In order to allow more flexibility, the debt portion of the CFO could be structured with a revolving credit facility provided by a syndicate of banks. But in such a case, the investors base would normally be limited to credit institutions and the liquidity on the revolving facility might be lower compared with that available on notes.

(7) A liquidity line or a cash reserve

Flexibility can also be offered to the transaction through a liquidity line, which would usually rank very senior in the waterfall of the payments and which would be provided by a very well rated institution. Alternatively, a cash reserve could be structured at initial closing in order to guarantee the timely payment of expenses.

(8) A minimum portfolio at closing

Usually, transactions offered to the market already consist of a minimum portfolio that will limit the negative carry. However, this also means that the fund manager must find a partner that can warehouse the first investments before the closing of the CFO and the simultaneous transfer of the investments to the SPV. One would need to assess a value of the existing portfolio to be transferred to the structure.[22]

(9) Secondary transactions

In addition, the investment guidelines may allow investments in secondary transactions that will allow earlier realizations. Particular attention should then be given to the fact that no clawback clause should be in the secondary agreement.

(10) An over-commitment strategy

The CFO manager may use an over-commitment strategy, under which it will commit more capital than it has available, in order to maximize the amount invested in private equity and help defray the drag associated with holding cash during the long investment period. An over-commitment strategy is based on the assumption that early distributions can be used for late drawdowns. In practice, a liquidity line will be put in place to ensure that capital calls will be met.

19.5.3   Interest rates

In CDO transactions where the assets bear fixed interest and the liabilities pay floating, the interest rate mismatch is typically hedged within the CDO structure. However, investments in private equity assets do not bear any interest, while the debt part of the CFO has running coupons. In addition, some fixed-income investors look for floating coupons (usually in the form of a spread over Euribor or Libor) and others look for fixed coupons. But, due to the uncertainty of the timing of the investment and divestment and the related notional amounts,

---

[22] When an existing portfolio of private equity funds is transferred at closing to the SPV, a 'fair value' review is performed by a third-party valuation service provider.

interest rate hedges are very difficult to put in place and not necessarily very efficient in a CFO transaction. As such, CFOs try to attract different classes of investors by issuing fixed, floating and zero-coupon bonds that mitigate the risk of performance due to variation in interest rates (see the description above on SVG Diamond II).

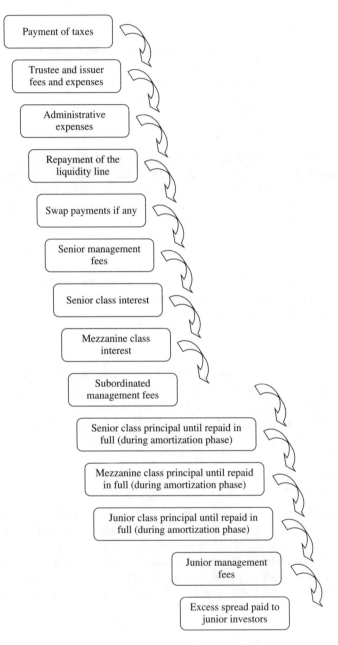

Figure 19.8   CFO's standard waterfall

19.5.4 Currency

Investment guidelines of CFOs will often allow for investments in various regions with different currencies, typically in USD, EUR, GBP or CHF. Depending on the strategy of the fund manager, and its envisaged geographical diversification, the CFO might issue some tranches in different currencies for amounts representing approximately the geographical split envisaged by the manager. This could limit the currency risk that otherwise would be difficult to hedge efficiently for the same reasons explained above regarding the hedge of the interest rate risk.

19.5.5 Liquidity

Most underlying private equity assets are illiquid, with a secondary market inhabited largely by opportunistic investors. Secondary sales, particularly when transacted under a pressurized time horizon, often occur at deep discounts. As such, private equity investing is necessarily a buy-and-hold strategy. This renders difficult to put in place certain structural mitigants available in other areas of structured finance, such as over-collateralization triggers[23] that would cause specific amortization events if available assets fall below a given cushion over outstanding debt. However, in certain structures, a stop of commitment or the sale of assets under a tight time frame is used to fund debt amortization as a form of pre-emptive deleveraging. Because such actions might not be feasible in the case of private equity, accurate benchmarking of its long-term performance is of added importance.

19.5.6 Waterfall

Distributions from the realization of the private equity investments follow a waterfall which typically is as shown in Figure 19.8.

19.6 EXTERNAL RATING

19.6.1 Rating approach

Private equity CFO ratings are not fundamentally different from the rating of more conventional securities. It is generally a credit opinion that assesses a probability of default of the underlying instrument. Importantly, ratings are not investment recommendations and the rating agencies do not provide a guarantee against loss.

Typically, private equity CFO transactions are rated by one or more of the major international rating agencies – Moody's, S&P and Fitch. They have all developed approaches to assigning credit ratings to notes issued by private equity securitizations. They had to develop or adjust their standard approaches to better capture risk factors specific to private equity, such as the limited availability of information, uncertain nature of underlying cash flows, limited secondary market and quality of private equity fund management.

The rating of CFO transactions also includes a legal review. As per other securitization transactions, CFOs need to ensure the bankruptcy-remoteness of the SPV, the security over the collateral to the benefit of the investors, and the enforceability of all the contracts between

---

[23] The over-collateralization measures the excess of the assets' value over the outstanding debt.

the various parties. In order to do so, rating agencies usually require a legal opinion from reputable law firms on the legal documentation.

19.6.2   The management review

As limited partners review the fund managers during their due diligence exercises, rating agencies see as a critical part of the rating process the quality review of the CFO's asset manager and notably its track record, sourcing ability, operational processes, research capabilities, infrastructure but also its credit quality.

The analysis of the track record is traditionally done via benchmarking. Its objective is to judge whether the drivers for success in previous funds are applicable for the future, taking changes in the market into account. Furthermore, managers should be able to demonstrate historical performance through various market cycles, the ability to execute a relatively consistent investment strategy.

Since access to top-performing private equity firms is often limited, rating agencies pay particular attention to the managers' sourcing ability, i.e. access to the whole market and, especially, to sought-after funds to prevent any negative selection bias.

Last but not least, rating agencies also analyze in detail the alignment of interests between the manager and the investors, which often occurs through subordination of some of the management fees and an investment in an equity piece of the transaction.

19.6.3   Surveillance

During the surveillance period, rating agencies will reassess the rating of the various notes, mostly based on the actual composition of the underlying portfolio and its performance. This exercise could trigger a confirmation of the rating, an upgrade of the rating if the transaction is performing better than expected, or a downgrade in the opposite situation. The surveillance takes into account all the parameters of the transaction, including the security of the credit enhancer if applicable. For example, the Princess transaction was downgraded when Swiss Re, the credit enhancer, was downgraded.

In transactions where the underlying portfolio is not entirely known at closing (transactions allowing a ramp-up period), the surveillance will focus on the compliance with the eligibility criteria set at closing.

The surveillance is based on reports produced by the fund manager, the trustee, etc. These reports need to be accurate, complete and sent on time so that the surveillance can be done properly. They must be precise and should report the value of the various private equity assets, including a qualitative description, the allocation of the proceeds in accordance with the waterfall, the calculation of the various triggers if any (over-collateralization, etc.), the compliance with the eligibility criteria, etc. Rating agencies will also review the fund manager on a periodic basis, with a particular focus on 'style drift'. This is where the fund manager changes its investment strategy outside its stated objectives. Style drifts are more likely to occur when the private equity assets are performing poorly, when there are still significant resources unallocated, when the manager follows a too opportunistic approach, or when the investment opportunities are scarce.

APPENDIX 19A

Table 19.6 Existing transactions

Transaction	Arranger	Investment advisor	Closing date	Total amount (million)	Maximum over-commitment	Tranche	Amount (million)	%	Ccy	Expected maturity	Legal maturity	Moody's	S&P	Fitch	Price
SVG Diamond Private Equity II Plc	Nomura	SVG Advisers Limited	March 2006	EUR500	140%	A-1	55.0		EUR	2013	2024	Aaa	AAA	AAA	6MO Euribor + 55 bps
						A-2	71.6	23%	USD	2013	2024	Aaa	AAA	AAA	6MO Libor + 55 bps
						B-1	76.5		EUR	2014	2024	Aa2	AA	AA	6MO Euribor + 90 bps
						B-2	40.0	22%	USD	2014	2024	Aa2	AA	AA	6.06%
						C	47.8	8%	USD	2014	2024	A1	A+	A+	6MO Libor + 210 bps
						M-1	43.0		EUR	2014	2024	Baa1	BBB	BBB+	6.90%
						M-2	20.3	12%	EUR	2014	2024	Baa1	BBB	BBB+	8.41%
						Equity	175.0	35%	EUR	n/a	n/a	NR	NR	NR	n/a
TENZING CFO S.A	BNP Paribas	Invesco Private Capital	December 2004	$212	125%	A	55.0	26%	USD	2010	2018	Aaa	NR	AAA	6MO Libor + 70 bps
						B-1	16.0	20%	USD	2011	2018	Aa2	NR	AA	6MO Libor + 140 bps
						B-2	21.0		EUR	2011	2018	Aa2	NR	AA	6MO Euribor + 140 bps
						C	33.0	16%	USD	2011	2018	A2	NR	A	6MO Libor + 240 bps

Table 19.7 (Continued)

Transaction	Arranger	Investment advisor	Closing date	Total amount (million)	Maximum over-commitment	Tranche	Amount (million)	%	Ccy	Expected maturity	Legal maturity	Moody's	S&P	Fitch	Price
						D-1	8.5	10%	USD	2012	2018	Baa2	NR	BBB	6MO Libor + 360 bps
						D-2	10.0		EUR	2012	2018	Baa2	NR	BBB	6MO Euribor + 360 bps
						Equity-1	42.7	28%	USD	n/a	n/a	NR	NR	NR	n/a
						Equity-2	13.0		EUR	n/a	n/a	NR	NR	NR	n/a
SVG Diamond Private Equity plc	Nomura	SVG Advisers Limited (formerly Schroder Venture International)	September 2004	EUR400	140%	A-1	40.0	21.25%	EUR	2013	2026	Aaa	AAA	AAA	6MO Euribor + 90 bps
						A-2	55.0		USD	2013	2026	Aaa	AAA	AAA	6MO Libor + 90 bps
						B-1	58.5	20%	EUR	2014	2026	Aa2	AA	AA	6MO Euribor + 160 bps
						B-2	26.3		USD	2014	2026	Aa2	AA	AA	6MO Libor + 160 bps
						C	15.0	3.75%	EUR	2014	2026	A2	A	A	6MO Euribor + 240 bps
						M-1	40.0	20%	EUR	2015	2026	Baa2	n/r	BBB	Private Placement
						M-2	49.0		USD	2015	2026	Baa2	n/r	BBB	Private Placement
						Equity	140.0	35%	EUR	n/a	n/a	NR	n/r	n/r	n/a

Name	Arranger	Manager	Date	Size		Tranche	Amount	%	Currency			Moody's			Coupon
NEW ECONOMY DEVELOPMENT FUND S.A	Deutsche Bank	Westport Private Equity Ltd	August 2003	EUR150	n/a	A	105.0	70%	EUR	2013	2013	n/r	A	A	6MO Euribor – 2 bps
SILVER LEAF CFO 1 SCA	Deutsche Bank	DB Capital Partners	May 2003	$484	n/a	Equity	45.0	30%	EUR	n/a	n/a	n/a	n/r	n/r	n/a
						A-1	76.0	25%	USD	2013	2013	Aaa	AAA	AAA	6MO Libor + 125 bps
						A-2	35.0		EUR	2013	2013	Aaa	AAA	AAA	6MO Euribor + 125 bps
						B-1	49.0		USD	2013	2013	Aa2	AA	AA	6MO Libor + 185 bps
						B-2	6.0	17%	EUR	2013	2013	Aa2	AA	AA	6MO Euribor + 185 bps
						B-2	20.0		EUR	2013	2013	Aa2	AA	AA	5.36%
						C-1	10.0		USD	2013	2013	A2	A	A	6MO Libor + 550 bps
						C-1	20.6	9%	USD	2013	2013	A2	A	A	9.29%
						C-2	10.0		EUR	2013	2013	A2	A	A	9.35%
						D-1	25.0	5%	USD	2013	2013	Baa2	BBB	BBB	11.54%
						E	17.0	4%	USD	2013	2013	Baa2	n/r	n/r	n/a
						Equity	194.0	40%	USD	n/a	n/a	n/a	n/r	n/r	n/a

20
J Curve Exposure

An industry expert described the thinking of institutional investors in Japan as follows: 'When I meet pension funds and discuss the feasibility of private equity investment, it is always the J Curve that is the hurdle to be overcome.'[1] Indeed, we strongly feel exposed to the J Curve, although – as we discussed – it is not representing the 'true' fair value of a private equity fund and just reflects an incomplete valuation model. The deep pessimism during early years of private equity funds investments or during market downturns is as unjustified as the excitement about apparently spectacular returns during later stages of a fund's lifetime. Many organizations' dynamics may come into play where senior management turnover is faster than the typical lifetime of funds, and where for under-performance predecessors are blamed while the incumbent managers want to reap all the praise. Typical investors used to the daily ups and downs of stock markets apparently find it difficult to get to grips with an asset class like private equity that usually only shows its true return potential after more than five years.

Regarding a particularly successful group of investors in private equity funds, the endowments, Lerner *et al.* (2004) suggested that their impressive track record to a large degree be due to good re-investment decisions. These researchers believe that endowments may enjoy superior returns not only because of better selection skills, but also because their early involvement gave them a 'seat at the table' or a 'first-mover's advantage' with the superior fund managers that allows them to continue to invest in subsequent funds of private equity firms that are closed to new investors. From this observation and from the discussions in our book, we put forward the hypothesis that in private equity and particularly in venture capital successful investment strategies play out and show their potential only after a number of fund generations, i.e. in 'evolutionary time'. Unfortunately, psychologically humans do not appear to be prepared to think in such time horizons. Moreover, against this background the institutional private equity market as we know it today is still very young, and a famous quote from the first premier of the People's Republic of China from 1949 until his death in January 1976, Zhou Enlai, springs to mind. When being asked about the impact of the 1789 French Revolution he is supposed to have said: 'It's too early to tell'.

20.1 CULTURAL INFLUENCES

For private equity we like to draw a parallel with wine. While it is quite common to grow at one time, say, wheat and the other time corn on the same piece of land – or even leave it

---

[1] Quoted from Chikusei Partners (2004).

idle from time to time – one cannot switch in and out from and to winemaking. A vineyard has to be set up properly, and cultivated consistently over many years. As with wine, there are good vintage years for private equity and bad ones. The winegrower will not know in advance which ones will be spectacular and which ones will only be good for vinegar. Nevertheless, to make good use of his resources, he needs to participate in all vintage years regardless, because the good years will – according to historical observation – compensate for the bad years. To be successful as an investor in private equity funds as well as a winemaker you need to be passionate about it.

Probably it is not far-fetched to assume a cultural influence in the widest sense on an institution's decision to become active in venture capital. As we discussed, also from a limited partner's perspective a significant share of venture capital's value proposition is founded in real options – e.g. co-investments or side funds, to name a few. To exercise such real options limited partners would need to follow a venture capitalist's modus operandi, which may not be possible in all cases. At the end of the day, institutions have to convince their own investors to become active in this asset class. Particularly university endowments may have a closer affinity to venture capital, as they relate to the commercialization of the very R&D and leading edge technology their faculty and students produce. Additionally, either as entrepreneurs or as financers, alumni are involved. Likewise, the interest of family offices in venture capital is not all that surprising, as such offices often represent successful entrepreneurs who 'made it', are even business angels and who see this sector of the economy with great sympathy. Typical institutional investors tend to invest when current returns are high and grow disillusioned when returns begin to decline, but there are limited partners that take another perspective. To quote the investment manager of a US family office, 'we are investing on behalf of a generation that is not born yet'. Such investors do not have the need to sell off assets to generate liquidity, and for them illiquidity is largely a matter of indifference.

20.2 BLURRED BOUNDARIES

During the 2006 World Economic Forum, Apax's CEO Martin Halusa voiced the opinion that within 10 years one could expect $100 billion private equity or, how others phrased it, 'juggernaut' funds. The newspapers' average reader may have the impression that private equity is just about mega-firms like Blackstone, Carlyle, KKR or Permira. The boundaries with other asset classes are becoming increasingly blurred, as some of these players are even venturing out into the hedge fund sector. It is the sheer volume of capital that can be put in motion by such mega-buyout groups that draws the public attention to this asset class. What we have been witnessing in the years since 2000 may to some degree be comparable to the 'junk bond revolution' in the USA during the 1980s and the public concerns voiced at that time, but sooner or later things will go back to normal. For these mega-buyouts over time returns are likely to come closer to public market levels, because this is essentially the area where they are operating. In a crowded landscape they need to bid against each other and with so many limited partners on board one would expect that this even becomes an own 'semi-public' and 'semi-efficient' 'club market' with even some decent liquidity.[2]

[2] For example, Apollo Management did not follow the IPO route of rivals like the Blackstone Group, probably because it was not too keen on the publicity that would come with a public listing. According to a Wall Street Journal report on 12 July 2007, it is foreseen to have Apollo Shares traded on a platform operated by Goldman Sachs and limited to institutional investors.

However, the mega-buyouts are definitely not representative for the private equity market and instead we are currently observing a growing segmentation of the buyout sector. Also, mid-stage buyouts have been growing and becoming more professional. There are simply enough inefficiencies, for example in the European economies, that offer sustainable opportunities for teams that have a good local network and are familiar with national law, tax and regulation.

20.3   LIMITED SCALABILITY

Venture capital is driven by innovation, but innovation is not as quickly scalable as investors and policy-makers would like it to be. The role of R&D expenditure in the development of the US VC industry cannot be under-estimated. While the cause–effect relationship between R&D and venture capital is difficult to assess, US sector-level data suggests that, at the aggregate level, it may be innovation activity that leads to the development of VC and not vice versa. Indeed, some researchers cast doubts on the hope of increasing investment into new ventures simply by increasing the supply of risk capital, and suggest that promoting innovation by increasing R&D expenditure can be more effective. For example, in the USA the funding of university research has not only led to valuable innovation but also created large numbers of graduates with advanced degrees in the sciences and engineering. Universities like MIT and Stanford have played important roles in the development of the VC industry and of Silicon Valley. Comparable observations hold for another country where venture capital is flourishing, Israel. And in Israel as well as in the USA, the broad impact of defense-oriented research – often of a 'blue sky' nature – on their VC industries cannot be under-estimated.

A very small number of transactions such as Yahoo or eBay made up the vast majority of the US VC industry gains between 1996 and 2000. On average there is not much more than one 'mega deal' like Skype per VC fund generation and the high-quality VC firms are highly likely to monopolize such type of deals. Therefore, stimulating venture capital requires committing to the best rather than trying to promote many mediocre teams.

20.4   END-GAME?

Harvard's Josh Lerner sees the following possible end-game: he expects the emergence of truly global private equity players that raise funds from large pools of money from institutions with less exalted return expectations. The mega-buyout firms' spectacular growth mentioned above is consistent with this prediction. Then there will be a 'robust fringe' of niche players in private equity.

How would this 'robust fringe' look? Various observations help us to put some hypotheses forward. Certainly, private equity funds are of great interest for institutions with long-term liabilities, such as insurers or pension funds. Whether the increasingly accepted and institutionalized buyout funds should still be considered as an 'alternative' investment is open to debate. However, due to their very nature VC funds will remain one of the truly alternative asset classes, but insurers and pension funds have simply too much capital to allocate to the VC market that would be unable to absorb such large amounts profitably. Therefore mainly medium-sized sophisticated investors, such as endowments or larger family offices, appear to have the long-term perspective, the right 'bite size' and the commitment for sustainable success in venture capital.

Moreover, endowments and family offices can keep long-term 'excess capital' that they do not have to return, for example to shareholders in the form of dividends; for them, private equity's illiquidity does not matter. Indeed, particularly in the USA, endowments and family offices are avid investors in alternative assets – as such institutions are not constrained by regulatory requirements cases, with up to 30% of the assets allocated to this activity documented. This class of investors is missing in many economies, which may be part of the explanation why most governments find it so difficult to kick-start a VC industry.

As Gottschalg (2007) observed, '*[m]aybe it is time to admit that private equity can create substantial value but does not always*'. Not every institutional investor appears to be in a position to generate value in this asset class, and to some degree it is an art. Venture capital is often described as a 'cottage industry' that is repeatedly criticized for its apparent lack of controls and inefficiency. However, a major part of our work aimed to describe this industry structure – with independent firms regularly raising new funds in the form of limited partnerships with an asymmetric sharing of risks and rewards – as a text book and time proven response to dealing with uncertainty. The efficiency, scalability and strong controls associated with modern large corporations are traded off against the flexibility of and communication within small teams that allow a much quicker adaptation to changing market conditions and newly arising opportunities. Mimicking nature and like cells multiplying and mutating, new fund management teams tend to branch out of established firms once new opportunities are perceived.

It is difficult to see how technical innovation could be pursued without having a framework that allows financial innovation as well. In fact, we feel concerned regarding recent attempts from policy makers to introduce heavy handed regulation aiming to structure what should rather be better kept as flexible as possible. We see regulation targeting VC funds and their set-up as misguided: how can a regulator replace the expertise of investment professionals without severely hampering the flexibility of the VC industry? It is rather the investors into VC funds, i.e. the limited partners, that should be forced to put the proper controls in place and that should be 'qualified' in more than a purely financial sense before being allowed to invest in such alternative assets. To draw a parallel to the complexity of modern air traffic: compared to the seemingly simple road traffic the higher standards for qualification and training of pilots contributed to a much better safety record for the airline industry. Likewise limited partners can manage portfolios of seemingly high risk investments in VC funds in a reasonably 'safe' way provided that they have put an adequate control framework in place. We hope that our works can help to create such a framework.

References

Akerlof, G. (1970) The market for 'Lemons': Quality uncertainty and the market mechanism. *The Quarterly Journal of Economics*, August, **84**(3): 488–500.

Alden, C. (2005) Looking back on the crash. *Guardian*, 10 March.

Allchorne, T. (2004a) Fund-of-funds: are the smart guys selling up? *European Venture Capital Journal*, September.

Allchorne, T. (2004b) Secondaries: a diversifying market. *European Venture Capital Journal*, November.

Allen, D., Lynch, T. and Bushner, E. (2001) *Accessing venture capital and private equity through fund of funds* Wilshire Associates. Available from www.altassets.com [accessed 2 August 2007].

AltAssets (2001) *Institutional Investor Profiles*. Various Interviews. AltAssets, London. Available at http://www.altassets.com [accessed 16 September 2006].

AltAssets (2002a) *The Limited Partner Perspective*. AltAssets, London. www.altassets.com.

AltAssets (2002b) *Institutional Investor Profiles: Volume I*. AltAssets, London.

AltAssets (2002c) *Institutional Investor Profiles: Volume II*. AltAssets, London.

AltAssets (2003a) *Institutional Investor Profiles: Volume III*. AltAssets, London.

AltAssets (2003b) *The Fund of Funds Market – A Global Review*. AltAssets Research Paper.

AltAssets (2004) *Institutional Investor Profiles*. Various Interviews. AltAssets, London. Available at http://www.altassets.com [accessed 16 September 2006].

AltAssets (2005) *Institutional Investor Profiles*. Various Interviews. AltAssets, London. Available at http://www.altassets.com [accessed 16 September 2006].

AltAssets (2006a) *Institutional Investor Profiles*. Various Interviews. AltAssets, London. Available at http://www.altassets.com [accessed 16 September 2006].

AltAssets (2006b) *Limited Partner Roundtable. Knowledge Wharton*. Wharton Private Equity Club, 2 May. Available at http://www.altassets.com/features/ arc/2006/nz8529.php [accessed 2 March 2006].

AltAssets (2006c) *VCM, Golding Capital Close Second Mezzanine Fund of Funds on €238m*. AltAssets, London, 28 July.

Amis, D. and Stevenson, H. (2001) *Winning Angels: The 7 Fundamentals of Early Stage Investing*. Pearson Education Ltd, London.

Andrews, D., Linnell, I. and Prescott, C. (1999) *Rating Preference Stock and Hybrid Securities of Financial Institutions*. Financial Institutions Special Report, Fitch Ratings.

Ang, A., Rhodes-Kropf, M. and Zhao, R. (2005) *Do Funds-of-Funds Deserve Their Fees-on-Fees?* Columbia Business School, 11 July.

Apax Partners (2006) *Unlocking Global Value. Future Trends in Private Equity Investment Worldwide*. Apax Partners, London.

Aragon, L. (2003) *Limited Partners Put Fund-Raisers Under Microscope*, 29 September. Available at www.evcj.com/evcj/1060714607660.html [accessed 4 October 2006].

Åström, A. and Alvarez, A. (2004) *Fee Structures in Pan-European Real Estate Investment Vehicles.* Aberdeen Property Investors Nordic. Available at http://www.ipdindex.co.uk/downloads/events/AndersAstrompaperVienna2004.pdf [accessed 6 January 2006].

Avery, H. (2006) Private equity FoFs take off. *Euromoney*, July.

Avida Advisors (2005) *Private Equity and Hedge Funds – An Upcoming Symbiosis of Two Different Asset Classes?* Avida Advisors Private Equity Info, July.

Axelrad, J. and Wright, E. (2001) *Distribution Provisions in Venture Capital Fund Agreements.* Fund Services Group. Wilson Sonsini Goodrich & Rosati, 5 August.

Axmer, D. (2005) When great minds don't think alike. *Hedge Funds Review*, October.

Baddeley, M. (2005) *Housing Bubbles, Herds and Frenzies: Evidence from British Housing Markets.* University of Cambridge, Centre for Economic and Public Policy. CEPP Policy Brief No. 02/05, May.

Bakman, L. (2005) *Modelling Search: Toward a Search Portfolio Perspective.* Paper, DRUID Tenth Anniversary Summer Conference, Copenhagen, Denmark, 27–29 June.

Basel-Stadt (2004) *Bericht der Parlamentarischen Untersuchungskommission zur Aufklärung der Vorkommnisse bei der Pensionskasse des Basler Staatspersonals sowie bei weiteren von der Finanzverwaltung verwalteten Fonds.* Grosser Rat des Kantons Basel-Stadt. Report No. 9413, 20 December. Available at http://www.grosserrat.bs.ch/geschaefte_dokumente/_/berichte/bericht_puk_pensionskasse.pdf [accessed 29 May 2006].

Beauchamp, C.F. (2006) *An Empirical Examination of 'Learning' Within the Private Equity Industry.* Mississippi State University, 19 May. Available at http://www.fma.org/SLC/DSS/Beauchamp FMA.pdf [accessed 14 June 2006].

Beinhocker, E.D. (1997) Strategy at the edge of chaos. *McKinsey Quarterly*, No. 1.

Beinhocker, E.D. (2006) *The Origins of Wealth.* Random House, London.

Bell, T.H. (2005) Steady as she booms. *Private Equity Annual Review.*

Berg, M.L. and Fisch, P.E. (2005) Multi-investor funds play significant role. *New York Law Journal*, 30 November.

Bernheim, B.D. and Whinston, M.D. (1997) *Incomplete Contracts and Strategic Ambiguity.* Harvard Institute of Economic Research Working Paper 1787.

Bernstein, P. (1996) *Against the Gods: The Remarkable Story of Risk.* Wiley, New York.

Biggs, B. (2006) *Hedgehogging.* John Wiley & Sons, Hoboken, NJ.

Bivell, V. (2006) . . . *Damn Lies, Statistics and Venture Capital Statistics.* Conference paper, OECD Global Conference on Better Financing for Entrepreneurship & SME Growth, Brazil, 29 March.

Blaydon, C., Wainwright, F. and Sorrentino, T. (2003) *Note on Private Placement Memoranda.* Center for Private Equity and Entrepreneurship, Tuck School of Business at Dartmouth University. Case #5-0012, 18 August. Available at http://mba.tuck.dartmouth.edu/pecenter/research/pdfs/Private_placement_memo.pdf [accessed 16 January 2006].

Bogner, I.G., Kuusisto, M.B. and Tegeler, D.W. (undated) *A Checklist of Legal and Regulatory Issues for Private Equity Funds of Funds.* Dow Jones, Private Equity Funds-of-Funds State of the Market.

Bokhari, F. (2007) Promising year ahead for Islamic bonds. *Financial Times*, 8 January, p. 6.

Borel, P. (2004) *Making Private Equity Work.* Private Equity International. November.

Borel, P. (2005) Zug to the future. *Private Equity Manager*, May.

Boucher, C. (2003) *'Winners Take All Competition', Creative Destruction and Stock Market Bubble.* University of Paris-Nord, January.

Brands, S. and Gallagher, D.R. (2003) *Portfolio Selection, Diversification and Fund-of-Funds.* Sydney School of Banking and Finance, The University of New South Wales.

Braun (von), E. (2000) *Selektion und Strukturierung von Private Equity Fonds-Portfolios.* Munich, IIR Private Equity & Venture Capital Konferenz.

Breslow, S. and Gutman, P.S. (2005) *Hedge Fund Investment in Private Equity.* Practical Law Company, June. Available at http://www.altassets.com/features/arc/2005/nz7645.php [accessed 3 November 2005].

Brierley, A. and Barnard, B. (2005) *Listed Private Equity – Bridging the Gap.* Report, DrKW Investment Trust Research. Dresdner Kleinwort Wasserstein, 25 November.

Brown, E. and Berman, P. (2003) Take my venture fund – please! *Forbes*, 23 June.

Bruce, R. (2005) Is 'fair value' good, bad or simply ugly? *Financial Times*, 16 June.

Brull, S. (2003) Not-so-private equity. *Institutional Investor Magazine*, 19 August.

Burgel, O. (2000) *UK Venture Capital and Venture Capital as an Asset Class for Institutional Investors.* BVCA, London.

Burgelman, R.A. (2002) *Strategy is Destiny: How Strategy-making Shapes a Company's Future.* Free Press, New York.

Burns, A. (2002) *Apocalypse Roulette: The Fall of Long-Term Capital Management.* Australian Foresight Institute, November.

Bushrod, L. (2004) To co-invest or not to co-invest? *European Venture Capital Journal*, April.

Business Week (2003) E.BIZ 25 – Architects – Michael Moritz, Sequoia Capital. *Business Week*, 29 September.

Butler, R. (2006) A gut feeling that risk is good. *Realdeals*, 1 June.

Bygrave, W.D., Hay, M. and Peters, J.B. (1999) *The Venture Capital Handbook.* Pearson Education Ltd, London.

Byworth, A.M. (2005) *Qualities of a Good Limited Partner.* CDC Presentation, 7 February. Available at http://www.altassets.com/features/arc/2005/nz6292.php [accessed 9 February 2005].

Capital Eyes (2002) *Clawbacks Ahead.* Bank of America Business Capital bi-monthly e-newsletter on leveraged finance, August. Available at http://www.bofabusinesscapital.com/resources/capeyes/a08-02-114.html?month=8&year=2002 [accessed 23 November 2006].

Capital Eyes (2003) *Mezzanine Debt – Another Level to Consider.* Excerpt from a Fitch Ratings report on Mezzanine Debt, August. Available at http://www.bofabusinesscapital.com/resources/capeyes/a08-03-176.html [accessed 9 January 2007].

Carroll, A. (2006) Carried interest to be paid deal by deal. *RealDeals*, 1 June.

Case, J. (2000) LTCM: rigorous empirical testing ground for modern theories of financial mathematics. *SIAM News* **34**(3).

Chakravorti, B. (2003) Bet, reserve options or insure? Making certain choices in an uncertain world. *Ivey Business Journal.*

Chancellor, E. (1999) *Devil Take the Hindmost – A History of Financial Speculation.* Penguin Putnam, New York.

Chen, J. (2000) *Economic and Biological Evolution: A Non-equilibrium and Real Option Approach*, July. Available at http://ssrn.com/abstract=250235 [accessed 27 February 2006].

Chen, J. (2003) *An Analytical Theory of Project Investment: A Comparison with Real Option Theory*, June. Available at http://ssrn.com/abstract=336380 [accessed 27 February 2006].

Cheung, L., Howley, C. and Kapoor, V. (2003) *Rating Private Equity CFOs: Cash Flow Benchmarks.* Research, Standard & Poor's, January.

Chikusei Partners (2004) *Japanese Institutional Investments in Private Equity – Experience and Future Trends.* Chikusei Partners Ltd. and Mitsubishi Research Institute, Inc. April.

Choi, S.-Y., Stahl, D.O. and Whinston, A.B. (1997) *The Economics of Electronic Commerce.* Macmillan Technical Publishing, Indianapolis, IN.

Choudhury, M. (2001) Islamic Venture Capital – A Critical Examination. *Journal of Economic Studies* **28**(1): 14–33.

Cochrane, J.H. (2005) The risk and return of venture capital. *Journal of Financial Economics* **75**(1).

Cohen, E.A. and Gooch, J. (1991) *Military Misfortunes – The Anatomy of Failure in War.* Vintage Books, London.

Conner, A. (2005) Persistence in venture capital returns. *Private Equity International*, March.

Constantinides, E. (2004) Strategies for surviving the Internet meltdown. *Management Decision* **42**(1).

Conza, M.A. (2002) *PIPE Transactions.* Testa, Hurwitz & Thibeault, 23 July. Available at http://www.altassets.com/knowledgebank/learningcurve/2002/nz2856.php [accessed 23 August 2006].

Cope, G. (2005) *Issues and Policy Framework for the Development of Self-sustainable Venture Capital Markets in Europe.* Luxembourg School of Finance, MSc thesis, April. Available at http://www.altassets.com/pdfs/lsf_euro_vc_development.pdf [accessed 1 March 2006].

Copeland, T. and Antikarov, V. (2003) *Real Options – A Practitioner's Guide.* TEXERE. Thomson, New York.

Costabile, S. (2006) *Successfully Overcoming Challenges in Private Equity Manager Selection.* Presentation, AIG Global Investment Group.

Courtney, H. (2001) Making the most of uncertainty. *McKinsey Quarterly,* No. 4.

Covitz, D. and Liang, N. (2002) *Recent Developments in the Private Equity Market and the Role of Preferred Returns.* Division of Research and Statistics, Board of Governors of the Federal Reserve System.

Cowley, L. (2002) Swiss fund-of-funds: leading the way. *European Venture Capital Journal,* April.

CPEE (2004) *Limited Partnership Agreement Conference.* Tuck School of Business at Dartmouth, Center for Private Equity and Entrepreneurship. Proceedings, 20–21 July. Available at http://mba.tuck.dartmouth.edu/pecenter/research/pdfs/LPA_conference.pdf [accessed 13 September 2006].

Das, S. (2005) *Credit Derivatives CDOs & Structured Credit Products,* 3rd edn. Wiley Finance, Singapore.

Davies, J. (2005) Cover story: telephony. *Real Deals,* 6 October.

Davies, P.K. (2002) Strategic Planning Amidst Massive Uncertainty in Complex Adaptive Systems: the Case of Defense Planning. RAND graduated School. Available from www.rand.org/about/contacts/personal/pdavis/davisICCS.html [accessed 23 April 2007].

Dawkins, R. (2000) *The Blind Watchmaker.* Penguin Books, London.

DEH (2001) *Socially Responsible Investment: Your Questions Answered – An Information Guide for Superannuation Trustees and Fund Managers.* Australian Government Department of the Environment and Heritage, July. Available at http://www.deh.gov.au/settlements/industry/finance/publications/respon-investment.html [accessed 13 July 2006].

Demaria, C. (2005) The convergence of alternative asset classes: a dead end. *360 Journal,* January. Available at http://www.360journal.com/Archives/Alterinv.php [accessed 23 August 2006].

DeMiguel, V., Garlappi, L. and Uppal, R. (2004) *How Inefficient Are Simple Asset-Allocation Strategies?* Available at SSRN: http://ssrn.com/abstract=676997.

DePonte, K. (undated) *Emerging Managers: How to Analyse a First Time Fund.* Research guide, Probitas Partners. Available at www.probitaspartners.com/news/due_diligence_managers.pdf [accessed 9 February 2007].

Dequech, D. (1999) On some arguments for the rationality of conventional behaviour under uncertainty. In Sardoni, C. and Kriesler, P. (eds), *Keynes, Post-Keynesianism and Political Economy.* Routledge, London.

Derman, E. (2004) *My Life as a Quant – Reflections on Physics and Finance.* John Wiley & Sons, Chichester.

Devenow, A. and Welch, I. (1996) Rational herding in financial economics. *European Economic Review,* No. 40.

Diamond, J. (2005) *Collapse – How Societies Choose to Fail or Succeed.* Penguin Books, London.

DiCarlo, L. (2001) Incubators on life support. *Forbes,* 18 January. Available at http://www.forbes.com/2001/01/18/0118main.html [accessed 14 January 2007].

Diego Arozamena (de), A. (2006) *CDO Spotlight: Global Criteria for Private Equity Securitization.* Research, Standard & Poor's, January.

Dimov, D. and Murray, G. (2006) *The Determinants of the Incidence and Scale of Seed Capital Investments by Venture Capital Firms.* University of Exeter, 18 August. Available at http://www.sobe.ex.ac.uk/respapers/Dimo&Murray_May06.pdf [accessed 21 August 2006].

Dinneen, P. (2004) *Emerging Markets Private Equity: Performance Update.* IFC Conference, 6 May. Available at http://www.ifc.org/ifcext/cfn.nst/AttachmentsByTitle/Patricia+Dinneen/$FILE/Panel4-PatriciaDinneed.pdf [accessed 1 February 2006].

Durrani, M. and Boocock, G. (2006) *Venture Capital, Islamic Finance and SMEs – Valuation, Structuring and Monitoring Practices in India*. Basingstoke Hampshire, New York.

Economist (2000) Money to burn. *The Economist*, 27 May.

Economist (2004a) The new kings of capitalism. *The Economist*, 25 November.

Economist (2004b) Once burnt, still hopeful. *The Economist*, 25 November.

Economist (2005) *Size Matters – Buy-outs are all the Rage*. 29 January–4 February.

Economist (2006a) Unhappy hunting grounds. *The Economist*, 4 February.

Economist (2006b) A barbarian no more. *The Economist*, 30 May.

Emerson, J. (2003) *The Blended Value Map – Tracking the Intersects and Opportunities of Economic, Social and Environmental Value Creation*, October. Available at http://www.compartamos. org/images/dynamic/chapters/109/Blended %20Value %20Map %20vCorta.pdf [accessed 16 August 2006].

EMPEA (2005) *New Funds of Funds Increase Options for Emerging Markets Private Equity Investors*. Emerging Markets Private Equity Association, 20 March. Available at http://www.empea. net/docs/Emerging_Markets_Private_Equity_Issue_1.pdf [accessed 31 October 2005].

Ennis Knupp & Associates (2005) *The Ohio Bureau of Workers' Compensation – Private Equity Valuation*. Final Report, 28 December.

Ernst & Young (2005) *IFRS Stakeholder Series: 'How Fair is Fair Value?'* May 2005. Available at http://www.ey.com/global/download.nsf/International/AABS_-_IFRS_-_How_Fair_is_Fair_Value/ $file/Global_Home.SServices-Solutions.Assurance-Advisory_How_Fair_is_fair_Value.pdf [accessed 16 June 2005].

Erturk, E., Cheung, L. and Fong, W. (2001) *Private Equity Fund of Funds: Overview and Rating Criteria*. Standard and Poors Publication.

European Commission (2003) *Benchmarking Business Angels*. European Commission – Enterprise Directorate-General. Best Report, No. 1.

EVCA (2004) *Further Comments to the Basel Committee: The Risk Profile of Private Equity and Venture Capital*, 6 February. Available at http://www.evca.com/images/attachments/tmpl_26_art_ 94_att_498.pdf [accessed 4 August 2005].

EVCA (2005a) *IFRS and the Private Equity Industry – Discussion Paper No 1*, April. Available at http://www.evca.com/images/attachments/tmpl_9_art_107_att_771.pdf [accessed 2 August 2005].

EVCA (2005b) *IFRS and the Private Equity Industry – Discussion Paper No 2*, September. Available at http://www.evca.com/images/attachments/tmpl_9_art_116_att_892.pdf [accessed 17 November 2005].

EVCJ (2004) *Securitisation: Still early days,* March. http://www.ventureeconomics.com/evcj/protected/ sectorreps/finance/1070549707736.html.

FAZ (2006) Permira zurück an der Weltspitze. *Frankfurter Allgemeine Zeitung,* 4 July.

Flag Venture Management (2001) *The Right Level of Diversification*. Venture Insights 1st Quarter, Flag Venture Management Special Report.

Fleischer, V. (2004) *Fickle Investors, Reputation, and the Clientele Effect in Venture Capital Funds*. UCLA School of Law, Law-Econ Research Paper No. 04–14, 2 October. Available at SSRN: http://ssrn.com/abstract=600044 [accessed 5 May 2006].

Fleischer, V. (2005) *The Missing Preferred Return*. UCLA School of Law. Law & Economics Working Paper Series, No. 465, 22 February.

Forbes (2004) *Interview with Guy Kawasaki: Does An Entrepreneur Need An M.B.A.?*, 17 March. Available at http://www.forbes.com/columnists/2004/03/17/cx_gk_0317artofthestart.html [accessed 30 November 2005].

Forrester, P. (undated) *Private equity collateralized debt obligations: What? Why? Now?* Available at http://www.mayerbrownrowe.com/privateinvestmentfund/news/art_forrester_cdo.PDF [accessed 30 March 2007].

Foster, D. and Kaplan, S. (2001) *Creative Destruction: Why Companies That Are Built to Last Underperform the Market*. Currency.

Fraser-Sampson, G. (2006a) *Multi Asset Class Investment Strategy*. John Wiley & Sons, Chichester.

Fraser-Sampson, G. (2006b) It's time for European venture to go green. Realdeals, 15 June.

Fraser-Sampson, G. (2007) *Private Equity as an Asset Class*. John Wiley & Sons, Chichester.

Freear, J., Sohl, J. and Wetzel, W. (2002) Angels on angels: financing technology-based ventures – a historical perspective. *Venture Capital*, No. 4.

Frey, P. (1998) *Stufenweise Finanzierung und Neubewertungsproblematik von Venture Capital Projekten*. Diplomarbeit, Universität Sankt Gallen, 1 September.

Friedman, R.M. (2005) *Essential Terms of Fund Foundation*. Presentation, The 2005 Private Equity Strategic Financial Management Conference, 19–20 July.

Fruchbom, P. (2005) GPs on LPs. *Private Equity International*, June.

FT MU (2006a) Mastering uncertainty part 1: seeking shelter from the storm. *Financial Times*, 17 March.

FT MU (2006b) Mastering uncertainty part 2: be prepared for the extreme. *Financial Times*, 24 March.

FT MU (2006c) Mastering uncertainty part 3: don't get swept away by change. *Financial Times*, 31 March.

FT MU (2006d) Mastering uncertainty part 4: the search for common meaning. *Financial Times*, 7 April.

Fukuyama, F. (1995) *Trust – The Social Virtues and the Creation of Prosperity*. Free Press Paperback Edition 1996, New York.

Gasparino, C. (2005) *Blood on the Street*. Free Press, New York.

Gaudron, J.-M. (2005) Skype/eBay – le coup de maître. *Paper Jam*, November.

Geller, J.A. (2006) *Hedge Funds: Gatecrashers at the Party*. Presentation at EVCA Symposium 'Shaping the Future', 16 June.

Geltner, D. and Ling, D. (2000) *Benchmark & Index Needs in the US Private Real Estate Investment Industry: Trying to Close the Gap*. RERI study for the Pension Real Estate Association, Hartford, CT.

Gilson, R.J. (2003) Engineering a venture capital market: lessons from the American experience. *Stanford Law Review* **55**(April). Available at http://ssrn.com/abstract=353380 [accessed 9 February 2006].

Ginsberg, A. (2002) *Truth, or Consequences – Academic Researchers are Helping Policy Makers and Practitioners Understand the Problems Facing the Venture Capital Industry*. The Berkley Center for Entrepreneurial Studies. Available at http://entrepreneurship.mit.edu/Downloads/IRBerkley02.pdf [accessed 14 June 2006].

Goepfert, D. (2003) *Interpellation zur Anlagepolitik betr. Pensionkasse*, 3 April. Available at www.sp-bs.ch/gr/anzg_2003/anzg_223.php [accessed 21 March 2005].

Gold, J. (2006) *The Best Things Come to Those Who Wait . . .* AltAssets, 14 June. Available at http://www.altassets.com/features/arc/2006/nz8830.php [accessed 15 June 2006].

Goldstein, D.A. (2005) *Convergence in Action*. White & Case LLP Publications, April. Available at http://www.whitecase.com/publications/pubs_detal.aspx [accessed 28 August 2005].

Gompers, P.A. (1995) Optimal investment, monitoring, and the staging of venture capital. *Journal of Finance*, No. 50.

Gompers, P.A. (2007) Venture capital. In Eckbo, E. (ed.), *Handbook of Corporate Finance: Empirical Corporate Finance*, Vol. 1. Handbooks in Finance Series, Elsevier/North-Holland, Amsterdam.

Gompers, P.A. and Lerner, J. (1999a) *The Venture Capital Cycle*. MIT Press, Cambridge, MA.

Gompers, P.A. and Lerner, J. (1999b) An analysis of compensation in the U.S. venture capital partnership. *Journal of Financial Economics* **51**.

Gompers, P.A. and Lerner, J. (2001) *The Money of Invention – How Venture Capital Creates New Wealth*. Harvard Business School Press, Boston, MA.

Gottschalg, O. (2007) Performance assessment: what we know and what we don't know. *Private Equity International*, January.

Grabenwarter, U. and Weidig, T. (2005) *Exposed to the J Curve*. Euromoney Books, London.

Granito, A. (2006) Growing pains. *Private Equity International*, October.

Gray, S. (2006) In the face of a growing investment divide. *Private Equity News*, Annual Review 2005, January.

Grundt, M. (2003) *Private Equity als Anlagekategorie einer Versicherung.* Diplomarbeit, Fachbereich Wirtschaft, Hochschule Wismar, April.

Guilhem, M. (2006) Wages: the promises of carried interest. *Private Equity.*

Haemmig, M. (2003) *The Globalization of Venture Capital – A Management Study of International Venture Capital Firms.* Verlag Paul Haupt, Bern.

Hamilton, I. and Walton-Jones, K. (2005) *Freedom of Information Act 2000: The Implications for Private Equity Funds.* AltAssets, 12 October.

Hamilton, N., Knox, A. and Utley, F. (2006) *Securitisation of Private Equity Fund of Funds,* 28 January. http://www.taneo.gr/Eng/HomePage_Eng.aspx.

Hancock, J. (2004) Venture capital secrecy is lifting. *The Baltimore Sun*, 2 February.

Hatch, R. and Wainwright, F. (2003) *Note on Private Equity Asset Allocation.* Tuck School of Business at Dartmouth, Center for Private Equity and Entrepreneurship. Case #5-0015, 18 August.

Heikkilä, T. (2004) *European Single Market and the Globalisation of Private Equity Fundraising: Barriers and Determinants of Foreign Commitments in Private Equity Funds.* Master of Science in Engineering thesis, Helsinki University of Technology.

Helft, M. (2006) A kink in venture capital's gold chain. *New York Times,* 7 October.

Hickey, J. (2006) A new level of finance. *The Financial Times*, 16 May.

Hickson, C.R. and Turner, J.D. (2005) *Partnership.* School of Management and Economics, Queen's University Belfast.

Hollenberg, C. (2006) Enter the hedge funds. *Private Equity International,* Restructuring and Turnaround Supplement, November.

Glyn A. Holton, G. (2004) Defining risk. *Financial Analysts Journal*, November, **60**(6): 19–25.

Hough, J. (2003) *Is Amazon Overvalued?*, 20 October. Available at http://www.smartmoney.com/pricecheck/index.cfm?story=20031020 [accessed 31 October 2006].

Hovhannisian, K. (2001) *Exploring on the Technology Landscapes: Real Options Thinking in the Context of the Complexity Theory.* International School of Economic Research, Università degli Studi di Siena. Paper presented at the DRUID Winter Conference at Aalborg, Denmark, 17–19 January 2002.

Hsu, D.H. and Kenney, M. (2004) *Organising Venture Capital: The Rise and Demise of American Research & Development Corporation, 1946–1973.* Available at SSRN: http://ssrn.com/abstract=628661.

Hutchings, W. (2002) Parallel perfects art of co-investment. *Financial News,* 6 September.

Hutchings, W. (2003) *Vontobel Cuts Private Equity Exposure.* Private Equity Funds and Investors, efinancialnews.com.

Hwang, M., Quigley, J.M. and Woodward, S.E. (2005) *An Index For Venture Capital, 1987–2003.* Contributions to Economic Analysis and Policy: Vol. 4, Issue 1, Article 13. Available at http://www.bepress.com/bejeap/contributions/vol4/iss1/art13 [accessed 28 June 2007].

Inderst, R. and Muennich, F. (2003) *The Benefits of Shallow Pockets.* London School of Economics, London.

Jaeggi, A.P. (2005) *Successful Risk Management for LP's Private Equity Portfolios.* Presentation, Super Investor, 17 November.

James, D. and Walton, G. (2004) *2004 Persistent Worlds Whitepaper.* International Game Developers Association Online Special Interest Group. Available at http://www.igda.org/online/IGDA_PSW_Whitepaper_2004.pdf [accessed 14 October 2006].

Junni, P. (2007) *Dynamic Aspects of the Relationship between Venture Capital Firms and their Limited Partners.* Swedish School of Economics and Business Administration, Department of Management and Organisation. Available at http://cms.cffnet.de/uploads/media/Corporate_Governance_I_Junni.pdf [accessed 14 February 2007].

Kalra, R. *et al.* (2006) *Going Public with Private Equity CFOs.* Fitch Ratings, February.

Kaneyuki, M. (2003) *Creative Valuation Techniques for Venture Capital Fund Reporting*. Finanz Betrieb.

Kaplan, S.N. (1999) *Accel Partners VII*. Case Study. Graduate School of Business, University of Chicago.

Kaplan, S.N. and Schoar, A. (2005) Private equity performance: returns, persistence and capital flows. *The Journal of Finance* **60**(4): 1791–1823.

Kaplan, S.N., Sensoy, B.A. and Strömberg, P. (2002) *How Well Do Venture Capital Databases Reflect Actual Investment?* University of Chicago, Graduate School of Business, September. Available at http://gsbwww.uchicago.edu/fac/steven.kaplan/ research/kss1.pdf [accessed 28 August 2006].

Karsai, J. (2004) *Can the State Replace Private Capital Investors? Public Financing of Venture Capital in Hungary*. Institute of Economics, Hungarian Academy of Sciences, Budapest. Discussion Paper 9. Available at http://www.econ.core.hu/doc/dp/dp/mtdp0409.pdf [accessed 14 February 2006].

Kat (2002) *The Dangers of Using Correlation to Measure Dependence*.

Keijzer, M.W. (2001) *Private Equity Holding AG – Neue Ausrichtung*. Private Equity Holding AG. Presentation for Press Conference, Zürich, 16 October.

Kempf, A. and Memmel, C. (2003) Parameterschätzungen in der Portfoliotheorie: Ein analytischer und simulationsgestützter Vergleich. *Die Betriebswirtschaft* **63**.

Kenney, M., Han, K. and Tanaka, S. (2004) The Globalization of Venture Capital: The cases of Taiwan and Japan. In Bartzokas, A. and Mani, S. (eds) *Financial Systems, Corporate Investment in Innovation and Venture Capital*. Cheltenham, UK and Northampton, MA: Edward Elgar, 52–83.

Kießlich, U.P. (2004) *The Secondary Market for Private Equity Funds*. Diploma Thesis. Wirtschaftliche Hochschule für Unternehmensführung. Vallendar. 2 August.

Kinsch, A. and Petit-Jouvet, G. (2006) Funds of private equity funds valuation – a sum of equals? *Private Equity International*, June. Available at http://www.ey.com/global/content.nsf/ Luxembourg_E/media_press_articles_Funds_of_Private_Equity_funds_valuation_a_sum_of_equals [accessed 26 June 2006].

Kogelman, S. (1999) *The Importance of Asset Allocation in Managing Private Equity Commitments*. Investment Management Research, Goldman Sachs Client Research and Strategy Group.

Kogut, B. and Kulatilaka, N. (1994) Options thinking and platform investments: investing in opportunity. *California Management* Review **36**.

Kohn, M. (2003) Business management in pre-industrial Europe. Draft chapter of *The Origins of Western Economic Success: Commerce, Finance, and Government in Pre-Industrial Europe*. Dartmouth College, Department of Economics. Working paper 03–10, July.

Kolotas, P., Kearns, P. and Le Merre, M. (2003) *New Economy Development Fund S.A. ('TANEO')*. Report – Structured Finance, Fitch Ratings, 5 August.

Kreutzer, L. (2006) OMERS sees opportunities in past disadvantages. *Dow Jones Private Equity Analyst Newsletter* **XVI**(4). Available at http://privateequity.dowjones.com/products/docs/pea_sample.pdf [accessed 15 October 2006].

Kuan, J., Snow, D. and Thomson, A. (2007) Proudly Off-Market. *Private Equity International*, Fund Structures 2007. Issue 6.

Kubr, T. (2004) Routes to liquidity. *Private Equity International*, April. Available at http://www. capdyn.com/publications/private-equity-international-kubr-apr2004.pdf.

Lantz, P., Ramstedt, N. and Stebrant, J. (2001) *Valuation Procedures for Portfolio Investments – A Comparative Study between Investment Companies in Sweden, the United Kingdom and the United States*. Graduate Business School, Göteborg.

Lerner, J. (2005) *The Limited Partner Performance Puzzle*. Harvard Business School. Presentation, Super Investor 2005.

Lerner, J. and Schoar, A. (2002) The illiquidity puzzle: theory and evidence from private equity. *Journal of Financial Economics* **72**(1).

Lerner, J., Schoar, A. and Wong, W. (2004) *Smart Institutions, Foolish Choices?: The Limited Partner Performance Puzzle*. HBS working paper.

Lhabitant, F.-S. (2004) *Hedge Funds – Quantitative Insights*. John Wiley & Sons, Chichester.

Lhabitant, F.-S. and Learned, M. (2002) *Hedge Fund Diversification: How Much is Enough?* FAME Research Paper No. 52, July. Available at http://www.gloriamundi.org/picsresources/rb-ll.pdf [accessed 30 January 2006].

Lindroth, J. (2006) HarbourVest secondaries deal in jeopardy as courts called in. *Realdeals*, 26 January.

Lipowski, A. (2005) *Periodicity of Mass Extinctions Without an Extraterrestrial Cause*. Research Paper. Adam Mickiewicz University, Poznan, Poland, 13 March.

Litvak, K. (2004) *Governance through Exit: Default Penalties and Walkaway Options in Venture Capital Partnership Agreements*. University of Texas, Law and Economics Research Paper No. 34, October. Available at http://ssrn.com/abstract=613142 [accessed 5 May 2006].

Livingston, J.S. (1971) The myth of the well-educated manager. *Harvard Business Review*, January–February.

London, S. (2006) The advantages of private equity eroded by its own success. *Financial Times*, 15 February.

MacFadyen, K. (2005) A clearer picture. *Private Equity Annual Review*.

MacFadyen, K. (2006) Brothers in arms. *Private Equity International*, May.

MacKenzie, D. (2003) Long-term capital management and the sociology of arbitrage. *Economy and Society*, No. 32.

Maginn, J. and Dyra, G. (2000) *Building Private Equity Portfolios*. Summit Strategies Group.

Malerba, F. (2005) *Innovation and the Evolution of Industries*. CESPRI Working Paper No. 172, Università Commerciale Luigi Bocconi, Milan, July.

Marcelino, J. (2006) *How to Monitor Risk in the Private Equity Asset Class: PEH Case Study*. Masters thesis, Ecole de Commerce Européenne, Lyon.

March, J.G. (1991) Exploration and exploitation in organizational learning. *Organizational Science* **2**(1).

Mathonet, P.-Y. and Monjanel, G. (2006) Valuation guidelines for private equity and venture capital funds: a survey. *Journal of Alternative Investments*, Fall.

Matter, S. (2005) *Besonderheiten beim Management von Private Equity 'Evergreen'-Strukturen*. Bundesverband Alternative Investments e.V.

Maxwell, R. (2003) *Hurdle? What Hurdle?* AltAssets.

Maxwell, R. (2004) *Success and Succession*. AltAssets, 4 June. Available at http://www.altassets.net/features/arc/2004/nz4981.php [accessed 5 December 2006].

Mayfield, R. (2004) *Ross Mayfield's Weblog – Power Laws and Private Equity*. Available at http://ross.typepad.com/blog/2004/03/power_law_and_.html [accessed 25 January 2006].

McGee, S. (2006) Leap of faith. *Investment Dealers' Digest*, 24 April.

Meek, V. (2004) New direction for Swiss listed PE funds? *European Venture Capital Journal*, April.

Meyer, T. (2006a) *OECD Technical Workshop on Private Equity Definitions and Measurements*. Issues Paper, SME Financing Gap, Vol. 2. Brasilia Conference Proceedings, OECD, Paris.

Meyer, T. (2006b) *Shall We Dansu? – Investments into Japanese VC Funds as a Special Case of FDI*. Unpublished manuscript.

Meyer, T. and Mathonet, P.-Y. (2005) *Beyond the J Curve: Managing a Portfolio of Venture Capital and Private Equity Funds*. John Wiley & Sons, Chichester.

Moise, M. *et al.* (2003) *Silver Leaf CFO 1 SCA*. Fitch Ratings Presale Report.

Moody's (1996) *The Binomial Expansion Method Applied to CBO/CLO*. Moody's Investors Service.

Moody's (2004a) *Tenzing CFO S.A. – Pre-sale Report*, December.

Moody's (2004b) *SVG Diamond Private Equity plc – Pre-sale Report*, July.

Moody's (2006) *SVG Diamond Private Equity II plc – Pre-sale Report*, January.

Morrow, M. (2005) The SOX appeal of going private. *Business Week*, 29 November. Available at http://www.businessweek.com/investor/content/ nov2005/pi20051129_4238_pi015.htm [accessed 25 January 2007].

Mowbray Capital (2005) *Upper Quartile is the Best Measure of European Venture*. Fact sheet, Mowbray Capital LLP. Available at http://www.mowbraycapital.com/downloads/factsheets/MCUpperQuartileMeasure.pdf [accessed 1 February 2006].

MPI (undated) *Fund Directors' Responsibility for Valuation, Pricing and Liquidity: A Business Perspective*. Report, Mutual Fund Governance Consulting. Available at http://www.mfgovern.com/reports/3-valuationprice.html [accessed 2 January 2007].

Murray, G.C. and Marriott, R. (1998) Why has the investment performance of technology-specialist, European venture capital funds been so poor? *Research Policy* **27**: 947–976. Available at http://ifise.unipv.it/Publications/RP-VCmodel.doc [accessed 17 February 2006].

Nattermann, P. (2000) Best practice doesn't equal best strategy. *The McKinsey Quarterly*, No. 2.

NBAN (2004) *Business Angel Finance 2003/2004 – Where Companies Find Development Capital and Investors Find Business Opportunities*. National Business Angels Network. Available at http://www.internetprnews.com/xpress/41/vppfiles/NBAN %20Angel %20Directory %202003 %20to %204.pdf [accessed 20 November 2006].

Norsk Vekst (2006) *Full seier i voldgiftssak for Norsk Vekst ASA mot tidligereforvaltere forhindret betydelig tap av verdier for aksjonrene*. Press release, 15 August. Available at www.norskvekst.com/binary?id=57227&download=true [accessed 28 July 2006].

Nuttycombe, D. (1994) Pac-Man, Tetris – and Now It's Doom's Day. *The Washington Post*, 10 October.

Oren, T. (2003) *VC Disclosure, IRRs and the J Curve*. June 18. www.pacificavc.com/blog/2003/06/18.html [accessed 2 August 2007].

Ormerod, P. (2005) *Why Most Things Fail*. Faber & Faber, London.

Ormerod, P., Johns, H. and Smith, L. (2001) *Creative Destruction and System Fitness: An Agent-based Model of Evolving, Fitness Maximising Firms and the Implications for Public Policy*. Volterra Consulting Ltd, December.

Otterlei, J. and Barrington, S. (2003) *Alternative Assets – Private Equity Fund of Funds*. Special report, Piper Jaffray Private Capital.

Pearce, R. and Barnes, S. (2006) *Raising Venture Capital*. John Wiley & Sons, Chichester.

Pease, R. (2000) *Private Equity Funds-of-Funds – State of the Market*. Research Report, Asset Alternatives Inc., Wellesley, MA.

Phalippou, L. and Gottschalg, O. (2006) *The Performance of Private Equity Funds*. Working Paper, HEC. Available at http://www.hec.fr/hec/fr/professeurs_recherche/ upload/cahiers/CR852.pdf [accessed 11 November 2006].

PREA (2005) *Reporting and Valuation Committee Meeting*, 11 March. Available at www.prea.org/about/rvminutes031105.pdf [accessed 17 March 2007].

Primack, D. (2005) Ohio to release portfolio company valuations. *Private Equity Week*, 16 December. Available at http://www.privateequityweek.com/pew/freearticles/1122125009679.html [accessed 1 February 2006].

Private Equity Analyst (2003) Secondary firms start to play a regenerative role in industry. *Private Equity Analyst* **13**(5).

Private Equity International (2005) The guide to private equity fund investment due diligence. *Private Equity International*.

Private Equity International (2006) Orphans in the portfolio. *Private Equity International*, May.

Private Equity Online (2004) *Past Performance: Your Best Guide to the Future*. PrivateEquity Online.com, 16 March. Available at http://www.prequin.com/article.aspx?articleid=11 [accessed 1 September 2006].

Private Equity Spotlight (2004) *Special Feature: The UK Freedom of Information Act. Private Equity International*, March.

Private Equity Spotlight (2005) *PEI Welcomes Clarity in FOIA Legislation. Private Equity International*, October.

Probitas Partners (2003) *Secondary Activity in Private Equity Investing*. Research Report, Fall.

Probitas Partners (2005) *A Look in the Rear Mirror. Alternative Investment Market Environment*. Probitas Partners, Summer.

Raschle, B. (2001) *Diversification.* Adveq Management. Available from www.altassets.com [accessed 2 August 2007].

Rasila, T., Seppä, M. and Hannula, M. (2002) *V2C or Venture-to-Capital – New model for Crossing the Chasm between Start-up Ventures and Venture Capital.* E-Business Research Center, Working Paper.

Red Herring (2006) Ohio disclosure rattles VCs. *Red Herring,* 30 January.

Reyes, J. (2003) *Benchmarking Private Equity in Today's Environment.* Thomson Venture Economics. Available at http://www.ventureeconomics.com/vec/download/evcainstitute2003.ppt [accessed 16 January 2006].

Rice, M.P., Wickham, P.G. and Masaki, K. (1997) *Partnerships Between Japanese and American Venture Capital Firms: An Explanatory Study.* Frontiers of Entrepreneurship Research 1997 Edition. Lally School of Management and Technology, Rensselaer Polytechnic Institute. Available at http://www.babson.edu/entrep/fer/papers97/sum97/rie.htm [accessed 14 November 2005].

Rösch, M. (2000) Investieren in Risikokapital muss nicht überaus riskant sein. *Finanz & Wirtschaft,* 5 July.

Rouvinez, C. (2003) Diversity scoring for market value CDOs. *Credit Risk,* May.

Rouvinez, C. (2005) The value of the carry. *Private Equity International,* July/August.

Rouvinez, C. (2006) Top quartile persistence in private equity. *Private Equity International,* June.

Roxburgh, C. (2003) Hidden flaws in strategy. *The McKinsey Quarterly,* No. 2.

Russel, M. (2006) *Behavioural Economics and the World of Private Equity.* Presentation, PCG Asset Management, Geneva.

Sahlman, W. (1990) The structure and governance of venture-capital organisations. *Journal of Financial Economics* **27**.

San José, A., Roure, J. and Aernoudt, R. (2004) *Business Angels Academies: Unleashing the Potential for Business Angel Investment.* Submitted to Gate2Growth Academic Network (unpublished).

Sanditov, B., Kool, C. and Cowan, R. (2001) *Mutual Illusions and Financing New Technologies: Two-Sided Informational Cascades.* University of Maastricht, 10 December.

Scardino, J. (2004) *Past Performance a Guide to Likely Future Performance in Private Equity. Private Equity Monitor.* Initiative Europe Ltd, Redhill, UK.

Schmidt, D. and Wahrenburg, M. (2003) *Contractual Relations between European VC-Funds and Investors: The Impact of Reputation and Bargaining Power on Contractual Design.* Johann Wolfgang Goethe Universität, Frankfurt. Center for Financial Studies, CFS Working Paper No. 15.

Seeteboun, H.-M. (2006) *The Pattern of Power Escalation between Managers and Investors in Private Equity Funds.* Available at http://pluto.huji.ac.il/~chanamuriel/power%20 escalation%20in%20pe%20funds.pdf [accessed 14 February 2007].

Sheehan, M. (2005) Portfolio for sale. *Venture Capital Journal,* June.

Singleton, G. and Henshilwood, G.L. (2003) *Avon Pension Fund – Developing a Strategy for Private Equity.* Available at http://www.bathnes.gov.uk/Committee_Papers/Pensions/pn030328/12zAppendix1.htm [accessed 11 January 2006].

Skypala, P. (2007) Secondaries attract private equity. *Financial Times,* Fund Management Supplement, 12 March.

Small, E. (2002) *Clawback Arrangements – The Investor Strikes Back. Edwards & Angell,* 10 September. Available at http://www.altassets.net/knowledgebank/learningcurve/2002/nz2990.php [accessed 6 October 2006].

Smith, P. (2005) Hedge funds take on private equity bidders in YBR sale. *Financial Times,* 8 April.

Smith, J.K., Smith, R.L. and Williams, K. (2000) *The SEC's 'Fair Value' Standard for Mutual Fund Investment in Restricted Shares and Other Illiquid Securities.* Working Papers in Economics, Claremont Colleges, 1 November.

Snow, D. (2006) An asymmetric success story. *The Private Equity Fundraising Compendium,* November.

Snow, D. (2006) Separation Anxiety. *Private Equity International,* May.

Snow, D. (2007) Public performance. *Private Equity International*, January.

Solnik, B. (2006) *The Contribution of Behavioral Finance to Understanding Asset Pricing and Investment Choices.* Presentation, June.

Sørheim, R. (2003) The pre-investment behaviour of business angels: a social capital approach. *Venture Capital* **5**(4).

Sormani, A. (2003a) Back to square one: asset allocation. *European Venture Capital Journal*, May.

Sormani, A. (2003b) Fund-of-funds: a bubble burst? *European Venture Capital Journal*, September.

Sormani, A. (2003c) Mezzanine: the hottest ticket in town. *European Venture Capital Journal*, 4 December. Available at http://www.ventureeconomics.com/evcj/protected/sectorreps/finance/1070549493265.html [accessed 14 November 2006].

Sormani, A. (2004) Turnarounds: an acquired taste. *Private Equity Week*, 27 May. Available at http://www.privateequityweek.com/evcj/protected/mthlyfeatures/1070549946483.html [accessed 2 January 2007].

Sormani, A. (2005a) Turnarounds: is it worth it? *European Venture Capital Journal*, June.

Sormani, A. (2005b) Fund-of-funds: working to stand. *European Venture Capital Journal*, August.

Sormani, A. (2005c) Hedge funds: a good fit? *European Venture Capital Journal*, September.

Sormani, A. (2005d) Working to stand out from the crowd. *European Venture Capital Journal*, September.

Stacey, R. (1996) *Complexity and Creativity in Organizations.* Berrett-Koehler, San Francisco.

Standard & Poor's (2003a) *Silver Leaf CFO 1 SCA Research*, March

Standard & Poor's (2003b) *The New Economy Development Fund S.A. (TANEO) Research*, May

Standard & Poor's (2004) *SVG Diamond Private Equity plc Research*, August.

Standard & Poor's (2006) *SVG Diamond Private Equity II plc Research*, January.

Statman, M. (2002) *How Much Diversification is Enough?* Leavey School of Business, Santa Clara University.

Stein, T. (2002) The next generation. *Venture Capital Journal*, 1 June. Available at http://www.probitaspartners.com/news/news_vcjournal060102.html [accessed 5 December 2006].

Stross, R.E. (2000) *eBoys: The First Inside Account of Venture Capitalists at Work.* Crown Business.

Stowers, R. (2004) *'Socially Responsible' Investing and Pension Funds: Welcome Reform or Fiduciary Nightmare?* American Enterprise Institute for Public Policy Research. Available at http://www.aei.org/events/filter.all,eventID.832/summary.asp [accessed 16 August 2006].

Stulz, R.M. (2000) Why risk management is not rocket science. *Financial Times*, Mastering Risk Series 10, 27 June.

Sull, D.N. and Escobari, M.E. (2005) *Success Against the Odds: What Brazilian Champions Teach Us About Thriving in Unpredictable Markets.* Available at http://news.ft.com/cms/5be686a6-93ee-11da-82ea-0000779e2340.pdf [accessed 27 February 2006].

Susinno, G. (2005). *Shortcomings in Advise versus the Art and Science of Investing in Hedge Funds.*

Sweeney, G. and Taylor, J. (2002) *Co-Investment Strategies.* WR Hambrecht, San Francisco.

Sweeney, G. *et al.* (2001) *Private Equity Sub-asset Allocation.* WR Hambrecht, San Francisco.

Swensen, D.F. (2000) *Pioneering Portfolio Management – An Unconventional Approach to Institutional Investment.* Simon & Schuster, New York.

Swensen, D.F. (2005) *Unconventional Success – A Fundamental Approach to Personal Investment.* Free Press, New York.

Takahashi, D. and Alexander, S. (2001) *Illiquid Alternative Asset Fund Modelling.* Yale University Investments Office.

Taleb, N.N. (2005) *Fooled by Randomness*, 2nd edn. Random House, New York.

Tegeler, D. and Poindexter, J. (2007) *General Partner Carry Ecoonomics – An Overview. Private Equity International.* Fund Structures 2007. Issue 6.

Tett, G. (2003) *Saving the Sun.* HarperCollins.

Thomson, A. (2006a) Carry conflicts. *Private Equity International.*

Thomson, A. (2006b) Out in the cold. *Private Equity International*, March.

Tierney, J.F. and Folkerts-Landau, D. (2001) *Structured Private Equity – An Old Market Becomes an Emerging Asset Class.* Deutsche Bank Global Markets Research, Frankfurt.

Toll, D. (2001) *Private Equity Partnership Terms and Conditions.* Research Report, Asset Alternatives.

Tracy, T. (2006) Super funds offer reduced-fee sidekicks. *Dow Jones Private Equity Analyst Newsletter* **XVI**(4). Available at http://privateequity.dowjones.com/products/docs/pea_sample.pdf [accessed 15 October 2006].

Tredegar Corporation (2002) *Annual Report.* Available at http://www.tredegar.com/ PDF/02report.pdf [accessed 21 June 2005].

Tricks, H. (2005) Equity funds fight to maintain privacy. *Financial Times*, 17 January.

Udovitch, A. (1962) At the Origins of the Western Commenda: Islam, Israel, Byzantium? *Speculum – A Journal of Mediaeval Studies* **XXXVII**: 198–207

Udovitch, A. (1986) Kirād. The Encyclopedia of Islam – New Edition, Leiden-New York, E.J. Brill, V.

Ueda, M. and Hirukawa, M. (2006) *Venture Capital and Industrial 'Innovation'*, May. Available at http://www.csom.umn.edu/Assets/63413.pdf [accessed 28 July 2006].

Wakin, J. (1993) Mudāraba. The Encyclopedia of Islam – New Edition, Leiden-New York, E.J. Brill, VII.

Warburton P. (2006) *Getting Flexible: New Strategies for Whole-of-Fund Carried Interest.* Ashurst's Investment Funds Group, April.

Ward, D. (2005) *Adopting the US Model in Europe.* MTI Partners, Presentation, Super Investor 2005.

Waters, R. (2005) The biggest gains are concentrated in a handful of funds. *Financial Times*, London, 16 February.

Weaver, R.N. (2003) *Clawbacks and Returns – What's the Right Hurdle Rate? What's the Right Preferred Return?* Institute of Fiduciary Education.

Weidig, T. and Mathonet, P.Y. (2004) *The Risk Profiles of Private Equity.* EVCA, Brussels.

White, M.C. (1999) *Business Valuation Techniques and Negotiations.* White & Lee LLP.

Wiegers, E. (2003) Wenn das Wagnis zum Verhängnis wird. *Wochen Zeitung*, 11 November. Available at http://www.woz.ch/archiv/old/03/37/6052.html [accessed 29 March 2005].

Wietlisbach, U. (2001) *Examining the Latest Developments & Potential of the Securitisation of Private Equity Portfolios.* Presentation, Super Investor 2001, 6 November.

Wilshire (2005) *Quarterly Newsletter.* Wilshire Private Markets Group, Spring.

Winograd, B. (2002) *Hamlet and Modern Portfolio Theory.* Prudential Investment Management.

Wipfli, D. (2002) *Wachstumsfinanzierung mit Private Equity.* Presentation, Partners Group, 30 September.

Woods, B. (2003) The myth of the New Economy. *E-Commerce Times*, 2 June. Available at http://www.ecommercetimes.com/story/20685.html [accessed 29 May 2006].

Worthington, R.L., Hurley, M.P., Fuller, T.G., *et al.* (2001) *Alternative Investments and the Semi-Affluent Investor.* Undiscovered Managers, Research Report, July.

Yoder, J. (2005) *Effective Endowment Management.* Presentation, CAIS/NYSAIS Business Affairs Conference, 4–6 May.

Young, C. and Meek, V. (2001) *The Direct Route*, 29 June. Available at http://www.altassets.com/ features/arc/2001/nz89.php [accessed 5 October 2006].

Zheng, Y., Liu, J. and George, G. (2006) *The Value of Capabilities and Networks in Technology Start-ups.* Available at http://www.london.edu/assets/documents/PDF/ George_2006_ on_valuation_of_capabilities_in_start-ups.pdf [accessed 7 February 2007].

Index

Page references in *italics* refer to Figures and Tables

Index compiled by Annette Musker